Cambridge History of Medicine

EDITORS: CHARLES WEBSTER AND CHARLES ROSENBERG

Medicine and society in Wakefield and Huddersfield
1780–1870

Medicine and society in Wakefield and Huddersfield

1780–1870

Hilary Marland

Wellcome Unit for the History of Medicine
University of Oxford

Medisch-Encyclopaedisch Institut
Vrije Universiteit, Amsterdam

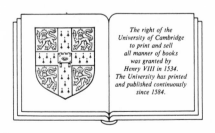

The right of the
University of Cambridge
to print and sell
all manner of books
was granted by
Henry VIII in 1534.
The University has printed
and published continuously
since 1584.

CAMBRIDGE UNIVERSITY PRESS

CAMBRIDGE

NEW YORK   NEW ROCHELLE   MELBOURNE   SYDNEY

Published by the Press Syndicate of the University of Cambridge
The Pitt Building, Trumpington Street, Cambridge CB2 1RP
32 East 57th Street, New York, NY 10022, USA
10 Stamford Road, Oakleigh, Melbourne 3166, Australia

First published 1987

Printed in Great Britain at the University Press, Cambridge

British Library cataloguing in publication data

Marland, Hilary
Medicine and society in Wakefield and Huddersfield 1780–1870 –
(Cambridge history of medicine)
1. Medical care – England – West Yorkshire – History
2. Social medicine – England – West Yorkshire – History
I. Title
362.1′09428′1   RA418.3.G7

Library of Congress cataloguing in publication data

Marland, Hilary
Medicine and society in Wakefield and Huddersfield 1780–1870
(Cambridge history of medicine)
Based largely on the author's thesis (PhD) – University of Warwick, 1984
Bibliography
Includes index
1. Social medicine – England – Wakefield (West Yorkshire) – History – 18th century.
2. Social medicine – England – Wakefield (West Yorkshire) – History – 19th century.
3. Social medicine – England – Huddersfield (West Yorkshire) – History – 18th century.
4 Social medicine – England – Huddersfield (West Yorkshire) – History – 19th century.
5. Medical care – England – Wakefield (West Yorkshire) – History – 18th century.
6. Medical care – England – Wakefield (West Yorkshire) – History – 19th century.
7. Medical care – England – Huddersfield (West Yorkshire) – History – 18th century.
8. Medical care – England – Huddersfield (West Yorkshire) – History – 19th century.
9. Wakefield (West Yorkshire) – History. 10. Huddersfield (West Yorkshire) – History.
I. Title. II. Series. [DNLM: 1. Charities – history – England. 2. History of Medicine,
18th Cent. – England. 3. History of Medicine, 19th Cent. – England. 4. Public Assistance –
history – England. 5. Socioeconomic Factors – England. WZ 70 FE5 M34m]
RA418.3.G7M28 1987   362.1′09428′15   86-20786

ISBN 0521 32575 7

To my parents and Sebastian

Contents

Contents ix

List of tables

List of maps and figures

List of appendices

List of abbreviations

HPL	Huddersfield Public Library (Kirklees District Archives and Local Studies Department)
HRI	Huddersfield Royal Infirmary (Postgraduate Library)
WDA	Wakefield District Archives (JGC Private Collection of Mr John Goodchild, District Archivist)
WYCRO	West Yorkshire County Record Office
C	Census Enumerators' Books
PMD	*Provincial Medical Directories*
AR HD	Annual Report, Huddersfield Dispensary
AR HI	Annual Report, Huddersfield Infirmary
AR WD	Annual Report, Wakefield Dispensary
AR WI	Annual Report, Wakefield Infirmary
Ms	Manuscript source (all sources are printed unless otherwise stated)

Parliamentary Papers

PP	Parliamentary paper or return
SCME 1834	Report from the Select Committee on Medical Education, PP, 1834, XIII (602).
SCMPR 1844	Report from the Select Committee on Medical Poor Relief. Third Report, PP, 1844, IX (531).
SCMR 1854	Report from the Select Committee on Medical Relief, PP, 1854, XII (348).
QRSM 1880	Abstracts of the quinquennial returns of sickness and mortality experienced by Friendly Societies for periods between 1855 and 1875, PP, 1880, LXVIII (517).

Newspapers

HHEx	*Halifax and Huddersfield Express*
HHE	*Huddersfield and Holmfirth Examiner*
HC	*Huddersfield Chronicle*
HE	*Huddersfield Examiner*
LI	*Leeds Intelligencer*
LM	*Leeds Mercury*
WHJ	*Wakefield and Halifax Journal*
WE	*Wakefield Express*
WJ	*Wakefield Journal and West Riding Herald*
WS	*Wakefield Star*
WRH	*West Riding Herald and Wakefield Commercial and Agricultural Journal*

Preface

This volume is based largely on a University of Warwick PhD thesis, *Medicine and Society in Wakefield and Huddersfield 1780–1870*, which was submitted in September, 1984. In revising the thesis, some sections have been reduced, others expanded or altered (especially Chapter 4 and the Conclusion). Notes and references have been revised and updated.

The book examines the formation and evolution of medical provisions in the two West Yorkshire communities of Wakefield and Huddersfield, one of its primary aims being to demonstrate the potential value of local studies in increasing our understanding of the development of systems of medical care, and of those who ran and serviced these facilities. The survey covers both 'institutional' facilities, namely hospital and dispensary provisions and Poor Law medical services, and 'self-help' agencies in the form of friendly society provisions for the sick and 'fringe' or 'peripheral' medical practices. The structural, professional and social development of medical communities in the two towns is also discussed at some length. A further motivation behind the project was to obtain as wide a picture as possible of the main sources of medical relief available during the late eighteenth and nineteenth centuries in the two West Riding towns.

Towards this end, a wide range of qualitative and quantitative sources were utilised, to include Poor Law material (pre- and post-1834), the records of medical charities and friendly societies, census returns, newspapers, trade and medical directories, and parliamentary reports and returns. The use of such a combination of material was found to give a better indication of the range of facilities available and their relative importance. Questions relating to the availability of and access to medical provisions were brought very much to the fore. One of the main conclusions arising from the application of this methodology is that the emphasis which has been given to institutional provisions would seem to have been misplaced. The importance of previously neglected options for medical care, the friendly society and 'peripheral' forms of treatment, have been stressed. Leading on from this, it can be suggested that self-help forms of medical relief, as compared with those 'provided' by the wealthy classes for the poor, were of much greater significance than has been assumed.

The true value of local studies to medical history can only be realised if the formation of medical provisions, and the personnel who serviced them, is examined against the backdrop of the communities in which they evolved. An effort has been made to link both the growth of institutional medical care and the progress of self-help forms to the histories of Wakefield and Huddersfield, their social, civic and economic developments during the late eighteenth and nineteenth centuries. The leading role of the layman in creating a demand for, and in the setting up and evolution of, medical provisions has also been stressed. It is hoped that an analysis of these factors will lead to a greater understanding of how and why medical facilities developed as they did, and to a clearer insight into the relationship between medicine, history and society.

I have received much assistance from the staff of many record offices and libraries while preparing this volume. Special thanks are due to the staff of the West Riding County Record Office, the Wakefield District Archives and the Kirklees District Archives and Local Studies Department, in particular Mr Michael Bottomley, Mr John Goodchild and Miss Janet Burhouse. I am especially grateful to Mr John Goodchild, Wakefield District Archivist, for making a large number of items from his private collection available to me. I am also grateful for the assistance of the librarians of the Wellcome Institute Library, the Public Record Office, the British Library, the Doncaster Public Library and the Warwick University Library, especially for the large amount of help given by the ladies dealing with Inter-Library Loans. My thanks also go to Dr C. S. Ward, Consultant Anaesthetist of the Huddersfield Royal Infirmary and ex-President of the Huddersfield Medical Society, for making the records of the Society available for my use.

My PhD supervisor, Dr J. Obelkevich, of the Centre for the Study of Social History, University of Warwick, read the many drafts of my thesis and made a great number of useful suggestions.

I also had several beneficial discussions with Dr Joan Lane, especially in the early stages of the project. I am particularly grateful to my two thesis examiners, Dr Tony Mason and Ms Margaret Pelling, for reading the thesis so exhaustively, and for making so many valuable suggestions, many of which I have attempted to incorporate into this volume. Thanks are also due to Dr Charles Webster of the Wellcome Unit for the History of Medicine at Oxford for encouraging the publication of the book, to the Cambridge University Press, and to the referees, whose comments were of great help in the final preparation of the book. I am obliged to the Economic and Social Research Council for providing funding for the first three years of the project and during the year 1986.

Last, but certainly not least, I would like to thank my family for their encouragement, and my husband, Sebastian, for his patience and constant support at all stages of the project.

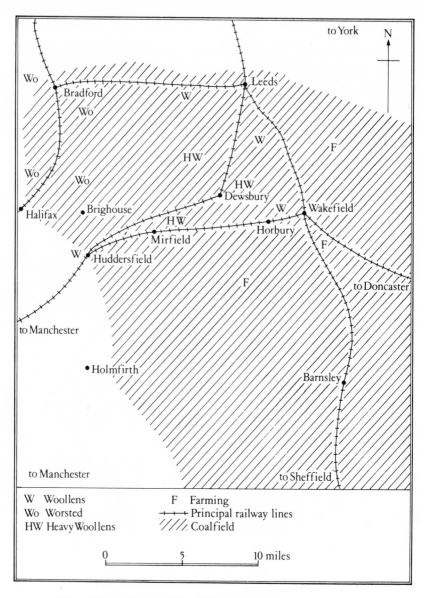

Map 1. The industrial West Riding, circa 1880.

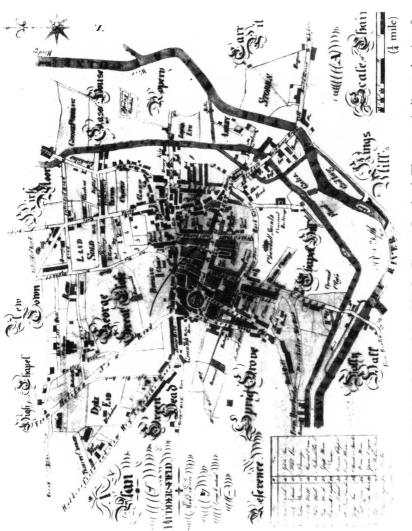

Map 2(a). A plan of Huddersfield made in 1826, by George Crosland. The arrow indicates the site of Huddersfield Dispensary, 1814–1831. (Reproduced courtesy of West Yorkshire Archive Service.)

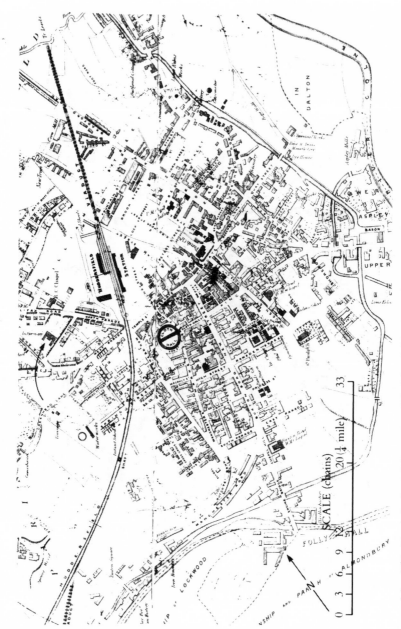

Map 2(b). Hardy's plan of the town of Huddersfield, 1850. The arrow indicates the site of Huddersfield Infirmary from 1831. (Reproduced courtesy of Kirklees Libraries, Museums and Arts.)

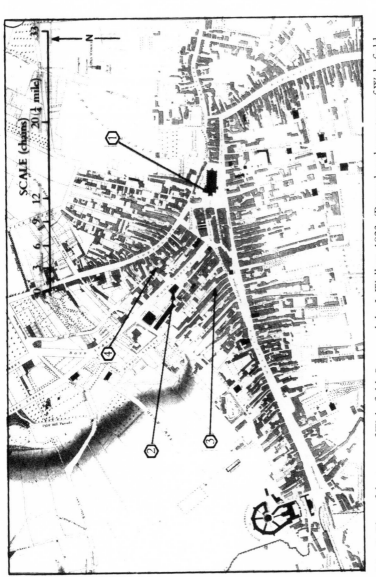

Map 3. Plan of the town of Wakefield. Surveyed, by J. Walker, 1823. (Reproduced courtesy of Wakefield Metropolitan District Libraries.)

As the basic structure of Wakefield changed very little during the nineteenth century, this map can be taken as being fairly representative of the period 1787–1879.
Sites of the Wakefield Dispensary and Infirmary:

1. 1787–1821 Northgate (west end of Wakefield Parish Church), 2. 1821–1831 Music Saloon, Wood Street. 3. 1831–1854 Barstow Square. 4. 1854–1879 Dispensary Yard, Northgate (including in-patient wards after 1854).

1

Introduction

During the last few decades the study of the history of medicine has begun to follow a number of interesting new directions. Previously the subject was regarded in extremely narrow terms. Method was based on a collection of facts arranged either chronologically or thematically;[1] emphasis remained with 'histories of technical achievement, of medical institutions, of progress of treatment against disease, and of the medical or allied professions'.[2] Most studies implied that medical developments took place in a vacuum, uninfluenced by wider social, economic, political or legislative changes. The process of moving away from studies of prominent medical practitioners, major medical institutions and theoretical and technical developments has now begun. There is a clearer understanding that scientific advances 'did not immediately translate into advances in medical practice',[3] and that 'great men' in medicine were by no means representative of (and in terms of impact and numbers probably by no means as important as) the medical profession as a whole. Prestigious voluntary hospital foundations tell us little about the sum total of medical facilities for the poor. Studies of institutional provisions as a whole leave out the large, 'grey' area of self-help medicine.

The field of the 'social history of medicine' still covers a great deal of uncharted ground, and much work needs to be done before a greater understanding is achieved concerning the relationship between medicine, history and society. Many areas suffer from neglect. Pioneering studies, such as Woodward's investigation into the voluntary hospital movement, undertaken in the early 1970s, have tended not to have been followed up.[4] Emphasis has remained with institutional provisions: in England, hospital and Poor Law medical services. Self-help agencies in the form of sick clubs and friendly societies, fringe and folk medicine and self-medication have received much less attention. Even within the boundaries of institutional medicine, research has shown a clear bias; towards in-patient hospital facilities and medical services under the New Poor Law. The more informal medical service provided under the Old Poor Law, and the numerically more significant out-patient and dispensary facilities have been comparatively neglected. There is still a geographical bias in favour of London and other major population centres. Emphasis to some extent remains with the 'important', 'accessible' and 'famous', rather than with the 'typical'.

Perhaps one of the most serious defects of investigations into medical history has been a failure to examine medical men and services in the context of the community, although it is acknowledged that local studies could add much to our understanding of the development of agencies of medical care. In the words of George Rosen, for example,

The social history of health and disease is . . . more than a study of medical problems . . . It requires as well an understanding of the factors – economic conditions, occupation, income, housing, nutrition, family structure and others – which create or influence health problems, and of the ways in which they operate.[5]

Medical services did not evolve in isolation. To take the setting up of hospitals, their establishment was determined only partially, often very partially, by perceived medical needs. Just as important were the motivations of the lay groups who financed these enterprises. As will be shown in Chapter 4, a wide variety of motivations could influence the setting up of these institutions: civic pride, a desire to control the labour market, fear of epidemic disease, social ambition, religious impulses and humanitarianism. All had more to do with social and economic rather than medical concerns, and with lay rather than medical groups.

P. Branca has suggested that the social history of medicine involves three layers: great medical personalities at the top, patients or prospective patients at the bottom, and the ordinary practitioner in the middle.[6] To this sub-division I would add a further layer, which also occupied something of an intermediate position: the interested layman. The importance of lay, usually middle-class, groups in directing medical services will be stressed throughout the following chapters. As suggested above, medical charities were just as dependent upon lay organisational and financial support as upon the co-operation of local medical men. It was often laymen who campaigned for the establishment of these institutions, and invariably they provided the greatest proportion of financial support and determined policy-making, including admissions policies.

The influence of lay groups within medical charities had its parallels in other medical services. Poor Law medical relief was directed by lay overseers and vestries, and after 1834 by the Boards of Guardians, assisted by the lay relieving officer. Friendly society and sick club provisions were determined by the initiatives of their lay, this time usually working-class, membership. The survival, development and growth of various types of fringe medicine was influenced by the changing demands of the population for these forms of treatment. In a similar way, the growth of the 'regular' medical profession and changes in practice were not determined solely by intra-professional developments in training, qualifications and ethics. Rather, the evolution of the medical profession was influenced very much by changing demands for medical care and the creation of new posts, both emanating from lay groups, especially the middle classes. The middle classes not only produced a demand for the services of medical men, in particular the general practitioner; they also helped to fill it. As will be demonstrated in Chapter 7, recruitment of medical practitioners took place in most cases from middle-class groups.

In the past, medical historians have made a limited selection and use of available sources, and this explains in part at least the emphasis which has been placed on institutional medicine and eminent personalities. This survey has attempted to examine as wide a range of source material as possible, to include the records of the Poor Law administration, medical charities and friendly societies, census data, trade and medical directories, newspapers, parliamentary papers and miscellaneous data relating to both 'regular' and 'fringe' medical practitioners. The use of such a variety of data was found to give a clearer picture of the range of options available, and their relative importance, in particular throwing more light on friendly society facilities and fringe medical practices. The project attempted both to look at new sources and to examine old sources in a new way. For example, while hospital reports have been used quite extensively by historians, little use has been made of subscription lists, which were frequently attached to annual reports. These lists give information on the social and occupational composition of supporters of medical charities, data which are not normally available elsewhere. The value of subscription lists in providing this information and in giving clues as to the motivations of those funding these institutions will be emphasised in Chapter 4. Until recently, parish documents, in particular overseers' accounts, were not regarded as a viable source for the study of medical history. Here they were found to be a reliable and unique source of information on medical relief under the Old Poor Law. In the last few years, meanwhile, census enumerators' books have attracted 'legions of historians and social scientists seeking a long-term historical perspective for their studies'.[7] The Wakefield and Huddersfield census returns proved to be valuable (especially when used in conjunction with trade and medical directories) in giving data on the numbers and social composition of medical men. They also provided, albeit in a limited form, information on various groups of fringe practitioners, an aspect of medical history for which data are extremely scarce. More details on sources and the problems implicit in the use of different forms of evidence are given in the appropriate chapters. But it should be emphasised here that the suggestion of R. S. Roberts that 'it is no longer appropriate to rely on any one sort of evidence or any one sort of approach'[8] in the study of medical history has been taken very much to heart. While an effort has been made to be selective, and to achieve a balance between qualitative and quantitative data, a wide range of primary source material has been utilised.

The selection of Wakefield and Huddersfield, two medium-sized communities, as subjects for the study was in part determined by the methodological approach. It was felt to be possible to look at a large number of sources relating to medical provisions and agencies only within the context of two 'manageably-sized' communities. This also facilitated an analysis of the towns' social and economic developments. Other factors also influenced the selection of Wakefield and Huddersfield. The choice was determined in part by the need to readjust the balance of studies towards the provinces and smaller communities.

Detailed studies of the evolution of medical facilities in urban settings provide information for comparison with other nineteenth-century communities with diverse economic and social backgrounds. But Wakefield and Huddersfield also provide us with an interesting comparative study in their own right. Wakefield, a traditional market and service centre, which experienced only a slow rate of population growth and a retarded industrial development during the nineteenth century, responded in a very different way in the provision of medical care compared with Huddersfield, a fast-growing and dynamic textile town. The diverse experiences of the two communities in terms of population growth, industrial development, town functions, political, social and civic activities will be discussed in Chapter 2, and throughout the following chapters we will return to the issue of how these factors influenced medical services and personnel in Wakefield and Huddersfield.[9]

One aim of this project was to sum up the relative importance of the different medical services and providers of medical treatment which emerged during the late eighteenth and nineteenth centuries. This comparison will be returned to in the concluding chapter (Chapter 9). Primarily, it will be suggested that the bias in the amount, quality and accessibility of source material, and, leading on from this, a bias in the selection of data, has resulted in the least important forms of medical provision being emphasised: that is, institutional forms, hospitals and Poor Law (especially post-1834) medical services.

Chapters 3 and 4 will examine the main forms of institutional provision in Wakefield and Huddersfield. Chapter 3 will look at official provisions, created through the medium of the Poor Law. Under the Old and New Poor Law administrations, medical relief was provided on a very small scale in both communities, although Wakefield, faced with a shortage of other forms of institutional medical relief, moved with greater rapidity towards the setting up of some form of basic health service for the poor. Similarly, only a small proportion of the populations of the two communities gained admission to hospitals and dispensaries. Statistically, the percentage taken as in-patients was negligible. Numerically, out-patient and dispensary facilities (comparatively neglected provisions) were of far greater importance, and their relative significance will be examined in Chapter 4. But it is not on the amount of medical relief offered that Chapter 4 will mainly focus. Rather, emphasis will be placed on the motivations of those setting up medical charities in the two communities: the social composition of support, the pressures leading to the establishment of these facilities, what their supporters hoped to achieve and their success in fulfilling their ambitions.

As already suggested, institutional provisions were perhaps of less significance than self-help and 'alternative' sources of relief, which will be focused on in Chapters 5 and 6. Chapter 5 will look specifically at the type and amount of medical relief provided by friendly societies in the two communities during the nineteenth century. A wide variety of fringe forms of medical treatment were utilised by the populations of Wakefield and Huddersfield, and not just the poorer inhabitants. In Chapter 6 it will be demonstrated how older forms of fringe practice, self-medication, folk healing and the utilisation of midwives, for instance, were bolstered in the nineteenth century by a wide range of new alternatives and person-nel, including medical botanists, chemists and druggists, hydro-pathy and an ever-increasing range of patent medicines. During the nineteenth century, use of these alternatives did not, as we might expect, diminish. Rather, they flourished, and apparently provided a large proportion of the population with sources (possibly for many the only sources) of medical relief. Chapters 5 and 6 will switch the emphasis to self-help medicine, but throughout the study an effort will be made to give some emphasis to the role of patients and potential patients in and their reactions to the various medical services.

Each chapter will look in passing at the providers of the different forms of medical treatment. But it is only in Chapters 6, 7 and 8 that a detailed analysis will be made of these groups. Chapter 6 will look at those on the periphery of medical life, the unqualified fringe practitioners, who included not only the traditional healers, but also predominantly 'commercial' groups, the 'market place' quack, the spa doctor, and the chemist and druggist. The 'regular' medical profession will be examined in some detail in Chapters 7 and 8. Emphasis has been placed on examining the 'medical community' as a whole, rather than any eminent practitioners who might have emerged during the nineteenth century. Chapters 7 and 8 will not only look at intra-professional developments, but also at the relationship between supply and demand, expressed in terms of practice-building opportunities and posts. The social position of medical men will also be examined, together with their efforts to improve both their professional and social status.[10]

2

Wakefield and Huddersfield: aspects of their economic, civic and social activities, circa 1780 to 1870

Wakefield and Huddersfield, while both situated in the West Riding woollen district at a distance of only thirteen miles from each other (see Map 1), developed in very different ways during the eighteenth and nineteenth centuries. By the late eighteenth century Wakefield had evolved into a regional market and service centre of some importance, and was,

. . . considered as one of the handsomest and most opulent of the clothing towns, being inhabited by several capital merchants, who have costly and elegant houses. It is large and populous, and possesses a considerable share of business.[1]

By early in the nineteenth century it could be described as being 'in many civil matters, the capital of the West Riding',[2] having the principal court for the election of Members of Parliament, a registry of deeds and wills, a prison, the office of the Clerk of the Peace, and, after 1818, the County Lunatic Asylum, all institutions utilised by the whole region. While Wakefield reached something of a peak in its material prosperity by late in the eighteenth century, the nineteenth century ushered in a period of 'gradual decline'.[3] The stagnation of the clothing industry was perhaps the most serious aspect of this decline, but it was paralleled by a more general quiescence in the community's other economic activities, institutions and social and cultural life.

For Huddersfield, by contrast, the nineteenth century, particularly the first decades, was a period of remarkable expansion and increasing prosperity (at least for a small proportion of the community). The basis for this growth was the woollen industry. Huddersfield (whose involvement in the woollen industry dated back to the thirteenth century) was just as much a product of the textile industry as Bradford and Leeds and the classic cotton mill towns of Lancashire, situated just over the Pennines. Huddersfield's massive population growth and its apparent upsurge in civic pride (reflected in a spate of church building, the foundation of numerous voluntary societies, and the initiation of local government and public health reform early in the nineteenth century) was linked closely to the development of, and the wealth produced by, the woollen industry. Wakefield's demise and Huddersfield's fruition were noted as early as the 1830s. In 1832 it was remarked that while Wakefield was still noted for its markets and commercial interests, '. . . as a town for manufactures it has declined, . . .'.[4] Five years later Huddersfield was described as '. . . a populous, flourishing, and handsome market town, which has more than doubled its magnitude, and greatly improved its appearance, since the year 1811'. While

Little more than a century ago, the population and wealth of Huddersfield did not amount to more than one-half of either Halifax or Wakefield, . . . now it is equal, if not superior, to the larger of them, ...[5]

In 1849 an article in the *Morning Chronicle* remarked that Huddersfield

has sprung up entirely within the last sixty years. Previous to that time it was but an insignificant cluster of irregularly built lanes. The town of Huddersfield is a species of minor capital of the broad and fancy cloth-working districts of Yorkshire; . . . .[6]

Wakefield and Huddersfield differed in many other aspects. While Wakefield remained a bastion of Tory/Establishment interests, Huddersfield developed as a centre of Liberalism and Non-Conformity during the late eighteenth and nineteenth centuries. The formation of governing bodies in the two communities also followed very different lines of development, Wakefield being incorporated in 1848, Huddersfield not until twenty years later. Both towns experienced upsurges of working-class discontent during the late eighteenth and nineteenth centuries, but they tended to be more severe and protracted in Huddersfield, largely due to structural changes in the textile industry. During this period there were 'fewer explosions of popular violence'[7] in Wakefield than elsewhere in the West Riding.

These differing patterns of development will be looked at more closely in the following pages. This chapter will concentrate on those aspects of civic and economic activity which would appear to have had an influence upon the development of medical provisions (as suggested in Chapter 1). Section 2.1 will examine the population growth and economic evolution of the two communities, Section 2.2 aspects of their civic life (local government, voluntary society activity, religion and politics), Section 2.3 activities in the field of public health and disease prevention, and the final Section (2.4) manifestations of distress and popular discontent.

2.1 Population growth and economic development

The West Riding experienced a remarkable increase in population during the late eighteenth and nineteenth centuries. Between 1700 and 1801 the estimated population per square mile of the Riding more than doubled from 91 to 212.[8] In the next thirty years the population increased from just over half a million to a little under one million.[9] By 1831, only two counties, Middlesex and Lancaster, had more inhabitants than the West Riding. The story of the massive growth of individual towns within the Northern manufacturing districts is well known. In the decade 1821 to 1831, for example, the population of Leeds increased by 47.7 per cent, that of Sheffield by 40.5 per cent and that of Bradford by 65.5 per cent. By 1831, Leeds had 123,000 inhabitants compared with 53,000 in 1801. Bradford, the fastest growing city in the first half of the nineteenth century, increased its population eightfold between 1801 and 1851. By 1851 Bradford had 103,778 inhabitants.[10]

Wakefield and Huddersfield shared in this phenomenon, Huddersfield in particular experiencing very spectacular growth rates. Between 1700 and 1800 Huddersfield grew from a sprawling and 'miserable' village with a population of less than 1,000 into a town of 7,268 inhabitants. In the first decades of the nineteenth century the town continued to expand significantly. Natural increase was boosted by migration into Huddersfield from neighbouring parts of Yorkshire and Westmorland, and to a lesser extent Ireland, in the 1830s and 1840s, the migrants being attracted by the Huddersfield textile industry.[11] The population of Huddersfield grew by over 30 per cent in every decade between 1801 and 1851. Between 1811 and 1821 it increased by 37.4 per cent; in the following decade by over 43 per cent (see Table 2.1). In the first seventy years of the nineteenth century Huddersfield's population increased fivefold (or by an average of 27.5 per cent per decade).[12]

Table 2.1. *The population of the Wakefield and Huddersfield Townships, 1801–1871.*

	Wakefield		Huddersfield	
Date	Population	Percentage increase over preceding decade	Population	Percentage increase over preceding decade
1801	8,131		7,268	
1811	8,593	5.7	9,671	33.1
1821	10,764	25.3	13,284	37.4
1831	12,232	13.6	19,035	43.3
1841	14,754	20.6	25,068	31.7
1851	16,989	15.1	30,880	23.2
1861	17,611	3.7	34,877	12.9
1871	21,076	19.7	38,654	10.8
Average percentage increase 1801–1871		14.8		27.5

Source: W. Page, *The Victoria History of the Counties of England. A History of the County of York*, Vol. III (1913), Table of Population, 1801–1871, p. 525.

Wakefield's population growth was rather less remarkable. Unlike Huddersfield, which underwent considerable spatial expansion during the century, Wakefield's population growth was largely contained within the town boundaries which were in existence at the end of the eighteenth century. By the turn of the century Wakefield with 8,131 inhabitants was larger than many of its neighbours, including Huddersfield. But failing to profit by either its late eighteenth-century leadership position in the woollen trade or from the coming of the 'railway age', its population increased just two and a half times (an average of 14.8 per cent per decade) between 1801 and 1871. Its growth amounted to half that experienced by Huddersfield.[13]

The population growth of the two communities was linked closely to their very different economic developments during the nineteenth century. By the late eighteenth century the livelihoods of both towns were tied very much to the clothing industry. However, while the story of Huddersfield's economic development in the nineteenth century was, on the whole, one of progress, Wakefield's was one of recession. The middle Calder Valley, including its principal town, Wakefield, did not share fully in the industrial development of the West Riding in the early nineteenth century, to some degree constituting 'an enclave of relative economic backwardness'.

Something like a 'poor man's frontier spirit', seems to have pervaded the economic atmosphere in the areas dominated by the towns of Leeds, Huddersfield and Halifax in the early nineteenth century, but the business mood of Wakefield appears to have been characterised by a devotion to the preservation of order, stability, and memory.[14]

To say Wakefield stagnated during the nineteenth century is perhaps something of an exaggeration. But certainly the town failed to exploit its natural advantages: a plentiful local supply of coal, excellent transport and communications facilities (by early nineteenth-century standards), including a nodal site on the River Calder, and a head start in both the production and marketing of cloth.

Since the Civil War Wakefield had 'enjoyed an uninterrupted course of tranquillity and prosperity',[15] its inhabitants being principally engaged in the woollen trade and agriculture. During the eighteenth century the town's woollen trade became especially prosperous, being dominated by three families of 'merchant princes', the Heywoods, Milnes's and Naylors.[16] The town was particularly important as a 'dressing' and 'finishing' centre. Undyed and unfinished goods were sent to Wakefield before being despatched to London or the continent. A Cloth Hall, specialising in white cloths, was built as early as 1710. Though initially prosperous, by mid-century, the Cloth Hall had lost out to fierce competition from Leeds. However, Wakefield continued to be of importance in the manufacture of broadcloths and 'tammies'[17] throughout the eighteenth century, and in 1778 the Tammy Hall (or Piece Hall) was opened for the sale of tammies, white cloths and blankets. Again the Hall flourished for a short period, but then fell foul of competition, this time the trade migrating from Wakefield to Halifax and Bradford.

The failure of Wakefield to expand commercially was blamed by nineteenth-century commentators on its dominance by a local and inert aristocracy. From the mid-eighteenth century onwards Wakefield had developed into a sought-after residential town, attracting '. . . persons in the higher classes, unconnected with trade; . . .',[18] who did little to forward the town's economic activities or to encourage entrepreneurial initiative. The Reverend C. E. Camidge, Vicar of Wakefield, suggested in 1866 that the town's share in woollen production had gradually become smaller because the aristocracy, who had already made their fortunes, refused to permit factories and workshops to be established in Wakefield:

> . . . they were well content to ride in their carriages and four, and attend the markets in other towns, but would not have the manufactures brought to Wakefield. Indeed they went so far as to have inserted in the indentures of apprenticeship, that those thus bound should not exercise their trade, etc. within seven miles of Wakefield.[19]

The attitude of the leaders of the Wakefield community, F. J. Glover suggests, forced small clothiers, who typically purchased small quantities of wool and then worked it up into finished cloth in their own homes, to seek marketing outlets elsewhere.[20] Manufacturers migrated to Leeds, Bradford, Halifax and Huddersfield, and to a lesser extent to the smaller Calder communities of Batley, Dewsbury and Heckmondwike. During the early nineteenth century many Wakefield merchants were forced out of business because of intense competition from manufacturers based in other textile towns of the region and because of the collapse of the European market. The Naylor family, formerly leading merchants in Yorkshire, typified the failure of the Wakefield merchants to adapt to the changing economic situation and new opportunities, refusing to manufacture, hesitating to enter the American market and clinging to out-of-date trading practices. The Naylors were declared bankrupt in 1825.[21]

In spite of the generally negative response to changes within the textile industry, a small number of Wakefield's inhabitants became involved in the woollen and worsted trade during the nineteenth century, some with much success, and several large worsted mills and dyehouses were established in the town and neighbourhood. By 1832 there were a total of ten woollen and five worsted mills in the Parish of Wakefield.[22] The partial failure of Wakefield's textile industry was tempered by the development of other economic activities, including rope manufacture, wire making, brewing and malting, boat building, agricultural implements and machine manufacture, iron founding, and soap and chemical industries. There were, in addition, many large collieries in the Wakefield area, producing for both domestic and industrial markets. In the year 1872 the Wakefield coal district contained fifty collieries and produced 1,080,195 tons of coal.[23] Wakefield was also surrounded by prosperous farming country. The speciality was market gardening, and Wakefield became a centre of supply for many of its densely populated neighbours.

The chief basis of the town's prosperity, however, was its extensive markets and trade in corn, malt and wool. By the early nineteenth century Wakefield had the largest corn market in the North of England. The town enjoyed good water transport facilities, and, during the century, excellent railway links were established, which enabled a further development of its commercial functions. The market places were extended several times during the nineteenth century to accommodate the increased volume of trade. A weekly market was held every Friday, when a great deal of business was transacted in corn and wool, the latter coming from all over the country to be disposed of to manufacturers in the surrounding districts. Cattle and sheep fairs were also held, and in the 1860s still ranked as 'the first in the north of England', with an average of 800 cows and 6,000 sheep changing hands in one day.[24]

While Wakefield's story during the nineteenth century was, in part at least, one of lost opportunities and lack of enterprise, which resulted in a retarded rate of material growth, Huddersfield's was one of initiative and dynamism. Huddersfield, situated in the Colne Valley, enjoyed great natural advantages for manufacturing purposes in the form of large coal supplies and numerous streams for water power. The town capitalised on its early start in the clothing industry, and built upon the technical skills of an experienced workforce and the entrepreneurial skills of its merchant-manufacturers. New men were attracted to the town, and many small manufacturers, possessing little capital, got the chance to thrive. The textile industry accommodated both small-scale entrepreneurs, dealing with one or two production processes, and the merchant-manufacturers, combining all stages of manufacture and anxious to install the new machinery.

Huddersfield's communications and transport facilities were initially poor and constituted a major barrier to the development of any commercial enterprises. The first improvement in transport arrangements was the rendering of the River Calder navigable from Wakefield to Halifax in the second half of the eighteenth century, which established water carriage facilities within a few miles of Huddersfield. In 1780 a short canal link, the Ramsden Canal, was made from the River Calder to Huddersfield, and a direct connection formed with Halifax, Dewsbury, Wakefield, Leeds, York and Hull. In 1811 a canal link was established westwards through the Pennines to Manchester and Liverpool by means of the Huddersfield Canal. This remarkable and costly feat of engineering 'converted the Colne Valley from a blind alley into a corridor between the manufacturing districts of the West Riding and South Lancashire'.[25] The Canal was crucial to the great expansion of industry in Huddersfield and the rest of the Colne Valley. Improved road transportation, followed by the coming of the railway to Huddersfield in the 1840s, largely superseded the canal system and further improved communications and channels of trade, attracted manufacturers to the district, and increased the town's prosperity.

By the late eighteenth century '. . . the chief occupation of the people, both of Huddersfield and the scattered district around, was the manufacture of cloth. Every house had its loom and its spinning wheel . . .'[26]. In 1768 a large Piece Hall was erected to accommodate small manufacturers by Sir John Ramsden, which was extended by his son in 1780. In 1795 John Aikin remarked that 'the trade of Huddersfield comprises a larger share of the clothing trade of Yorkshire, particularly the finer articles of it'. The town was 'peculiarly the creation of the woollen manufactory, whereby it has been raised from an inconsiderable place, to a great degree of prosperity and population'.[27] Aikin's comments became of increasing validity during the nineteenth century. By the 1830s Huddersfield had become one of the four 'principal seats and emporiums of the Yorkshire woollen manufactures'.[28]

A number of manufacturers took advantage of the new inventions in the textile industry which appeared around the turn of the century and enlarged their units of production. However, most production remained domestic and small scale well into the nineteenth century. In 1790 there were a total of three wool textile mills in the Parish of Huddersfield, by 1810 fourteen and by 1830 32.[29] Crump and Ghorbal describe in their *History of the Huddersfield Woollen Industry* how, by the 1830s, wool was manufactured by a whole range of concerns, from numerous small-scale clothiers 'up to considerable firms, who later built the upland mills and weaving sheds around or near their warehouse and domestic premises'. Most of the mills in the area evolved from domestic bases.

In some cases the manufacturer gathered a few hand looms into his warehouse and there formed a loom shop that was the embryo of the modern mill. In other cases the mill grew out of a dyehouse or a finishing shop . . . it was mainly the merchant-manufacturer, evolved from the clothier, who amalgamated the three branches of the industry into one organisation. When he gathered round the scribbling mill the warehouse and dyehouse of the clothier and the dressing shops of the croppers, with perhaps a few jennies and hand looms, he created a new unit that soon became known as a factory.[30]

The building of mills for woollen cloth production attained high levels in the 1830s, 1840s and 1850s. Between 1833 and 1838 the number of mills in the West Riding increased from 129 to 606,[31] most of which were erected in the districts dominated by Leeds and Huddersfield. A contemporary remarked of the latter town in the early 1830s that 'there are more new mills building (here) than in any other part of Yorkshire'.[32]

Overall cloth manufacture flourished throughout the nineteenth century in Huddersfield, despite several severe trade depressions (of which more pp. 45–49). Wool dominated production, of broad- and narrow cloths, worsteds, tweeds, serges, kerseymeres, cords, and so on. In the 1820s and 1830s the 'fancy trade' was developed in the town and high-quality fancy goods came to be a vital component of the Huddersfield textile industry. The fashion which prevailed in the mid-nineteenth century for coat cloths of light and mixed fabrics was a source of great prosperity to the town, and an injury to the fine broadcloth manufacturers of Leeds and other textile centres. The Huddersfield Cloth Hall, which was extended in 1848, continued to do an immense amount of business throughout the century. It was attended weekly by about 500 manufacturers from the country plus a large number with warehouses in Huddersfield.[33]

By the second half of the nineteenth century, cotton production was also on the increase, and a number of silk spinning mills had been established in the district. Although textiles dominated production, other industries developed during the century, in particular, engineering, card making, and the manufacture of dyestuffs and chemicals, largely offshoots of the woollen industry. There were also a number of large collieries in the area.[34] A weekly market for cattle, corn, pigs and provisions flourished during the nineteenth century. Local agriculture, formerly undeveloped, was given an impetus by the massive population growth in Huddersfield and the surrounding villages, with particular emphasis coming to be placed on wheat and barley production.

2.2 Civic life

By the late eighteenth century Wakefield had reached something of a peak in its civic as well as economic life. By this time its inhabitants had established a number of schooling provisions and voluntary and philanthropic organisations, including the Dispensary in 1787, and several important episcopal and dissenting churches. From 1797 a newspaper, the *Wakefield and Dewsbury Journal*, was published in the town (a second paper, the *Wakefield Star and West Riding Advertiser*, appearing in 1803). Acts for improving the town were passed in the late eighteenth century, and during the same period the market place was resited in Westgate and Assembly Rooms opened. Further civic developments did take place during the nineteenth century, but, by this time, Wakefield could already look 'back to a rich and colourful past'.[35] An elegant new corn exchange was opened in 1837 and a new market place in 1847. Many important voluntary societies were founded early in the nineteenth century; for example, the House of Recovery (1826), the Mechanics' Institute (1820), and the Philosophical and Literary Society (1826), and, in the 1820s, Public Buildings were opened in Wood Street. Lancastrian, National and Church Sunday and day schools were founded during this period to supplement existing charity schools. There was a renewed spate of church building, particularly by Non-Conformist sects, and the first slow steps were taken towards improving the health of the town.

In contrast, at the beginning of the nineteenth century, Huddersfield was in all senses a new community, still little more than a village, supporting few of the institutions or functions normally associated with town life. In the first decades of the century Huddersfield embarked upon its most important period of urban development, a time marked by a massive upsurge in civic activities and consciousness. These developments were linked very closely to the population growth and economic expansion experienced by the town in the first decades of the nineteenth century. They were also closely associated with an influx of pioneering individuals, in particular cloth manufacturers – 'The Huddersfield notables were men who had come into the town, grown with it, moulded it, had their opportunities and perceptions enlarged by it'.[36]

During the first decades of the nineteenth century the appearance of Huddersfield was much improved, the market place rebuilt and modern streets erected. New churches and chapels were founded, most notably the Trinity Church (1819), the Queen Street Wesleyan Chapel (1819) and the Ramsden Street Independent Chapel (1825). A Subscription Library was set up in 1807 and a Philosophical Society in 1825. A National School was opened in 1819, becoming the first schooling provision for poor children in the town. It was followed by a spate of Church schools in the 1830s and 1840s, and in 1845 a second National School was opened at Seedhill. In 1814 the General Dispensary was established, the Infirmary in 1831. In the late 1830s the Huddersfield College and the Collegiate School were founded, followed in 1841 by a Mechanics' Institute. In 1820 the first serious steps towards improving the government of Huddersfield were taken when an Act for 'lighting, watching, cleansing and improving' the town received royal assent. In 1848 a second Improvement Act was granted to Huddersfield. In 1850 the Conservative *Huddersfield Chronicle and West Yorkshire Advertiser* became the first newspaper to be published in the town, closely followed by the Liberal *Huddersfield and Holmfirth Examiner* in 1851. A number of important banking houses were set up in the town in the 1820s and 1830s, and, in 1853, what was to become a highly successful Chamber of Commerce was initiated. In 1845 the *Leeds Mercury* described Huddersfield in glowing colours as '. . . a town of first rate importance, which despite many obstacles has advanced in commercial and social enterprise beyond any in the United Kingdom . . .'.[37]

Local government

The development of institutions for the governance of the two communities took very different forms during the nineteenth century. While Wakefield received its Charter of Incorporation as early as 1848, the inhabitants of Huddersfield had to wait a further twenty years before they obtained the power to elect a Corporation. Huddersfield was unique for its domination by the Ramsden family of Byram Hall, Lords of the Manor and owners of much of the land on which the town was built. The Ramsdens influenced not only the growth and development of the town,[38] but also patterns of voting and religious worship.

Common to the systems of local government in both towns for much of the century was a basic failure to come to grips with problems faced by communities experiencing expansion and change, in particular a large growth in population. Serious pressure was put on already inadequate services for cleansing the towns, providing water supplies, systems of sewerage and waste disposal, and poor relief. The antiquated local government bodies in existence in both towns at the beginning of the nineteenth century were unwilling or legally incapable of adapting to the needs of the communities. The extended authority granted to these bodies during the course of the century only went a small way towards equipping them with the powers required to undertake reform, and could do nothing to overcome barriers of conservatism and inertia.

Up until 1820 the government of Huddersfield was divided between a 'Court Leet' (formally granted to the Ramsden family in the seventeenth century) and the Parish Vestry. While the Vestry had a general power of supervision over the affairs of the Parish (including the administration of the Poor Law), the Court Leet had rather an ill-defined and vague set of powers. Amongst the duties performed by the Court Leet was the appointment of a miscellaneous set of officials, including a Constable, an Inspector of Weights and Measures and a Collector of dead cats, dogs and vermin from the rivers! The Court Leet had no power to levy a rate, and its power was challenged in 1812 and again in 1816 when the inhabitants of the town appointed, in Vestry meetings, a Constable and an Assistant Constable. Neither the Vestry nor the Court Leet had any control over matters of public health.

The first improvement in the government of Huddersfield occurred in 1820 when an application was successfully made to Parliament for an Act for the better 'Lighting and Watching of the town'. The preamble to the Act remarked that

. . . the town of Huddersfield is large and populous (approaching 13,000) and a place of considerable trade, and is also a great thoroughfare for travellers, and some of the streets, lanes and other public passages within the said town, are not lighted or watched, and all of them are not properly cleansed, but are subject to various nuisances, ...[39]

The Commissioners were to meet every three weeks or in an emergency and were to be responsible for the lighting, gas supply, watching and cleansing of Huddersfield. Some progress was made under the Commissioners. They established an efficient police force and improved the appearance of the town. In 1822, gas was introduced to Huddersfield by a private company under the authority of the Commissioners. But the Commissioners' jurisdiction was restricted to a small area of the town (to within 1,200 yards of the old cross in the market place). Moreover, the appointment of the Commissioners had to be approved by the Lord of the Manor, Ramsden. He, together with several other family members, served on the Board, and consequently the town's major landlord also controlled its most important local government body.[40] Another development, albeit a minor one, took place in 1840 when a Board of Highway Surveyors was appointed by the inhabitants of Huddersfield at a Vestry meeting, with powers to keep existing roads in good repair.

By the 1840s the inhabitants of Huddersfield had become increasingly dissatisfied with their system of local government. In contrast with the progress made in other civic and economic spheres, local government remained ineffectual. An application made in 1841 by a group of influential inhabitants for a Charter of Incorporation was rejected, but in 1848 a major step forward was taken with the passing of the Huddersfield Improvement Act. By this Act the government of the town passed to 21 Improvement Commissioners, of which only three were appointed by the Ramsden family. The remaining eighteen were elected annually by the ratepayers, with six retiring each year in rotation.

This Act widened the constitutional basis of local government and gave the Commissioners much greater powers to institute improvements. However, its application was confined to the old boundary set out in the 1820 Act (which included a population of 24,100 out of a total of approximately 30,000 inhabitants). On its circumference many villages and hamlets formed their own local government boards. Moreover, all small ratepayers were excluded from the election process, while the cumulative vote gave larger ratepayers a preponderance in the elections.[41] The Liberal-dominated Improvement Commissioners constituted the local government of the town for a period of twenty years, and, while never willing reformers, during this time they performed a number of useful services. They opened a new cemetery at Birkby on the outskirts of town, paid special attention to the cleansing of lodging houses, set up a large model lodging house in 1854 at a cost of £6,000, constructed new streets, laid down eight miles of main sewers and established an effective police force.

The fact that the jurisdiction of the Commissioners was confined only to the central part of Huddersfield, while its outskirts were expanding rapidly, proved to be a major problem. By the mid-1860s the population of the urban area around Huddersfield was approximately 72,000, with over eleven boards administering its local affairs. The necessity of giving one body the powers to govern this large conurbation formed one of the main considerations in the renewed agitation for a Charter of Incorporation in 1867. The application was supported by the Improvement Commissioners, who, in May, 1867, passed a resolution to authorise their own extinction. A petition in favour of incorporation was signed by 4,933 ratepayers with a rateable value of £106,782. Just over 2,000 ratepayers with a rateable value of only £16,750 were against the application.[42] The poorer ratepayers opposed incorporation, because it promised ambitious and expensive proposals for local improvement. Despite this opposition, in July, 1868 the Borough of Huddersfield was incorporated. The Borough embraced a population of 72,455 and contained twelve wards, with fourteen Aldermen and 42 Councillors. The first Mayor to be elected was the Liberal Charles Henry Jones, JP (great uncle of Asquith). The new Corporation entered quickly and enthusiastically into its work, taking over the town's water supply from the Waterworks Commissioners (1869) and the privately-owned gas works (1872), constructing large new reservoirs (1876 and 1881) and appointing the town's first Medical Officer of Health (1873).

Wakefield had received its Charter of Incorporation twenty years before Huddersfield in 1848. But the town faced similar problems of organisation, particularly in the implementation of sanitary and related improvements, for much of the nineteenth century. Wakefield had taken its first steps towards putting its government on a sounder basis during the late eighteenth century. On account of the 'very ruinous condition of the streets, lanes, alleys, and passages'[43] in the town, a petition was addressed to Parliament, resulting in the Act of 1771, which transferred the government of Wakefield from the Lord of the Manor to a Board of 161 Commissioners. In 1796 a second Improvement Act was implemented. These Acts resulted in minor improvements in the drainage and sewerage of the town and in the state of the streets and market. Private gas works were set up in 1822 and waterworks by an Act of 1837.

By the late 1840s, however, there was much dissatisfaction with the governance of the Street Commissioners. In 1847 a committee was appointed to take the necessary steps to apply for a Charter of Incorporation in consequence of the town's defective arrangements with regard to paving, draining, lighting, sanitary regulations and policing. Following the granting of a Charter in 1848 the government of the Borough was shared by two executive bodies, the Corporation and the Street Commissioners. The latter body of 48 Commissioners still carried out the provisions of the two Improvement Acts, and therefore remained responsible for the paving, sewering, cleansing and lighting of the town, while the newly-formed Corporation confined itself to police functions! The Commisioners, an oligarchic and self-interested group, were incapable of implementing major policy changes, especially with regard to public health provision.

Spending had increased on street improvements and lighting and watching from approximately £800 to £900 per annum in the early nineteenth century to £1,360 in 1845. But the limitations on the amount of rates to be levied of 2s in the pound, and on money to be borrowed to not more than £5,000, were serious barriers to improvement. The jurisdiction of the Commissioners was, moreover, confined only to a small portion of the Township. In 1850 out of the 15½ miles of roads and streets contained within the Wakefield Township, only 3½ miles were controlled by the Street Commissioners. The Highway Surveyors managed a further 4½ miles, while the remaining 7½ miles were not subject to any public superintendence. Other townships in the Borough of Wakefield neither contributed to nor derived any benefit from the application of local Acts. These Acts gave the Street Commissioners only a permissive power to pave the streets and form sewers, and there was no way they could enforce these provisions on private owners of property. Perhaps the most serious obstacle in the way of improvement, however, was the inertia of the Commissioners. While minutes of meetings held in the 1840s show their awareness of the fact that the Improvement Acts were no longer adapted to the needs of the town, there is no evidence of the Commissioners taking any steps to amend the deficiency.[44]

The question of introducing a new Improvement Bill, which would cover the whole Borough of Wakefield and give the power to levy a general rate, was first proposed by the inhabitants of the town in 1845. The Bill that was finally proposed by the Corporation in 1848 never passed into law due to opposition within the town and the failure of the Street Commissioners even to consider the proposals. The Corporation's next move was to petition the Board of Health, setting forth the bad sanitary state of the town, the insufficiency of local Acts and the failure of the Street Commissioners to tackle Wakefield's growing problems with any effectiveness. In 1849 a Sanitary Committee composed of Council members examined the town, and drew up a report in May, 1850. In the following year the Board of Health held an inquiry in Wakefield. Finally, in 1853, the powers of the Commissioners passed to the Wakefield Town Council, who were constituted a local Board of Health. This step did not appear to herald any particular improvement in the governance of the town and, as shall be seen later, progress in the field of public health reform was especially slow and faltering.

Charitable and voluntary society activity
Throughout the nineteenth century Wakefield and Huddersfield contained a high proportion of middle-class inhabitants. This was especially the case in Wakefield, where this sector was made up of businessmen and service groups. Wakefield's main functions as a market and service centre for the West Riding were reflected in its occupational composition. Lawyers were a large and thriving group, and there were also considerable numbers of agents, bankers, accountants and members of the medical profession, some of whom were employed by the asylum or county prison.[45] Using Armstrong's social classification scheme, in 1851 7 per cent of the population of Wakefield could be described as 'Professional', and a further 21 per cent as 'Intermediate', a broadly middle-class group, employing between one and 25 workers.[46] The stability of the middle class in terms of size was reflected in enumerations of registered electors. In 1832 722 inhabitants of Wakefield were registered as being qualified to vote (5.9 per cent of the population). By 1865 the figure was 1,189 (6.1 per cent).[47]

Huddersfield reputedly had a high proportion of middle-class inhabitants compared with other textile towns, this group largely being made up of merchants and manufacturers. The registers of electors reveal that proportionally the middle class more than kept up with the town's population growth. In 1832 there were 415 electors on the register (2.2 per cent of the town's population), in 1847 there were 1,085 voters (3.9 per cent) and by 1865 2,172 (5.9 per cent).[48] In 1851, 11 per cent of Huddersfield households employed resident servants.[49] By 1872 one family in every ten employed at least one female domestic servant.[50] The size and composition of the middle class proved to be more than a determinant of electoral behaviour. It also influenced the type and amount of voluntary society activity undertaken in the two communities.

Both Wakefield and Huddersfield developed the usual range of social, educational, religious and charitable organisations common to nineteenth-century towns, and both were influenced by the Evangelical Movement and Non-Conformist revival of the early nineteenth century, which acted as stimuli to charitable effort and church and school building programmes. By mid-century both towns had their share of schooling provisions for the young, adult education institutes, visiting, temperance and benevolent societies, and a wide range of social and cultural organisations designed for the better-off members of the community, many with a denominational bias. Wakefield had a head start in the founding of charities and other societies, with a considerable number being set up in the eighteenth century or earlier, institutions typical of the pre-industrial period: almshouses, charity schools, a Free Grammar School and private benefactions for the poor. Most of these earlier foundations fell under the control of the Governors of the Wakefield Charities, a body of fourteen townsmen, distinguishable mainly for their conservatism (political and otherwise) and their support of the Established Church.

Huddersfield's voluntary societies and charities were founded, almost without exception, in the early and middle decades of the nineteenth century. In spite of its later start, Huddersfield was able to catch up and even overtake Wakefield in many areas of voluntary activity. In this sphere, as with economic enterprise, the townsmen of Huddersfield showed more dynamism and initiative than their Wakefield counterparts, and, in terms of size and status, Huddersfield's societies were frequently superior. Medical charitable activity provides a good example of this trend. The Wakefield Dispensary (1787) was founded almost thirty years before a similar charity was established in Huddersfield (1814). The Wakefield Dispensary, however, received little support from the inhabitants of the town, barely sufficient to enable its survival and certainly too little to allow for an expansion of its facilities. On the other hand, the Huddersfield institution flourished and expanded. The enthusiasm engendered by the Huddersfield Dispensary was sufficient to support the foundation of an Infirmary in 1831. It was not until the mid-1850s, meanwhile, that hospital provisions on a very limited scale were set up in Wakefield.[51]

The dynamism of the inhabitants of Huddersfield and the large amount of support voluntary activity could command was reflected in other fields. Huddersfield's growing number of inhabitants created a greater need for private charities and amenities; the wealth produced by the woollen industry, meanwhile, was available to fund these enterprises. The Huddersfield Mechanics' Institute, for instance, was founded in 1840, mainly through the efforts of one individual, Mr Frederick Schwann, a successful local manufacturer, Unitarian and temperance reformer. It soon outgrew its first building and in 1860 a new purpose-built Institute was opened in Northumberland Street at the cost of £4,000. By 1859 the Institute had around 780 scholars and 51 teachers.[52] The Huddersfield Mechanics' Institute was reputedly one of the best in England, and by the 1870s it had around 1,500 members.[53] Meanwhile, the Huddersfield College, founded in a similar way in 1838 on the initiative of Mr William Willans, a leading local Non-Conformist and Liberal, developed into one of the finest colleges in the country. Wakefield also supported a successful Mechanics' Institute, which by 1842, following a poor start, had 248 members and by 1866, 744. In 1855 the Institute raised sufficient money, chiefly by means of a bazaar which brought in £3,000, to purchase the Music Saloon for their use.[54] However, it could not match the Huddersfield Institute in either size or reputation. Nor did Wakefield have institutions to compare with the Huddersfield College or other Huddersfield cultural and educational societies. With respect to Sunday school provision, Huddersfield was ahead of Wakefield by the mid-nineteenth century. In 1841 Wakefield had a total of sixteen Sunday schools (of all denominations) with 2,876 scholars. Huddersfield, meanwhile, had 21 Sunday schools and 5,205 scholars.[55]

For our purposes medical charities are of special interest, and a discussion of the Wakefield and Huddersfield Dispensaries and Infirmaries and the Wakefield Fever Hospital will follow in Chapter 4. Aside from these institutions, the provision of medical facilities on a charitable basis was limited in Wakefield and Huddersfield. Both had lying-in charities founded in the early nineteenth century: the Wakefield Female Benefit Society[56] and the Huddersfield Ladies Benevolent Association. These organisations, run by committees of middle-class ladies, aimed to provide linen, other necessities and small payments for lying-in women. Neither apparently provided much in the way of actual medical assistance. Apart from the lying-in charities, several visiting and provident societies, which were often attached to churches or chapels, provided a degree of financial and medical aid to the sick poor. The Huddersfield Provident Union Society, for example, which was connected to the Independent Chapel, was established for the relief of the sick, the support of the aged and to pay for the funeral expenses of those attached to the Chapel. This and similar church-linked societies operated on the basis of both providence (with small contributions being made on a regular basis by the poor) and philanthropy (with financial support also coming from wealthier members of the congregation).

The Huddersfield Benevolent and Visiting Society (1830) sought both to provide religious instruction and to relieve distress and sickness. Emphasis was placed very much, however, on the offering of spiritual as opposed to temporal aid. In only a limited number of cases were the Society's officers prepared to give material assistance to the sick or to call in a medical attendant.[57] This balance in favour of spiritual assistance was apparently typical of most visiting societies. The 'saving of souls' was also the prime objective of the Wakefield Town Mission, although some material and medical relief was provided for the 'deserving' poor, and the Mission did acquire the services of a gratuitous physician, surgeon and dispenser of medicine. The reports of the charity placed emphasis on the spiritual rather than the material benefits received by those visited. In the annual report for 1852, for example, one of the visitors reported that she had visited thirteen families and ten sick persons:

One of these is that of a man in deep poverty, sinking under the influence of disease. I was thankful, through one of the Deacons of Zion, to get some pecuniary relief for him, and, at the same time, presented to his mind the great things of God. Two others, who are consumptive, are, I trust, progressing in the knowledge of the truth as it is in Jesus, and will be ready whenever their Master calls.[58]

Visits to the sick on behalf of the Mission ran into thousands every year, but pecuniary aid and medical treatment appear to have been offered only on rare occasions (as in 1849 when the Mission was made responsible for the distribution of funds to families afflicted by cholera).

Religious life

During the nineteenth century the West Riding (while below the national average for church attendance) had large congregations compared with other industrial regions, and, out of the West Riding, Wakefield and Huddersfield had the highest levels of both church attendance and accommodation. In 1841 Edward Baines recorded high levels of church and chapel accommodation in Wakefield and Huddersfield (see Table 2.2). The towns also recorded high figures for general attendance in the 1851 religious census. The national index of attendance on census day, March 30, 1851 was 61, and this index was exceeded in only fourteen towns throughout the country with over 10,000 inhabitants. All of these with the exception of Wakefield and York were South of the Trent. Meanwhile, the index of attendance for towns with a population of more than 10,000, 49.7, was exceeded in just 21 communities, including Huddersfield. Compared with other Yorkshire towns, church attendance in Wakefield and Huddersfield was extremely high. Wakefield's index of attendance of 71.1 was the highest recorded in any Yorkshire town and Huddersfield came third with an index of 59.6. (York fell in between with a figure of 62.3. Leeds had an index of 47.7, Bradford 42.7, Halifax 41.4 and Sheffield 32.1.) Wakefield had sittings for 70.9 per cent of its population (24.9 per cent Anglican and 46.0 per cent Non-Conformist), Huddersfield for 51.1 per cent (18.8 and 32.3 per cent).[59]

Wakefield and Huddersfield had high rates of both Anglican and Non-Conformist sittings and attendances. Out of a total of 29 towns situated in the chief manufacturing districts in 1851 only Wakefield and Huddersfield could claim church attendance in excess of an index of 25 for both Anglicans and Non-Conformists.[60] The Established Church fared especially well in Wakefield throughout the eighteenth and nineteenth centuries. As early as 1724 Defoe had observed that 'here is a very large (Parish) church, and well filled it is, for here are very few dissenters'.[61] In 1851 the Established Church accounted for 49.6 per cent of attendances in Wakefield, Non-Conformists 47.5 per cent and Catholics 2.9 per cent. In Huddersfield (in common with most other cotton and woollen towns of the North) Non-Conformists accounted for the highest proportion of attendances, with 52.8 per cent of the total. Anglican congregations made up 43.3 per cent of attendances, Catholics 3.9 per cent.[62] By the 1870s Huddersfield had nine episcopal churches and twenty large dissenting chapels, Wakefield seven and ten respectively. Both had one Catholic church.

As shown in Table 2.2, the inhabitants of Wakefield and Huddersfield supported a wide variety of Non-Conformist sects, although Methodism came to have the most outstanding influence on the religious life of both communities during the late eighteenth and nineteenth centuries. By the mid-nineteenth century the major Non-Conformist sects were represented in both towns – Methodists, Baptists, Congregationalists, Quakers and Catholics. The founding of Catholic churches coincided with an influx of Irish into Wakefield and Huddersfield. A Catholic church was opened in Wakefield in 1828. In the same year a Catholic mission was established in Huddersfield, and the Catholic Church of St Patrick's was completed in 1832. In Huddersfield, a number of Protestant businessmen subscribed to the building fund, an indication of the value they placed on Irish labour.[63]

Methodism had an enormous impact on the religious life of Wakefield and Huddersfield. The story of the progress of Methodism in both towns is one of growth and fragmentation. Huddersfield had been strongly Methodist ever since the days when Henry Venn, the Vicar of Huddersfield (1759–1777), had encouraged and supported Wesley on his visits to the town. Wesleyan Methodism made considerable progress in the late eighteenth century, but the formation of the New Connexion in 1797, the first major secession, constituted a serious setback to the Wesleyans. In the Huddersfield circuit membership fell from 1,714 to 949 between 1797 and 1799 due to the success of the New Connexion.[64] In 1814 the High Street New Connexion Chapel was opened in Huddersfield with accommodation for 700. It was rebuilt in 1865 with 1,500 sittings. The New Connexion, with its more democratic

Table 2.2. *Denominational summary of Wakefield and Huddersfield in 1841.*[1]

| Denominations | Wakefield Parish – pop. 28,321 | | | | | Huddersfield Borough – pop. 25,068 | | | | |
| | Church and chapel accommodation | | | Sunday schools | | Church and chapel accommodation | | | Sunday schools | |
	Sittings before 1800	Sittings since 1800	Total sittings	Total teachers	Total scholars	Sittings before 1800	Sittings since 1800	Total sittings	Total teachers	Total scholars
Episcopalians (Anglicans)	3,534	4,150	7,684	91	806	1,620	3,316	4,936	200	1,672
Baptists		600	600	20	70		700	700	10	150
Catholics		400	400	10	86					
Friends	450		450			600		600		
Independents	950	1,150	2,100	157	1,047		2,800	2,800	126	853
Wesleyan Methodists	471	3,540	4,011	223	1,180		4,710	4,710	174	1,005
New Connexion Methodists									176	780
Primitive Methodists		908	908	87	525		1,088	1,088		
Unitarians	700		700	8	120		650	650	50	170
Various		230	230						190	575
Total	6,105	10,978	17,083	596	3,834	2,220	13,264	15,484	926	5,205

Non-Conformist Total	2,571	6,828	9,399	505	3,028	600	9,948	10,548	726	3,533
Total accommodation and Sunday school attendance as a percentage of the population in 1841			60.3		13.5			61.9		20.8
(Non-Conformist Total)			(33.2)		(10.7)			(42.2)		(14.1)

[1] The figures given here are for Wakefield *Parish* and Huddersfield *Borough*.
Source: E. Baines, *The Social, Educational, and Religious State of the Manufacturing Districts*, Table No. IV, Denominational summary of large towns.

structure, proved to be very popular in the manufacturing areas, in particular Sheffield, Leeds, Nottingham and Huddersfield, all towns which had radical associations during the nineteenth century. As E. P. Thompson has suggested, it was probably most popular amongst artisans and weavers tinged with Jacobinism, and, in Huddersfield, members of the New Connexion came to be known as 'Tom Paine Methodists'.[65]

Between 1810 and 1820 Primitive Methodism began to make an impact in the town and a Huddersfield circuit was formed in 1824. Primitive Methodist chapels were opened in 1834 and 1847. Yet, in spite of the competition, Wesleyan Methodists still made up the largest Non-Conformist congregations in the town. By 1840 there were two Wesleyan chapels in Huddersfield which together had accommodation for 3,500 people. The Queen Street Wesleyan Chapel, with 2,000 sittings, was proclaimed as the largest in the country when it was opened in 1819. By mid-century Huddersfield had the strongest Wesleyan congregation in the West Riding, and certainly the one which had grown most rapidly since 1814.[66] By 1851 the total attendance at Methodist chapels in the town represented 34.7 per cent of all church attendances.[67]

The development of Methodism in Wakefield followed similar lines. Wesley also preached with great success in the town, and the first Wesleyan chapel was opened in 1801. However, the New Connexion movement had little influence in Wakefield. Instead, the nationally unimportant Wesleyan Reformers became a significant force, to some extent taking over the position of the Wesleyan Methodists. The Primitive Methodists also had an important impact, the first Wakefield circuit being formed in 1822, the first chapel being erected in 1823. Despite severe losses from the Wesleyan Connexion around the 1850s (and not all those leaving the Wesleyans joined another Methodist denomination), attendance at Methodist chapels in the town in 1851 accounted for 27.7 per cent of all church attendances.[68]

The story of the growth of Methodism is a remarkable one. Perhaps even more remarkable is the fact that, in both Wakefield and Huddersfield, the Established Church managed to adapt to the challenge of Non-Conformity and retain a high level of support throughout the nineteenth century. By the late nineteenth century the parish churches of the two communities still held many worshippers. In Huddersfield this was due in part to the influence of the

Ramsden family, who acted as patrons to the Parish Church throughout the eighteenth and nineteenth centuries. It was also due to the efforts of Anglicans in both communities to increase church accommodation, in particular the number of free sittings. In 1816, for example, Benjamin Haigh Allen, a man with close links with the Evangelical Movement and a personal friend of Wilberforce, proposed that a new church should be built in Huddersfield. He argued that the lack of church sittings was aiding the rapid growth of dissent in the town. Allen gave the land upon which the church was built, paid £12,000 for its erection, and contributed £4,000 for its endowment.[69] In 1819 the Trinity Church was completed, with accommodation for a congregation of 1,500, one-third of which were free sittings. In 1836 the Parish Church was rebuilt. By 1841 there were a total of 4,936 Anglican sittings in the town shared between the Parish Church of St Peter (1,620 sittings) and four other churches. By 1870 a further four churches had been built in Huddersfield and its out-townships, and, by 1872, the Establishment proportion of church accommodation was given as 34.8 per cent.[70] Wakefield made a similar response to the challenge of dissent. By 1841 there were a total of 7,684 Anglican sittings, and between 1839 and 1857 four new churches were consecrated in the town. The Anglican influence was further reinforced in 1888 when Wakefield became the capital of a new diocese.

Political activity

Wakefield and Huddersfield were created boroughs by the 1832 Reform Act, obtaining the privilege of sending one representative to Parliament. The towns showed very different patterns of voting behaviour during the nineteenth century. The politics of Huddersfield were dominated on a popular level by Radicalism, in voting behaviour by Liberalism, or rather until the third quarter of the century by Whig interests. Between 1832 and 1868 a total of fourteen borough elections were held in Huddersfield, and a Whig or Liberal candidate was elected at every one of them (see Table 2.3(b)). The Whig candidates were frequently nominees of the Ramsden family, and in early contests Huddersfield was depicted as a pocket borough. Whigs obtained much of their support from the merchant manufacturers,[71] and were typically supporters of free trade and opponents of the extension of the franchise and factory reform.

Table 2.3(a). *Parliamentary contests in Wakefield, 1832–1865.*

Date of election	Registered electors	Successful candidate	Votes	Party	Other candidates	Votes
December, 1832	722	Daniel Gaskell, Esq.		Lib-Reformer	Returned without opposition	
January, 1835	617	Daniel Gaskell, Esq.	277	Lib-Reformer	Hon. W. S. Lascelles (Cons.)	220
July, 1837	713	Hon. W. S. Lascelles	307	Cons.	Daniel Gaskell, Esq. (Lib.)	281
July, 1841	837	Joseph Holdsworth, Esq.	328	Lib.	Hon. W. S. Lascelles (Cons.)	300
1842	On petition, Mr Holdsworth was declared unduly elected (as having been, at the time of the election, Returning Officer of the Borough), and Mr Lascelles seated in his place.					
July, 1847	780	George Sanders, Esq.	392	Cons.	Geo. W. Alexander, Esq. (Lib–Voluntaryist)	258
July, 1852	848	George Sanders, Esq.	359	Cons.	W. H. Leatham, Esq. (Lib.)	326
March, 1857	967	J. C. D. Charlesworth, Esq.		Cons.	Returned without opposition	
April, 1859	952	W. H. Leatham, Esq.	406	Lib.	J. C. D. Charlesworth, Esq. (Cons.)	403
July, 1859	On petition, Mr Leatham was declared unduly elected, and the writ suspended.					
February, 1862	1,059	Sir J. C. D. Hay	456	Cons.	Richard Smethurst, Esq. (Lib.)	425
July, 1865	1,189	W. H. Leatham, Esq.	507	Lib.	Sir J. C. D. Hay (Cons.)	457

Source: Poll Book of the Wakefield Borough Election, 1865, p.v, WDA (Local Collection W.324).

Table 2.3(b). *Parliamentary contests in Huddersfield, 1832–1868.*

Date of election	Registered electors	Successful candidate	Votes	Party	Other candidates	Votes
December, 1832	415[a]	Captain Lewis Fenton	263	Whig	Captain Joseph Wood (Lib–Radical)	152
January, 1834	489[a]	John Blackburne, K.C.	234	Whig	Michael T. Sadler (Tory–Factory Reformer)	147
					Captain Joseph Wood (Lib–Radical)	108
January, 1835	350[a]	John Blackburne, K.C.	241	Whig	General Johnson (Radical)	109
July, 1837	630[a]	Edward Ellice	340	Whig	Richard Oastler (Tory–Radical–Factory Reformer–Anti-Poor Law)	290
1837	624[a]	W. R. C. Stansfield	323	Whig	Richard Oastler (as above)	301
July, 1841		W. R. C. Stansfield		Whig	Returned without opposition	
July, 1847	1,085	W. R. C. Stansfield	524	Whig	Mr Cheetham (Lib–Voluntaryist)	487
July, 1852	1,400	W. R. C. Stansfield	625	Whig	William Willans (Lib.)	590
1852		On petition, Mr Stansfield was unseated				
April, 1853	1,268[a]	Lord Goderich	675	Lib.	Joseph Starkey (Cons.)	593
March, 1857	1,413[a]	Edward Akroyd	823	Whig	Richard Cobden (Lib.)	590
April, 1859	1,539[a]	E. A. Leatham	779	Lib.	Edward Akroyd (Whig)	760
July, 1865	2,172	T. P. Crosland	1,020	Whig	E. A. Leatham (Lib.)	791
March, 1868	1,900[a]	E. A. Leatham	1,111	Lib.	W. C. Sleigh (Cons.)	789
November, 1868		E. A. Leatham		Lib.	Returned without opposition	

[a] Total number of votes cast.

Sources: D. F. E. Sykes, *op. cit.*, pp. 363–378; C. P. Hobkirk, *op. cit.*, p. 3.

Their challengers were often Radicals, men such as Michael Sadler standing in 1834, Richard Oastler in 1837 and Richard Cobden in 1857, who in most cases stood on a Tory ticket. The Radical candidates were consistently the favourites of the non-voters, and on some occasions these men, standing for such issues as factory reform, extension of the franchise and opposition to the New Poor Law, did surprisingly well at the polls. In 1837 Richard Oastler came closer than any other Radical candidate to winning the election when he polled 301 votes against his opponent, the Whig W. R. C. Stansfield, who collected 323 votes. In 1859 Edward Aldam Leatham, a junior member of the Wakefield banking firm and a prominent Quaker and Liberal, was elected in spite of the combined opposition of the Whigs and Conservatives, and 'the sway of the Whig party in Huddersfield was broken for ever'.[72] From 1859 to 1886 Mr Leatham held the seat save for a period of three years, 1865 to 1868, when he was ousted by Thomas Pearson Crosland.[73]

In Wakefield the pattern was very different, with a more equal division between support for the Liberal and Conservative parties on the part of both the electorate and non-voters. In 1832 the Liberal and Reformer, Daniel Gaskell, was elected as Wakefield's first representative, holding his seat until 1837, when he was defeated by the Conservative, Lascelles. The seat was retained by Conservative candidates until 1865. In 1841 the Liberal candidate, Holdsworth, was elected and then unseated on petition. In 1859 the Conservative deadlock again appeared to have been broken when W. H. Leatham was elected with a majority of three votes. He too was unseated shortly after as a result of a Tory petition. In 1865 Leatham finally won back the seat for the Liberals. From 1832 onwards, however, the vote had been in many cases almost equally divided between Liberal and Conservative candidates, the latter in some cases winning by only a very small majority. (See Table 2.3(a).) Compared with the rest of the West Riding the town had a high Conservative poll, and as late as the 1880s Wakefield was the only constituency in the urbanised West Riding outside Leeds and Sheffield to have an average Unionist poll above 50 per cent.[74]

2.3 Public health and disease

Wakefield and Huddersfield were frequently sketched in glowing colours by contemporary observers in local directories and histories. In the late eighteenth century an American visitor to Wakefield described it, for example, as

> . . . a clothing town wherein appear evident tokens of wealth and taste in building, the avenues to it delightful, . . . the lands here abouts excellent and under the most improved cultivation. The Westgate Street has the noblest appearance of any I ever saw out of London, ...[75]

By the mid-nineteenth century Wakefield was still being represented as an 'opulent and handsome market town'.[76] In 1844 Engels referred to Huddersfield as 'the handsomest by far of all the factory towns of Yorkshire and Lancashire, by reason of its charming situation and modern architecture, . . .', while in the late 1860s Huddersfield was portrayed as 'one of the prettiest and cleanest manufacturing towns in the West Riding, – if not the whole Country', 'well paved, drained, and lighted' with 'many fine buildings'.[77] On the other hand, health reports and accounts of more critical contemporaries pointed to serious problems of overcrowding in sub-standard dwellings, a variety of nuisances, defective sanitary arrangements and inadequate water supply, problems faced by the majority of both towns' inhabitants for most of the nineteenth century.

In terms of living and sanitary conditions Wakefield and Huddersfield seem to have fared better than many of the larger manufacturing towns. The horror stories of Bradford, Sheffield and Manchester were duplicated to a lesser extent in these smaller communities. While facing many of the difficulties common to nineteenth-century manufacturing centres, chief amongst which was a massive population pressure on existing public amenities, Wakefield and Huddersfield experienced them in a much less acute form. The out-townships of Wakefield and more particularly Huddersfield continued to support large industrial populations, which tended to reduce pressure on the town centres. Slum conditions remained confined to streets, courts and smaller districts, such as Wakefield's Nelson Street, Westgate Common and East Moor, and Huddersfield's 'Hell Square' (at the junction of Upperhead Row and Westgate), Windsor Court and Castlegate, all notorious for their appalling conditions and as sites for serious outbreaks of epidemic disease. Spatial separation on a class basis was less advanced in Wakefield and Huddersfield than in the larger manufacturing towns, although there were clear contrasts between certain

Table 2.4. *Mortality rates in selected*
West Riding towns in 1842.

	Deaths	Deaths per thousand
Huddersfield	1 in 55.6	18.0
Halifax	1 in 48.3	21.7
Wakefield	1 in 41.1	24.3
Bradford	1 in 39.8	25.1
Sheffield	1 in 39.0	25.6
Leeds	1 in 36.5	27.4
Average for the West Riding (1839)	1 in 47.6	21.0

Sources: G. C. Holland, MD, *The Vital Statistics of Sheffield* (London and Sheffield, 1843), p. 105; W. Ranger, *op. cit.*, Appendix, p. 67; First Annual Report of the Registrar-General, PP, 1839, XVI (187), Appendix.

areas. In Wakefield high-status St John's was populated by 'aldermen, solicitors and merchants'; speculatively built Lower York Street, 'a mixture of terraces, cottages, and some back-to-back houses', was the residence of 'clerks, tailors and schoolmasters'; Nelson Street, 'seventeenth-century terraced houses infilled with back-to-back dwellings', was the home of 'labourers, rag gatherers and prostitutes'. In Huddersfield the poor lived immediately east and west of the town centre, while the middle classes 'avoided ill drained river valleys, preferring high ground upwind of the town centre'.[78]

Mortality rates for Huddersfield were lower than those experienced by many of its neighbours. In 1822 the number of deaths in Huddersfield was estimated by Dr Walker as one in 54 of the population (or 18.5 in a thousand), a figure which compared with one in 40 (25:1000) for Leeds.[79] By 1842 Huddersfield's mortality rate had become even more favourable compared with other West Riding towns. Wakefield, on the other hand, experienced surprisingly high rates of mortality. The figures cited for Huddersfield in the Registrar-General's Report of 1846 were less promising, although the prevalence of typhus in the town pushed up the death rate for this year; one in 49 for males and one in 52 for females,[80] but were still good compared with other manufacturing centres. Mortality rates for Wakefield were subject to large fluctuations, but on the whole were considerably worse than those of Huddersfield, and comparable with those of larger manufacturing towns. In 1841 one estimate put the rate at one death for every 41 inhabitants (24.5:1000), in 1845 one in 39 (25:1000).[81] Between 1838 and 1848 the number of deaths in Wakefield averaged out to one in 35.6 (28:1000).[82]

For our purposes one of the most important determinants of the success of local government bodies in the two communities was their impact on problems related to public health. As seen in the last Section, Wakefield became incorporated in 1848 and appointed a local Board of Health five years later. Yet progress in this field appears to have been slower than that made in Huddersfield from the mid-nineteenth century onwards under the authority of the Improvement Commissioners. In spite of the apparently greater problems faced by Huddersfield's governing bodies in terms of population pressure, the town received more favourable reports on its sanitary condition than its smaller neighbour. The local government bodies of both towns did make some progress during the first three-quarters of the nineteenth century in the field of sanitary reform (although it was only in the last decades of the century that really concerted efforts began to be made). Progress was, however, at best steady and at worst painfully slow, and the failures of local government in this field had a detrimental effect on the health of the inhabitants of the two towns for much of the century.

Although contemporary reports on the town should not be taken too literally, Huddersfield seems to have fared comparatively well in terms of sanitary and living conditions (especially when we remember the enormous population increase experienced by the town in the early decades of the century). The town, which by nature was 'extremely ill supplied with water for domestic purposes', received an improved supply from springs situated four miles from the town following the establishment of a Waterworks Company in 1827. The town's first major reservoir was completed in 1829. In 1845 a new Water Act was obtained, which empowered the Commissioners to extend the Waterworks. Between 1846 and 1848 around £26,000 was expended in laying pipes and constructing a large reservoir at Longwood.[83] The Second Report into the State of Large Towns and Populous Districts, published in 1845, gave

Huddersfield a relatively favourable write-up.[84] The Report commented that the dominance of the Ramsden family over the town had brought some benefits: most of the streets were of ample width, well arranged and paved, efforts were made to impose building regulations, and much of the main sewerage had been attended to.

Despite the joint progress made by the Ramsden trustees (especially following the tightening up of the management of the Estate in the early 1840s) and the Improvement Commissioners, much remained undone. In 1844 Engels noted that

> It is notorious that in Huddersfield whole streets and many lanes and courts are neither paved nor supplied with sewers nor other drains; that in them refuse, debris, and filth of every sort lies accumulating, festers and rots, and that, nearly everywhere, stagnant water accumulates in pools, in consequence of which the adjoining dwellings must inevitably be bad and filthy, so that in such places diseases arise and threaten the health of the whole town.[85]

The 1845 Report largely concurred with this summary. Neglect of sanitary problems, the Report claimed, resulted directly in outbreaks of fever and a low level of general health. The Report added that the proprietors of private houses were unwilling to foot the expenses of linking up their property to the main sewer. It also pointed to the existence of many nuisances in the town centre, including the usual array of pigsties, dunghills and open privies.[86]

In spring, 1847, during an epidemic of typhus, the Board of Surveyors and Improvement Commissioners appointed an Inspector of Nuisances, Mr William Stocks. Following reports citing several houses belonging to Improvement Commissioners as nuisances, Stocks was dismissed. He had been in office only four months, but during this short period he had served notices on a total of 500 nuisances, including 128 privies, 24 cesspools, 119 rubbish and ash heaps, 27 pigsties, 131 drains and twelve manure heaps, all requiring to be removed, abated or altered.[87] At the public health inquiry held in 1848 to decide upon the necessity of granting Huddersfield a new Improvement Bill, supporters of the Bill complained of the lack of sewerage in the town (only one-quarter of the houses in Huddersfield had, critical witnesses claimed, any drainage), nuisances, poor housing, inadequate cleansing of the streets and a severe shortage of privies. All these factors resulted in a low state of health, especially amongst the poor, and a high incidence of epidemic disease, in particular typhus fever. Joshua Hobson, one of the key witnesses, described the town as a 'mess of incongruities, irregularities, and bad arrangements', Huddersfield being 'pre-eminently a town of courts; and the dwellings of the workers are almost invariably, . . ., built back-to-back'.[88]

The new Board of Commissioners who came into power following the 1848 Inquiry performed a number of useful acts which served to improve the health of the town. The 1848 Act gave the Commissioners extensive powers to improve the sanitary state of Huddersfield, to lay down sewers, widen roads, pave and clean streets and to prevent and remove nuisances. In 1853 the costs of improvements in progress and in contemplation were estimated at £50,000. In the year ending April, 1852 the Commissioners expended £13,644, in the following year £14,828.[89] Perhaps the most important contribution of the Commissioners during their twenty years in office was the laying down of eight miles of main sewers. By the late 1860s, however, much remained to be done. The mortality rate of Huddersfield during the years 1865 to 1868 had risen from totals in the 1840s of approximately 18 per thousand of the population to 24 per thousand.[90] This rate still compared quite favourably with an average of 26.7 per thousand given for the West Riding in 1865. (The national average for the decade beginning 1861 was 22.5 per thousand.)[91]

After 1868 the newly-established Huddersfield Corporation tackled the sanitary problems of the town with some enthusiasm. A Sanitary Committee was set up in 1868 and the first Medical Officer of Health appointed in 1873. The first report of the Sanitary Inspector, delivered in 1869, alluded to the still defective sanitary state of the town and its detrimental effect upon the health of the population. For example,

Groups of nuisances, of the most flagrant kind, met your inspector on every hand. In one case I found sixteen houses, with an average population of five in each, say 80 persons, with only one privy and no ashpit . . . .
The condition of the River and Canal during the past summer and a portion of autumn has been very bad indeed. The stench arising from both of them has been fearful, and cannot have had otherwise than a very prejudicial effect upon the health of the inhabitants . . . it is when the river enters the neighbourhood of the populous districts, and as it passes through the town, that its objectionable and obnoxious condition is most manifest.

More optimistically the Report showed an awareness of the need to deal with these defects as rapidly as possible:

Sanitary science has proved that epidemic, endemic, and contagious diseases have their origin in the infraction of those physical laws and conditions upon which life and health depend, and that 'a great amount of the sickness and mortality in this country depends upon preventable causes'. Believing this I have carefully gone over the Borough with a view to the removal of such nuisances as were most injurious to the public health.[92]

The first MOH, Dr Pritchett, showed a similar awareness of such problems, and his tasks came to include the inspection of dwellings and water supply, and the monitoring of movements of disease. By July, 1873 Pritchett was able to report that the mortality rate for the preceding month had fallen to an average of 16.2 per thousand for the whole Borough.[93]

In Wakefield, the scare resulting from the cholera outbreak of 1849, and to a lesser extent the typhus epidemic of 1846–1847, prompted the Town Council to apply for a Public Health Act for the town. (During the 1849 cholera epidemic it had been left very much to the Board of Guardians to implement sanitary improvements.[94]) The Report linked to the application for a Public Health Act was published in 1852.[95] It pointed not only to the inadequacy of local government control and the ineptitude of the Street Commissioners, but also to poor standards of sewerage, drainage, nuisance removal, housing, water supply and the appalling state of the common lodging houses. For example, it was reported by one of the medical witnesses, Mr Milner, that out of nine districts, comprising 2,707 houses and 13,074 inhabitants, only eight yards and courts had 'good' drainage. In sixteen cases it was 'middling' and in 144 'bad'. (The definition of 'bad' was given as referring to an open gutter or water on the surface of a court or street.) Out of 13,074 people 650 lived in well-drained localities; nearly 12,500 where drainage was partial or non-existent.[96] The Report concluded that the town from its general characteristics of climate and situation, and a general striving for cleanliness by most of its inhabitants, ought to have been 'remarkable' for the general good health of the population,

. . . but that such is not really the case; for although the mortality of Wakefield is below that of some of the neighbouring towns, it is considerably above that of others; and that the real cause of this excessive mortality is to be found in the generally defective nature of the existing sanitary arrangements.[97]

Evidence brought forward relating to specific districts had been especially damning. For example, an inquest held on two cholera victims in September, 1849 had returned a verdict of death from Asiatic Cholera. The Jury had added,

That the street called Nelson-street within the borough of Wakefield, in which they lived, for want of drainage, from foul and improperly constructed privies, from the accumulation of filth and matter of an offensive description, the crowding together in the houses of a much greater number of persons than they ought to contain, . . . is now, and has long been in a state highly dangerous to the public health.[98]

In 1853 the Wakefield Town Council was constituted as the local Board of Health. In spite of this change, and the criticism of the 1852 Report, progress in the field of public health reform was slow. After the struggle to wrest the power to implement sanitary improvements from the Street Commissioners, the Council proved to be just as inept. In 1870 a report was made to the Medical Officer of the Privy Council by Dr John Netten Radcliffe outlining the 'insanitary state' of Wakefield. Both *The Lancet* and the *Medical Times and Gazette* published the Report in part. *The Lancet*[99] expressed particular anxiety about the fact that an average-sized and reasonably wealthy town, which in theory should have enjoyed good sanitary conditions, was in such a poor state. The *Medical Times and Gazette* called the Report 'shocking'.[100] The Report stated that the drainage of Wakefield was still extremely partial, privy accommodation and nuisance removal inadequate, slum housing widespread and the water supply appalling. The water supply of the town was picked out for special criticism. One of the sources of water derived from the River Calder four miles above Wakefield was, the Report claimed

. . . simply ponded sewage, with the added refuse of various manufactories, dye, and other works, which pour into the beck streams of many-coloured and various stinking abominations . . . the town pours into the current, conspicuously to sight and smell, its own especial collective streams of nastiness. Seeing or knowing this, it is not to be wondered at that many of the inhabitants prefer to run the risk arising from the use of water obtained from surface wells rarely altogether safe from the danger of excrementitious contamination.[101]

The Report placed the blame for the defective state of the sanitary arrangements with the local health authority, which was 'grossly in fault'.

Wakefield and Huddersfield were afflicted with the usual range of endemic and epidemic diseases which plagued nineteenth-century towns, chief amongst which were typhus, typhoid and other fevers, diseases of the respiratory and digestive organs (diarrhoea, dysentery, tuberculosis, pneumonia, influenza, and so on) and diseases of childhood. Deaths amongst children were especially high. Between 1837 and 1847 total deaths in Wakefield from all causes amounted to 3,161. Of these 1,402 (44.4 per cent) occurred amongst children aged under five.[102] (See Appendix 1.)

One of the chief witnesses to the 1848 Huddersfield Inquiry, Joshua Hobson, radical journalist, Chartist and public health campaigner, cited in his evidence the returns of the District Registrar, relating to the number and causes of deaths in the town. Towards the end of 1846 there had been much sickness in Huddersfield, 'chiefly in those parts which are notorious for their want of drainage and their general crowded and filthy conditions'. In the quarter ending December, 1846 the number of deaths in the Huddersfield District had been 306, more than twice the figure recorded for any other quarter since 1841. In 1847 the aggregate total for the whole year was 867 deaths. Ninety seven were attributed to typhus, 91 to phthisis, 32 to scarlatina, 38 to pneumonia, 31 to whooping cough, 25 to diarrhoea, nineteen to smallpox, thirteen to bronchitis and seven to influenza. (Other causes of death were not given.)[103]

Serious outbreaks of typhus prompted the setting up of the Wakefield House of Recovery in 1826,[104] and in 1847 the Huddersfield Board of Guardians took the unprecedented step of establishing a Temporary Fever Hospital to deal with typhus cases. In 21 weeks a total of 106 paupers were admitted and treated for typhus fever.[105] Cases of contagious disease accounted for a high proportion of cases treated by both the towns' dispensary charities and Poor Law medical officers.[106] In some years normally endemic diseases erupted in an epidemic form. In 1837, for example, there was a serious outbreak of influenza in Wakefield (and nationally). John Cryer, a Wakefield bookseller, recorded in January, 1837 that

. . . the influenza has been general in the town and every part of the neighbourhood. Last Sunday not less than eleven people lay dead of it in different parts of the town; all the places of worship displayed the effects of it. One day last week there was a lessened attendance of fifty children at the Lancastrian school on account of it. So many persons in so small a time were never known to die as within the last few days.[107]

Even in a 'normal' year, when no serious outbreaks were recorded, deaths from disease remained high. In 1845, for example, zymotic diseases accounted for 103 out of the 407 deaths recorded in Wakefield. Forty three were attributed to measles, seventeen to scarlatina, twelve to typhus and ten to diarrhoea. Tubercular diseases accounted for 73 deaths, lung diseases, including bronchitis, pleurisy, pneumonia and asthma, for 41 deaths, and diseases of the brain, spine and nerves 38.[108] Between 1838 and 1848 deaths from zymotic diseases accounted for 24 per cent of all deaths in the Borough of Wakefield.[109]

In terms of shock and the short-term impact upon mortality rates, the cholera epidemics of 1832 and 1849 had a major effect on the two communities, particularly Wakefield, which suffered badly in both outbreaks. In 1849 the number of deaths in Wakefield was pushed up from an average of 376 (over the previous five years) to 499.[110] In 1832 Huddersfield escaped relatively unscathed, but in Wakefield 62 deaths were recorded from the disease, with a high proportion occurring in the House of Correction.[111] The first case of Asiatic Cholera recorded in Wakefield occurred on 24 June, 1832. John Scaife, a horse keeper at the Strafford Arms coach office, was taken ill at 6.00 am and died by mid-afternoon, despite, as one observer claimed, having been attended by sixteen local doctors.[112]

The Wakefield Board of Health, set up specifically to deal with the threat of cholera, had made some efforts to prepare for such an occurrence. They had been meeting weekly since April, had taken a house for use as a cholera hospital, attempted to clean up some of the town's worst trouble spots, and distributed blankets, clothes and soup to the poor. The wife and children of the first victim were removed immediately to the cholera hospital, the bedding and clothing of the deceased were burnt, the premises fumigated. The body, following a post-mortem examination, was interred on the same evening. The Board and local inhabitants appear to have been optimistic about their chances of containing the disease, which they claimed had been brought to the town by bargemen on the river. The local press warned that cholera was only likely to attack persons with 'drunken or vicious habits' and those who resided in the least cleanly localities, who were therefore 'predisposed' to the disease.[113]

Initially the outbreak did confine itself to the House of Correction. The second case to occur was that of a prisoner, James Petty, who became ill on the same day as the first victim and died the following day. In July, 1832 Dr Crowther reported that there had been 71 cases of cholera in the prison, and that fifteen prisoners had died. The governor of the prison, Mr Edward Shepherd, also contracted the disease and died on 19 August.[114] As the number of cases in the House of Correction were falling off, the disease began to make progress in the town itself. Towards the end of August it was reported that since 24 June there had been a total of 115 cases, with 35 deaths.[115] By late September the cholera outbreak was virtually over, although there were a few isolated cases and fatalities in October. Between June and September there had been 153 cases and 56 deaths (75 cases and 36 deaths occurring in the town itself).[116]

In July, 1832 the *Leeds Mercury* lamented that they had to add Huddersfield 'to the list of infected places'.[117] However, the outbreak in Huddersfield was both short term and mild. In late July the *Mercury* announced that while thirty cases had been reported in the neighbourhood of the town, few had been recorded in Huddersfield itself. The total number of deaths was given as eleven, out of which seven occurred in the Workhouse,[118] situated one mile from the town centre. The disease lingered on until September, but was almost completely confined to the Workhouse and a group of houses adjoining it.

The 1849 epidemic took an even higher toll in Wakefield, resulting in 241 deaths, of which a large number occurred in the Lunatic Asylum. Cases of Asiatic Cholera were first reported in the House of Correction in January, but the main attack began in September. During the 1832 outbreak there appears to have been little criticism of local government agencies. In 1849, however, much of the blame for the severity of the attack was laid at the door of the Street Commissioners. The *Leeds Mercury* reported that the want of a cholera hospital in the town was much felt 'and the wretched substitute of some cottages in Nelson-street, the most unhealthy and degraded part of the town, is a disgrace to the inhabitants, and a gross injustice to the poorer class of sufferers'.[119] The Board of Guardians proved to be the most active agency during the 1849 outbreak. In the first few months of the year they carried out a big clean-up operation in the town, whitewashing and cleansing many dwellings, and removing large numbers of nuisances. By October the epidemic had reached the Wakefield Asylum, and within one month out of the 600 inmates over 100 had died of cholera. The devastating attack was blamed largely on the establishment's 'wretched drainage'.[120]

Huddersfield also suffered more severely in the 1849 outbreak. Again isolated cases of cholera were reported in January, but the main thrust of the attack came between August and October. The epidemic was confined to well-known trouble spots, areas of town where there was a continually high incidence of disease. Birkby, the vicinity of the Workhouse, and Johnny Moor Hill at Paddock were very badly affected. Altogether a total of 52 deaths were recorded from Asiatic Cholera in 1849.[121] Seventeen of the deaths occurred at Johnny Moor Hill, 'the poorest and most filthy part of the village (Paddock), . . . a place notorious for the prevalence of fever and other forms of disease'. Out of the nineteen houses situated there with a total of 110 inhabitants there were twenty cases of cholera and 32 cases of diarrhoea.[122]

2.4 Distress and popular movements

Wakefield and Huddersfield, in particular the latter community and its surrounding villages, were scenes of much working-class distress and a series of popular uprisings during the eighteenth and nineteenth centuries. The late eighteenth century and the period of the Napoleonic Wars were punctuated by food riots, in most cases a direct result of distress caused by rising food prices and shortages of basic commodities. During the first decades of the nineteenth century discontent continued to manifest itself in connection with rising prices and periods of trade depression and unemployment. But during this period popular discontent and uprisings came also to be linked more and more to political issues. Both towns were important centres of Luddism, bases for demonstrations in favour of Reform, centres of support for reforming factory legislation, and in the 1830s and 1840s strongholds of Radicalism and Chartism. The weavers of the district were especially active in the latter movement. Huddersfield was, in addition, the scene of an almost insurrectionary resistance to the New Poor Law and a noted centre of Owenism and trade union activity.

The turn of the nineteenth century was a period of depression for the working class, which was particularly severe in the West Riding.[123] In 1783 when the price of wheat reached 60s a quarter, there were corn riots in Bradford, Halifax and Huddersfield, the rioters demanding an immediate reduction in the price of corn. In 1795 the population of Wakefield was anonymously invited to impose popular prices on commodities brought to the market. In 1799, following a disastrous harvest, a soup kitchen was opened in Huddersfield to supply the poor at 1d a quart. By this time the distress was so great that in November of the same year gangs of half-starved workers seized the town's corn warehouses, and distributed their contents at what they considered to be a fair price, while the women of Huddersfield rioted over the price of potatoes. By 1799 inflation and shortages had pushed the price of wheat up to £6 15s 0d a quarter. Meanwhile, wages in the woollen industry were only around 16 to 18s a week for men and 5 to 6s for women: 'The poorer classes lived on barley, bran, and pea meal, when they could get it'.[124] In May, 1800 there were bread riots in Wakefield, and again in March, 1801 the authorities feared riots, provoked by rising food prices, would take place in Leeds and Huddersfield. In 1801 famine prices were aggravated by underemployment. In Huddersfield, for example, trade was 'extremely dead'.[125]

Perhaps more serious for the authorities was the fact that protest over prices began to be combined with demonstrations against the constitution and the Combination Acts. There were rumblings of Jacobinism in the region in the years following the French Revolution.[126] In 1800 an anonymous warning to the constables of Wakefield ran 'Take care of your life, damn King George . . . and Billy Pitt, may hell be their portion . . .'.[127] In spring, 1801 protest meetings took place in Wakefield and other towns in the region, which coincided with the suspension of Pitt's two Acts, and in 1802 it was reported to Earl Fitzwilliam, Lord Lieutenant of the West Riding, that committees opposed to the Combination Acts were meeting in Wakefield.[128]

Food riots did in fact continue well into the 1840s in the West Riding, but came to be of less significance compared with protests relating to the introduction of machinery, poor working conditions, low wages and efforts to achieve wider political objectives. High prices and poor wages, exacerbated by trade depression, did, however, remain features of working–class life for much of the early nineteenth century. In January, 1820 it was found necessary to set up a subscription charity in Wakefield to relieve distress amongst its poor; to provide bread, oatmeal and soup at reduced prices. Although the appeal was not widely answered by the inhabitants of the town, enough money was raised to relieve about 4,000 persons for eight weeks.[129] In the same year many of the inhabitants of Huddersfield were said to be destitute of food and clothing and suffering the 'severest distress'.[130] In January, 1820 the Earl of Dartmouth donated £300 towards relieving the poor of the town.[131]

In the late 1820s and 1830s there was a severe depression in the Huddersfield fancy trade. A committee of masters established in 1829 that over 13,000 people out of a population of 29,000 subsisted on 2d a day per head when the wage was divided between all family members. It was estimated that in Huddersfield 660 inhabitants earned 6s 11d per week, 421, 3s 6d, 2,439, 2s 9d and 13,226 only 1s 3d.[132] This was, however, a 'curious depression', during which the output of cloth exceeded that of any previous period and the condition of the workers was bluntly attributed to 'the abominable system of reducing wages'.[133]

Still in the 1830s and 1840s the weaving district of Huddersfield and its environs contained a large population of utterly depressed outworkers, subsisting on the poorest diet. 'They do not know what it is, many of them', declared Richard Oastler, 'to taste flesh meat from year's end to year's end . . . and their children will sometimes run to Huddersfield, and beg, and bring a piece in, and it is quite a luxury . . .'.[134] In 1842 it was estimated that 3,196 out of the 25,000 inhabitants of Huddersfield had an average income of 8d per person per week![135] Between 1852 and 1853 a young married couple, both Huddersfield handloom weavers, kept an account of their earnings. Over 104 weeks the woman earned £24 10s 0d or 4s 8½d weekly, her husband £66 7s 7d or 12s 9d weekly, making a total of 17s 5½d per week for their joint labour.[136]

Wages varied considerably within the woollen industry, and this somewhat complicates the picture. In 1800 Mr Gott, a Leeds manufacturer and a pioneer of the factory system, estimated that in the woollen industry men could earn 16 to 18s per week, women 5 to 6s, young children 3s, older children (aged fourteen to eighteen) 5 to 6s and old men 9 to 12s.[137] Around 1825 the wages of Huddersfield handloom weavers ranged from 9s to 17s, the wide margin being due to the irregularity and varying qualities of work.[138] Some highly skilled and specialised sectors of the workforce received high wages. For example, in the 1850s slubbers were paid something in the region of 27s per week, mule spinners 28s and tenterers 26 to 30s.[139] For the majority of the workforce, the weavers, piecers, knotters and burlers, they remained low for much of the century. Between 1832 and 1850 the average wages of male woollen weavers increased from 20s per week to just 21s.[140] As late as 1870 female burlers in the Huddersfield area received only 8 to 9s per week, male wool and piece dyers 18s and cloth dressers 20s.[141]

Distress combined with the introduction of machinery into the textile industry culminated in the Luddite uprisings of the early nineteenth century, perhaps the most serious manifestation of popular discontent to affect the West Riding. The Luddite rising commenced in Nottingham in March, 1811 when rioters destroyed stocking frames. Luddism in Yorkshire and Lancashire was triggered off early in 1812 by the example of the Midlands. Wakefield and Huddersfield were both involved in the movement, in particular the latter, which became one of the chief centres of Yorkshire (and indeed Northern) Luddism. In January, 1812 rumours of impending trouble became so great that the manufacturers of Wakefield placed guards in their mills and a nightly watch was established. By February nightly attacks were being made in the Huddersfield district on gig mills and shearing frames. In January, for example, the Oatlands Mill, Huddersfield, which contained the new cropping machines, was set on fire. In late February the finishing shops of Joseph Hirst and William Hinchliffe of Huddersfield were destroyed, and in the following month machinery was broken at Vickerman's Mills in Huddersfield.[142] In March it was claimed that 'there were 2,782 Sworn Heroes bound in a Bond of Necessity in the Army of Huddersfield alone'.[143] Well-organised attacks were linked with emphatic threatening letters to local manufacturers who dared to introduce the obnoxious machinery.

Many of the smaller manufacturers in the region, faced with an impotent magistracy and military and the hostility of public opinion, gave way and removed the shearing frames. By April, 1812 it became clear that if the Luddites wished to go further they must attempt to destroy the few substantial mills that were still holding out. In late March two mills near Leeds were successfully attacked, and on 9 April Joseph Foster's large cloth factory at

Horbury, near Wakefield, was sacked and cropping machines broken by a contingent of 300 Luddites. The next major attack was on Rawfolds Mill in the Spen Valley. Its proprietor, William Cartwright, was determined to crush the Luddites and protected the mill with armed workmen and soldiers. Around 150 Luddites attacked the mills, led by George Mellor, a young cropper from a finishing shop at Longroyd Bridge, near Huddersfield, a recognised 'King Ludd' of the district (and the son–in–law of Captain Wood). The Luddites were, however, forced to retreat, following a number of deaths and injuries on their side.

Cartwright's example infused a new spirit into the local manufacturers and magistrates. William Horsfall, a manufacturer of Ottiwells, near Huddersfield, for example, armed his workforce and had a cannon mounted in his mill. He vowed that he would 'ride up to the saddle girths in Luddite blood'. The Luddites struck the mill on 27 April, but the attack failed, and Horsfall was assassinated in revenge. When news of Horsfall's death became general, the magistrates redoubled their efforts to capture the leaders of the movement, and millowners stepped up their precautions against attack. The death of Horsfall in fact signalled the end of the Luddite challenge in Yorkshire. The leaders were rounded up, a number were executed or transported, and the movement soon died away.[144]

The death of the Luddite movement was not followed by either an abatement of distress or of popular uprisings. There were sporadic outbreaks of machinery breaking throughout the West Riding, and in 1817 and 1820 there were abortive uprisings in the Huddersfield area. Operatives in the Wakefield and Huddersfield districts were also involved in the Plug Riots of 1842, a year of both great distress and Chartist agitation. Boilers were plugged and machinery shut down at a large number of Huddersfield mills, including Messrs Brooks, Meltham Mills, Stables of Crosland Mills, David Shaw, Son and Co., Beaumont, Vickerman and Co., and John Brook and Sons, Armitage Bridge.[145] This was one of the last instances of law breaking and uprising in the West Riding, and gradually more peaceful forms of protest became prevalent.

The decades of the 1830s and 1840s were ones of almost continual political and popular agitation in the manufacturing districts of the North, movements in which the inhabitants of Wakefield and Huddersfield were very much involved. The early 1830s witnessed campaigns for the Reform and Ten Hours Bills, the late 1830s the Anti-Poor Law Movement. In the 1840s came the agitation of the Anti-Corn Law League and the Chartist movement. In May, 1832, for example, a county Reform meeting held at Wakefield by the Leeds Reformers attracted over 100,000 people.[146] Following the passing of the 1832 Reform Act there was a revival of trade unionism in the region. In 1832 the Operative Builders' Union was formed in Huddersfield, becoming the only union in British history to unite all the building crafts in one body.[147] The district was very much involved in the campaign for reforming factory legislation in the 1830s. Short-Time Committees were organised in the spring of 1831 in Huddersfield, Leeds, Bradford and Keighley, and in June of the same year a group of operatives entered into an alliance with Richard Oastler, uniting his particular brand of Tory paternalism with their Radicalism. The Factory Movement was fiercely resisted by a large and influential group of Huddersfield manufacturers.

In 1837 the Huddersfield Short-Time Committee was mobilised against the implementation of the New Poor Law. In Wakefield opposition to the new administration was moderate and short lived, but in Huddersfield it reached almost insurrectionary proportions. In common with many other Northern towns, ratepayers, Poor Law administrators and populace objected strongly to the 1834 Act, which threatened central interference, an end to out-relief and the introduction of the hated workhouse test. Popular resistance combined with the refusal of the Huddersfield magistrates to help launch the new system and the reluctance of Poor Law administrators to implement the required changes. In 1836 a Poor Law Commissioner was burned in effigy, and mobs repeatedly surrounded the meeting place of the Huddersfield Board. On one occasion the meeting was invaded by a crowd led by Richard Oastler to prevent the transaction of further business.

The organisation of the Factory Movement turned its full force against the New Poor Law. In the Huddersfield area every township appointed a committee from which a delegate was sent to a general committee, which planned a campaign for the whole district. The activities of this and other local committees were co-ordinated by the West Riding Anti-Poor Law Committee presided over by William Stocks, a Huddersfield yarn dealer and a long-standing Ten Hours campaigner (and future Inspector of Nuisances). The Huddersfield Board of Guardians was dominated by members opposed to the New Poor Law, and they refused to proceed to the election of a Union Clerk. The new administration was in theory implemented in Huddersfield in 1837, but the foot-dragging resistance of the Guardians and popular mistrust and resentment of the new regime continued for many years.[148]

3

Poor Law medical relief

Unlike several of the forms of medical relief to be considered in the following chapters, Poor Law medical services have received considerable coverage by historians.[1] Emphasis has, however, generally been placed on the period following the introduction of the New Poor Law in 1834. Moreover, historians have tended to assume that however bad medical provision was during the first years of the New Poor Law administration, it marked the beginnings of a period of improvement on the pre-1834 system. The story of medical relief under the new administration is depicted as one of steady (or at times painfully slow) progress, a result of the appointment of higher calibre medical attendants, better workhouse facilities for the sick, and more generous interpretations of the Orders of 1842 and 1847, which attempted to standardise medical relief. These improvements are said to have culminated in the Metropolitan Poor Law Act of 1867,[2] which although limited to London, 'paved the way for further development in the provinces'.[3]

The provision of medical relief for the destitute was selected for special condemnation by the 1834 Commissioners. Amongst other things, they criticised the contract and tender systems of appointment, the low quality of medical personnel and the lack of formality surrounding medical relief. Yet the report of 1834 'recommended no alteration in the current practice of dealing with the destitute sick by Outdoor Relief and domiciliary medical treatment; and did not even provide for any sick persons in the Workhouses'.[4] The 1834 Commissioners took one step forward and two steps backward with regard to arrangements for medical relief. While condemning the defects of the old system, they failed to suggest what could be put in its place.

In fact medical relief was mentioned in only one clause of the new

Act, which gave the Justices of the Peace power to order medical assistance to be given in cases of sudden illness. There was no specific provision for medical relief on a regular basis. The General Medical Order of 1842 endeavoured to standardise practice, especially with regard to the appointment of medical officers. The Order stipulated that medical officers should hold a double qualification, one of which should be from one of the Colleges of Physicians or Surgeons, the other from a university or the Society of Apothecaries. It also laid down maximum limits for the acreage and population of each medical district of 15,000 acres and 15,000 inhabitants. The Order abolished the tender system of appointments, and instructed that medical officers should appoint substitutes and that a list of permanent paupers should be drawn up, consisting of the sick, infirm and old, who were entitled to medical relief at all times. The General Consolidated Order of 1847 regulated comprehensively all aspects of medical relief, although in effect it merely standardised existing practices. Legislatively then little changed during the decades following the introduction of the Poor Law Amendment Act.

In practice progress was even slower than the legal developments would suggest. The 1842 Order was widely evaded. The limits placed on the size and population of medical districts were frequently exceeded, medical appointees were in many cases inadequately qualified, and the Guardians ignored the provisions for the permanent employment of medical officers.[5] Outdoor medical relief was strictly minimised, while provisions for the sick in workhouses were at best adequate, at their worst appalling. Little evidence has been given by historians to show that there were any substantial improvements in medical relief until the 1860s, that is, until thirty years after the passing of the new Act.

If conditions for the destitute sick were so poor during the first decades of the new administration, it seems hardly credible that they could have been much worse prior to 1834. This assumption will be discussed with reference to Poor Law medical relief in the Wakefield and Huddersfield areas before and after the enactment of 1834, circa 1780 to 1870. The chapter will be divided into two parts. The first Section will look at pre-1834 medical relief, the second Section at medical services under the New Poor Law. Under both the old and new administrations the provision of medical relief by the Poor Law authorities was limited in the North, especially when compared with other parts of the country. But in the Wakefield and Huddersfield districts medical services do appear to have deteriorated after 1834 in a number of ways. Medical relief under the New Poor Law was administered more sparingly; the use of other medical agencies, dispensaries, infirmaries, sick clubs, and so on, as supplements to Poor Law services diminished, as did the range of medical personnel employed. The newly-appointed medical officers got a worse deal with regard to remuneration and workload, which probably was reflected in the standard of treatment they provided.

A few points should be made before proceeding with the discussion of medical services, the first referring to the problem of evidence. The Old and New Poor Law administrators have left us with very different sets of historical evidence. Before 1834 the most useful sources are the overseers' account books, which give details of expenditure, including payments to medical practitioners and other medical expenses. The account books were checked by local magistrates and ratepayers, and therefore constitute a fairly reliable source of evidence. Unfortunately, few overseers' accounts have survived for the Townships of Wakefield and Huddersfield themselves, but there is an abundance of material on adjacent townships, which after 1837 came to be included in the new Unions based around Wakefield and Huddersfield.[6] These accounts are supplemented by vestry minute books, and medical bills and contracts, drawn up between overseers and doctors.

Evidence used for the period after 1834 includes the minute books of the Huddersfield Board of Guardians,[7] nineteenth-century parliamentary inquiries into the provision of medical poor relief,[8] the accounts of the Boards of Guardians, correspondence between the central administration and the Wakefield and Huddersfield Boards, and local newspapers. The minute books and accounts, while detailing the salaries paid to medical officers, and the sums spent annually on vaccination, midwifery cases, subscriptions to medical charities and lunacy accounts, give little further evidence of the 'kind' of medical treatment provided. There are few details of the number of visits medical men made to the sick or of the types of medicines and other relief they dispensed. Any supplementary relief to the sick given in the form of extra food, alcoholic stimulants, bedding, fuel or additional money payments are not listed separately, and are therefore indistinguishable from other payments for out-relief.

Nineteenth-century Poor Law administration in the North, not least the provision of medical services, was unique in several ways. The increasing cost of poor relief in the early part of the century, together with the massive population growth of the region, prompted Poor Law administrators in many West Riding townships to tighten up their systems of relief. During the first few decades of the nineteenth century many townships set up select vestries with up to twenty elected members, 'substantial householders', plus the vicar, churchwardens and overseers as ex-officio members. The select vestries differed little in function or composition from the Boards of Guardians set up after 1834. Some townships also appointed salaried officers to supervise poor relief, the most usual appointee being the assistant overseer.[9] A Select Vestry was established in Huddersfield early in the nineteenth century. Wakefield did not set up a select vestry, but poor relief was administered by a committee of ratepayers, which dated back to before 1819.[10] Meanwhile, several neighbouring townships had opted for select vestry administration by the 1830s: for example, Mirfield in 1819, Dewsbury in 1820 and South Crosland in 1828. South Crosland, with only 2,000 inhabitants, also appointed a standing overseer in 1828 at a salary of £24 per annum.[11] By 1830 the West Riding had a total of 161 select vestries, with about one-quarter of the Riding's townships having implemented this administrative change.[12]

Payment of relief was carefully regulated under the new administrations, and the cost of poor relief fell in the West Riding in the decades prior to 1834, tending to be much lower than in other counties. By 1831 poor relief in the West Riding cost only 5s 7d per head of the county's population compared with 18s 3d in Suffolk, 16s 6d in Wiltshire and 15s 4d in Norfolk. Between 1817 and 1822 the cost of poor relief in the Riding had fallen by 31 per cent. Expenditure dropped further from a figure of £252,000 in 1833 to £180,000 in 1837.[13] By 1834 many Northern townships had adopted the system of using the workhouse as a deterrent to the idle and dissolute; others made relief to the able-bodied dependent upon their performing tasks of work. In Huddersfield, for example, the able-bodied were employed in street cleaning, and the workhouse deterrent was also utilised before 1834.[14]

By 1834 poor relief in the West Riding was on the whole efficiently administered and cheap, and well adapted to local patterns of poverty. Poor Law administrators in this and other Northern regions saw no reason why the 1834 Act should be any concern of the North. The 1834 Commissioners had after all been most concerned with the corrupt and inefficient administration of poor relief in the agrarian South, and had largely ignored the special problems of the Northern manufacturing districts.[15] Chief amongst these problems were the seasonal and large-scale periods of unemployment, which followed in the footsteps of trade depression, particularly in the textile industry. Large numbers of normally independent workers were thrown temporarily onto the poor rate or public and private charity. The normal practice adopted by the overseers during these periods was to make small payments of out-relief to tide the unemployed over the period of depression. Under these circumstances the last thing the Poor Law administrators of the North wanted was to bring this large group into the workhouse, depriving them of their independence and causing them to become a permanent burden on the poor rate. The size of the problem can be judged by the fact that during 1842, a year of 'severe and widespread distress', more than 11,000 people, over one-tenth of the population of the Huddersfield Union, were in receipt of parish relief.[16]

The policies of Northern administrators were at complete variance with the ideology of the 1834 Act, which placed emphasis on the principle of 'less eligibility' and the workhouse test. The 1834 Act deterred Guardians from paying out-relief to the able-bodied, insisting that this group, on application for assistance, should be brought into the workhouse. This important division in both opinion and practice brought the manufacturing districts of the North into fierce conflict with the Poor Law Commissioners, and resulted in massive opposition to the new Act by both the Poor Law administrators and magistrates and the working class. The 1834 Act was opposed in Wakefield and Huddersfield, resistance being especially strong in Huddersfield.[17] The medical profession of Wakefield and Huddersfield forwarded petitions to the Poor Law Commissioners, opposing changes in the system of providing medical relief to the poor. The inhabitants of Huddersfield also sent a petition appealing for a total repeal of the Poor Law Amendment Act, as did several other local townships, including Horbury, Almondbury, Deighton, Lindley, Linthwaite and Mirfield.[18]

The final point to be made here, and the most important for our purposes, is that medical relief in the North, including the West

Riding, was given only on a small scale throughout the nineteenth century. The introduction of the Poor Law Amendment Act made little difference to the amount of medical relief provided for the poor of this area. In 1843 the cost of Poor Law medical relief in the West Riding was calculated at 1d per head of the population. This was less than anywhere else in the nation. The average for the country was $2\frac{1}{2}$d per annum, and the cost of medical relief was highest in Essex at 6d per head.[19] The low cost of medical poor relief in the North was referred to in every nineteenth-century parliamentary inquiry on the subject. The reasons given for this phenomenon never varied: the existence of a strong network of medical charities, including many dispensaries, and large numbers of friendly societies and medical clubs, and a greater tendency on the part of the poor to resort to quack medicine and the druggist.[20] The low cost of medical care (and indeed all other forms of poor relief) was also attributed to the more independent character of the Northern labourer, who was unwilling to look to the parish for medical assistance. In 1839 Mr Power, Assistant Poor Law Commissioner for the West Riding of Yorkshire and Lancashire, stated that the low cost of medical relief under the old administration in his region was due to

A close spirit of economy in relieving the poor on the part of the assistant overseers and vestries: a great degree of hardihood and independence in the mass of the people; the existence of numerous clubs and societies, providing against the contingency of sickness, and embracing large numbers of the operative classes; . . . .[21]

A further reason for the low cost of medical relief in this region, and one referred to rather less by contemporaries, was that, despite the dislocations caused by trade depressions in the North, it was far wealthier than many Southern and Midland regions. Overall, there was less poverty and fewer permanent paupers.

3.1 Medical relief under the Old Poor Law

In 1839 Mr Power summed up the provision of medical poor relief in the West Riding and Lancashire under the Old Poor Law thus:

. . . with scarcely any exception, through the whole district, the medical relief, of which any distinct account could be found in the township books, bore an extremely small proportion to the population, and to the general expenditure on the poor.[22]

In evidence given to the 1844 Select Committee Report on Medical Poor Relief it was maintained that before 1834 the amount spent on medical relief in the North was one-sixth of that expended in Southern and Midland counties.[23] In the Wakefield and Huddersfield areas (and probably throughout much of the North) Poor Law medical relief was the least important form of medical provision in existence for the poor throughout the nineteenth century. In Wakefield, Huddersfield and their surrounding townships medical relief did not normally exceed 5 per cent of total poor relief expenditure, or 2d per head of the population.

The 1844 inquiry and other nineteenth-century reports on poor relief also remarked upon the complete absence of 'systematic' medical relief in the Northern manufacturing districts. It is true that arrangements for the medical relief of the destitute varied from township to township in the North. But by early in the nineteenth century many townships had developed rudimentary systems of dealing with medical relief, which were reasonably well adapted to their large populations and the pattern of poverty in the region. Provisions existed on a small scale for the relief of the sick in the workhouse. However, in common with other forms of relief, most medical assistance was given to the outdoor poor, those who could normally manage on their wages, but who in times of depression and unemployment, or in special circumstances, such as the birth of a child or the sickness of a family member, were forced to turn to the parish.

Medical relief was provided through the payment of doctors' bills on behalf of paupers and others thought eligible for this form of assistance. This was organised in various ways. In some cases the parish would pay medical men for individual patients, usually after a bill had already been run up. In January, 1815, for example, the Overseers of South Crosland paid Thomas Jessop two guineas 'his bill for Doctoring Matthew Oldfield' and £4 5s to Joseph Taylor for 'Doctoring and attending upon Joseph Thornton'.[24] Another method was to allow a number of doctors to run up yearly or half-yearly accounts for their treatment of the destitute. In 1812 the Mirfield Overseers paid three local medical practitioners almost £78 for attendance during the year: Dr Taylor £13 8s, Dr Kitson £23 15s and Dr Green £40 15s.[25] For those of the poor believed capable of paying something towards their medical expenses, the parish authorised part payment of medical bills. Finally, a few parishes, usually larger ones, chose to appoint a doctor under contract to supply medicine and advice to all those deemed eligible by the overseers. The method of relief adopted varied from parish to parish, and not infrequently the different methods of paying for medical assistance existed together within one parish. In some cases a contract surgeon was appointed, and at the same time individual bills were paid to other medical practitioners.

Medical contracts drawn up under the Old Poor Law were apparently very much alike. In them the doctor agreed to provide medical attention and drugs for a specified time in return for a fixed payment. Certain items were commonly excluded: smallpox vaccination, midwifery cases and broken bones. For the last two, fixed prices per case were often agreed upon. In June, 1773, for example, the Wakefield Overseers (catering for a Township population of about 7,500) drew up the following contract with Benjamin Stocks, apothecary:

June 3^d 1773 'Agreed wth Mr Ben^n Stocks to Serve this House and all out Pentioners, wth medicines, & to Deliver all the Women that requires his assistance, within this House, for Twenty Guineas a Year; it is allso agreed That he be allow for attendg all persons wth Broaken Bones; and half a Guinea for Delivering each Person out of the House, that the Overseers appoint him to attend as Witness our Hands the Date above . . . .[26]

By early in the nineteenth century the Overseers of Mirfield, a large clothing village with 5,000 inhabitants, situated midway between Wakefield and Huddersfield, had also made it their usual practice to employ a contract surgeon. Competition between Mirfield practitioners for the post was keen. In 1813 the Overseers decided that Mr Kitson was entitled to

. . . the greatest proportion of medical assistance allowed to Poor Persons and paid by the Parish on the Ground that he has resided longer in the Township and pays a greater proportion of Poor Rates than either of the others and also is ready and willing to come forward with the first in the Parish in any Subscription tending to relieve the distress of the Poor.[27]

In later years the Overseers fluctuated between the policies of appointing a single contract surgeon for the poor and dividing the contract up between the various applicants. Either way competition for the post no doubt enabled the Overseers to keep medical costs down, although compared with post-1834 appointments the Mirfield Overseers were not ungenerous. In 1816 Mr Kitson was paid £50 for attendance on the poor. He was paid separately for journeys

out of town and midwifery cases. In 1818 Mr Parker was paid £30
for the year, and in 1820 Mr Hoyle £22 10s. In 1822 it was resolved
that Messrs Kitson, Parker and Hoyle should take the contract 'in
rotation at the sum of Forty Pound pr year for the term of three
years'.[28] The contracts were in theory to cover most medical
assistance, the exception being midwifery cases: 'women wanting
assistance at delivery Shall have a Choice in the Doctor'.[29] In
practice, however, the Overseers appear not to have forced the poor
to obtain medical relief from the contract surgeon. In 1818, for
example, although the contract was given to Mr Parker, at least
three other regular practitioners ran up medical bills, which were
settled by the Overseers.[30] The most liberal overseers, usually in
small townships, paid paupers sums of money, presumably to
enable them to seek medical assistance where they chose. In July,
1795 the Overseers of South Crosland paid 8s 6d to 'William
Beaumont wife for Husband Doctors Bill'. In 1800 they paid Nancy
Taylor and Sarah Dyson 3s and 4s 6d respectively 'to go to Doctor
with'.[31]

In most cases the Overseers had little choice in their selection of
medical men, especially if they wished to employ one resident in
their particular township. Normally they employed the nearest
available medical practitioners, always surgeons,[32] supplementing
their services with 'specialists' from Wakefield and Huddersfield in
more serious cases. During the first decade of the nineteenth
century the Overseers of Stanley Township, near Wakefield, ran up
medical bills with three Wakefield surgeons, Messrs Mitchell,
Statter and Stott.[33] All three had well-established surgical/general
practices, and were the nearest alternatives, there being no resident
doctor in Stanley. In Mirfield the Overseers rotated medical
appointments between the three or four resident village surgeons.
Before 1834, for reasons of convenience, cost and lack of alternatives, pauper patients were usually treated by the same medical
personnel as private patients. Contracted posts provided a steady
and often substantial source of income for a medical man, while the
fees paid for individual cases were frequently equivalent to those
paid by private patients. Either way Poor Law appointments prior
to 1834 seem likely to have been attractive to local medical practitioners.

The most usual cases treated by Poor Law medical appointees
were broken limbs and other injuries, fevers, children's diseases and

chronic diseases of old age, rheumatism, dropsy, chest infections, and so on. Regular medical men shared obstetric cases with the midwife, the midwife probably attending over half of all pauper confinements. Common items of medical expenditure listed in the account books were for the setting of fractures, bleeding, ointments, salves and a wide variety of pills and medicines, plus charges for visits to the sick. In most townships and in most years midwifery expenses (together with the costs of maintaining lunatics) topped the list.

The attendance of regular, qualified doctors was supplemented by the services of a wide range of 'fringe' practitioners. Indeed, one of the most interesting aspects of medical relief under the Old Poor Law was its variety. Payments were recorded in the Overseers' account books to a large number of fringe personnel, including a variety of local healers, bonesetters, doctresses, and most commonly midwives. Sums of money were also given to enable the poor to visit more distant specialists, spas, and in a few cases the seaside. In October, 1784, for example, the Mirfield Overseers paid 2s 6d to the 'Boansetter for Bet. Swift' and in April, 1795 10s 6d 'To Milnes Wife for Cureing John Child Children'.[34] In the early nineteenth century the Overseers of South Crosland, near Huddersfield, authorised payments, usually of several shillings, to enable the sick of their Township to visit the Whitworth[35] and Denby doctors, and 'pd Samuel Holstead wife £3 10s to go to Blackpool for the benefit of her eyes'.[36] In 1788 all eight delivery cases paid for by the Huddersfield Overseers were attended by midwives.[37] It is difficult to be precise about the extent to which fringe medical personnel were employed. The status of medical practitioners is not always clear from entries in account books. In some cases regular medical men were distinguished by the title 'doctor', in other cases they were referred to simply as 'Mr' or even by their first names, Thomas Jessop, Joseph Taylor, and so on. But it appears that up until the early decades of the nineteenth century at least half of the pauper deliveries, in and out of the workhouse, were attended by midwives. Meanwhile, something like one-quarter of all medical complaints were treated by fringe personnel.

Medical treatment by qualified and unqualified practitioners was further supplemented by the services of local medical charities. The overseers ran up bills or paid subscriptions to the infirmaries at Leeds and York to enable them to send more serious cases to these establishments for treatment. As early as 1751 the Overseers of the Wakefield Township paid £1 2s 6d to 'Wm Webster for admittance into the Infirmary & for expenses to carry him to Yorke'.[38] In 1810 the Mirfield Overseers paid 4s for 'Sheard Betty to go to Infirmary', in 1818 8s for 'Jno Muffitts Son to go to the Infirmary' and in 1820 1s 6d to Wm Wilman for the same purpose. The Mirfield Overseers also paid out large sums to maintain a blind boy at the Liverpool School for the Blind. In 1815 the payments totalled £5 and by 1817 £12.[39]

The removal of sick paupers to a distant medical institution was an expensive business for the overseers. In addition to paying either a subscription or a bill for maintenance, travelling expenses were incurred, plus charges for providing the patient with clothing, linen and other necessities, and in some cases funeral costs. Because of the expense, the sick poor were normally only sent to an infirmary as a last resort, in many cases after considerable sums had already been spent on medical attendance, drugs and nursing. In December, 1821, for example, the Overseers of Horbury, near Wakefield, made arrangements for William Procter's wife to be sent to the Leeds Infirmary. She apparently had been ill for some time, and the Overseers had already spent several pounds on nursing and medical attendance:

December 24, 1821	£ s d
Rebecca Coope for attending W. Procter's Wife	6 6
Journey to Leeds Infirmary with a Recommendation for Wm Procter's Wife	2 6
Letter from Leeds Infirmary	5
Wm Procter's Wife	1 0
Expenses to Leeds Horses Cart with Wm Procter's Wife	5 0
To Bedgown making for W. Procter's Wife	6
Wid. Chappell for making Lint Shoes for W. Procter's Wife	1 4

In this case the treatment received at the Leeds Infirmary appears to have been successful, and in January, 1822 a payment of 3s 9½d was recorded to 'Samuel Bainds for W. Procter's Wife from Leeds'. No further expenses were recorded in the Overseers' account books for Mrs Procter.[40]

The rigid admission policies maintained by many medical charities acted as a further limitation on the transference of paupers to these institutions. Almost without exception medical charities received more applications for admission than they could handle. Infirmaries operated very much on a 'first come first served' basis, or restricted admissions to more serious and acute complaints. Some excluded paupers altogether. Despite these limitations, overseers in the Wakefield and Huddersfield areas found it beneficial to continue to subscribe to medical charities up until the mid-1830s. In 1830, for example, the Ossett Overseers paid a six guinea subscription to the Leeds Infirmary,[41] and in 1835 the Wakefield Township's subscriptions to the Leeds Infirmary and Ilkley Bath Charity together totalled £13 5s 3d.[42]

Following the establishment of medical charities closer to home – the Wakefield Dispensary in 1787, the Huddersfield Dispensary in 1814 and Infirmary in 1831, and the Wakefield House of Recovery in 1826 – local parishes frequently opted to subscribe to them. However, the policies of these charities regarding the admission of paupers varied considerably during the late eighteenth and nineteenth centuries. During the 1790s the Overseers of the Wakefield Township paid an annual subscription of £30 to the Dispensary.[43] This seemingly accounted for the bulk of medical relief paid for out of the rates in this decade, the Dispensary being expected to treat all sick paupers in return for this large subscription. By the early nineteenth century, however, this policy had been dropped, and the Wakefield Overseers no longer subscribed to the Dispensary. Nor apparently did the Overseers of the Wakefield Township or any other local townships take advantage of the provisions for the admission of paupers to the Wakefield House of Recovery. After 1837, on the other hand, the Wakefield Board of Guardians came to make extensive use of this facility. A number of local townships did subscribe to the Huddersfield Dispensary and Infirmary under the old administration. In return for a subscription of three guineas per annum, overseers obtained the privilege of having one in-patient or two out-patients on the charity's books at a time.[44] The townships taking advantage of this facility were generally those with small populations, who perhaps found charitable subscriptions relieved them to some extent from the necessity of employing medical officers. By 1831 four townships subscribed to the Infirmary – Farnley Tyas (population, 900), Netherthong (1,000), Heckmondwike (3,000) and Linthwaite (2,500). The Overseers of the Huddersfield Township (population, 19,000) appear not to have been subscribers.[45]

The largest item of expenditure in the category of medical relief during the nineteenth century was payment for the care and maintenance of lunatics. Because mental illness was usually either long term or permanent, it constituted a specially expensive form of relief. Up until the early nineteenth century the usual practice with regard to lunatics was to maintain the least harmless and disruptive in either their own homes or in lodgings, or, if no other alternative could be found, in the parish workhouse. The more dangerous cases were sent to local private asylums or to Bethlem. In 1775, for example, the Overseers of Horbury Township moved Jno. Hoyle from the Workhouse to 'Bedlam'.[46] These more expensive alternatives were, however, avoided where possible. By the early nineteenth century the weekly charge for maintaining a pauper lunatic in a private institution could amount to between 9s and 12s.[47]

In 1818 the West Riding County Lunatic Asylum was established at Wakefield, and it became more usual for local overseers to send violent or troublesome cases to this institution for incarceration and/or treatment. The maintenance of lunatics at Wakefield became a huge financial burden for the ratepayers. By the 1820s the Overseers of Horbury Township spent something in the region of £20 per annum for the maintenance of lunatic paupers at Wakefield.[48] In 1830 the Overseers of Ossett, near Wakefield, paid £8 8s 6d for the maintenance of just one patient in the Wakefield Asylum for 26 weeks, at the rate of 6s 6d a week.[49] Expenses for the maintenance of lunatics belonging to the Mirfield Township amounted to between £60 and £80 per annum by the 1830s, accounting for well over half of all medical expenses.[50] By 1835 Wakefield Township's lunatic asylum account came to a massive £233. Total expenditure on medical relief during the year amounted to £358, with asylum fees making up 65 per cent of the total.[51]

Another common method of providing medical relief for the pauper or near-pauper in the North was through the payment of admission fees and subscriptions to sick clubs and friendly societies. The preponderance of friendly societies in the Wakefield and Huddersfield districts made this a viable alternative for local overseers,[52] and the practice seems to have been fairly widespread. The Horbury Overseers, for example, kept up the friendly society subscriptions of a number of individuals during the 1820s.[53] In 1820 the Mirfield Overseers paid a total of £3 5s for club subscriptions on behalf of ten individuals, which accounted for almost 10 per cent of the year's total medical expenses of £36.[54] The payment of friendly society subscriptions relieved overseers from the responsibility of giving out-relief to the sick, as friendly societies paid a small weekly dole to sick members. By early in the nineteenth century a few societies also made provision for sick members to be attended by a club surgeon.[55] The payment of friendly society subscriptions by parishes may have been, as Gosden suggests,[56] largely confined to the preservation of the membership rights of sick and aged members, who were likely to become a major burden on the poor rates. But overseers may also have been willing to keep up the subscriptions of members faced with temporary financial difficulties, or even have paid subscriptions on a more permanent basis. For something in the region of 10s a year, the overseers could relieve themselves from the burden of paying out-relief (and in some cases from supplying medical attendance and drugs) to potential candidates for sick relief.

Under both the Old and New Northern Poor Law administrations only a very small proportion of relief was provided in the workhouse. In normal circumstances only the old, infirm and helpless were taken into the workhouse. In the Wakefield and Huddersfield areas the old poorhouses were usually small and ill-adapted for the admittance of more than a small number of paupers. During the 1780s there were generally between 25 and 35 paupers at any one time in the Mirfield Workhouse; by the 1820s between 20 and 30.[57] Expenditure on indoor relief was also low. In the early nineteenth century the Mirfield Overseers normally spent something in the region of £300 to £400 on indoor relief compared with £1,500 to £2,000 on out-relief. Medical relief to indoor paupers was also comparatively limited. If a contract surgeon was employed, the contract normally included attendance at the workhouse and the delivery of female indoor paupers. Otherwise medical attendance was provided for in the same way as outdoor medical relief, through the payment of doctors' bills. The most frequent indoor medical expenses were for midwifery cases. Other bills were run up for the bleeding of indoor paupers, the treatment of injuries, for leeches and a variety of pills and potions. In 1778, for instance, the Mirfield Workhouse diary and account Book recorded expenses totalling only £2 2s 9d for medical relief and associated expenses:[58]

		£	s	d
Jan^ry 12	To Rose Gooder for laying Elin Thornton		2	6
Feb^ry 27	To Mr Ismay for churching[59] Elin Thornton		1	0
April 23	To Roas Gooder for laying Ann Vevers		2	6
	To Dr Ladley for cuering Alse Firth of veneral diseas		15	0
June 30	Dr Lee for bleding Jo Smith			3
Aug^st 24	To a Bottall of Dr Lee for Mer^m Holdsworth		1	6
		2	2	9

In 1802 the total expenses for the medical relief of indoor paupers in the Mirfield Workhouse came to £2 3s 1d, including 19s for midwifery cases:[60]

		£	s	d
Jan 18	Itch Salves		1	0
March 27	To Molly Holroyd for Delivering Mary Sykes		2	6
April 15	To Inman Leg Setting & a Rubbing Bottle		3	6
	To Jona^n Milner Horse to Carry Inman to Lockwood.[61]			8
April 29	To Doctor Taylor for Ben. Inman leg Dressing Bottle & Salve		2	0
	To a Box of Pill 6d To Drugs for Eye Waters 4d			10
June 12	To Doctor Taylor for Jane Hirst Arm & Inman Leg		3	6
June 21	To Doctor Taylor for Jo Smith Thum 2s 6d our Exps 3d		2	9
June 23	To Doctor Kitson for Delivering Eliz^h Sykes		10	6
Aug 16	To Gibson of Bradley for Curing Crabb Hand[62]		2	0
Sept 7	a Rubbing Bottle 6d			6
Oct 16	To Churching of Secker		1	0
	To Molly Holroyd for Delivering Do		2	6
Oct 21	To Doctor Jubb as per Bill		6	10
Dec 8	To Quick Silver 6d			6
Dec 31	To Amy France for Delivering Ann Fawcet		2	6
		2	3	1

The total cost of medical relief, both in and out of the workhouse, generally amounted to very little. In 1788 the medical bills run up by the Huddersfield Overseers accounted for just over 3 per cent of outdoor relief.[63] In 1811 expenditure on medical relief made up less than 4 per cent of indoor and outdoor relief in the Mirfield Township.[64] In 1835 the Wakefield Overseers expended just over £358 on medical relief out of a total expenditure of £6,037 (5.9 per cent). If we deduct the sum of £233 spent on the maintenance of lunatics in the Wakefield Asylum, the amount spent on medical relief falls to just over 2 per cent of the total expenditure.[65]

Cost-conscious overseers were anxious to find ways to reduce expenditure on the sick. This explains their willingness to make the treatment of sick paupers the responsibility of sick clubs, medical charities and contract surgeons. It also explains, in part at least, why overseers were ready to employ fringe medical personnel to treat the sick. In rural districts lacking a qualified resident doctor, resort to local fringe practitioners may have been the only alternative to sending for a more distant (and therefore more costly) medical attendant. In many cases the poor may also have preferred the ministrations of a local healer, and there was a long tradition of seeking assistance from these individuals.[66] Of more importance to the overseers, however, was the fact that fringe practitioners often cost less than a regular doctor. In the late eighteenth and early nineteenth centuries, for example, midwives charged between 2s and 5s for a delivery, compared with a surgeon's fee of 10s 6d or a guinea for more complicated cases. Meanwhile, local healers generally made more moderate charges for treatment than a regular practitioner, although the fees paid to them could vary from a couple of shillings to perhaps a pound in more difficult cases. Broken limbs were an expensive item, and when treated by a regular medical man would cost as much as 10s to a few pounds. This item was normally excluded from medical contracts. Bone-setters, who usually charged something in the region of a few shillings, were frequently employed to treat this category of complaint. In some cases fringe practitioners may have been remunerated according to the success of their treatment. The accounts suggest that payments could be dependent on the practitioner effecting a cure, rather than merely giving treatment. In addition, fringe personnel were generally paid by 'case', whereas payments to qualified medical practitioners were usually made on an itemised basis, with separate charges for visits and medicines. In this way, large bills could be run up, often amounting to several pounds, for one course of treatment.

While overseers attempted to pare medical costs to a minimum, they do seem to have been aware of the long-term advantages of providing effective medical relief. A large short-term outlay on medical treatment could prevent sick or injured persons from becoming a permanent burden on the poor rate. In individual cases medical relief could be both humane and generous. Payments for medical attendance and medicines were frequently backed up with extra assistance: the payment of out-relief, the provision of food, alcoholic stimulants, fuel, clothing and bedding, and in many cases attendance by a nurse, often a female pauper. Payments to nurses for washing and attending on the sick were common items in overseers' accounts. These forms of assistance, although not strictly medical, were vital supplements to medical relief, which was often more generous than is first apparent. In the year 1788–1789, for example, the Huddersfield Overseers expended only £7 3s 8d on medical assistance; for midwifery cases, doctors' bills, medicine, and so on. But in addition to this a further £8 0s 10d was spent on supplements to medical care: out-relief 'for being poorly', rum, funeral and lying-in expenses. The supplementary expenses included the large payment of £2 3s 10d for '16 Weeks pay at 2s to Samuel Burn for a Child Nursing at Burstal and other Expenses'.[67]

Midwifery expenses normally included not only the cost of a midwife or a surgeon to attend at the delivery, but also the payment of a lump sum towards the expenses of buying clothes and other necessities for the child. The usual payment was half a guinea to a married couple and a guinea to an unmarried woman. Additional out-relief was often paid, especially to the unmarried, together with grants of extra food, blankets or alcoholic beverages. Expenses for 'churching' were also paid by the overseers. If the child died at birth or soon after, which was a frequent occurrence, the overseers undertook to pay the funeral expenses. In May, 1784, for example, the Huddersfield Overseers paid, in addition to expenses for a midwife, 5s for a filiation order for Sarah Denby and one guinea for her month's lying-in. In 1785 they paid 2s to Dame Tomlinson for delivering Hannah Finsley, 5s in out-relief, and a week later 1s 4d for 'Finsley Child Funeral'.[68]

Considerable sums could be spent on individuals or families, some of whom seem to have been almost continually afflicted with sickness. Between May, 1784 and March, 1785, for example, the Overseers of the Huddersfield Township expended large sums on the Hudson family, assisting them with childbirth expenses and sick relief for Nat. Hudson, who appears to have been a constant burden on the poor rate:[69]

			£	s	d
1784	May 9	John Marshall Wife midwife for Nat. Hudson Do.		2	0
	May 16	Rachel Hudson Going to Church after Lying in			9
	,,	Rachel Hudson Shoes		3	6
	May 30	Itch Salve & Brimstone for Nat. Hudson			7
	July 25	A Godfrey Bottle[70] for Rachel Hudson child			6
	Aug 15	Natt Hudson to Whitworth Doctor		5	0
	Sept 5	Nat Hudson wife Bleeding			3
1785	March 14	Nat. Hudson 2 yd flannel		2	0
	March 28	Self and Wife Bleeding			4
	,,	to Doctor for Nat		2	0
				16	11

Large sums could also be expended on individual courses of treatment. In the winter of 1797 to 1798, for example, the Mirfield Overseers ran up several doctors' bills totalling £1 2s 5d treating Fanny Hirst, an indoor pauper, who died in January, 1798:[71]

			£	s	d
1797	Dec 5	To Doctor for Fanny Hirst		5	6
1798	Jan 19	To Fanny Hirst from Denby Doctor		4	5
	Jan 23	To Fanny Hirst hurreying to Church		2	
	,,	To Hearse & Church Dues		2	9
	Feb 14	To Doctor Kitson as p. Bill for Fanny Hirst		12	6
			1	7	2

In 1801 they spent almost £3 on medicines, wine, brandy and bleeding for a female workhouse inmate, Betty Oates (out of total medical expenses of £16 12s 5d).[72] In September, 1817 Mr Wilks, surgeon to the Huddersfield Dispensary, was paid £9 by the Overseers of Mirfield Township 'for attending Mathew Hirst and cutting of [*sic*] his Leg'. In March, 1819 they paid Mr Wooler, surgeon, £9 15s 3d for attendance upon one Sam. Gile. In this case the accounts do not specify what the treatment was for, although it is likely that again this was a primary operation.[73]

There are three striking features about medical relief under the Old Poor Law in Wakefield, Huddersfield and other local townships. The first characteristic is that the outlay on this form of relief was small in comparison with total expenditure on relief and in relation to costs per head of the population. Secondly, where medical relief was given it was frequently generous, and backed up with the payment of out-relief and the provision of nursing attendance and other forms of assistance. The final feature worth noting is that a wide variety of medical relief was given to the sick, including not only treatment by regular doctors and payments for drugs, leeches, appliances, and so on, but also provisions for attendance by unqualified personnel, midwives and nurses, and for admittance to local medical charities and friendly societies.[74]

3.2 Medical relief under the New Poor Law

The Poor Law Amendment Act of 1834 has been designated by historians as a distinct watershed in the provision of medical services for the poor, marking the beginning of an improved and widening range of facilities. The Wakefield and Huddersfield Unions were both created under the provisions of this Act in 1837. The Wakefield Union embraced seventeen townships under the direction of a Board of 22 Guardians. Huddersfield Union comprised the four parishes of Huddersfield, Almondbury, Kirkburton and Kirkheaton, which included a total of 32 townships and a massive population of 100,000. The Board of Guardians consisted of 36 persons (including five elected for Huddersfield). The Township of Chevit was later added to the Wakefield Union, and by 1853 the population totalled 48,900. By this date the Huddersfield Union included 123,843 inhabitants. The Wakefield Union covered over 34,662 acres, the Huddersfield Union a massive 68,640 acres.[75]

From 1837 onwards the Wakefield Board of Guardians was dominated by farmers from the country districts, plus small groups of manufacturers, merchants, tradesmen and professional men. The Huddersfield Board was more divided, although farmers also made up an important element, reflecting the rural character of the scattered Union. In later decades, however, manufacturers became an increasingly significant group. In 1850 farmers still dominated the Board: out of the 41 Guardians elected there were fourteen farmers, ten merchants and manufacturers, six tradesmen, four professional men, two gentlemen and one vicar (plus three whose occupations were not recorded and one vacancy). By 1870 manufacturers had become the most important group, their numbers having doubled to twenty. There were also eight farmers, seven gentlemen, two tradesmen and two estate agents on the Board (plus one vacancy). By 1870 many of the townships in the Huddersfield Union were represented by leading business and civic figures.[76]

The application of the 1834 Act in Wakefield and Huddersfield did lead to some major changes in the provision of medical services, although apparently not usually in the right direction. Perhaps the most distinctive feature was a narrowing of the range of facilities made available under this category of relief. The introduction of the new Act did not result in any significant rise in expenditure on medical relief. Rather the reverse when we take into account the large population increases experienced by the Wakefield and Huddersfield Unions. In the year 1834–1835, for example, the medical expenses of the Wakefield Township totalled £358. By 1858 its half-yearly expenditure on this category of relief came to £192 (or approximately £400 for the whole year). Spending on certain items had actually fallen. In 1834–1835 the amount spent on surgeons' salaries and bills totalled a little over £86 (1½d per head of the population). By 1858 the salary bill for the Township amounted to just £40 per annum, plus £7 for supplementary bills (just over ½d per head of the population).[77] As late as 1863 the total medical expenses of the Huddersfield Township amounted to only £296 (less than 2d per head of the population). Excluding expenses for the maintenance of lunatics of £126, the amount spent per head of the population falls to 1d. The proportion of the total expenditure of the Township spent on medical relief was 2.7 per cent, excluding the maintenance of lunatics 1.6 per cent.[78]

Certain forms of medical relief which had been utilised under the old administration disappeared altogether with the introduction of the new Act. After 1837 the district medical officers became the sole suppliers of medical treatment. The practice of allowing doctors to run up individual bills for the treatment of paupers ceased, except in very exceptional cases, as did the employment of fringe practitioners. The Poor Law medical officer took over the majority of obstetric cases, which under the old administration had been very much the preserve of the midwife. The system of keeping up friendly society subscriptions for the poor also ceased, although the framers of the new Act hoped that the streamlining of medical services after 1834, the principle of 'less eligibility' and the restriction of medical relief to paupers would encourage the working classes to take up friendly society membership on their own behalf.[79] All in all the provision of medical relief under the new administration became more formalised and far more strictly regulated.

The chief agent in the provision of medical relief under the new system was the Poor Law medical officer.[80] After 1837 the Wakefield and Huddersfield Unions were divided up into seventeen and twelve medical districts respectively, and a medical officer appointed for each district to supply *all* medical attendance and drugs to those considered eligible by the Guardians and relieving officers. The Huddersfield Board of Guardians appointed medical officers on a fixed salary basis. The Wakefield Board used the tender system up until 1842.

Under the old administration it seems that doctors, even those not employed under contract, had some say in deciding who was eligible for medical treatment. In many cases the overseers paid bills which had already been run up by the medical practitioner. The medical man was not only allowed to judge the medical eligibility of cases, but on occasion he advised the overseers as to the suitability of those in receipt of medical assistance for other forms of relief. In 1833, for example, Thomas Martin, surgeon, sent a note to the Overseers of Honley Township certifying the eligibility of one of his medical cases for relief.[81]

This is to Certify to the Committee & Overseers of Honley that I have attended Jon[n] Crosland of Gully in Wooldale for nearly 3 Weeks, of an Inflammation of the Lungs and Dropsy, & that he is a fit person for reliefe from the Township. I think that he will not require it long, as witness my Hand this 29th Mar: 1833   Tho[s] Martin
                                                                                  Surgeon

Under the New Poor Law the medical officers lost all the powers that they might have had to authorise medical treatment, and certainly had no influence in directing other forms of relief. Medical authorisation became the preserve of the newly-appointed relieving officers, who based their decisions on the financial position of the applicant rather than on medical criteria. The only groups entitled to apply directly to the medical officer for assistance were the aged, infirm, permanently sick or disabled paupers who were included on the medical relief lists, drawn up by the medical officers in response to the 1842 Medical Order. If a medical officer took it upon himself to give medical assistance to persons not included on the medical list without an order from the relieving officer, he ran the risk of not being remunerated for his services. Similarly, the recommendations of medical officers for extra food, alcoholic stimulants, fuel and clothing had to be passed by the relieving officer. This system not only led to a shift in emphasis from medical to social and financial criteria in determining who should obtain medical relief, but also to the substitution of a slow and cumbersome method of directing relief. The sick pauper now had to apply first to the relieving officer to obtain an order for medical relief and take the order to the medical officer, who was then, and only then, authorised to attend the patient. In practice this often led to delay in obtaining treatment.

The formalisation of medical relief under the New Poor Law does not seem to have resulted in improved relationships between the medical officers and Boards of Guardians. While under the old system relationships between doctors and overseers appear on the whole to have been good, under the new administration relationships between the two parties seem to have been at best unfriendly, at worst positively acrimonious. The minute books of the Huddersfield Board of Guardians devote more space to disputes over salaries, the payment of medical bills, the size of medical districts, and so on, than to any other aspect of medical relief.

Following the implementation of the 1842 Medical Order the Huddersfield Union was redivided into sixteen medical districts. Salaries ranged from £40 for the Huddersfield North District, which included the Workhouse (with a population of over 25,000) to £12 for Marsden District (with a population of 2,400).[82] Complaints concerning remuneration were frequent and in some cases led to the resignation of medical officers. Between the implementation of the Order in 1843 and 1850 five medical officers resigned and there were four major disputes over salaries (plus four vacancies resulting from the deaths of medical officers). In 1847 an attempt was made by the Guardians to make all medical appointments annual, which would have given them greater control over salaries, but this move was overruled by the Poor Law Commissioners. However, the Guardians were able to keep several of their medical appointees subject to annual re-election until the late 1860s, ignoring an order of 1855 by which the Poor Law Board made it 'imperative' upon the Huddersfield Guardians to make future appointments permanent.[83]

The most serious dispute during this period arose between the

Huddersfield Guardians and the medical officer for the Huddersfield North District, Mr T. R. Tatham.[84] The dispute, which began in 1847, was widely reported in the local press and leading medical journals, Tatham receiving much support from *The Lancet*. The argument centred around two issues: Tatham's salary, and his claim for extra remuneration in respect of his duties in attending the Temporary Fever Hospital during the 1846–1847 typhus epidemic. The dispute over Tatham's salary was finally resolved in July, 1847, following a great deal of quibbling on the part of the Guardians. His salary was doubled from £40 to £80,[85] for which Tatham was expected to administer medical relief in a district with a population of over 25,000, and attend at the Huddersfield Workhouse.

The second area of contention took much longer to resolve, the dispute lasting from February, 1847 to June, 1848. Over this period Tatham won the support of the press and the medical profession, and even some backing from the Poor Law Board. Meanwhile, the case resulted in much adverse publicity for the Huddersfield Board of Guardians. Tatham claimed expenses of over £100 for his attendance at the Temporary Fever Hospital and his treatment of over 160 typhus cases, many of which had been sent from other medical districts in the Union.[86] The Board, after much consideration, offered Tatham £42, which they claimed would 'amply remunerate' him for his extra services.[87] Tatham eventually obtained legal assistance and took the case to court. The court found in Tatham's favour and the judge strongly condemned the behaviour of the Huddersfield Guardians. The judge was, however, unable to order them to compensate Tatham because of a technical detail, the Guardians having failed to note in their minutes the request that Tatham attend at the Fever Hospital.[88] Public sympathy in Huddersfield was so great that a subscription was opened to reimburse Tatham for his expenses in attending at the Fever Hospital.

The Guardians of both the Wakefield and Huddersfield Unions attempted to keep the wages of medical officers to a minimum. In 1850 the amount paid by the Guardians of the Huddersfield Union for medical officers' salaries, plus charges for vaccinations, pauper deliveries and extra cases, totalled £646 18s 6d (1¼d per head of the Union population). In 1856 the wage bill for all seventeen medical districts of the Wakefield Union amounted to only £214 (including £40 for the Wakefield District, with a population of 16,990), and that of the Huddersfield Union to £488 (including £80 for the Huddersfield North District).[89] Expenditure on salaries in both Unions in this year averaged out to approximately 1d per head of the population. Examples of salaries and additional expenses paid to the medical officers of the Huddersfield Union in 1850 are given in Table 3.1. The Table shows the payments made in the two Huddersfield Districts, in two of the smaller medical districts of the Union, and two of the larger districts, held conjointly by one medical officer.

In defence of the Guardians, the change-over to the new administration did result in increased expenditure for some items of medical care. Before 1837, for example, the amount charged for the setting of fractures was worked out in individual cases between overseer and surgeon, and usually amounted to something in the region of 10s to £1, or to several pounds in more difficult cases. Bonesetters were also employed, with their more moderate charges of a few shillings. Under the 1842 Order the fee was fixed at £1 for the treatment of dislocations or fractures of the arm, and £3 for simple fractures or dislocations of the leg, making payment for these commonly occurring cases a considerable item of expenditure.[90]

In most cases the Guardians of the two Unions kept within the limits of 15,000 acres and 15,000 inhabitants laid down for medical districts by the 1842 Order. The Boards of Guardians did have more difficulty complying with the regulations regarding qualifications and residence requirements. In the remoter and smaller medical districts it was often impossible to find a resident medical man with the stipulated qualifications, who was willing to accept the small salary offered. But on the whole the medical officers seem to have been reasonably well qualified, differing little from the calibre of men appointed under the old administration. Indeed, in many cases the same doctor was appointed district medical officer as had served under the Old Poor Law.

Others of those appointed in the Wakefield and Huddersfield Unions in the late 1830s and 1840s were young and newly-qualified practitioners. Some apparently saw Poor Law appointments as a first step in their professional careers, and soon moved on to better posts and private practice. These men usually obtained appointments in the Wakefield or Huddersfield Districts, or in one of the larger and more accessible medical districts of the Unions. Others, who, while frequently obtaining their appointments when recently

Table 3.1. Samples of medical officers' accounts to the Board of Guardians of the Huddersfield Union for the year 1850.

Name of medical officer	District	Population of district	Salary	Vaccination account[a]	Midwifery account[b]	Extra cases	Total £ s d
Mr Tatham	Huddersfield North	25,018	80 0 0	25 5 6	3 0 0	13 0 0	121 5 6
Mr Clarke	Huddersfield South	5,858	31 0 0	22 2 6	—	7 0 0	60 2 6
Mr Goodall	Lockwood + Almondbury[c]	7,992 + 8,125	35 0 0	18 7 6	1 0 0	—	54 7 6
Mr Roberts	Slaithwaite	4,730	30 0 0	8 15 6	—	4 0 0	42 15 6
Mr Hesslegrave	Marsden	2,665	12 0 0	2 11 0	—	—	14 11 0
	Huddersfield Union	123,843	395 15 0	207 3 6	6 0 0	38 0 0	646 18 6[d]

[a] Rate for vaccination 1s 6d.
[b] Rate for midwifery cases 10s 0d.
[c] Two medical districts.
[d] Excluding charges for postages of £21.
Source: Minute Book of the Huddersfield Board of Guardians, Vol. 7, 19 April, 26 July and 18 October, 1850, 24 January, 1851, Ms HPL (P/HU/M).

qualified, also hung on to them for many years, some until their retirement from practice or death. These were typically men, who, while building up a respectable practice in the villages or small townships in which they resided (and sometimes obtaining other professional appointments, most usually as certifying factory surgeon, police and prison surgeon, or railway surgeon), never aspired to the best medical appointments or town practices. Often they were the only medical practitioners in their localities, and it was natural that they should not only provide a service to paying members of the community, but also to the destitute via the Poor Law agencies.

The Wakefield and Huddersfield posts attracted an especially high calibre of medical men, in spite of the low salaries and the heavy workload associated with these positions. The appointments provided a good introduction to the local community, and brought medical practitioners into contact with a potential group of clients, the Board of Guardians and their connections. For a younger man appointment to the Wakefield and Huddersfield Medical Districts offered opportunities for acquiring experience and building up a professional reputation. Surgeons to the Huddersfield Medical Districts included William James Clarke, Samuel Knaggs, George Winter Rhodes and T. R. Tatham. All had obtained the double qualification of MRCS/LSA and all built up successful private practices in the town and were later elected honorary surgeons to the Huddersfield Infirmary.[91] Of these four only T. R. Tatham was unable to fulfil his professional ambitions in the town. He left Huddersfield for Nottingham in 1863, following disputes with the Poor Law Guardians in the late 1840s and with the committee of the Huddersfield Infirmary in the early 1860s.[92]

In Wakefield members of old, established medical families dominated Poor Law medical posts. These often junior members frequently held two or more appointments. Although in terms of remuneration Poor Law posts offered little, monopolisation of these appointments could help to prevent outsiders from setting themselves up in practice in the town. In 1841 the Wakefield Board advertised for tenders from local medical practitioners for the various townships in the Wakefield Union, 'which proposals must state a gross sum for which the Candidates will undertake to attend all sick Paupers residing within the respective Townships'.[93] Mr Ebenezer Walker was appointed medical officer for Ardsley

East and Alverthorpe-with-Thornes; Mr John Burrell for Walton and Sandal Magna. Mr William Statter (nephew of Squire Statter, who served under the Old Poor Law) was chosen as medical officer for Warmfield-cum-Heath, Messrs William and Samuel Holdsworth for Stanley, and Mr Edward Taylor, a member of one of the town's most eminent surgical families, was appointed medical officer for the Wakefield Township and Union Workhouse.[94] Messrs Ebenezer Walker and Henry Horsfall, members of two influential surgical families, served as medical officers to the Wakefield Medical District and Union Workhouse (a separate post after 1852) in the 1850s and 1860s.[95]

The worst difficulties were experienced by the Huddersfield Board in their efforts to fill posts in the more isolated parts of their enormous and scattered Union. In part, these were difficulties of their own making. They showed a keen reluctance to offer acceptable salaries for districts which, while not usually densely populated, covered large areas and could involve much travelling and inconvenience for medical appointees. In many cases there was only one candidate for these appointments, which offered salaries of something in the region of £15 to £20 per annum. As a consequence these posts were often filled by local men (although sometimes they did not reside in the district itself) who did not fulfil the requirements concerning qualification as laid down in the 1842 Order. The usual problem was that candidates only possessed one of the required qualifications of LSA or MRCS (or a medical degree), but not both. In 1843 no less than seven of the medical officers appointed in the Huddersfield Union were not duly qualified according to the 1842 Medical Order, most of them holding the LSA alone.[96]

In many cases it was clearly impossible for the Board of Guardians to appoint medical men who were both duly qualified and resident in the appropriate district. Usually the Poor Law Commissioners (and, after 1847, Poor Law Board) were willing to compromise. In 1845, for example, Mr John Roberts was appointed medical officer to the Linthwaite District of the Huddersfield Union. John Roberts was not duly qualified according to the 1842 Order. The Guardians justified his appointment on the grounds that, except for his son, James Roberts, who was already medical officer for Slaithwaite, he was the only resident medical man in the District. The Board considered it desirable that the poor should have a medical officer resident amongst them, and stressed that Roberts was 'an old

Established and qualified Practitioner'. The appointment was approved by the Poor Law Commission.[97] In some cases appointments were made conditional upon medical practitioners acquiring the necessary qualifications. In later decades the situation regarding qualifications improved. By the 1860s, for example, only one or two medical officers were not fully qualified according to the 1842 Order.[98]

Of course qualifications tell us little about the fitness of medical men to fulfil their duties, their conscientiousness or their compassion towards the poor. Complaints against medical men, usually on grounds of neglect, were fairly frequent and occasionally of a serious nature. In some cases they led to the dismissal of medical officers, as in 1841 'in consequence of great dissatisfaction being felt by Paupers requiring Medical Relief in the District of Mr Machill'.[99] In 1848 Mr Joseph Hesslegrave, medical officer to Marsden, was dismissed on the order of the Poor Law Board, following his failure to attend on two paupers, one of whom had died. However, when his post was re-advertised, Hesslegrave applied, forwarding to the Board of Guardians a memorial on his behalf from several of Marsden's most influential ratepayers. Hesslegrave was re-elected to the Marsden District, and the appointment approved by the Poor Law Board.[100] In 1858 Mr Roberts, medical officer for Golcar, was merely reprimanded by the Guardians for his refusal to attend upon the children of Rebecca Taylor, in spite of receiving a note from the relieving officer. Three of the children had died from scarlet fever, without ever having been attended by a medical practitioner.[101]

Because both the Wakefield and Huddersfield Unions adopted the practice of paying their medical officers a fixed salary rather than by case, there is little evidence on the total number or type of cases treated. There is no reason for supposing that the nature of cases differed much from those treated under the Old Poor Law except, as shall be demonstrated later, the number of obstetric cases attended by medical officers declined substantially. Treatment of injuries, including fractures, and fever cases probably still accounted for most of the medical man's workload. Between March, 1843 and March, 1844 Mr T. R. Tatham claimed that he had treated 127 patients in the Workhouse and 180 out-patients, making a total of 307 for the year, or 1.2 per cent of the population of his Medical District. This total included 24 bleedings and 209 dressings of wounds. Altogether Tatham maintained that during the year he

Table 3.2. *Medical cases and vaccinations in the Huddersfield Township and Huddersfield Union during the half-year ended March, 1861.*

| Districts | Medical cases | | | Estimated percentage of the population receiving Poor Law medical relief p.a. | Vaccinations | Estimated percentage of the population vaccinated p.a. |
	Workhouse	District	Total			
Huddersfield North District	48	284	332		204	
Huddersfield South District		136	136	3.0	70	1.8
Paddock District[a] (Huddersfield)		56	56		40	
Huddersfield Union	105	1,172	1,277	1.94	1,551	2.36

[a] Paddock District was created out of the Huddersfield South District in 1850.
Source: A Statement of the Accounts of the Huddersfield Union, 1861–1873. Medical Cases and Vaccinations during the Half-Year ended March, 1861, HPL (P/HU/Cfo).

had made a total of 1,633 visits to the sick. His salary was then £40 per annum, which in this year averaged out to 2s 6d per case, and less than 6d per visit, including expenses for medicine.[102] In the year 1844–1845 Tatham attended 325 cases (1.3 per cent of the population of his District) and in 1846–1847, when typhus was prevalent in the neighbourhood, 582 cases (2.3 per cent).[103] The number of medical cases and vaccinations attended to in the half-year ending March, 1861 in the Huddersfield Districts and Union as a whole is given in Table 3.2. Between March, 1850 and May, 1851 Mr E. Walker, surgeon to the Wakefield Medical District, claimed to have treated a total of 791 cases, almost 5 per cent of the population of 16,500 within his District. His salary of £40 averaged out to just over 1s per case. Walker specified the type of illness treated over this period, which had consisted in the main of fever cases. Over fourteen months there had been 207 cases of continued fever, 95 of diarrhoea, 31 of whooping cough, 30 of smallpox and 416 'other diseases', which presumably included injuries and surgical cases.[104]

Workhouses tended to remain very much as they had been under the Old Poor Law administration in the West Riding: small, uncomfortable, often insanitary, and in general sloppily organised. Wakefield, however, opted to build a purpose-built workhouse in 1851 at the cost of £8,000, with room for 360 paupers. The Workhouse was usually only half full, accommodating between 150 and 200 paupers at a time during the 1850s (or approximately 0.4 per cent of the Union population of almost 50,000). However, this was a considerable increase on the numbers accommodated in the old workhouse in George Street. (On census day, 1851, for example, a total of only 67 paupers had been resident in the old workhouse.[105]) The new Workhouse, situated in Park Lane, and described as 'a large and handsome brick building',[106] had hospital wards for the admission of pauper invalids, including fever cases.

The Huddersfield Guardians fiercely resisted the attempts of the central administration to persuade them to embark on a programme of workhouse building. Rather the Board continued to rely on five old parish poorhouses, situated in Huddersfield, Golcar, Almondbury, Honley and Kirkheaton, which together had accommodation for only 250 inmates (or 0.2 per cent of the Union population of 124,000 in the 1850s). The Huddersfield Workhouse, which offered the most generous provisions for the sick, could only accommodate a maximum of forty patients. In the 1860s as few as 200 medical cases per annum were treated in all the Union workhouses (including the old and infirm, disabled and lunatic cases). As early as the year 1849 a committee selected from the Board of Guardians had reported on the inadequacy of workhouse arrangements. All five workhouses were inconvenient, cramped, poorly constructed and damp, 'a very inferior substitute for a good Workhouse'. They also provided insufficient accommodation. The committee recommended the building of one Union workhouse, which they believed would provide both a more effective and cheaper alternative.[107] It was not until 1862 and 1872, however, that new and improved workhouse facilities, with provisions for the sick, were opened near Huddersfield at Deanhouse and Crosland Moor.

Even these facilities had very limited provisions for the sick, Deanhouse accommodating a total of only 22 sick paupers.

Provisions for sick inmates were very limited in the Huddersfield Union workhouses, and conditions in general appear to have been bad. During the 1846–1847 typhus outbreak Mr Tatham reported that fever patients were lying three to a bed in the Huddersfield Workhouse.[108] Conditions were so overcrowded that patients had to be removed to other Union workhouses and a Temporary Fever Hospital. The Commissioners in Lunacy complained repeatedly during the 1850s and 1860s about conditions in all the Union workhouses for lunatics, the sick, and indeed all other occupants. In 1848 the *Leeds Mercury* had reported on the shocking conditions in the Union workhouses, the Huddersfield Workhouse being in every respect, the report claimed,

wholly unfitted for a residence for the many scores that are continually crowded into it, unless it be that we desire to engender endemic and fatal disease. And yet, this Huddersfield poor-house is by far the best in the whole union. It is a palace itself compared with some of the hovels into which the poor are crammed in other parts of the district.[109]

Another newspaper report of 1848 stated that typhus victims in the Huddersfield Workhouse

lay in overcrowded wards, often for weeks, on bags of straw or shavings crawling with lice, without a change of linen or bed clothes. Forty children shared one room, eight yards by five, and were crowded from four to ten in a bed. The Guardians, divided in town and country factions, and at loggerheads with their medical officer, failed to inform themselves of the state of the workhouse or to take any remedial action.[110]

During the same year the Poor Law Board ordered their Inspector to Huddersfield to examine the state of the Workhouse. Mr Tatham reported to the Inspector that during the typhus epidemic

. . . owing to the contaminated state of the wards, patients who had been convalescent had relapses of fever and have since died; by the contaminated state of the wards I mean the water closet which was completely full for three or four weeks, and in April it overflowed and ran down the walls into the passage below; another cause of contamination was the children who were rubbing in [sic] for the itch; . . . the hospital was extremely filthy, the floors were filthy. I don't think they had been washed down throughout the hospital, from the time of its being opened; marks of uncleanliness presented themselves nearly everywhere; . . . [111]

In 1857 a special committee appointed by the Guardians reported that the lack of classification in the hospital wards of the Huddersfield Workhouse had led to 'abandoned women' with diseases of a 'most loathsome character' being mixed up with idiots, young children and even lying-in cases. The hospital accommodation was crowded, damp, insanitary and 'utterly unfit' for lodging sick inmates.[112] Under pressure from the central administration, the Guardians did take some steps towards improving conditions during the 1850s and 1860s, but they were slow and unenthusiastic reformers, and little was done to ensure better standards for the workhouse sick until the last quarter of the nineteenth century. A report on West Riding workhouses made by Inspector Cane on behalf of the Poor Law Board as late as 1867 stated that arrangements for the reception of infectious diseases, medical attendance, nursing and the general care of the sick, for ventilation, drainage and water supply, and the bedding, food and clothing of inmates were still most unsatisfactory. Huddersfield was one of the worst offenders, there being an 'entire insufficiency' of accommodation, especially for the sick. Here 'puddings were boiled in the same copper as the foul linen was washed and boiled in'. There was a shortage of pauper nurses; those employed were unable to read the labels on medicine bottles, even though they were trusted to administer drugs.[113]

Provisions for lying-in women in the Huddersfield Union workhouses were also appalling for much of the century, especially as the workhouses tended to become more overcrowded. After 1842 midwifery cases had to be paid for separately by the Boards of Guardians. The Huddersfield Board pared expenses to a minimum, paying medical officers the lowest rate of 10s per case, and only on very rare occasions agreeing to pay extra for especially long and difficult deliveries. Between June, 1843 and June, 1844 only 87 deliveries were attended by medical officers for the whole Union, and the number seems to have fallen off further in later decades. According to the medical officers' accounts for 1850, only twelve domiciliary deliveries were attended by them during this year. In the half-year ending September, 1850 only two confinements took place in the Wakefield Union Workhouse.[114]

The policy of the Wakefield and Huddersfield Boards of Guardians regarding the maintenance of lunatics remained very much as it had been under the Old Poor Law, with paupers only being removed to an asylum as a last resort. Efforts were made by the Guardians to maintain pauper lunatics in the workhouse to save on expenditure. The 1851 census enumerators' books recorded fourteen 'pauper idiots' as resident in the Wakefield Workhouse, and five in the Huddersfield Workhouse.[115] During the half-year ending March, 1861 a total of 62 'lunatics and idiots' were 'relieved' in the Huddersfield Union workhouses. On census day, 1861 fourteen were resident in the Huddersfield Workhouse (12 per cent of the 113 inmates).[116] The census returns also recorded small numbers of 'pauper idiots', 'imbeciles' and 'persons slow in intellect' who resided in lodgings or with their family, and who were supported by the rates. Troublesome or violent paupers were removed to the County Asylum at Wakefield or, if this was full, to the Lancashire or Cheshire County Asylums or one of several private asylums. The principal private asylums utilised were Haydock Lodge in Lancashire and Fisherton House in Wiltshire. The Haydock Lodge Asylum catered specially for the massive overflow of pauper lunatics from the county asylums of Lancashire, Cheshire, Staffordshire, Leicestershire and the West Riding of Yorkshire. By 1846 it was licensed to receive 400 pauper inmates.[117]

Payments for the maintenance of lunatics remained the largest item in the category of medical expenditure, and became more and more costly as the century progressed. By 1850 the Huddersfield Union spent almost £600 on the maintenance of lunatics at the Wakefield Asylum alone. Out of this the Township of Huddersfield expended £125 for the care of eight pauper patients.[118] By the 1860s expenditure had increased to well over £1,000 per annum. In 1860, for example, 57 of the inmates of the Wakefield Asylum were chargeable to the Huddersfield Union at a cost of £1,290.[119] In 1861 the cost of maintaining lunatics in asylums amounted to £1,432 or 6 per cent of total expenditure. By 1868 the lunatic asylum account of £2,614 made up approximately 10 per cent of all Union expenditure.[120] In 1858 the Wakefield Union expended just over £300 on the maintenance of lunatics in asylums. This compared with an expenditure of £1,325 on out-relief and a total expenditure of £3,754 for the year. The maintenance of lunatics, therefore, accounted for 8 per cent of all expenditure.[121]

The Guardians of the Wakefield and Huddersfield Unions kept up some subscriptions to medical charities in order to gain access to the special services that they could provide (and the payment of such subscriptions was sanctioned by an Order of the Poor Law Board in 1851). Presumably the Guardians were most interested in obtaining treatment for pauper accident cases, and other emergencies, which would otherwise entail the payment of extra fees to the medical officers. However, subscriptions were generally small scale, and relationships between the Boards of Guardians and administrators of the charities were poor for much of the century. The Wakefield Dispensary (and after 1854 Infirmary) had a policy of excluding paupers. If patients in receipt of poor relief were admitted to the charity, the usual practice was to discharge them immediately, or to transfer them to the Workhouse or the medical officer for Wakefield. In 1854–1855, for instance, ten pauper patients were removed to the Workhouse.[122] In the annual report for the year 1859–1860 the committee warned subscribers against letting their tickets of recommendation fall into the hands of 'improper objects', '. . . amongst other classes, those who may have been in the receipt of parish relief, ought to be supplied with medical aid, not from this institution, but by the Surgeons appointed by the Board of Guardians'. The committee also suggested that those not in receipt of parish relief might still apply first to the relieving officer, who was in a position to authorise grants of food, clothing and fuel, etc. to the sick, facilities the Infirmary was unable to provide. They concluded that with increased care in the distribution of tickets the institution could confer its benefits on '. . . the most deserving of the poor, and avoid the risk of being used merely as a relief of the general poor rate'.[123]

The officers of the Huddersfield Dispensary and Infirmary were prepared to admit paupers for treatment on the payment of an annual subscription by the Boards of Guardians. However, the Infirmary Board was involved in a number of disputes with the Guardians of both the Wakefield and Huddersfield Unions over the payment of maintenance expenses, the size of subscriptions and the removal of deceased paupers.[124] The Huddersfield Board of Guardians did keep up their subscription of five guineas per annum to the Huddersfield Infirmary for much of the century, which entitled them to keep two in-patients or four out-patients on the books at a time. The Wakefield Board of Guardians, unable to obtain admission for paupers to the Wakefield Dispensary and Infirmary, paid subscriptions in some years to the Huddersfield charity, although their contributions were spasmodic. The Wakefield

Guardians also took advantage of provisions for the admission of pauper patients to the Wakefield House of Recovery in return for a weekly payment of several shillings for maintenance. In 1838 the Wakefield Board of Guardians paid out £4 13s for the maintenance of two paupers suffering from typhus fever (for a total of thirteen weeks, averaging out at 7s a week per patient).[125] During 1847, 50 out of the 71 patients admitted to the House of Recovery were sent by the Wakefield Guardians.[126] The Wakefield Board also subscribed to the Leeds Infirmary and Ilkley Bath Charity, while the Huddersfield Guardians sent a small number of patients to the Manchester Eye Institution, the Doncaster Deaf and Dumb Institution and the York and Liverpool Schools for the Blind. Taken together, however, these subscriptions amounted to very little. In 1850 the Wakefield Union paid out only £18 12s to charitable institutions.[127] In 1860 the Huddersfield Board spent approximately £25 on subscriptions and the maintenance of paupers in medical charities.[128]

One area of potential influence, which, while not linked directly to medical relief, had very close associations, was the field of preventive medicine. In 1834 the Poor Law Unions came to provide the first administrative coverage of the whole nation, and it was not until 1888, through the county councils, that local government agencies came to provide a similar coverage. For this reason the Boards of Guardians were soon utilised by central government to implement a number of reforms associated with health. The first, and perhaps most successful, imposition of this kind was vaccination. In 1840 an Act was passed which provided via the Poor Law agencies a vaccination service for the entire population. The district medical officers were to act as vaccinators, being paid a separate per capita fee of 1s 6d. In 1841 a further Act was passed emphasising the non-pauperising nature of the vaccination service, and finally in 1853 vaccination was made compulsory. Public vaccinators were appointed in the Wakefield and Huddersfield Unions in 1840. In 1858 £30 was spent on approximately 400 vaccinations in the Wakefield Township alone.[129] Between October, 1840 and June, 1841 1,222 vaccinations were performed in the Huddersfield Union.[130] This set the pattern, and in the future large numbers of people were vaccinated annually by the Poor Law medical officers. In the year 1850, 2,763 persons were vaccinated in the Huddersfield Union at a cost of £207 3s 6d. Throughout the 1860s more than £200 was expended per annum in the Huddersfield Union on over 2,500 vaccinations.[131]

By the Nuisance Removal and Diseases Prevention Act of 1846 the Guardians became responsible for controlling nuisances and epidemics outside the boroughs. In Wakefield the Board made some effort to remove nuisances, especially before and during the 1849 cholera epidemic. Their efforts in this direction were applauded both in the local press and by witnesses to the 1851 public health inquiry. In the first months of 1849 the Wakefield Board attempted to improve the sanitary state of the town, cleaning up some of the worst areas of Wakefield and instituting lime-washing programmes. In several instances they applied the provisions of the Nuisance Removal and Diseases Prevention Act. The Board also took responsibility for providing medical relief for the poor. The expenses of the Guardians during the 1849 cholera epidemic totalled £1,011, including £837 for medical officers' bills. The greatest part of the expenses were run up in the Borough of Wakefield itself.[132] The efforts of the Wakefield Board in the field of preventive medicine were, however, hampered by the Street Commissioners; their powers were insufficient to enforce the removal of nuisances or to take more drastic action, as, for example, in the provision of sewers. Following the setting up of the Wakefield Board of Health in 1853, the authority of the Board of Guardians in this field diminished.

In 1848 the Huddersfield Board of Guardians constituted themselves as a Sanitary Committee, and the medical officers were requested to make inspections of their districts and report any nuisances. In December, 1848 an assistant was employed to serve notices respecting nuisances. Large numbers of nuisances were reported to the Board by both the medical officers and local inhabitants. A rather smaller number of nuisance notices were served, and in very few cases the assistant overseers directed to arrange their removal. Although some nuisances were either removed or abated, the Guardians merely scratched the surface of the problem. They proved to be half-hearted sanitary reformers, and a nationwide lack of response by the Boards of Guardians was reflected in the 1855 Nuisances Removal Act, which removed the Guardians' responsibility in the field of preventive medicine. The government was, however, forced to restore these powers to the rural Guardians in 1860. After 1860 there was some confusion concerning the jurisdiction of the Huddersfield Board of Guardians in the area of nuisance removal, but they attempted to avoid responsibility where possible. By this time many local townships had set up their own Boards of Health, and these, together with the Improvement Commissioners, appear to have taken over most duties with respect to nuisance removal and sanitary reform.[133]

The Huddersfield Board of Guardians' forays into the control and treatment of outbreaks of epidemic disease were also marked by a lack of enthusiasm and parsimony. During the 1847 outbreak of typhus fever the Guardians reluctantly committed themselves to setting up a Temporary Fever Hospital, complete with a nursing staff, largely made up of paupers. When cholera broke out in 1849 at Paddock, near Huddersfield, the Board of Guardians reacted, by their standards at least, with some speed. They ordered that a temporary cholera hospital be built, carried out house-to-house visitations, printed notices on how to avoid the cholera and authorised medical men to treat those thought to be suffering from the disease at the expense of the Board.[134] The bill finally presented by medical men for the treatment of cholera cases totalled almost £270, which caused something of a panic amongst the Guardians. They rescinded the order regarding free medical treatment in October, and when local medical men began to demand payment of bills, the Board began to quibble about charges run up for persons in 'good circumstances'. The Guardians issued notices to the public requesting that those of them able to pay for medical assistance should do so, instead of allowing the expense to be charged to the poor rates. They also threatened to make public the names of all those refusing to comply with the above request! The cholera hospital was hastily sold in November. The expenses run up by the Guardians during the epidemic totalled just over £500, half of that expended in Wakefield, which they regarded as something of a financial disaster, although it represented only a fraction of total expenditure for the year.[135]

Concluding remarks

The most crucial point to be re-emphasised here is that spending on Poor Law medical relief was low under both the old and new administrations in the areas around and including Wakefield and Huddersfield, and probably throughout much of the North. The

most significant change wrought by the introduction of the Poor
Law Amendment Act of 1834 was not linked to the amount of
medical relief, but to the ways in which it was administered. The
wide variety of medical agencies resorted to before 1834 has been
pointed to in the first Section. Under the Old Poor Law (and other
historians have noted this tendency)[136] there is evidence to suggest
that where medical relief was given, it could be both humane and
generous. Before 1834 townships were usually small, and close
personal links were maintained between paupers and the relief
agencies. The Old Poor Law administrators, meanwhile, showed
an awareness of the need to treat short-term illness or injury 'as an
insurance against persistent illness and ultimate dependence but also
in order to maintain a standard of provision which had become
accepted as the necessary minimum'.[137] They seem also to have
been aware of the needs of the poor, and, in an age when medical
treatment was in most cases merely palliative, understood the
importance of providing as a supplement to medical aid, additional
food, alcoholic stimulants, fuel, bedding, nursing attendance and
extra financial assistance.

In many cases economy and humanity coincided, an occurrence
which presumably satisfied both the ratepayer and the relieved. The
payment of friendly society subscriptions, especially on a temporary basis, for example, offered overseers a cheap means of 'insurance'. For the poor it offered a form of 'independence' and avoid-
ance of pauperisation. Resort to the midwife or fringe practitioner
provided a cheap alternative for the overseers, and often a preferred
form of treatment for the poor. The payment of medical bills on an
individual basis could, especially in the case of smaller parishes, cost
less than the employment of a contract surgeon. It gave the poor,
meanwhile (within certain limits of cost and accessibility), the
freedom to choose their own medical attendant.

After 1834 many of these old forms and practices were swept
away. The employment of fringe personnel and midwives ceased
immediately, as did the payment of friendly society subscriptions
and the provision, even in a very basic form, of domiciliary nursing
facilities. The practice of paying subscriptions to medical charities
continued, but subscriptions were on a small scale, and poor
relationships between the Boards of Guardians and committees of
these charities worked against the development of co-operation
between the two agencies. One continuum under both the old and

new administrations was that most medical assistance was given as out-relief rather than in the workhouse.

The imposition of vast administrative units in place of the old townships appears to have had its negative effects. The inauguration of the New Poor Law was marked, especially in Huddersfield, by resistance and opposition. During the first years of the new administration the Huddersfield Board of Guardians showed a particular reluctance to implement the orders of the Poor Law Commission. The Poor Law Commissioners in some cases attempted to enforce their orders; in others left well alone, and allowed the Guardians a large degree of autonomy. On the whole, orders relating to medical relief appear to have been followed, but the interpretations of the Board of Guardians were not marked by generosity.

The formation of the Wakefield and Huddersfield Unions to a large extent destroyed the relationship which had formerly existed between pauper and relief agency. Policies were implemented and orders for medical relief given without regard to individual cases. Under the New Poor Law medical relief was meant for the destitute alone, not for all the needy. The system which had existed under the Old Poor Law of giving medical relief to those who were in temporary need or, who while applying for medical aid, did not require other forms of relief, disappeared under the new regime. Application for medical relief after 1834 equalled pauperisation.

Accounts of medical relief under the New Poor Law have tended to stress the parsimony of the Boards of Guardians. The period after 1834 was also marked by a hardening of attitudes on the part of the Poor Law medical officers. Under the Old Poor Law there is a suggestion that medical men kept their charges down, perhaps in some cases treated poor patients gratis.[138] Power claimed that those providing medical assistance felt under an obligation to keep bills to a minimum, referring to

> . . . a disposition on the part of the medical men to make moderate charge upon the township for attending upon pauper patients, properly distinguishing between the latter and a more wealthy class of patients, and not presuming too far upon the competency of the township to supply the difference.[139]

After 1834 the giving of free medical relief may have continued, but was hardly encouraged by the attitude of the Boards of Guardians (especially in Huddersfield), and their poor relationships with the medical officers. As appointees of centralised Boards, the status of medical men under the New Poor Law was very much that of employees. They lost much of the influence that they had enjoyed under the old administration in directing medical and other forms of relief. The close working relationship between the township surgeons and overseers was not replaced by a similar relationship between medical officers and the Boards of Guardians. Meanwhile, the creation of large medical districts, and the practices of allowing medical men to take responsibility for two or more districts and to reside outside these districts, assisted in the breakdown of the old relationship between surgeon and pauper. After 1834 the Poor Law medical officers became increasingly concerned with increasing their rates of remuneration and raising their status within the Poor Law system, with little success in the period up to 1870. A system of directing medical relief was implemented under the New Poor Law where the Boards of Guardians and relieving officers were dominant. This is reflective of a more general tendency for the layman to play an increasingly dominant role in the organisation of medical treatment during the nineteenth century. This tendency has its parallels with respect to other medical facilities, and will be referred to again in the following chapters.

By 1870 Wakefield and Huddersfield showed very contrasting levels of progress in the provision of medical relief, with Wakefield moving with far greater rapidity towards the establishment of a modern, non-pauperising health service. The Wakefield Board of Guardians opened their enlarged and improved workhouse facility as early as 1852. The first indication of the impact of the new Union Workhouse, with its facilities for the sick, was the closure of the House of Recovery in 1854. The officers of the House of Recovery, which was intended to serve a wider social group than paupers, felt that their role in the provision of a hospital service for fever cases had been superseded by the new workhouse provisions.[140] The importance of workhouse facilities for the sick was also reflected in the employment after 1852 of a medical officer whose duties covered workhouse attendance only.

In Huddersfield the Guardians were reluctant to enlarge their workhouse facilities for any class of pauper, or to take on the responsibilities of providing a hospital service. There was no separate workhouse medical officer and the standard of nursing attendance remained low, usually being provided by paupers and even 'idiots'. Despite the campaigns of the medical officer to the Huddersfield North District, Mr Tatham, and the Poor Law Commission and Board, facilities were not much extended or improved. In 1862 a new Union workhouse, Deanhouse, was finally opened, but by the late 1860s it was still only capable of accommodating 44 sick paupers.[141] In the fields of public health and disease prevention too, the Huddersfield Guardians lagged far behind the Wakefield Board.

A higher proportion of the population of Wakefield received medical treatment via the Poor Law. In 1844 Henry Rumsey estimated that 2.9 per cent of the population of the Wakefield Union received Poor Law medical relief, an average of 1,282 per annum. In the Huddersfield Union an average of 1,600 patients, 1.47 per cent of the population, were treated annually by Poor Law medical officers. The medical officers of the Wakefield Union also had smaller medical districts. In 1844 the average population to each medical officer was 3,952 in Wakefield, 6,807 in Huddersfield.[142] With small fluctuations, the figures cited by Rumsey for 1844 probably provide an accurate indication of the amount of medical relief provided by the two Unions up until the final quarter of the nineteenth century.

The better achievements in Wakefield may have been a reflection of a more liberal attitude on the part of the Wakefield Board with regard to their responsibilities and spending on medical relief. Dominated by one social and occupational group of farmers, the Wakefield Board may have been more united in policy direction than their Huddersfield contemporaries, divided as they were between town and country factions. However, in a similar way to the Huddersfield Board, the Wakefield Guardians do seem to have been anxious to pare medical costs (for example, medical officers' salaries) to a minimum. A more likely explanation is that the small scale of the Wakefield medical charities (to be discussed in the following chapter), combined with the reluctance of the committee of the Dispensary and Infirmary to admit paupers or to extend their scale of operations beyond the Township boundaries, forced the Wakefield Guardians into action. In Huddersfield the existence of hospital and dispensary provisions on a larger scale may have relieved the Guardians to some extent from their responsibilities in the field of medical provision. In 1844 Rumsey calculated that 5,905 persons were treated by the Huddersfield Dispensary and

Infirmary. In Wakefield the total number admitted to the Dispensary and House of Recovery in the same year amounted to only 728, one-eighth of the Huddersfield figure.[143]

The importance of medical charities as a relief on Poor Law agencies, however, should not be exaggerated. Medical charities were designed to treat a different class of patient, and even subscribing Boards of Guardians were only able to maintain a few patients at a time in these institutions. On the other hand, the significance of the friendly society and alternatives to 'institutional' medicine, the chemist and druggist, the quack doctor and local fringe practitioner,[144] as a relief on Poor Law medical services has probably been underestimated. There does seem to have been a decline in the 'quality' and range of Poor Law medical relief offered after 1834. But medical relief under both the old and new administrations was insignificant in terms of the proportion of the population relieved and compared with other forms of medical provision.[145]

4

The medical charities of Wakefield and Huddersfield: case studies in charitable motivation

And now, great Architect of earth and skies,
Deign on our work of Charity to smile!
To thee the incense of our prayers shall rise,
That we may raise the top-stone of our pile,
Unmarked by injury, in those that toil.
Oh! may our hearts with streams of kindness flow,
Rich as the waters from the fount of Nile –
Making the sick man's frame with health to glow,
And cheering those that droop beneath the weight of woe![1]

The 'philanthropic spirit' of the Victorian age found concrete expression in a large number of organised charities, dealing with an ever-widening range of social problems: the relief of poverty, the education of the poor, the abolition of vice and intemperance, the care of orphans and the aged, the spread of the Christian gospel, and the provision of medical care. There has been a considerable outpouring of historical research on both individual charities and charitable work in specific fields. However, explanations of the motives of those behind philanthropic enterprises, their expectations and the services they hoped to provide, remain unsatisfactory.

David Owen has provided us with perhaps the broadest and most comprehensive study of charitable enterprise to date.[2] But he fails to grapple with questions concerning the social origins of the philanthropic (with the exception of leaders in the field of charity), their interests and aspirations. And indeed there is little consensus of opinion amongst historians as to the dynamics behind charitable work. The explanations that have been offered tend to refer to an assortment of influences: humanitarian impulses, religious motivation, social pressures from an unruly working class, paternalistic ideals, and a preference for voluntary, as opposed to state, action.

Derek Fraser, for example, has suggested that charity can be seen as a response to four types of motivation: a fear of social revolution, a humanitarian concern for suffering, a satisfaction of some psychological or social need, and a desire to improve the moral tone of the recipients.[3]

Alternatively, Best has argued that through several centuries the wealthy classes developed an ethos of what he labels 'prudential charity'. By the nineteenth century large sums of money had been invested in the establishment of institutions designed to relieve the most unbearable pressures of poverty, to form in the poor a law-abiding and politically quietist frame of mind, and to open to the more capable or morally deserving of them some means of self-elevation.[4] R. J. Morris, meanwhile, has suggested that the development of voluntary societies, including charitable organisations, can be seen as an attempt by the middle classes to solve the problems which emerged in industrial towns during the nineteenth century. Through voluntary societies the middle classes endeavoured to cool class conflict between themselves and the poor, mitigating distress and spreading middle-class values. These activities also provided a basis for the unification of the middle class otherwise divided by sectarian, social and party splits.[5]

In recent years historians have attempted to explain philanthropy, and a whole range of other ruling-class activities, by structuralist theories relating to society as a whole. Chief amongst these are the 'harmony model' of paternalism and the 'conflict model' of social control. The theory of paternalism centres around the phrase that 'property has its duties as well as its rights'. The wealthy, socially superior and conscientious paternalist was to perform three principal sets of duties: ruling, guiding and helping the poor (including acts of charity). In the last decade social historians have approached 'a whole range of the activities of power groups as exercises in devising mechanisms of social control which conditioned and manipulated the propertyless masses into accepting and operating the forms and functions of behaviour necessary to sustain the social order of an industrial society'.[6] Supporters of the theory of social control share in the basic assumption that the social order was maintained, not just by legal systems and the police, but through a wide range of social institutions and activities, including leisure, education, charity, religion, poor relief, and so on. The mechanisms of both paternalism and social control negate the role of the working classes in creating their own values and institutions. Both theories have been of significance, not just because of the number of historians who have supported them, but because of the debate they have aroused. The themes of paternalism and social control shall be taken up later in this chapter (pp. 145–159). It will be argued that while these theories could explain in part the motives of the philanthropic, they were secondary to more pragmatic considerations.

Studies of charitable enterprise have concentrated on London and other large cities, to the detriment of smaller communities with their differing social structures and patterns of poverty. Investigations to date have also favoured national movements or major charities. Studies of medical charities, for example, have been almost entirely devoted to the oldest and most famous eighteenth-century foundations, and are heavily concentrated on large population centres, in particular London.[7] In the case of nationwide charitable associations emphasis has been placed on central organisations, rather than local branches. We have ended up with a view of policies and aims expounded from central headquarters, by well-versed spokesmen. Much is known of the (at least stated) motives of philanthropists as put forward by leaders in the field of charity, churchmen and important social reformers. Far less is known of those who organised or financed smaller charitable enterprises in their own localities, putting into action the sentiment that 'charity begins at home'. These groups were clearly less verbal than their more auspicious contemporaries. Numerically, however, and in terms of their total financial contributions, these 'small-time' philanthropists were often of greater importance. Moreover, they must also have had some anxieties or sympathies which induced them to give financial or organisational support to local charities, which should be explained.

In this chapter the three major Wakefield and Huddersfield medical charities will be examined: the Wakefield House of Recovery or Fever Hospital (founded in 1826), the Clayton Hospital and Wakefield General Dispensary (referred to as the Wakefield Dispensary and Infirmary) (1787) and the Huddersfield General Dispensary and Infirmary (1814). The period under discussion will date from their initiations through to the last quarter of the nineteenth century, and in the case of the Fever Hospital, until its closure in 1854. It will be shown how the aims and expectations of the supporters of these enterprises were consolidated, and how the charities adapted to the needs of the community as they perceived them.

The reasons for attempting such an analysis are twofold. Firstly, an insight into the motives and ambitions of the groups involved in the support of these institutions could form a basis for comparison with other philanthropic enterprises, and for an analysis of the theories which have been put forward to explain philanthropy, including those of social control and paternalism. As infirmaries (and other medical charities) became 'one of the main avenues for provincial philanthropic activity', being common to both 'major population centres and country towns',[8] they constitute good examples for a study of charitable enterprise. Secondly, it can be argued that the influence of those organising and financing medical charities was perhaps more important than medical opinion and practice, and that such groups warrant detailed analysis. During this era medical charities were dominated by lay interests and money; lay officers controlled the admission policies of these institutions, lay finance, the size and field of operations. Policy-making then was directly influenced by the aims and ideals of lay philanthropists.[9]

This chapter will be divided into four sections. Section 4.1 will look at the organisation, funding and success rate of the charities, in terms of the number of patients admitted and cured. In Section 4.2 an analysis will be given of the type of persons active in the support of the Wakefield and Huddersfield Infirmaries. Most hospital histories (and histories of charities) have discussed, often in some detail, the individuals prominent in the initiation, running and funding of the institution: presidents, patrons, major benefactors, and so on. The second Section will focus on the activities and backgrounds of some of the most important patrons of the Wakefield and Huddersfield Infirmaries, those who donated large sums of money to the charities or who played an important organisational role. However, this Section will also attempt to take the analysis of the philanthropic further, by looking at the social characteristics and background of the 'average' subscriber to the two infirmaries.

The third Section (4.3) will discuss the aims of the charities as espoused by their patrons. What motivated those who gave up time or money to promote the interests of the infirmaries? Did they expect some kind of return for their efforts, and if so, in what form?

The most useful source for a discussion of this kind was found to be the printed annual reports of the institutions,[10] which devoted much space to explaining the purposes of the charities and the priorities of their patrons. Sets of rules also threw some light on the objectives of the charities, as did newspaper accounts of meetings and other activities. Minute books proved to be a disappointing source of evidence. The minutes were mainly devoted to listing attendances at meetings and to accounts of expenditure. Although decisions taken at committee and general meetings were recorded, little background was given to the decision-making process or of the opinions of those present. Little is known of the relationships which evolved between donors and recipients in charitable institutions, and the third Section will also take a brief look at those who came to be on the receiving end of charity in the two infirmaries. How were patients selected, and in what ways, if any, were attempts made to regulate their behaviour following admission?

The final Section (4.4) will examine the role of women in these institutions. Division of labour and exclusion from certain activities on the basis of sexual criteria were usual features of charitable enterprises. However, the part played by women in running and, more particularly, financing the Wakefield and Huddersfield Dispensaries and Infirmaries during the nineteenth century was significant, even if it was secondary to male contributions. The Wakefield House of Recovery was exceptional in that it was managed solely by women, who determined its policies and field of activity, and it will receive particular attention in this Section.

4.1 Organisation, funding, admissions and success rate

Before proceeding further, it would appear to be useful to make a few remarks concerning the way in which the three Wakefield and Huddersfield medical charities were funded and organised. My remarks will be kept brief, as the government and financial organisation of these institutions were comparable with those of most other eighteenth- and nineteenth-century medical charities, and these aspects of hospital history have been adequately covered elsewhere.[11]

All three institutions were managed by elected officers, a President, Vice-Presidents, a Treasurer and an Honorary Secretary, and a committee. The committee was selected from the governors of the charities[12] (while the medical officers served as ex-officio members). Meetings of the governors were held annually to hear the report of the committee, to check the accounts, and to elect a new committee for the following year. In addition, special general meetings were occasionally held to deal with any unusual business: fund-raising campaigns, plans to extend the operations of the charity, or, more usually, to elect new officers and medical personnel. Most of the day-to-day management of the charities devolved on the committee, which met monthly to deal with accounts, the ordering of drugs, food and other necessary items, the appointment of staff and business relating to the admission, conduct and care of patients. By the mid-nineteenth century the two infirmaries had also found it necessary to appoint weekly committees, which were chosen at each monthly committee meeting. The weekly board, in co-operation with the medical officers, dealt with the admission of patients. They were also responsible for inspecting the hospital; checking the wards, the state of provisions, the conduct of the servants and nurses, and so on.

Most of the funding of the Wakefield and Huddersfield medical institutions came from charitable sources. In common with most dispensaries and infirmaries of the period, they were in theory to be supported mainly by annual subscriptions. The subscribers gained the privilege of recommending patients in return for, and in proportion to, their contributions.[13] (Initially a half guinea subscription to the Wakefield Dispensary entitled a subscriber to recommend three patients annually; a guinea subscription to the Huddersfield Dispensary allowed the subscriber to keep one patient on the books at a time.) Other vital sources of income included donations, legacies and congregational collections. These sources were supplemented by the profits of various fund-raising events: for example, bazaars, concerts, balls and lectures. The Wakefield Charity Ball, for instance, was an important source of annual income for both the Dispensary and the House of Recovery for much of the nineteenth century,[14] while a bazaar held for the benefit of the Huddersfield Infirmary in 1831 raised over £1,500.[15] In 1820, £400, the profits of a Music Festival held in Wakefield, was divided in equal proportions between the Church, the Lancastrian Schools and the Dispensary.[16] When Cook's Olympic Pavilion opened in Wakefield in 1822, the profits of an evening's performance of riding skills and of the first week's lessons, a total of £10, were donated to the funds of the

Dispensary,[17] and in 1827 Dr Alexander paid £10 to the Wakefield Dispensary, the receipts from the publication of his pamphlet on phrenology.[18]

By the mid–nineteenth century it had become a common practice for the officers of the Wakefield and Huddersfield Infirmaries to invest surplus funds in railway debentures and other stock. These investments yielded an important and, in normal circumstances, regular source of income. By 1866 the interest on investments in the Huddersfield Waterworks, the Woodhead Road, the Mersey Docks, three railway companies and government stock brought an annual income of over £800 to the Huddersfield Infirmary, almost 20 per cent of the charity's total receipts.[19] A further innovation in the funding of the two infirmaries came in the 1870s with the advent of the Hospital Saturday Fund, made up of working men's subscriptions, collected in their places of work. In the year 1876–1877 workpeople's subscriptions to the Huddersfield Infirmary amounted to £428 (9 per cent of the total income).[20] Other miscellaneous and non–charitable sources of income included apprenticeship fees (which were paid to the charity rather than to the medical officer), payments by Poor Law officials, fines awarded by the magistrates, and small receipts for the sale of surgical appliances and drugs. By the third quarter of the nineteenth century small sums were also paid by patients in a position to contribute something towards the cost of their treatment and board.

It is difficult to give anything more than a very general impression as to what constituted an 'average' income for the medical charities of Wakefield and Huddersfield. Of the three, the Wakefield House of Recovery had the most stable income, it being usually somewhere in the region of £300 per annum. The receipts (and expenditures) of the Wakefield and Huddersfield Infirmaries were subject to quite dramatic fluctuations, although the overall tendency was for them to increase during the nineteenth century. The receipt of a large legacy or a canvass for new subscribers could provide a major boost to income. Alternatively, a depression in trade or the deaths of long–standing supporters could lead to serious financial setbacks.

The Huddersfield Dispensary, which from its initiation in 1814 operated on a much bigger scale than the Wakefield institution, also commanded larger sources of income. In the ten months following the opening of the Huddersfield Dispensary £958 was received, mainly in the form of donations and subscriptions.[21] In the same year the receipts of the Wakefield Dispensary amounted to only £115.[22] Following the establishment of in-patient facilities, the funds of both charities increased. The Huddersfield Infirmary opened in 1831, and by 1835 its income had risen to £1,350.[23] By 1856, two years after the addition of in-patient facilities, the total income of the Wakefield Infirmary amounted to almost £700.[24] By the year 1870–1871 the incomes of the Wakefield and Huddersfield Infirmaries totalled £1,250 and £4,230 respectively.[25]

The success of medical charities rested of course not just on their philanthropic achievements, on which this chapter will concentrate, but on the number of patients that they were able to treat and cure. Hospital histories have tended to concentrate on in-patient treatment, which accounts, in part at least, for the pessimistic interpretations of the contributions of hospitals to the falling mortality rates of the nineteenth century.[26] In-patients, however, accounted for a far smaller number of admissions than out- or home-patients to most infirmaries of this period, and, although something of a side issue to this chapter, this would appear to be a useful point to emphasise the overriding numerical importance of out-patients. One of the most outstanding features of the Wakefield and Huddersfield medical charities was the great emphasis placed on out- and home-patient treatment. Both charities started out as dispensaries, treating several hundred out and home cases per annum, in many cases successfully. But even when they expanded into infirmaries, numerically out-patients continued to make up by far the most important category of admissions. As late as the year 1860–1861, for example, 351 in-patients were admitted to the wards of the Huddersfield Infirmary compared with 5,680 out- and home-patients (that is, sixteen out- and home-patients to every one in-patient).[27] The difference between the various categories of patients was even greater in the Wakefield Infirmary. In 1860–1861 only sixteen in-patients were admitted compared with 1,488 out-patients (93:1). By the year 1870–1871 the number of in-patient admissions to the Wakefield Infirmary had increased to ninety, but out-patient admissions had also doubled to 2,934 (33:1).[28] Between 1831 (and the addition of in-patient wards) and 1871 the ratio of in- to out-patients admitted to the Huddersfield Infirmary averaged out at one to fifteen. Between 1854 and 1871 the ratio for the Wakefield charity averaged out at one to 53![29] Home-patients generally accounted for around half of the Wakefield charity's

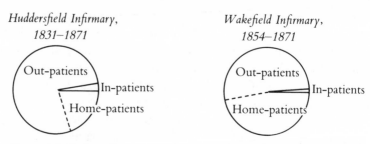

Figure 4.1. Ratios of in-, out- and home-patients admitted to the Wakefield and Huddersfield Infirmaries.

out-patient admissions. Meanwhile, approximately 20 to 30 per cent of the out-patients treated by the medical officers to the Huddersfield Infirmary were attended in their own homes. The ratios of out-, home- and in-patients admitted to the two institutions are shown in Figure 4.1.

The reasons for this bias in admissions are straightforward. Out- and home-patients cost less to treat, and involved none of the major capital expenditure associated with the construction and fitting out of infirmary wards. In 1833 the committee of the Huddersfield Infirmary computed that in-patients cost an average of £3 7s per head, out-patients 3s. Put another way, one in-patient cost as much to treat, feed and otherwise maintain as 22 out-patients. In 1862 Dr Holdsworth, physician to the Wakefield Infirmary, estimated that every additional bed provided by the charity would cost £20 to £25 per annum.[30] Moreover, there was no effective upper limit on the admission of out and home cases, except that determined by the ability of the medical staff to cope (and to a much lesser extent than with in-patients, financial limitations). This bias in favour of out-patients was apparently shared to a greater or lesser extent by most nineteenth-century medical charities, for the same reasons as those cited here, to facilitate an expansion in the numbers admitted and increased value for money.[31] Many, like the Wakefield and Huddersfield foundations, began life as dispensaries; others originated as infirmaries, whose out-patient (and more particularly, casualty) departments expanded during the century.

All in all, both institutions expanded the scale of their operations significantly during the nineteenth century.[32] In the first few decades following its foundation the Wakefield Dispensary admitted between 400 and 500 patients per annum. By 1850–1851 admissions were up to 1,115.[33] Although the addition of in-patient facilities after 1854 had little impact on total admissions, by 1862–1863 they first passed the 2,000 mark, with 2,143 in- and out-patients being accepted for treatment during this year.[34] By 1870–1871 admissions totalled 3,024.[35] Figure 4.2(a) demonstrates what these admission figures meant in terms of the proportion of the population treated. During the late eighteenth century and the first decades of the nineteenth century the institution treated something in the region of 5 per cent of the population of the town per annum. Following a period of fluctuation in the mid-nineteenth century, the proportion of the population treated began to rise steadily, passing the 10 per cent mark in the early 1860s. Figure 4.2(a) also provides a striking illustration of the relative importance of out- and in-patient admissions.

The Huddersfield Dispensary and Infirmary was from the outset a more 'important' institution in terms of wealth, support and numbers treated. In addition, the charity took patients from a wider geographical area, so although its impact was greater, it was also more diffuse. (Approximately one-third of out-patients and one-half of in-patient admissions were accepted from districts beyond the limits of the Huddersfield Township.) In the year following its foundation, 1814–1815, 1,141 out-patients were admitted.[36] By as early as 1820–1821 intake had increased to over 2,000, and by the next year it had passed the 2,500 mark.[37] Following the opening of the new purpose-built infirmary building in 1831, with facilities for the treatment of several hundred in-patients per annum, admissions continued to rise. By 1850–1851, a total of 6,644 patients were treated.[38] A peak in the number of admissions was reached around mid-century. Thereafter they declined slightly (perhaps linked to a fall-off in the number of accident and infectious disease cases as much as to a ceiling on admissions). Admissions averaged out at 5,787 out- and 377 in-patients per annum between 1855 and 1870.[39] The proportion of the population admitted to the charity, and the relationship between in- and out-patient admissions, is shown in Figure 4.2(b). Correcting the figures to take into account the large percentage of admissions taken from beyond the Township boundaries, it can be seen that the proportion of the population of Huddersfield admitted for treatment fluctuated around the 10 per cent mark throughout the nineteenth century.

These admission figures give a favourable impression of the

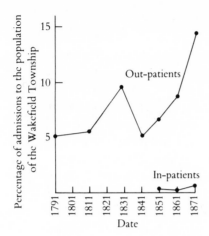

Figure 4.2(a). In- and out-patient admissions to the Wakefield Dispensary and Infirmary shown as a percentage of the population of the Wakefield Township, 1791–1871.

E = *estimate.*

Date	Population	Number of out-patients	Number of in-patients	Admissions shown as a percentage of the population of the Wakefield Township	
				Out-patients	In-patients
1791	8,066 E	418	—	5.18	—
1801	8,131	—	—	—	—
1811	8,593	482 (1812–1813)	—	5.61	—
1821	10,764	—	—	—	—
1831	12,232	1,180	—	9.65	—
1841	14,754	722[a]	—	4.89[a]	—
1851	16,989[b]	1,115	39 (1854–1855)[b]	6.56	0.23
1861	17,611	1,488	28 (1861–1862)	8.45	0.16
1871	21,076	2,934	90	13.92	0.43

[a] The sharp fall-off in admissions appears to be linked to severe financial difficulties during the 1840s.
[b] Estimate for 1854–1855 (population estimated at 17,300).
Source: Annual Reports of the Wakefield Dispensary and Infirmary.

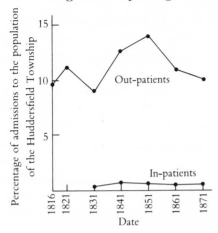

Figure 4.2(b). In- and out-patient admissions to the Huddersfield Dispensary and Infirmary shown as a percentage of the population of the Huddersfield Township, 1816–1871.

E = *estimate.*

Date	Population	Number of out-patients[a]	Number of in-patients[b]	Admissions shown as a percentage of the population of the Huddersfield Township	
				Out-patients[a]	In-patients[b]
1816	11,477 E	1,074	—	9.36	—
1821	13,284	1,518	—	11.43	—
1831	19,035	1,667	69	8.76	0.36
1841	25,068	3,128	192	12.48	0.77
1851	30,880	4,181	187	13.54	0.61
1861	34,877	3,787	176	10.86	0.50
1871	38,654	3,848	230	9.95	0.60

[a] Figures corrected by one-third to exclude patients admitted from beyond the Township boundaries.
[b] Figures corrected by one-half to exclude patients admitted from beyond the Township boundaries.
Source: Annual Reports of the Huddersfield Dispensary and Infirmary.

impact of the medical charities on the communities, but they must be qualified in two ways. Firstly, there is little guarantee of the accuracy of such figures, drawn up by hospital administrators, anxious to demonstrate the success of the charities and to encourage support. Patients were frequently counted more than once, and even Dr Walker, physician to the Huddersfield Infirmary, freely admitted that he had 'little confidence' in the accuracy of patient lists.[40] Out-patient figures were particularly susceptible to imperfect registration. Secondly, as will be seen in Section 4.3., there was considerable bias in the nature of the cases accepted and treated by the medical charities. Accident and epidemic disease cases received preferential treatment, while 'chronic' cases were commonly excluded.

The impact of the charities cannot of course be measured solely in terms of numbers admitted. It is also vital to examine the success rate of the charities in terms of cures. The results for out-patients were consistently more successful than for in-patient treatment, and this adds further weight to the argument emphasising the importance of out-patient facilities. In the Huddersfield Dispensary's first year in operation, for example, out of the 1,141 patients treated, 762 or 67 per cent were 'cured or relieved', while only 24 or 2 per cent died.[41] Similar results were obtained throughout the nineteenth century, with slight fluctuations from year to year depending upon the type of case admitted and the prevalence of epidemic disease in the town. In 1870–1871 5,772 out-patients were treated. 77 per cent were cured or relieved and 115 or 1.9 per cent died.[42] Averaging out all the out-patient figures available for the Huddersfield Dispensary and Infirmary between 1814 and 1870, we arrive at a rate of 'cured and relieved' of 77.7 per cent (62.4 per cent 'cured'). The mortality rate over this period was 1.8 per cent.[43] Comparable results were achieved by the Wakefield Dispensary and Infirmary. In 1790–1791, the first year where results are available, 418 patients were admitted. 376 or 90 per cent were cured or relieved, ten or 2.5 per cent died.[44] In 1870–1871 of the 2,934 out-patients treated, 85 per cent were cured or relieved; the mortality rate was 1.9 per cent.[45] Between 1787 and 1870 an average of 85.1 out-patients were 'cured or relieved' (70.6 per cent 'cured'); the average mortality rate was 3.5 per cent.[46] After circa 1840 both institutions recorded declining rates of cure, although mortality rates remained roughly the same. It is possible that as out-patient admissions grew, the medical officers came under increasing pressure, and that the quality of care and success rates fell. It is also possible that the fall-off in those categorised as 'cured and relieved' was due to more accurate and realistic classification and record-keeping. However, by the decade 1860–1870 the Wakefield and Huddersfield Infirmaries could still record rates of 'cured and relieved' in the order of 79 and 71 per cent respectively. Meanwhile, mortality rates averaged out at 3 and 2.4 per cent.[47]

The results for in-patient treatment in both institutions were rather less favourable. Between 1854 (and the addition of in-patient facilities) and 1870 the mortality rates in the Wakefield Infirmary averaged out to 9.94 per cent for in-patients and 3.18 per cent for out-patients. Between 1831 and 1870 the comparative rates for the Huddersfield Infirmary were 6.06 and 1.8.[48] This was in part a result of the insanitary conditions which prevailed from time to time in the hospital wards, and which led to the spread of infectious disorders.[49] But a far more important causal factor was the severity of the cases admitted as in-patients, most often serious accident and surgical cases, which carried with them a high risk of death. In the first year when patients were taken into the Huddersfield Infirmary, 1831–1832, 108 of the 137 cases admitted (79 per cent) were cured or relieved, while four patients died, giving a mortality rate of only 2.9 per cent.[50] The mortality rate did rise during the century parallel to an increase in in-patient admissions and to the growing severity of the cases. In some years the rate peaked 9 or 10 per cent. In a more 'typical' year such as 1865–1866 out of the 384 in-patients admitted 29 (7.6 per cent) died. 52 per cent were cured and 28 per cent relieved or made out-patients. (The remainder had either discharged themselves, absconded or remained under treatment.)[51] The Wakefield Infirmary achieved similar results following the admission of in-patients in 1854, although rates of both cure and death tended to be subject to very large fluctuations. The percentage of patients cured ranged between 60 and 90 per cent, with the mortality rate varying from zero to 19 per cent! Overall, especially when we remember the overriding numerical importance of out-patients, the results of both charities were reasonable.[52] It should also be remembered that these institutions frequently offered the only available source of relief to those admitted, especially with regard to cases requiring surgery.

While operating on only a small scale, the Wakefield House of

Recovery was largely successful, with the majority of its admissions being either 'cured' or 'relieved'. The mortality rate from typhus fever, the most usual class of admission, was approximately 14 per cent (compared with the usual typhus mortality rate of 25 per cent).[53] During the charity's 28 years in existence approximately 700 cases were admitted. The number of cases treated fluctuated from year to year. The highest numbers of admissions were recorded in epidemic years, when the institution became of special value. In 1837–1838, for example, 98 cases were admitted, in 1846–1847, 107.[54] The charity's overall contribution (as pointed out by contemporaries) was, however, not to be estimated solely on the basis of admissions and cures, but by the benefit of removing infected individuals from their homes, thereby curtailing the spread of disease in the community.

4.2 Supporters

Major patrons

A number of individuals made significant contributions of time, money or both towards the support of the Wakefield and Huddersfield Infirmaries. These men[55] either filled honorary posts, devoting many years of active service to the institutions, or donated very large sums of money. Their contributions made them influential in determining policy-making and the scale of operations. From this outstanding group of men, whose charitable work certainly went beyond any 'call of duty', a few individuals have been selected for special attention.[56]

The first of these, James Campey Laycock, became one of the Huddersfield Infirmary's longest-serving officers. He was Secretary to the institution from 1821 until 1860, and President from 1860 until his death in 1885. Altogether he worked for the charity for a period of 64 years. J. C. Laycock had trained as a solicitor and established himself in legal practice in Huddersfield in 1820. The practice flourished, and he quickly became very active in the business, public and philanthropic affairs of the town. Laycock was an original shareholder of the Huddersfield Banking Company, founded in 1827, and for over sixty years he gave his services and advice to the Huddersfield and Upper Agbrigg Savings Bank, first in the capacity of Honorary Secretary, and then as a member of the

Board of Management. He was also Chairman to the Huddersfield Gas Company for a great number of years. His first public appointment was as Clerk to the Justices in 1828. On the incorporation of the Borough in 1868 Laycock was appointed Clerk to the Borough Bench. He was first a nominal Whig, but in later years became a moderate Conservative. However, in contrast with his activities in public and legal affairs, Laycock never became prominent in the political life of the town.

Laycock was a staunch Churchman and was largely instrumental in the rebuilding of the Huddersfield Parish Church in 1836. He assisted in the project to build day schools in connection with the Church, and was Secretary and Treasurer to the Managers of the Day Schools from 1841 to 1884. For over forty years he was a teacher and superintendent of the Parish Church Sunday Schools. He gave £300 towards the building of new Parish Church Schools in the town and laid the foundation stones of them in 1879. Laycock was one of the founders of the Huddersfield Collegiate School (1837), a conservative institution, which made provision for middle-class education on a religious basis. He was a trustee and governor to the School for over fifty years. Laycock was active in the Church Missionary Society and was President of the Huddersfield Branch of the British and Foreign Bible Society.[57]

Soon after his arrival in Huddersfield Laycock became closely associated with the affairs of the Dispensary. In 1821 he was appointed Co-Secretary to the institution, and in 1837 Honorary Secretary. For fifty years he was responsible for the voting of an annual donation of 25 guineas by the Huddersfield Banking Company to the charity. Laycock was an annual subscriber and made several small donations to the Infirmary on his own account. His financial contributions, however, never amounted to very much. Yet, as a rule money was not something the Huddersfield Infirmary was really short of. What was very important to its functioning was organisational energy, and Laycock's special contribution to the charity was as a conscientious worker. He was actively involved in the day-to-day running of the institution and in its business affairs, and (as is confirmed by the minute books) he was rarely absent from weekly and monthly committee meetings. Laycock vigorously supported the movement to establish an infirmary in Huddersfield; he served on the Infirmary Committee, and played a large part in organising fund-raising and the building and staffing of the institution. In 1858 a specially commissioned portrait of Laycock was hung in the Board Room in recognition of his great services to the charity.

In Laycock's funeral sermon, given in February, 1885 at the Parish Church, the Reverend J. W. Bardsley stressed the importance of men such as Laycock in the development of a young community (such as Huddersfield) and in the consolidation of new public and philanthropic institutions (such as the Infirmary).

. . . our departed friend has written upon the portals of every institution with which he was associated the indelible writing of honour and good-ness, of purity and truth, and in so doing he has lengthened the cords and strengthened the stakes of commercial, professional, and philanthropic enterprise.[58]

The Infirmary Board added their tribute to Laycock's contributions to the town in the following resolution.

. . . the Board desire to record their sense of the great loss the Infirmary has sustained in the death of its president . . . The death of so eminent a townsman will be widely deplored, but nowhere will it be more deeply felt than at this Infirmary, with which he has so closely identified himself, and to which he had rendered such long and valuable services.[59]

In contrast to individuals such as Laycock, who devoted time and energy to the running of the Infirmary, others avoided active involvement, but instead donated large sums of money to the charity. One such individual was Mr Charles Brook, a prosperous cotton thread and silk manufacturer, and proprietor of Meltham Mills, near Huddersfield. Just before his death in 1869 he donated the massive sum of £30,000 for the erection of a Convalescent Home at Meltham in connection with the Huddersfield Infirmary.[60] Mr Brook was about to retire to his home in Leicestershire and in leaving the district

. . . was desirous of leaving behind some memento of the past, and of the interest he has taken in regard to the welfare and prosperity of the people, more especially those in this district, with whom, for so long, he has been associated in business.[61]

His 'solicitude' for the charity was further evinced by a legacy of £1,000 for the benefit of the Infirmary.[62]

Brook had, however, shown little previous interest in the development and running of the Infirmary. His involvement had gone only as far as the payment of an annual subscription, a donation of fifty guineas towards the Infirmary Building Fund and the acceptance of the honorary title of Vice-President in 1831.[63] It is also interesting to note that Brook had originally offered the Convalescent Home to the town of Huddersfield rather than to the Infirmary. Because of legal restraints the Corporation was forbidden to acquire property as far outside their Borough boundaries as Meltham, and the gift was subsequently offered to the Infirmary. Brook's lack of interest in the affairs of the Infirmary reflected his general non-participation in public and charitable affairs. However, Brook appears to have been generous in his financial support of local charities and was an annual subscriber to many of them. He paid for the erection of a Church at Helme (near Huddersfield), and in 1861 he contributed £100 towards the erection of a new building for the Mechanics' Institute. He was reputedly a very liberal private benefactor.[64]

Some men combined generous financial contributions with an active interest in the affairs of the medical charities. J. C. D. Charlesworth of Chapelthorpe Hall, near Wakefield, one of the largest coal proprietors in the West Riding, gave both forms of support to the Wakefield Infirmary. He was a trustee to the charity for many years, and its President from 1855 until his death in 1880. Charlesworth keenly supported the project to provide larger, purpose-built accommodation for the charity and shortly before his death he laid the foundation stone of the new infirmary building. Charlesworth (together with other members of his family) was one of the institution's most important benefactors. In 1859 he donated £46 in aid of a Special Improvement Fund. In 1863 he gave £50 towards the Prince Albert Memorial Fund (to build an additional ward), and in 1871 £500 to the Endowment Fund for the benefit of the proposed new hospital building.[65]

Charlesworth was active in local public and political affairs, and patronised several other Wakefield charities. His efforts in these directions reflected his background of a 'typical' Tory landed gentleman. Politically he was a 'true blue', and in 1857 was returned as the Conservative member for Wakefield. (He was defeated in 1859 by the Liberal candidate, Leatham.) He was a JP and a Deputy Lieutenant for the county, a member of the West Riding Police Committee, a Visitor of Private Asylums, and Colonel of the Wakefield Volunteers. Charlesworth was also a Past Master of the

Wakefield Lodge of Freemasons and President of the Wakefield
Men's Conservative Club. He was a keen sportsman, President of
the Cricket Club and Chairman of the Hunt Committee. Charlesworth was a rigid Churchman, and prominent in the support of
Wakefield Parish Church and his local church at Sandal.[66]

The Wakefield Infirmary's most important nineteenth-century
benefactor, indeed the founder of the institution, was Thomas
Clayton, a retired Wakefield businessman. Clayton did not fit in
any way into the genre of the traditional landed gentleman, represented by men such as Charlesworth. He was 'middle class', a
Liberal and keen supporter of Edward Baines and Lord Morpeth, a
Non-Conformist and a tradesman, albeit a successful one. Thomas
Clayton had been in business as a tallow chandler, but had been able
to retire in 1826, then aged only forty. Until 1848 he played very
little part in local affairs. In this year Wakefield received its Charter
of Incorporation, and Clayton was elected as one of the town's first
Aldermen. In 1854 he was chosen as Mayor, and in the same year,
then aged 68, he married for the first time. His bride, Eliza Stead of
Huddersfield, was the widow of a local merchant and the sister of
William Willans, a leading Huddersfield Congregationalist and an
active supporter of the Huddersfield Infirmary.[67] The marriage
apparently produced a marked change in his lifestyle, and 'exercised
a most beneficial influence on Mr Clayton during the remainder of
his life'.[68] First of all, the marriage was responsible for a change in
his style of worship. Until 1854 Clayton had not attended any place
of worship on a regular basis. Rather he had practised as a Berean or
Bible Christian, studying the scriptures at home. Following his
marriage he became a regular attender at the Congregationalist
Zion Chapel in Wakefield. The second, and for our purposes most
important, change wrought by his marriage, was an increased
liberality towards charitable institutions, in particular the Wakefield
Dispensary and Infirmary.

Clayton had been a subscriber to the charity and a committee
member for many years, but not a financial supporter of any great
significance. The first of many important gifts to the charity was
made in 1854, when he bought three houses in Dispensary Yard,
Northgate, and presented them to the Dispensary Committee.[69]
This addition to the accommodation enabled the charity to admit
in-patients for the first time, and in consequence an addition was
made to the title of the institution, to become 'The Wakefield

General Dispensary and Clayton Hospital'. In 1862, following several more large donations by Clayton, the name was changed again to give more prominence to the part he had played in its development, to 'The Clayton Hospital and Wakefield General Dispensary'. It became one of the few hospitals in England to be named after a benefactor.[70] In 1865 Clayton headed an Endowment Fund for the benefit of the charity with a contribution of £1,000.[71] In 1867 the Infirmary Committee rewarded Clayton's contributions to the charity in the time-honoured way; a special subscription was set up to procure a portrait of Thomas Clayton, which on completion was displayed in the Infirmary Board Room, alongside those of Colonel Charlesworth and John Binks, Honorary Secretary to the charity from 1860 to 1890. The appeal commented that a portrait would '. . . be at once a memorial of Mr Clayton, as founder of the Hospital and a great benefactor to it, and also as a Wakefield man worthy of being kept in remembrance by the present and future residents of the town and its neighbourhood'.[72]

By the time of his death in 1868 Clayton had donated a total of well over £1,800 to the Infirmary, and a legacy provided for the further annual payment of £300 to the charity. The legacy, however, would only continue to be paid if two conditions were complied with. The first of these was that no chaplain should be attached to the Hospital, but that entry to visit patients should be available to ministers of all persuasions. The second condition, or rather set of conditions, stipulated that the legacy would collapse if the hospital ever ceased to be supported by voluntary contributions or if the name was altered. The legacy would also cease if an attempt was made to transfer the institution to the Governors of the Wakefield Charities (a staunchly Conservative/Church of England organisation) or any other body, or if the nature of the government was changed.[73] The legacy continued to be paid until 1948. In the eighty years between Clayton's death and the nationalisation of the health service the charity received a total of £18,000 from the legacy.[74]

Although the Infirmary was Clayton's favourite charity, he also supported many other philanthropic enterprises, both in the town and further afield. Between 1854 and 1868 he made liberal contributions to the Zion Chapel Sunday School, the Wakefield Town Mission, the British and Foreign Bible Society, the Ragged School and several other local charities. In his will Clayton bequeathed large sums of money to a variety of charities, including the London Missionary Society, the Doncaster Deaf and Dumb Institution, the York School for the Blind, the Harrogate Bath Hospital and the Royal National Lifeboat Association.[75]

Subscribers

It is tempting to continue with the discussion of the individuals cited above, and to propose psychological or ideological reasons for their benevolence. But even with a greater amount of evidence, conclusions of this nature would be largely guesswork. More importantly, these prominent benefactors do not give a complete or representative picture of the background or concerns of the average philanthropist. The Wakefield and Huddersfield Infirmaries obtained their 'bread and butter' support from a large number of individuals, with diverse social and occupational backgrounds. These were the people who paid annual subscriptions to the charities, often for many years, who made smaller donations or bequests (of tens or even hundreds of pounds), who served from time to time on committees, canvassed support, involved themselves in fund-raising on a small scale, or performed other less conspicuous services for the benefit of the institutions. Annual subscriptions normally made up the charities' most important source of income. In 1834–1835, for example, small annual subscriptions to the Huddersfield Infirmary (usually one or two guineas) totalled £869, seven times the amount received in large donations or legacies. In 1865–1866 the Wakefield Infirmary received £515 in subscriptions, over six and a half times the total sum from donations.[76]

Lists of annual subscribers provide the most complete enumeration of individuals giving their support to the two infirmaries, or indeed to any charitable enterprise. Brian Harrison has suggested that much quantitative information might be obtained from rigorously investigating a few selected charities. Balance sheets and subscription lists were pointed to as being especially worthy of analysis.[77] Yet, on the whole, studies of philanthropy have made surprisingly little use of evidence taken from subscription lists. Prochaska made a limited use of them for a selection of charities between the years 1790 and 1830, to arrive at percentages for women subscribers and the amount of their contributions.[78] Otherwise they have been neglected, and their value unrecognised. This neglect is surprising for several reasons. They are reasonably prolific, usually being attached to the annual or press reports of charitable institutions. Moreover, the data they give tends to be reliable. Charitable institutions were dependent upon public goodwill, support and money, in particular regular annual subscriptions. Personal details of subscribers and the amount of their subscriptions were carefully recorded by the charities' officers, and omissions avoided, to ensure that no contributor would be offended, or potential subscribers deterred. Subscription lists provide us with evidence of the numbers and social composition of those supporting philanthropic enterprises, information which is usually unobtainable elsewhere.

An analysis has been made of the subscription lists of the Wakefield and Huddersfield Dispensaries and Infirmaries for a few selected years. These lists give the name, address and sex of subscribers, and the amount of each individual's contribution. From the lists we can obtain information on the total number of subscribers, the percentage of male and female subscribers, and the number of churchmen, societies, firms and companies making annual contributions to the charities. Using subscription lists in conjunction with nineteenth-century trade directories, individuals could also be matched up with their occupations.

The advantages of subscription lists have already been referred to. But there is a reverse side of the coin, and analysis of these lists is not without its problems. The length of the lists makes the task of identifying individual contributors formidable. By the mid-1860s the Wakefield Infirmary had over 400 annual subscribers, the Huddersfield Infirmary more than 800.[79] This problem is compounded by the difficulty of tracing the occupations of subscribers in directories which were often (especially in the first half of the nineteenth century) arranged by trade, rather than alphabetically by name. In addition, the classification of occupations in trade directories is occasionally inaccurate or out of date, and invariably vague. The terms 'merchant', 'manufacturer', 'shopkeeper' and 'gentleman' could encompass a wide range of incomes and social standing. The label 'shopkeeper', for instance, covered an extremely diverse group. To take one example, chemists and druggists, who were fairly active supporters of the two infirmaries, embraced a wide range of income levels and social status. Subscribers from this group, however, did tend to represent the more wealthy elements of the shopkeeping community. Chemists subscribing to the Huddersfield Infirmary included Henry Fryer, a single man who employed one female domestic servant and two assistants in his shop in the Market Place. George Hall, a married man with three children, meanwhile, employed two domestic servants, three apprentices and two general servants in his town centre chemist's shop. Hall resided at Longwood House, Fartown, on the outskirts of Huddersfield, where he farmed 92 acres and employed five farm labourers.[80] A further problem is that many individuals fell into more than one occupational group.[81] Analysis of the subscription lists, therefore, can only give us a broad indication of the occupational and class groups who developed an interest in medical charity.

The occupational analysis has been confined to male subscribers. Most women subscribers were effectively 'unemployed', although there were a few exceptions. Proprietresses of academies, shops, inns and small business concerns appeared occasionally on subscription lists. Most often, however, the women whose names appeared on the lists were the wives, daughters or sisters of male subscribers. The percentage of males who could be matched up to an occupation ranged between 72 per cent and 90 per cent. Of those left unidentified, a considerable proportion resided at a distance from Wakefield and Huddersfield, and in effect fell out of the range of this study.[82] The survey of subscribers has been limited to inhabitants of the two towns and the immediate neighbourhood.

Most subscribers lived in Wakefield or Huddersfield. Subscribers earned the privilege of recommending patients for treatment, and those living within close proximity of the charities tended to have more opportunity to exercise this privilege, and by implication more incentive to give their support. Most patients admitted to the two institutions also resided within the town boundaries of Wakefield and Huddersfield. The rules of the Wakefield Infirmary even stipulated that the benefits of the charity '. . . shall be extended to the poor residing in Wakefield or the neighbourhood, . . .', and that no patient would be visited at home who resided more than one mile from the Market Cross. The regulations of the Huddersfield Dispensary and Infirmary made no such stipulations, stating only that the institution was intended to give aid to the sick poor of the 'district'.[83] The wider geographical scope of the institution was reflected in its full title of 'The Huddersfield and Upper Agbrigg Infirmary'. From the outset the Huddersfield charity was far more liberal in its admission policies, at least as regarded geographical restrictions. Large numbers of patients were admitted from outlying villages, and such places as Holmfirth, Brighouse, Dewsbury, Mirfield and Kirkburton. In the year 1874–1875, for example, 23 per cent of out-patients and 42 per cent of in-patients were admitted from outlying districts.[84] This admissions policy could only be put into action if there were a sufficient number of subscribers to recommend patients living outside Huddersfield. The committee of the Huddersfield Infirmary were active in soliciting support from more distant areas, and, as is shown in subscription lists, generally they were able to attract considerable support from outlying villages and towns at some distance from Huddersfield.

The occupation analysis indicates that support for the two infirmaries came predominantly from the middle classes, especially commercial groups, and this could be seen as part of a middle-class effort to increase their influence in the communities. Important landowners and members of the local gentry did make financial contributions to the Wakefield and Huddersfield Infirmaries. Yet numerically, and not infrequently in terms of the value of their contributions, they were outclassed by merchants, manufacturers, and even tradesmen. It is hardly surprising, when we consider the predominance of the clothing industry in the region, to find that those most frequently leading the field in support of these charities, particularly in Huddersfield, were textile merchants and manufacturers. Other commercial groups, principally wine and spirit merchants, brewers and maltsters, corn merchants and ironfounders, were also well represented. In addition, a broad group of tradesmen were prominent on the subscription lists, including stationers and printers, grocers, drapers, ironmongers, druggists, innkeepers and individuals connected with the building trade, master joiners, builders, painters, plumbers, and so on. Meanwhile, farmers were conspicuous only by their almost complete absence from the lists.

Professional groups varied in their degree of support. Members of the legal profession appeared frequently on the lists, together with a smaller number of architects, bank managers, accountants, surveyors and agents. The medical profession on the whole was poorly represented, and usually it was only the medical officers to the institutions who subscribed. Only three doctors subscribed to the Wakefield Dispensary in the year 1852–1853 out of a total of 26 Wakefield medical practitioners (12 per cent), compared with 24 members of the legal profession out of a total of 50 (48 per cent).[85] Vicars made up a small percentage of subscribers. But we should not underestimate their importance, as they were often active in promoting congregational collections, making their personal contributions through this medium. 'Lower middle-class' groups, teachers, clerks and commercial travellers, also made up a small proportion of subscribers. The group classified as 'gentlemen' was consistently responsible for a large portion of the institutions' financial support, accounting for up to 15 per cent of all annual subscriptions to the Wakefield and Huddersfield Infirmaries. Many of those labelled as gentlemen in the trade directories had in fact retired from a commercial or professional calling. Others were major land or property owners.

The Wakefield Dispensary's subscription list for the year 1852–1853 provides us with a 'typical' example of the occupational make-up of contributors to these charities. The total number of subscribers was 187, out of which 147 (79 per cent) were male. 124 of these male subscribers (that is, 84 per cent) could be identified in the trade directories. A large cross-section of retailers accounted for 20 per cent of all identified male subscribers, a group dominated by grocers, druggists, printers and stationers, and drapers. Members of the legal and 'service' professions (including barristers, attorneys, agents and surveyors) made up the next largest group, 19 per cent of the total. 'Gentlemen' accounted for 15 per cent of subscriptions, corn merchants and maltsters 13 per cent, and textile merchants and manufacturers 10 per cent. Eight per cent were vicars, 4 per cent bankers and 2 per cent members of the medical profession.[86] More detailed breakdowns of the occupational groupings of subscribers to the two dispensaries and infirmaries in the years 1830–1831 and 1865–1866 are given in Tables 4.1 and 4.2. The breakdowns shown in the tables appear to be fairly representative of the general pattern of subscribers' occupations throughout the nineteenth century. The majority of subscribers to the House of Recovery were female, and will be discussed in Section 4.4.

Table 4.1. *Occupational groupings of subscribers to the Wakefield and Huddersfield Dispensaries, 1830–1831.*

Occupation groups	Wakefield Dispensary		Huddersfield Dispensary	
	Number in group	Percentage of total	Number in group	Percentage of total
Merchants and manufacturers	47	31.1	70	48.3
Tradesmen	46	30.5	37	25.5
Service groups and businessmen[b]	6	4.0	4	2.8
Legal profession	18	11.9	8	5.5
Medical profession	4	2.6	5	3.4
Clergymen and ministers	6	4.0	5	3.4
Builders and contractors	1	0.7	0	0
Clerks	1	0.7	2	1.4
Schoolteachers	0	0	0	0
Farmers	0	0	0	0
Gentlemen	22	14.6	14	9.7
Others	0	0	0	0
Totals[a]	151	100	145	100

[a] The totals refer to the number of identified males, not the total number of male subscribers. 151 out of the 168 (90 per cent) male subscribers to the Wakefield Dispensary were identified; 145 out of 192 (76 per cent) for the Huddersfield Dispensary.
[b] To include bankers, surveyors, agents, architects, accountants, auctioneers, etc.

Table 4.1(a). *Breakdowns of the occupational groupings of merchants and manufacturers and tradesmen, for subscribers to the Wakefield and Huddersfield Dispensaries, 1830–1831.*

(i)	Wakefield Dispensary		Huddersfield Dispensary	
Commercial and manufacturing sub-groups	Number in group	Percentage of total	Number in group	Percentage of total
Textile manufacturers	20	42.6	60	85.7
Corn merchants	15	31.9	0	0
Brewers and maltsters	5	10.6	2	2.9
Wine and spirit merchants	5	10.6	3	4.3
Dyers, chemical, soap and oil manufacturers	0	0	0	0
Ironfounders and machinery makers	0	0	2	2.9
Colliery owners	2	4.3	1	1.4
Timber merchants	0	0	1	1.4
Others	0	0	1	1.4
Totals	47	100	70	100

(ii)	Wakefield Dispensary		Huddersfield Dispensary	
Tradesmen sub-groups	Number in group	Percentage of total	Number in group	Percentage of total
Drapers, hosiers, tailors, etc.	7	15.2	7	18.9
Grocers, tea dealers, etc.	12	26.1	7	18.9
Butchers	2	4.3	0	0
Booksellers, stationers, printers, etc.	2	4.3	4	10.8
Druggists	8	17.4	4	10.8
Jewellers, watch-makers, etc.	1	2.2	0	0
Ironmongers	2	4.3	2	5.4
General dealers	1	2.2	0	0
Building trades	6	13.0	3	8.1
Innkeepers, hoteliers	4	8.7	8	21.6
Curriers	0	0	2	5.4
Others	1	2.2	0	0
Totals	46	100	37	100

Sources: 17th AR HD, 1830–1831; 44th AR WD, 1830–1831; Parson and White, 1828; White, 1837.

Table 4.2. *Occupational groupings of subscribers to the Wakefield and Huddersfield Infirmaries, 1865–1866.*

Occupation groups	Wakefield Infirmary		Huddersfield Infirmary	
	Number in group	Percentage of total	Number in group	Percentage of total
Merchants and manufacturers	91	29.2	272	53.2
Tradesmen	101	32.4	124	24.3
Service groups and businessmen	17	5.4	27	5.3
Legal profession	19	6.1	22	4.3
Medical profession	6	1.9	13	2.5
Clergymen and ministers	18	5.8	15	2.9
Builders and contractors	3	1.0	10	2.0
Clerks	14	4.5	2	0.4
Schoolteachers	3	1.0	1	0.2
Farmers	3	1.0	4	0.8
Gentlemen	34	10.9	21	4.1
Others	3	1.0	0	0
Totals[a]	312	100	511	100

[a] 312 out of 359 (87 per cent) male subscribers to the Wakefield Infirmary could be identified; 511 out of 706 (72 per cent) for the Huddersfield Infirmary.

Table 4.2(a). *Breakdowns of the occupational groupings of merchants and manufacturers and tradesmen, for subscribers to the Wakefield and Huddersfield Infirmaries, 1865–1866.*

(i) Commercial and manufacturing sub-groups	Wakefield Infirmary Number in group	Wakefield Infirmary Percentage of total	Huddersfield Infirmary Number in group	Huddersfield Infirmary Percentage of total
Textile manufacturers	20	22.0	218	80.1
Corn merchants	23	25.3	4	1.5
Brewers and maltsters	10	11.0	6	2.2
Wine and spirit merchants	4	4.4	6	2.2
Dyers, chemical, soap and oil manufacturers	10	11.0	12	4.4
Ironfounders and machinery makers	9	10.0	13	4.8
Colliery owners	5	5.5	2	0.7
Timber merchants	3	3.3	3	1.1
Others	7	7.7	8	2.9
Totals	91	100	272	100

(ii) Tradesmen sub-groups	Wakefield Infirmary Number in group	Wakefield Infirmary Percentage of total	Huddersfield Infirmary Number in group	Huddersfield Infirmary Percentage of total
Drapers, hosiers, tailors, etc.	22	21.8	20	16.1
Grocers, tea dealers, etc.	13	12.9	21	16.9
Bakers, confectioners	3	3.0	3	2.4
Butchers	5	5.0	7	5.6
Booksellers, stationers, printers, etc.	9	8.9	7	5.6
Druggists	11	10.9	7	5.6
Jewellers, watch-makers, etc.	4	4.0	3	2.4
Ironmongers	4	4.0	7	5.6
General dealers	3	3.0	4	3.2
Building trades	9	8.9	11	8.9
Innkeepers, hoteliers	10	9.9	14	11.3
Curriers	2	2.0	5	4.0
Others	6	5.9	15	12.1
Totals	101	100	124	100

Sources: 35th AR HI, 1865–1866; 79th AR WI, 1865–1866; White, 1866.

4.3 Motivations

The founding of the medical charities
An account of the setting up of the dispensaries and infirmaries in Wakefield and Huddersfield forms a good starting point for a discussion of the motivations of those supporting these charities. The promoters of these institutions set out in their appeals for support the basic reasons as they saw them for the establishment of medical facilities for the poor in the two communities. The Wakefield Dispensary was set up in 1787, becoming only the seventh dispensary to be founded in the provinces, and the first to be established in West Yorkshire. Its predecessors had been founded, in most cases, in what were by late eighteenth-century standards, major centres of population: Bristol (in 1775, with a population of 100,000), Liverpool (1777, 35,000) and Newcastle (1777, 20,000).[87]

There are no obvious reasons why a dispensary should have been set up in Wakefield in this particular year. There was no significant increase in the population of the town in the late eighteenth century (it being less than 8,000), and no noticeable deterioration in the health of the inhabitants (marked, for example, by an increase in epidemic disease or in industrial accidents). However, its establishment did coincide with a discernible fall in living standards and an era of depression.[88] Medical services for the poor of Wakefield, meanwhile, were lacking just as much as elsewhere. The nearest infirmaries were at Leeds (nine miles from Wakefield) and York (29 miles), and these charities would only admit patients living at a distance in exceptional cases. Meanwhile, Poor Law relief was very limited and the provision of medical aid by friendly societies still in its infancy.[89]

The enthusiasm of a few local clergymen, doctors, gentlemen and businessmen was directly responsible for the founding of the Wakefield Dispensary. The first two groups were already well acquainted with the condition of the poor, and the Vicar of Wakefield, the Reverend Michael Bacon, became the charity's first President, and the town's two leading medical men, Drs Richardson and Dawson, the Dispensary's first medical officers. The first committee was composed of members of the town's leading families, including merchants, bankers, professional men and local 'gentlemen'. Wakefield's three leading mercantile families were all involved. Mr John Naylor became the charity's first Treasurer, and members of the Milnes and Heywood families served on the committee. The Dispensary was initially located in rented houses in Northgate on the west side of the Parish Church. In 1821 it moved to a room under the Music Saloon, in 1831 to a house in Barstow Square and in 1854 to Dispensary Yard, Northgate. (See Map 3.)

The setting up of the Dispensary may have been due, at least in part, to humanitarian considerations, or to the desire of certain individuals for the prestige which active involvement in a charitable enterprise conferred. A more likely reason was that its establishment was closely linked to considerations of civic pride. Wakefield was after all the administrative, judicial and electoral headquarters of the West Riding. And as seen in Chapter 2, Wakefield reached something of a peak in its economic and civic development in the late eighteenth century. The last quarter of the eighteenth century was an economic boom period, and much money was available to fund charitable enterprise. This period was also marked by a phase of church building, and the founding of other civic and charitable institutions.

Whatever motivations led to its establishment, they appear to have ceased to be of any importance by the first half of the nineteenth century. During this period the charity literally limped along, facing an almost continual lack of support and shortage of funds, large debts and frequent threats of closure. The officers of the Dispensary blamed the extension of the 'field of charity' in Wakefield, and the competition for support this engendered, for the poor state of funds.[90] Others pointed to the bad management of those in charge.[91] During the first decades of the nineteenth century there appeared to be an almost complete lack of interest on the part of the public in the survival of the charity. In 1810, for example, it was reported that no meeting of the Dispensary Committee had been held for four years because Tuesday, the day on which the committee was supposed to meet annually, was '. . . so inconvenient, that many of its members cannot attend; so that when a meeting has been called, not more than two or three have usually attended . . .'.[92] This decline in support and interest can be closely linked to the general economic and social stagnation which took place in Wakefield during the first half of the nineteenth century. It can also be linked to personal financial disasters such as the collapse of the Naylor family's cloth business and of several large banking firms, representatives of which had sat on the committee and made substantial financial contributions. The most surprising aspect of this period is that the charity survived at all. By 1810 over £80 was owed to the Treasurer.[93] In 1816 a meeting was held to determine the 'future continuance' of the institution, and in 1827 the committee pointed to the ever-increasing debt owed to the Treasurer, '. . . an increase, which threatens it with dissolution at no very distant period, unless the liberality and benevolence of the more opulent part of the inhabitants interpose to prevent so great a calamity!'.[94]

Despite the wavering support the Dispensary received from the inhabitants of Wakefield, sufficient funds were raised to get it through each successive crisis, and the institution was able to operate in much the same way for almost seventy years, with several hundred individuals being treated annually as out- or home-patients. In the year 1814–1815, for example, 474 patients were admitted for treatment, in 1842–1843, 693.[95] By the mid-nineteenth century the charity was functioning in a much more satisfactory way. Its financial position had improved to such an extent, by an increase in annual subscriptions, donations, and congregational collections, that there was even a surplus of funds in some years. At last, in 1851 the committee could report to the Dispensary's supporters on the '. . . growing prosperity and efficiency of the Institution'.[96]

It was not until 1854 that the charity extended itself into an infirmary. Surprisingly enough, considering the financial problems already faced by the Dispensary, the addition of wards for in-patients was proposed as early as 1829. The issue was first raised by the Dispensary's surgeons, who claimed that more serious surgical cases could be better attended in hospital wards, rather than at the patients' own homes. Their intentions of extending the operations of the charity were, however, resisted by the senior physician to the Dispensary, Dr Crowther. He argued that provision for surgical patients was not necessary in a town such as Wakefield where accidents by machinery were still relatively uncommon, and that the establishment of wards would lead to the impoverishment of other local charities, in particular the Fever Hospital. Whether Crowther's arguments won the day, or whether the charity's precarious financial position curtailed any hopes of expansion, is not clear, but the idea of admitting in-patients was shelved for another decade.[97]

In 1840, at the annual meeting of subscribers, it was agreed that there was a necessity to 'fit up' a few wards for the purpose of admitting patients requiring surgical aid. A sub-committee was even appointed to inquire into the cost of such a provision. The subscribers were apparently confident in the success of their venture, and the *Wakefield Journal* commented '. . . nor have we the slightest doubt that when an appeal to the public is made, that ample means will be readily granted to that institution to enable it to extend its general usefulness'.[98] Applications were made to the local nobility, gentry and clergy, and the Earls of Harewood and Fitzwilliam consented to give the appeal their support.[99] The institution was still bedevilled by financial difficulties, however, and in 1842 the project to establish surgical wards was again abandoned.

By the mid-nineteenth century the need for in-patient facilities was recognized by both lay supporters and medical men alike. (Dr Crowther, one of the scheme's loudest opponents, died in 1849.) Accident cases occurred far more frequently, a direct result of an increase in the number of coal mines, railways and factories in the area. Even so, it seems unlikely that a hospital would have been set up in Wakefield had it not been for the liberality of its founder, Thomas Clayton. He not only donated the houses which came to accommodate the in-patient wards in 1854,[100] but financially he carried the institution through its first few difficult years. In 1864, for example, the Infirmary Committee reported a deficit in the annual income of £300. Clayton 'bailed' the charity out by setting up an Endowment Fund, headed with a contribution of £1,000.[101]

By the time of Clayton's death in 1868 the charity had been placed on a much more secure financial footing. The number of subscribers had more than doubled since 1854, to over 400, and approximately quadrupled since the early 1840s, and the institution had been able to attract a large number of wealthy patrons, such as the Charlesworths, Gaskells, Foljambes and Pilkingtons.[102] The Endowment Fund yielded an annual interest of several hundred pounds, and income from other sources, such as congregational collections, donations and legacies, had increased significantly. In 1868 the total income of the charity was £935.[103] In the late 1860s the Clayton

Hospital finally entered upon a new era of widespread support and financial security.

The Huddersfield Dispensary and Infirmary experienced a far more rapid development than its Wakefield counterpart. From the opening of the Dispensary in July, 1814 it enjoyed a greater degree of support and relative freedom from financial problems. The Dispensary was established ostensibly to commemorate the ending of the Napoleonic Wars. But its foundation probably also owed something to the anxiety of local doctors and employees of labour about the dearth of medical provisions for the poor of the district. The War had caused considerable distress in the manufacturing districts, and as a result the poor had become more dependent than ever upon charitable relief.

The more influential inhabitants of Huddersfield may also have been concerned about the fact that they were falling behind other West Riding towns in the provision of medical services. By 1814 there were general infirmaries in Leeds (1767) and Sheffield (1797), and dispensaries in Halifax (1807), Wakefield (1787) and Doncaster (1792). Reference has been made in Chapter 2 to the importance of the first few decades of the nineteenth century to Huddersfield's development. The rapid population increase was paralleled by industrial growth and efforts to improve the town, including the founding of new churches, education institutes and charities, and progress in sanitary reform. The establishment of the Dispensary in 1814 fits in closely with this pattern of improvement, dynamism and increasing civic pride.

The first Dispensary Committee was almost exclusively composed of local manufacturers, including John Fisher (silk spinner), Robert Firth (machine maker), J. M. Ridgway (woolstapler), Henry Stables (woollen merchant and manufacturer), Thomas Atkinson (cloth manufacturer), two members of the Battye family (cloth manufacturers) and John Hannah (merchant and manufacturer). The first Treasurers were Messrs Brook and Sons, woollen merchants and manufacturers.[104] There were no clergymen on the committee, and, while the Dispensary attracted some early aristocratic patronage (Sir John Ramsden was the first patron to the institution, Sir Joseph Radcliffe, Bart., the first President), the initiative for the establishment of the charity came almost exclusively from prominent members of the local business community and employees of labour, particularly those involved in the textile industry. The chief purposes of this group were eloquently expressed in the Second Annual Report of the institution, published in 1816.

> If it be universally admitted that the genuine Wealth of Nations consists not more in a numerous than in a healthy Population, doubtless whatever tends to promote it becomes of infinite Importance . . . The Committee are more immediately led to this Remark, by observing that the far greater Number of the Patients cured during the last Year, consists of Children and Adults who have not passed the meridian of Life . . . If it be our Duty to guard the Poor from the frequent ill Effects of defective Food and Clothing, of ill ventilated Abodes, or dangerous Callings; as well as our Interest as much as possible to arrest the spread of Infection, which commonly has its rise in the Abodes of Poverty, this Charity imperiously calls for your Support.[105]

In the first ten years the medical officers of the Dispensary treated a grand total of 17,579 'objects'.[106] By 1824 admissions generally added up to well over 2,000 per annum. Most admissions were epidemic disease or accident cases, which were treated in a rented house in Packhorse Yard.

Within ten years the officers and committee of the Dispensary were already pressing for the establishment of hospital facilities in the town. In 1823 the committee expressed concern about the fact that subscriptions were failing to keep up with the increased number of applications for treatment, due directly to the massive population growth of the district. The committee saw this as an 'auspicious' point '. . . to draw the Attention of the Governors to the Expediency of providing a Fund for the Erection of Wards, for the Reception of a limited Number of In-Patients: more especially for those frequent Accidents arising from the extensive Use of Machinery.[107] In 1824 an appeal was set up to raise funds for the projected hospital, and a sub-committee was appointed to consider the cost of such an expansion in facilities. The sub-committee, which had been assisted in its estimates by Dr Turnbull, physician to the charity, reported back to the governors that a suitable building for the Dispensary and for twelve to fifteen beds could be built and equipped for around £2,500, and that the annual expenditure of such an institution would be in the range of £800 to £900.[108]

The appeal was given further impetus by a 'melancholy accident', which took place in Huddersfield in April, 1825. Sixteen workmen, employed in the erection of the new Congregationalist chapel in Ramsden Street, were killed or seriously injured when the platform they were working on collapsed, throwing them to the ground from a height of over fifty feet. This incident brought home to the public the necessity of making some provision for the reception of urgent accident cases in Huddersfield itself, and revived the campaign to raise funds for the proposed infirmary.[109] Mr Samuel Clay, a Huddersfield linen draper, entered into the fund-raising effort with particular gusto. Within one week in May, 1825 Clay obtained, by personal application to 'his wealthy neighbours', donations amounting to £3,329 and the promise of annual subscriptions totalling £100 towards the support of an infirmary.[110] Clay's efforts marked a significant turning point in the campaign and much of the credit for the founding of the Infirmary must go to him.[111]

The Dispensary's medical officers also entered into the campaign with some enthusiasm. The physicians to the charity, Drs Turnbull and Walker, wrote and circulated pamphlets advocating support for the project. In his appeal to the population of Huddersfield Dr Turnbull outlined the main purposes of the proposed extended institution: to isolate and treat those suffering from contagious diseases, and to reduce the distress caused to the poor by sickness in the family, which led often to debt, 'moral despair' and a reliance on the parish. The rapid increase in the population of the district, Turnbull added, 'principally engaged in sedentary and unwholesome occupations', had aggravated the above problems.[112]

However, little significant progress was made with the project until 1828. At the annual meeting of subscribers in June, and later at a general meeting of the inhabitants of the town, held at the George Hotel in October, it was resolved

That as the present building is not adequate to the wants of the sick poor, in this district, it is the unanimous opinion of the meeting, that the time is arrived, when an Infirmary should be erected, on such a scale, and of such dimension, . . . as may be co-adequate with the resources and wants of the district . . .

By October, 1828 donations and subscriptions to the project totalled £7,678, which the Dispensary Committee believed was adequate to pay for the erection of the building. The committee was confident that the sum of £900 per annum could be raised for the maintenance of the institution.[113] An Infirmary Committee was appointed to organise the erection of a suitable building and to continue the fund-raising effort. The Infirmary Committee was composed predominantly of manufacturers, plus a few members of the legal profession, local gentlemen and one or two tradesmen (and the Dispensary's medical officers). In 1829 a plot of land was leased on the New North Road from the Ramsden family and an architect appointed. In June of the same year the foundation stone of the 'Huddersfield and Upper Agbrigg Infirmary' was laid by Sir John Charles Ramsden. Two years later to the day the building was opened, with much ceremony, for the reception of patients. The total cost of the building and its fitting out had amounted to £7,500. The scale on which the charity came to operate in 1831 exceeded the earlier expectations of its promoters. The Infirmary building was much bigger than anticipated, it was purpose built, needed a large number of staff to cope with the increased work load, and in many years cost well over £1,500 to run, twice the estimate of the founders.

Aims and ambitions

An examination of the motivations and ambitions of the supporters of the two infirmaries and the House of Recovery, as expressed in annual reports and other relevant documents, initially confronts us with an apparently wide assortment of impulses and aims: religious, social, economic, pragmatic and humanitarian. A closer look at the evidence, however, suggests that the emphasis lay very much with practical rather than ideological or humanitarian concerns. The main expedient was to provide a cheap and efficient form of medical relief for the sick poor, particularly those suffering from contagious diseases, which threated to invade the homes of the wealthy, and accident cases, suffered for the most part by employees of local manufacturers.

The main reason cited for the setting up of infirmaries in the two towns was to cope with the enormous growth in accident cases, resulting in particular from the increased use of machinery in the region. This was of the greatest importance in Huddersfield, where a rapid population growth had been paralleled by an expansion of the factory economy, particularly in the textile industry. The Fourteenth Report of the committee of the Huddersfield Dispensary, for instance, had drawn 'the attention of the Subscribers to the expediency of providing a suitable building, for the reception of a limited number of In-patients: . . . the population of the district has rapidly increased, and with it an extension of machinery, and an increased risk of life and limb: the number of accidents has been appallingly great during the last few years . . . .'.[114] At the ceremony for the laying of the foundation stone of the Huddersfield Infirmary in 1829 J. C. Ramsden, MP stressed that 'in a manufacturing county, where machinery is necessarily extensively employed, the working classes are exposed to a much greater danger than in an agricultural district, or one less populously inhabited. It is in great measure to provide against casualties of this nature, that Infirmaries become necessary'.[115] In the Wakefield area the growth in the number of mining concerns increased the incidence of industrial accidents. In both towns the expansion of the railway network in the mid-nineteenth century resulted in a large number of accident cases, involving both passengers and railway workers.[116]

Accidents consistently accounted for a large proportion of all the cases treated by the two hospitals, and for the vast majority of in-patient admissions. Indeed the in-patient departments came to cater almost exclusively for surgical and accident cases. The committee of the Huddersfield Dispensary had given great priority to accident cases, which were the only category to be admitted without a subscriber's recommendation.

Accidents, when they befall the objects of the charity, are *immediately* admitted under the care of the surgeon of the week, *without a letter of recommendation*, on application at the dispensary, or on being brought within the limits for visiting patients (their emphasis).[117]

This policy continued following the addition of in-patient wards. By the end of the Huddersfield Infirmary's first working year 137 in-patients had been admitted, including eighteen cases of fracture, many severe. Twelve amputations had been performed, together with various other 'important' operations.[118]

In the year 1846–1847 379 accident cases were admitted as in- or home-patients out of a grand total of 6,709 admissions.[119] In 1857 the committee of the Huddersfield Infirmary reported that the mortality rate of in-patients had increased considerably during the previous year (to over 6 per cent) due to the admission of many 'terrible accident cases', and in 1864 they drew the attention of the subscribers to the 'excessive number' of cases of scalds, fractures and severe accidents.[120] In 1864 T. Holmes reported that accident cases still made up the majority of in-patient admissions, although they had become less severe in recent years, due in part to a reduction in railway accidents. While the railways were under construction in the Huddersfield area one of the Infirmary surgeons claimed to have performed eleven primary operations in fourteen days! In 1862, 93 in-patients were admitted following accidents and injury, out of a total of 328 (28.4 per cent). Out of the 328 admitted 39 died (11.9 per cent). Five of the deaths had resulted from 'machinery accidents', three from 'railway accidents', two from 'ordinary accidents' one from 'injury by a cart shaft', three from burns and scalds and two from lacerations of the foot! When Holmes visited the Infirmary, out of the thirty surgical cases in the hospital wards (out of 38 in-patients) seven were accident and seven 'acute' cases, including three cases where amputations had been performed.[121] In the year 1873–1874 a total of 518 in-patients were admitted to the Huddersfield Infirmary. Of these 174 were accident cases (34 per cent). Eighteen of the 32 deaths occurring amongst Huddersfield Infirmary in-patients in the year 1880–1881 were accident cases. In the same year, 1,736 'casualties' were treated as out-patients.[122]

The revised set of rules drawn up by the committee of the Wakefield Infirmary following the addition of wards in 1854 stated that in-patient admissions would be limited to surgical and accident cases. In a similar way to the Huddersfield charity, cases of 'sudden emergency or accidents' could be admitted without a recommendation, although one was to be secured following the admission.[123] The Wakefield Infirmary admitted a total of 68 in-patients during the year 1865–1866. Sixty (88 per cent) were surgical or accident cases, including 29 fractures, nine wounds, three dislocations and ten contusions.[124] Between 1863 and 1871 a total of 267 fracture cases alone were taken into the wards of the Wakefield Infirmary (over 45 per cent of in-patient admissions).[125] Once the policy of admitting a high proportion of accident cases was taken up, it became self-perpetuating; accident cases quickly filled up the few available beds, and were tedious to treat.

 Promoters of the charities stressed the importance of the treatment of accident cases in commercial districts such as Wakefield and Huddersfield in their annual reports and appeals for support. This provision, they claimed, not only relieved the employer from the burden of providing for his injured workers, but rapidly restored the workman to his calling, a factor of special importance in an area 'whose local Prosperity is so intimately interwoven with the Maintenance of the Health and Strength of the laborious Poor'.[126] Special appeals were made by the officers and committees of the two infirmaries to obtain financial support from those who reaped most benefits from the charities: factory owners, and railway and mining companies. The *Leeds Mercury*, for instance, noted in 1847

Our attention has been called to the great number of cases from accident that have of late been brought to the Infirmary, and to the great drawback they must necessarily cause upon the funds of the institution. Now that so many railway works are in progress in the neighbourhood of Huddersfield, it ought to become a matter of serious consideration on the part of the contractors and sub-contractors, that they have an imperative duty to perform in contributing liberally to the funds of the Infirmary, in order to meet the extra charges that now fall upon it, in consequence of the unavoidable accidents that occur in the construction of railway works.[127]

The annual report of the Infirmary for the same year remarked

During the last six months 31 cases have been admitted as in-patients for injuries received on the railways now forming in this neighbourhood. Many of these have been of a severe and complicated nature – requiring a long course of treatment – and the cost to the charity has been necessarily large. Perhaps, however, no class of cases shows the value of an Infirmary more strikingly than railway accidents. Where otherwise could they obtain that prompt and efficient aid so essential to their proper management?[128]

During 1847 a deputation had been organised to wait on the different railway companies operating in the area to request an increase in subscriptions. Several companies agreed to this, and in fact the subscriptions paid by railway companies to both the Wakefield and Huddersfield Infirmaries increased during the nineteenth century, albeit slowly. By 1859 the Wakefield Infirmary received £10 per annum from the Lancashire and Yorkshire and Great Northern Railway Companies, by 1861 £15. In 1856 the Huddersfield Infirmary received £15 in subscriptions from the same sources.[129]

The most notable increase in subscriptions and donations came from local industrialists and employers of labour, especially those involved in the Huddersfield textile industry. By 1831 13 per cent of subscriptions to the Wakefield Dispensary were paid by textile merchants and manufacturers. In Huddersfield the figure was 41 per cent. The actual number of textile manufacturers subscribing to the Wakefield charity remained steady, but as a proportion of the total subscribers they had declined to just 6 per cent by 1866. The percentage of subscriptions paid by textile manufacturers to the Huddersfield Infirmary, meanwhile, remained level at between 40 and 45 per cent throughout the mid-nineteenth century. In both towns, but in particular Wakefield, with its more diverse industrial base, many subscribers were involved in manufacturing concerns other than textiles: for instance, coal mining, machinery making, brewing and chemical manufacturing. Taken together (with textile manufacturers) this group accounted for over a quarter and a half of all subscriptions to the Wakefield and Huddersfield Infirmaries respectively by 1866.[130] (See Tables 4.1 and 4.2.)

For a subscription of just a few guineas per annum an employer of labour could cover himself against accidents in the workplace, a much cheaper alternative to providing adequate safety precautions, employing a factory surgeon or paying for the medical treatment of employees on an individual basis. A survey of the large number of accident cases reported in the local press indicated that many of those gaining admission to the infirmaries were employees of subscribers, most being injured in their place of work. In July, 1860, for example, two accident cases, which had been treated in the Huddersfield Infirmary, were reported in the *Huddersfield Examiner*. The first case was that of a young man, Frederick Marsden of Kirkburton, who was crushed while unloading timber at the goods shed at Huddersfield station. He was taken to the Infirmary, but died two days after his admission. The second case was that of Elizabeth Middleton, an eleven-year old mule piecer, employed in the factory of Messrs George Crosland and Sons, Lockwood. The girl fell into an unprotected steam pipe in a fulling room. She was also taken to the Infirmary, but was so badly scalded that she died within a few days.[131]

A large proportion of hospital admissions and all of the admissions to the Wakefield House of Recovery were infectious disease cases. The two infirmaries normally did not admit these cases as in-patients, but treated them as out- or home-cases. In the year 1815–1816 over 750 of the 1,600 admissions (47 per cent) to the Huddersfield Dispensary were cases of infectious disease. The most frequently occurring diseases were smallpox (331 or 21 per cent of admissions), scarlatina (246, 15 per cent), scrofula (45, 3 per cent), phthisis (21, 1.5 per cent) and whooping cough (16, 1 per cent).[132] In 1824 the report of the Huddersfield Dispensary claimed that the 'extraordinary prevalence of Small Pox, during the Year, swelled the amount of patients as well as the proportion of deaths, ...'.[133] The report of the Dispensary for 1826–1827 noted an enormous rise in the number of patients, which exceeded the total for the previous year by over 800. It blamed this increase on the distress in the area and on the 'prevalence of Measles, which raged for several months amongst the Children of the Poor, and was a fertile source of Infant Mortality'.[134] In the year 1857–1858 typhus and typhoid raged epidemically during the winter months and pushed up admissions to nearly 6,000.[135] As late as 1873–1874 86 cases of zymotic disease occurred amongst home-patients to the Huddersfield Infirmary (almost 10 per cent of cases).[136]

The value of the institutions in treating disease cases was estimated in several ways. First of all fast and efficient medical treatment could in many cases result in a speedy recovery for those afflicted. Quick intervention could also prevent the spread of the disease to other family members and the community at large. The committee of the House of Recovery laid emphasis on both these factors, adding that removal from an unhealthy home environment was often sufficient to prompt recovery. Dr Crowther of Wakefield pointed out the special value of the House of Recovery and similar institutions thus:

The Utility of this Institution (the House of Recovery) is not to be estimated, like other medical Charities by the number of patients admitted and cured, but by the number of lives which have been saved, by avoiding exposure to Infection. One patient sent in the early stage of the disease from a large family, may prevent the Illness of the whole family, and the Death, perhaps of several of them.[137]

Perhaps a more important consideration for the wealthy classes was the danger of the spread of epidemic disease into their homes. The committee of the House of Recovery outlined this threat very succinctly:

. . . we trust the public will see that by supporting the Fever Ward, it is not only performing an act of the greatest humanity, under circumstances of peculiar exigence and distress, but is at the same time conferring a positive benefit on themselves, by being able to crush a disease in its birth, which might otherwise very shortly creep into their own dwellings, to the destruction of themselves and their dearest connections.[138]

Although disease usually originated in the poorer areas of town, in its spread it was no discriminator between classes, and typhus fever, smallpox, measles, and so on, still attacked the middle and upper classes in large numbers. (Even the Royal Family were afflicted with typhoid fever and diphtheria.)[139] During an outbreak of influenza in 1833, for instance, Clara Clarkson of Alverthorpe Hall, Wakefield (a subscriber to both the Fever Hospital and Dispensary), noted in her diary that most of her family had contracted the disease. She also reported that someone in 'every family' in Wakefield had been afflicted with influenza, sometimes the whole family. Clara Clarkson also recorded many cases of smallpox, typhoid and consumption amongst members of her own class.[140]

Fear of infection from servants was particularly strong. The committee of the House of Recovery soon latched on to this special anxiety. In their Sixth Report they noted

In many instances of late, Typhus Fever has first attacked the Servants in respectable families; when their immediate removal to the House has, *in every instance*, been attended by the happy result of security to the remainder, in addition to the gratification afforded to the minds of Masters and others, by having such sources of well-founded anxiety and alarm removed from the presence of their families (their emphasis).[141]

The committee of the House of Recovery undertook to treat servants and remove them from the home. Special rates were offered for the treatment of subscribers' servants. Non-subscribers were to pay 1s 6d per day, subscribers just 1s. Between 1826 and 1854, 75 (11 per cent) of the 696 patients admitted to the House of Recovery were servants or apprentices. In 1839, for example, nine out of the 49 admissions were servants, in most cases of subscribers. In April of this year the Reverend Garvey, the husband of a subscriber, sent a domestic servant afflicted with typhus fever to the House: in 1841 he sent two more servants, this time suffering from continued fever. Employees of local manufacturers and shopkeepers also accounted for a high proportion of admissions. Railway workers, meanwhile, made up one of the highest single categories of admissions. Between 1837 and 1847, for example, 34 employees of the various railway companies operating in the Wakefield area were admitted to the charity.[142]

The committees of the medical charities referred frequently to the practical advantages of shifting employers' responsibilities for the medical care of their workers or servants on to medical charity. They also stressed the economy of these institutions. In particular they emphasised that the medical and lay officers, through personal contact with the applicants for relief, were able to discriminate between 'deserving' and 'undeserving' persons. Moreover, in comparison with other charities, medical charity removed a root cause of distress, sickness or injury, instead of merely relieving distress on a temporary basis. The Fifth Report of the Huddersfield Infirmary remarked

The Board trust it will not be necessary to dwell on the importance of Infirmaries; wherever they have existed, experience has shown that they combine advantages rarely to be secured by the most liberal exercise of private charity – Here the benevolent may find a channel in which their bounty may flow without suspicion of abuse – situated in a district, abounding in machinery, open night and day to pressing cases of accident this Infirmary has already been a blessing to the surrounding poor.[143]

Again in 1863 the committee of the Huddersfield Infirmary stated

Such an application of charity is not subject to the abuses and imposition that too often attach to the relief of mere destitution. It husbands the resources of society when viewed in reference to the mitigation of suffering, the speedy return of the workman to his labour, and the probable diminution of the loss of life.[144]

Ideas of 'maximum utility' and 'value for money' in return for a modest subscription in the 'Joint-Stock bank of Charity'[145] seemed likely to appeal to the commercial classes of Wakefield and Huddersfield. The strong link between sickness and poverty was also pointed out. Illness could lead to the pauperisation of a family, and hence to a permanent drain on the poor rate. Voluntary contributions were put forward as being preferable to an increase in the poor rate or in the impositions of central government, which offered none of the attractions or returns of a charitable investment.

Humanitarian and religious considerations played some part in both the winning of support for the charities and presumably in motivating the philanthropic. However, while appeals to the humanitarianism of the public were widely utilised, they were normally linked with and secondary to practical considerations. The 36th Report of the Huddersfield Infirmary provides a typical example of this 'combined' appeal.

So long as a labouring man or mechanic is under the influence of neglected disease, he is circulating means of contagion to others, and instead of a producer is perforce a consumer; at the same time being himself unnaturally consumed. If we compare the painful, costly and pernicious results, as they fell upon the whole community as well as on individuals, of a few hundred such sufferers, with the opposite effects of their being restored to their families and callings, the argument statistically due to sound enlightened economy as well as fellow feeling benevolence of medical institutions, is irresistible.[146]

There appears to be a relative absence of purely altruistic concerns. This is not to say that supporters of the medical charities felt no sympathy with the plight of the poor or with those who were admitted as patients, but it does seem the donor expected, and indeed received, more from the charities than the satisfaction of performing an act of kindness.

For the more religiously inclined the performance of acts of charity held out the promise of ultimate salvation, and the committees of the two infirmaries appealed on many occasions to the 'Christian benevolence' of the public. In 1852 the committee of the Wakefield Dispensary declared in their annual report,

An Institution whose benefits are acknowledged by all, should not be suffered to languish for want of funds. Every Christian man should feel himself called upon to contribute to it according to his ability; every Christian congregation should remember it in their offerings to God . . . . Days of darkness and sorrow must sooner or later be the portion of us all, but 'blessed is he that considereth the poor, the Lord shall deliver him in time of trouble'.[147]

Similarly, in 1868 the committee of the Huddersfield Infirmary offered the following spiritual comfort in their annual address.

To all those who have, by means of this House of Mercy, contributed towards the alleviation of the languishing bed of sickness, it will be no small satisfaction in their suffering and dying hour, to meditate upon the generous retrospects of here and there the hard pillow of destitution soothed, a pang of physical affliction gently assuaged, and sorrow lightened and relieved through the instrumentality of this great Christian Charity.[148]

A number of financial and other practical advantages could accrue from active involvement in such voluntary societies as the Wakefield and Huddersfield Infirmaries. Important practice-building opportunities were gained by the doctors who became active in these institutions as medical officers and committee members.[149] Almost without exception parliamentary candidates and those involved in local politics at least subscribed, or, preferably, held official posts or served on the infirmary committees. Subscribers to the Wakefield Dispensary in 1853, for instance, included fourteen Councillors, four Aldermen and the Mayor of Wakefield, John Gregory. Alderman Robert Hodgson was President of the charity, Alderman Clayton an Auditor and committee member, and Councillor Ash a committee member. The Member of Parliament for Wakefield, George Sanders, also served on the Dispensary Committee.[150] Large numbers of bankers and members of the legal profession became involved in financing and running these charities, often filling the posts of Honorary Secretary or Treasurer. John Battye, an attorney, became the first Secretary to the Huddersfield Dispensary in 1814, while J. C. Laycock, by profession a solicitor, served the Huddersfield Dispensary and Infirmary for many years, first as Honorary Secretary, then President. Members of the Leatham banking family acted in the capacity of Treasurers to the Wakefield Dispensary and Infirmary for a great number of years. Contacts formed through the medical charities may well have brought clients to these groups.

Merchants and tradesmen, meanwhile, may have utilised meetings of the charities to make business contacts, and one very real advantage gained by tradesmen was the formation of business contracts with the charities themselves. The institutions required large quantities of such items as drugs, groceries, milk, linen and alcoholic beverages, and where possible goods required by the infirmaries would be purchased from subscribing tradesmen. An early resolution of the committee of the Huddersfield Dispensary instructed that drugs be ordered 'equally and impartially off each Druggist who subscribes to the institution, as long as quality and prices are approved of'.[151] Arrangements such as these clearly worked both ways. The tradesman could secure a large order, but low prices and discount would be expected in return. For example, two-guinea annual subscriptions were deducted from the bills of three York druggists in 1817 by way of a discount. Competition and tenders for goods were also encouraged. In 1831 arrangements were made for the provisioning of the newly-established Huddersfield Infirmary. Goods were to be supplied by Messrs Carr,

Joshua Walker, Black, Wilson, Law Walker, Joshua Hammond, Thomas Firth and George Bates, all subscribers to the institution. The Infirmary was to be supplied with water for five guineas per annum, which the Waterworks Commission undertook to subscribe to the charity.[152]

Samples were taken of all tradesmen supplying goods and services to the Huddersfield Dispensary and Infirmary in the years 1825–1826, 1855–1856 and 1865–1866. In 1825–1826 52 per cent of those trading with the institution were also subscribers, and in 1855–1856 and 1865–1866, 58 per cent. It was not uncommon for tradesmen to be elected to the committees of the Infirmaries, which were responsible for selecting suppliers and ordering goods for the use of the charities. The committee of the Huddersfield Infirmary for the year 1855–1856, for example, included Law Walker, butcher, W. P. England, chemist and druggist, and Joseph Brook, stationer, printer and bookseller, and printer of the charity's annual reports.[153]

Numerous social advantages were also gained through involvement in medical charities. Complicated scales of privileges were drawn up to allocate the power of making recommendations according to the size of the financial contribution.[154] The performance of acts of charity, not least the distribution of recommendations to 'deserving objects', played a status-giving or status-maintaining role. The donor was put in a position of prestige in the eyes of those who benefited from his benevolence, and, more importantly, in the eyes of his contemporaries, the medical charities acting as 'a conspicuous symbol of the charitable impulses of the rich, and as a spur to the gratitude and submission of the poor'.[155] This may have been especially important to middle-class groups, actively seeking social advancement and acceptance by the local élite.

Subscribers' names appeared in newspaper reports and the printed annual reports of the charities, alongside those of the local aristocracy. They gained the right to vote in the election of medical staff, lay officers and committees, and the chance to serve themselves in one of the latter capacities. Social prestige was attained through attendance at fund-raising events, where one gained the opportunity to rub shoulders with the local élite. For example, the Wakefield Charity Ball, held annually in aid of the Dispensary and House of Recovery, was generally 'supported by the chief families in the town and neighbourhood',[156] the Fitzwilliams, Pilkingtons,

Armytages, and so on, together with other middle- and upper-class subscribers. The public ceremonials and private banquets, which marked the opening of the infirmaries, important additions to facilities or a jubilee, were occasions not only for much mutual 'back-patting', but also for a gathering of the local élite. Poems were even composed to celebrate these occasions, to praise both the institution of charity and the charitable.[157]

As Davidoff has suggested, provincial town society depended very much on the relationship between middle-class and county groups. Where there were no dominant local aristocratic families, or where the London Season and other attractions of national society drained away aristocratic attendance and interest, then professional and business people took over.[158] This was partly the case in Wakefield and especially Huddersfield, where active involvement in local charities had been largely taken over by the middle classes. In Wakefield this process was speeded up by the demise of several of the most important old merchant families early in the nineteenth century. Huddersfield, meanwhile, with the notable exception of the Ramsden family, had never had strong connections with more traditional landed interests or the old merchant classes, it being very much the spawning ground of a new and dynamic commercial class. However, the local aristocracy of the districts surrounding both towns still showed sufficient interest to make financial contributions and to participate occasionally in public events. Indeed, the medical charities provided a forum for some accommodation between town and country, the newly rich and powerful commercial and professional groups and the traditional ruling and landowning élite. Many of the motives which John Pickstone has suggested as being responsible for the upsurge of medical charities in the eighteenth century were still valid a century later.

Perhaps the movement has to be seen as part of the social dynamics of the country town, a means of social integration between landowners and townsmen, a means of demonstrating benevolence to the lower classes . . . They provided a focus for the charitable middle class, an object for civic pride and an exemplar of those mutual obligations of rich and poor which many wished to encourage.[159]

The Wakefield and Huddersfield medical charities gained the support of a cross-section of religious and political groups: church and chapel, Whigs and Tories. Leading representatives of various religious denominations in both Wakefield and Huddersfield were active in the charities: in Wakefield, for example, the Quaker Leathams, the Wesleyan Gaskells and the Congregationalist Thomas Clayton co-operated with the staunchly Anglican Charlesworths and Tews. Within the confines of this chapter it has been impossible to closely identify the patterns of denominational support amongst subscribers to the charities. However, they do seem to have been fairly representative of the patterns of religious worship in their respective towns, with an almost 50:50 division between church and chapel in Wakefield, and a much stronger

Table 4.3. *Voting patterns of subscribers[a] to the Wakefield and Huddersfield Dispensaries and Infirmaries in selected elections.*

(i)	Voting pattern of subscribers to the Huddersfield Infirmary			Voting pattern of the Huddersfield public	
	Votes for each candidate	Percentage of votes	1834 Huddersfield Poll candidates	Votes for each candidate	Percentage of votes
	88	54	John Blackburne (Whig)	234	48
	19	11	Captain Wood (Liberal–Radical)	108	22
	57	35	Michael T. Sadler (Tory-Reformer)	147	30
	164	100	Totals	489	100

(ii)	Voting pattern of subscribers to the Wakefield Dispensary			Voting pattern of the Wakefield public	
	Votes for each candidate	Percentage of votes	1837 Wakefield Poll candidates	Votes for each candidate	Percentage of votes
	54	59	Hon. W. S. Lascelles (Tory)	307	52
	37	41	Daniel Gaskell (Liberal)	281	48
	91	100	Totals	588	100

(iii) Voting pattern of subscribers to the Wakefield Infirmary		Voting pattern of the Wakefield public		
Votes for each candidate	Percentage of votes	1862 Wakefield Poll candidates	Votes for each candidate	Percentage of votes
55	53	Sir J. C. D. Hay (Conservative)	456	52
48	47	Richard Smethurst (Liberal)	425	48
103	100	Totals	881	100

Sources: 4th AR HI, 1834–1835; 43rd AR WD, 1830–1831;[b] 73rd AR WI, 1860–1861; A Copy of the Poll. Borough of Huddersfield, 1834, HPL (B.324); Wakefield Borough Election. Poll Book, 1837, WDA (Local Collection W.324); Poll Book of the Wakefield Borough Election, 1862, WDA (Local Collection W.324).

[a] The figures are for subscribers whose voting behaviour, as recorded in the Poll Books, could be identified.

[b] The annual report for 1830–1831 was the only report extant for the 1830s and 1840s, and was, therefore, the closest obtainable for a comparison with the 1837 Poll.

Non-Conformist element in Huddersfield.[160] The Wakefield and Huddersfield Infirmaries also drew support from both Liberals and Conservatives, again including leading representatives of each party: in Wakefield the Liberal Gaskells, Leathams and Holdsworths, and the Tory Charlesworths, Haighs, Wormalds and Westmorlands. The voting patterns of subscribers to the Wakefield and Huddersfield charities have been compared with general voting behaviour, as recorded in the Poll Books, for a selection of borough elections, which seemed to be fairly typical of the nineteenth century: the 1834 Huddersfield election, and the 1837 and 1862 Wakefield elections. The results are given in Table 4.3.[161] Although the samples are small, they indicate that the political biases of subscribers to the charities broadly paralleled political opinion in the towns as a whole. In Huddersfield, however, much less support was registered by subscribers for the Radical Wood[162] (although the difference in percentages was divided almost equally between the Whig Blackburne and the Reformer Sadler). The

Huddersfield Infirmary did also attract a small number of Radical supporters, including the Chartist Lawrence Pitkeithley and Richard Oastler. In Wakefield, meanwhile, the voting behaviour of subscribers tended to be biased more towards Conservatism than was the case for the town as a whole.

Not all Wakefield and Huddersfield charities and voluntary associations provided a basis for the unification of middle- and upper-class groups, otherwise divided on economic, party or denominational grounds. It has been suggested that in the West Riding the second quarter of the nineteenth century was marked by 'a struggle for power within urban communities and a contest for supremacy between town and country'.[163] Meanwhile, Pickstone has observed that 'in the close-fought urban politics of the nineteenth century, control over the various town institutions was important, especially when a town had not yet been incorporated'.[164] Such struggles were likely to have been more prevalent in Huddersfield, which was only incorporated in 1868 (compared with Wakefield in 1848). And, indeed, two of Huddersfield's most important 'local government' agencies, the Improvement Commissioners and the Board of Guardians, were rent by major divisions, the first, although dominated by the Liberal–Whig interest, along political lines, the second into town and country factions. Voluntary efforts could be similarly divided, the most notable example being the setting up of two rival colleges run respectively by Non-Conformists and Churchmen: the Huddersfield College (1838) and the Collegiate School (1837). In Wakefield splits such as these were seen less within local government bodies, but were still prevalent amongst voluntary organisations. The Wakefield Mechanics' Institute, for instance, was a strongly Liberal/Non-Conformist preserve; the rival Church Instruction Institution was dominated by Churchmen and Conservatives. The Wakefield Governors of the Charities were a staunchly Establishment group, while the Benevolent Society was dominated by Wesleyans. Both towns, meanwhile, supported the usual array of Church and Non-Conformist schooling provisions.

To a large extent (at least in Wakefield and Huddersfield) medical charities appear to have been able to cut across social, ideological, political and religious differences. This may well have been because medical charities, unlike educational, missionary or visiting societies, were largely apolitical and non-denominational in their

functions and aims. Moreover, the promoters of medical charities
needed a good deal more financial backing than most other philanthropic concerns, and could not afford to confine their appeal to
specific groups. While towns of this size and wealth might be able
to support rival colleges, education institutes and small-scale charitable enterprises, it is very unlikely that financial backing could be
given to two large medical institutions.[165] More than many other
voluntary societies, the Wakefield and Huddersfield Infirmaries
provided the basis for the kind of unification of the middle classes
that Morris has found in mid-nineteenth century Leeds.[166] The
necessity for the wealthy classes to find such a basis for unity was
also a common theme of the annual reports of the charities and of
appeals for support. In 1863 the annual report of the Huddersfield
Infirmary stated

It (medical charity) knits closer the bond that should unite all classes of a
community; and amid the jarring and discord occasioned by political and
religious dissension, such an Institution forms a truly attractive field – a
green spot in the wilderness – on which all sects and parties may, for a time,
forget the points on which they differ, and devote themselves to labours of
love and humanity, on the obligation of which they are all agreed, and the
performance of which, while it relieves the objects of their common care;
binds them together as brethren and friends.[167]

The position of the patients: social control or paternalism?

At least until the late nineteenth century there appears to have been
very little room in medical charities for working-class participation.
The poor were excluded from involvement in the government,
policy-making and financial support of these institutions. Meanwhile, control over admissions remained largely in the hands of the
lay subscribers, rather than the medical officers, the physicians and
surgeons generally being only allowed to keep one or two patients
on the books at a time. The letter of recommendation was offered
as a potential inducement to subscribers, and in normal circumstances admissions were determined by social rather than medical
criteria.

Many of the exclusions referred to in standard hospital histories,
of children, pregnant women, fever and chronic cases,[168] do not,
however, seem to have been applicable in the Wakefield and
Huddersfield Infirmaries and Fever Hospital. Fever cases and
chronic complaints, while rarely being treated as in-patients, made

up the largest percentage of out- and home-cases in the two infirm-aries. Pregnant women were occasionally treated as home-patients, while children were regularly admitted as in- and out-patients. In the year 1838–1839, for example, children under ten years old accounted for 16 per cent of the 3,568 out-patient admissions and 8 per cent of the 336 in-patient admissions to the Huddersfield Infirmary.[169]

Exclusions were more likely to be applied on the basis of social criteria. Paupers, for example, could not be sent to the infirmaries by means of the normal channel of subscribers' recommendations. Rather they had to be directed by the Boards of Guardians, who would undertake to pay for them on a weekly basis, and to remove them in the case of death. Patients who were members of sick clubs (which did not subscribe to the charities)[170] or those considered too well off to be 'deserving' were ordered to pay something towards their keep and treatment, or were dismissed. Meanwhile, cases of venereal disease were rigorously excluded, except where the patient could prove himself or herself married and of 'good character'.

The process of admission, treatment and discharge was geared to inculcating feelings of gratitude and dependence in patients. Firstly, the potential patient was expected (if able) to go in person to a governor to request a recommendation. After being subjected to rigorous admission procedures and checks by both the governor and admissions board, he faced the possibility of being dismissed as an 'improper object' of the charity. Subscribers repeatedly had their attention drawn to the necessity of exercising great caution in the handing out of recommendations. In 1830, for example, the com-mittee of the Huddersfield Dispensary found

... it is still necessary to recommend increased attention to the selection of objects, and while they willingly concede, that it is better that in a few instances the Charity should be abused, than that one case of real suffering should go unrelieved, yet it is of the last importance, that improper objects should be excluded, and that all obtain recommendations in their own neighbourhoods, where their circumstances are known, ...[171]

In 1853 the committee of the Huddersfield Infirmary found it necessary to place a list of questions concerning the patients' circumstances on the forms of recommendation;

And as a check against imposition this Board urges upon the notice of the Governors the propriety of requesting explicit answers to such printed queries before they give Out Recommendations, in order that the accuracy of the statements may be tested in such manner as may be thought expedient.[172]

Little information is available on the social status and occupations of those admitted as patients. No patients' books have survived for the Wakefield and Huddersfield Infirmaries during this period. Nineteenth-century census returns, however, did list the occupations of hospital patients, and the occupations of the small number of in-patients resident in the Huddersfield Infirmary on census day in 1841 and 1851 are given in Table 4.4. The patients' book of the Wakefield House of Recovery, meanwhile, provides a complete record of all admissions to the charity between 1826 and its closure in 1854. Table 4.5 gives details of the occupations of patients admitted to the House of Recovery in 1838 and 1847, two fairly typical years in terms of the class of patient admitted, although atypical in terms of the high number of admissions (and high number of paupers and vagrants admitted in the epidemic year of 1847). The samples shown in the Tables, although small, give some indication of what the officers and subscribers to the medical charities classified as 'deserving'. A large proportion of patients were either servants or employees in factories and workshops.[173] Presumably, in many cases they were sent directly to the charities by their employers, who were frequently subscribers with the power to recommend patients. The fact that servants were regularly admitted should be emphasised, as it has been assumed that this group was commonly excluded from medical charities.

Once admitted, either as an in- or out-patient, the recipient would face a barrage of rules concerning his behaviour while receiving treatment from the charity. The normal procedure was for rules to be read to the patient on admission. In case a reminder was required, the rules were also hung in wards and waiting rooms. One of the duties of hospital visitors was to ensure that patients were abiding by the rules, and not causing trouble to the medical or other staff. If any rules were broken, the offender was liable to immediate expulsion. Patients could be discharged for irregular attendance, immoral behaviour or poor conduct. Disobedience to the medical officers was also punishable by expulsion. The rules of the Wakefield Dispensary stipulated

That the Patients shall attend regularly, shall conform to the Regulations inserted in the Letters of Recommendation, and shall behave with pro-

Table 4.4. *Occupations of Huddersfield Infirmary in-patients on census day, 1841 and 1851.*

	1841		1851	
Occupations	Number	Percen-tage of total	Number	Percen-tage of total
Textile workers:	18	60.0	11	39.3
1841 1851				
Weavers 6 2				
Piecers 2 4				
Cloth				
dressers 0 2				
Burlers 2 0				
Winders 2 1				
Croppers 1 0				
Others 5 2				
Factory workers				
(unspecified)	2	6.7	0	0
Agricultural				
labourers	2	6.7	0	0
General labourers	0	0	2	7.1
Watermen	2	6.7	0	0
Shoemakers	0	0	1	3.6
Tailors	0	0	1	3.6
Building trades	2	6.7	3	10.7
Hawkers	1	3.3	1	3.6
Servants	1	3.3	3	10.7
Children				
(no occupation)	2	6.7	5	17.9
Female				
(no occupation)	0	0	1	3.6
Total	30	100	28	100

Source: Census Enumerators' Books, Huddersfield, 1841 and 1851.

Table 4.5. *Occupations of patients admitted to the Wakefield House of Recovery in the years 1838 and 1847.*

Occupations	1838		1847	
	Number	Percentage of total	Number	Percentage of total
Servants and apprentices	7	13.2	3	4.1
Railway labourers	7	13.2	3	4.1
Male factory workers (unspecified)	0	0	2	2.7
Female factory workers (unspecified)	3	5.7	5	6.8
Spinners	1	1.9	1	1.4
Labourers (unspecified)	3	5.7	8	10.8
Bricklayers	2	3.8	1	1.4
Watermen	1	1.9	0	0
Joiners	1	1.9	0	0
Cobblers	0	0	3	4.1
Tailors	2	3.8	0	0
Hawkers	1	1.9	1	1.4
Dyers	1	1.9	0	0
Female gardeners	0	0	1	1.4
Military pensioners	0	0	1	1.4
Lodging house keepers	1	1.9	1	1.4
Irish vagrants	0	0	22	29.7
English vagrants	0	0	4	5.4
Polish vagrants	0	0	1	1.4
Tramps	0	0	1	1.4
Paupers	0	0	3	4.1
Children (no occupation)	17	32.1	3	4.1
Females (no occupation)	6	11.3	10[a]	13.5
Total	53	100	74	100

[a] Including one mason's wife, who it was noted in the patients' book 'should pay'.
Source: Wakefield House of Recovery. Register of Patients, 1826–1854, Ms WYCRO (C235/5/1).

priety, or be instantly dismissed, and when cured the Patients shall inform the recommending subscriber.[174]

The rules for in-patients to the Huddersfield Infirmary, meanwhile, insisted

That they (the patients) strictly observe the directions of their Physicians and Surgeons; and also of the Apothecary, the Matron, and the Nurses. . . . That no men patients go into the women's wards, nor women into the men's; . . . That there be no cursing, swearing, rude or indecent behaviour, on pain of expulsion after the first admonition. . . . That there be no playing at cards or any other game. . . . neither shall spirituous liquors, nor any provisions, be introduced by the patient or their friends.[175]

Rules of this nature were apparently common to all nineteenth-century medical charities. At first sight these regulations appear severe, but in principle some differ only in degree from those enforced in present-day hospitals. The main difference is that today these codes of conduct go largely unspoken, while the nineteenth-century infirmary committees found it necessary to bring these regulations very much to the notice of the patient. The officers and committees of these charities may have wished to instil habits of obedience, regularity, sobriety, duty and good moral behaviour into their patients by means of strict regulations. However, it is just as likely that they believed the imposition of such rules was necessary to the smooth functioning of the institutions.

On discharge, following the termination of treatment (and not necessarily a cure), patients were required to make some formal expression of gratitude, by letter or in person, to the recommending governor. Failure to do so was liable to result in future exclusion from the charity. Unpleasant as these expressions of gratitude might have been for those who had to make them, they were part and parcel of philanthropic activity during the eighteenth and nineteenth centuries, and apparently did not carry with them any 'sinister' connotations. Rather expressions of gratitude gave the supporters of these charities a feeling of gratification, the 'luxury of doing good'. In an annual address to subscribers in 1853, for example, the committee of the Wakefield Dispensary drew the attention of their supporters to

. . . the decreasing number of patients, discharged for non-attendance, as an evidence not only of an increasing sense on the part of the Patients themselves of the benefits conferred by the Institution, but also of their gratitude towards its promoters.

In the previous year 59 patients had been discharged for non-attendance, but 'during the past year hardly one-half of that number have adopted this ungracious method of relieving themselves from attendance'.[176]

The promoters of the charities expressed remarkable confidence in a Divine support and approval of their particular brand of good works. Their charities, they believed, had been singled out for special approval, a fact which was evidenced by their prosperity and success. In 1870 the committee of the Huddersfield Infirmary humbly acknowledged '. . . with devout gratitude, the blessing of Almighty God on this House of Mercy'. In their report for the previous year the committee had reviewed the steady growth of the charity,

. . . and thankfully recognise in the work the hand of Him from whom all goodness emanates and they likewise hope that the poor recipients of His bounty participate in this feeling, and may be led to know that, though 'the sorrows of death encompassed them, He heard their voice!'[177]

Presentiments of the imminent salvation of patrons on account of their good works, and hopes of inculcating a religious revival amongst patients, were expressed in the reports of the institutions. These expressions tended to reflect the notion that the social structure was a creation of Divine Providence, and that the poor should be contented with the humble lot to which God had assigned them, ideas that were also common to nineteenth-century sermons.[178] The more fervent supporters of these charities may have wished to impose their own brand of Christianity and sense of Christian duty on those admitted as patients. While the poor received bodily treatment from the medical staff, they would also receive spiritual aid and instruction. These motives were hinted at during the ceremony for the laying of the first stone of the Huddersfield Infirmary, when the Vicar of Huddersfield, the Reverend J. C. Franks, offered a prayer for the future patients of the charity:

Give them unfeigned repentance for all the errors of their life past, and steadfast faith in thy Son Jesus; that their sins may be done away by thy mercy, and their pardon sealed in heaven, before they go hence, and are no more seen.[179]

The imparting of spiritual comfort and religious instruction were amongst the duties taken up by women visitors.[180] Clergymen were also given access to wards to conduct services and offer religious instruction and 'other spiritual assistance to the Patients'.[181] Patients who were well enough were expected to attend church services, and were 'recommended' when discharged to offer thanks in their respective places of worship. Links were established between the medical charities and local churches and chapels through the medium of congregational collections. One of the privileges obtained by clergymen undertaking to preach sermons and collect in aid of the institutions was the right of recommending patients from their flocks. Presumably only those suitably attentive to their religious obligations could gain a recommendation from such a source.

On the face of it there appears to have been ample opportunity for religious indoctrination (and, after all, gratitude to God for His Divine support of the charities and gratitude to the patrons for their financial and practical support were not so far apart, especially when control over admissions and religious indoctrination was in the hands of the same group). But, in fact, the encouragement of a religious awakening amongst patients seems to have been seen by the majority of supporters only as a fringe benefit. Clergymen and those keen on spreading the Gospel were allowed to carry out their work, but religious reform was not one of the main activities of the charities. Meanwhile, the only group who were likely to be influenced in this way were in-patients, who made up a very small proportion of admissions. Moreover, it is not inconceivable that in some cases the religious reformers were preaching to the converted (and, after all, church attendance was high in both towns).[182] Those of the patients who wished to see a clergyman or receive spiritual aid were able to follow their own religious inclinations, and clergymen of all sects were given access to patients. (One of the stipulations attached to Clayton's legacy was that clergymen and ministers of all denominations would be admitted freely to the wards of the Wakefield Infirmary.)

In a similar way there appears to have been little inclination to insist on the acceptance of other middle-class value systems and forms of behaviour, although the reports of the medical charities occasionally contained strong expressions of the need to contain the poor and keep them in a position of deference. For example, in 1816 the committee of the Huddersfield Dispensary pointed out 'how much it is likely to add to the Contentment and even *Subordination* of the Poor, to find that they are so protected when overtaken with

Affliction'.[183] Statements such as these, however, tended to coincide with periods of depression or working-class discontent.

When economic depression or social unrest threatened the medical charities stepped up their appeals for support, in order, as they saw it, 'to meet this threat'. In 1826 the Huddersfield Dispensary faced one of the most serious crises in its history, when the bankruptcy of its Treasurers led to 'the wreck of their resources'. This personal disaster coincided with a general depression, and 'the disastrous crisis, which spread its oppressive gloom over the whole empire, and was felt in all its violence in this district, contributed to swell the amount of applicants to the Dispensary'. Appeals were made to obtain more subscriptions and collections in different places of worship, and the response was sufficient to enable the charity to continue to function. The committee remarked at the termination of this difficult year,

Great as have been the sufferings of the poor, from want of employment, how much greater would they have been, had not this Institution been still enabled to continue its aid to the Sick poor. And it is satisfactory to know, whatever other distress was felt by the labouring classes, no part of it arose from a want of the means of medical relief.[184]

Similarly, in 1855, during another period of economic difficulties, the committee of the Wakefield Dispensary noted

A period of protracted depression and high prices lie before the working classes, to which it is impossible to look forward without anxiety; surely at such a time all charitable institutions should be extended not contracted.[185]

The anxieties of the wealthy classes during periods of depression or social dislocation could be justified by the outbreaks of popular discontent which erupted throughout the West Riding during the first half of the nineteenth century. Food riots continued into the 1840s and Wakefield and Huddersfield were centres for Luddite insurrections, Anti-Poor Law and Factory Act agitation and Chartism.[186] Through the operation of ameliorative charities, it was claimed, bonds could be formed between the classes and order maintained. Periods of acute poverty for the working classes could be tided over without the threat of serious social dislocation.

The geographical gulf between rich and poor, as described by Stedman Jones for London in the second half of the nineteenth century,[187] did not develop in Wakefield and Huddersfield, at least

during the first three–quarters of the century. In Huddersfield, and
to a much lesser extent in Wakefield, there was some movement in
the second half of the nineteenth century to new suburbs and villa
areas on the outskirts of the towns but this process by no means
matched the segregation on class lines of London and the larger
manufacturing towns (such as R. J. Morris's mid–nineteenth-
century Leeds). Towns such as Huddersfield retained a 'preindust-
rial' structure until late in the century, the centre being occupied by
high-status groups, residing in large houses with servants, many of
whom were engaged in 'dealing' and the professions. Still in 1880
most areas of town contained a mixture of rich and poor (and
Catholic and Protestant).[188] Personal links between the classes in
both towns remained strong, and contact between employer and
employee was maintained within relatively small-scale workshops
and mills. Many local businessmen and shopkeepers still lived on
their business premises, and retained strong social links with their
employees and servants.

Could support of medical charity then have been an expression of
the paternalism of local manufacturers and employers of labour as
discussed by Joyce and Roberts?[189] Despite, or because of, the small
scale of many workshops, and the survival of close links between
master and men, industrial development in the West Riding was
less conducive to the formation of industrial paternalism than
Joyce's Lancashire. As Joyce himself states, as 'a consequence of
later and less complete mechanisation in West Riding textiles,
together with the attendant delay in urban growth, the economic
organisation of industry . . . was far less favourable to the emergence
of industrial paternalism'. Rather the factory economy of the region
was characterised on the one hand by exploitation on the part of the
employer, on the other hand by independence on the part of the
workforce.[190]

Examples do exist of 'good' employers in the Wakefield and
Huddersfield areas, many of whom did show some 'paternalistic
characteristics'. In 1841, for example, John Naylor, a Wakefield
cloth manufacturer, was praised in the local press for his 'Good
Example to Employers'. Not only had he set up a library for his
workforce, but he had also kept his workmen employed during the
recent depression in the woollen trade.[191] Naylor was an active
supporter of the Wakefield Dispensary; his father, also John Naylor,
had been the institution's first Treasurer. A Parliamentary Com-

mission of 1845 praised the efforts of Messrs Stansfeld and Briggs, owners of collieries at Flockton, near Huddersfield, to improve the working and 'mental' conditions of their workforce. Amongst other things, they had set up a Horticultural Society, a Temperance Society, evening classes and a Sunday school, and organised sports and other 'rational recreations'. Earl Fitzwilliam and the Charlesworth family also received praise for the good working and housing conditions, and facilities for education and recreation, that prevailed at their collieries.[192] All three colliery owners were supporters of their local medical charities.

Just as many, if not more, examples exist of poor working conditions, exploitation of the workforce and evasion of the Factory Acts by employers of labour in Wakefield and Huddersfield. The very same people who supported the exploitative factory system were frequently patrons of the medical charities. In Huddersfield opposition to the Factory Acts was particularly strong, and in 1831 a group of Huddersfield factory owners presented a petition to Parliament against a proposed Bill to reduce the hours of labour for factory children. The petitioners included the Stables family, the Starkey Brothers, Jonas Brook and Brothers (including Charles Brook, who founded the Meltham Convalescent Home), Thomas Nelson, Henry Brook, the Roberts Brothers, Thomas Kilner and John Hannah. All of this group gave financial support to the Huddersfield Infirmary, several served as committee members. Legal assistance for the petition was supplied by none other than J. C. Laycock, one of the Infirmary's foremost supporters.[193] In 1837, Mr Benjamin Lawrence Clarkson, a Wakefield woollen manufacturer and patron of the Wakefield Dispensary, was prosecuted for forging certificates to show school attendance for children under the age of thirteen.[194] In 1834 one Joseph Schofield, a Huddersfield Liberal, Dissenter, millowner and supporter of the Huddersfield Infirmary, was fined for employing children without age certificates and for working a girl thirteen hours continuously. Richard Oastler found numerous other instances of exploitation and brutality amongst Huddersfield millowners.[195]

The harsh and in many cases dangerous working conditions which prevailed in many workplaces also accounted directly for a large number of industrial accidents and a gradual decline in the health of the workforce. The 1833 Parliamentary Inquiry into factory conditions, presided over by Mr Sadler, heard evidence, for example, from a seventeen-year-old Huddersfield factory hand, Joseph Habergam, who testified to the appalling conditions, particularly for young children, in three local textile mills: George Addison's Bradley Mills, Mr Brook's Upper Mills and Mr William Firth's, Greenhead, near Huddersfield. In addition to the long hours of labour children had to endure, Habergam cited instances of illnesses caused by dust, deformities resulting from long hours of labour, fines and beatings by overlookers and numerous accidents, which not infrequently resulted in death. For Habergam, factory work had resulted in a serious deformity of his limbs. At the age of seventeen he was forced to give up work. He received a recommendation from Mr Bradley Clay, a Huddersfield rope manufacturer, for admission to the Huddersfield Infirmary, and his case was serious enough to warrant a transfer to the Leeds Infirmary (on the recommendation of Richard Oastler). Mr Hey of the Leeds Infirmary and Dr Walker of the Huddersfield Infirmary concluded that, as a result of factory work, Habergam would be permanently crippled. Cases such as Habergam's could be multiplied.[196]

While 'it is difficult to imagine a system of health care better designed to make clear the 'bonds of attachment' within society',[197] it is unlikely that medical charity was inspired chiefly by either ideas of paternalism or social control. Some representatives of the local landowning or manufacturing classes may have been motivated in part by notions of paternalism. But almost certainly this was not the case for the majority of these groups. Any paternalism which might have existed was generally of a very stinted kind; a small annual contribution to medical charity hardly cancelled out the exploitation of the workforce which took place in many factories and workshops of the region, or the apparent lack of concern about poor housing, education and living conditions.

More than many other forms of philanthropy, medical charity gave the donor the chance of personal contact with the recipient, and the opportunity to monitor his or her behaviour and to create a situation of dependency. A similar relationship is described by Anne Summers, which evolved through the voluntary visiting of the poor: 'The poor had nothing to offer in return except gratitude and good behaviour . . . by and large the relationship was one of clientage; and as such it left the poor with very little dignity'.[198] Yet, however great the opportunities were for imposing some form of control on patients, these efforts do seem to have been secondary to the practical purpose of providing a cheap[199] and efficient medical service for sick and injured members of the local workforce.

Even if those promoting these charities wished to impose a system of control and an acceptance of middle-class values on the poor, it is not clear that these efforts would be crowned with success. We have no idea of how those treated in these institutions reacted to any patterns of behaviour which might be forced upon them. The working classes of the region, however, enjoyed a reputation for independence, and if medical charities came to be associated with dominance and control, they might well have sought medical relief elsewhere, or have gone without medical assistance.

Annual reports stressed the need to 'win the confidence' of the poor, and, after all, the success of medical charities rested in the first place on poor people seeking medical aid in these institutions. When the Wakefield Infirmary was established in 1854, the committee drew the attention of the subscribers to the need of vigorously supporting the institution from the outset;

... during the ensuing year the first impression will be formed in the public mind. A feeling in its favour or a prejudice against it will probably be permanently fixed among the labouring classes: should it be allowed to languish it will probably fail and the result will be deeply regretted, it being 'discreditable to the public spirit and charitable feeling of WAKEFIELD'.[200]

The patrons of medical charities were in some respects in competition with various self-help provisions. The better-off members of the working class could turn to the friendly society for medical aid, while the chemist and druggist, local healer and quack provided alternative sources of medical treatment for all stratas of society.[201] Meanwhile, the 'conforming' patient might just as well be thumbing his nose at the establishment, taking what he needed from the charity, giving the appearance of conformity, but in fact taking little notice of efforts to improve his conduct or impress upon him his dependence on his betters for something even as basic as health care. Also, it is not inconceivable that the patients already shared in many of the values of orderly and moral behaviour stressed by the patrons of the charities.

Moreover, the patients were not completely powerless. Complaint procedures existed and were utilised from time to time.[202] Patients were discharged from the charities far more at their own request, than because of 'irregular conduct' or as 'improper objects'. In the year 1865–1866, for example, 45 patients were discharged from the Huddersfield Infirmary at their own request, six absconded and only one was dismissed as an 'improper object'. Between 1855 and 1871 only five in-patients were discharged for 'irregularity'.[203] At the beginning of the last quarter of the nineteenth century the setting up of Hospital Saturday Funds in Wakefield and Huddersfield gave working men collectively similar privileges to individual subscribers. Both infirmaries had received small amounts from collections of workpeople from the mid-nineteenth century onwards (and rather more commonly, the fines imposed on workmen by their employers). In the final quarter of the century, with a good deal of encouragement from the infirmary committees, the collection of contributions in factories, mines and other places of work became better organised, and for the infirmaries, more fruitful.

During the 1870s the committee of the Wakefield Infirmary began to solicit workpeople's subscriptions in earnest. In the annual report for the year 1872–1873 the committee commented

It is a source of gratification to see that among this years receipts, . . . are several sums from bodies of workpeople, the class deriving the benefit of the Institution. The Committee hopes that the example thus set may be followed by the *employees* in other Establishments (their emphasis).

In this year collections had been received from the Calder Soap Works, the Lancashire and Yorkshire Railway (Goods Guards), Victoria Colliery and two local mills.[204] The first organised Hospital Saturday took place in 1875 and raised, 'to the great surprise and gratification of the committee, the magnificent sum of £549'. This contribution represented over 24 per cent of the total income for the year, exceeding the figure for donations and legacies (£229 or 10 per cent), congregational collections (£291 or 13 per cent), interest on investments (£312 or 14 per cent) and even annual subscriptions (£448 or 20 per cent).[205]

In 1876 the foundation stone was laid of the new Clayton Hospital. It was arranged that the event should coincide with Hospital Saturday to provide a special stimulus to the labouring classes. And indeed the collections made by workpeople in this year totalled £712 (which the President, Colonel Charlesworth, made up to £1,000). The committee of the Infirmary were so impressed that it was agreed that provision should be made for two members of the

Hospital Saturday Committee to become ex-officio members of the General Committee.[206] By 1881 the committee concluded that the support of the Hospital Saturday Fund had 'become indispensable to the carrying on of the Hospital, . . .'. By this year contributions were received from over 120 firms, factories and mines in Wakefield alone.[207]

The amount received by the Huddersfield Infirmary from this source also increased in the fourth quarter of the century, albeit slower and with less apparent enthusiasm than in Wakefield. This was perhaps due to the more radical nature of the Huddersfield workforce, and the poor relationship existing between employer and employee, which may have resulted in a disassociation from the philanthropic efforts of the manufacturers. In 1872–1873 only £126 was received from workpeople's contributions and the committee remarked that

It is desirable . . . that the working classes, upon whom the Infirmary has a special claim for support, should identify themselves more thoroughly with it and increase its funds to such an extent as to claim a share in the management of it, through their representatives.[208]

By 1877 the committee could in fact report a large increase in workpeople's subscriptions, chiefly a result, they claimed, of meetings which had been held at the Infirmary by representatives of mills and workshops in the district. The delegates had been impressed by the provisions made by the Infirmary and '. . . a hearty willingness was expressed by all present to do all in their power to bring the claims of the Institution before their fellow-workmen, with a view to their contributing more liberally in future'. In 1877 workpeople's contributions totalled £428, a result of the setting up of committees to collect funds and the establishment of an Infirmary Saturday.[209] By the year 1880–1881 the Infirmary received over £700 from 110 workshops in the Huddersfield area.[210]

The setting up of the Hospital Saturday Funds and the co-opting of representatives of working men on to the infirmary committees marks a turning point with respect to the participation of the working classes in the control and financing of these institutions, which existed primarily for their benefit. Before the final quarter of the nineteenth century, if we wish to find instances of working-class self-help and independence in the provision of medical care, we must look outside the system of medical charity to friendly societies, sick clubs and 'alternative' medical provisions.

4.4 Women and philanthropy

The place of women in the charitable enterprises of Victorian England has created much interest in recent years. It has been concluded that philanthropy was normally male dominated, that the scope of women was limited, and that distinctions were enforced between men's responsibilities and those thought suitable for women. Yet the role of women as financial contributors and charity workers did expand throughout the nineteenth century. They extended their traditional role of visiting the poor, broke into new fields, such as prison reform and missionary work, and became active in some pressure group activities: for example, anti-slavery and the campaign against the Contagious Disease Acts. They were also able to break into the field of institutional charity, a formerly all-male preserve, either by persuading committees of management to give them the opportunity to serve or by establishing their own societies.[211] Within voluntary institutions, however, their efforts were channelled into different spheres from those of their male counterparts, away from government and financial decision-making, towards the activities of fund-raising, religious teaching and domestic management. These efforts, which maintained strong links with nineteenth-century ideals of domesticity, family life and moral improvement, came to be directed mainly towards women and children of the poorer classes.

Comparatively little is known of the scope of women's involvement within individual institutions, and even less of the type of women likely to participate in philanthropic enterprise, their financial and social status. In this Section a brief analysis will be given of the social and economic status of female participants in the three most important Wakefield and Huddersfield medical charities (the two infirmaries and the House of Recovery). This will be followed by an examination of the kinds of activity that these women became involved in.

The 'stereotyped' charitable woman is well documented in literature, and this stereotype has retained a surprisingly high level of acceptance in studies of nineteenth-century philanthropy. The philanthropic woman was depicted as being a member of the upper or middle class, with sufficient wealth to enable withdrawal from the workplace, and to a large extent from the home, and to employ several servants. For example, Hannah More portrayed the archetypal nineteenth-century charitable 'lady' in *Coelebs in Search of a Wife*, published in 1809,

Mrs. Stanley said, 'I have often heard it regretted that ladies have no stated employment, no profession. It is a mistake: charity is the calling of a lady; the care of the poor is her profession. Men have little time or taste for details. Women of fortune have abundant leisure, which can in no way be so properly filled up, as in making themselves intimately acquainted with the worth and the wants of all within reach'.[212]

Hannah More insisted that women were particularly suited to charitable activity because of their free time, acquaintance with domestic needs and sympathy with female complaints. Emotional or personal factors have often been grafted on to these characteristics: deprivation of alternative outlets for organisational or other talents, lack of fulfilment in marriage or the loss of a child being common examples. Possession of leisure is now seen as a prerequisite for involvement in philanthropic effort, even if this is qualified by the notion that this involvement did lead to the sacrifice of free time, devotion of energy and a necessary development of expertise.[213] Spinsters and childless women are seen as being especially well placed to develop charitable interests. Thus, we have arrived at a largely negative and cynical view of women's motives for charitable involvement: 'For many a leisured (and perhaps bored) wife or spinster, charity had its recreational and creative aspects'.[214]

This conception arises in part from the characterisation of middle-class Victorian women, and from a misunderstanding of the income levels of those involved in charitable enterprise. What is often described as 'middle class' – separation of the home from the workplace, the employment of a minimum of three servants and the development of the 'paraphernalia of gentility', including an idle and ornamental wife – only encompassed the upper bracket of this social group. The reality for most women of this class was quite different. Many middle-class families, relying on an income of between £150 and £300 per annum,[215] could afford only one or two servants, and the women of the household often had a heavy domestic workload, particularly those with large families. Meanwhile, living 'over the shop' or near to one's business premises was the norm for many middle-class families in towns such as Wakefield and Huddersfield, and conceivably many women were actively involved in the running of such businesses. Tight budgeting was a common factor in household management, an area which increasingly became the responsibility of women. Often there would be little to spare for charity.[216] As the usual organisers of household expenditure,[217] women may have had a large say in determining where they would make charitable contributions, on behalf of themselves and their family. Moreover, the everyday experience of dealing with domestic concerns and the raising of children equipped these women with skills which could be of great use in charitable institutions.

Female supporters of the Wakefield and Huddersfield medical charities came largely from the same social groups as the male subscribers identified in Section 4.2. Indeed married couples often shared an interest in medical charity. In 1830, for example, well over half (64 per cent) of the female subscribers to the House of Recovery were members of families who also supported the Wakefield Dispensary, with these women often subscribing to both charities.[218] The fact that these women frequently enjoyed some degree of independence in making charitable contributions is evidenced by the fact that where both partners subscribed, they are in many cases recorded separately on subscription lists, and it was not uncommon for women's contributions to exceed those of their husbands. Women's payments to medical charities made up a high percentage of total contributions, and this is without taking into consideration the very real possibility that in some cases their payments were covered by their husband's name on subscription or donation lists.

The typology of the charitable woman as a 'frustrated spinster' is brought into question by the fact that the majority of women supporting and working for these charities were married. In 1830, 63 per cent of female subscribers to the Wakefield Dispensary and 75 per cent of those subscribing to the House of Recovery were married. By 1841 the proportion of married women subscribing to the latter institution had reached 87 per cent.[219] It is not unreasonable to speculate that many of those recorded as single had not yet reached a marriageable age. Late marriage was after all fairly common amongst the middle class during the nineteenth century,[220] and many of the single women listed were the daughters of other subscribers. Most lady visitors to the medical charities were married women. Indeed, when some knowledge of household management was necessary for active involvement in this capacity, the exertions of less experienced single women may well have been discouraged.

Women of the upper class did lend their support to the medical charities, particularly the wives of members of the local gentry and landowners. Their names appear as patronesses or heading subscription or donation lists. For example, the Patronesses to a charity ball held in aid of the Huddersfield Infirmary in 1849 included the Countess of Dartmouth, the Countess of Zetland, Lady Harriet Ramsden, Lady Radcliffe, Lady Ramsden and the Hon. Mrs Ramsden. Amongst the Patronesses to the annual Wakefield Charity Ball in 1870 were Countess Fitzwilliam, Countess de Grey and Ripon and four other female representatives of the local aristocracy.[221] Often the philanthropic efforts of the upper class were limited to the payment of monetary contributions and allowing their names to be used as an incentive to potential supporters. Much of the real work (and funding) was undertaken by middle-class women, from a commercial or professional background. The founding ladies of the Wakefield House of Recovery, for example, included Mrs Sharp, the wife of the Vicar of Wakefield, the daughters of a coal proprietor, a woolstapler and a civil engineer, and the wives of a physician and a merchant. In addition, the institution obtained the support of the wives of several local gentlemen: Mrs J. P. Heywood (Wentworth House), Mrs Gaskell (Thornes House) and Mrs Hague (Stanley Hall). Mrs Heywood, the wife of a local magistrate, acted as Treasurer to the institution from its founding to its closure in 1854. In 1830, a typical year, subscriptions to the House of Recovery were received mainly from the wives of solicitors, clerks, merchants and tradesmen (for example, linen drapers, stationers, druggists, grocers, ironmongers and innkeepers).[222] Employments of these sorts covered a wide range of possible income levels and social standing, but did not preclude the possibility of an important sacrifice of time and money by members of these occupation groups.

The activities of women are rarely mentioned in the minutes or rules of the medical charities. But financial records show the magnitude of women's monetary contributions, and references to women volunteers in annual and press reports enable us to build up a picture of their roles as workers, fund-raisers, and, in the House of Recovery, officers. The first decades of the nineteenth century witnessed a significant rise in the number of charitable institutions which admitted women visitors. When the Huddersfield Infirmary opened in the third decade of the century, one of the first actions of the officers was to give access to women visitors. In 1859 the Wakefield Infirmary followed suit, five years after provision was made for the reception of in-patients. Prochaska maintains that, to

gain access to charitable institutions, these women would have had
to be well placed financially and socially, and have some special
service to offer.[223] The first lady visitors appointed to the Wakefield
Infirmary were the wives of prominent townsmen and supporters
of the charity. The list included the wife of the Vice-President, the
Rev. Canon Camidge, Mrs Clayton, wife of the institution's most
important benefactor, and Mrs Gill and Mrs Secker, the wives of a
local gentleman and a merchant. Knowledge of domestic management, skills in dealing with servants and the ability to provide
comfort and religious instruction were amongst the requirements
sought after. But if specialised knowledge and wealth were prerequisites for lady visitors, the same also holds good for male
officers to the charities. No man would ever be appointed to a
position of prominence in a medical charity unless he was a member
of the local élite or was in possession of special abilities, organisational energy or sufficient wealth to provide a lead in financial
support.

Female visitors were responsible for two main areas of work: the
provision of 'Christian attention' to the patients and supervision of
domestic management. As the size and functions of the medical
charities expanded, and admissions increased, there was a parallel
growth in domestic concerns and in women's activities. A large
proportion of admissions to both infirmaries were female. For
example, in the year 1838–1839 245 males and 91 females (27 per
cent) were admitted to the Huddersfield Infirmary as in-patients.[224]
Female visitors, therefore, became necessary to deal with the needs
of women patients. The rules for the management of these institutions contained few details relating to domestic affairs, and it is
likely that women's involvement in this sphere became an agreeable
proposition to the all-male committees. Women's experience in
dealing with female servants was particularly sought after. These
women, often armed with the experience of visiting the poor in
their own homes, brought to the medical charities ideals of domestic
economy and harmony, and the ability to exercise a 'proper moral
influence' over servants and patients alike.

A lady visitor in an hospital or Asylum, should be to that institution what
the kind judicious Mistress of a family is to her household – the careful
inspector of the economy, the integrity and the good moral conduct of the
housekeeper and other inferior servants.[225]

The duties of lady visitors to the Huddersfield Infirmary came to include the provision of linen and household items, running a patients' library and supervision of the matron, nurses and domestic arrangements. Ladies were also responsible for setting up a fund to provide patients and other poor persons with flannel waistcoats. In 1855–1856, for example, over £52 was collected for this purpose, and 570 waistcoats made by the ladies and patients in the Infirmary, which were distributed by the medical officers amongst the poor.[226] The application of household skills could be of great value, and it is likely that higher standards of patient care were maintained in institutions which appointed lady visitors. Through the creation of a clean environment, thorough ventilation, warmth and adequate nutrition much could be done to relieve a patient. Indeed, improvements in these areas could have been more conducive to recovery than medical treatment. Women's involvement as visitors then could even be seen as a partial determinant of the success rate of a medical charity.

Nor should we underestimate the importance of women as religious reformers, at least in the eyes of those promoting these charities. It has already been pointed out that the inculcation of Christian duties and the 'saving of souls' were professed (although not the most important) aims of these charities, and a tenet in appeals for support. As F. K. Prochaska has related, in many charitable institutions, and in particular medical charities, women concentrated on dispensing large doses of scripture and 'pursuing souls to the bitter sweet end'.[227] The offering of spiritual comfort was one of the roles allocated to women visitors, who bombarded the patients with gifts of Bibles, prayer books, psalms and religious tracts, and such uplifting publications as *The Christian Magazine* and *The Gospel Trumpet*. For example, in 1859 Miss Thomas donated a large print book of psalms, and Mrs Laycock several books and tracts, for the benefit of in-patients to the Huddersfield Infirmary. In 1864 Mrs Allen provided a monthly supply of *The Gospel Trumpet*, and in 1866 Mrs F. R. Jones donated two 'handsomely bound' copies of *A Pilgrim's Progress*.[228]

Parallel to the expansion of woman's role in the internal management of voluntary institutions, they became increasingly important as both financial contributors in their own right and fund-raisers. Women subscribed to the medical charities of Wakefield and Huddersfield in significant numbers, and often made large donations and benefactions. In the year 1830–1831, for example, 12 per cent and 23 per cent of the subscribers to the Huddersfield and Wakefield Dispensaries were female. The proportion of female subscribers fluctuated throughout the century; by 1865–1866, for example, they accounted for 13 per cent and 7 per cent of subscriptions to the Wakefield and Huddersfield Infirmaries.[229] Any fall off in subscriptions on the part of women was, however, more than compensated for by an increase in donations and legacies during the second half of the nineteenth century.

In the year 1855–1856, for example, Miss E. Broughton collected £40 in donations for the Wakefield Infirmary, and of the £46 14s 2d raised in donations in 1856–1857, £32 11s 8d (70 per cent) was contributed by women, either through personal canvasses or individual donations. In 1829, £300 towards the building of the Huddersfield Infirmary was donated by Mrs Whitacre of Woodhouse, and in 1843 Mrs Cocker of Huddersfield presented £100 to the Huddersfield Infirmary.[230] Women frequently left large legacies to the infirmaries, although on the whole they were smaller than those endowed by their male counterparts. In 1829 a legacy of £500 was received by the Huddersfield Dispensary from Miss Flanson of Paddock, near Huddersfield. In 1862 the Huddersfield Infirmary was endowed with a legacy of £50 by the late Miss Susan C. Raistrick, and in 1866 one of £87 from Mrs Betty Roberts of Delph, near Huddersfield.[231] These figures are not untypical, and donations paid by women were occasionally sufficient to earn them the privilege of becoming life governors. Life Governors to the Huddersfield Infirmary included Lady Radcliffe and the Honourable Mrs Ramsden. The Misses Broughton, Mrs Parker and Mrs Clayton were Life Benefactors to the Wakefield Infirmary.

Fund-raising activities came to be very much the preserve of women during the nineteenth century. They undertook the personal canvassing of subscriptions and donations, and the organisation of fund-raising events; bazaars, concerts and balls, in aid of the institutions. For example, in the year 1858–1859 the Treasurer of the Huddersfield Infirmary recorded the receipt of a contribution of £4 15s, the proceeds of a Bazaar of Work, contributed by 'a few Young Ladies, pupils of the Misses Wood, Fitz-Wm. St. West'.[232] In 1828 a bazaar for the benefit of the Fever Hospital and Wakefield Dispensary was organised by the Ladies Committee of the former charity. The proceeds totalled £440.[233] A striking example of the success of female fund-raising activity was the massive £1,500 made at a bazaar in aid of the Huddersfield Infirmary in May, 1831.[234] This function was organised almost entirely by the ladies of Huddersfield and the surrounding districts, assisted by Dr Walker, physician to the Huddersfield Dispensary.

Perhaps an even more striking example of a successful fund-raising event was the annual charity ball, organised in Wakefield for the benefit of the Infirmary and the House of Recovery. This event was notable not so much for the sums it raised, although in some years these were considerable, but for the fact that it was organised annually by the all-female committee of the House of Recovery for a period of over 25 years (from 1828 to 1854). (After the closure of the House of Recovery, the ball continued to be organised by the committee and medical officers of the Wakefield Infirmary.) The arrangements were 'entirely Directed' by the Ladies Committee through the Honorary Secretary, Miss Anne Brown, and on her retirement in 1836, by Miss Heald. They selected the patrons and patronesses from the chief supporters of the ball in the district, advertised the event in the press and arranged the fittings and refreshments.[235] In 1828 the profits of the ball including donations totalled £209 (the sale of 338 tickets raising £169).[236] Even in years when the profits from the ball were low, they still represented an important source of income for both charities. In 1841, for example, the profits of the ball totalled only £76. The £38 paid to each institution represented over 16 per cent of the income of the House of Recovery in that year, and 23 per cent of that of the Wakefield Dispensary.[237]

The financial contributions of women seem to have been eagerly accepted, and gave them similar social advantages to those enjoyed by men. They were given the opportunity to rub shoulders with members of the local élite, while the appearance of their names on subscription lists conferred upon them the attributes of prestige, gentility and benevolence. But women's financial offerings did not carry with them the same privileges extended to male subscribers. No woman ever served as an officer or on a committee of either infirmary during the first three-quarters of the nineteenth century. Therefore, they had no way of influencing financial decision-making or of determining policy. However, they did hold similar privileges with regard to voting and recommending patients.

Women were not as a rule admitted to elections, but were allowed to vote by proxy or by letter. It is difficult to assess how far they made use of these facilities. Accounts of voting results at the elections of medical officers, however, suggest that most votes were utilised, and there are notes of patients, often female, being admitted under the recommendations of women subscribers to the two infirmaries.

F. K. Prochaska has described what he calls an 'explosion' of female societies during the period 1790–1830,[238] which coincides with the founding of the House of Recovery in 1826. The charities which Prochaska describes share several features with the Wakefield institution: a high percentage of women subscribers (usually over 80 per cent of the total number of subscribers), a low degree of male involvement, and the formulation of policies determined largely by women. The House of Recovery, however, merits special attention by virtue of its uniqueness; medical charities run by women were at least rare, probably exceptional, during this period. The sole running of the charity, with the exception of the provision of medical treatment and drawing up of annual reports, a task undertaken by the medical officers, was the responsibility of women. Throughout the institution's history, from 1826 to 1854, no man sat on a committee or became an officer. Even the onerous task of Treasurer became the preserve of a woman, Mrs Heywood, who was responsible for investments and handling large sums of money. Women elected their own officers and committees, and chose the medical staff and servants:

The power of Electing and Removing the Physicians and Surgeons, of Appointing a Committee of Management, and of Making and Repealing Rules, shall be vested in the General Meeting of Trustees; . . . '.[239]

Although control over admissions was placed largely in the hands of medical men, subscribers could make recommendations. Women consistently accounted for over 80 per cent of subscriptions to the charity. Responsibility for recommending 'suitable cases' for admission, and for initial contact with patients of both sexes, therefore, usually devolved on women. While the medical side of the charity was left very much to the medical officers, the supervision of household concerns and of servants was undertaken by the Ladies Committee. Committee meetings were held every month to receive the matron's report and to direct the ordinary business of the house.

The officers and committee were also responsible for the organisation of fund-raising events, including the annual charity ball, and for soliciting subscriptions. Although in some years the annual report expressed regret at having to limit admissions, there were fewer complaints about shortages of funds or the need for increased economy than in the reports of the Wakefield and Huddersfield Infirmaries (particularly the former). Women accounted for by far the largest proportion of the regular income from subscriptions: 82 per cent in 1830 and 84 per cent in 1841.[240] From time to time donations or legacies were received from female supporters, and in some cases these could be very generous. In 1831, for example, Mrs Johnstone donated £25 to the institution, and in 1840 Mrs Heywood, Treasurer, gave £99.[241]

Despite the fact that the House of Recovery only operated in an ordinary house, 'in a not very eligible situation' with 'very moderate sized wards, with no corridors for ventilation, no separate bath rooms or lavatories, . . . and one nurse, who was herself on more than one occasion laid up in a fever', the charity was very successful. The case-mortality from typhus fever in the House of Recovery was approximately half the usual rate: about 86 per cent of the patients admitted were sent away cured.[242] When the charity was wound up in 1854 it was not due to any financial or medical failure. Rather, the opening of the new Union Workhouse in Wakefield in 1852, with facilities for the admission of fever cases, coupled with a general decline in the incidence of fevers, substantially diminished the need for a fever hospital. In the face of a rapid fall off in admissions and the beginnings of a decline in financial support, the officers and committee of the House of Recovery opted for closure.

The efforts of the women involved in the running of the charity were applauded by the Wakefield medical profession. They received praise for both their philanthropic achievements and the high standards they maintained within the institution. Dr T. G. Wright, physician to the charity, suggested that the ladies who established the Fever Hospital, '. . . deserve record as a group of earnest philanthropists, to whose indefatigable labour the suffering poor of the town were long and largely indebted'.[243] Another Wakefield physician, Dr C. Crowther, gave even higher praise to the committee of ladies, who managed the institution in '. . . a very economical and efficient manner'. In a large bequest he left land and money for the establishment of a second fever hospital in the town. The following recommendation was made to future managers of the charity.

I recommend the Governors to imitate the Ladies in the management of the Fever Hospital, and to call to their Aid, if they find it expedient to do so, a Committee of that sex, subject to the appointment of the Governors.[244]

What is also significant and unusual about the House of Recovery is that, unlike Prochaska's female societies, which dealt mainly with the needs of women and children, the women active in this charity came into regular contact not only with the diseased poor, but with the poor of both sexes. Almost equal numbers of male and female patients were admitted to the institution,[245] at a time when there was considerable opposition to contact between middle-class women and working-class men, and when women's philanthropic work was being restricted by the demand that they direct their efforts solely towards women and children.

Members of the Ladies Committee and ordinary subscribers to the House of Recovery were involved in other local philanthropic enterprises. Several committee members were also on the committee of the Wakefield Female Benefit Society, founded in 1805 to provide assistance to poor lying-in women, which was an 'all female' society in terms of both support and beneficiaries.[246] Other committee members and subscribers worked for and financed various local missionary and benevolent societies: the Wakefield Town Mission, the Benevolent Society and the Bible Society, for instance. In these organisations, however, their role was limited to making financial contributions, visiting the homes of the poor to dispense advice and spiritual comfort, and fund-raising activities. They were totally excluded from the decision-making processes. The story was much the same in Huddersfield. The House of Recovery was the only organisation in either town where women directed policy-making and finance, and dealt with the poor of both sexes.

The activities of women in the Wakefield and Huddersfield Infirmaries were also basically restricted to their traditional roles of visiting and funding. However, their contributions should not be underestimated. It has already been suggested that as visitors women could influence an improvement in the management and cleanliness of the wards. Their financial contributions, meanwhile, could be crucial, especially during the periods of financial crisis often referred to in the reports of these institutions. The contributions of women, often derived from a private source of income, may have been more stable than those of male patrons. Finally, there is little to suggest that women's involvement in policy-making would have led to any significant changes in the way the infirmaries were funded and organised, or indeed in their aims. The motives of the Ladies Committee of the House of Recovery seemed to differ little from those of their male counterparts on the infirmary committees. Emphasis was placed on preventing the spread of infectious diseases, particularly to the homes of the rich, on admitting only 'proper objects' (and insisting on payment by improper ones), on sound and efficient management and economy.

Concluding remarks

Clearly it is impossible to put forward a mono-causal explanation for the founding and continued support of the Wakefield and Huddersfield medical charities, and it has not been the purpose of this chapter to do so. Such a simplified conclusion could only be achieved by a crude reductionism. The promoters of the charities showed a willingness to resort to a variety of appeals in order to win support and approval of their work, and the charities obtained the backing of a wide range of social and occupational groups, each presumably with their own sets of ambitions and expectations. We should not expect a clergyman to support medical charity for the same reasons as a large employer of labour, a tradesman, a member of the legal profession, a doctor or a middle-class woman. Different groups supported the Wakefield and Huddersfield medical charities for different reasons, be they pragmatic, social, altruistic, out of a sense of Christian duty, or a combination of these motivations. This was one of the advantages of medical charity; it could attract a wide cross-section of support, each individual or group taking what they wanted out of it, and altering their degree of practical or financial input accordingly. It was also less likely to be hampered by sectarian or religious divisions (compared, for example, with missionary or educational work).

Neither is a multi-causal theory of charitable endeavour, which makes no attempt to place motivations in any order of importance, satisfactory. A good deal of support for the Wakefield and Huddersfield medical charities came from commercial groups, in particular manufacturers. In one sense this is not very surprising, as commercial groups made up one of the largest occupational sectors in both towns, especially Huddersfield. However, the existence of such groups does not imply automatic support for philanthropic enterprise in general and medical charity in particular. In Huddersfield merchant-manufacturing groups were responsible not only for the greatest proportion of financial backing, but also for the direction of policy-making and the day-to-day running of the Infirmary. This dynamic and wealthy group emphasised rational and practical aims, the provision at a low cost of an efficient and selective form of medical treatment for the working class, whose labour was crucial to the functioning of the local economy. The manufacturing elements appear to have been able to win support for their policies from other social and occupational groups, while leaving room for the expression and fulfilment of other aims and expectations. The straightforward practical purposes of medical charities had a broad potential appeal. The problem of treating sick employees and servants concerned a large proportion of the community's wealthier inhabitants. The more specialised problem of dealing with accident cases was not directly relevant to all the patrons of the Huddersfield Dispensary and Infirmary. However, it was relevant to the smooth functioning of the local economy, which touched most pockets. Meanwhile, the wealthy classes were unanimous in recognising the dangers which could result from the spread of epidemic disease, and were anxious to curtail this threat. A medical provision for the poor of the town was clearly a necessity, and charity, with its numerous side benefits, offered an attractive alternative.

Support for the Wakefield medical charities was shared more equally between a cross-section of social and occupational groups. Although manufacturers made an important contribution (especially when we remember that their role in the town's economy was far less significant than in Huddersfield[247]), tradesmen, professional and service groups and 'gentlemen' were also well represented as both financial contributors and policy makers. Less emphasis was placed on the treatment of persons injured at their place of work than in Huddersfield. The reports of the Wakefield Dispensary and Infirmary also reveal that their framers were less clear about the purpose of the institution and about the methods they should adopt in order to win support. The divided nature of the charity's support was paralleled by vague policy statements. This lack of single-mindedness guaranteed, in part at least, a wide cross-section of support. But the fact that the governance of the charity was never in the hands of one dominant group may go part way towards explaining its more ineffective role as an agency of medical relief.

The Wakefield and Huddersfield Infirmaries and House of Recovery seem to have functioned largely on the principle of self-interest, with practical considerations taking precedence over altruistic motivations. The charities acted as ameliorative institutions, relieving the acute distress occasioned by sickness or injury, becoming particularly active during periods of local economic depression or when social unrest threatened. But they in no way attempted to deal with any of the root causes of poverty and distress (with the exception of some minor forays into the field of public health[248]), in spite of the fact that the patrons of these charities seem to have been well aware as to what these root causes were. The First Report of the Huddersfield Dispensary, for example, in appealing for support, eloquently described the conditions of the working class of the district during the period of the Napoleonic Wars.

Often is the poor Man doomed to struggle, at the same Time, with Penury and Disease, with his Bodily Afflictions aggravated by the Wants and Cries of his helpless Family. It is his Lot to be more exposed to the incidental Causes of Disease, to the Changes and Inclemency of the Weather, immured, perhaps, in a confined Situation, with defective Food and Clothing; or engaged in laborious and, frequently, unhealthy Employments; and liable, at all Times, to accidental Injuries.[249]

Emphasis has been placed in this chapter upon the necessity of looking not only at the stated motivations of the philanthropic, but also at their social and economic backgrounds. Only then can we obtain a true impression of their aims and ambitions. Without some knowledge of the backgrounds of the patrons to the Huddersfield Dispensary the above quotation could be interpreted as an expression of humanitarianism; the operation of medical charity as an exercise in disinterested benevolence.

There would also appear to be a strong case for looking at the functioning of medical charities against a backdrop of local social and economic conditions (as outlined in Chapter 2). Medical charities, in a similar way to all other voluntary institutions, did not function in a vacuum. The setting up of the dispensaries and infirmaries and the Wakefield House of Recovery was linked closely to local social problems, the state of the towns' economies, the level of civic pride, the emergence of dynamic individuals, and so on. These factors go a long way towards explaining the relative success of the Huddersfield Dispensary and Infirmary, which developed in a go-ahead social, civic and economic setting. The substantial population increase made such a provision all the more necessary. Money, largely from the textile industry, was available to fund the enterprise. Huddersfield's enterprising merchant-manufacturers were able to harness this wealth and provide a powerful and effective leadership.

In a similar way, the difficulties faced by the Wakefield Dispensary and Infirmary during the early and mid-nineteenth century were tied very much to the general decline of the town, particularly the slowing down of its industrial growth. There was less money available to fund charitable enterprise, less incentive for providing medical relief on a large scale and no strong leadership group emerged to direct fund-raising or policy-making. It was only in the 1850s and 1860s that the charity entered a period of financial and managerial security. This improvement in its position was closely associated with a local economic upturn, an apparent resurgence of civic pride and the interest of a number of eminent and wealthy individuals (such as Clayton and Charlesworth), ready to give a lead in both the government and financing of the institution.

Interestingly enough, up until the mid-nineteenth century, of the two Wakefield medical charities, the House of Recovery could be said to have been far more successful in terms of both the funds it commanded and its management. While operating in the same social and economic climate as the Dispensary, the House of Recovery enjoyed several advantages over the other charity. Its aims were simple and clear: to remove the threat of epidemic disease from the community. Its management was controlled by a small group of women, who also provided most of the funding. The policies and aims of the committee were well-defined, unambiguous and unchanging throughout the period of the charity's existence.

This chapter has perhaps created rather a static picture of both the aims of the patrons of the Wakefield and Huddersfield medical charities and their actual functions. But in fact the charities did appear to be remarkably resistant to change and adaptation to developments in the local situation (with the exception of economic downturns or social unrest), and more specifically to the evolution of new health problems. As Charles Webster has remarked, 'it can be by no means assumed that infirmaries were created, expanded and adapted in accordance with the needs of local communities, or even that advocates of modest medical improvements could rely on support from the wealthier classes who traditionally supported medical charities'.[250] One of the main reasons behind the narrow and static interpretation of the role of the medical charities was the fact that the organisation and admission's policy of these institutions remained firmly in the hands of laymen, with the medical staff playing only a secondary part in policy direction for the first three-quarters of the nineteenth century.[251] Throughout this period the supporters of the medical charities of Wakefield and Huddersfield limited themselves largely to the treatment of accident and epidemic disease cases, and to the admission of 'the deserving and useful poor', a policy dominated by social and economic rather than medical considerations, which took little account of the larger-scale health problems created by industrial society.

5

Medical relief and the friendly societies

Friendly societies were the largest and probably the best organised group of working-class institutions to evolve during the eighteenth and nineteenth centuries. They were composed of groups of men, and to a much lesser extent women, who collected together to insure themselves against the three major calamities that could befall the labouring classes: sickness, unemployment and death, with its associated threat of a pauper funeral. Combined with these insurance functions, friendly societies, which normally were based at a local public house, offered possibilities for socialising, by means of club nights, annual outings and feasts. Some friendly societies, typically those recruiting their members from one trade, acted as trade unions in disguise, especially during the period of the Combination Acts (1799–1824). Even these organisations, despite their differences in function and aim, combined their clandestine trade union activities with the provisions of a typical friendly society.

The traditions of the friendly society or 'box club' reached far back into the eighteenth century; many highly organised clubs existed by the 1750s. But the nineteenth century witnessed an enormous increase in both the number of members and of societies, as they apparently adapted with some success to the new demands and scale of industrial life. The earliest type of friendly society to evolve was the local organisation, taking its membership from a small neighbourhood, and formulating its own set of regulations and scales of benefit. After circa 1830 the affiliated orders came to be of more significance compared to the local societies. The Manchester Unity of Oddfellows and the Foresters grew especially fast from the 1830s and 1840s. Though organised in local courts and lodges, the affiliated orders developed a central administration, and a uniform code of rules and scale of benefits. They also tended to be more stable financially than the local societies.

English friendly societies underwent a remarkable expansion in the nineteenth century, especially in the second and third quarters of the century, 'the classical age for the foundation of friendly societies'.[1] By mid-century 'nearly half the adult male population' was reputed to belong to a friendly society.[2] The membership of friendly societies increased from an estimated 648,000 in 1793 to 704,350 in 1803, 925,429 in 1815, and to over four million in 1872. Meanwhile, the number of societies grew from 9,672 in 1803, with funds of one million pounds, to over 32,000 in 1872, with funds of nearly twelve million.[3] The membership of the Manchester Unity of Oddfellows alone increased from 248,000 persons organised in 2,039 lodges in 1845 to 497,000 members in 3,074 lodges in 1875. By 1872 friendly societies had four times as many members as trade unions and twelve times the membership of co-operative societies.[4] By the last quarter of the nineteenth century there was a vast network of friendly societies throughout the country; every average-sized town had several affiliated national societies, as well as numerous local societies.

This chapter will examine the role played by friendly societies in providing sick pay and medical care for their members. Although we are only dealing with one function of the friendly society, it is necessary to mention some of the more general problems which arise in any study of their activities. The most serious problem is the lack of reliable statistical evidence on nineteenth-century friendly societies. In spite of this difficulty, however, an attempt will be made to estimate the proportion of the population opting for friendly society membership. Without such an estimate we cannot hope to assess their value as agents of medical relief. Also it is necessary to make some judgement regarding the social make-up of friendly societies, an area of contention for both contemporaries and historians. Were these organisations made up of individuals from the lower end of the labour market, whose only other alternatives when sick would be to apply for poor relief or to a charity? Or were friendly societies patronised by well-paid artisans, tradesmen and members of the 'labour aristocracy', who could even have afforded private medical treatment? Linked to this question is the debate about the role of friendly societies as class institutions.

Did the development of the friendly society movement signify a striving by the working classes for independence and self-help? Or did friendly societies merely provide a cheap form of insurance for the comparatively well-off?

Wakefield and Huddersfield shared in the common features of friendly society development in Northern England, where these organisations had their greatest impact. Friendly societies in these two communities, therefore, make suitable case studies for an examination of the role of this movement in providing medical relief for the poorer classes. A survey of friendly societies in the two towns in the late eighteenth and nineteenth centuries has been undertaken, using extant sets of rules, reports, minute books and membership lists. Parliamentary returns, especially those concerned with the registration of friendly societies, have also been referred to. Of special interest is the first quinquennial report on sickness and mortality in friendly societies, which was drawn up in 1880.[5] Parliamentary inquiries which touched on friendly society provisions, and the reports and descriptions of contemporaries relating to these organisations, were also consulted. At best, these sources can produce only a sketchy picture of friendly society provisions and very scanty statistical evidence. Many records of individual societies have disappeared. The returns of registered societies are notoriously incomplete, while the majority of societies chose not to register at all. Meanwhile, the evidence of contemporaries was biased towards the affiliated orders, ignoring the still significant local societies.

The discussion in this chapter will be organised into four sections. Firstly, an attempt will be made to assess the number and percentage of the population joining friendly societies in Wakefield and Huddersfield (therefore providing themselves with this form of medical cover). In the next Section we will briefly examine the social composition of friendly societies, and the motives of those who joined these fraternities. Thirdly, the organisation of medical relief by friendly societies will be examined. How much sickness benefit did members receive? How long was benefit continued? Did friendly societies also provide medical attendance and medicines? What was the quality of this medical treatment? Following on from the above, in the fourth Section it will be suggested that the nature of medical assistance provided by friendly societies could tell us something about the type and duration of sickness to which the poor were most usually subject.[6] The chapter as a whole will tend very much towards the descriptive. This can be justified by the fact that most aspects of the friendly society movement have been only scantily covered, while the part played by these organisations in providing medical relief for the poor has been almost totally ignored by historians.[7]

5.1 Membership

Friendly societies embraced a larger proportion of the working class than any other eighteenth- or nineteenth-century institutions, and, as Perkin suggests, they can be therefore considered as the most typical of all the working–class bodies formed to respond to the problems of industrialisation.[8] This proposition would seem to be confirmed by the fact that friendly societies grew most rapidly in the period and areas of fastest industrial (and population) growth, developing heavy concentrations in Lancashire, Yorkshire and other industrial regions of the North and Midlands. In the predominantly agricultural counties the impetus to form friendly societies, and their success if initiated, was much less.[9]

Contemporaries, while recognising the enormous significance of friendly societies, were unable to form accurate conclusions as to the precise number of members or their true functions. Friendly societies showed much secretiveness and evasiveness in the face of upper-class inquiries. Henry Rumsey complained of such difficulties while collecting information on the amount of medical relief provided by sick clubs and friendly societies, which he gave as evidence to the Select Committee on Medical Poor Relief in 1844. Inquiries on the subject were 'disliked by the working classes and by the surgeons of the clubs'.[10] A series of benevolent acts, beginning with the First Friendly Society Act of 1793, offered protection of funds at law through the registration of societies with the magistrates. However, large numbers of clubs failed to register, because of 'hostility to the authorities, parochial inertia, or through a deep secretiveness'.[11] Because of the failure of registration, contemporaries were unable to compute membership numbers with any accuracy, or to assess the class of person friendly societies attracted. This lack of reliable data provides similar problems for historians.[12]

The manufacturing districts of Yorkshire were amongst the areas most active in the establishment of friendly societies. Already, by the turn of the century, a return for the West Riding showed the area contained a registered 492 friendly societies, with 59,000 members. Many of these were in the larger industrial towns. Sheffield had forty societies, Leeds 26, and Halifax fifteen.[13] The large number of friendly societies (together with the wider availability of medical relief via charitable institutions) was cited as an important reason for the comparatively low cost of Poor Law medical relief in the North during the nineteenth century. Witnesses to nineteenth-century parliamentary inquiries repeatedly affirmed the independence of the labouring classes in the North, their inclination towards self-help, enthusiasm for friendly societies and their reluctance to look to the parish for medical assistance.

In common with many other West Riding manufacturing towns, large percentages of the populations of Wakefield and Huddersfield became members of a friendly society. In 1803 five friendly societies were recorded in Wakefield, and four in Huddersfield. Total membership was given as 246 and 900 respectively. In Wakefield, therefore, approximately 3 per cent of the population were friendly society members, in Huddersfield 12 per cent. By 1815 the number of registered friendly society members in the two towns had increased to 725 and 1,401. This represented percentage increases in membership of 195 and 56 in just over ten years. Expressed as a proportion of the population, in 1815 7.5 per cent of persons residing in the Wakefield Township, and 12.2 per cent of those living in Huddersfield, were members of a friendly society.[14] While in Wakefield friendly society membership outstripped population growth, in Huddersfield, with its far higher rate of population increase, the percentage of the population taking up membership remained static.

Friendly societies were not just popular in the towns. The villages surrounding Wakefield and Huddersfield also boasted large friendly societies. In 1815 Horbury, near Wakefield, with a population of just under 2,500, had one registered friendly society with 406 members (approximately 16 per cent of the total population). South Crosland, situated four miles south of Huddersfield, with a population of approximately 1,500, had two registered societies by 1815, with a total of 360 members (or 24 per cent of the population). Saddleworth, a distance of fourteen miles from Huddersfield (and part of the Huddersfield Union after 1837), had fourteen societies, with a total of 3,207 members (24 per cent of the population), including one female society with 499 members.[15] These estimates already indicate an impressive level of friendly society membership. But it is important to note that these figures only cover the membership of registered societies. Considering that many societies failed to register, or made incomplete returns, we can safely assume that membership was much higher.

By 1844 it was estimated that more than one in eleven of the population of Wakefield were members of some kind of friendly society.[16] By 1866 Huddersfield was reputed to have a total of 83 friendly societies (although only about ten had bothered to register).[17] Wakefield and Huddersfield both shared in the growth of the affiliated orders after 1830. By 1840 there were twenty courts of Ancient Foresters alone in the Wakefield area, and thirteen in and around Huddersfield. In 1840 approximately 480 Foresters were meeting in Wakefield's public houses. In the same year about 110 members of Royal Shepherds Sanctuaries (a Branch of the Royal Foresters) were recorded in the Huddersfield Township. In mid-nineteenth century Honley (a distance three miles south of Huddersfield) there were flourishing societies of Ancient Druids, Modern Druids, Foresters, Free Gardeners and Shepherds. The Honley branch of the Ancient Order of Foresters alone had 110 members.[18]

Individual societies in the area recorded overall increases in membership during the nineteenth century. Admittances and withdrawals, and lapses in the payment of subscriptions, seem to have been subject to short-term fluctuations in economic conditions. The Grand United Order of Oddfellows, Cleckheaton, for example, had only thirty members in 1826 (a year of depression). By 1839 the figure had risen to 194 (although many of these were listed as 'unfinancial', that is, failing to pay their subscriptions). Between 1819 and 1859 approximately 170 men joined the Saddleworth Sanctuary of Royal Shepherds.[19] The reports of the Wakefield British Friendly Union Society show both a steady increase in membership and a strengthening of the Society's financial position during the mid-nineteenth century. In 1847 there were 43 members and a balance of £206. By 1862 membership had risen to 83 and the balance had more than quadrupled to £920.[20] By the 1860s the 'typical' Wakefield and Huddersfield friendly society had between 50 and 100 members; in exceptional cases between 100 and 200 (see Table 5.2).

5.2 Social composition

There are a variety of opinions, held both by nineteenth-century commentators and present-day historians, concerning the social composition of friendly societies. One group with particularly strong views on the subject were nineteenth-century medical practitioners. Members of the medical profession saw friendly societies as one barrier in their fight for higher professional status and commensurate remuneration. Friendly societies not only paid their surgeons badly, but they also involved them in degrading undercutting practices and the hated contract system. Perhaps of even more importance, doctors saw friendly societies as a direct threat to their private practices and incomes, believing that many of those who subscribed to these organisations could well afford to pay for medical treatment. The membership of friendly societies, according to doctors, was largely made up of tradesmen, small farmers, artisans and even members of the middle class. As late as 1868 a *Lancet* editorial complained that the sick clubs '. . . include many persons whose social level is above that of the class for whom the benefits they are capable of dispensing were intended'.[21]

A number of historians hold similar views on the social make-up of friendly societies. Perkin, for example, has suggested that in the first half of the nineteenth century friendly societies were composed of the labour aristocracy, who were paid 50 to 100 per cent more than labourers.[22] Gilbert, meanwhile, has pronounced that friendly societies '. . . made no appeal whatever to the grey, faceless, lower third of the working class. Friendly society membership was the badge of the skilled worker'.[23] At the other extreme, it has been suggested by one economic historian that the working classes were driven into friendly societies, not because it appeared to them as the most dignified way of securing medical help and funeral benefits, but because there was no other way of avoiding pauperisation.[24] Neither of these two extremes seems viable. There was simply an insufficient number of well-paid artisans to account for the total membership of friendly societies. The 'labour aristocracy' made up only approximately 10 to 15 per cent of the working class. Meanwhile, even a conservative estimate of friendly society membership would put it at well over 15 per cent of the adult male population. More liberal estimates would put the figure at nearer 50 per cent, especially in the manufacturing districts. This large deficit in membership must have been filled by some other group or groups. On the other hand, it is unlikely that those faced with imminent pauperisation could have afforded the weekly subscription of even as little as 3d a week, which friendly society membership usually demanded.

The truth probably lies somewhere between the two extremes. Gosden has proposed that the major affiliated orders originated and afterwards recruited amongst the better-paid groups of working men, which seems likely in view of their higher rates of admission, subscription and benefits. Up to 1850, Gosden suggests, the Manchester Unity of Oddfellows recruited most strongly amongst such occupation groups as textile workers, printers, carpenters and other members of the building trades, small craftsmen and tradesmen (blacksmiths, butchers, tailors and shoemakers, for example).[25] E. P. Thompson, meanwhile, ascribed friendly society membership to a wide cross-section of the working class, to include small tradesmen, artisans and labourers, with the greatest proportion of membership being made up of artisans.[26] Rumsey, in his evidence to the 1844 parliamentary inquiry on medical relief, suggested that the rate of medical officers' remuneration was a reliable indication of the composition of the society. When the sum exceeded 2s 6d per head, the members were often of a 'superior' description: small tradesmen, shopkeepers, office workers, and so on. The Oddfellows, Rumsey claimed, belonged chiefly to this class. Societies paying this rate or less, in fact the majority, were composed by implication largely of members of the 'ordinary' labouring classes.[27]

Probably for the artisan class, membership of a friendly society was almost mandatory, and the major affiliated orders took most of their members from the better-paid artisan groups, plus some small tradesmen and white-collar workers. Meanwhile, local societies and less important affiliated orders (who paid lower benefits and were less likely to appoint a medical attendant) were made up predominantly of labouring men. The activities of the affiliated orders in Wakefield and Huddersfield reflected some superiority in their membership. Rates of admission and subscription were in general higher in the affiliated orders. They normally took the trouble to register, and they rarely folded up because of a lack of funds. They also tended to play a more prominent role in the public affairs of the towns.

Until the passing of the Poor Law Amendment Act in 1834,

paupers and near-paupers were also admitted into friendly societies in Wakefield and Huddersfield. Their admission fees and weekly or monthly contributions were paid by the overseers of the poor, who presumably found it cheaper and more convenient to make arrangements with a club for the relief of the sick poor, than to pay out-relief and the expenses of medical treatment out of the rates. Evidence was found in overseers' account books of the payment of 'club' subscriptions in Huddersfield, Wakefield and other local townships from the late eighteenth century up until circa 1834, and indeed it appears to have been a fairly common practice.[28]

Evidence on the occupations and social status of friendly society members is unfortunately extremely rare (with the exception of the membership of the major affiliated orders). An examination of the records of societies in and around Wakefield and Huddersfield produced only a few items giving this kind of information. A contribution book of the Royal Shepherds Sanctuary, Huddersfield, listed the names, ages, occupations and residences of those becoming members of the Sanctuary between 1832 and 1841. Of the twenty individuals joining the society between these dates, sixteen were textile workers (weavers, spinners and slubbers, etc.), two were joiners and two were tailors. The low rates of benefits reflected the relatively low status of the membership. Dole in the case of sickness was just 6s a week for the first thirteen weeks, and 3s a week thereafter. The contribution book of the Perseverance Lodge of the Independent Order of Oddfellows (Huddersfield District), meanwhile, included details of the ages, occupations and dates of admission of the 38 members of the Lodge, listed for the purposes of making a return for the 1861 quinquennial returns. The relatively higher-status, but diverse, membership was composed of twelve members of the textile industry, six members of the building trade, five shopkeepers, three shoemakers, two printers, two bookbinders, two merchants, a salesman, warehouseman, groom, pillmaker, labourer and a manufacturer. Benefits were also higher, 10s for the first twenty weeks, and 7s 6d for the second twenty weeks.[29] A few societies took members from just one trade, such as the Huddersfield Friendly Society of Journeymen Joiners and Carpenters and the Warehousemen's and Clerks' Providential Association. These societies, which appear to have been designed for a 'better class' of member, were, however, comparative rarities, and it is reasonable to assume, in an area so dominated by the cloth industry, that textile workers made up a substantial part of friendly society membership.

Closely linked to the question of the social composition of friendly societies is the debate over their role as class institutions. What did those who became members hope to get out of involvement in these fraternities? Were friendly societies seen merely as an efficient method of obtaining medical and other benefits, or did they embody some form of socio–political aim? The wealthier classes of the nineteenth century came to regard the activities of friendly societies with some ambivalence. On the one hand, they were acclaimed as agents of working-class self-help and independence; their progress was encouraged by the nineteen paternal acts of parliament passed between 1793 and 1875. In particular, friendly societies were valued for reducing the burden of poor rates. The 1834 Royal Commission on the Poor Laws expressed admiration of the principles upon which friendly societies conducted the payment of benefit to members. They also hoped that by '. . . introducing an equivalent degree of strictness into the giving of poor relief, they would persuade more members of the working classes to subscribe to friendly societies'.[30]

On the other hand, friendly societies were also regarded as possible sources of political and industrial insubordination. Any organisation which involved large numbers of the working class meeting together out of the gaze of the upper classes aroused suspicion. The fact that many friendly societies operated in an atmosphere of secrecy and exclusiveness heightened fears. In 1830, for example, an anonymous Huddersfield pamphleteer criticised friendly societies for their secrecy, their financial and legal insecurity, their wastage of money and their secret oaths. If labouring men insisted on joining a friendly society (contrary to his counsel), he recommended entering one that had been registered, that had no oaths or secrets, that had a secure financial policy (that is, one which required large payments and offered small benefits) and one which would not tempt young men into drunkenness and dissolute practices![31]

The friendly societies in Wakefield and Huddersfield apparently did not involve themselves in political activities. Involvement in local events was also rare, but when it did take place, it reflected co-operation with, not opposition to, the ruling classes. At the opening of the Huddersfield Infirmary, for example, the participation of local friendly societies in the ceremonial was encouraged by the Infirmary Committee. A Huddersfield lodge of Oddfellows noted in a letter to the nearby Deighton Lodge that all the secret orders in the town had received invitations to attend, '. . . for which occasion they are all trying to make the best show. We are determined to make as good an appearance as any of them'. Members were encouraged to attend the function on horseback, and to wear their scarves and medals. A good attendance was called for to show the United Order '. . . is not only respectable but numerous also'.[32] Many fraternities attended at the opening ceremony in June, 1831, including lodges of Oddfellows, Royal Foresters, the Ancient Order of Shepherds (around 4,000 persons from throughout the West Riding) and various local societies.[33] Local friendly societies (as shall be seen on pages 195–196) became regular contributors to the Huddersfield Infirmary. By the 1870s the annual Friendly Societies' Demonstration made several hundred pounds per annum for the institution. In the year 1880 the sum of £328 13s 6d was received from the committee of the Huddersfield, Brighouse and Rastrick Friendly Society Demonstration.[34]

Activities such as these reflected support rather than opposition to the ruling groups in the local community, and lends some weight to Perkin's argument that friendly societies were '. . . non-revolutionary, ameliorative organisations designed to mitigate by mutual insurance the insecurities of the competitive system without in any way seeking to overturn it'.[35] Although friendly societies worked within the system, and indeed embodied ideals and functions that the upper classes approved of, principally those of self-help and rate-saving, they were organisations established for and financed and run by the working classes. There is little to suggest there being much interference in the initiation and running of friendly societies by members of the upper classes,[36] and, as Thompson suggests, the strength of the movement was due to '. . . a high degree of working-class endeavour'.[37] It was working-class members who imposed the strict regulations which came to be typical of friendly societies. The emphasis was on self-discipline, community purpose and even the highest Christian motives. The main, and far from revolutionary, purposes of friendly societies should not be forgotten, to offer relief to the sick, unemployed and bereaved.

It having pleased the Almighty Governor of the Universe to place us here in a State of Dependence upon each other & he having interwoven in our Natures that pleasing Sensation of Sympathy and Social Love which teaches us to pity and commiserate the misfortunes of our Fellow Creatures and to alleviate them as far as lies in our power. We the members of an Institution called a Free Gift have united ourselves together for the sole purpose of relieving those of our Brother members who shall have the misfortune to be rendered incapable of following their regular Employments through Sickness Lameness or any other Calamity, and of supporting themselves and perhaps a numerous Family.[38]

Strict rules were formulated and apparently rigidly enforced to regulate secrecy, attendance, the duties of officers and even dress at club meetings. The Wakefield Lodge of Oddwomen, for example, stipulated

Every member of this Socy shall keep her seat & behave herself in a peaceable decent and modest manner and keep good order during Lodge Hours or Committee meetings. Nor shall any one be allowed to swear or utter any profane or provoking language one towards another or give any unpolite or indecent Toast or Sentiment, or indecent or immodest songs . . . or do any act or thing derogatory to this Socy under the Penalty of being expelled . . .[39]

Some societies went further than this, and laid down regulations concerning the behaviour of members outside of club activities. Fines were imposed for offences such as quarrelling, swearing, talking out of order, lateness or refusal to accept an office, which could be more exacting than those imposed by a factory owner on his employees. The Wakefield Free Gift Society, for example, imposed fines for causing a quarrel (4d), talking after being called to order three times (4d) and questioning a decision to allow benefit to a member (1s for the first offence, 2s for a second, and 3s or exclusion for a third offence).[40] The Wakefield Benevolent Brief fined any members resident in the Township of Wakefield, who failed to attend a meeting or to send a contribution of 6d, 1s. The penalty for declaring secrets or transactions of the Brief was 2s, for swearing, fighting, gaming or quarrelling in a meeting 2s 6d, for smoking 6d, and for refusal to accept office 4s.[41] The behaviour of friendly society members was controlled just as closely as that of recipients of Poor Law medical relief or patients in a charitable institution.[42] The difference of course was that the 'social control' placed on friendly society members was not imposed from above and outside the working classes. Rather, it was a code of conduct and regulation of their own creation.

5.3 Medical relief and sickness benefits

The assistance given to sick friendly society members generally took two main forms. Firstly, a weekly benefit was paid to those too sick to follow their usual employment. This was the most important form of relief during the nineteenth century, and accounted for the largest proportion of friendly societies' disbursements. Secondly, some societies took it upon themselves to provide medical attendance for sick members by means of a club doctor. Both forms of relief were in many cases confined to the subscribing member. His wife, children and other dependents were often ineligible for aid.

Upon becoming ill, a member was expected to give notice to the steward or another official of the society. The fact that a member was sick had normally to be certified by an official of the society, a medical practitioner, a clergyman, or another approved witness.[43] Following confirmation of sickness, the member became entitled to a weekly benefit of something in the region of 10s a week. Payment of the benefit would continue at this rate for a prescribed period, provided the member was still certified as sick, a fact that was checked at weekly or fortnightly intervals. At the end of this period, usually of six months' duration, the benefit would be substantially reduced. The Wakefield Golden Fleece Lodge of Loyal Ancient Shepherds, for example, paid 10s per week sick money for the first six months. In the second six months it was halved to 5s a week.[44] The Friendly Society at Almondbury (two miles from Huddersfield) stipulated in its rules, drawn up in 1810, that if a member was '. . . visited with sickness or other affliction, insomuch as to confine him to his room, . . .' he shall be paid 9s weekly. When he became able to 'walk out' the member was allowed 6s a week, so long as he remained unfit to work.[45] After the termination of a year's illness most societies again reduced the benefit; an amount was often fixed at the discretion of their officers or committees. Similarly, if a member became permanently incapacitated a reduced weekly allowance would be paid. The committee of the Wakefield Female Benefit Society resolved in 1810, for example,

Whereas Mary Clarkson, a Beneficiary Member has now been ill two years and confined to her Bed, and . . . has been paid the first year full allowance, and the 2^d Year Walking allowance: It is resolved – that she be allowed and paid the sum of one shilling a Week out of the sick fund until her recovery or Death. And it is further resolved that she be paid out of the private fund as a present the sum of ten shillings and sixpence this Quarter in addition to the one shilling per week; the same to be paid by two instalments.[46]

The Wakefield Free Gift Society paid 4s a week to members afflicted with permanent lameness, blindness or any other incurable disease (and to those aged over seventy). Chronically ill members were permitted to employ themselves without losing their benefit, providing they did not earn above 6s per week.[47]

Friendly societies apparently tried to exclude high-risk categories from membership. Only certain age groups were admitted as members. Typically the upper age limit was forty, the lower seventeen. Scales of admission were frequently drawn up which differentiated between age groups. Admission rates to the Wakefield Lodge of Loyal Ancient Shepherds, for example, varied from 12s 6d for those aged between eighteen and 35 to 20s for the 39–40 age range.[48] Most societies also insisted that an individual should be in good health when he entered into membership. For example,

No person shall be admitted a member of this Brief, but such as shall be at the time of admission, of a sound constitution, as also his wife free from all lameness, sickness, and disorders whatforever . . .[49]

If the person entering the society attempted to deceive the members as to his state of health, he would be henceforth excluded. Intake was often limited to a small geographical area, and soldiers, seamen and militia men were usually excluded.

Before being entitled to any payment of benefits, a member had to have paid an entrance fee and to have subscribed a fixed sum weekly or monthly to the society for a minimum period, usually of several months' duration. Subscription rates varied from club to club, but were usually higher in the affiliated orders. Members of the Wakefield Society of Oddwomen paid an entrance fee of between 5s 6d and 10s 6d, and 6d a month in contributions. Their rates of sickness benefit were also low, just 2s a week. The Almondbury Friendly Society demanded an entrance fee of 3s 6d and a contribution of 2s 9d every quarter. Meanwhile, members of the Golden Fleece Lodge of Loyal Ancient Shepherds paid 1s 6d per month in subscriptions.[50] In some local societies the size of contributions was determined by the number of members sick. The Free Gift Society of Wakefield, for example, asked members to pay 3d a week for every sick member up to a limit of 1s a week.[51]

The Wakefield Female Benefit Society differed fundamentally from most other Wakefield and Huddersfield friendly societies, in that it was supported by both beneficiary and non-beneficiary members, the latter having most say in the management of the Society. At the first meeting of the Society in July, 1805, 177 honorary members offered their support, and 57 beneficiary members were admitted. The Society was directed by a committee of middle-class ladies, and it was this committee which determined the rules of the Society and the allocation of benefits. The Benefit Society combined the functions of most friendly societies, including the payment of allowances to sick members, with those of a lying-in charity. Special payments were made to lying-in members, and a sub-committee was set up to organise loans of linen.

The Society also maintained two funds. The first was made up of the contributions of beneficiary members. The second and largest fund was a 'private' one, supported by the subscriptions and donations of honorary members. The Society did in fact become extremely wealthy. In 1818 the rules of the Society were registered, and its funds, therefore, came to be protected by the law. By 1831 funds totalled over £2,400.[52] Money from the private, charitable fund was paid out regularly to members.[53] Income from the beneficiary members' fund never seems to have been sufficient to meet the payment of allowances. The payment of subscriptions by beneficiary members seems to have been more of a token gesture, rather than a real effort to provide benefits to sick and pregnant members. Such payments may have been enforced by the committee in order to impose a semblance of 'self-help' and providential behaviour.

The Huddersfield Co-operative Trading Friendly Society, established in 1829, and enrolled under the Friendly Societies Acts in 1838, provides us with a more 'typical' example of a friendly society, in that it was supported and directed solely by beneficiary members. The objects of the Society were, however, more ambitious and wide ranging than was usually the case for friendly societies, and it presumably attracted a 'better class' of member.

The objects included assisting members to find employment, the purchasing or renting of land and buildings for the use of the Society, the establishment of a co-operative store, the erection of dwellings and schools to house and educate members, and the relief of sick members. Rates of admission to the Sick Brief were 2s for members aged under fifty and 10s for those aged over fifty. Persons aged 55 and over were not admitted. The subscription rate was 1s a month and a member would become entitled to the benefits of the Brief two months after his entrance. No person was admitted to the Brief

. . . but who is in good health, having the proper use of all his limbs, and not subject to any hereditary complaint, so as at certain times of the year to render him unable to follow his usual occupation.

The Brief was governed by a President, two Inspectors and a committee of seven members, who were chosen in rotation. The President was to receive notice from sick or lame members, and pass on this information to the Inspectors, who would visit the sick once a week to check on their state of health and pay their allowances. If the sick member resided more than two miles from Huddersfield, a certificate of sickness was to be signed by a doctor or two 'respectable' witnesses. Members unable to follow their employment because of sickness or any 'providential' accident were allowed 10s a week for up to six months. If the indisposition continued, members would be paid 5s for the following six months. After the termination of a year's illness, the President would call a general meeting of the members to determine the rate of any further allowances. When a sick member was so far recovered as to be able to resume his usual employment, he was to give notice to the President within three days. Failure to comply with this rule led to a 2s fine or exclusion. If a member of the Brief feigned illness in order to receive an allowance, he would be excluded henceforth.[54]

Those friendly society members who applied for benefit were subject to both the general regulatory statutes of the society (of which there were usually many) and rules specifically concerned with the receipt of sickness money. A member was normally denied benefit if it was suspected that his illness resulted from misconduct or carelessness. The West Riding of Yorkshire Provident Society ruled, for example, that 'no member shall be entitled to claim from the funds in respect of any sickness or accident brought on or occasioned by gross intemperance or immorality'.[55] The Prince Albert Lodge of Ancient Druids at Thurstonland, near Huddersfield, stipulated that no member would receive any benefit from the Lodge for any 'hurt or sickness' occasioned by

... drinking fighting or attending dog fighting cockfighting bullbaiting or mankind fighting with each other, wrestling the veneral [sic] disease or attending any demoralizing game or place unless in the capacity of Peace officer ... or by carrying or firing a Gun except it be in the military service selfe defence or the protection of Property ...[56]

The Almondbury Friendly Society added hunting and playing at football to a similar list.[57] Benefits were also discontinued if sick members went out at untimely hours, frequented pubs or gaming houses, took violent exercise, laid wagers or became intoxicated. The West Riding of Yorkshire Provident Society even stipulated that

... No member receiving sick allowance shall leave home, except with the approval of the medical officer, who shall prescribe, in writing, upon the sickness paper, the hours at which he may walk out for air or exercise; and in all cases upon leaving home without such permission, he shall not be allowed to receive any sick allowance nor claim medical aid on account of the same illness.[58]

Although many of these prohibited activities were clearly unsuitable for the sick, they also suggest that an attempt was being made to enforce strict codes of moral behaviour and discipline on members. Members were also encouraged to report breaches of rules by others. Robert Firth, a member of the Deighton Lodge of Oddfellows, wrote in 1832 of

... having seen Brother John Gledhill intoxicated with Lickours [sic] and at the same time Laying Sick and Receiving Sick Money from this Lodge No 156 and having Rowld [sic] upon the ground ... I Beg leave to move that the case of John Gledhill Be investigated and the subject Be Brought Before the consideration of the Lodge No 156 Being A Breach of the 20 & 21 By Law.[59]

In addition to paying sick benefits some friendly societies appointed club doctors to attend their members. This 'attendance' normally covered advice, and possibly medicine, but until late in the nineteenth century it was very unlikely to include surgical operations or other more specialised treatment. The employment of club doctors became more common during the nineteenth century, and this practice may have been given a boost by the passing of the Poor Law Amendment Act in 1834, which placed more stringent restrictions on the receipt of medical relief.[60] By the mid-nineteenth century medical attendance was recognised as one of the normal benefits which membership of a friendly society should confer. Again the affiliated orders took the lead in this movement. By mid-century individual courts of the Ancient Order of Foresters appointed their own medical officers, and the Manchester Unity of Oddfellows included amongst its objects the provision of medicine and attendance. In societies which remained without the facility of their own medical attendant, sick members were presumably expected to pay for medical treatment, if it was felt to be necessary, out of their sick benefit.

Medical practitioners were selected by friendly society members to provide medical attendance and medicines at so much per head of membership. Remuneration of medical men was normally low, in the region of 2s to 3s per head per annum in most cases, and members frequently complained that the attendance they received from their club surgeon was of a poor quality. H. W. Rumsey, drawing on evidence from the returns of medical men based in forty large English towns, reported to the Select Committee on Medical Poor Relief in 1844 that

The whole system of medical attendance in clubs is generally complained of in these returns as defective and unsatisfactory in the highest degree. . . . I should say the members of sick clubs are not generally satisfied with their medical attendant. They like to have the power of electing him. They expect him to walk in their annual processions, and they thank him for his services at their club feasts, but individually they often complain that they are not sufficiently supplied with medicines and attendance.[61]

Rumsey went on to stress that the post of surgeon to a friendly society could not be remunerative if members were properly attended. A Gomersal Poor Law Guardian (serving in the Dewsbury Union of West Yorkshire) stated in 1854 that club members did not normally receive medical care of a high standard.

I do not think they obtain as satisfactory medical attendance as the paupers do. I have heard many complaints by the members of the clubs, of neglect on the part of their medical man.[62]

If the medical care given by friendly society surgeons was of such low quality, it is surprising that a growing number of people opted for membership of these organisations during the nineteenth century. Medical men complained bitterly throughout the century about the low salaries paid by friendly societies, while those they attended grumbled about inadequate treatment. A large friendly society with a membership of around 200 would still only pay a salary of approximately £20 to £30 to their surgeon. Societies of this size were rarities, and payments of £10 to £15, or even as little as £5 (for societies with fifty members), were apparently typical. Yet it is doubtful that the standard of medical care was very low, or indeed much different from that offered by the Poor Law authorities. After all, complaints of low payment, too low for a conscientious medical practitioner to even cover his expenses, let alone make any sort of profit, were also common amongst Poor Law medical officers. Rates of payment to Poor Law medical officers often averaged out at only 2s to 3s per *case* and a few pence per visit, while if we estimate the level of sickness amongst friendly society members to be approximately 20 per cent (see Section 5.4), then the rates paid to society surgeons could be calculated at around 10s per case. Moreover, friendly society members not only selected their own medical attendant, but also had the power to dismiss him if he proved unsatisfactory. Membership of a friendly society presumably gave the individual the 'right' to complain about his medical attendant (just as today the English tax payer grumbles about his National Health Service doctor). Rumsey also suggested in his report that friendly society members'

. . . dissatisfaction is, I dare say, frequently unfounded and unjust; but the consciousness that their medical contractor is underpaid makes the members naturally suspicious about the due fulfilment of the contract.[63]

In Wakefield and Huddersfield at least, friendly society surgeons were apparently not the 'lower order of practitioners, half-educated, ill-conditioned men, who are of no benefit to the community' that Rumsey speaks of. It is true that the top medical men of the locality, those with the wealthiest private practices and hospital posts, did not normally take up appointments as club surgeons. It is also true that competition for these posts involved doctors in undercutting practices.[64] But these positions were frequently filled by either newcomers to the area or recently-qualified men, who saw friendly society appointments as one way of establishing themselves in the locality and as a means of support, albeit a limited one, while they built up a private practice. If they hoped to establish a practice in the area, it would be expected that they would try to provide at least a reasonable level of medical care for their friendly society patients, even if this resulted in personal financial loss. The individuals who took up friendly society appointments often held, in addition, the position of Poor Law medical officer or that of surgeon to the volunteers, police, prison or local assurance societies. William Dean of Slaithwaite, near Huddersfield, for instance, held all of these posts. In addition, he acted as Registrar of Births and Deaths for Slaithwaite and as Chairman of the Local Board of Health. William Henry Thornton of Horbury, near Wakefield, combined the position of friendly society surgeon with the posts of Union medical officer, police surgeon and surgeon to several local assurance societies. On paper at least, Thornton was excellently qualified, being an MRCS (1849), LSA (1850), MB (London, 1850) and MD (London, 1853). John Bradshaw of Huddersfield also gave his services as a friendly society surgeon from time to time during the mid-nineteenth century. In addition, he held two rather more prestigious appointments, as a certifying factory surgeon and as honorary surgeon to the Huddersfield Infirmary.[65]

There is little evidence either way to show whether or not friendly societies employed fringe medical personnel to treat their sick members, although P. S. Brown claims that numerous friendly societies appointed herbalists.[66] Friendly society records contain very little information concerning their medical attendants; most of the details relating to club surgeons were extracted from the *Provincial Medical Directories*, which only listed returns from qualified practitioners. Although fringe practitioners could have been attractive from the point of view of cost, friendly societies may have avoided using them because they could detract from the status of the society, or because their employment seemed to be in contradiction with their ideals of 'maximum utility' and 'providential behaviour'. However, there may have been much hidden medical attendance by fringe personnel, paid for out of members' dole money, and as such facilitated directly by friendly societies.

To supplement the services of the club surgeon, many friendly societies made arrangements with local charitable dispensaries and hospitals to obtain the medical treatment which these institutions could offer to their members. The rules of both the Wakefield and Huddersfield Infirmaries made provision for the treatment of members of subscribing friendly societies,[67] and several local societies came to make use of this facility. This made it possible for friendly society members to receive medical aid not covered by their medical attendant, in particular operations and other surgical treatment. In the year 1831–1832, the inaugural year of the Huddersfield Infirmary, six local friendly societies paid an annual subscription to the charity: the Holmfirth Benevolent Society, the Foresters Royal Court, No. 29, Marsden, the Old Friendly Society, Holmfirth, two lodges of Oddfellows and a lodge of Ancient Shepherds. By 1855–1856 thirteen societies subscribed, and by 1865–1866 sixteen.[68] In addition to, or instead of, annual subscriptions, some friendly societies paid donations to the infirmaries. In 1859 the Huddersfield Foresters Society promoted a congregational collection at the Parish Church, which raised £10 4s, and donated a further sum of £10 6s to the funds of the Infirmary. In return, the Infirmary Committee resolved that the Society should have the privilege of having one in-patient and two out-patients on the books at a time for a period of six years. In 1866 a Huddersfield lodge of Oddfellows donated £70 to the Infirmary, and became entitled in return to recommend six out-patients or three in-patients, presumably for a similar period.[69] The reports of the Wakefield Infirmary first record a payment by a friendly society in the year 1858–1859, of one guinea by the Ossett Lodge of Oddfellows. By 1865–1866 six friendly societies paid annual subscriptions to the charity.[70]

5.4 The nature of illness experienced by friendly society members

The payment of benefits to sick members accounted for by far the greatest proportion of friendly society expenditure. Indeed, the paying out of this type of benefit was perhaps the most important function of these organisations. The arrangements made for the disbursement of sick relief by friendly societies took into account the likelihood of long-term, chronic sickness, resulting in protracted or even permanent unemployment. Sickness was normally talked of in terms of months and years, rather than days and weeks. Most friendly societies appear to have supported a small number of 'permanently sick' members, and many friendly society members were recorded as being sick both for long periods and at frequent intervals. In 1839, for instance, the Huddersfield Royal Shepherds Sanctuary, No. 99, paid out a total of £3 6s to A. Beaumont of Paddock, who was certified as sick from 12 July to 20 September of that year. Beaumont was also recorded as being sick in 1837, 1841, 1842, 1844 and 1846 (eight weeks in the last year).[71] During the year 1861–1862 the Wakefield branch of the British Friendly Union Society recorded that £21 had been expended on sickness benefits. Of this, Henry Rhodes received payments totalling five guineas for sickness in March (two weeks), April (four weeks) and May (four weeks). John Heald was recorded sick several times between August and December, and received a total of £6 12s 6d in benefits.[72] The chronic, long-term nature of the illnesses suffered by friendly society members may also explain why the appointment of medical officers took second place to the payment of sickness money. Little is known of the type of sickness experienced by members, but complaints such as rheumatism, influenza, inflammation of the chest, throat and eyes, bowel disorders, heart disease and minor injuries seem to have been fairly common.[73] A medical man could do little to 'cure' these kinds of disorder, and the patient may have seen the payment of a regular weekly benefit as being of more value than medical treatment.

Sickness then was often long term and chronic. In addition, quite a high proportion of friendly society members appear to have been subject to bouts of illness. In 1838 43 out of the 194 members of the Grand United Order of Oddfellows, Charity Lodge, Number 97, Cleckheaton, were recorded as being sick. (It is possible that some of those listed as sick had been counted several times.) Between 1864 and 1871 the same Lodge recorded aggregate sickness of between seventeen weeks or an average of 1.5 days per member per annum, and 93 weeks three days or nearly 7.5 days per member per annum (1864 and 1871). The average number of days sickness per member over this period was 4.4 days per annum.[74]

The main avowed purpose of the West Riding of Yorkshire Provident Society, which was set up and registered in 1857, and based in Leeds, was to deal with long-term illness amongst its members. The officers of the Provident Society claimed that the failure of many benefit societies was due to a lack of attention to the laws of sickness and mortality. The Society made provision not only for old-age pensions, life insurance and ordinary sick allowances, but also for protracted illness and assurance against severe accidents, '. . . founded upon the latest information as to the laws of sickness and mortality'. The Society, which limited its operations to the West Riding, was managed by a council based in Leeds, district boards and branch committees, and was composed of honorary and beneficiary members. The management of the society was in the hands of the upper- and middle-class honorary members. The council itself was made up of eminent and wealthy individuals, including The Right Honourable The Earl of Ripon, The Very Reverend Dr Hook and two MPs, and several important Wakefield and Huddersfield men were included on the Society's provisional committee.[75] Visiting committees, also composed of honorary members, were appointed by each branch to report on the state of members receiving sick allowances. Medical officers, who had to be qualified practitioners and members of one of the Royal Colleges of Physicians or Surgeons or LSAs, were selected by the members from a list of practitioners who had been approved by the council. The medical officers were to examine applicants for life and sickness insurance, and to attend members requiring medical assistance and supply them with medicines.

The Society was supposedly specially adapted to the requirements of the working classes. A graduated scale of payments was set up according to age, and the largest allowances possible were paid without endangering the funds of the Society. An attempt was made to make the provisions of the Society within reach of the 'ordinary' labouring man, but in fact the contributions were too high for all but the best-paid artisans to afford. For example, to secure 10s per week during sickness for a twelve-month period (in payments and benefits to continue for life) persons aged twenty were to pay 6d per week or 1s 11d a month, a person aged 35, 3s 1d a month and a person aged fifty, 6s a month. Combined benefits were also available to cover sickness, old age and death. For example, for 2s a week a person not exceeding 21 years of age could secure 10s a week in sickness benefit, 10s a week pension after the age of 65, and £50 at death.[76]

The return of a local medical practitioner, given as evidence in the 1852 Wakefield health report, quoted figures from three unidentified Wakefield friendly societies over a ten-year period. These figures also indicated fairly high levels of sickness (4.5 days sickness per member and almost 20 per cent of members off work by

Table 5.1. *RETURN from three clubs in Wakefield during a period of ten years (c. 1840–1850).*

Number of members		5,260	
Number off work by sickness		1,040	
Number of days work lost by sickness		23,489	
Number of deaths		47	
Percentage of members off work by sickness		19.77	
Number of days sickness per man sick		22.5	
Number of days sickness per member		4.465	
Number of days sickness per 1,000,000 living		8.930	
	£	s	d
Amount raised	5,272	18	0
Expended in sick relief	2,195	16	7
Expended in medical attendance	855	9	2½
Burial fees, public house expenses, etc.	2,221	12	2½

W. R. MILNER

Source: W. Ranger, *op. cit.*, Evidence of W. R. Milner, Esq., p. 88.

sickness), and long periods of average sickness (22.5 days per man sick). The return also demonstrated the relative importance of sick benefits and payments for medical attendance. Although statistically imprecise, the return has been reproduced in full in Table 5.1.

Nineteenth-century parliamentary returns also gave evidence of high levels of sickness amongst friendly society members. A return of an unidentified, registered Huddersfield friendly society for the years 1846 to 1850 gave its average annual membership as fifty. The average number of weeks sick over the same five-year period was 42, or 5.9 days sick per member per annum. The return of a large Wakefield society, with an average of 160 members a year, gave similar results. The number of weeks sick between 1846 and 1850 averaged out at 178, or 7.8 days sick per member per annum. In 1849, for example, there was an aggregate of 260 weeks sick, and membership for that year totalled 185. The number of days sick per member averaged out to 9.8.[77]

The first quinquennial return of sickness and mortality, drawn up in 1880 and covering the years 1860 to 1875, indicated similar levels of sickness amongst friendly society members. (This return also showed something of the nature of the employment followed by

Table 5.2. *Membership and sickness in selected Wakefield and Huddersfield friendly societies, 1860–1870.*

| | | | Number of members in returns classified according to their occupation | | | |
| | | | Light labour | | Heavy labour | |
Name of society	Date of establishment	Five years ending with	With exposure	Without exposure	With exposure	Without exposure
Huddersfield						
Wesleyan Methodist FS	1840	1860	4	56	2	6
Perseverance Lodge MU	1840	1865	3	66	3	5
Manoah Tent Court IOR	1838	1870	8	37	2	5
Court Conquerer AOF	1837	1870	1	19	1	3
Court Kosseth AOF	1853	1865	1	7	20	0
Peace and Prosperity Lodge	1851	1865	1	19	2	3
Richard Oastler Lodge OD	1852	1865⎱	1	31	17	14
		1865⎰	11	13	14	4
NIOOF Heart of Honesty Lodge	1864	1865	4	55	13	23
Strangers Refuge Lodge MU	1847	1870	5	56	8	24
Victory Lodge MU	1816	1870	29	156	13	41
Wakefield						
Wesleyan Methodist FS	1832	1865	1	29	5	7
Hope at the Fountain Lodge GUOOF	1845	1865	—	52	27	3
Old Oak at Home Lodge	1844	1865	3	14	10	7
		1870	4	21	13	9
Prince Alfred Lodge MU	1830	1870	3	29	27	12
Court Village United AOF	1836	1865	—	26	11	12

[a] The Heart of Honesty Lodge had only been established for one year.
Source: QRSM 1880.

friendly society members, breaking occupations up into four categories, viz., light and heavy labour, both with and without exposure.) Extracts from the returns of a selection of Wakefield and Huddersfield friendly societies are given in Table 5.2. The sample

Special class	Number of members		Amount of sick pay during the five years		Number of days sick per member during the five years	(per annum)
	At beg. of five years	Entered during five years	Weeks	Days		
	58	10	212	0	18.71	(3.74)
	61	16	283	0	22.10	(4.42)
	33	19	156	5	21.10	(4.22)
	19	5	74	5	18.71	(3.74)
Miners 3	21	10	60	0	11.61	(2.32)
	24	3	110	5	24.63	(4.93)
	55	10	206	2	$\{$ 15.88	$\{$ (3.18)
Miners 5	—	49	51	4	$\{$ 6.33	$\{$ (1.27)
	—	95	155	5	9.84	(9.84)[a]
	76	17	232	0	15.00	(3.00)
Miners 18	179	78	1,264	0	34.43	(6.89)
	38	4	391	0	55.86	(11.17)
	47	35	263	2	19.27	(3.85)
Miners 10	37	7	257	0	35.05	(7.01)
Miners 11	36	20	222	2	27.79	(5.56)
Miners 5 Mariners 2	68	10	507	2	39.03	(7.81)
	26	23	159	5	19.57	(3.91)

demonstrates a wide variance between societies with respect to the number of days sick per member. The figures range from 9.84 days sick per member per annum for the newly-established Huddersfield Heart of Honesty Lodge of Oddfellows and the average of 11.17 for the Wakefield Wesleyan Methodist Friendly Society, to 2.32 days for the Huddersfield Court Kosseth Lodge of Oddfellows. The average for the sample was 5.4 days sick per member per annum.[78] It could be argued that these figures indicate relatively low levels of sickness. However, these are averages, and taking other results and indications of the survey into consideration, it is likely that these averages disguise much long-term sickness amongst a *proportion* of friendly society members. Such a tendency was also revealed in a study of Preston friendly societies made in 1843. While the number of days sick *per member* of the eleven societies surveyed averaged out to eight days, the average *per man sick* was over six weeks per annum. The proportion of friendly society members recorded as sick averaged out at 20.9 per cent for the eleven societies, and the average payment to each sick person at £2 8s 10d.[79]

Concluding remarks

Nineteenth-century observers and historians have pointed with great frequency to the financial instability of friendly societies.[80] Many friendly societies, in particular local fraternities, broke up in the nineteenth century because of a lack of funds or bankruptcy, a result of mismanagement, an over-generosity in the payment of benefits or a failure to attract a sufficient number of young and healthy members to support the sick and aged. Yet, although the century certainly witnessed many personal and community tragedies, caused by the collapse of societies, overall they grew and prospered for the first three-quarters of the nineteenth century. Most Wakefield and Huddersfield societies continued to function throughout the nineteenth century, and indeed the funds of a number of them were in a flourishing condition by the third quarter of the century. For example, in 1862 the Wakefield British Friendly Union Society recorded a balance in the funds of £920. Throughout the 1870s the membership and income of the Prince Albert Lodge of the Ancient Order of Druids, Thurstonland, near Huddersfield, increased steadily. In 1873 there were 87 members and a balance of £570, and in 1876 96 members and a balance of £606.[81]

During the last quarter of the century, however, a financial malaise began to creep over even some of the largest and best-organised societies. Improvements in medical and sanitary science, and in the standard of living of the working class, caused an increasing number of their members to live well into old age. While the death rate fell amongst friendly society members, sickness claims rose. The speedy killer diseases of the first half of the nineteenth century, typhus, cholera, influenza and diseases of the digestive organs, were replaced by the lingering illnesses of tuberculosis, cancer, and respiratory and circulatory diseases. As Gilbert has remarked, in the last quarter of the century friendly societies experienced a phenomenon that would not be fully understood until after the First World War, that increased length of life did not necessarily equal better health.[82] It seems likely that friendly societies had always catered for chronic illnesses, and as these became more common, demands upon them grew. Meanwhile, the decline in the birth rate in the last part of the nineteenth century resulted in a shortage of young members. A failure to understand and respond to these changes, and increased competition for young members through the offer of larger benefits, marked the decline of friendly societies.[83]

However, the late eighteenth century and the first three-quarters of the nineteenth century, the period with which we are most concerned, could well be described as the 'golden age' of friendly societies. Despite certain shortcomings, such as the limitation of relief to subscribing members (excluding their dependents) and to 'low-risk categories', during this period friendly societies provided a good and fairly cheap system of medical relief for large numbers and a wide cross-section of the lower classes. It seems likely that friendly societies were forced to adapt to the problems of large-scale unemployment in the Wakefield and Huddersfield areas (and that lapses in the payment of subscriptions were not responded to by exclusion), as they continued to attract members from affected trades, particularly the textile industry. In addition to attracting the membership of a wide group of artisans and labourers, up until circa 1834 many paupers received medical cover via the friendly societies.

The emphasis which friendly societies placed on the payment of benefits, rather than on providing medical attendance and medicines, was in many cases well adapted to the needs of their members. The nature of the illnesses suffered by friendly society members was, as has just been indicated, typically long term, seasonal and chronic. While medical science could do little to cure such cases (at least for much of the nineteenth century), the payment of a regular benefit could go a long way towards relieving the member and his family, providing them with a small income and removing them one step further from the threat of pauperisation. The fact that friendly societies catered for chronic cases is of particular importance, as it was this type of case which was most commonly excluded from medical charities, and which was treated most stringently by the Poor Law authorities. The friendly society movement was one of the most significant examples of self-help on the part of the working classes to emerge during the nineteenth century. These fraternities gave their members a degree of choice in selecting their medical attendants and some control over their own health, and led to a decreased reliance upon charity and poor relief.

6

Fringe medical practice

The establishment of dispensaries and infirmaries, the extension of friendly society medical facilities and the provision of a formal channel of medical relief through the agency of the New Poor Law in theory gave the poor of the nineteenth century more access to medical treatment than they had ever had before. Those wealthy enough to pay for private medical care, meanwhile, were able to choose from a large selection of attendants, including a growing range of specialists, as the number of qualified medical personnel increased during the century.[1] Yet rich and poor alike continued to resort to a variety of 'unorthodox' sources of medical aid in the case of sickness. The nineteenth century saw not only the survival of the traditional fringe practitioner, the folk healer, the wise woman, the bonesetter and the quack, but also witnessed the flourishing of other para-medical groups: for example, chemists and druggists, patent medicine vendors and medical botanists.

In the growing urban settlements of the West Riding the fusion of town and country/traditional and modern in many aspects of life was reflected in the wide array of alternatives to orthodox medical treatment. Belief in the ancient ideas of disease transference, the healing power of springs and wells and in old folk remedies existed side by side with the new 'sciences' of hydropathy, homoeopathy, phrenology and medical botany, apparently without conflict. Despite the proliferation of new forms of para-medical treatment, traditional fringe practices remained popular during the nineteenth century. In some cases new ideologies and treatments were grafted on to existing practices, leading to their transformation or refinement. In this way, for example, ancient healing wells and springs were developed, with the aid of hydropathic theories, into the extensive spas and bathing establishments of the nineteenth century. The use of fringe medicine then did not, as we might expect, diminish in the nineteenth century. Rather the combination of old and new elements led to an overall increase in the range and amount of medical alternatives.

This chapter will look at alternative forms of medical treatment and the extent to which they were used by the populations of Wakefield and Huddersfield. Numerical evidence relating to fringe practice in the two communities will be examined in section 6.1. In Section 6.2 different forms of fringe practice, including folk healing, quackery, medical botany, water cures and the 'medical' activities of chemists and druggists, will be discussed, and reasons sought for the continuing and even growing popularity of fringe medicine. Following the definition suggested by Roy Porter, we shall distinguish between orthodox medicine and fringe medicine on the grounds of legal and professional inclusion and exclusion, rather than on any objective judgement as to the quality of treatment given, its scientific standing or its success rate.[2] All the alternatives to be discussed here were provided by legally unqualified, 'non-professional' personnel.[3]

The existence and use of fringe practices was a countrywide phenomenon, but it was especially widespread and important in the manufacturing districts of the North. Contemporaries could not fail to be aware of the popularity of alternative medicine with the poor of this region. This fact (together with the existence of strong networks of medical charities and friendly societies) was used to explain the relatively low cost of medical poor relief.[4] The Northern labourer was depicted as being more self-reliant than his Southern and Midland counterparts. Independence in obtaining medical treatment could be seen as one more aspect of the self-determination of the 'sturdy' Northern labourer, which was realised through such mediums as the Mechanics' Institute, the friendly society, the trade union and other working-class organisations. The Northern labourer was also depicted by contemporaries as being more willing to submit to the lure of unqualified medical personnel and self-medication.

Members of the medical profession were also quick to point to the relative strength of the quack in the Northern manufacturing towns. This region was of special concern in their efforts to discredit and stamp out unqualified practice. The large number of letters and articles appearing in major medical journals on this subject reflected this concern. For example, a leading article in *The Lancet* in 1857 drew attention to the problem of the unqualified practitioner in the North.

Such persons exist in numbers which would surprise those less conversant with the real state of the case than ourselves. Hanging about the suburbs of town, infesting its central parts, and acting ostensibly as druggists, these people absorb much money and destroy many lives and much health. But the north is the favoured habitat of such individuals; and more especially the manufacturing districts of Lancashire and Yorkshire.[5]

What the belligerent medical profession and other nineteenth-century commentators usually failed to point out is that the practice of resorting to unorthodox forms of medical treatment was not confined to the poor. The better off (as shall be demonstrated later), who could after all afford to experiment, supplemented attendance by regular medical practitioners with various forms of unorthodox treatment.

Nineteenth-century commentators also failed to offer much in the way of numerical evidence to back up their statements about the extent of unqualified practice. The medical journals, for example, mostly confined themselves to attacks on individual quacks and their misdemeanours. Nineteenth-century observers presumably faced similar difficulties in retrieving figures as the historian faces today. Until recently medical history has mainly been concerned with the orthodox practitioner and institutional forms of medical provision. The unqualified practitioner has been pushed into comparative obscurity. This fact is compounded by the dearth of sources relating to alternative forms of medicine. The quack, with his ambiguous social, medical and legal position, left few records of his activities. Novels, diaries and contemporary histories, however, do go a short way towards illuminating the lifestyles of unqualified practitioners, while census enumerators' books and town directories offer us limited numerical evidence on this group. The local press of the nineteenth century, meanwhile, featured advertisements by different elements of the medical fringe, in particular the chemists and druggists, which give further clues as to their activities. Medical journals of the period also constitute an important, albeit heavily biased, source of information, especially with reference to the competition of the unqualified to regular practitioners.

6.1 Numerical evidence

The starting points for a collection of numerical data have been the census returns and nineteenth-century trade directories. These sources are not without their problems, and neither appears to show the true extent of unqualified practice. All in all the numerical data tends to understate the size of the medical fringe. It is unlikely that the small groups of fringe practitioners recorded in the census enumerators' books and directories would have aroused the concern or interest of laymen and the fury of the medical profession, especially when it is remembered that fringe practice was supposed to have reached a peak in the North. While figures for certain para-medical categories, notably chemists and druggists, dentists and opticians, appear to be fairly reliable, the totals obtained for other groups were very low. The trade directories were also inconsistent in what they chose to include. They omitted such groups as quacks, medicine vendors and midwives from their listings, while including other fringe practitioners: for example, bonesetters, herbalists and medical botanists.

More categories are represented in the census enumerators' books, although the classification of fringe groups seems to have varied from census to census, and the totals given for unqualified practitioners are again lower than we might expect. Although the practice of quack medicine was not strictly illegal, followers of this employment may not have wished to declare their true means of livelihood on an official return. One suspects that the majority of fringe practitioners did not appear on the returns at all. Many, after all, were itinerant, and may have been missed by the enumerator, or have avoided him. Others gave false or inaccurate descriptions of their occupations. For example, it is possible that those deriving an income from the sale of drugs, with or without medical advice, were included in the vague categories of 'hawker', 'traveller' or 'salesman'. Meanwhile, some individuals, presumably unable to live off what they earned from medical practice, combined doctoring with another trade. Others carried out a variety of para-medical services. In 1851 the extravagantly named Anthony Bernasconi Chevalier de la Barre, then resident in Huddersfield, described himself in the returns as an engineer and dentist. At other times he had adopted the labels of 'physician', 'surgeon', 'aurist' and 'oculist to the King of France'. The 1861 enumerators' book for Wakefield

Township recorded John Mitchell as a dentist, optician and jewel-ler.[6] Others, in particular women, may not have regarded them-selves or have been classified as medical personnel. This was the group who carried out doctoring on a part-time basis, as a favour or paid service to family or neighbours, who passed on remedies, helped procure abortions, attended at births and nursed the sick. Some of this 'less visible' group may have given their services free or at least very cheaply. Other part-time healers had recourse to the sale of remedies or to occasional practice as a source of extra income.

The 1841 occupation abstract taken from West Riding census returns gave unimpressive figures for most para-medical groups. Only the chemists and druggists were well represented, with a total of 643 for the county (including eighteen female druggists). The totals for Wakefield and Huddersfield were 21 and 23 respectively. The results for other fringe groups were surprisingly low. Only two medical botanists were returned for the whole of the West Riding, along with eight dentists, three herbalists, six leech dealers and bleeders, four medicine vendors, two quack doctors and 22 midwives.[7] An analysis of the 1851 census for the West Riding has produced similar results: 314 chemists and druggists, 28 dentists, twenty midwives, nine medicine vendors, nine medical botanists and four quack doctors throughout the whole region.[8]

Compared with the county as a whole, Wakefield and Hud-dersfield appear to have had their fair share of fringe practitioners in relation to their size. Data has been extracted for the two towns from the census returns of 1841, 1851, 1861 and 1871, and from a selection of nineteenth-century trade directories, dating from 1822 to 1870.[9] The complete results of the analysis are given in Tables 6.1 and 6.2. Defects in the source material (as already suggested) mean the figures given are unlikely to be precise or complete, but at least what they do suggest is that certain groups of para-medical person-nel survived well into the middle decades of the century. There was even an increase recorded in some categories. The chemists and druggists showed the largest gains in both towns. In 1822 there were six listed in Wakefield and five in Huddersfield. By 1861 the figures, according to the census returns, were 21 and eighteen respectively.[10] While the populations of Wakefield and Hud-dersfield had risen by 64 per cent and 163 per cent, the number of druggists had increased by over 250 per cent in both towns. Other groups also became better represented as the century progressed. In

Table 6.1. *Number of para-medical personnel in Wakefield and Huddersfield between 1822 and 1870 (extracted from trade directories).*

Para-medical occupations	1822		1828		1837		1847		1853		1861		1866		1870	
	W	H	W	H	W	H	W	H	W	H	W	H	W	H	W	H
Chemists and druggists	6	5	10	6	13	9	20	14	19	16	19	17	19	21	18	19
Homoeopathic chemists (botanic)	—	—	—	—	—	—	—	—	—	1[a]	—	1	—	1	1	1(1)
Patent medicine vendors	—	2	1	1	—	1	—	—	—	—	—	—	—	—	1	—
Herbalists	—	—	—	—	—	—	—	—	2	—	1[b]	1	2	2	4	5
Medical botanists	—	—	—	—	—	—	—	—	—	1	—	4	—	—	—	—
Apothecaries (unqualified)	—	—	1	—	—	—	—	—	—	1	—	1	—	—	—	—
Bonesetters	1	—	1	—	1	—	—	—	—	—	1	1[c]	1	—	1	—
Opticians	—	—	—	1	—	—	—	—	—	—	—	1	1	1	4	1
Dentists	—	—	—	—	1	—	1	1	4	5	4	4	5	5	4	7
Bath proprietors	—	—	—	—	—	—	1	—	—	2	1[b]	1	1	1	1	—

W – Wakefield.
H – Huddersfield.

[a] David Butler, homoeopathic dispenser.
[b] Edward Morrison, herbalist, galvanist and bath proprietor.
[c] George Haigh, spinal doctor.

Source: Trade directories: Baines, 1822, Parson and White, 1828, White, 1837, 1847, 1853, 1861, 1866 and 1870. (See Bibliography for complete references.)

1847 there was one resident dentist each in Wakefield and Huddersfield, whose services were presumably supplemented by travelling dentists. By 1866 both towns had five resident dentists.[11] No quack doctors appear on the 1841 census returns for either town, but by 1861 four had the temerity to declare themselves as such, three in Wakefield and one in Huddersfield.[12] As the century progressed new categories appeared in the enumerators' books and trade directories, including herbalists, homoeopathic chemists, medical botanists and in Wakefield a single phrenologist. According to *White's Directory* for 1861, and the census returns for the same year, the population of Huddersfield was served by seventeen

Table 6.2. *Number of para-medical personnel in Wakefield and Huddersfield in 1841, 1851, 1861 and 1871 (extracted from census enumerators' books).*

Para-medical occupations	1841		1851		1861		1871	
	W	H	W	H	W	H	W	H
Chemists and druggists	14	11	15	19	21	18	18	25
Herbalists/herb sellers	—	—	—	1	1	1[a]	1	4
Medical botanists	—	—	—	1	—	6	1	2
Hawkers/travelling doctors	—	—	4	2	1	—	—	1
Quack doctors	—	—	—	1	2	1	—	—
Apothecaries (unqualified)	—	—	—	1	—	—	—	—
Bonesetters	—	—	—	1	—	—	—	—
Midwives	—	1	—	—	—	1	—	1
Opticians	—	—	1	1	1	1[a]	1	1
Dentists	—	—	1	2	4	4	3	8
Homoeopathists	—	—	—	—	—	—	—	1
Phrenologists	—	—	—	—	—	—	1	—
Turkish bath keepers	—	—	—	—	1	—	—	1

W – Wakefield.
H – Huddersfield.
[a] James Daley of Huddersfield combined the activities of optician and herbalist.
Source: Census Enumerators' Books, Wakefield and Huddersfield, 1841, 1851, 1861 and 1871.

chemists and druggists, six medical botanists, two herbalists, one quack doctor, one homoeopathic chemist, a spinal doctor, an optician, a Turkish bath proprietor, and several local mineral spas.[13]

6.2 Forms of fringe practice

Evidence of the widespread use of unqualified medical personnel has been found in the pre-1834 Wakefield and Huddersfield overseers' accounts. A surprising aspect of medical relief under the Old Poor Law in the West Riding (as seen in Chapter 3) was the diversity of both the treatment and medical personnel utilised by the overseers. Contracts were made from time to time in Wakefield, Huddersfield and other nearby townships with qualified medical men to supply the poor with treatment and drugs for a fixed payment. Supplementing this was the payment of individual bills to medical men, including unqualified practitioners. Payments to local bonesetters, healers and doctresses appear frequently in the accounts, and sick paupers were occasionally paid lump sums to enable them to visit distant spas and specialised fringe practitioners. Midwives and 'nurses' (often female paupers) were employed extensively to attend sick and lying-in paupers. Patent and 'popular' remedies also constituted major items of expenditure.

In July and August, 1784 the accounts for Huddersfield Township included payments of 2s for a midwife, 6d for a Godfrey Bottle for Rachel Hudson's child and 5s to Nat. Hudson, affected by the 'Itch', to enable him to visit the Whitworth Doctor.[14] The accounts of the Overseers of Mirfield, a clothing village situated midway between Wakefield and Huddersfield, show that a large proportion of the money paid out for the sick went to fringe practitioners, midwives and nurses and as subscriptions to sick clubs. In 1792 the Overseers paid 7s 6d to 'the midwife' for three deliveries, 10s 6d 'To Robt Crowther for setting Wid. Tattersall Thigh' and one guinea 'To Robt Green for Curing Oates wife'. These were the only medical expenses recorded in this year.[15] In April, 1807 Wid. Jubb was paid one guinea for 'Curing Gladhill' and in July, 1818 Jas. Booth was paid one pound for going twice to Buxton to take the waters.[16] It was also the occasional practice to pay medical bills which had already been run up by the poor, or to give a lump sum towards medical treatment. Presumably in these cases the choice of attendant was left to the patient.

The employment of unqualified personnel may have been a response on the part of the overseers to the preferences of the poor for a certain type of medical practitioner, at a time when there was still little to choose between the ministrations of 'regular' doctors and unqualified individuals. Probably of greater importance to the Poor Law authorities and ratepayers, however, was the fact that the use of fringe practitioners represented a considerable saving of expense. For example, during the late eighteenth and early nineteenth centuries a midwife charged only 2s to 5s for an attendance, compared with the surgeon's fee of 10s 6d or one guinea for a difficult or time-consuming case. The rates of remuneration offered by the overseers, meanwhile, could sometimes have deterred qualified men from making contracts to supply medical aid. At times the overseers may have been unable to obtain the services of professional doctors, and have been forced to turn to the fringe practitioner as the only source of available (and cheap) medical treatment. Whatever their motives, the overseers, who were after all an 'official' agency, gave their sanction to the widespread treatment of paupers by unqualified practitioners. As seen in Chapter 3, only a small proportion of the poor received medical assistance through the medium of the Poor Law. However, it can be assumed that fringe practitioners, with their advantages of cheapness, easy access and familiarity, were also resorted to by many of the poor who were not in receipt of poor relief.

The use of fringe medicine was not, however, a practice confined to the pauper or near-pauper. Independent labourers, artisans and the wealthy classes were also drawn in large numbers to the quack, local healer and the druggist's shop. As a Leeds surgeon remarked caustically to *The Lancet* in 1854,

Nor is the druggist system confined to the poor, for very many indeed of the middle classes go to the druggist first, and only send for the surgeon when a certificate of the cause of death seems likely to be wanted for the registrar.[17]

The wealthy were especially attracted by the water cure, and during the nineteenth century visits to spa establishments by this class became regular and frequent. The new 'sciences' of mesmerism, phrenology, homoeopathy and medico-galvanism also proved to be popular with this group. Lectures in Wakefield and Huddersfield on these subjects were numerous and well attended. Phrenology appears to have been especially popular. Dr William Ellis and Dr Alexander, both superintendents of the Wakefield Asylum in the early nineteenth century, were very active in publicising phrenology. Ellis founded a Phrenological Society in the 1820s, while Alexander delivered lectures on the subject at the Wakefield Dispensary. Such eminent speakers as Spurzheim and Matthew Allen visited the town in the 1820s.[18] About 150 people subscribed to the publication of a pamphlet on phrenology by Disney Alexander in 1827, including Earl Fitzwilliam and many other local notables.[19] In 1852 lectures on the subjects of both mesmerism and phrenology still attracted 'numerous audiences' at St Paul's National School, Huddersfield.[20]

The middle and upper classes, in a similar way to the poor, had also built up a stock of family remedies for less serious ailments. Philanthropic women, who took upon themselves the task of visiting and nursing the sick, were in a particularly good position to develop simple medical skills and a repertoire of homely remedies. These women could be seen as carrying on a long healing and caring tradition amongst their poorer neighbours, a tradition which had been continued for many centuries by the wealthy mistress of the household, local gentlewomen and the wives of clergymen. Doctors' bills, meanwhile, could be a burden even to the middle classes, and it seems they were prepared to try self-medication or the services of fringe doctors and chemists and druggists before calling in a regular medical practitioner.

Self-medication

In the words of Roy Porter, 'self-diagnosis and dosing were routine amongst all ranks of society, and laymen regularly dispensed medicine to friends, family and servants'.[21] Clara Clarkson of Alverthorpe Hall, Wakefield, provides us in her reminiscences with good illustrations of how she and other members of her family treated minor complaints. Herb teas were taken for tiredness and colds, yeast and port wine for sore throats, hot flannel and bran bags for aches and pains, and oil of cloves and brandy for toothache.[22] The naturalist and traveller, Charles Waterton, Squire of Walton Hall, near Wakefield, and member of one of the oldest families in the county, was an advocate of far more radical forms of self-medication. He became a great enthusiast of bleeding, and made extensive use of the lancet on himself and others. In 1800 Waterton caught pneumonia, and during his treatment he was bled by Mr Hey, the eminent Leeds surgeon. Waterton was so taken with the treatment that he learnt to bleed himself, and towards the end of his life he reported that he had bled himself 136 times.[23] Throughout his life Waterton fasted rigorously (recommending a diet of bread and weak tea without milk), purged himself frequently and dosed himself with various pills and potions when ill. Waterton also enjoyed passing on medical advice to others. He recommended that travellers should carry with them bark, laudanum, calomel, jalap and, most important, a lancet. In case of illness Waterton advocated sulphate of quinine, two grains in the morning, and two in the evening, 'an invaluable medicine', which although used every day, 'never requires to be increased'.[24] He had his own prescriptions and

Mr Waterton's Pills were famous in Walton and the neighbourhood. During the 1849 cholera epidemic Waterton gratuitously distributed amongst the poor of Leeds and adjoining townships a powder which he claimed was highly beneficial in cases of cholera.[25] Despite the adversities suffered during his travels in South America, and the hardships he imposed upon himself by means of his strict regimen and radical forms of self-medication, he enjoyed an extraordinarily active life until the age of 83.

While Waterton's remedies represent an extreme form of self-medication, they were apparently not unique. Interesting examples of the survival of traditional, and sometimes 'radical', folk remedies are contained in a booklet, written by James Hirst, a Huddersfield weaver, between 1836 and 1892.[26] In this booklet, entitled *Notable Things of various Subjects*, Hirst recorded details of the local weather, instances of longevity and other items of interest to him, including medical recipes. The recipes contained plant extracts, herbs, and more curious components, such as dung of cat and earthworms. The remedies would, Hirst claimed, cure a wide variety of complaints from headaches and sore eyes to stone, cancer and jaundice. For example,

The juice of ground ivy snuft up into the nose out of a spoon or a saucer purgeth the head marvellously and takes away the greatest and oldest pain thereof that is. This medicine is worth gold though it be very cheap. I have known them that have had marvelous [*sic*] pains in the head almost intolerable for the space of a dozen years and this helped them presently and never had the pain since they took this medicine.

Pottage made of the leaves and roots of strawberries being eaten fasting certain days of them that have the jundice [*sic*] doth help them perfectly – This was the secret of a certain monk wherewith he got marvelous much money.

Earthworms slit and cleansed and washed from their slimy and earthy matter (half a dozen of them at least) and cut in pieces or chopped and a good mefs of pottage made thereof, made with oatmeal and water, and so much every day eaten by them that have the black jundice, for the space of twelve days or longer, no doubt it will perfectly cure them thereof, though it be past cure, or else a spoonful of the powder made of them in March or any other time when you can catch them taken every day so long, in a little draught of any drink doeth perfectly cure the same – This is very true and hath been oftentimes proved it hath helped some in four days or five days.

Hirst's remedies contain elements of traditional folk healing practices. For example, emphasis is placed on making up the recipes at certain times of the year, week or day, and on following a closely prescribed ritual.

An egg laid on a Thursday and emptied and filled with salt and set in the fire remaining there untill [sic] it may be made into powder and then cankered teeth rubbed with the powder thereof it both kills the canker and the worms that eat the teeth and destroys them – Proved.

It cannot be said with any certainty that these recipes were used. They may have been recorded purely as curiosities. Hirst, however, maintained that the effectiveness of the remedies had been proved, and that some of them were very popular. Also it should be pointed out that most of the recipes, although certainly not palatable, were usable, in that they were composed of (mostly) harmless, easily obtainable, cheap or even free ingredients.

A similar example of the survival of 'homely' remedies is provided in the form of a recipe book, written in 1818 by James Woodhead of Netherthong, near Huddersfield.[27] Woodhead's recipes, almost forty in number, were based less on traditional folk healing rituals and contained more 'standard' ingredients, herbs and simple, easily obtainable medicaments, but like Hirst's they covered a wide range of ailments, including jaundice, consumption, 'obstructions', various aches and pains, nervous complaints and blindness. The booklet also contained a recommendation for 'Widow Welch's Pills', 'for young women', a well-known abortifacient, and a recipe for female pills, composed of iron, aloes and antimony. To give just two examples of Woodhead's remedies:

for looseness boil sweet dock roots and take a quantity of tea and take 1 table spoon-full every three or 4 hours. Or boil a hand-full of Logwood and take the same quantity.   tried
For Inflamed Eyes
Take flowers of Woodbinding or what we call honeysuckle to simmer them in A pot with sum [sic] water then strain the flowers out, add A little Lump Sugger [sic] and alum let them all simmer together then Bottle it for use   Dr Radclieff

In the same way as Hirst, Woodhead maintained that many of the recipes had been tried and tested.

The widespread use of homely remedies is illustrated by the frequency with which chemists and druggists advertised a willingness to make up family recipes. For example, in 1804 G. B. Reinhardt, a Wakefield druggist, promised that

Those Families who may honor [*sic*] him with their Commands, may depend upon having every Article in the Medical Department, as Genuine as at the Apothecary's Hall, London: . . .[28]

Advertisements of this nature were common throughout the nineteenth century. In 1839 G. Hackforth, chemist and druggist, announced to the Wakefield public that he had taken new premises in Kirkgate, which he intended to open as 'A Family Medicine Warehouse, and General Drug Dispensary'.[29] In 1855 John Handley, also of Wakefield, a member of the Pharmaceutical Society of Great Britain, promised those who would entrust him with their family recipes that they would be carefully compounded under his own superintendence, using the best quality articles.[30] Compounding family recipes remained a crucial part of the chemists' business throughout the nineteenth century. Judging by the way it was emphasised in their advertisements, it was probably a more important component of the chemists' trade than the making up of doctors' prescriptions.

The literate section of the population could increase their stock of recipes, and indeed improve their knowledge of many aspects of medical care. Roy Porter, for example, describes how the *Gentleman's Magazine* was used as a forum for the exchange of medical advice and remedies during the eighteenth century, and how it seemed to be generally assumed that the 'reader was likely to be prescribing for himself and his circle' and that he was 'not a little au fait with medical theories'. Remedies from standard medical publications appeared together with folk and herbal recipes in the *Magazine*.[31] A wide range of cheap and easily obtainable books and tracts dealing with the subjects of self-medication and the 'preservation of health' were available in the eighteenth and nineteenth centuries. Some of these were the contributions of various fringe elements (medical botanists, herbalists, mesmerists, and so on); others were the work of orthodox practitioners, anxious to see an improvement in the general health of the population, which tended to emphasise 'regimen' rather than 'treatment'. Some of these works became very famous, such as Buchan's *Domestic medicine*,[32] which went through numerous editions following its publication in 1769, coming to rival John Wesley's *Primitive physic* in popularity. Altogether, Buchan's work remained influential for something like 150 years. There were also a large number of similar, but less well-known books on the market. In 1811, for example, the

Huddersfield printer and publisher, J. Lancashire, produced *The Villager's Friend & Physician*,[33] priced 6d. This long pamphlet offered advice on exercise, diet, drinking, bathing, clothing and even the education of children! It also recommended remedies for common complaints, such as fevers, croup, dropsy, measles, smallpox, sore throats and earache. Similar ground was covered by Dr Alexander of Wakefield in his tract, *An Answer to the Enquiry, if it be the duty of Every Person to study the preservation of his Health, . . .'*,[34] which was designed especially for those too poor to obtain medical advice, those living at great distances from medical practitioners, and those who were 'frequently indisposed from trifling causes'.[35]

Health guides written by orthodox practitioners tended to recommend self-help only up to a certain point. In the case of serious illness, they strongly advocated calling in a regular practitioner. They were also fiercely opposed to quackery and fringe practices. For example, the anonymous author of *The Villager's Friend & Physician* warned,

Avoid, for your life's sake, the ignorant quack who deals out advertised nostrums. Nor less necessary is it to shun the empiric who assumes the character of the regular practitioner, and does to sport with the lives of his fellow creatures, by dispensing medicines in the most critical cases, without a knowledge of the principles of science.[36]

Dr Wright of Wakefield warned against the fraud, deceit and imposture of the quack, and in particular his utilisation of standard remedies without discrimination, in a popular pamphlet published in 1843. He particularly attacked the 'universal specifics', such as 'Morison's Pills', which were sold in Wakefield marketplace and which in his experience had caused paralysis and mental derangement. Wright suggested some simple remedies for minor complaints as a safeguard against quackery.[37]

Sedentary fringe practitioners
Those who chose not to heed advice of this nature, did not necessarily turn to the itinerant quack and vendor of medicines in the case of illness. Continuing a centuries-long tradition, they looked instead to the expertise of neighbours, old wives and local healers. Many popular healers lived quietly in the community, offering herbal remedies and folk practices, which had been handed down through the generations. Their healing functions may have

sometimes owed more to considerations of prestige and tradition than to economic motives. Some of these healers became specialists in certain types of treatment or ailments: for example, aurists, eye doctors, abortionists, bonesetters and leech women. The latter not only supplied regular doctors with leeches, but frequently became experts in blood letting themselves. Sally Oldfield of Honley, near Huddersfield, 'a cheerful, bustling dame', was one such expert,

. . . ready to answer every call of sick emergency, and learned in knowledge of all bodily ailments. With what dread we watched her fearlessly handle the snake-like horrors known as leeches that were destined to perform such bloody-thirsty deeds upon our trembling bodies, whilst she tried to disarm our fears by humourous jests or soothing words![38]

Sally Dunkirk of Slaithwaite, near Huddersfield, long experienced in treating sickness of all kinds, developed a special talent for dealing with the mentally ill. She was so well regarded that her expertise was called on not just in Slaithwaite, but in many adjoining neighbourhoods. A local inhabitant, describing Slaithwaite life in the 1860s, wrote

Any bad case of fever, or lunacy, of exceptional emergency, was a call for Sally's services. In such cases she became general, and house maid, doctor, and nurse, friend and physician all in one . . . A most useful woman was she for the times in which she lived . . . If her treatment failed to restore the patient to normal health it was a case forthwith to be sent to a lunatic asylum. Her fees were never much more than a liberal supply of home-brewed beer, unrestricted stock of good 'bacca', and the indispensable long clay pipe, with a good 'table', and implicit obedience to her orders.[39]

Other fringe practitioners in the Slaithwaite district included David Balmforth, a noted 'toothdrawer' and the local dentist, and Richard Horsfall of Merrydale (known in the area as 'Merrydale Dick'), who became well known in the locality for healing wounds, bruises, sores and dislocations.[40]

Midwives can also be included in the category of 'sedentary' fringe practitioners. Evidence on this group is very limited: as seen in Table 6.2, for example, very few women declared themselves as midwives in the census returns.[41] Since early in the eighteenth century man-midwives or accouchèurs had effectively pushed women out of middle- and upper-class practice, and the status of the midwife had consequently declined. However, for the majority of poor women during the nineteenth century, assistance at childbirth was still provided by a midwife. A few working-class women would call in a druggist or surgeon to attend at a birth, but this alternative was too expensive for most of this class (7s 6d to a guinea). Midwives were valued for more than their low charges; for just a few shillings the midwife would take care of the mother and baby for a few days after the confinement, undertake household tasks and even look after the husband and other children. The local midwife, usually a respectable widow or married woman with several children of her own, was well known in the community, frequently very experienced and did not normally use instruments in deliveries.

Overseers' accounts provide us with one of the few pieces of concrete evidence on the employment of midwives. Before 1834 midwives appeared more in overseers' accounts than any other category of medical attendant, and were employed for at least half the deliveries paid for from the poor rate (both in and out of the workhouse). Midwives were employed in many cases on a regular basis by the overseers, although generally they were paid by case. Rates of payment varied between 2s and 5s throughout the late eighteenth and early nineteenth centuries. In March, 1788 Dame Haigh was paid 6s by the Overseers of the Huddersfield Township for delivering three poor women. In the first years of the nineteenth century the Mirfield Overseers employed Molly Holroyd on a regular basis as a midwife. In addition to a twice-yearly wage of three guineas, she was paid 2s 6d per delivery. By 1800 the Overseers of South Crosland were paying 4s for each delivery attended by the midwife.[42] Following the introduction of the New Poor Law this avenue of employment became theoretically closed to the midwife, as midwifery cases were taken over by the newly-appointed Poor Law medical officers. In effect, however, the medical officers dealt with very few obstetric cases, which may have aided the survival of the midwife.[43]

The overseers' accounts also testify to the survival of female practitioners into the late eighteenth and early nineteenth centuries; not just midwives and nurses, but a number of 'wise women', surgeonesses and doctresses, who carried out medical practice as a commercial undertaking. These women were employed in considerable numbers by the overseers, sometimes as part of a husband and wife team, such as the Jubbs of Mirfield, who were both engaged in medical practice. Otherwise they worked alone, frequently specialising, for example, in bonesetting, the cure of 'sore legs' or in the treatment of children. For instance, in the late eighteenth century the Mirfield Overseers employed Eliz[th] Rishworth to 'cure legs', and in October, 1787 'Jonas Law wife' received one guinea for 'setting Kellit Leg'.[44]

One of the most interesting individuals to practise medicine in nineteenth-century Wakefield was Joseph Crowther, who carried on the traditional art of bonesetting. He practised in the Wakefield area from early in the nineteenth century until the mid-1860s, when his practice was taken over by one Sarah Crowther, presumably his daughter. Crowther, like most local fringe practitioners, was comparatively poor, living all of his life in Westgate Common, one of the least salubrious parts of Wakefield. Yet his activities, like those of his predecessors, were famed throughout Yorkshire, his family having 'exercised the art, from father to son, time out of mind'.[45]

In 1850, following two severe falls, Squire Waterton, then aged 68, called in Joseph Crowther, who had been recommended to him by his gamekeeper. Despite attendance by qualified surgeons, one of Waterton's arms remained stiff and deformed, causing constant pain, and he had even considered amputation. Crowther's diagnosis reflected badly on the efforts of the surgeons. Waterton's elbow and shoulder were still out of joint, his wrist badly damaged and the whole arm shrunk. The treatment, as recorded by Waterton, was somewhat drastic. Following 21 days of embrocations, stretching, pulling, twisting and jerking, Crowther cured the shoulder and wrist. The last act was one of 'unmitigated severity'. The bonesetter 'smashed to atoms' the callus[46] which had formed in the dislocated elbow joint, 'the elbow itself cracking, as though the interior part of it had consisted of tobacco-pipe shanks'. Within days, however, Waterton could claim that the arm was completely recovered. The total fee paid to Crowther is not mentioned, but Waterton gave him a £5 note as a bonus.[47] Following the completion of his treatment, Waterton gave his impressions of bonesetters and their work.

Let me hasten to give you a true idea of a bonesetter. He is not a quack; he pretends to cure no diseases. He sells no new medicine. His sole occupation is to set bones and put joints to rights and to let blood and draw teeth.

Formerly, when surgery in England was not so mature as at present, and surgeons not so numerous, the bonesetter was in great practice . . . But, in our times, the surgeon has usurped the office of the bonesetter and he gets all the cases in higher life which can afford to pay him. Whereas the bonesetter, making very low charges, draws all the disabled poor to him and he has twenty times more operations to perform than the surgeon.

Waterton had been in the practice of sending the poor of his neighbourhood to Mr Wheatman of Carlton, near Pontefract, an 'excellent bonesetter', who died in 1847, three years before Waterton had his operation. Wheatman told Waterton that he normally treated over 500 cases a year. 'This made him perfect and nothing used to astonish me more than the clear manner in which he pointed out the nature of the case and the determined manner in which he put it to rights.'[48]

Itinerant fringe practitioners

It was not only the local fringe practitioner, who resided and worked within the community, that survived into the nineteenth century. A variety of itinerant quack doctors[49] and medicine vendors periodically visited Wakefield, Huddersfield and the surrounding villages. The travelling quack moved from town to town, inhabiting inns and lodging houses, and making his appearance on market days to sell medicines, pull teeth, and to diagnose and treat a wide range of ailments. As a nineteenth-century observer of the Huddersfield area reminisced,

In those days quack doctors were very much in evidence. I well remember them visiting the neighbourhood attired in shabby half worn black suits including a frock coat, and top hat. They were very loquacious and talked glibly about the lungs and the kidneys, and the blood and stomach, and all the ills of which the flesh is heir to, and for which they had never-failing remedies and certain cures, with samples available at the moment, and ready to supply a stock of medicines which every family ought to possess.[50]

The itinerant quack, who usually lacked any kind of local reputation or established clientele, was very much a showman, and dependent on the generation of publicity. He would announce his forthcoming visits by means of handbills or advertisements in the local press. In August, 1847, for example, many hundred copies of a pamphlet entitled *The whole art of preventing and curing diseases, and of enjoying peace and happiness both of body and mind to the longest possible period of human existence . . .* were circulated amongst the market people of Huddersfield. The author's own pills were recommended to those who wished to attain this happy condition.[51] Mrs Drummond of Leeds, who was obviously something of a success story in the West Riding, advertised extensively in the local press during the mid-nineteenth century. Mrs Drummond (who claimed the titles MRCS and MD) was based in Leeds, and from this base in the auspicious Park Square, she frequented various West Riding towns, accompanied by her assistant 'doctors'. One of her assistants came to Wakefield every Friday, market day, for consultations. The services he offered included the fixing of artificial teeth and the chance to purchase Mrs Drummond's Famed Herbal Tonic and Aperient Canada Pills, which would cure 'any' disease or debility, including stomach complaints, colds, coughs, consumption, jaundice, gout, fever, scrofula, scurvy, rheumatism, piles, cancer, incontinence, smallpox, tumours, ulcers, worms, ague, hysterical fits, wasting, lowness of spirits, pimples, bad breath and poor sight![52]

Quack doctors appear to have followed two main lines of tack in promoting their services and products. Some, like Mrs Drummond, offered cures for all ills; others (in a similar way to local healers) claimed to be experts in specialised treatments. For example, during the mid-nineteenth century Mr Clarkson advertised his expertise in curing 'bad legs' in the West Riding press. He claimed to operate on a 'no cure, no pay' basis, and pledged to be able to perform more cures in twenty cases 'than any other man in Europe' or to forfeit £50 to charity.[53] These practitioners frequently specialised in the treatment of venereal diseases, individuals such as Mr Wilkinson of Leeds, who had devoted his studies for many years 'to the successful treatment of diseases where secrecy and expert practice is required'. 'Wilkinson's Purifying Drops' could be obtained from Mr Dewhirst, chemist, New Street, Huddersfield. The Drs Henry claimed to be able to 'eradicate every species of Venereal Infection' and to effect 'perfect cures' in a week. One of the Drs Henry could be consulted twice weekly at 3 Albion Street, Huddersfield.[54]

Up until the third quarter of the nineteenth century most oculists, dentists, aurists and other para-medical groups could be categorised as itinerant fringe practitioners. Before then they had no recognised training or qualifications.[55] The majority of dentists, for example (although they might be based in a large town), earned their living by making visits around a circuit of towns, attending on certain days or weeks at each place. Their businesses were carried on in public houses, hotels and in the back rooms of shops. In April, 1810 Mr Northern, surgeon dentist, advertised in the *Wakefield Star* that he

Respectfully informs the Ladies and Gentlemen of Wakefield and its Vicinity, that he intends making his periodical visit on MONDAY the 24th Inst. and may be consulted at Mr. HADFIELD'S Spirit merchant, until the 8th of May – Afterwards at his house in Leeds.[56]

Mr Moseley, surgeon dentist of London and Hull, 'respectfully announced' in 1841 that in compliance with the requests of his patients, he would attend at various towns in the West Riding for a limited period. He would visit Huddersfield on Mondays and Tuesdays, where he could be consulted at Mr Thomas Herring's, saddler. He would also attend at Mr Gray's, Wood Street, Wakefield on Fridays.[57] Similarly, in 1849 the following advertisement appeared in the *Leeds Mercury*.

THE LADIES' DENTIST. – RETURN TO BRADFORD – CHEVALIER BERNASCONI DE LA BARRE . . . has returned from Switzerland and Italy. Apply as before 156, Briggate, Leeds; or at 62, Portland Crescent, (Private Residence). Attendance at Bradford, punctually every Monday and Thursday, at his Rooms, Mr. Barrow's, Watchmaker, Bank Street; Wakefield every Friday; inquire at Nichols and Sons, Booksellers.

In the next issue of the *Mercury* de la Barre added that he would also attend every Tuesday at the Imperial Hotel, Huddersfield.[58]

Mr Swift, aurist, attended at many towns in Lancashire and Yorkshire during the mid-nineteenth century, treating eye and ear complaints. In 1841, for example, he arranged to visit the Victoria Tavern, Huddersfield, on 9 November, and the Bull and Bell, Leeds, on the 10th and 11th. His drops for deafness were obtainable at Mr Swift's, chemist, Huddersfield.[59] Mr Child, who specialised in the cure of blindness and who claimed to give 'advice gratis', regularly visited a number of West Riding towns from his base in Birmingham.[60] Meanwhile, the services of chiropodists were also available on an itinerant basis. In 1831 Mr A. Davidson, 'surgeon-chiropodist' (who claimed to be qualified from the Royal College of Surgeons, Berlin), declared himself 'ready to undertake the eradication of corns, bunions, defective nails, etc.' at Mr Woore's, King St, Huddersfield, or at the houses of those 'who may honour him with their commands'.[61]

In many cases itinerant fringe practitioners depended more on their wits and techniques of salesmanship to earn a living, than on any medical skill they might or might not possess. In this way they differed from their more stationary counterparts, whose livelihoods depended on their continued success in treating members of a local community. The itinerant quack was also more likely to be of doubtful respectability, and to be involved in cases of malpractice or dupery. In May, 1854 W. Freeland, an itinerant vendor of 'speedy cures for all diseases', was brought before the magistrates at the Wakefield Court House. He was not summoned, however, in connection with his activities as a medicine vendor, but on a charge of being drunk and incapable. The defendant stated that he had come from Cleckheaton 'to place his infallible cure in the hands of the inhabitants of Wakefield as were so unfortunate to be bodily afflicted, and so weak in mind as to spend money on his wares'. The *Wakefield Express* reported that the inhabitants of Wakefield were generally awake to that sort of dupery, and that Freeland had not been very successful. Freeland was unable to pay the fine and court costs, which amounted to 19s, and the *Express* remarked cynically that his stock would soon be disposed of if he could not raise the money, '. . . and a good opening will be afforded for an enterprising fellow to begin business in a new line'.[62]

Except where malpractice by unqualified practitioners led to serious injury or death, or where trickery was practised on a large scale, the authorities appear to have ignored them. Random sampling from nineteenth-century Quarter Sessions Indictment Books turned up only a few cases involving fringe practitioners, and these were usually cases of fraud rather than malpractice.[63] One such case was the trial at Wakefield Court House in 1857 of a travelling quack, William Langley Riley, who was charged with obtaining money on false pretences. Riley, a Wakefield labourer, had been travelling around the countryside in a conveyance under the designation of 'Drs. Langley Riley and Co.'. Riley had used an original method of duping the public. He had pretended to be a medical officer from the Royal Botanical College of Health in London, who had been sent by the Government for the special benefit of the poor. He had professed to his 'beneficiaries' that he was dispensing medicine gratis, charging only for the Government stamp. A large medicine chest was produced in court containing spurious drugs. However, despite the evidence brought against him by several witnesses, Riley was acquitted.[64]

Medical botany

While the traditional quack doctor continued to thrive during the nineteenth century, this period also witnessed the emergence of a new form of fringe practice, medical botany. Although followers of medical botany claimed to have no connections whatsoever with 'quack' medicine, it was usually practised by unqualified personnel, initially as a form of self-help medicine, by the 1860s more frequently on a commercial basis. The system of medical botany became very popular in the middle decades of the century, especially with the working classes and in Northern England. Medical botany, which had close links with herbalism, was imported from America by Dr Isaiah Coffin, who in the 1840s organised the Friendly Botanic Society of Great Britain and local societies in several Northern towns, including Huddersfield, Halifax, Brighouse and Manchester.[65]

Part of the success of the movement was due to the emphasis placed on self-medication, and Coffin's promise to make 'every man his own physician'. The treatments were simple and based largely on herbal remedies. (The herbs Coffin used were chiefly *Lobelia inflata* (an emetic) and Cayenne pepper (a counter-irritant and gastric stimulant), which were combined with the administration of herb teas, warmth and a nutritious diet.) Components of the remedies became easily obtainable during the mid-nineteenth century from the agents of Dr Coffin, and handbooks were available to explain the treatment of a wide variety of common ailments. Medical botanists were actively opposed to the treatments and monopoly position of the medical profession, which helps explain the appeal of the movement to a working class already disenchanted with and suspicious of regular medical practitioners. Coffin maintained that the remedies of regular doctors were worse than useless, and delighted in pointing out cases of malpractice and divergences between methods of treatment on the part of qualified medical men. In contrast to the 'mysteries' of orthodox medicine, Coffin's remedies were, he maintained, empirical, natural, easy to comprehend and apply, and effective.[66]

It was not only the medical aspect of Coffinism which appealed to the working man. The organisation of recruitment also helped account for the success of the movement. As John Pickstone has suggested, the recruiting methods adopted by Coffin 'took the characteristic form of social and religious movements aimed at the industrious classes'.[67] Methodism, vegetarianism and the Temperance Movement, for instance. Much of the support for medical botany came from working men involved in these movements. Coffin made lecture tours of towns and encouraged the formation of local societies, members of which had to possess his book, *The Botanic Guide to Health* (priced 6s), and be proposed and seconded by two members. The democratic organisation of these societies (which had much in common with friendly and co-operative societies and trade unions) also attracted the working classes. There was an elected committee, whose responsibility it was to see that sick members were visited and prescribed for. Meetings often began with a lecture by one of the members or a visitor. Members also got the chance to give an account of successful treatments and to report on any difficult cases they had come across. Agents were appointed by the society to keep a store of medicines and relevant books.

Medical botany became popular in Wakefield and, more especially, Huddersfield (where Methodism, teetotalism and working-class political movements were also of greater significance) during the mid-nineteenth century. The Huddersfield Botanic Society was one of the first to be established, and in 1845 the members presented Dr Coffin with an inkstand,

. . . as a small token of respect and esteem, for your professional abilities, and gratitude for the dispensation of the plain and simple, yet invaluable, principles contained in your system of Medical Botany . . . – a system which *we* have fully proved by experience to be in perfect unison with *nature*, as well as by the many astonishing cures affected not only by you, but by many of our own Members, and persons who attended your Lectures when delivered in this town.[68]

Agents set themselves up in Huddersfield to supply the necessary herbs and a growing range of patented preparations. By the 1860s, for example, two Huddersfield booksellers offered for sale Dr Coffin's Indian Pills, '. . . the best Family medicine ever offered to the public . . .', priced 1s 1½d per box. In 1866 T. N. Swift, chemist and druggist, begged

. . . to inform the public that he is the appointed agent of Dr. Skelton, of London, of whom may be had all Dr. Skelton's preparations, and also every variety of Herbs used in Medical Botany.

T. N. Swift, 51, King St, Huddersfield.[69]

By the 1860s there were at least six botanic practitioners in the town.[70] While hotly denying any links with quackery, some of them made claims similar to those of the most ambitious quack doctor. In 1861, for example, the following advertisement appeared in the *Huddersfield Examiner*.

NEVER DESPAIR – But go and CONSULT Mr. J. L. FIRTH, MEDI-CAL BOTANIST, 38, Buxton Road, opposite the Co-operative Stores, Huddersfield, on all DISEASES incident to the Human Frame, namely, Consumption, Asthma, Coughs, Colds, Rheumatism, Jaundice, Liver Complaints, Gravel, Gout, Scrofula, Scurvy, Dysentery, Diarrhoea, Dropsy, Female Irregularities, Erysipelas, Indigestion, Spasms, Cramp, Nervous Debility, Bilious Complaints and Febrile Diseases in all forms.[71]

Two botanic practitioners established commercial dispensaries in Huddersfield. Mr Booth, proprietor of one of these establishments, imitating a common quack technique, supplied testimonials from grateful patients in his advertisements, such as those of 'W. HOL-LINS, Bradford Road, Huddersfield, cured of gravel, and pain in the back in two days' and Mr George Holmes of Lockwood, near Huddersfield, who was cured of dropsy with one bottle of medicine!'[72] J. Wildes, proprietor of the Huddersfield Botanic and Eclectic Dispensary, offered, in addition to 'Botanic and Eclectic' treatments, vapour and shower baths, priced 1s, and from four to ten o'clock on Saturdays, for the benefit of the working class, 6d. He also offered prospective customers free medical advice on Wednesday and Thursday mornings, although medicines would still be charged for.[73] In addition to the six resident botanic prac-titioners (compared with 23 regular doctors in 1861), Huddersfield was also visited by a number of itinerant medical botanists. For example, in 1868 Mr R. Bean (for twenty years assistant to the eminent botanic practitioner, Dr Skelton) was available for consul-tation every Wednesday at Mr T. N. Swift's, chemist and druggist, Cross Church Street, Huddersfield.[74]

By the 1860s medical botany appears to some extent to have moved away from the ideal of self-help medicine practised by the working man. Not only had it become more commercial, but it also had fallen into the genre of 'quack' medicine, with its emphasis on patented cure-alls, on extensive advertisement, often with excessive claims, and on treatment by personnel who regarded medical botany as a means of livelihood, including itinerant practitioners.[75]

The water cure

One form of medical treatment embraced by quack practitioners and orthodox medical men, and utilised by both rich and poor, was the water cure. This method of treatment was adapted and modernised during the late eighteenth and nineteenth centuries, becoming if anything more popular. The notion of the healing power of water had very ancient origins. Many holy wells and springs dated back to the pagan era, and several English spas, Bath and Buxton, for example, were popular in Roman and Medieval times.[76] Some of the wells and springs in the Wakefield and Huddersfield areas were of antique, if not ancient, origin. The water of St Helen's Well, Honley, near Huddersfield, for example, was for centuries reputed to possess many curative properties. In Wakefield St Swithin's Well, Kirkthorpe Well, New Wells and California Well were valued for their health-restoring powers. In 1827 a new spa was discovered at Stanley, near Wakefield, which had similar properties to Malvern Water. The water was reputedly good for kidney and bladder infections and for body sores. The recommended dose was 'two tumblers before breakfast'.[77] The ancient St Swithin's well was still used by local inhabitants in the eighteenth and nineteenth centuries. The water was believed to be effective in curing many complaints, especially tubercular diseases, weakness and scorbutic illnesses. In the late eighteenth century the old folk method of disease transference was still widely practised at St Swithin's well, and as a twentieth-century local medical man and sceptic remarked,

. . . when the well was open it was near the hedge on which used to be hung bits of rag with which people had washed. They were left hanging under the delusive idea that as the rags wasted away so would the part affected, which had been washed therewith, proceed to mend and become sound.

Whether effective or not, the well was still popular with Wakefield people in the middle decades of the nineteenth century, and the Reverend Samuel Sharpe, Vicar of Wakefield, was in the habit of bathing there.[78]

The science of hydropathy gave the water cure a fresh rationale, although the system of treatment it embodied did not really offer much that was new. On the whole hydropathy emphasised 'natural' and gentle remedies: rest, a sensible diet and moderate habits, combined with bathing and drinking large quantities of spa water.

Hydropathy differed from the other fringe practices already discussed, in that it did not face the united resistance of all 'regular' doctors. However, it opposed, and was opposed by, the traditional allopathic practitioners of medicine. As John Smedley explained in his introduction to *Practical Hydropathy* in 1861,

The medical profession generally look with contempt on Hydropathy, believing we have no sound principles for the basis of our action, such as they suppose they have in their counter-irritants, setons, issues, mercurial ointment, their soothing narcotics, stimulating quinine, steel mixtures, colchicum, . . . They cannot believe mere water can have either the powerful or curative effects of their severer applications, or produce such quick results.[79]

The system did win partial and complete converts from the medical profession. Some orthodox practitioners embraced the system of hydropathy *in toto*, becoming spa doctors or proprietors of bathing establishments. Others, while not seeing hydropathy as a cure for all ills, believed the emphasis placed on fresh air, bathing and relaxation could be beneficial, especially for those with delicate constitutions or convalescent patients. In common with other systems of medical treatment of ambiguous status (homoeopathy and mesmerism, for example), both qualified and unqualified medical practitioners were involved in hydropathic medicine, in promoting spas and in treating visitors to these establishments.

The inhabitants of Wakefield and Huddersfield participated in the spa treatment's new wave of popularity during the nineteenth century. Local springs and wells were developed into bathing establishments, while several of the spa establishments already in existence gained a new lease of life. In 1832, for instance, the 'once celebrated' cold bath at Kirkthorpe, Wakefield, was reported to have been repaired and put into 'excellent condition' for the reception of bathers.[80] The wealthier inhabitants of Wakefield and Huddersfield visited more distant spas, the most popular being Harrogate, Buxton and Ilkley. To a greater extent than other types of fringe medicine, the water cure became popular with the wealthy (although the poorer classes, as shall be seen later, were not totally excluded). This popularity was in part due to the mildness of hydropathic treatment compared with the radical regimes imposed by allopathic practitioners. But it was also a result of the pleasing social life associated with spa towns, which by the nineteenth century had been toned down from the rowdy and burlesque social activities of the previous century, to a dignified round of 'at homes', tea parties, card games and promenades. A. B. Granville noted during his tour of Northern spas in 1841 that Harrogate had two distinct seasons, the town being inhabited first by persons of a lower social class, and then in August by a more aristocratic clientele. In July Harrogate was, wrote a correspondent of Granville,

. . . as yet, full of clothiers from Leeds, and cutlers from Sheffield, besides all the red noses and faces in England collected together. There is not a livery-hat in the place but our own, and ours, at present, is the only 1£ 1s subscriber on the books at the sulphur well; showing the caliber [*sic*] of the company, who cannot afford more than five or ten shillings, and most of them the half of the smaller sum. But Sheffield and Leeds will soon loom homewards, and then, they say, better company will come.

Granville's informant proved correct.

At the close of that month (July) the Spa season properly begins, and this lasts till Doncaster races. Before that time, carts and gigs empty their gatherings daily. Coroneted chariots, britzschkas, and postchaises, ply about in abundance, after that, bringing their more noble cargoes of aristocratic visitors.[81]

The better-off inhabitants of Wakefield and Huddersfield frequented the spa towns in high season. Clara Clarkson of Wakefield, for example, went once or twice a year, usually in May and September, to Harrogate or Ilkley. In latter years she came to prefer Ilkley. In 1876 (then aged 65) she spent two month-long vacations in Ilkley. Although the town had, as she described it, 'changed astonishingly', with the addition of many new buildings and villas, and an increased influx of visitors, she was still able to spend her days quietly, pleasantly and uneventfully.[82] However, the cost of spa treatment was prohibitive for the majority of the population. By 1884, for example, the bill for a Wakefield couple for one week's baths and medical attendance at the Ilkley Spa totalled £4 10s 6d.[83]

The proprietors of spa establishments in the neighbourhoods of Wakefield and Huddersfield did their utmost to attract custom away from their more opulent (and usually more expensive) competitors. They claimed that both the quality of the water and the range of facilities were equal to, if not better than, those of more distant spas. Much in fact was done to improve the facilities of local spas, and to create a social atmosphere which would attract a wealthy clientele. In 1827, for example, a large spa baths was established by a company of subscribers at Lockwood, half a mile south of Huddersfield, on the site of an old sulphur well, where

> The existence of mineral springs had suggested to the speculative mind dreams of an English Baden, or at least of another Harrogate. The river was spanned with a rustic bridge, grounds were laid, and a Bath Hotel opened its doors.[84]

In 1831 the proprietors declared that the spa

> . . . combines every requisite to comfort and invigorate the weak and sickly. The Spa Water is generally known and highly esteemed for its Medicinal qualities; in particular it has been found highly beneficial in Glandular, Rheumatic, Gouty, Dyspeptic, Scorbutic, and all kinds of cutaneous Complaints.

They claimed that the baths were the 'most complete' in the West Riding, and added that lodgings in Lockwood and Huddersfield were excellent and terms moderate.[85] Granville reported in 1841 that the water, although mild in composition, was also believed by locals to be effective in curing many disorders, particularly those of the skin.[86] The baths were enlarged and improved several times during the nineteenth century. In 1852, for example, the swimming bath was roofed, and in 1860 facilities were made for improving the filling and warming of the baths and an additional slipper bath was opened.[87] By the 1860s there were facilities for swimming, warm, Buxton, shower, vapour, sulphurous, fumigating and shampooing baths. According to local observers, the baths became increasingly popular in the middle decades of the century. In 1833 over 10,000 baths were taken at the Lockwood establishment. In the 1867 season there were almost 30,000 bathers.[88]

The commencement of the bathing season in the locality, which took place in the first week of May, was promoted as an important social event. The opening day of the Slaithwaite Spa (established in 1825), which by the 1860s was known locally as the 'Harrogate of the district', was one of 'Slawit's' great days.

> It was a time anticipated and remembered for music and dancing and fine ladies and gentlemen; the elite of the Colne Valley were on view on this occasion, and patrons and visitors made their appearance at their best.[89]

At the 35th Anniversary of the Slaithwaite Baths in 1861, for example, afternoon tea was taken, followed by a concert. Speeches were made by Slaithwaite worthies, including the schoolmaster and the local medical practitioners, William and Thomas Dean, praising the water cure in general, and the Slaithwaite Spa in particular.[90] By the 1860s the Spa offered a wide range of facilities: in addition to numerous kinds of baths, there were pleasant grounds and walks and two bowling greens. Clients could either pay for individual baths (the charge, for example, in 1852 for a swimming bath was 6d, for a shower bath 1s, for a Buxton bath 1s 6d, and for a hot bath or vapour bath 2s) or make an annual subscription. The subscription fee for one person for a season during the 1850s and '60s was 12s 6d, and for a family 25s.[91]

It was not only the wealthy classes who availed themselves of the water cure. The poor clearly could not afford charges of this kind, but they were not completely excluded from the benefits of bathing. This class had made long use of local springs and wells both as a water supply and for bathing. In the early nineteenth century the labouring classes of the Huddersfield area frequented springs situated at Holmfirth, Kirkheaton, Lockwood and Slaithwaite. The water at Slaithwaite had, for example, '. . . long been beneficially used by the inhabitants in cutaneous, rheumatic, and other diseases, before the erection of the present commodious baths'.[92] The poorer classes continued to visit those springs which had not been taken over and developed for the wealthy, and which therefore cost nothing to use. In addition, they gained some access to the newly-established bathing establishments. A large proportion of the visitors to the Lockwood and Slaithwaite spas during the nineteenth century were said to be mechanics and factory workers.[93] The higher wage earners of these groups may well have been able to afford the bath charges. Meanwhile, subscription charities were set up by wealthy clients for those too poor to pay for themselves. At the Slaithwaite establishment, for example,

. . . the need for so powerful an aid in freeing the poorer classes of their community from troublesome and disabling disorders, have so convinced the wealthier inhabitants of the advantages to be derived from the gratuitous distribution of mineral water to the afflicted poor, that a subscription charity for that purpose has been established at the Spa. This is as it ought to be, and the propagation of this information ought to stimulate others to follow the benevolent example at other watering-places.[94]

By the mid-nineteenth century most major spas also had subscription charities attached to them to enable the sick to visit their establishments gratis. It also became a general practice for hospitals and dispensaries, and to a lesser extent Boards of Guardians, to make annual subscriptions to these charities, which made it possible for them to send their own patients for treatment. The Wakefield Board of Guardians, for example, subscribed to the Ilkley Bath Charity, while in 1853 the governors of the Huddersfield Infirmary authorised the payment of annual subscriptions to the medical charities at Harrogate, Buxton, Ilkley and Southport.[95] From then on patients were sent regularly by the Infirmary's medical officers to watering places as part of their cure or to convalesce. In 1870 the Huddersfield Corporation took over the Lockwood Spa, renaming it the 'Lockwood Public Baths', offering baths at much reduced rates for the labouring classes and children – for example, a warm bath cost 2d, and for up to four children aged below eight years 4d.[96]

So far nothing has been said of the significance of sea bathing as a health cure. Seaside holidays for rich and poor alike became more popular in the mid- and late nineteenth century, especially as the railways began to facilitate cheap and easy transport to the coast.[97] The favourite resorts of the inhabitants of Wakefield and Huddersfield included Scarborough, Southport and Blackpool. The sea-bathing holiday shared many features of the spa cure, with emphasis on relaxation, fresh air and bathing. While a visit to the seaside was more likely to be seen as a vacation than a health cure, it was also popular with convalescent patients, the chronically sick and those with weak constitutions. Sea bathing was advocated by many regular practitioners. Patients were sent to sea-bathing charities by the governors of the Huddersfield Infirmary as an alternative to spa treatment on the recommendation of the institution's medical officers. Dr Walker, physician to the Infirmary, was also very active in the campaign to set up a sea bathing infirmary on the West coast for the benefit of the poor, to be supported by charitable subscriptions and the Poor Law Unions. The treatment that could be supplied by such an institution, Walker claimed, would be especially beneficial in more 'tedious cases', for example, scrofula, rheumatism, spinal disease and paralysis.[98]

Chemists and druggists

Numerically chemists and druggists made up the most important group of para-medical personnel from the early nineteenth century onwards. The most obvious function of the chemist was to make up

Table 6.3. *Ratio of chemists and druggists to qualified medical practitioners, 1822–1870*

	Chemists and druggists (shops)		Qualified medical practitioners (physicians)		Ratio of chemists and druggists to qualified medical practitioners	
Year	Wakefield	Huddersfield	Wakefield	Huddersfield	Wakefield	Huddersfield
1822	6 (6)	5 (5)	18 (6)	13 (3)	1:3.0	1:2.6
1828	10 (9)	6 (5)	20 (6)	14 (3)	1:2.0	1:2.3
1837	13 (12)	9 (9)	19 (4)	17 (3)	1:1.5	1:1.9
1847	20 (19)	14 (14)	25 (6)	21 (3)	1:1.3	1:1.5
1853	19 (17)	16 (15)	26 (7)	22 (5)	1:1.4	1:1.4
1861	19 (18)	18 (17)	22 (4)	23 (4)	1:1.2	1:1.3
1866	19 (18)	22 (20)	19 (5)	21 (3)	1:1.0	1:0.95
1870	19 (19)	21 (19)	18 (3)	21 (3)	1:0.95	1:1.0

Source: Trade directories: Baines, 1822, Parson and White, 1828, White, 1837, 1847, 1853, 1861, 1866 and 1870.

the prescriptions of qualified medical men, but they combined a number of 'fringe' activities with this function. The willingness of chemists to make up family remedies has already been referred to. In addition, they offered for direct sale to the public a wide range of drugs and chemicals, and constituted the largest group of stockists and suppliers of patent medicines. They were also actively involved in the counter-prescribing of drugs, including many of their own remedies.

From the seventeenth century onwards the traditional pharmaceutical practitioners, the apothecaries, had been extending their role as dispensers of drugs, and turning to general medical practice. This transition was speeded up by the passing of the Apothecaries' Act in 1815. In the late eighteenth and nineteenth centuries the number of chemists and druggists increased, partly in response to population growth, especially in urban areas, but also to fill the gap left by the apothecaries as they devoted more time to medical practice.[99] The towns of Wakefield and Huddersfield were no exceptions to this development. The title 'apothecary' had all but disappeared from early nineteenth-century town directories, as this group was absorbed into the category of 'surgeon'. This change in terminology, and actual practice, was paralleled by a considerable growth in the number of chemists and druggists, as shown in Table 6.3. In 1780, for example, there were just two chemists' shops in Huddersfield; by 1837 there were nine, and in 1870 nineteen.[100]

The increase in the number of chemists and druggists in Wakefield and Huddersfield, which was most significant in the middle decades of the nineteenth century, could have been the result of three developments. The first possibility was that a growing number of medical practitioners abandoned their dispensing functions during this period, and turned the making up of prescriptions over to chemists, which led to an increased volume of trade for this group. Secondly, their increase could be explained quite simply by the population growth of the two communities, which resulted in a larger market for the chemists and druggists' services. The final possibility was that the inhabitants of the two towns made *growing* use of the chemists' services, and thus facilitated a rise in their numbers.

Although there was an increase in the number of qualified medical practitioners in Wakefield and Huddersfield during the nineteenth century, it did not keep pace with the growth in the number of chemists and druggists (see Table 6.3). A nationwide survey, using information extracted from the 1841 census returns, concluded that there was one chemist and druggist in Great Britain to every two medical practitioners.[101] By the 1850s and 1860s the proportion of chemists and druggists was even higher. In 1822 there was one chemist and druggist to every three medical practitioners in both Wakefield and Huddersfield. By 1866 the ratio was one to one. The unequal growth experienced by these two groups was partly offset by the tendency of doctors to turn the function of dispensing over to the druggist during the mid-nineteenth century. Up until then it was not uncommon for individuals to combine the activities of a surgeon–apothecary and druggist. For example, in 1810 M. Barber of Wakefield, 'Surgeon, etc.', not only offered his services 'IN EVERY DEPARTMENT OF HIS PROFESSION', but also kept a chemist's shop in the town centre, where he dispensed his own prescriptions and those of other medical men. In 1842 William Rowlandson of Wakefield, 'Surgeon, Chemist, etc, etc', begged '. . . most respectfully to inform the inhabitants of this Town and Neighbourhood, that he has opened an Establishment for the Dispensing of Medicine, where he intends carrying on the Business of a Chemist and Druggist, in all its branches'.[102] Although pharmacy did not pass out of the hands of the medical profession, by the middle of the century the roles of the two medical groups had tended to become more sharply delineated, and the chemist could expect to take over some of the business of dispensing prescriptions.

Although the increased trade which came in from making up doctors' prescriptions was an obvious boon to the chemist, it is inconceivable (especially when we remember that there was one chemist to *every* medical practitioner in the 1860s) that the chemist could have survived solely on his income from this source.[103] Of course no chemist attempted to do this. A typical chemist's shop would, in addition to a wide range of pharmaceutical preparations, stock a selection of toilet articles, tobacco, snuff, tea, coffee, and other foodstuffs, oils, herbs and dyes. In some cases the chemist combined with his pharmaceutical enterprises the activities of a grocer, bookseller, tea or lead merchant. In the early nineteenth century, for instance, G. B. Reinhardt of Wakefield carried on the businesses of 'Chymist, Druggist, Tea–Dealer and British Wine Merchant'. W. P. Lockwood, chemist, who advertised extensively in the Wakefield newspapers during the mid-nineteenth century, offered to the public drugs, pharmaceuticals and miscellaneous articles connected with the trade, plus a range of cosmetics, hair dyes, perfumes, candles, spices, pickles, sauces, herbs, Italian goods, and so on. In addition he acted as agent to several insurance companies.[104] Thirteen of the nineteen individuals listed as chemists and druggists in the 1853 Wakefield town directory were also in business as tea dealers.[105] In 1854 Henry Crowther set himself up in business in Wakefield both as a chemist and dentist.[106]

The sale of chemicals, the ingredients of remedies, patent preparations, family medicine chests and the chemists' own special 'cure alls' also came to be staple parts of the chemists' trade during the nineteenth century. The increased turnover of these items was in part a natural response to the population growth of the nineteenth century. But also there appeared to be an increased demand for the chemists' services from the public. This growing demand is testified to by the fact that the number of chemists and druggists *more* than kept up with the population growth of Wakefield and Huddersfield during the early and mid-nineteenth century (see Table 6.4 and Figure 6.1).

Table 6.4 and Figure 6.1 demonstrate that the ratio of chemists and druggists to the populations of Wakefield and Huddersfield increased significantly in the early and middle decades of the nineteenth century. In 1821 there was approximately one druggist to every 2,700 inhabitants in Huddersfield. By 1871 the ratio was

Table 6.4. *Ratio of chemists and druggists to the populations of Wakefield and Huddersfield, 1821–1871.*

	Township population		Number of chemists and druggists		Ratio of chemists and druggists to the population	
Year	Wakefield	Huddersfield	Wakefield	Huddersfield	Wakefield	Huddersfield
1821	10,764	13,284	6	5	1:1794	1:2657
1831	12,232	19,035	11 E	7 E	1:1112	1:2719
1841	14,754	25,068	14	11	1:1054	1:2279
1851	16,989	30,880	15	19	1:1133	1:1625
1861	17,611	34,877	21	18	1:839	1:1938
1871	21,076	38,654	18	25	1:1171	1:1546

E = estimates derived from trade directory listings for 1828 and 1837.

Sources: Census Enumerators' Books, Wakefield and Huddersfield, 1841, 1851, 1861 and 1871; Baines, 1822, Parson and White, 1828, White, 1837. (The discrepancies between the figures given here and in Table 6.3 are due to the use of census data in addition to trade directories in Table 6.4.)

one druggist to every 1,500 inhabitants. In Wakefield over the same period the ratio fell from one druggist to every 1,800 people to one for every 1,200 inhabitants in 1871. Wakefield was better served numerically by chemists and druggists throughout the century, but in both towns the increase in their numbers proportionally far outstripped population growth.[107]

The importance of the chemist's role in selling medicines directly to the public, and in particular his counter-prescribing activities, was testified to by the growing concern it aroused amongst contemporaries, especially the medical profession. In 1853, for example, a leading article in the *Medical Times and Gazette* remarked,

. . . we reflect, that already the Profession is yearly deprived – we might almost say robbed – of thousands of pounds by pharmaceutists, who prescribe over their counters or even boldly visit patients at their own homes.[108]

Again the Northern manufacturing districts were pointed to as areas where the practice of resorting to the druggist's shop had reached a peak. In 1844 H. W. Rumsey stated in his evidence to the Select Committee on Medical Poor Relief that in Wakefield '. . . probably from 4,000 to 5,000 poor resort annually to druggists', that is, approximately one-third of the population.[109] A surgeon describing the extent of unqualified practice in the Leeds district

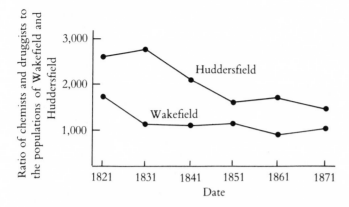

Figure 6.1. Ratio of chemists and druggists to the populations of Wakefield and Huddersfield, 1821–1871.

complained in a letter to *The Lancet* in 1854, that the 'lower' extreme of a surgeon's potential practice was effectively closed to him by the prescribing druggists.

These people sell to the working class for a few pence whatever to themselves seems fit and proper for all manner of diseases, never leaving their crowded shops, and of course living at no expense for horse, carriage, taxes, &c, while *all their receipts are in ready money*. But when the patient has spent all his ready cash, what then? Why he goes to the regular practitioner, where he gets credit for months, years, or very frequently *for ever* (his emphasis).

Meanwhile, he added, very many of the middle class also resorted first to the druggist in the case of illness.[110]

With few restrictions on the sale of drugs, chemists (and as shall be seen later, virtually anybody else) were able to sell their wares unimpeded throughout the nineteenth century. The involvement of chemists, and other retail groups, in the sale of drugs directly to the public is illustrated by the massive 'over-the-counter' sale of opium preparations in the nineteenth century.[111] The widespread use of opiates, in particular their administration to children, aroused the concern of both the medical profession and the interested layman.

The habit thus introduced has become to an alarming degree prevalent, especially in the manufacturing counties, . . . and is not confined to infants suffering from disease, but is also extended to those in a state of health, in order to ensure their more easy management when their mothers are absent from home.[112]

Opiates were not only obtainable from chemists and druggists' shops, including the most respectable establishments,[113] but also from quacks and medicine vendors, and other retailers, including the ubiquitous corner shop and even the pub. Opium and its derivatives were also contained in large numbers of patent cures and infant-calmatives. Wakefield and Huddersfield were in no way immune to the problems associated with the use of opiates, although Dr Walker of the Huddersfield Infirmary maintained that the charity was responsible for saving the lives of a large number of children who had been dosed with narcotics.[114]

Atkinson's Infant Preservative seems to have been a local favourite, but vast quantities of Godfrey's Cordial, Peace and Steedman's Soothing Powders For Children, plus preparations of the suppliers' or customers' own creation, were sold by chemists and other retailers in the two towns. In 1843 Dr Wright of Wakefield fiercely condemned the use of Godfrey's Cordial and other 'Soothing Syrups'.

These baneful medicines contain *Laudanum*, or some other preparation of *Opium*, which ought never to be administered, but with the utmost caution, to the young. And yet, to such a dreadful extent is the practice, of lulling and stupefying their sickly and restless infants, indulged in, by ignorant, idle, and vicious mothers, that these *Godfrey's Cordials* and *Soothing Syrups*, and a similar nostrum called *Peace*, are prepared wholesale by most druggists, . . . and I have been informed, that several hundred pounds in weight of these pernicious compounds are made and sold annually in this Town, besides the stamped medicines of similar effect (his emphasis).

Wright went on to describe the cycle of doping, feeding with 'trashy' food, abdominal disease and more doping, until 'the *Peace* of Death at length releases the little sufferer. This is no imaginary picture, but one drawn from practical experience amid the diseases of the poor'.[115]

The use of narcotics and the doping of infants with opiates were common forms of self-medication. Both self-medication and the assistance of fringe personnel were also much resorted to in birth control and the procurement of abortions. There was also a large amount of literature produced on the subject. Midwives and wise women (or 'grannies' as they were popularly known) offered advice and more practical assistance, especially in inducing abortions, and many traditional methods, the use of herbs, instruments and the 'controlled fall', remained widespread. Most birth control techniques remained inaccessible to the poor during the nineteenth century for reasons of cost and convenience, and abortion continued to be used as a basic, though extremely unreliable and dangerous, method of family control. Techniques of birth control and abortion were widely used in areas where industrial employment was available to women, particularly in the textile districts, such as Wakefield and Huddersfield. The workplace provided a forum for the exchange of information, remedies and practical assistance.[116] Birth control appliances and abortifacients were available from quacks, patent medicine vendors and chemists' shops. A wide variety of herbs and drugs could be cheaply and easily purchased which were utilised in the procurement of abortions, including tansy, pennyroyal, gin and salts, iron and aloes, turpentine, quinine, and later in the century lead. Quinine, for example, was used both as a spermicide and to induce abortion. Chemists and druggists also acted as suppliers of a wide range of 'French' or 'female' pills, which were claimed to cure 'suppression of the menses' and 'female irregularities', preparations such as Velnos' Vegetable Syrup, Widow Welch's Pills and Frampton's Pill of Health, all obtainable in Wakefield and Huddersfield. Frampton's Pill of Health was especially widely advertised in the two towns, and indeed throughout the West Riding, during the mid-nineteenth century, claiming to remove 'all Obstructions in females'. In 1839, for instance, it was offered for sale by England and Fell, chemists of Huddersfield, and by six Wakefield chemists and druggists, and presumably the actual number of stockists was much higher.[117]

In a similar way to other nineteenth-century retail groups (and fringe practitioners), the chemists and druggists of Wakefield and Huddersfield made extensive use of advertising techniques to promote their products. They did this by distributing trade cards and through the medium of the local press. Newspaper advertisements were aimed in part at the local medical profession, guaranteeing accuracy in the compounding of prescriptions and a high quality of drugs. But the general public formed a more important target of advertising campaigns. When W. Clater commenced business in

Wakefield in 1827, for example, he placed the following advertisement in the local paper.

W. Clater
Chemist and Druggist
Market Place, Wakefield

Respectfully informs the *Nobility, Gentry, and Inhabitants* of Wakefield,
and its Vicinity, that he has commenced Business in the above place, and
has laid in an entire, fresh, and extensive Assortment of all kinds of Drugs,
Chemicals, and Galenicals (my emphasis).[118]

When Charles Spivey of Huddersfield retired from his chemist's
business in 1860, he returned thanks, not to the medical profession,
but '. . . to the Inhabitants of Huddersfield and neighbourhood for
their liberal support during many years he has been amongst them,
. . .'. He recommended that the same support be given to his
successor in business.[119]

Chemists also used sales drives to increase their turnover of
particular products, especially patent medicines and their own
preparations. In 1810, for example, R. Elliot of Huddersfield
brought several of his own specialities to the public notice:

The following Valuable Medicines prepared by

R. ELLIOT,

Chemist and Apothecary, Huddersfield, are strongly recommended to the
Public.
Elliot's Restorative and Healing Tincture
Elliot's Family Cordial
The Ceylonian Powder
Elliot's Lozenges[120]

When G. B. Reinhardt took over the chemist's shop of his late
father in 1832, he advertised that business would be carried on as
usual in the same premises,

. . . whereat may be had, as usual, faithfully prepared from the Recipes of
the late G. B. Reinhardt, his invaluable Medicine, BALSAM of
HOREHOUND, for curing Coughs, Colds, Asthmas, Hooping Coughs,
Declines, and Consumptions. Also (opportunely) his truly valuable and
never failing Medicine for the Cholera Morbus, or Vomiting and Purging;
and also his excellent medicines for Worms; all which Medicines, from
trial and experience, have obtained very high reputations, and can only be
prepared by G. B. Reinhardt, as he is the sole possessor of his late Father's
Recipes.[121]

Chemists and druggists were the largest group of stockists and vendors of patent medicines in Wakefield and Huddersfield.[122] In many cases they were the sole suppliers of certain remedies. In the mid-nineteenth century, for example, Dr Locock's Pulmonic Wafers, Holloway's Ointment and Dr Bright's Pills of Health for both sexes were obtainable from F. Cardwell and G. E. Smith in Wakefield and W. P. England in Huddersfield. Denis's Celebrated Family Pills for digestive complaints, asthma, sick headaches, etc., were available from England of Huddersfield and Lawton, Mountain and Cardwell of Wakefield, while M. Sweeting's Toothache Elixir was retailed exclusively by R. S. Alderton of Wakefield and C. Spivey of Huddersfield. In 1839 Mr Smith informed the 'afflicted' of Wakefield,

. . . that Mrs. HAIGH has appointed him to sell her valuable Ointment, which will be found very efficacious in the following Diseases, viz. – Relief in Cancers, Abscesses, Bad Breasts, Swellings and Tumour, Wounds, Ulcers, etc. etc . . . . The Proprietor of the above Ointment being well aware of its unrivalled efficacy, wishes it to be made generally known The Ointment may also be had at her residence, in the Little Bull Yard, Westgate, Wakefield.[123]

Chemists and druggists did not, however, enjoy anything like a complete monopoly in the retail of medicines and patent preparations. Competition for custom existed not only between the qualified and unqualified medical practitioner, but also between the various fringe elements. The chemist faced stiff competition from quack doctors and itinerant medicine vendors. As the *Pharmaceutical Journal* grumbled in 1846,

. . . as the law now stands every man who has a 'doctor's shop', with coloured bottles, is a Chemist and Druggist. The itinerant quack doctors . . . are, according to law, Chemists and Druggists. Although they periodically frequent the markets, they (also) have Druggist's shops, and enjoy the same legal privileges as a Member of the Pharmaceutical Society.[124]

The public could also obtain drugs and patent medicines from a variety of other retailers: stationers, newspaper proprietors, grocers, butchers and publicans, to name but a few. The traditional corner shop, situated typically in the poorest areas of towns, sold drugs and patent preparations, and was much resorted to by a predominantly working-class clientele. Booksellers, stationers and printers, with their easy access to advertising facilities, were always major suppliers of patent medicines. In the early nineteenth century the Hurst family, booksellers, stationers, printers and proprietors of the *Wakefield and Halifax Journal*, advertised and sold a wide selection of patent remedies to their readers. In 1816, for example, the *Wakefield and Halifax Journal* advertised Botanical Bitters, prepared by Dr Harmstrong, for the cure of cholera morbus, bowel disorders, bilious and liver complaints, heartburn, jaundice, worms, and so on, priced 11s for a pint bottle or 22s a quart. This preparation was also retailed by Mr Nichols of Wakefield and Mr Smart of Huddersfield, both stationers and booksellers. In just one issue of the *Wakefield and Halifax Journal* in January, 1827, its proprietors advertised for sale at the *Journal* office Butler's Acidulated Cayenne Lozenges (in 2s and 4s 6d boxes), Butler's Pectoral Elixir for coughs, colds and asthma (in 1s 1½d and 2s 9d bottles), Perry's Essence for tooth- and earache (1s 1½d and 2s 9d), Solomon's Drops for 'impure' blood, skin eruptions, scrofula, dropsy, 'venereal taints', etc. (11s and 33s a bottle), Mr Lignum's Improved Vegetable Lotion for Scorbutic eruptions (2s 9d), Mr Lignum's Scurvy Ointment (1s 9d) and Marshall's Universal Curate for all sores, burns, ulcers, cancerous tumours, ringworm, St Anthony's Fire, and so on (1s 1½d and 2s 9d).[125] A more unlikely stockist of patent medicines was Mr Hollingshead, a Huddersfield draper, who acted as agent for the sale of John Kaye's Worsdell's Pills, '. . . the most extensively established Family Medicine of the present day' (sold in boxes costing 1s 1½d, 2s 9d and 4s 6d). Worsdell's Pills were supplied in other Yorkshire towns during the 1840s by a variety of shopkeepers, including booksellers, grocers, tailors and hairdressers.[126]

This large group of non-pharmaceutical medicine suppliers were seen, not surprisingly, as a major problem by the druggist. But the chemists and druggists' own lack of specialisation led to difficulties in eliminating competition from other retail groups and the itinerant hawkers of medicines. The *Pharmaceutical Journal* complained in 1843.

The indiscriminate sale of drugs by unqualified persons would produce much less injury to the credit and interests of the regular Druggists, if the public had the means of forming a correct estimate of the value of the articles they purchase, and of the qualifications of the parties concerned. But unfortunately in most country towns not only is every Grocer or

Oilman a Druggist, but almost every Druggist is a Grocer or Oilman. The Druggist has no badge or credentials to designate his superior qualification: in fact, he is not *of necessity* more qualified than the Grocer. The blue and red bottles in the windows are common to all; and this is the criterion understood by the public as indicating what is called 'a doctor's shop'.[127]

Concluding remarks

The eighteenth century has often been epitomised as 'the great age of quackery', but the nineteenth century was perhaps an even more important epoch for fringe practice. Those who wished to resort to alternative medicine found a wider range of practitioners and treatments than ever before. The traditional folk healers and itinerant quacks survived, while new fringe practices developed. The fringe practices which have been discussed here form by no means an exhaustive list. Homoeopathy, mesmerism, medical galvanism and phrenology, for instance, which combined 'scientific' theories with an ambiguous medical status, also had their influence, even in provincial towns such as Wakefield and Huddersfield. By the 1860s, for example, several chemists and druggists in both towns specialised in homoeopathic preparations, and during the same decade 'Roman or Turkish Baths' were opened in Wakefield and Huddersfield. In 1871 a single phrenologist was recorded in the Wakefield census returns, and in Huddersfield a female homoeopathist.[128] Several individuals set themselves up as medical galvanists during the middle decades of the nineteenth century. Samuel Braithwaite, for instance, a Wakefield optician and watchmaker, branched out into the manufacture of 'Electro-Galvanic machines' in the 1850s, which he promoted as curative agents 'in Paralysis – Indigestion – Fits – Nervous complaints and other forms of long standing disease'.[129]

The boundaries between fringe and core medicine were frequently vague; both regular and fringe practitioners, for example, became involved in hydropathic medicine and homoeopathy. For this reason (and because of a lack of reliable figures) it is difficult to be precise about the numbers of fringe medical personnel and about what really constituted fringe practice. Several medical men made their appearance in Wakefield and Huddersfield during the nineteenth century, who, while claiming to be 'legally' qualified, were of dubious social and professional status. In a similar way to

the traditional quack, they advertised extensively and made excessive claims with regard to their medical skills. In the 1820s, for
example, Doctor Dunn, who claimed to be a graduate of an 'ancient
University' and a Member of the Royal College of Surgeons,
London, set himself up in practice at Mr Blakeney's, a Wakefield
boot and shoemaker. Dunn claimed particular success in curing eye
and ear disorders. In addition, Dunn promised to cure ruptures,
cancers, scurvy, scrofula, all kinds of fits, nervous complaints, loss
of appetite, indigestion and all disorders of the stomach and bowels,
consumptions, asthma, gout, sore legs, rheumatism, and so on *ad
infinitum.*[130]

A Dr Cavania advertised in a similar vein in the West Riding press
in the 1860s and 1870s. He had branch establishments in Leeds and
Wakefield, and attended at Huddersfield each Tuesday. Again his
status was somewhat dubious. He professed to be a member of the
University College of Physicians and Surgeons, Philadelphia, and
late of the Lordsmith Street Hospital, Chesterfield, and General
Medical Institute, Sheffield. However, he had no British qualifications, and Cavania adopted advertising techniques which broke all
professional codes of conduct:

WHY SUFFER FROM DISEASES, WHEN IMMEDIATE RELIEF
CAN BE OBTAINED by applying to DR. CAVANIA, M.D., . . .
consult a Doctor of a quarter of a century's practical experience, and whose
successful treatment of all diseases has gained for him a world-wide
reputation . . . the miraculous cures daily bring persons and letters from
all parts of England; diseases in the blood are cured so that there is no
return, and this too without cutting or burning . . .

Cavania also added the testimonials of some of his satisfied customers to his advertisements; for example, of John Barras, sexton at
West Ardsley, near Wakefield, who was cured of an acute and
crippling case of 'sore legs' in ten weeks, following two months'
unsuccessful treatment by regular doctors. Also cited was the case
of Mrs Housley of Lofthouse, near Wakefield, afflicted with an
abdominal abscess and extreme debility, who had been given up as
incurable by two surgeons. As the testimonial graphically
explained, Mrs Housley

. . . suffered from a large abscess, the size of a child's head, . . . about a
foot in circumference; quarts of thick matter were discharged; she was in
great agony, . . . and was losing flesh daily; was so weak she could not

walk, and had to be taken to Dr. Cavania in a carriage, more dead than alive. In a few days she found relief, and in six weeks the abscess was healed up, in two months able to walk, in twelve weeks quite restored to her health and retained her flesh, and able to attend to her family. It is her husband's wish and her wish that this should be published. (Signed) HOUSLEY.[131]

Individuals such as Dunn and Cavania are difficult to classify. Their qualifications may well have been invented. On the other hand, they may have had a medical training and have practised 'regularly' before opting to seek their fortunes on the medical fringe. Whether they saw themselves as regulars or fringe practitioners, it is certain that they would have been labelled as quacks by the medical profession.

The medical profession carried on a fierce campaign against fringe practice, in particular the quack doctor, throughout the nineteenth century. Although they effectively pushed unorthodox practitioners towards the periphery of medical practice, they were not able to wipe them out. The sedentary local healers, whose practices tended to be much less 'aggressive' than those of their itinerant contemporaries, were also more difficult to detect. Except in cases where they were accused of malpractice, this group remained unmolested by the regular medical practitioner. Meanwhile, the more flamboyant itinerant quacks were pushed (literally) into the market place to compete as they would for customers. They retaliated against the attacks of regular practitioners by developing their marketing skills, becoming in effect 'small-time entrepreneurs'.[132] The quack advertised his services and products in the press and in handbills and posters to a greater extent than ever before. Dr Wright of Wakefield claimed that quacks had not only become more common in the nineteenth century, but also more successful. He described how the quack doctor's 'zany' had been replaced by bills and adverts, which were 'ten times more efficient'.[133]

It was not just the itinerant quack who sharpened up his techniques of salesmanship, other fringe groups taking advantage of the commercial boom of late eighteenth-century England. The consumption of medicines, always large, was given a further boost by this boom. Many fringe elements, spa proprietors, chemists and druggists, medical botanists, and so on, came to rely more and more on newspaper advertisements for publicising their services, benefiting from a further growth in provincial newspapers during the nineteenth century. Chemists and druggists developed more competitive retailing techniques, basing themselves in central locations, setting up attractive window displays, and offering customers competitive prices and special offers. A glance at any nineteenth-century provincial newspaper, meanwhile, illustrates the 'big sell' techniques of the patent medicine vendors, their promotion of brand names and distinctive packaging, their offers of money-saving bargains through the purchase of bigger quantities. Medicines and medical treatment became another commodity, to be bought and bargained for. A *Lancet* editorial of 1857, which attempted to analyse the popularity of quack medicine in the manufacturing districts of Yorkshire and Lancashire, remarked that

Large towns consist almost entirely of operatives who look upon physic as a trade, – and a poor one too, – who have not the ability to form any opinion as to the proficiency of their betters in point of general education – who rather like some one of their own class – who have a strong belief in a natural gift for doctoring, and, above all, believe most fervently in cheap physic, cheap advice, and cheap visits.[134]

The extension of the railway network may also have worked to the advantage of fringe practitioners. It made the itinerant more mobile, while potential customers could travel with greater ease to the more distant spa or specialist.

'Alternative' medicine of course embraced many different systems of treatment and a wide variety of personnel, each with their own attractions and disadvantages, and this factor makes it difficult to talk about reasons for the success of the fringe in terms of generalities. The sedentary folk healer, who was less likely to 'actively' solicit custom, based his or her popularity largely upon tradition, familiarity, accessibility, and not infrequently medical skill. The quack doctor, meanwhile, was able to utilise either new 'scientific theories' or more traditional remedies, backing his claims to medical skill up with magical tricks, psychological comforts and advance publicity. Fringe practitioners, without the restraints of orthodox medicine's efforts to implement a strict code of ethics, could promise more to the potential patient. Many offered speedy 'wonder' cures. John Kaye of Dalton Hall, near Huddersfield, for instance, proclaimed his Worsdell's Pills, which purified the blood, drained the system of impurities and improved indigestion, as the 'best' antidote to sickness (all for 1s 1½d to 4s 6d a box):

. . . we have no hesitation in saying (fearless of contradiction), that there never was a medicine which, for the short time it has been before the Public has wrought cures so numerous and striking.[135]

In 1840 the Doctress Broadbent of Leeds invited all sufferers from diseases to avail themselves of the opportunity of being 'permanently and effectively cured'. The Drss promised that her methods of treatment were very different from the practice of 'the faculty', her 'grand object' being '. . . gently to assist Nature in her efforts by the judicious and peculiar administration of the simplest Medicines – chiefly British Herbs', which directly opposed the usual system of treatment, which 'racks, debilitates, and ultimately destroys the constitution'.[136] Fringe practitioners frequently claimed to be able to cure where the regular practitioner had failed, imposed time limits on the cure, and promised to drop charges once that time limit had been exceeded.

A quick recovery was an important consideration, especially for the working class, who were soon reduced to poverty if members of their family, in particular the breadwinner, became sick. The medical profession, meanwhile, were unable to shake off the poorer classes' suspicion of both their treatments and motives, and fears of 'experimentation' and 'body stealing' remained widespread. Self-medication and the adoption of such techniques of treatment as those offered by herbalists and medical botanists fitted in with the working-class repudiation of all 'priesthoods', the prevalence of popular science and self-education, teetotalism and working-class political movements, all popular in Wakefield and Huddersfield. The medical profession was as yet an insecure establishment, and, compared with traditional practices and practitioners, a novel one. Orthodox medicine had not yet proved itself any more successful than alternative remedies, and the scientific argument in favour of limiting practice to the qualified was not very convincing. Fringe medicine frequently offered more attractive forms of treatment, in many cases being far less drastic and painful than the regular allopathic methods. Even if they did not effect a cure, fringe remedies, such as those offered by herbalists, hydropathists and homoeopathists, could do little harm to a patient. Many alternative systems also emphasised prevention and treating 'the whole person', aspects which account for the continuing popularity of 'alternative medicine' today. The present-day 'inadequacies' of orthodox medicine and the fact that alternative systems continue to offer many attractions, not least the ability to direct one's own health care and to avoid drug-based treatments, represents a continuum from the nineteenth-century situation, when the effectiveness of orthodox medicine was much more questionable.[137] It should also be stressed that in the eighteenth and nineteenth centuries fringe personnel offered treatment in cases where the regular medical profession avoided involvement: for example, in the procurement of abortions, birth control, the treatment of VD and the provision of opiates on demand. The treatment of chronic illnesses, rheumatism, chest complaints, 'sore legs', and so on, was also specialised in by many fringe elements. Treatment of these ailments could prove to be extremely costly when treated on a regular basis by qualified medical men, and it was particularly difficult to gain admission to medical charities or to obtain Poor Law medical assistance in such cases.

It is important to re-emphasise here that during the eighteenth and nineteenth centuries the layman still played a dominant role in determining his health care and in directing his medical treatment. This applied to both regular and alternative practice, and was a privilege not necessarily confined to the wealthy classes. Those resorting to fringe practices, however, probably had more control over how they were treated. The reputation of fringe practitioners came from the public alone, not from their professional peers, and they had to establish a name for themselves with that public (even, as was frequently the case with itinerant quacks, if this was only very short-lived) and show themselves adaptable to changing demands. It was easy enough for a consumer to switch to another supplier of medicines, a spa which offered better facilities, or to a new and more enterprising fringe practitioner, perhaps somewhat easier than moving from one regular practitioner to another. For those of the poor receiving 'institutional' relief, meanwhile, no choice of attendant would be offered.

Cost is another factor to be considered, and on the whole fringe medicine did offer a cheap substitute for orthodox medical treatment. Many remedies, especially those based on herbs, cost nothing to use; patented preparations or the remedies prepared by chemists cost as little as a few pence to several shillings. Meanwhile, the fees charged by fringe personnel (although subject to variance and not often advertised) were usually low. Frequently advice was given gratis provided that it accompanied the sale of medicine. In addition, many fringe elements, particularly local healers, combined a 'caring' function with their healing activities. Meanwhile, by the mid-nineteenth century the minimum fee charged for *one visit* (excluding medicines) by a regular practitioner was approximately 2s to 5s; more complicated courses of treatment could cost upwards of several guineas.[138] The middle classes wished to keep their doctors' bills to a minimum, and were apparently ready to try cheaper (and frequently more 'promising') alternatives. However, although it has been suggested here that many of the middle and upper classes resorted to fringe practitioners, their largest and most consistent pool of custom was the poor and working classes. While a small number of unqualified healers made a handsome living practising amongst the wealthy, most lived and worked with the poorer sections of society, where they were accessible in terms of location and culture. For the poor resort to a druggist's shop, a local healer or market-place quack was often the only form of treatment affordable. Too poor to pay for a regular doctor, it was the only way of avoiding the stigma of applying for poor relief or to a medical charity, or of appealing to the private benevolence of a regular medical practitioner. On a more positive note, it often constituted a 'preferred' form of medical relief.

7

The medical profession in Wakefield and Huddersfield: occupational and social characteristics

The nineteenth century has been depicted by medical historians as the most important epoch in the development of the 'modern' medical profession. Far-reaching legislative and structural changes were embodied in the Apothecaries' Act of 1815 and the 1858 Medical Act, the most significant structural development being the disappearance of the 'pure' physician, surgeon and apothecary, and their replacement by the general practitioner of medicine. These changes were accompanied by attempts on the part of the medical profession to achieve higher standards of training, qualification and practice. Concerted efforts were also made to improve the status of the profession, raise the level of entrants and to formulate codes of behaviour between medical practitioners, efforts directed, in part at least, towards ensuring that the practice of medicine was recognised as a 'gentlemanly' calling. Attempts to eliminate the competition of the unqualified were linked to the above aspirations, as medical men sought not only to increase the size of their practices, but also to achieve for themselves a monopoly over medical treatment.

Few localised case studies have been undertaken to test the more general conclusions reached on the changing structure and practices of the medical profession during the nineteenth century.[1] Little is known of how legal and structural changes affected medical communities or individual practitioners, or of the rank-and-file provincial medical man. Nor have the attempts of local groups of medical men to organise and raise their professional status received much attention, especially outside the capital. Likewise, little is known about the social characteristics of medical men; their incomes,[2] standards of living, status in the community and ability to integrate with local élite groups.[3]

This and the following chapter will attempt to answer some of these questions with reference to the medical communities of

Wakefield and Huddersfield. This chapter will concentrate on the occupational and social characteristics of medical practitioners. Section 7.1 will examine the career structures of medical practitioners in the two towns: their numbers, qualifications, practices and appointments; if and how these changed during the nineteenth century. Did, as is often claimed by historians and nineteenth-century medical practitioners, the profession become overstocked during this period? Did practice-building and job opportunities improve, decline or merely change? Did the nineteenth century witness the demise of the 'pure' physician, surgeon and apothecary and the rise of the general practitioner? It will be suggested that the growth in the middle-class market and changing job opportunities encouraged the rise of the general practitioner of medicine, and that in place of the tripartite division medical men could be seen as being ranged along a scale according to their training, practices and appointments.

The social characteristics to be discussed in the second Section (7.2) reflected and reinforced this scale. Few attempts have been made to analyse the social and economic position of medical men, except for the most famous and prominent, and indeed data on this subject are scarce. Professional success and social status were, however, closely related. The second Section will look at the social characteristics of Wakefield and Huddersfield medical men: their origins, incomes, household structures and place of residence. These characteristics reflected the successes or failures of medical practitioners in winning appointments and patients. It will be demonstrated that social status and family background were crucial to the career prospects of medical men.

Chapter 8 will look at the ways in which medical men attempted to further themselves professionally and socially. The nineteenth century witnessed a burgeoning of medical societies, set up to deal with both scientific and professional concerns. As will be shown in the first Section of Chapter 8, these efforts were by no means confined to the metropolis and larger provincial towns; smaller communities of medical men could also support such activities. Nor, unfortunately for the profession, was intra-professional conflict confined to communities with large medical populations. As will be illustrated in Chapter 8, even within small provincial communities such as Wakefield and Huddersfield conflict between medical men was rife. The first Section will also focus on one of the key issues upon which all medical men were able to unite – efforts to rid themselves of the competition of the unqualified practitioner. The relationship of the medical practitioner with the middle classes and local élite groups was of great importance in determining both his professional success and social standing. The involvement of medical men in the affairs of the two communities (in particular their activities in local voluntary societies) will be focused on in the second Section of Chapter 8. This discussion, it is hoped, will shed further light on the position of medical men in the social order of the nineteenth century.

Emphasis will be placed throughout this and the next chapter on the mid-nineteenth century, a period for which more data are available, and which has been depicted by both contemporaries and historians as an important epoch of consolidation for the profession. By this time most structural and legal changes had been worked through, and doctors were able to concentrate more on efforts to improve their social and professional status. The advantages of examining the professional and social development of the medical profession against the background of two very different communities will also be emphasised. As will be seen, the economic climates and social structures of Wakefield and Huddersfield partially determined the careers and social and civic activities of medical practitioners.

Concentration on two 'middle-sized' communities has facilitated the use of a wide selection of the large (almost unmanageable) range of quantitative and qualitative evidence available. From 1847 onwards an annual directory of medical practitioners was published, giving details of the qualifications and appointments of regular doctors. Census returns and trade directories give further information on the numbers, professional qualifications and social characteristics of medical men. The growing number of medical journals which appeared during the nineteenth century provide the historian with information on the issues, both scientific and professional, closest to the hearts of the medical profession. All these sources have been referred to. Material relating specifically to Wakefield and Huddersfield was also consulted. The records of medical charities and medical societies were of particular value. Newspapers, the memoirs of local medical men, the records of voluntary societies and occasional sets of doctors' bills served to give a more rounded picture of the social and occupational activities of medical men.

7.1 Occupational characteristics

Numbers
The number of medical practitioners in Wakefield and Huddersfield increased steadily during the first half of the nineteenth century. Their numbers failed, however, to keep up with the large population growth of the two towns. By 1780 Wakefield already had nine resident medical practitioners: three physicians and six surgeons and apothecaries. In the same year three qualified surgeon-apothecaries were listed as being resident in Huddersfield.[4] By 1822 Wakefield had eighteen medical practitioners, Huddersfield thirteen. A peak in numbers was reached in Wakefield in the 1850s, when a total of 26 practitioners resided in the town. In Huddersfield the largest number of medical men was recorded in the early 1860s, when they totalled 23. By the 1870s the number resident in both towns was in decline,[5] despite the fact that the populations of Wakefield and Huddersfield continued to rise.[6] (See Tables 7.1(a) and (b) and Figure 7.1.)

Taken alone these figures do not mean much. How did they compare with totals for other towns, and more significantly did the number of medical practitioners in Wakefield and Huddersfield keep pace with the demand for medical treatment in the nineteenth century? The data given in Tables 7.1(a) and (b) and Figure 7.1 indicate that (excluding an increase around the turn of the century), the ratio of medical practitioners to the populations of both towns diminished progressively. Between 1821 and 1871 the population of Wakefield increased by some 96 per cent. By 1871, however, the number of medical practitioners in the town had actually fallen below the 1821 figure (from eighteen to seventeen). Between 1821 and 1871 Huddersfield's population rose by a massive 191 per cent. Over the same period the number of doctors in practice rose from thirteen to 21. This, however, represented a percentage increase of only 62. In the decade of Huddersfield's largest population growth, 1821 to 1831 (43 per cent), only one more doctor established himself in practice in the town.

Clearly the number of medical practitioners did not keep up with the general population growths of Wakefield and Huddersfield. However, it should be remembered that by far the greatest population growth took place amongst those classes who could by no means afford the services of a private medical practitioner, the labouring classes and the poor. It was to the upper and middle

Table 7.1(a). *The increase of Wakefield and Huddersfield medical practitioners and Township populations, 1780–1871.*
E = estimated population.

Year	Qualified medical practitioners (per cent increase)		Township populations (per cent increase)			
	Wakefield	Huddersfield	Wakefield		Huddersfield	
1780	9	3	8,000	E	3,500	E
1821	18 (100)[a]	13 (333)[a]	10,764	(25.7)[a]	13,284	(73.7)[a]
1831	21 (17)	14 (8)	12,232	(13.6)	19,035	(43.3)
1841	24 (14)	18 (29)	14,754	(20.6)	25,068	(31.7)
1851	26 (8)	21 (17)	16,989	(15.1)	30,880	(23.2)
1861	24 (−8)	23 (10)	17,611	(3.7)	34,877	(12.9)
1871	17 (−29)	21 (−10)	21,076	(19.7)	38,654	(10.8)
Total increase 1821– 1871	−1 (−5.6)	8 (61.5)	10,312	(95.8)	25,370	(191.0)

[a] These are percentage increases over a forty-year period.
(As a wider range of sources have been utilised in the compilation of Tables 7.1, the figures differ from those given in Table 6.3.)

Table 7.1(b). *Ratio of Wakefield and Huddersfield medical practitioners to the population, 1780–1871.*

Year	Ratio of practitioners to Township populations	
	Wakefield	Huddersfield
1780	1:889	1:1167
1821	1:598	1:1022
1831	1:582	1:1360
1841	1:615	1:1393
1851	1:653	1:1470
1861	1:734	1:1516
1871	1:1240	1:1841

Sources: Medical Register for the Year 1780; Census Enumerators' Books, Wakefield and Huddersfield, 1841, 1851, 1861 and 1871; Trade directories: Baines, 1822, Parson and White, 1828, White, 1837, 1853, 1861 and 1870 (see Bibliography for complete references); *Provincial Medical Directories,* 1847–1872.

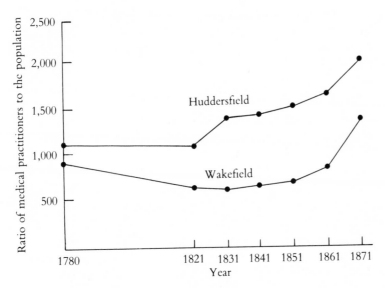

Figure 7.1. Ratio of Wakefield and Huddersfield medical practitioners to the population, 1780–1871.

classes that the medical practitioner turned for his main source of custom and income, and these groups grew more steadily during the nineteenth century. The medical men of the two towns were probably more than capable of supplying the demand for private medical treatment, despite the overall increase in population. In terms of practices there was a limit to the number of doctors Wakefield and Huddersfield could accommodate.

Using data taken from the occupation abstract of the 1841 census,[7] the number of medical men in Wakefield and Huddersfield could be compared with totals for other West Riding towns. The number of medical practitioners in the West Riding in 1841 was given as 778.[8] Of this total, 56 were classified as physicians and 722 as 'surgeons, apothecaries and medical students' (over the age of twenty). It is hardly surprising to find that Leeds and Sheffield, the towns with the largest populations and boasting major hospitals, numerous other medical charities and medical schools, also supported the largest number of doctors. 130 medical practitioners resided in Leeds; 87 in Sheffield (including fourteen physicians in both towns). Thirty practitioners resided in Bradford, including one physician. Only ten medical men resided in Barnsley, none of whom were recorded as physicians, while Doncaster provided employment for thirteen medical men, including one physician. Wakefield and Huddersfield both had 22 resident practitioners (including three physicians in each town).[9] These figures become more meaningful when they are examined together with the populations they served. Table 7.2 shows the ratios between medical practitioners and the populations of selected West Riding towns in 1841 and 1851. The figures suggest that the larger and more completely industrialised towns of Leeds, Sheffield, Bradford and Huddersfield had less favourable ratios than the smaller market and service centres of Wakefield and Doncaster. Wakefield had the most favourable ratio of one medical practitioner to every 671 inhabitants, approximately half that of Sheffield with one doctor to every 1,277 inhabitants in 1841.

Similar information was extracted from the 1851 census returns for the West Riding by Sigsworth and Swan.[10] They recorded a total of 538 practising doctors (physicians, surgeons, apothecaries and general practitioners) and 132 unqualified assistants, apprentices and pupils. The ratio of medical practitioners to the population of the Riding was given as 1:2539. These results indicate that a decline in numbers had taken place since 1841 and that the ratio of practitioners to the population had become less favourable. The 1851 total of 538 represents a decline of 31 per cent from the 1841 figure of 778. The number of inhabitants in the West Riding to every medical practitioner had increased by over 70 per cent. Sigsworth and Swan also recorded the least favourable ratios of medical practitioners to town populations in the larger urban communities. (See Table 7.2.) Bradford had the least favourable ratio in 1851, followed by Leeds and Sheffield. The medium-sized textile towns of Halifax and Huddersfield had more favourable ratios. The smaller, predominantly market/service towns of the West Riding had the best ratios: for example, Wakefield had a ratio of 1:653, Pontefract 1:959 and Ripon 1:760. In Leeds and Bradford the ratio of doctors to the populations of the towns had gone down markedly since 1841. In Leeds there were half as many doctors to the inhabitants as in 1841. In Bradford the ratio of doctors to the population had declined by a massive 142 per cent.

Type of practice
Sigsworth and Swan have suggested that the much more favourable ratios for market towns may be explained partly by the fact that

Table 7.2. *Ratio of medical practitioners to the populations of selected West Riding towns in 1841 and 1851.*

Place	Total number of resident medical practitioners in 1841 (physicians)	Population in 1841	Ratio of medical practitioners to the population 1841	1851
West Riding	778 (56)	1,154,101	1:1483	1:2539[b]
Sheffield Parish	87 (14)	111,091	1:1277	1:2082[b]
Bradford Township	30 (1)	37,765	1:1259	1:3052[b]
Leeds Borough and Town	130 (14)	152,054	1:1170	1:2426[b]
Huddersfield Borough and Township	22 (3)	25,068	1:1139	1:1470
Halifax	67 (3)	130,743	1:1951[a]	1:1399[b]
Doncaster Borough	13 (1)	10,455	1:804	1:670
Wakefield Township	22 (3)	14,754	1:671	1:653

[a] The figures given for Halifax in 1841 cover the whole Parish, including many outlying villages and rural areas.
[b] These figures are taken from the computations of Sigsworth and Swan.
Sources: 1841 Census, Occupation Abstract, PP, 1844, XXVII (587); White, 1847, 1853; E. M. Sigsworth and P. Swan, *op. cit.*, pp. 37–38.

doctors living in these communities also served the surrounding countryside. They point to the large number of grooms employed in market towns as evidence to support their contention. There may be some truth in this suggestion. Several Wakefield practitioners, for example, extended their practices to the surrounding villages and countryside. Indeed, some seem to have concentrated on an out-of-town practice. By early in the nineteenth century, for example, the Walkers, an eminent surgical family, had built up a very respectable country practice, while continuing to base themselves in the centre of Wakefield. The town's senior surgeon, Edward Taylor, also had many patients residing at a distance from Wakefield, and in 1810 he became the first doctor in the area to 'set up a gig'.[11]

Practices such as these, however, were by no means confined to smaller communities. Medical men in the larger, industrialised towns of the region often had far-flung practices. Indeed, as their wealthier clientele moved out of town centres to new suburban areas and out-townships, doctors were forced to either follow their migration or extend the geographical limits of their practices.[12] The most eminent medical men of the region, in particular those with honorary hospital appointments, were usually based in the largest towns and cities. They served as medical advisors to the wealthiest West Riding families, either in the capacity of consultant or family doctor. Dr Simpson, a Bradford physician, recorded in his diary for the year 1825 making many visits on horseback to his more distant patients.[13] In the first half of the nineteenth century Squire Waterton of Wakefield employed both Mr Horsfall of Wakefield and Dr Hobson of Leeds as his regular medical attendants. Mr Hey, surgeon to the Leeds Infirmary, was called in to treat more urgent cases of illness or when a second opinion was necessary.[14] Indeed, Hey appeared to have been called to Wakefield on a regular basis by a number of the town's doctors. The practices of medical men then, regardless of the type of town in which they established themselves, were apparently not confined to their place of residence.[15] (And, as will be seen in Section 7.2, the employment of grooms may well have had as much to do with considerations of prestige as notions of practicality.)

A more straightforward explanation for the favourable ratios of doctors to the populations of smaller market towns is to be found in the social make-up of these communities. Market and service towns were industrially less developed than their larger neighbours. Rather, their economies were based on trading and service functions, and as such they were likely to attract a high proportion of middle-class inhabitants, the basis of a medical practitioner's private practice. Wakefield had a large proportion of middle-class inhabitants throughout the nineteenth century, while Huddersfield, which enjoyed something of an intermediate position in terms of the doctor/patient ratio, had a large middle-class population in comparison with other textile towns.[16] Those towns with the most rapid population growths, such as Bradford and Sheffield, also had higher proportions of poorer inhabitants, unable to afford the services of a medical practitioner. As the proportion of poorer inhabitants in large urban communities increased during the nineteenth century, so did the ratio of medical practitioners to the population decline. A large number of physicians was also indicative of a substantial middle- and upper-class clientele. Only the wealthy could afford the services of the more expensive physician,[17] and this class of practitioner was best represented (in proportion to the population) in the smaller market towns of the region. In 1841 Bradford, with a population of 37,765, had only one physician, Leeds had fourteen (one to every 10,861 inhabitants) and Wakefield three (one to every 4,918 inhabitants).

Other local factors may also explain the presence of large numbers of medical practitioners. A number of lucrative and prestigious posts, for example, attracted medical men to Wakefield in the early nineteenth century. In 1818 the West Riding Lunatic Asylum opened in Wakefield, and came to provide a number of honorary and paid appointments. Several medical men combined attendance at the Asylum with private practice. The institution expanded several times during the century, offering some full-time paid posts for those intending to specialise in the treatment of insanity. By the mid-nineteenth century approximately one-third of all medical practitioners resident in Wakefield were full-time employees or part-time honorary attendants at the Asylum. Meanwhile, the prison, the House of Recovery, the Dispensary and Infirmary, and a number of smaller charitable enterprises offered paid or honorary medical posts. The number of doctors devoting themselves to full-time private practice in Wakefield was, therefore, much lower than the figures might first suggest. During this period far fewer posts were on offer in Huddersfield. Only the Dispensary, set up in 1814, provided one paid and four honorary medical appointments.

One of the most frequent and serious complaints to crop up amongst nineteenth-century doctors related to the overstocking of the medical profession. Competition for paying patients was keen. As early as 1783 the Huddersfield medical profession was considered to be overcrowded, when R. B. Batty transferred from Huddersfield, where two other surgeon-apothecaries practised, to Dewsbury, where there was no competition.[18] At this time there were just over one thousand inhabitants to each of the three medical practitioners. Dr Simpson of Bradford also complained of this development in 1825.

The medical profession is quite overstocked . . . and since the Peace situations have become very difficult to meet with . . . Compared with trade a profession is good for nothing. There are in Bradford three Physicians and ten Surgeons, besides most of the villages in the vicinity have one Surgeon & some of them two. I don't believe that there is full employment for more than one Physician and six Surgeons . . . We are surrounded by towns filled with Physicians & these at no great distance. Halifax is eight miles off where there are four Physicians, Huddersfield eleven miles and four Physicians, Wakefield fourteen miles & five Physicians, . . . medical men are ill paid here & liable to numerous bad debts. If I had a son to bring up to a profession I certainly should make the choice of the law.[19]

In 1854 a Leeds general practitioner pointed to the problem faced by 'well-taught, talented young surgeons, who are trailing along a dull round of poverty and disappointment', cut off from the 'upper' extreme of practice by the physician, and the 'lower' extreme *and* the middle classes by the quack and prescribing druggist.[20]

Medical practitioners have left little evidence relating to the geographical range or size of their practices. But it seems that few doctors were able to devote themselves to full-time private practice. A small number in each town dominated private practice: Drs Richardson, Crowther and Wright, for example, built up the best medical practices in Wakefield during the nineteenth century. Large numbers of medical men also held honorary or paid appointments, ranging from the prestigious posts of medical officer to the local infirmary through to the more lowly positions of Poor Law medical officer and friendly society surgeon. Most practices also included a certain amount of unpaid medical work amongst the poor. Witnesses to various nineteenth-century parliamentary inquiries into medical relief claimed that most medical men 'expected' to provide some gratuitous medical relief to the poor. Some practitioners even set aside a few hours each week when they would attend the poor gratis (although medicines were probably still charged for). In 1809 Samuel Marshall, surgeon, offered free advice to the poor of Wakefield between 10.00 am and 1.00 pm on Tuesdays and Thursdays. William Rowlandson, also of Wakefield, gave a similar service on Mondays and Fridays in the 1840s.[21] In 1825 the Huddersfield Medical Society went as far as drawing up a scale of charges based on the incomes of patients. Those occupying houses of £30 rental per annum (or upwards) were to be charged not less than 1s each day for visits, those renting houses at between £15 and £30, 6d, and those 'occupying houses at a Rent under fifteen pounds per annum shall be charged for visits or not according to the discretion of the practitioner'.[22]

During the nineteenth century there were three main methods by which a medical men could set himself up in practice.[23] Generally the best situated individuals (as will be demonstrated in Section 7.2) were those who could enter the practice of their father or other relatives, or those able to marry into a medical family. Those without family connections had to buy a medical practice or set up a new practice, ideally in an area where there was little competition. Practices, which could cost as much as several hundred pounds, were purchased from medical men who were about to retire or move to another area. The newly-arrived (and frequently newly-qualified) practitioner took the practice in good faith, hoping to inherit patients and a 'good professional reputation'. In 1809 when Richard Milner, surgeon, purchased his second practice, that of the late Mr Holdsworth, he placed the following advertisement in the Wakefield press:

R MILNER.
MEMBER OF THE ROYAL COLLEGE OF SURGEONS
IN LONDON
BEGS Leave to inform the Inhabitants of Wakefield and the Vicinity, that he has taken the House in Kirkgate, lately occupied by Mr. HOLDS-WORTH, Surgeon, etc; and respectfully Solicits the Support of the Public in general, and of the late Mr. Holdsworth's Friends in particular.
Mr. Milner has been in Practice at Sherburn since January 1802 – to which Neighbourhood, he can, with Pleasure, refer for his Professional Character.[24]

Milner's career progressed well in Wakefield. He remained there until his death in 1825, and his son William R. Milner also practised successfully in the town. W. R. Milner was appointed apothecary to the Dispensary in 1832 and resident surgeon to the House of Correction in the 1840s. He also acted as Secretary to the Wakefield Medical Society during the mid-nineteenth century.[25] In 1822 Mr Rutter took over the practice of the late Mr Birkett, surgeon. In advertising his intention of setting himself up in the town, Mr Rutter begged

. . . to inform the Inhabitants of WAKEFIELD and its Vicinity, especially those who so liberally supported his Predecessor, that he has commenced the Practice of SURGEON, APOTHECARY, and MIDWIFERY, in all their Branches, in the House lately occupied by Mr. B., and trusts he shall be found worthy to receive a continuance of their Patronage.[26]

Another way of obtaining a practice, or rather a share in a practice, at a smaller cost and at less risk was to form a partnership, preferably with an established medical practitioner. A partnership offered the young practitioner an effective means of introduction and a chance to obtain some experience; for the older, established man a means of lessening his workload. In 1831, for example, articles of agreement were drawn up between George and William Holdsworth, who became partners in equal proportions in the 'business or profession of a Surgeon & Apothecary & Accoucheur' for a period of seven years. The partnership was dissolved in 1837 'by mutual consent'.[27] There are numerous examples of partnerships in the two towns, especially for the first half of the nineteenth century (when the profession was most overstocked): in Wakefield, for example, between Stott and W. Walker, surgeon-apothecaries, during the first two decades of the century, and in the late 1820s between Stott and Dunn, R. Milner and Bennett in the 1820s, and Dawson and Heald in the 1830s and early 1840s. Most partnerships were dissolved amicably after a few years, the younger partners then setting up in practice alone, frequently in the same town. After riding out the first few difficult years in practice with a partner, many of these individuals achieved some success. Dunn and Bennett both had successful practices in the town, Bennett also being appointed surgeon to the Wakefield Asylum.[28]

The rise of the general practitioner (and consultant?)
The above examples indicate that by early in the nineteenth century medical practitioners were offering their services in more than one branch of medicine. Traditionally medical historians have relied upon a tripartite classification into physicians, surgeons and apothecaries as a framework for the analysis of the medical profession.

The medical profession in early nineteenth-century England consisted, in brief, of three distinctly organised, legally defined status groups practicing 'the profession of physic', 'the craft of surgery', and the 'apothecary's trade'.[29]

Even if this was a precise definition for the eighteenth century, and this indeed is highly questionable,[30] by very early in the nineteenth century it had ceased to be a useful guide for explaining either the structure of the profession or the activities of its members. The three licensing bodies of the Royal Colleges of Physicians and Surgeons and the Society of Apothecaries had little relevance to the majority of medical practitioners, particularly those residing in the provinces. The number of licensed physicians, for example, was insignificant. In 1800 there was a total of only 179 Fellows, Licentiates and Extra-Licentiates in England. By 1847 this number had increased to 683, but even then licensed physicians accounted for less than 5 per cent of all medical men in England. Only 23 per cent of provincial physicians had bothered to affiliate themselves with the College by 1850.[31] A larger number of practitioners held surgical licences – 8,000 by the mid-nineteenth century, and the LSA – between 1815 and 1834 approximately 7,000 were granted.[32] The controlling councils of all three bodies, however, were dominated by small, powerful and self-interested élites, which throughout the century made little or no effort to represent the interests of the majority of the medical profession.

The law continued to recognise the three groups as distinct entities, and the tasks these groups were supposed to perform were strictly defined. The practice of physicians, for example, was held to be

. . . properly confined to the prescribing of medicines to be compounded by the apothecary, and in superintending operations performed by surgeons in order to prescribe what was necessary to the general health of the patient, or to counteract any internal disease.[33]

But by very early in the nineteenth century few medical men could afford the luxury of confining themselves to one branch of practice. The 'general practitioner', who combined medical advice with surgical practice, and in some cases pharmacy and midwifery, was becoming commonplace, especially in the provinces. Irvine Loudon has suggested that the traditional divisions between medical men already meant little in the eighteenth century 'because the type of practice adopted by an individual was dictated most of all by the competition and opportunities for business in his chosen area of practice'.[34] As early as 1783 the majority (82.3 per cent) of medical men listed in the *Medical Register* were described as 'surgeon-apothecaries'. In Yorkshire there were 233 surgeon-apothecaries (79 per cent) compared with 42 physicians, eight 'surgeons only' and eleven 'apothecaries only'.[35]

The continuing rise in the number of general practitioners in the early nineteenth century could be seen in part at least as resulting from the rapid overall increase in the number of medical personnel during the same period. Competition for patients became keen, and, unable to survive through the practice of one branch of medicine, the doctor was forced to diversify. In 1813 it was estimated that there were approximately 12,000 general practitioners in England and Wales;[36] by 1834 the figure was put at between 12,000 and 14,000 (or about one general practitioner to 1,000 inhabitants compared with one to 2,280 in 1974).[37] Witnesses to the Select Commmittees of 1834 and 1847–1848 on medical education and registration testified to the fact that there were hardly any medical men, even in London, who could confine their practices to pure medicine or surgery. In his evidence to the 1834 inquiry John Yelloly, MD, LRCP and former physician to the London Hospital, stated:

In London, the number of well-employed physicians is exceedingly small; and in the country, the largest towns have hardly more than two or three who are very well employed; so that whether employment of physicians has diminished or not of late years, it is perfectly clear that the general practitioner has infinitely the much largest part of the practice, both in London and in the country.[38]

Medical historians now tend to agree with the contention that the most important structural and practical change to take place during the late eighteenth and nineteenth centuries was the replacement of the 'pure' physician, surgeon and apothecary by the general practitioner of medicine[39] (or in contemporary terminology the 'surgeon–apothecary'[40]). This development towards general practice was aided by two major legislative landmarks, the Apothecaries' Act of 1815 and the 1858 Medical Act. The 1858 Act in particular marked a concrete step towards creating more uniform standards of qualification and practice. The setting up of the Medical Register in 1858 established the concept of equal recognition of all regular practitioners before the law; the surgeon and apothecary became formally assimilated with the higher-status physician. The General Medical Council, also a product of the Act, began to busy itself with raising standards of education and regulating recruitment to the profession.[41] The education of students in hospitals and medical schools gradually improved during the nineteenth century. More demanding and realistic examinations became the rule as medical practitioners began to qualify in more branches of medicine.

Ivan Waddington has added a further dimension to the analysis of the structure of the nineteenth-century medical profession. He has proposed that the old tripartite division was slowly replaced by a new professional structure, based on a differentiation between general practitioners and consultants.[42] The growth of hospitals in the eighteenth and nineteenth centuries, he suggests, gave rise to a new class of consulting physicians and surgeons, who enjoyed many advantages over their colleagues without hospital posts. Consultants were able to attract large numbers of paying pupils, and their incomes from teaching alone could be considerable. Their ex-students, once established in practice, frequently passed on wealthy clients for consultations with their old teachers. Moreover, consultants were provided with a golden opportunity to become medical advisors to lay governors, their families and connections. As an additional bonus, the consultant had access to a large amount of 'clinical material' in the form of hospital patients, in an age when scientific research was becoming an increasingly important and prestigious activity. Not only, Waddington suggests, were consultants able to build up the best practices; they also came to dominate the key political offices, including the licensing bodies.

Qualifications were important indicators of structural change within the medical profession. Ideally from the best universities and hospitals, they could confer status on the medical practitioner and influence the size and quality of his practice. The title 'doctor' was especially sought after by both patients and practitioners. Overall, Wakefield and Huddersfield medical practitioners seem to have acquired a wider range and apparently higher standard of qualifications during the nineteenth century. After 1815 all medical men who wished to practise generally were required by law to take the examination of the Society of Apothecaries.[43] Many practitioners obtained a double qualification from the College of Surgeons and Society of Apothecaries. In 1834 3,500 members of the College of Surgeons (England) also held the LSA.[44] By 1848 it was estimated that there were between 14,000 and 15,000 general practitioners in England and Wales: more than half of these possessed the double qualification.[45] By 1851 over half of the medical practitioners in Wakefield and Huddersfield held a surgical diploma and the LSA. A further 10 per cent held a triple qualification.[46]

Information on the qualifications of medical men in the first decades of the nineteenth century is patchy. However, it is safe to suggest that up until circa 1815 it was usual for doctors to qualify in only one branch of medicine, even if they intended to become active in more than one branch. The majority of medical men in Wakefield and Huddersfield qualifying before 1815 held only a single qualification. Medical practitioners such as William Turnbull of Huddersfield, who graduated from Edinburgh University in 1814 as MD and became a Licentiate of the Royal College of Surgeons, Edinburgh, in the same year, are rare.[47] By the mid-nineteenth century the picture was very different. The wider variety of qualifications acquired by medical practitioners in the two towns began to reflect the range of medical tasks they intended to undertake. By 1851 approximately three-quarters of all medical practitioners in Wakefield and Huddersfield had acquired the LSA, an indication of the numbers practising generally. Over 80 per cent held a surgical diploma and 25 per cent a medical degree or physician's licence. By 1851 a minority of practitioners were qualified in just one branch of medicine. The most usual combination of qualifications was the LSA and a surgical diploma, which were held by over half of the medical men in both towns.[48] (See Tables 7.3(a) and (b).)

The results of a survey of the qualifications of Wakefield and Huddersfield medical practitioners for the years 1851, 1861 and 1871, showing the number of individuals holding each qualification and combinations of qualifications, are given in Tables 7.3(a) and (b). Between 1851 and 1871 the percentage of practitioners obtaining the LSA declined in both towns. The number holding a surgical diploma of some kind remained fairly constant, although the number of Licentiates and Fellows grew, especially in Wakefield. By 1871 more medical men had obtained a medical degree or a licence to practise medicine, particularly in Huddersfield, where the number of individuals with an MD or MB grew from four to eleven between 1851 and 1871. Many medical men acquired additional medical licences after they had been in practice for some years, hoping to improve their status and practices. The Licentiate of the Royal College of Physicians or an MD from a university not requiring residence were typical 'mid-career' qualifications. An increasing number of Wakefield and Huddersfield practitioners also acquired a Licence in Midwifery (the LM).

By the second half of the nineteenth century double or triple qualifications had largely replaced the single qualification to practise. Early nineteenth-century physicians, such as Drs Amory, Richardson and Crowther of Wakefield, with MDs from Cambridge and Edinburgh, for example, were replaced by individuals such as Dr Thomas Giordani Wright, LSA (1830, University College, London, and Edinburgh), MD (1831, Edinburgh and Ludg. Batavia), MRCS (1831, London), LRCP (1841, London), MRCP (1859, London).[49] In terms of the number of examinations passed and affiliation to the Royal Colleges, Wakefield and Huddersfield medical men appeared to be better and more widely qualified in 1871[50] than they had been at the beginning of the century or even twenty years before.[51]

The possession of certain qualifications did not necessarily indicate the nature of each individual's medical practice. For instance, Samuel Holdsworth of Wakefield obtained the double qualification of MRCS and LSA, the 'insignia' of a general practitioner, in 1835. Between 1836 and 1839 he served as house surgeon to the Wakefield Dispensary. In 1839 he obtained an MD from the University of Pisa. Despite the fact that he held qualifications in all three branches of medicine, Holdsworth described himself as a 'physician', and indeed was appointed as honorary physician to the Wakefield Dispensary and Infirmary in 1863.[52] The reverse was also common; medical men qualified in just one or two branches of medicine acted as general practitioners, combining surgery, medicine, pharmacy and midwifery, although not legally entitled to do so. Surgeons, lacking a licence to practise medicine, trespassed on the physician's preserve. Meanwhile, physicians undertook small surgical operations as part of their everyday practice.

By the early nineteenth century Wakefield and Huddersfield medical men were combining a wide range of tasks in their practices. In the first decades of the century Messrs Mitchell and Birkett functioned as 'surgeon–apothecaries and druggists', and in 1833 Mr Strafford advertised his services as 'Surgeon, Apothecary and Accoucheur' in the *Wakefield and Halifax Journal*.[53] A number of individuals combined medical practice with a chemist's business. In 1809, for example, M. Barber, Surgeon, etc., took

... the earliest opportunity of informing his Friends and the Inhabitants of Wakefield and its Vicinity, that he has studied SURGERY AND THE PRACTICE OF PHYSIC, in London, for several Years, under the ablest medical Professors, and having since had the Advantage of seeing extensive Practice, apprehends that his medical knowledge IN EVERY DEPARTMENT OF HIS PROFESSION, and his unremitting Attention, will secure the Confidence of those who may place themselves under his Care (his emphasis).

Table 7.3(a). *The qualifications of Wakefield medical practitioners, 1851, 1861 and 1871. (Number and percentage of medical practitioners holding qualifications in each branch of medicine.[a])*

Qualification	1851	1861	1871
LSA (LAH)	19 (73)	24 (80)	20 (65)
MRCS	22	28	19
LRCS	1	1	6
FRCS	—	2	3
Total	22 (85)	28 (93)	27 (87)
MD	5	6	7
MB	1	1	2
MRCP	—	2	2
LRCP	—	5	6
Extra LRCP	2	1	1
FRCP	—	1	1
LKQCP Ireland	—	1	1
LFPSG[b]	—	—	1
Total	7 (27)	10 (33)	14 (45)
LM	1 (4)	2 (7)	5 (16)
Combinations of qualifications:			
LSA and surgical diploma	14 (54)	17 (57)	12 (39)
LSA and MD or licence in physic	1 (4)	1 (3)	1 (3)
Licences in physic and surgery	1 (4)	2 (7)	3 (10)
Triple qualification to practise	3 (11)	6 (20)	7 (22)
Single qualifications:			
LSA	1 (4)	0	0
Surgical diploma	4 (15)	3 (10)	5 (16)
MD or licence in physic	2 (8)	1 (3)	3 (10)
Number in practice prior to 1815	3	1	0
Total number of medical practitioners surveyed	26 (100)	30 (100)	31 (100)

Table 7.3(b). *The qualifications of Huddersfield medical practitioners,
1851, 1861 and 1871. (Number and percentage of medical practitioners
holding qualifications in each branch of medicine.[a])*

Qualification	1851	1861	1871
LSA (LAH)	16 (76)	20 (74)	15 (58)
MRCS	16	16	13
LRCS	1	3	5
FRCS	—	1	—
Total	17 (81)	22 (81)	20 (77)
MD	4	7	9
MB	—	1	2
MRCP	—	1	1
LRCP	—	1	3
Extra LRCP	1	1	1
FRCP	1	—	—
LFPSG[b]	1	1	3
Chir. Coll. P & S, New York[b]	—	1	—
Total	5 (24)	9 (33)	13 (50)
LM	1 (5)	1 (4)	3 (12)
Combinations of qualifications:			
LSA and surgical diploma	12 (57)	16 (59)	11 (42)
LSA and MD or licence in physic	0	3 (11)	3 (11.5)
Licences in physic and surgery	1 (5)	3 (11)	6 (23)
Triple qualification to practise	2 (9.5)	1 (4)	1 (4)
Single qualifications:			
LSA	2 (9.5)	0	0
Surgical diploma	2 (9.5)	2 (7.5)	2 (8)
MD or licence in physic	2 (9.5)	2 (7.5)	3 (11.5)
Number in practice prior to 1815	3	2	1
Total number of medical practitioners surveyed	21 (100)	27 (100)	26 (100)

[a] Some practitioners held double qualifications in one branch of medicine:
for example, an MD (Edinburgh) and LRCP (London), or MRCS (England) and LRCS (Edinburgh).
[b] Counted as both a qualification in medicine and surgery.
Sources: Provincial Medical Directories, 1852–1872; Census Enumerators'
Books, Wakefield and Huddersfield, 1841, 1851, 1861 and 1871. For
details of medical licensing bodies and licences and degrees, see Appendix
9.

In 1810 M. Barber took over his late father's chemist's shop, adding the dispensing trade to his other lines of business.[54] Many general practitioners followed the old tradition of charging for medicines only well into the nineteenth century. The pharmaceutical side of the GP's business was often the most lucrative; midwifery, meanwhile, was generally regarded as the most time-consuming and worst-paid aspect of general practice. The combination of medical practice with the chemist's trade tended to decline slightly during the late nineteenth century.[55] But the practice of combining other branches of medicine continued.

Changes in nomenclature reflected developments in structure, although these tended to lag far behind practical changes. In particular medical men clung to the designations 'physician' and 'surgeon' long after they had become obsolete in describing the tasks they undertook (and these divisions continued to be used in trade directories for much of the nineteenth century). By early in the nineteenth century the description 'apothecary' had ceased to be used in trade and medical directories, and appeared only rarely in census returns (often referring, in fact, to unqualified individuals).[56] All Wakefield and Huddersfield medical men were classified in the 1841 census enumerators' books as 'physicians' or 'surgeons'. By 1851 the majority of medical men described themselves in the returns as 'general practitioners': two-thirds in Huddersfield and over a half in Wakefield. Those not in general practice now felt it necessary to state otherwise. Expressions such as 'practising as a physician' and 'consulting physician' were used to stress the purity of their practices.[57] This was especially the case for those medical men with honorary hospital appointments, which were in theory the preserve of 'pure' physicians and surgeons.[58]

The rise of the general practitioner has been closely linked to a widening demand for medical care on the part of the expanding middle class. While this group were unable to afford the fees charged by pure physicians and surgeons, they did demand qualified medical attention. George Birkbeck (by profession a physician) claimed in his evidence to the 1834 Select Committee that there was a tendency by the 'greater part' of the public to employ general practitioners. This he attributed to the better education of general practitioners, and to a change in the condition of society, which had become averse to the division of labour, and sought assistance in one individual, rather than the more expensive form of three.[59] The general practitioner, combining medical and surgical care, and frequently throwing in the services of dispenser and midwife, appealed to both the middle-class mentality and budget.[60] The middle-class populations of Wakefield and Huddersfield provided an important pool of custom for the general practitioner; a rather lesser source of clients for the more specialised consulting physicians or surgeons.

Middle- (and upper-) class families tended to rely for much of their medical treatment on general practitioners, although they were prepared to call in a specialised attendant in more severe cases of illness or where a second opinion was required. Clara Clarkson, a wealthy Wakefield spinster, for example, employed members of the Walker family, surgeons of Wakefield, for many years. Later in life Dr T. G. Wright became her regular medical attendant.[61] Early in the nineteenth century the Lees, prosperous Wakefield solicitors, employed Messrs Stott and Walker and Messrs Milner and Bennett, general practitioners, as family doctors. A bill paid to Stott and Walker in 1816 included payments for medicines, surgical attendance, inoculation and a tooth extraction! Payments were made to Milner and Bennett for the years 1822 to 1824 for pills, medicines, embrocations, plasters and for bleeding. The Lees also employed Dr W. H. Gilby to attend them after his arrival in Wakefield in 1825, helping him obtain a foothold in the town.[62] Between 1870 and 1884 Mr Whitely of Wakefield (himself a surgeon) employed a number of general practitioners, including William Statter and Thomas Walker, to attend upon his family. In most cases payments covered both surgical and medical attendance. In 1884 he also called in Dr T. G. Wright for a series of consultations.[63]

As Waddington himself suggests, his thesis would seem to have rather less relevance to smaller provincial towns, such as Wakefield or Huddersfield, where there was little chance of a doctor being able to confine himself to consulting work alone. Honorary dispensary and infirmary appointments did offer medical men the chance to build up a clientele from the lay officers and subscribers and their connections, but, as shown in Chapter 4, most of the support for medical charities came from middle-class groups, who were probably unwilling and even unable to expend large sums on medical care. What this potential client group demanded from their medical advisors (just like the rest of the middle class) were not the specialised services of consulting physicians and surgeons, but the more general range of services provided by a family doctor.

The practice of passing patients on to ex-teachers was also less common in smaller provincial towns. Few students and apprentices were trained at the medical charities of Wakefield and Huddersfield during the nineteenth century; in most cases only one or two at a time. Those who were taken on usually became the responsibility of the resident house surgeon, rather than the honorary physicians and surgeons, who after all only attended at the institutions once or twice a week. A large proportion of the pupils taken by the Wakefield and Huddersfield Infirmaries did not even complete their terms of apprenticeship, and when they did complete their training, they often moved to other towns to practise.[64] The fees for apprentices, meanwhile (which were quite high – about £150 for a three-year term at the Huddersfield Infirmary by mid-century), went directly to the charity's funds, rather than to the medical staff.

This is not to say that hospital appointments served no useful purpose. The small amount of consulting work available in the two towns was probably monopolised by the honorary medical appointees. Those who obtained these posts gained a stamp of approval from the lay governors and were automatically raised to a higher status than their professional brethren.[65] They were in many cases able to build up the best local practices. Honorary appointees also had far more access to clinical material than other practitioners and were able to gain reputations for expertise in specialised fields. What we find in effect is a group of medical practitioners, who, while not detaching themselves completely from other branches of medicine, by dint of their qualifications and honorary posts, were able to concentrate more on a consulting practice.[66]

Appointments

Clearly some form of medical hierarchy existed in provincial towns such as Wakefield and Huddersfield, but to make a hard and fast division into a consulting group with honorary hospital posts and ordinary general practitioners does not appear to be feasible or useful. Hospital appointments did, however, offer more practice-building opportunities than other posts, and were much sought after. Medical men themselves stressed the importance of obtaining them in order to succeed in private practice. When the Huddersfield Dispensary was set up in 1814 there was an undignified scramble amongst the town's medical men for posts. Mr Wilks, who was appointed senior surgeon to the charity, was strongly urged by a Halifax colleague, John Thomson, to apply for the position. Thomson claimed that those doctors who failed to get elected 'would rue the day as long as their professional life lasts'.[67] Similarly, in 1823 a 'sharp contest' took place for the two newly-created surgical posts to the Wakefield Dispensary. Messrs J. Horsfall and W. Dawson were appointed, obtaining 153 and 130 votes. The unlucky candidates, Messrs Bennett and Marshall, polled 76 and 62 votes respectively.[68]

What medical historians, preoccupied with the benefits of hospital appointments, have failed to point out is that a wide range of other employment opportunities existed for medical practitioners, offering prestige, salaries, or both, and giving a variety of practice-building opportunities. Even in smaller provincial communities such as Wakefield and Huddersfield there were a large, and through the nineteenth century a growing, number of openings as army, police and prison doctors, surgeons to factories, railway and mining companies, medical referees to assurance societies, certifying factory surgeons, friendly society surgeons and Poor Law medical officers (see Table 7.4). While the figures given in Table 7.4 are probably subject to inaccuracies, they do indicate an impressive increase in the number of posts available between 1828 and 1871, from sixteen to 40 in Wakefield and seven to 38 in Huddersfield.

Smaller (and not necessarily medical) charities in some cases appointed honorary medical officers. For example, the Wakefield Town Mission appointed a succession of medical officers to treat sick persons encountered while undertaking missionary work from its initiation in 1840. Dr Crowther was appointed the first consulting physician, Messrs E. Walker and Son the first gratuitous surgeons.[69] In 1861 Mr Samuel Knaggs, Esq. was elected honorary surgeon to the newly-opened Huddersfield and District Ragged and Industrial School.[70] In Wakefield the House of Recovery and Asylum offered further status-conferring honorary appointments and salaried posts. Other prestigious openings were created for medical men within the volunteer movement, which brought them into direct contact with leading local families. In 1860, for example, Frederick Greenwood was appointed honorary surgeon to the Huddersfield Rifle Corps. Other officers to be elected at the same time included T. P. Crosland, Esq. (gentleman and later MP for Huddersfield) as Captain, and the Thomas Brooks of Colne Villa and Northgate House (important local cloth manufacturers) as Lieutenants.[71] Greenwood had a long and important association with the volunteer movement in Huddersfield, becoming Lieutenant-Colonel of the 6th Huddersfield Volunteer Corps in 1868.

While friendly society and Poor Law posts did not confer much

Table 7.4. *Medical appointments in Wakefield and Huddersfield, 1828, 1851 and 1871.*

Appointments	Wakefield			Huddersfield		
	1828	1851	1871	1828	1851	1871
Number of medical practitioners (in Townships)	21	26	17	14	21	21
Honorary dispensary and infirmary posts[a]	7	11	5	5	6	7
Salaried dispensary and infirmary posts	2	2	2	1	1	3
Honorary asylum posts	3	4	2	0	0	0
Resident, salaried asylum posts	2	2	5	0	0	0
Poor Law medical appointments	1	2	3	1	3	4
Certifying factory surgeons	0	1	2	0	3	1
Surgeons to factories, mining and railway companies	0	0	6	0	0	2
Prison surgeons (salaried visiting and resident posts)	1	2	2	0	1	2
Police surgeons	0	0	2	0	0	3
Army surgeons	0	1	2	0	0	3
Assurance society referees	0	0	2	0	1	7
Friendly society appointments	0	1	2	0	1	3
Honorary medical attendant to charities	0	2	4	0	1	2
Municipal posts	0	1	1	0	0	1 (1873)
Total number of posts[b]	16	29	40	7	17	38

[a] In Wakefield including posts at the House of Recovery and Eye Dispensary.
[b] Returns to the *Medical Directories* were notoriously incomplete, and in all likelihood many of the totals are underestimates of the true number of posts (in particular for the category of friendly society appointments and for surgeons to factories and assurance societies).
Sources: Parson and White, 1828; White, 1853, 1870; *Provincial Medical Directories*, 1852, 1872.

in the way of material benefits or prestige, they provided footholds into medical practice and were seen as suitable openings for young general practitioners.[72] Appointment to the paid post of house surgeon to the local dispensaries and infirmaries provided a better opening, especially for young men. These posts also offered reasonable salaries (although they were regarded as 'full time'): in the 1830s the house surgeon to the Wakefield Dispensary was paid £80 per annum, by the 1870s £125.[73] Of more importance, these posts provided the newly-qualified practitioner with valuable practical experience and gave him a means of introduction to medical practice in the town. Upon terminating their appointments as house surgeon (usually after a period of about three years), many individuals established themselves in practice in Wakefield or Huddersfield. Often they were appointed to honorary posts at a later date.

For example, Thomas Abbey Bottomley qualified in 1851 and served as house surgeon to the Huddersfield Infirmary from 1851 to 1855. Afterwards he set up in practice in the town, and in 1865 was elected honorary surgeon to the Infirmary. Similarly in 1869, Thomas Brewer, former house surgeon to the Huddersfield Infirmary (1863–1868), was appointed to the post of honorary surgeon.[74] Others moved on to other towns to practise, often with some success. William Oxley obtained his first appointment as house surgeon to the Huddersfield Infirmary in 1856. He tendered his resignation in 1863, when the death of a relative gave him the opportunity of entering private practice in Rotherham. In the 1860s he was elected honorary surgeon to the Rotherham Dispensary.[75] Between 1867 and 1871 Lawson Tait, who later became famous for his obstetric surgery, and opposition to Lister, spent a beneficial period as house surgeon to the Wakefield Dispensary and Infirmary, after qualifying in Edinburgh in 1866 (LRCS). He had 'a mass of surgical material' at his disposal in Wakefield and took on the bulk of the operating. During this period Tait published prolifically on a wide range of surgical subjects and began to lay the foundations of his reputation as a surgeon of considerable talent. Incidentally, while in Wakefield Tait was called out in consultations as far away as Castleford, and apparently practised as both a physician and surgeon.[76]

Other posts, while perhaps offering less in the way of prestige or practice-building opportunities, provided a steady, and sometimes large, source of income. One such post was that of visiting surgeon to the Wakefield House of Correction. As early as 1814 it was resolved that William Walker should be allowed a salary of £120 per annum for attendance on prisoners plus £80 for medicines. By 1842 the surgeon's salary had been fixed at £250 per annum. In 1857 it was raised to £300, a considerable income by mid-nineteenth century standards.[77] This figure compared very favourably with other paid medical posts. In the mid-1850s a salary of only £40 per annum was paid to the Union officer for the Wakefield Township (which included payment for medicines!).[78] Henry Dunn served as visiting surgeon to the House of Correction for thirty years, receiving a salary of £250 per annum. Despite this commitment, he still had sufficient time to build up a respectable private practice and to serve as honorary surgeon to the House of Recovery.

Several medical men in Wakefield and Huddersfield (particularly those who acquired honorary appointments) were able to accumulate a large number of posts. William James Clarke of Huddersfield, for example, served as honorary surgeon to the Infirmary from 1853. He was also employed as medical officer to the South District of the Huddersfield Township and as surgeon to the County Police and Huddersfield Prison. In the early nineteenth century Dr William Thomas served as honorary physician to the Wakefield Dispensary, the House of Recovery and the Asylum, and as visiting physician to the House of Correction. William Dean of Slaithwaite, near Huddersfield, obtained posts as medical officer (at a salary of £30 per annum) and Registrar of Births and Deaths for the Slaithwaite District of the Huddersfield Union, as police surgeon, army surgeon, medical officer to several friendly societies and as medical referee to the Royal Assurance Company. In the 1850s Henry Horsfall of Wakefield was appointed medical officer to the Union Workhouse (at a salary of £25 per annum), surgeon to the headquarters of the West Riding Constabulary and medical officer to the Hatfield Collieries. During the 1860s Mr William Wood served as visiting surgeon to the Wakefield House of Correction and West Riding House of Refuge, as certifying factory surgeon, medical officer to the Lancashire and Yorkshire and the Manchester, Sheffield and Lincolnshire Railway Companies, and as medical referee to numerous assurance societies.[79]

A small number of medical practitioners, usually those who had already built up a practice and reputation, created their own appointments by setting up medical institutions. These could be either profit-making establishments or charitable enterprises. In 1855, for instance, Dr James George Atkinson of Wakefield set up a private asylum at Stanley, near Wakefield, for 'the care and education of persons of imperfect and defective intellect'.[80] Atkinson served as physician to the Wakefield Dispensary and Infirmary and the Wakefield Eye Dispensary over the same period, and presumably these appointments assisted him in his efforts to attract well-off paying patients to his establishment. The Eye Dispensary was itself established solely on the initiative of another Wakefield medical man, John Horsfall, Esq., surgeon to the Wakefield Dispensary. Horsfall set up the Eye Dispensary in 1841 'for the Relief of Poor Persons afflicted with Diseases of the Eye'. Horsfall styled himself 'Consulting Surgeon' and was assisted in his venture by his Dispensary colleague, Dr Atkinson, and by Mr Burrell, surgeon. Eye operations were performed and medicines dispensed gratuitously every Monday and Friday from 12.00 pm to 1.00 pm at the Eye Dispensary. The Vicar of Wakefield was President of the charity, and he, along with other Wakefield clergymen, dispensed recommendations for treatment.[81] Although Horsfall may well have based his venture on altruistic motives, he also obtained some practical benefits. In return for a few hours' work each week, he gained a reputation as something of a specialist and as a person of benevolence. He also gained access to a potential client group of clergymen and ministers.

By the mid-nineteenth century legal and structural developments, changes in medical education and qualifications and in the pool of custom and medical posts had brought the general practitioner very much to the fore. The number of honorary medical posts did not increase by much during the nineteenth century; nor had the limited amount of consulting work available in provincial towns such as Wakefield and Huddersfield given rise to a distinct, specialised class of consultants. Few medical men could honestly describe themselves as 'pure' consulting physicians or surgeons. Indeed, the number of honorary posts in Wakefield actually decreased significantly during the mid-nineteenth century, following the closure of the Fever Hospital (1854) and the turnover of the Asylum largely to paid staff, and this factor (together with the general fall off in the number of medical men qualifying) may explain the decline in the number of medical practitioners in the town after 1850. A wide range of other medical posts, however, had become available, which, while offering less in terms of prestige, provided salaries and practice-building opportunities. (See Table 7.4.) These posts, which typically demanded the services of an 'all-rounder', together with the increased middle-class demand for medical care, encouraged the development of the general practitioner of medicine.

However, wide divergences still existed between medical practitioners: their qualifications, appointments, and the size and quality of their practices. To lump them together under the category 'general practitioner' is just as misleading as to label them according to the tripartite classification. The medical men of Wakefield and Huddersfield could be seen as being ranged along a scale determined by their education, qualifications, appointments and practices (and, as will be demonstrated in the next Section, by their social status and family background). At the top end of the scale a few medical men in each town were able to build up practices which combined consulting work with attendance as family doctor on the wealthiest local families. Typically these men would monopolise the most important honorary appointments (and as will be shown in Chapter 8, they hung on to them for many years). In Wakefield, for example, this group included Drs William Thomas and Thomas Giordani Wright, honorary physicians to the Dispensary, Fever Hospital and Asylum, who combined attendance at these institutions with two of the best local practices.

Further down the scale were those who built up successful practices based on the expanding middle-class market, who perhaps held posts as prison, police, army or certifying factory surgeons or as assurance society medical referees. This grouping were likely to hold the double qualification of MRCS/LSA, in some cases adding a mid-career MD, a Licence or a Fellowship to augment their status and practices. Towards the bottom end of the scale were those holding the worst-remunerated Poor Law and friendly society appointments, which, while seen as suitable openings for young men, could also be regarded as 'dead end' jobs for the older practitioner. These individuals would usually be less well qualified and have a smaller share in the middle-class market, perhaps confining their practices to a predominantly lower middle- and working-class clientele.[82]

7.2 Social characteristics

The social characteristics of medical men, as might be expected, mirrored the occupational characteristics discussed in the first Section. The two sets of characteristics in fact acted very much upon each other. Wealth and social background influenced the kind of education a medical man could afford and the type of practice he would enter. In turn, the quality of his qualifications, practice and appointments determined income, lifestyle and social prestige. It was a cycle few medical men could break out of, and in Wakefield and Huddersfield medical practice appeared to fulfil a status-maintaining role, rather than being a means of upward social mobility. Several criteria which could tell us something of the living standards of Wakefield and Huddersfield medical men will be discussed in this Section, including household structure, servant employment, place and type of residence, and income levels. Although most of this group could be labelled 'middle class', there were significant variations in the social and financial positions of medical men in the two towns.

The lifestyles of doctors were in most (although not in all) cases dictated by their incomes from medical practice. A few individuals blessed with large private means (as shall be shown later) had no pecuniary motives for taking up the profession of medicine. Data relating to the living standards of all qualified medical men residing within the township boundaries of Wakefield and Huddersfield have been extracted from the census enumerators' returns for 1841, 1851, 1861 and 1871. The data collected were arranged in a form similar to that used by Brown in his analysis of Bristol medical men, as recorded in the census enumerators' books of 1851.[83] The sample resulting from this collection of information for Wakefield and Huddersfield medical practitioners was small, and the data could be reproduced in two tables (Tables 7.5 and 7.6).

Household structure
Table 7.5 gives details of household size and the position of the medical practitioner in the household, as head or otherwise. It also outlines the structure of households, following Laslett's definitions.[84] Over 20 per cent of all the doctors surveyed were single and resided alone, while a small number lived with usually unmarried siblings. The remainder were members of families. Sixty per cent of the doctors surveyed lived in simple families (that is, they were married, with or without children) and 10 per cent in extended families (with the addition of parents, aunts, grandchildren, nephews or nieces to the household). Most doctors presided over small households with four or less members, although the samples did include several large families, such as those of Dr T. G. Wright of Wakefield and Mr Samuel Booth of Huddersfield, who both had nine offspring living at home during the mid-nineteenth century.[85] The majority of medical practitioners (over three-quarters) in both towns, whether married or not, were described in the census returns as heads of households.

A small group of young practitioners resided with their parents.

Table 7.5. *The distribution of household size and the structure of households of Wakefield and Huddersfield medical practitioners, 1841–1871.*

W – Wakefield, H – Huddersfield
M – Married, Un – Unmarried, Wid – Widower
S – Solitary, NF – No Family (co-resident siblings), SF – Simple Family (married couples alone or with children, or widowers with children),
EF – Extended Family, MF – Multiple Family (two or more conjugal family units)

Census		Number of individuals	Relationship to head of household			Number of households of specified size[g]										Mean household size	Marital status			Structure of households				
			Head	Kin of head	Lodger	1	2	3	4	5	6	7	8	9	10+		M	Un	Wid	S	NF	SF	EF	MF
1841	W	22	22[a]	0	0	4	6	3	4	1	1	1	1	0	1	3.82	13	7	2	4	3	12	3	0
	H	18	14	2	2[c]	2	4	4	0	3	1	1	0	1	1	3.75	11	7	2	4	1	8	5	0
1851	W	24	22	0	2[d]	5	4	3	4	2	1	1	1	1	0	3.55	16	6	2	7	0	14	3	0
	H	16	12	2[b]	2[c]	0	3	4	2	1	1	1	1	0	1	4.50	12	2	2	1	1	12	2	0
1861	W	18	16	1	1[c]	3	3	2	2	3	1	1	0	0	2	4.41	11	5	2	4	1	12	1	0
	H	25	22	0	3[c]	3	2	4	5	3	2	2	1	0	0	4.00	16	7	2	6	2	15	1	1
1871	W	18	14	2	2[c]	2	2	4	2	2	3	0	0	0	1	4.00	11	5	2	4	1	11	2	0
	H	23	19	0	4[f]	2	4	7	0	1	2	1	1	1	0	3.79	13	6	4	6	3	13	3	0

[a] Including two medical practitioners, sharing one residence.
[b] Including William Robinson, residing in the household of his father, George Robinson, also a medical practitioner.
[c] Including the Huddersfield Infirmary's resident house surgeon.
[d] The two individuals not classified as heads were the house surgeon to the Wakefield Dispensary and the resident prison surgeon.
[e] One individual classified as a lodger was the Wakefield Infirmary's resident house surgeon.
[f] Including the Huddersfield Infirmary's resident house surgeon and assistant.
[g] Excluding all medical practitioners employed by and resident in institutions, and lodgers.

Source: Census Enumerators' Books, Wakefield and Huddersfield, 1841, 1851, 1861 and 1871. The Table is based on the definitions of household size and composition suggested by Laslett, in P. Laslett, *op. cit.*, pp. 28–32.

Table 7.6. *The number of resident servants employed by Wakefield and Huddersfield medical practitioners, 1841–1871.*

Census		Percentage of doctors employing servants	Number of servants						Mean
			0	1	2	3	4	5+	
1841	W	95	1	7	9	3	2	0	1.9
	H	92	3	3	9	1	0	0	1.5
1851	W	91	2	6	5	6	2	1	2.1
	H	100	0	6	5	3	0	0	2.2
1861	W	100	0	6	2	5	2	2	2.5
	H	91	2	8	7	5	0	0	1.7
1871	W	89	2	4	2	5	2	1	2.3
	H	85	3	3	9	5	0	0	1.8

The survey covered only heads of households and the kin of heads, excluding doctors residing in medical institutions.
Source: As for Table 7.5.

A few other individuals, again usually young men, lived in lodgings. Of the 20 per cent of medical men who resided alone, many were bachelors in their twenties and thirties. In some cases these groups may have chosen not to establish households, or at least not to marry, for reasons of convenience and cost. The data indicate that most doctors eventually married. Out of all the medical practitioners listed on the census returns between 1841 and 1871 approximately 70 per cent were or had been married. A large number of doctors, however, delayed marriage and taking on the responsibility of a family, perhaps wishing first to establish themselves in practice and ensure a stable income.[86] The gap between qualification to practise and marriage was often large. For example, in 1843 Thomas Ross, a Wakefield general practitioner, married Louisa Spawforth, daughter of a London wine merchant. He was then aged forty and had been in practice for almost twenty years. Dr William Thomas of Wakefield, a highly successful practitioner, was 56 when he entered into matrimony for the first time with Lucy Charlotte, the eldest daughter of the late General Sir Samuel Hawkes, GCH. Thomas had himself served as an army surgeon between 1806 and 1821, but by the time of his marriage in 1842 he had been practising in Wakefield for 21 years.[87]. Not all medical men married so well or so late, but for the majority there was a gap of several years between qualification and marriage.

Servant employment: its relation to income

Most doctors residing in Wakefield and Huddersfield employed domestic servants. Table 7.6 shows the number of living-in servants employed by medical practitioners between 1841 and 1871. Overall (with the exception of 1851) throughout the nineteenth century Wakefield medical men hired more servants than their Huddersfield contemporaries, indicating a higher standard of living. Most medical men employed between one and three resident domestics, while a few individuals found the need for four or five.[88] Those with honorary appointments ran the grandest households, employing on average twice the number of servants as medical men without honorary positions. T. G. Wright, honorary visiting physician to the Wakefield Asylum and House of Recovery, employed five servants in his household – a cook, a nursemaid, a housemaid, a waiting maid and a groom. Dr D. B. Kendell, honorary physician to the Wakefield Dispensary and Infirmary, hired four servants – a cook, nurse, housemaid and footman.[89] Beyond a certain level the employment of servants may have indicated a type of 'window dressing', the hiring of servants for prestige rather than practical purposes. The employment of male servants, such as grooms and footmen, in particular entailed a much larger expenditure on the wage's bill.[90]

Employment of domestic servants was not necessarily a close indication of wealth or high social status. By the mid-nineteenth century the number of middle-class families who could afford servants had greatly increased. The rise in the number of domestic servants was in fact much greater than the general population increase in this period. In 1801 there were approximately 100,000 domestic servants; by 1851 the number had risen to 1,300,000.[91] By mid-century Mrs Beeton was able to suggest that a typical middle-class home was not complete without at least three domestics – a cook, a parlourmaid and a nursemaid or housemaid.[92] Some historians of the middle class claim, on the other hand, that most middle-class families were unable to afford three domestics. Rather one general servant would be the norm.[93] The term 'middle class' clearly embraces a wide range of income levels, and it is difficult to suggest what precise criteria typified this group. Most of the doctors surveyed in Wakefield and Huddersfield could be classified as middle class, but the gradations in wealth and status this term covered were large, and this was reflected in the employment of domestic assistance.

The ability of medical men to employ servants could, however, indicate something about their social standing and incomes. *A New System of Practical Domestic Economy*, published in 1823, suggested that a family earning £200 per annum would be in a position to hire one maid, while those with an income of £700 per annum could employ four living-in servants, one man and three maidservants. An increase in income would be followed by a disproportionate increase in expenditure on servants' wages. The annual wage bill for a family with a yearly income of £200 would be in the region of £9 10s (5 per cent of income), while for those with an income of £700 per annum the bill would be about £81 (12 per cent of income).[94] The size of wage bills as a proportion of income did not increase by much during the mid-nineteenth century.

Very little information is available on the incomes of medical men during the nineteenth century.[95] One way in which we could estimate, albeit in a very tentative way, the financial position of doctors is by the number of servants they employed. For example, Dr T. G. Wright, with his five resident domestics, and Dr D. B. Kendell, with four servants, must have had incomes approaching £1,000 and £700 per annum respectively (although part of this may have come from other sources than medical practice). A large number of medical practitioners employed two female domestics, and we could estimate their incomes as being something in the region of £300 per annum. This fits in closely with the estimate of the nineteenth-century statistician, Baxter, who cited £300 as the average a doctor might have left after deducting £100 in expenses from his gross earnings in the late 1860s. £300 would afford a family in an industrial town two servants and a house of about seven rooms.[96] For example, George Holdsworth, surgeon-apothecary and certifying factory surgeon, resided in a small nine-roomed 'mansion' in St John's, one of the most auspicious parts of Wakefield. He employed two female domestic servants and a groom on a part-time basis. His expenditure on servants' wages in the early 1840s was somewhere in the region of £20 per annum, indicating a yearly income of approximately £300.[97]

Further down the scale of status and income were individuals such as W. R. Milner, who, as resident surgeon to the Wakefield House of Correction during the mid-nineteenth century, earned something in the region of £200 per annum. He employed one female servant to take care of himself and an unmarried sister.[98] Towards the bottom end of the scale medical practitioners typically made do with one general servant or housekeeper. Others managed without any resident servants, although these were a minority. And this group may well have employed living-out servants on a daily or weekly basis, which would not be indicated in the census returns. Less well-off medical men frequently relied on the services of their wives, unmarried female relatives and daughters. John Moxon of Huddersfield, for example, who started out in practice in 1823 as a 'surgeon and druggist', appeared at first to have relied on his unmarried sister and a female ward for the fulfilment of household tasks. By 1851, after dropping the dispensing part of his practice, he had prospered sufficiently to be able to afford one resident domestic servant.[99]

The practice of employing resident medical assistants and taking on living-in pupils and apprentices appears to have dwindled by the mid-nineteenth century. Most Wakefield and Huddersfield doctors had no resident assistants, although a few surgeons and general practitioners kept up the practice of apprenticing young men for terms of five or six years.[100] Medical practitioners, however, frequently took an active part in educating sons (or other male relatives) for the profession, taking them on as pupils in their practices. Of the eleven resident pupils recorded in the Wakefield and Huddersfield census enumerators' books for 1861, six were the sons or male relatives of the doctors in question. For example, Robert Hollings, general practitioner, had apprenticed his younger brother, Edwin, and Dr T. G. Wright had taken his eighteen-year-old son, Charles, as his pupil.[101] Otherwise, the traditional living-in apprentice was largely replaced by living-out pupils, who stayed with their families or in lodgings. (Many 'unattached' medical pupils and assistants appear in the census enumerators' books.) Except in the case of family members, taking on students or assistants does not seem to have been a particularly prestigious activity. Rather, it was a source of cheap labour, and, in the case of apprentices, a source of income (often as much as £40 per annum).

Residential patterns

Further indicators of the social status of medical practitioners were place and type of residence. The addresses of Wakefield and Huddersfield doctors were extracted from trade directories and census returns, and using this method it was possible to monitor where medical practitioners chose to live during the nineteenth century. The residential areas chosen by Wakefield and Huddersfield doctors between 1822 and 1870 are shown in Tables 7.7(a) and (b).

Residential patterns in nineteenth-century Wakefield and Huddersfield took very different forms. In Wakefield the pattern for the population as a whole and for medical practitioners was remarkably static. The town did not expand by much during the nineteenth century, and its relatively limited population growth was largely accommodated within the town boundaries that were in existence at the beginning of the century. There was a permanent concentration of doctors in the town centre, usually in the most pleasant areas. Westgate, for example, was already favoured by better-off medical men during the eighteenth century:

. . . at the bottom of Westgate, which is really well built and handsome enough, with a fine outlook . . . , live rich merchants, physicians, etc. . . . [102]

Westgate and Kirkgate, with their advantage of a central location, remained popular with medical men throughout the nineteenth century. During the mid-nineteenth century Southgate and South Parade were developed as highly sought-after residential areas, and many doctors, especially the more prosperous, took up residence there.

The residential patterns of medical men in Wakefield and Huddersfield shared two common characteristics. Firstly, doctors tended to live in the more salubrious parts of the towns, and, secondly, they followed the residential movements of their clientele. In Wakefield this meant remaining in roughly the same areas throughout the nineteenth century. In Huddersfield the picture was far more dynamic, and there were clear changes in the residential patterns of the providers of medical treatment during the nineteenth century (shown in Table 7.7(b)).

Throughout the century it is possible to trace a gradual movement by the wealthy from central locations to the (especially Western) outskirts of Huddersfield. By the third quarter of the

Table 7.7(a). *Patterns of residence amongst Wakefield medical practitioners, 1822–1870.*

Street or area of residence	1822	1828	1837	1847	1853	1861	1866	1870
Northgate	4	2	1	1	2	—	1	2
St John's	1	—	—	—	—	—	—	1
Westgate (incl. Market Street and Market Place)	5	7	6	8[a]	11	7	6	6
Kirkgate	4	8	6	7[a]	5	4	3	3
Wood Street and Bond Street	1	1	—	1	—	2	1	1
Westgate Common	1	—	1	—	—	—	—	—
Southgate	—	1	1	1	2	1	1	3
South Parade	—	—	2	4	3	2	2	1
Queen Street	—	—	—	1	1	—	—	—
West Parade	—	—	—	—	—	1	1	—

[a] Joseph Bennett, surgeon, had two properties, in Market Street, Westgate, and Ings Villa, Kirkgate.
Sources: Census Enumerators' Books, Wakefield, 1841, 1851, 1861 and 1871; Trade directories: Baines, 1822, Parson and White, 1828, White, 1837, 1847, 1853, 1861, 1866 and 1870.

century the abandonment of the town centre by many of the middle and upper classes had led to the formation of suburban and villa areas, and to an expansion of the villages surrounding Huddersfield. Doctors shared in this outward migration. The streets favoured by doctors early in the nineteenth century, New Street, King Street and Kirkgate, had been virtually abandoned by the middle decades of the century. In the 1830s and 1840s Queen Street, Buxton Road and High Street became more popular, representing a movement away from the town centre. The decades 1850 to 1870 saw another shift to the outskirts of town, as doctors took up residence in Ramsden Street, York Place, New North Road and Paddock. New North Road, 'the Kensington of Huddersfield',[103] was especially popular with medical men. The new Infirmary had been constructed there in 1831, and during the middle decades of the century it became the 'Harley Street' of the town, as a large proportion of doctors, usually the more successful, took up residence and established practices there. (See Maps 2.)

An analysis of the occupants of neighbourhoods where medical men resided, based on Kelly's 1857 street directory, adds weight to the idea that doctors tended to site themselves in the same areas as their potential clientele. Kelly's *Directory* gives a street-by-

Table 7.7(b). *Patterns of residence amongst Huddersfield medical practitioners, 1822–1870.*

Street or area of residence[a]	1822	1828	1837	1847	1853	1861	1866	1870
New Street	4	3	3	—	—	—	—	—
Westgate (incl. West Parade and Temple Street)	1	2	1	—	—	—	—	—
Kirkgate (incl. Cross Church Street)	2	2	1	1	1	—	—	—
King Street	2	4	4	—	—	—	—	—
Market Street (incl. Cloth Hall Street)	1	—	—	1	—	—	—	—
Beast Market	1	—	—	1	2	—	—	—
Upperhead Row	1	—	1	—	1	—	—	—
Longroyd Bridge	—	1	—	—	—	—	—	—
Queen Street	—	2	2	3	2	2	2	2
New House	—	1	—	—	—	—	1	—
South Parade	—	—	1	2	1	—	—	—
Buxton Road	—	—	2	2	1	1	2	1
High Street (incl. Albion Street)	1	—	1	2	1	1	—	—
Sheepridge	—	—	1	—	—	—	—	—
Ramsden Street	—	—	—	1	3	4	5	3
Mold Green	—	—	—	1	1	1	1	1
New North Road (incl. York Place and Brunswick Street)	—	—	—	2	7	7	5	6
Paddock	—	—	—	—	1	2	2	2
John William Street	—	—	—	—	—	1	1	1
Macaulay Street	—	—	—	—	—	1	1	1
Commercial Street	—	—	—	—	—	—	—	1
Lascelles Hall	—	—	—	—	—	1	—	—

[a] The streets are listed approximately as they occur from the centre of Huddersfield to its periphery.

Sources: Census Enumerators' Books, Huddersfield, 1841, 1851, 1861 and 1871; Trade directories as in Table 7.7(a).

street breakdown of the inhabitants of Wakefield and Huddersfield and their occupations. It is possible from this information to identify the fellow occupants of streets resided in by medical practitioners. Those physicians and surgeons with the wealthiest practices and honorary appointments usually lived in large premises and employed several residential servants. They also resided in the type of street inhabited by merchants, manufacturers, professional groups and gentlemen. For example, William Wood, a leading Wakefield physician (who employed a cook, housemaid, waiting maid and groom in the 1860s), resided in Cheapside, Westgate. There were seven other residents in the street: four woolstaplers, a cornfactor, a schoolmaster and a lady of independent means. Several eminent medical men lived in South Parade, Wakefield, together with attorneys, corn merchants and woollen manufacturers. By 1857 two physicians and two surgeons had taken up residence in New North Road, Huddersfield, Their neighbours consisted in the main of successful and wealthy professional and commercial families. Meanwhile, medical practitioners whose clientele presumably consisted mostly of tradesmen, shopkeepers, lower middle-class groups and artisans chose to live in business and shopping streets, rather than in purely residential areas.[104] We should not, however, take an analysis of this nature too far. Doctors were a fairly mobile group as regards residence. Meanwhile, many streets in both towns contained a mix of inhabitants. With the exception of a few very prosperous or very poor areas or streets, there was still no clear division according to class and income, and tradesmen and lower middle-class elements mingled with professionals, wealthy commercial groups and gentlemen. Doctors with a scattered or mainly country clientele may have also found it most convenient to remain in the town centre, rather than picking out one residential area as the location for their practices.

There was a wide diversity in the residences of medical men, although many of them lived in rented accommodation. Rented property varied from a couple of rooms over a shop (typically occupied by the 'surgeon-apothecary') to quite grand residences, such as the 'good dwelling house in Northgate, Wakefield occupied by William Holdsworth, surgeon containing a Breakfast and Dining-room, two kitchens, Drawing-room, and eight Bed-Rooms, Cellars, Stable, Coachhouse, Yard, and Garden, . . .', which served to accommodate Holdsworth, his wife, four children and three servants.[105] Westgate End House, Wakefield, served as a doctor's residence from the late eighteenth century. It was a large house with stabling for four horses, two coach houses and a surgery attached. It was occupied successively by the Walker family, Lawson Tait, and in the last quarter of the nineteenth century by Dr B. Kemp.[106]

Indications of wealth

Several doctors in Wakefield and Huddersfield were blessed with large private means, and were not fully dependent on an income derived from medical practice. Some inherited sums of money or property. Others, as seen above, married successfully, often to women from a commercial or professional background. In 1812 Richard Milner (following his arrival in Wakefield in 1809) married Sarah, daughter of the late Mr Robert Halliley, cornfactor. William Holdsworth, surgeon, entered into matrimony with Mary, the only daughter of Mr J. Atkinson, woolstapler of Wakefield, in 1831.[107] In 1871, during Lawson Tait's short residence in Wakefield, he married Miss Sybil Stewart, daughter of a Wakefield solicitor.[108] Other medical practitioners married into trading families. In 1813 Samuel Thomas of Wakefield, surgeon, married for the second time at the age of 41. His second wife, Miss Shaw, was the daughter of a Wakefield grocer. In 1839 Mr Joseph Bennett, surgeon to the Wakefield Asylum, married Miss Anne Sykes, niece of Mrs Shaw, proprietress of the Griffin Inn, Wakefield.[109]

Intermarriage within the medical profession was also fairly common. In 1820 George Sargent became partner to Mr Rowland Houghton, an eminent Huddersfield surgeon. Shortly after Mr Houghton died and Sargent succeeded to his large practice. In 1821 he married the late Mr Houghton's eldest daughter.[110] Similarly, in 1831 Mr Henry Dunn, a Wakefield practitioner, married Lucy Stott, second daughter of the late Thomas Stott, surgeon. Stott had been Dunn's senior partner. Dunn had served for several years as resident house surgeon to the Wakefield Dispensary, and had been appointed honorary surgeon to the House of Recovery in 1826. In addition to inheriting his father-in-law's practice, Dunn had also taken over his post as visiting surgeon to the House of Correction (at a salary of around £250 per annum). Dunn's union with Lucy Stott at the age of 27 capped an auspicious start to his medical career. The couple lived together in some apparent style in a large house in Market Street, with three female domestics and a groom.[111]

Those doctors able to afford it invested money in property or land. In 1796 Edward Taylor, surgeon and apothecary of Wakefield, purchased three acres of land on Wakefield Outwood from Thomas Smith, merchant, for £150, with the option to buy additional land at the rate of £50 per acre.[112] Another Wakefield surgeon, John Burrell, owned houses on South Parade. Dr Richardson had part shares in the 'valuable freehold establishment in Northgate, Wakefield, known as Elwick's Yard', consisting of dwelling houses, workshops, stables and gardens. George Holdsworth held shares in a number of railway companies, the Barnsley Canal and other stock, totalling approximately £2,000.[113] In the Huddersfield district medical men frequently supplied capital for financing house-building projects.[114] Several doctors also left land and property in their wills. Rowland Houghton left a large house in Rosemary Lane, Huddersfield, property in Corn Market, Northbar and Cross Church Street, and dwelling houses in Doncaster on his death in 1820.[115] In 1839 Squire Statter bequeathed, in addition to his surgical practice, messuages, lands and tenements situated in Sandal Magna and Wakefield to his nephew, William Statter.[116] By the will of the late Joseph Bennett, surgeon and general practitioner, which was proved in 1863, real estate in Wakefield, Stanley-cum-Wrenthorpe and New Zealand was bequeathed to his family. (His life was also insured for £2,000.)[117]

Those with alternative or supplementary sources of income were able to consider retiring from medical practice or taking up another profession. Dr William Dawson, Bachelor of Physic of Cambridge (1775), practised medicine in Wakefield from 1788 until 1794, when he became a senior partner in the firm of Dawson, Craven and Burrell, one of the first mercantile houses in the town. He discarded the title 'doctor' and retired from his post as honorary physician to the Dispensary, but continued to act as physician to his friends. Other medical practitioners were in a position to consider early or semi-retirement. In 1871, for example, Frederick Greenwood of Edgerton Lodge, near Huddersfield, then aged only 44, was recorded in the census returns and *Medical Directory* as being retired from practice,[118] although he continued to function in the capacity of certifying factory surgeon. It is conceivable that those possessing large private fortunes practised medicine only on a part-time or a consulting basis, as a charitable gesture for privileged acquaintances.

Dr Crowther of Wakefield fell into this fortunate category of wealthy medical practitioners. He succeeded to the principal medical practice in Wakefield in 1820 following the death of Dr Richardson, and married the sister of Joshua Smithson (later a wealthy railway owner) in 1825 at the age of 53. Crowther acted as visiting physician to the Wakefield Asylum for eight years and as honorary physician to the Dispensary for 54 years. Judging by his charitable contributions, Crowther was in no way dependent upon his income as a physician. During his lifetime he made many large contributions to charity, expending £4,592 alone on a project to build almshouses. On his death in 1849, £11,200 was bequeathed by Crowther for the establishment of an Almshouse for Dissenters and for the erection of a Fever Hospital.[119]

At the other end of the scale, some doctors found it difficult to survive in practice. Several Wakefield and Huddersfield medical men failed altogether; others apparently died in poverty.[120] A number of practitioners appear very briefly in town or medical directories before disappearing into obscurity, there being no record of them starting up in practice in other towns. The need for such an organisation as the West Riding Medical Charitable Society reflected the degree of poverty existing amongst medical practitioners. This Society was established in 1828 to relieve destitute medical men and their families, and was actively supported throughout the county. Representatives came from Wakefield, Huddersfield, Leeds, Bradford, Sheffield, Halifax and Doncaster. The first nine years were spent accumulating a fund of £2,000 from subscriptions, but from 1837 onwards the Society found itself in a position to distribute funds amongst some of 'their necessitous medical brethren'.[121] In the year 1845–1846, for example, nine destitute families were relieved, and in 1854–1855 £300 was distributed between sixteen families.[122] The Society was still very active in the third quarter of the century, indicating that the incidence of poverty amongst medical men had not declined. The main beneficiaries were doctors who had had to discontinue their practices because of ill health or other disabilities, and the widows and families of deceased medical men. Many doctors it seems were financially incapable of insuring themselves against the eventualities of sickness and death.[123]

Recruitment

Entrants to the medical profession in Wakefield and Huddersfield came mainly from middle-class families, that is, from professional or commercial backgrounds. Many were the sons of merchants and manufacturers, members of the legal profession, army officers and doctors. A smaller group of medical men came from a trading or, in rare cases, an artisanal background, or were farmers' sons. Typical recruits from wealthy commercial backgrounds were Samuel Mills of Huddersfield, son of William Mills, a local ironfounder, Oliveira Luis Fernandes, son of Jose Fernandes, a prosperous Wakefield corn merchant and brewer, and Sidney Alder of

Wakefield, son of Thomas, a landed proprietor and corn merchant.[124] Thomas Alder apprenticed his son to William Price of Leeds, surgeon and apothecary, in 1845. A large premium of £262 was agreed upon to cover a period of five years, during which time Sidney would be allowed to attend lectures at the Leeds School of Medicine, and also to assist as a dresser at the Leeds Infirmary.[125] The practice of medicine was typically taken up by the younger sons of commercial men, while the eldest sons followed in their father's footsteps. Samuel Mills, for example, had two older brothers – the first joined his father in the ironfounding concern, while the second entered the legal profession. Meanwhile, Sidney Alder's two brothers both settled for business as corn merchants. Upon qualification Sidney Alder became an army surgeon, while Samuel Mills set himself up in practice in Huddersfield, before moving to Lincoln in the mid-1860s.[126]

The second major avenue of recruitment was from the professional classes. Sons of legal practitioners, army officers or clergymen frequently took up the profession of medicine. The eldest son of John Edward Dibb, Deputy Registrar of Deeds at Wakefield, for example, trained to be a solicitor, while his second son, Edward Napier Dibb, became a medical practitioner.[127] The son of the Reverend John Coates, Vicar of Huddersfield (1791–1823), practised as a surgeon in Ashton-under-Lyne. The second son of Coates's successor, the Reverend J. C. Franks, was also intended for the medical profession, but died at the age of 25 before qualifying.[128] By the mid-nineteenth century there was some recruitment from less auspicious backgrounds. William Saville, for example, the son of a Wakefield pawnbroker, qualified as MRCS/LSA in 1852, after completing his training at the Middlesex Hospital. He established himself in what seems to have been a successful practice in Rotherham. He was appointed house surgeon to the Rotherham Dispensary, and in the 1860s honorary Dispensary surgeon and assistant surgeon to the 19th West Yorkshire Volunteers.[129] Walter J. Sykes and Alfred W. Lupton, the sons of the secretary to the Wakefield Waterworks and a retired Wakefield schoolmaster, both returned to the town to practise in the late 1860s. Sykes served briefly as house surgeon to the Wakefield Infirmary, before moving to Leeds to practise and to take up a post as Union medical officer. Lupton appears to have failed in practice; there are no records of his activities in the medical directories from the 1870s onwards.[130]

The largest source of recruitment was from the medical profession itself. Many sons of Wakefield and Huddersfield doctors followed their fathers into practice. Other male relatives of medical men, nephews, brothers and cousins, for example, took up the profession of medicine. They were often assisted by established family members; taken as apprentices and pupils, offered partnerships in practice or recommended to other medical practitioners. Not infrequently the sons (or other relatives) of Wakefield and Huddersfield doctors practised in the same town, eventually taking over the family concern. The eldest sons of Drs Thomas Giordani Wright and William Wood of Wakefield, and Messrs William James Clarke and Joseph Clough of Huddersfield, for example, followed their fathers into the profession. Two of these, William Dyson Wood and William Henry Clough, set themselves up in practice in Wakefield and Huddersfield respectively.

The third son of Samuel Knaggs of Huddersfield, Dr Francis Henry Knaggs, enjoyed a prestigious medical career. Born in Huddersfield in 1861 and educated at Huddersfield College and Guy's Hospital, Francis Knaggs held posts at Guy's, Moorfields Ophthalmic Hospital, Gloucestershire General Infirmary and Eye Institution, and at the Huddersfield Royal Infirmary. In 1889 he joined his father in his Ramsden Street practice, which he carried on after the latter's death, specialising in eye and ear affections and undertaking much consulting and operative work.[131] The Dyson family of Honley, who were descended from 'good yeoman stock of high local standing', followed the profession of medicine from grandfather to grandson during the nineteenth century, in the persons of John Dyson, Alexander Dyson and J. R. H. Dyson.[132] Connections between medical families in the two towns, complicated by intermarriage, were frequent.

During the late eighteenth and nineteenth centuries several families became prominent on the medical scenes of both towns, especially Wakefield. In Wakefield the Walkers (with six family members practising medicine), the Horsfalls, the Taylors and the Statters dominated general practice; in Huddersfield the Greenwoods and the Robinsons. These families, while not going quite as far as creating 'medical oligarchies', did enjoy many advantages over doctors without local connections and a medical background, who they were in direct competition with. The sons of medical practitioners were 'local boys', often being born and brought up in the same community. Their progress during medical training was noted in the press, and presumably found its way into local gossip. Upon qualification, they had an easier time building up a practice or were given a share in their father's practice, which they could expect to inherit on his death or retirement. For example, when Wakefield's senior surgeon, Edward Taylor, died in 1814 at the age of sixty, his practice (and property) were taken over by his son, Edward Taylor, junior, who advertised in the local newspaper that he

Begs to acquaint the Friends of his late Father, and the Public, that he intends pursuing the Profession, and shall feel grateful for a continuance of their Favours, so long enjoyed by his late Father, which it will be the object of his utmost endeavours to deserve.[133]

On the death of Squire Statter in 1839 his property and practice, and, by implication, his 'professional reputation' were bequeathed to his nephew, William. William had qualified in 1829 (LSA/MRCS). By the time of his uncle's death, although only aged 32, he had been in practice for ten years. During the early 1840s Edward Watson was taken as a partner into William Statter's Kirkgate practice. By 1851 the partnership had been dissolved, and William Statter had established himself in the up-market South Parade, with his wife and family, where he was attended by four resident servants. His professional standing, meanwhile, was enhanced by the acquisition of a medical degree in 1848. In 1854 he became a Fellow of the Royal College of Surgeons. William Statter was active in local cultural and charitable activities, and his prestige in the community was confirmed by his appointment as a Justice of the Peace in 1870.[134]

In addition to enjoying lucrative practices (and upper-class families seem to have preferred local men to 'foreigners'), medical families were often able to monopolise the best appointments, including the much sought-after honorary posts at local dispensaries and infirmaries. Judging by the number of times that this fact was referred to in testimonials and appeals for support by prospective candidates for these posts, being a local man (even with no medical connections) was a great advantage. If, in addition to this, the candidate came from a respected medical background, then his chance of success was multiplied accordingly. In Huddersfield, for example, the Robinsons and the Greenwoods together gained a partial monopoly over surgical posts to the Infirmary during the nineteenth century. To take the Robinsons, for example. George Robinson was appointed one of the first surgeons to the Dispensary when it was established in 1814. He continued to hold an honorary surgical post after the Infirmary opened in 1831, becoming senior surgeon, and in 1853 consulting surgeon. Altogether he acted as an honorary surgeon to the charity for fifty years. His son, William, qualified for medical practice in 1840, after completing his training at University College Hospital, London. Between 1840 and 1843 William held the paid post of resident house surgeon to the Infirmary. Following this valuable practical experience, William went into practice with his father. The partnership lasted until the death of the latter in 1865. In 1853 William was appointed honorary surgeon to the Infirmary, a post which he held until 1892, when he took up the position of consulting surgeon. In 1892 William's son, Dr F. W. Robinson, took over his post as honorary surgeon. The Robinson family practised in Huddersfield for most of the nineteenth century, and from 1814, without a break, held honorary dispensary and infirmary appointments.[135]

Despite a general rise in income in the second half of the nineteenth century, entry into the medical profession does not appear to have been a means of achieving upward social mobility. For wealthy families it was perhaps one method of consolidating their social standing. For successful businessmen, the entry of sons into the professions may have conferred prestige upon the family, but it is unlikely that medical practice brought exceptional financial rewards. As has already been suggested, recruits to the medical profession were taken largely from commercial and professional backgrounds. In turn, the sons of medical practitioners were frequently fed back into commercial careers, the army and the professions. The sons of Drs Amory and Richardson of Wakefield, for instance, both had successful army careers. The two eldest sons of Dr George Julius, who practised in Wakefield in the 1850s, entered the legal profession, the eldest as a solicitor, the second as an articled clerk. William, the second son of George Robinson, followed his father into medical practice, while his first son became a solicitor. Others went into commercial careers, such as George Remington Allatt, son of Richard Allatt, a Huddersfield general practitioner, who became a woollen merchant.[136] The daughters of medical practitioners also frequently married into commercial or professional families. For example, in 1822 the only daughter of the late William Mitchell, surgeon of Wakefield, married Thomas Foster of Horbury, a wealthy yarn manufacturer. The eldest daughter of William Starkey, general practitioner, married John Watson, a Wakefield solicitor, in 1839.[137]

Those medical practitioners fortunate enough to come from a wealthy middle-class background tended to prosper. Whether they had medical connections or not, they had access to a good and costly education and to well-off clients by means of family and business contacts and the 'old-boy' network. The two-way exchange between the medical profession on the one hand and non-medical professions and commercial undertakings on the other reflected a certain stability of income and social position on the part of groups involved in this interchange.

Doctors from more humble backgrounds were unlikely to flourish. The medical education they received was often inferior. They were less likely to have medical degrees and college affiliation. Moreover, they did not have the access to a wealthy clientele which their social superiors enjoyed. They had little contact or influence with local élite groups and were less likely to win good appointments. The sons of more lowly medical practitioners tended to be fed back into less attractive occupations, becoming tradesmen, small businessmen, clerks and shopkeepers. The father of Jonas Helliwell, a Huddersfield general practitioner, for example, earned his living as a tinner and brazier. Jonas Helliwell succeeded in practice to the extent that he survived, obtained a Poor Law post and was able to remain in Huddersfield. However, his practice does not appear to have been a lucrative one, and he did not obtain any well-paid or honorary appointments. His only son, William, did not enter the medical profession, but became a clerk to a woollen merchant. The eldest son of William S. Wade, an ex-army surgeon, who set himself up in practice in Wakefield in 1863, initially with only a moderate degree of success (perhaps linked to the scandal concerning Wade's marriage to a bigamist!), became a clerk to the Great Northern Railway Company.[138] Though a few individuals may have found the practice of medicine a lucrative undertaking, by which means they gained in social prestige, for the majority it involved little change in income or status.

Concluding remarks

The practice of medicine had presumably become a lucrative undertaking for families whose younger members continued to enter the profession. The fact that young men, with or without medical connections, took up medicine in growing numbers during the first half of the nineteenth century indicates that it *could* be a profitable career, despite the problems of overcrowding and of becoming established in practice (and for many of the middle classes, a lack of alternative employment opportunities). The cost of a medical education alone was sufficient to act as a deterrent in the absence of future financial rewards. Many Wakefield and Huddersfield medical practitioners had expensive educations. Thomas Giordani Wright, for example, obtained the triple qualification to practice in 1831, following training in London and Edinburgh, supplementing this with educational visits to Leyden and Germany. Others received part of their medical training in Paris, Pisa and Erlangen. Even the costs of obtaining the MRCS/LSA could be as much as £500 by mid-century. As has already been seen, an apprenticeship fee to either a medical practitioner or a medical charity alone could cost £150 to £200 in this period.[139] In 1842 it was suggested that a 'moderate general practice in London' earned £300 to £400 per annum.[140] The provincial counterpart earned rather less, perhaps £150 to £300 per annum, or even as little as £100. The incomes of medical men were said to have increased by the latter half of the nineteenth century, which coincided with a decline in their numbers. By the mid-1860s *The Lancet* estimated (probably optimistically) that 'a good practice' could gross £700–£1,000 annually, while a young energetic GP, even 'without connections', could expect £300 a year profit in a respectable London suburb. *The Lancet* also reported in the mid-1860s that most of the 300 doctors who had died in 1861 had bequeathed property.[141]

In a similar way to details relating to the size and range of medical practices, little information is available on either the charges made for medical treatment or the total income of medical practitioners. Fees for visits varied from a few shillings to the guinea fee charged by Dr Wright, Wakefield's leading physician in the second half of the nineteenth century. And, as has already been suggested, incomes from practice could vary from less than £100 to ten times that amount, even in small communities such as Wakefield and Huddersfield.[142] Salaried posts could provide an important source of income: even the low salaries of around £20 to £60 offered for Poor Law appointments could form an important addition to income, while the rates paid for such posts as surgeon to the Wakefield prison of £250 constituted a good living wage. However, even taking the possibility of obtaining posts into consideration, as Loudon has suggested, there were simply insufficient patients to go round throughout the nineteenth century.[143] For much of the nineteenth century there were only around 600 inhabitants to each medical practitioner in Wakefield; in Huddersfield the figure was approximately 1,300. The fact that some individuals succeeded in practice, even to the extent of achieving a very high standard of living, meant that others were condemned to poverty or failure.

It is difficult to define with any great precision the social characteristics of medical men. While the majority could be described as 'middle class', there were considerable divergences between the social backgrounds, incomes and lifestyles of this group. The analysis of social characteristics would seem to reflect and reinforce the axis along which medical men were seen to be cast in the first Section. At the top end of the scale were those with an expensive university training, honorary appointments and a share in the towns' best practices. This group employed large numbers of servants, lived in impressive villas in the best parts of town, and, as will be seen in Chapter 8, mixed freely with local élite groups. They were likely to have come from a wealthy, often medical, background; their sons either perpetuated the family interest in medical practice or were fed into the professions or a commercial career.

Further down the scale the 'average' and probably largest group of medical men lived on an income of approximately £200 to £300 per annum, rented a moderately-sized house and employed one or two resident servants. This group may have held honorary appointments, although in most cases not the most senior ones, or a variety of other salaried or non-salaried posts (such as army, assurance society, prison or certifying factory surgeon). Further down the scale again we find the 'lower middle-class' practitioner, who was often unable to set up a household or afford domestic assistance. These individuals came in many cases from inauspicious backgrounds, had received the cheapest forms of medical training, held the worst-remunerated Poor Law and friendly society posts, and based their practices on a largely working- /lower middle-class clientele.

Throughout the nineteenth century Wakefield tended to attract (and produce) a higher class of medical practitioner, in terms of qualifications (having more university educated and college-affiliated doctors) and social background. Medical men employed more servants in Wakefield, and apparently enjoyed grander and more 'gentlemanly' lifestyles than their Huddersfield contemporaries. This was partly a result of the larger number of honorary posts that were available in Wakefield, but was also closely linked to the social composition of the town, which not only gave medical men the opportunity to build up prosperous practices, but also gave them a chance to participate more fully in local élite activities. We shall return to this theme in Chapter 8.[144]

8

The medical profession in Wakefield and Huddersfield: professional and social activities

8.1 Professional activities

Historians generally agree that the nineteenth century saw most progress in the professionalisation of English medicine.[1] During this century medical men attempted to create a unified, homogeneous and high-status profession. Up until the nineteenth century the majority of medical men had been unable to legitimise their social, professional and intellectual positions. Medicine remained rather a low-status profession, surgery even more so, especially when compared with the other professions: the army, the church and law.[2] Structural changes (as seen in Chapter 7) were largely worked out by the mid-nineteenth century, and the legal closure of the profession to outsiders was achieved in theory by the 1858 Medical Act. The medical profession, however, had not achieved the unity that the 1858 Act would appear to suggest. Doctors failed to agree upon even the basics of diagnosis and treatment, on the value of different qualifications and to regulate relationships between themselves. During the nineteenth century, however, the medical profession did make some moves towards the fulfilment of the 'attributes' of an 'ideal profession': the development of a systematic body of theory, professional authority and the sanction of the community, the establishment of a code of ethics and the formation of a professional culture (based on medical institutions, places of education and professional organisations).[3]

This Section will look at the attempts of Wakefield and Huddersfield medical practitioners to achieve professional unity during the nineteenth century. Few historical studies have been made of professional bodies, and those that do exist are usually 'so thin and lacking in critical framework as to be of almost no use to succeeding scholars'.[4] Sociologists, meanwhile, have failed to agree on a definition as to what constitutes a 'profession' or on the main features which the process of professionalisation could be said to embody.[5] However, it is not my purpose here to enter into a theoretical discussion on the process of professionalisation. Rather this Section will concentrate on a pragmatic account of the attempts of provincial medical men to put into effect what *they understood* by the formation of a professional structure.

Until more work is completed on the subject of professionalisation by historians, we have to be satisfied with a fairly vague definition of the process. Using a definition suggested by Shortt, professionalisation will be denoted here as 'a process by which a heterogeneous collection of individuals is gradually recognised, by both themselves and other members of society, as constituting a relatively homogeneous and distinct occupational group'.[6] To this rather broad definition we could add, as Inkster suggests, some minimum criteria which must be fulfilled in the process of professionalisation.[7] These could include a uniform training and examination system, leading to recognised and legally-sanctioned qualifications, a consensus regarding codes of ethics and behaviour, the establishment of platforms permitting both the furtherance of medical science and the development of group consciousness, control over medical institutions and a monopoly of medical care through the elimination of unqualified elements.

The discussion in this Section will centre around three main themes of professionalisation. Firstly, we will look at the attempts of Wakefield and Huddersfield medical practitioners to unite and legitimise their professional status through the medium of medical societies. Although some progress towards professional unity was made through these mediums, conflict between individual medical practitioners remained rife throughout the century, and this Section will also look at some of the conflict situations which arose between Wakefield and Huddersfield medical men, expressions, in effect, of 'unprofessional' behaviour. The third and final area of discussion is closely related to the first two. In order to achieve the unification and closure of the profession medical men had to succeed in driving out unqualified competition. As one historian has put it, 'modern medicine did not arise in a vacuum; it established itself by denying legitimacy to competing practitioners and medical cultures'.[8] We will examine the attempts of qualified doctors in Wakefield and Huddersfield to eliminate the unqualified, and to achieve a practical application of the legal closure defined by the 1858 Act. It seems that this was one issue around which all medical men were able to unite, but which was of particular importance to provincial general practitioners, who suffered most directly from the competition of the unqualified. In Section 8.2 an analysis will be given of the 'extra-professional' activities of medical men in the two communities, and of the development of relationships between medical and lay groups.

Medical societies

One of the most important mediums through which attempts were made by medical men to further their professional aims was the medical society.[9] They were vital agents in the development of the modern medical profession, 'at the same time themselves transforming as the contingency arose'.[10] Medical book clubs, social clubs and scientific societies had existed in the eighteenth century, based usually in London or other large cities, and devoted mainly to intellectual, scientific and social exchange. But the nineteenth century witnessed an unprecedented growth of medical organisations, set up both to further scientific knowledge *and* to pursue professional goals. As Peterson suggests, the proliferation of medical associations in the first half of the nineteenth century was in part a result of 'the growth of a medical population in any given locale large enough to sustain activities designed to further professional intercourse and mutual assistance'.[11] The formation of these societies also reflected the failure of the London-based corporations to assist provincial practitioners in their struggle for professional unity and status. Provincial practitioners came to see their scientific, social and professional advancement as being dependent upon their own efforts to organise. It is significant that the Provincial Medical and Surgical Association, later the BMA, was set up in Worcester in 1832, rather than in a major centre, its chief purpose being to counter the powerful conservative interests of medicine in the metropolis.[12]

The scientific activities of medical societies were largely superseded by professional concerns during the nineteenth century. This is not to say that all scientific activity ground to a sudden halt, and societies directed more purely towards intellectual and scientific attainment were still set up by medical communities. The Manchester Medical Society, founded in 1834, had as its immediate objects the establishment of a library, and the holding of occasional meetings for mutual improvement and the advancement of medical science. A medical society was set up in York in 1832 'for the purpose of promoting and diffusing Medical knowledge'.[13] In Sheffield the Humane Society (1809) and the Medical and Surgical Society (1820) were established primarily to further scientific research. In 1828 two new medical societies were formed in competition with one another, which later developed into the Sheffield School of Anatomy and Medicine and the Sheffield Medical Institution.[14]

Groups of Wakefield and Huddersfield medical practitioners established medical libraries in the first half of the nineteenth century. A Medical Society was founded in Huddersfield in 1825,[15] which mainly concerned itself with scientific issues, and in 1854 a Microscopic Society was initiated in Wakefield 'for the cultivation of microscopic inquiry with reference to physiological and Medical Science . . .'.[16] Medical libraries in a strict sense cannot really be classified as 'societies'; their members rarely met together, and when they did, it was to discuss rules concerning membership and the circulation of books, rather than any scientific or professional issues. However, medical libraries did represent an instance of enterprise on the part of provincial practitioners, who normally had only limited access to medical books and journals. Medical libraries enabled them, if they felt so inclined, to keep abreast of the latest medical debates and developments.

The Huddersfield Medical Library was set up in 1814, coinciding with the establishment of the Dispensary. The Library had a permanent home in the Dispensary (and later Infirmary) from 1814 onwards. From 1823 it became usual for the resident apothecary of the Dispensary to be appointed Librarian. The stock of the Library was large, emphasis being placed on ordering new publications and on the circulation of current medical journals. Most Huddersfield practitioners were members, and special provisions for 'country' members, including reduced rates of subscription, enabled many doctors residing in outlying districts and villages to enjoy the facilities of the Library.[17] The Library was a boon not only to individual practitioners, but also to the staff of the Infirmary. In 1853 the Infirmary Board resolved

. . . that whilst this privilege has been useful to the profession, it has also been highly beneficial to the institution by providing it free of expense with an excellent library which for reference in urgent and difficult cases is of utmost value to the medical staff – and which by tending to keep up & promote professional improvement cannot but be advantageous to all who seek relief within these walls.[18]

The Huddersfield Medical Library was still functioning successfully in the early decades of the twentieth century.

The Wakefield Medical Book Club, which was initiated in 1830, differed fundamentally from its Huddersfield counterpart in that it never enjoyed a permanent home. Rather, it operated on the basis of a circulating library. Books were ordered by subscribers through a stationer and circulated amongst members. At annual meetings all books which had gone out of circulation were sold by auction. The disadvantage of this Club, therefore, was that it never built up a stock of books. Nevertheless, it also appeared to have been popular with medical practitioners: in 1830 over half of the Wakefield medical profession joined the Club, and it was still active in the mid-nineteenth century.[19]

The Huddersfield Medical Society was established in 1825 by the town's surgeons, who met together at the Dispensary (and later Infirmary) to discuss scientific matters, unusual cases and the fixing of fees for medical treatment. Initially the establishment of a uniform scale of charges appears to have been one of their main concerns. They were drawn up in some detail, fixing the fee according to class (based on the rental per annum of houses occupied by patients), time of visit (day or night) and the distance of the patient from the centre of Huddersfield. Lists of charges were also agreed upon for various cases. The charge for a simple fracture of the upper extremity was fixed at between 5s and 10s 6d according to class, for 'inserting a seton' 2s to 5s, for midwifery cases half a guinea to a guinea, for inoculation 2s 6d to 7s 6d and for 'consultation fees in Medicine and Surgery' 2s to 5s.[20]

In 1828 the basis of the Society was broadened. It was resolved at a meeting in May of that year that 'the physicians be Respectfully invited to join the Society'. The name of the association was consequently changed to 'The Huddersfield Medico-Chirurgical Society'.[21] Around the same time the emphasis of meetings changed. Discussions concerning fees became less frequent, and were replaced by scientific debate. The meetings tended to centre around difficult cases which members had come across, which revealed a certain degree of co-operation between participants in the debates. For example, at a meeting in February, 1829 the discussion revolved around a case under the care of Mr Greenwood of a child 'afflicted suddenly with a virulent and apparently spasmodic affection of the Heart or Trachea'. Mr Atkinson recommended doses of 'opil. camph. in conjunction with Digitalis', and at the following meeting Mr Greenwood reported that this treatment had appeared to bring some relief. At a meeting held in September of the same year the members discussed midwifery cases and the treatment of 'dangerous infantile disorders', and in August, 1833 there was a 'desultory conversation on Cholera, in which it was agreed that no settled mode of Treatment has yet been discovered for this disease that can be depended upon'.[22]

The Wakefield Microscopic Society also led to both increased social contact and heightened scientific activity amongst the town's medical practitioners. The Society was founded in 1854 by Messrs Dawson, Dunn, F. Horsfall and Milner and Drs Holdsworth, Wood and Wright. The seven founders could elect new members, who were required to pay an entrance fee of 2s 6d, on the condition that they possessed a 'good' achromatic microscope. Several more doctors joined the Society in the next few years; others came occasionally to meetings as visitors. The Society met fortnightly at members' homes in rotation. The individual hosting the meeting would decide in advance on a subject, and provide specimens and illustrations. Members of the Society examined a varied range of subjects, including tissue samples, human and cow's milk, blood and portions of diseased tissues taken from patients under their care. They also looked into food adulteration. In December, 1854, for example, members of the Society investigated arrowroot, mustards and starch as sold in shops, 'all of which were found to be more or less adulterated with wheat or other starches, cayenne pepper and turmeric powder'.[23] The Society subscribed to microscopic journals and purchased newly-published books on the subject. It was reconstituted in 1858 when 'persons not being members of the medical profession' became eligible for membership. This constitutional change resulted in a fall off in support by medical men, and membership appeared to become confined to the medical élite of Wakefield.[24]

Scientific interchange was not restricted to Wakefield and Huddersfield. Medical men visited other medical societies and infirmaries in the region or London to hear or give lectures and attend discussions, and vice versa. For example, medical men from as far away as Rochdale and Manchester attended meetings of the Wakefield Microscopic Society as visitors in the 1850s.[25] In 1829 Mr J. H. Abraham of Sheffield gave two lectures on the subject of pneumatics for the benefit of the campaign to establish an infirmary in Huddersfield.[26] In 1851 Mr J. Gracey of Manchester, Professor of Physiology, came to Clayton West, near Huddersfield, to deliver a lecture on the structure and vital functions of the human frame and laws of health.[27]

The Wakefield and Huddersfield medical professions' output of books, pamphlets, articles and correspondence to medical journals also increased during the nineteenth century. The proliferation of quality medical journals during the century offered growing opportunities to publish.[28] This fact no doubt encouraged provincial medical men to write up their scientific findings. In Wakefield and Huddersfield a wide cross-section of the medical profession wrote papers on a diverse range of subjects. For example, in the early nineteenth century Dr Alexander of Wakefield published pamphlets dealing with the subjects of croup, phrenology and self-help medicine.[29] P. A. Brady practised in Huddersfield in the late 1840s and early 1850s, and during this period he contributed papers on the medical profession and its educational system, the circulation of the blood, the treatment of cholera and the 'philosophy of physiology' to the *Medical Times*.[30]

The honorary physicians and surgeons attached to the Wakefield and Huddersfield Infirmaries contributed case notes and details of surgical procedures to medical journals. For example, in 1855 W. J. Clarke, honorary surgeon to the Huddersfield Infirmary, contributed notes to *The Lancet* on a case of strangulated hernia and its successful treatment by surgery, while the patient was under the influence of chloroform.[31] Dr John Taylor, formerly Professor of Clinical Medicine at University College Hospital, London, wrote papers on various medical subjects while attached as honorary physician to the Huddersfield Infirmary. Between 1847 and his death in 1852 he contributed articles on heart disease, gangrene, cholera and the system of appointments in voluntary hospitals to *The Lancet* and the *Medical Times*.[32] Examples of publications by Wakefield and Huddersfield doctors could be multiplied, but it suffices to say that a considerable and growing proportion of them, including general practitioners, wrote pamphlets and learned papers during the nineteenth century.

During the middle decades of the nineteenth century the profession became more interested in the regulation of medical ethics. This concern found expression in the editorials and correspondence of medical journals, in a spate of books on the subject and through the medium of professional associations set up primarily to regulate medical ethics. The Manchester Medico-Ethical Association, founded in 1847, was set up specifically to deal with ethical issues. Meanwhile, the BMA, established for more general purposes, founded a Medico–Ethical Committee in 1853. By the mid-nineteenth century the shift in emphasis to ethical concerns had apparently become something of a nationwide phenomenon. In 1852 the *Medical Times and Gazette* was able to refer to

. . . attempts made in different parts of the country to remedy some of the existing evils of the Profession by codes of law and rules of etiquette emanating from the members of the Profession itself. We are convinced that associations of medical men in our great towns will do much to strengthen our cause, to defend our just rights, and to correct abuses, provided that the members of such associations be guided only by pure and honourable motives, and the laws which they frame be devised with the sole view of promoting the general good.[33]

Medical ethics in this period could be defined as the regulation of relationships between medical practitioners, rather than between doctor and patient. The doctor-patient relationship received little attention either in publications or in the proceedings of medical societies. A great deal of energy was devoted on the other hand to the problem of regulating relationships between medical men.[34] This bias reflected the experiences of medical men in the everyday practice of their profession. Most conflict apparently arose not out of dealings with patients, but in their relationships with professional colleagues. The development of an interest in medical ethics could be seen as an attempt on the part of doctors to ease these tension-ridden relationships, and to reduce the amount of potentially very damaging intra-professional conflict.

Waddington suggests that the main pre-condition for this development was the breakdown of the patronage system in the nineteenth century. This breakdown was paralleled and partly facilitated by the widening of the market for medical services, as discussed in Chapter 7. The eighteenth century had been an age of patronage, which gave rise to a structure of client control, the aristocratic and wealthy client being the dominant partner in the client–practitioner relationship. Under patronage the doctor deferred to and identified with his patrons, rather than his professional colleagues. In the nineteenth century the medical man became less dependent upon the patronage of the very wealthy, as his clientele expanded to include a large proportion of the middle class, who were nearer to medical practitioners in both status and wealth.[35] Such an analysis should, however, not be taken too far, as it has also been seen in Chapter 7 (and elsewhere) how much medical men still depended upon laymen, this time largely middle-class groups, for both appointments and private patients. But it does seem that during the nineteenth century the patronage system broke down to some extent, and that 'colleague control', where the professional activities of practitioners were regulated by colleagues, took its place.

In 1852 a Medico–Ethical Society was set up in Huddersfield. It presumably evolved out of the earlier Medico–Chirurgical Society, and it retained close links with the Medical Library, also holding its meetings at the Infirmary. By the mid-1850s upwards of forty medical practitioners had enrolled in the Society. At this time approximately 25 medical men were in practice in the town, so the Society must have had a catchment area which extended well beyond the boundaries of Huddersfield. The Huddersfield Infirmary's medical officers dominated the Society: Dr Turnbull (senior physician) was President, George Robinson (consulting surgeon) Vice-President, Dr Scott (honorary physician) and Mr G. W. Rhodes (honorary surgeon) Honorary Secretaries and Messrs W. Greenwood, W. J. Clarke and William Robinson (honorary surgeons) committee members. Indeed, with the exception of four individuals, all the Medico–Ethical Society's officers were also honorary Infirmary staff.

In 1860 the aims of the Medico–Ethical Society were summed up thus:

The objects of this Society are to maintain proper professional usage and etiquette; to maintain the interests of the Profession; also the powers to correspond, as an Association, with other bodies or individuals on any subject involving mutual interests, etc., etc.[36]

Members of the Huddersfield Medico–Ethical Society took upon themselves powers which closely resembled, albeit on a local scale, those adopted by the GMC after 1858. The Society, dominated by the medical élite, attempted to regulate the behaviour and practices of medical men, and because it obtained the support of most (perhaps all) members of the local medical profession, the potential influence of the Society was considerable. The rules of the Society were extremely stringent, especially those regulating membership. The first section of the Bye-laws of the Society, which referred to disqualification from membership, ruled in 1852

No member shall practise, professed or exclusively, homoeopathy, hydropathy, or mesmerism.
No member shall, by advertisement or other improper means, solicit private practice.
No member shall be the proprietor of, or in any way derive advantage from, the sale of any patent or proprietary medicine, or in any way recommend its public use.
No member, who may keep an open shop, shall sell patent medicines, perfumery, or other articles than pharmaceutical drugs and preparations.[37]

The medical profession as a whole was normally enthusiastic about societies of this nature, and the compilers of the 1860 *Medical Directory* commented on the Huddersfield association in favourable terms.

This Society has been already of great advantage to the medical men of this district, and will, no doubt, be the means of cementing still closer the interests of each, and diminish or prevent the abuses so often complained of in the Medical Profession.[38]

It is not clear when a medical society first originated in Wakefield. Unfortunately no documentary evidence survives, but correspondence to medical journals indicates that the Wakefield Medical Society was active by the early 1850s. The Society was supported by the Dispensary medical staff, and its meetings were held in the Dispensary building, and it is possible that some form of professional association, perhaps an informal one, had existed in close connection to the Dispensary before this period. In a similar way to the Huddersfield Medico–Ethical Society, by the mid-nineteenth century it appears that the Wakefield Medical Society, despite any social or scientific benefits which might accrue from it, existed primarily to further professional goals. The Wakefield Society was very much involved in judging the professional behaviour of local medical men, giving vent in medical journals to expressions of support or disapprobation of the professional activities of their colleagues. The examples which will be given here are not designed to illustrate the rights and wrongs of each case. Indeed adjudicating the cases is difficult, not least because of the limited evidence available. Rather, they demonstrate the kind of professional issues that medical men were becoming concerned with by the middle decades of the nineteenth century, and how they tried to deal with them.

In 1851 a letter was forwarded to *The Lancet* by W. R. Milner, Secretary to the Wakefield Medical Society, deploring the behaviour of Mr William Thornton, a general practitioner, who resided at Horbury, near Wakefield. Thornton had, it claimed, offered in a circular letter to undercut any medical man in the district applying for the post of medical officer to local sick clubs. It had been resolved at an assemblage of the Wakefield Medical Society 'That this meeting regrets that any medical man should degrade the profession to which he belongs, by issuing such a document as the letter now read, . . .'. The editor of *The Lancet*, Wakley, added in apparent surprise (although he surely knew the extent to which undercutting was practised by sick club surgeons) 'Is it possible that the letter signed 'William Henry Thornton' *could* have issued from a medical practitioner?'[39]

Thornton answered his accusers in the following edition of the journal. He claimed that the Wakefield Medical Society had been '. . . grossly imposed on, . . . truth having been told to a certain extent, but not the whole truth'. According to Thornton, he had been the first victim of undercutting, by an established Horbury practitioner, Mr W. Kemp, a member of the Wakefield Medical Society. Thornton, who had only resided in Horbury for five months, apparently faced a problem common to many young and newly-qualified practitioners.[40] Although careful not to suggest any failure in the judgement of the membership of the Wakefield Medical Society, Thornton inquired,

. . . but I may ask, when the elder practitioner in a place stoops to such conduct, and cuts down prices, not only in clubs, but in private practice, how is the younger one to maintain them? I think it would be much better at once to prescribe gratuitously, a course which I shall most probably adopt if I find the lowering-price system is continued.[41]

Following Thornton's reply, the Wakefield Medical Society apparently dropped the subject, and left the two practitioners to argue the issue out between themselves. In the end it seems that experience (and the advantage of coming from an established local medical family) triumphed over youth, as Thornton left the Wakefield area a few years later. However, Thornton's career seems not to have been adversely affected by this early skirmish. After leaving Horbury, he established himself in what appears to have been a successful practice in Dewsbury. In the 1860s he held the posts of Union medical officer, police surgeon and medical referee to a number of assurance societies. He became a Fellow of the Royal College of Surgeons in 1868. By this time he had become something of an expert in the field of obstetrics, publishing regularly on the subject, and was a Fellow of the Obstetrical Society, London. Thornton's social position, meanwhile, was secured by his appointment in the 1860s as a Justice of the Peace for Dewsbury.[42]

Again, in 1854 the Wakefield Medical Society reacted to a problem of a professional nature. This time its members leapt to the defence of Mr Housley, an ex-Wakefield practitioner, who had been found guilty of negligence in his treatment of a fracture case. A series of resolutions passed at a meeting of the Society appeared in *The Lancet*. The defence of Housley was based largely on the members' impression of his early career in Wakefield, and of his professional bearing, rather than on any medical or surgical skills that he might or might not possess:

> . . . Mr. Housley, having passed his youth and the earlier part of his professional career in Wakefield, is well known to many of us, and we bear willing testimony to the kindness of his disposition, to his honourable feeling and conduct, to his ability, industry, and professional attainments.[43]

It is interesting that the members chose to defend Housley on these grounds. It suggests that professional integrity was seen as being very closely linked to a practitioner's performance of his medical tasks. Negligence was less likely to be practised by a 'respected' member of the medical community. The members of the Wakefield

Medical Society also objected strongly to the awarding of what they saw as excessive damages, claiming

... the jury must have been, to some extent, influenced by the marked prejudice which seems to operate against the members of our profession whenever they have to appear in a court of Justice, whatever may be the capacity in which they appear there.[44]

They warned that the chance of recovering large damages from a medical attendant might tempt patients to interfere with the treatment of injuries in order to issue a charge of malpractice. The members of the Society initiated a subscription in the area on behalf of the 'victimised' practitioner, and transmitted a copy of their resolutions and an expression of sympathy to Housley.

Wakefield medical men were not exclusively concerned with local issues. They also involved themselves in decisions taken at a national level, when these threatened their status or livelihood, showing their capacity to unite around issues that affected all concerned. The Wakefield Medical Society, for example, forwarded a memorial in 1852 requesting that any new charter granted to the Royal College of Surgeons should make two provisions: firstly, that in the election of the Council all Fellows should have the privilege of voting by balloting papers and not be compelled to attend in person, and, secondly, that all who were members at the date of the granting the proposed new charter should be equally eligible for the Fellowship as those members who had received their diplomas before 1843.[45]

In 1853 another memorial was forwarded to the Royal College of Surgeons by its membership in the Wakefield area, objecting to the proposal of the College to confer the degree of Licentiate in Midwifery (LM) on persons who had not previously taken any degree in medicine or surgery. The Wakefield practitioners saw the proposed measure as being 'unnecessary and mischievous'. They maintained that present Members of the College of Surgeons and holders of the LSA were 'amply sufficient' to treat obstetric cases. More than this, they feared competition from a class of practitioners, who had gone through a course of study inferior to that required by themselves. Not only would LMs deprive them of the obstetric cases that they had always treated, but, the petitioners claimed, they would also encroach on other branches of practice.

And this competition will be the more injurious, as it will spring from a class of persons who will have some pretence for holding themselves out to the world as qualified practitioners, and who will be so regarded by large classes of the community who know little and care less, about the distinction of Fellow, Member, or Licentiate, but who will be apt to regard all who have passed an examination at one and the same place as being on an equal footing; and it is little likely that those who take the licence in midwifery without having obtained the diploma of membership, will be unwilling to encourage the delusion, and to act upon it to our disadvantage.

The Wakefield surgeons not only feared the impact of direct competition; they also anticipated that the plan would lower the status of the profession.

We also fear that the introduction of an inferior class of practitioners into the College will have a tendency to lower the whole body in public estimation; for if, as is very possible, the tone of professional morality of the proposed Licentiates in Midwifery should be lower than that of Members of the College, any discredit attaching to that circumstance would, in the eyes of the public be to some extent shared by us.[46]

A number of Wakefield and Huddersfield medical men also became involved in regional or national campaigns and societies. Dr Walker, physician to the Huddersfield Infirmary, originated and spearheaded the campaign to establish a sea bathing infirmary on the Western coast for the benefit of the poor, which received much support from medical men throughout the West Riding, Lancashire and Cheshire in the 1840s. (The proposal appears, however, never to have been put into action.)[47] Several Wakefield and Huddersfield medical practitioners were active in the West Riding Medical Charitable Society. In 1836, for example, when the annual meeting of the Society was held in the Wakefield Court House, Dr Thomas of Wakefield was appointed one of the Vice-Chairmen. Dr Walker and Mr Sargent of Huddersfield and Messrs Dawson and Ross of Wakefield were chosen as Stewards.[48]

Large numbers of Wakefield and Huddersfield medical men became involved in regional, national, Scottish or London-based medical societies, especially in the second half of the nineteenth century. By the 1860s, for example, many had joined the British Medical Association. George Winter Rhodes (honorary surgeon to the Huddersfield Infirmary and Honorary Secretary of the Medico–Ethical Society) was an active member of the BMA and of the King's College Medical Society. Samuel Harris Armitage, a Huddersfield GP, was a member of the Royal Medical Society and a Fellow of the Royal Botanic Society. William Scott (also honorary surgeon and Secretary of the Medico–Ethical Society) was a Fellow of the Royal Medical and Surgical Society, London.[49] During his period as house surgeon to the Wakefield Infirmary (1867–1871) Lawson Tait kept up his involvement in a number of medical societies. He was a member of the Irish Surgical Society and the Dublin Obstetric Society, Honorary Member (late President) of the Hunterian Medical Society, Edinburgh, and a member of the BMA.[50] Tait also lectured to the Leeds Medical Club and attended meetings of the London Medical Society.[51] Again these examples could be multiplied, but they serve to show that provincial medical men were involved in professional activities which went beyond their community and local interests.

The activities of Wakefield and Huddersfield medical men reflected a heightened nationwide concern with professional issues. The medical journals of the day were enthusiastic about the efforts of local groups of medical men to defend their professional status and uphold strong codes of ethical behaviour. The journals were especially keen about societies such as the Huddersfield Medico–Ethical Society. An article which appeared in an 1852 issue of the *Medical Times and Gazette* declared 'full concurrence in the spirit which pervades this code of ethics drawn up by our Yorkshire brethren'. The article praised the Society for protecting the layman from the 'incompetent and illegitimate' practitioner, and for preventing 'grave offences against the etiquette of a noble and honourable Profession'.[52] The activities of the Huddersfield Society smacked very much of dominance by a self-appointed élite group, and the imposition of codes of behaviour based on the aims and opinions of this group. The emphasis of societies such as this lends some support to the contention of N. and J. Parry, that the factor of most significance in assessing the professionalisation of a group is the degree of control achieved by professional associations over their members.[53] The article in the *Medical Times and Gazette* pointed out the penalties of exclusion from societies such as that initiated in Huddersfield:

. . . the quiet yet firm exclusion of parties guilty of unprofessional conduct from the society of their brethren – their elimination, as it were, from the temple of science, – their exile from friendly intercourse, – is a punishment few can endure; and, if inflicted with judgement, it will soon have the effect of preventing a repetition of the offences.[54]

It was not only societies which concerned themselves with these issues. Individual medical men took it upon themselves to explain the difficulties besetting the medical profession, and to suggest remedies. P. Brady, a local general practitioner, summarised the situation as he saw it in Huddersfield and at a national level in an 1847 issue of the *Medical Times*.[55] He claimed that the status of the profession in the eyes of the public had never been at a 'lower ebb'. Brady blamed this on the education system, the low quality of medical students, the ease of obtaining diplomas to practise and the '. . . rapid increase of a class of members whose education, moral and intellectual, by no means adapts them for its pursuits'. Brady succinctly outlined many of the main grievances of medical men and the major causes of intra-professional dispute. A self-confessed enthusiast for the lancet, he criticised other local medical men, not only for following incorrect courses of treatment, but for mis-diagnosis in the first place. For example, Brady cited an instance of a case of pericarditis (heart disease) being treated by an unnamed Huddersfield doctor as pleurisy (inflammation of the lungs), and cases concerning the mismanagement (in Brady's opinion) of childbirth. In particular Brady attacked those practitioners who had an aversion to bleeding and other 'heroic' methods of treatment.[56] In so doing, he emphasised and exemplified one of the fundamental causes of disunity between medical men; a failure to agree on even the basics of diagnosis and treatment, a situation hardly calculated to give confidence to a prospective patient.

Brady also attacked the self-interest of medical corporations, the tender system and undercutting practised by medical men applying for Poor Law and sick club appointments, and the system of election in medical charities.

The system of interest and favouritism which invariably obtains in the election of physicians and surgeons to hospitals, dispensaries, etc., to the exclusion of real merit, must be abolished. We often hear expressions of surprise at the tortoise pace at which the art of medicine advances, but the wonder ceases when we witness the honours and emoluments of the profession conferred on the *protégés* of the powerful and influential, while intellects of the highest order not infrequently decline the hopeless and ignominious contests (his emphasis).

Brady did not confine himself to an attack on medical practitioners. He also blamed the low status of the profession on the lack of interest shown by laymen, not least an apparent absence of concern with high levels of mortality, and the efforts of medicine to combat these. Few laymen, he claimed, bothered to find out if and how their medical attendants were qualified; as a result the most ignorant and ill-informed members of the profession frequently gained the best practices. Brady apparently was not a man without grudges, feeling he had not achieved the success due to him. It goes without saying that he was not one of those well-favoured individuals who obtained hospital appointments. However, he did outline grievances felt by many members of the profession, and, like other correspondents to the medical journals, he saw the remedy for the evils which beset the profession in unity of action by qualified medical practitioners. He concluded his account with the following plea:

Let us, then, unceasingly agitate for the removal of the numerous and gross abuses under which the profession labours. Let us, by the perpetual exposition of our grievances, endeavour to enlist the sympathies of the public . . . but, above all things, let us never forget that all efforts must be futile and ineffective which are unaccompanied by those two essential requisites – unanimity of opinion and cooperation in action.[57]

Intra-professional conflict

The efforts of medical societies and pleas from individuals such as Brady did not, however, eliminate conflict from intra-professional relationships. Fracas between members of the profession, whether they be over methods of treatment or codes of conduct, punctuated the nineteenth-century medical scene in Wakefield and Huddersfield as much as everywhere else in the country. Even within medical societies themselves there were disputes concerning membership, attendance, precedence and regulations. Fines were instituted and frequently enforced in all the societies for non-attendance, lateness, failure to return books on time, and so on. Meetings of the Huddersfield Medico–Chirurgical Society frequently had to be cancelled because of the lack of attendance. In January, 1832 the only two members to turn up at the meeting were Messrs Greenwood and Hudson. In the minute book they recorded 'their surprise and regret that the other members should have so little regard to the objects of this Society, & to the mutual interests of each other, as to absent themselves so generally and so frequently from the monthly meetings'.[58] The minutes of the Huddersfield Medical Library record frequent and often bitter disputes over the payment of fines, and in 1865 some 'unpleasantness' arose from the want of a definite rule regulating the circulation of books and journals. It was resolved 'That Seniority of membership, should be the only principle of precedence recognized by the Society'.[59]

Outside the medical societies, accusations of undercutting and unfair competition were frequent causes of disputes over Poor Law and friendly society appointments. The Thornton–Kemp dispute discussed above was by no means untypical. Meanwhile, elections to dispensary and infirmary posts were typified by fierce rivalry, competition to win the support of the lay governors by means of personal solicitation and advertisement, and even the buying of votes. The competition for posts to the newly-inaugurated Huddersfield Dispensary in 1814 was, as the *Leeds Mercury* noted, 'marked by unpleasant Disputes'.[60] The election campaign resulted in Mr William Wilks being appointed senior surgeon. (The other surgical post was filled by George Robinson, the division of votes being Wilks 209, Robinson 174, Bradshaw 163 and Houghton 161.)[61] Before being appointed Wilks had made a speedy journey to Edinburgh to be examined by the Royal College of Surgeons. Without a diploma from this body, he would have been ineligible for the post of surgeon. This step was strongly urged by a Halifax colleague, John Thomson, physician to the Halifax Dispensary, who wrote a letter of introduction on Wilks's behalf to one of the examiners of the College. Before Wilks set off for Edinburgh, he received a letter from Thomson informing him of this action:

I ought sooner to have said Mr. Joseph Bell, my correspondent, is the youngest son of the late *Mr. Benjamin Bell*, the Author of the System of Surgery, and the *very best authority* and *best interest* in the place. I believe Mr. J. Bell, is an examiner. If not, he is as good as one of them, amongst them all and acquainted with them all. I don't believe they will ask you two questions, but this is *mum*. However easy your examination may be, do not either now, or at any time mention *that* I will write a letter of introduction to Mr. Joseph Bell by you . . . Bell's introduction will do your work (his emphasis).[62]

Thomson assured Wilks that if he took this step, and, on his return to Huddersfield, issued an advertisement offering himself for the post of surgeon, the appointment would be secured. Thomson also emphasised that if Wilks did not secure the post, the consequences for his future would be serious.

It is this conviction which makes me urge the importance of this step upon you. If the young men get in, depend upon it, they will in time rise, and they can only do so by rising on your and Mr. Houghton's ruin. *Your family therefore and any professional and private consideration* join me in urging this step (his emphasis).[63]

Competition for such posts was invariably fierce, and in 1833, in the run up to the election of a surgeon to the Huddersfield Infirmary, the committee resolved 'That a letter be sent to each of the candidates requesting them to abstain from buying votes for the occasion'.[64] Disputes between the medical staff of dispensaries and infirmaries following their appointments were also not unheard of. In 1853, for example, the committee of the Huddersfield Infirmary was forced to settle a question of precedence which had arisen between two recently-elected surgeons, Messrs Clarke and Tatham. The committee voted on the question, and decided Tatham was entitled to precedence over his colleague.[65]

In 1829 a dispute arose between the two physicians to the Wakefield Dispensary, Drs Crowther and Gilby, over the suitability of the Dispensary building. Dr Gilby denounced the building, situated under the Music Saloon in Wood Street, 'as a miserable and filthy hole, little better than a cell, and perfectly inadequate for its intended purpose'. Gilby's criticisms were supported by the surgical staff. Mr Horsfall, for example, declared that because of poor conditions it was impossible to perform any surgical operations in the Dispensary. Crowther, the senior physician, stated, on the other hand, that he found the building adequate and convenient, and was opposed to any move to a new location.[66] In 1832 the dispute flared up again following the death of the resident apothecary, Hodgson, of typhus fever. Gilby suggested that the apothecary might not have died had he resided in a healthier situation. Crowther, meanwhile, blamed Hodgson's death on his failure to consult other members of the Dispensary staff when taken ill. Hodgson, Crowther maintained, had mismanaged the treatment of the disease, dosing himself with contradictory medicines.[67] The argument between Crowther on the one hand, and Gilby and the surgical staff on the other, also centred around the viability of establishing surgical wards in the institution, an idea to which Crowther was strongly opposed.[68] The proposal to set up infirmary wards was in fact dropped for the time being, but Gilby and the surgeons appear to have made their point about the resiting of the Dispensary. Around this time the charity moved from its location under the Music Saloon to a new site in Barstow Square. Dr Crowther also failed to see eye to eye with several other of his medical brethren. He was, for example, involved in a fierce conflict with the Director of the Wakefield Asylum, Dr Corsellis, over the management of the institution. Crowther was

one of the old school of medicine and disliked any innovations, though for 8 years one of the physicians connected with the West Riding Lunatic Asylum, Dr. Corsellis then being the Director, between whom and Dr. Crowther there was little sympathy, partly on account of a book '*Observations on the management of Madhouses*' which the latter published in 1838, and which even his best friends regretted was ever issued from the press.[69]

Disputes between medical men were not just recorded in the pages of medical journals or confined to meetings of medical charities and societies. They were also reported in local newspapers, coming, therefore, to the direct notice of the public. The above disagreements between the medical officers of the Wakefield Dispensary were, for example, covered in some detail by the *Wakefield and Halifax Journal*. In 1860 two Huddersfield practitioners, Dr Clough and the anonymous 'MRCS', used the local press as a forum for their dispute over the status of their respective qualifications. The correspondence between the two, which continued for several weeks, centred mainly around Clough's use of the title 'doctor', which he had adopted on becoming a Licentiate of the Royal College of Physicians, Edinburgh, earlier in the year. 'MRCS' maintained that such a Licence did not give Clough the right to use this title; rather, only a university graduate was entitled to such a privilege. In turn, Clough accused 'MRCS' of sour grapes because he had 'discovered that my legal qualifications now are superior to his own'. Clough (who appeared to know the identity of 'MRCS') added in conclusion,

... when a man from private pique and acrimonious feeling towards me, represents to you that it is on public grounds only that he inquires about my license or title – prevaricates and falsifies the truth by slandering and misrepresenting me before the public – tis time such correspondence should cease, especially when such originates from an anonymous scribbler. I therefore (only) for the present, decline further correspondence. . . .[70]

Occasionally doctors produced and circulated pamphlets airing their grievances or attacking their colleagues. In 1864 T. R. Tatham, former surgeon to the Huddersfield Infirmary, published a series of letters which he had sent to the Infirmary Committee, making public his complaints against the institution. The correspondence was mainly directed against the lay governors of the charity, although Tatham also attacked several of the institution's medical officers, whom he accused of patrimony and 'trading in physic', stating that some of the medical officers 'I shall ever remember with esteem and regard, for others that feeling is remote'.[71] In particular, Tatham fiercely criticised the election of Mr Frederick Greenwood (son of William Greenwood, honorary surgeon) to the post of surgeon in 1862, claiming 'It savours strongly of a family pie!'[72]

For much of the nineteenth century relationships between medical men in Wakefield and Huddersfield were characterised, at least in part, by rivalries, hostility and petty jealousies. These disputes were potentially very damaging both to the images of individual practitioners and to the profession as a whole, and were hardly designed to inspire public confidence and trust. The stringent regulations of societies such as the Huddersfield Medico–Ethical Society appear more reasonable when they are seen in the context of a disunited and conflict-ridden profession. The promotion of a strict code of ethical behaviour, especially through the medium of local and national medical societies, was seen by medical men as an important method of regulating disputes, establishing procedures for their settlement and achieving at least the semblance of uniformity and unanimity.

The campaign against quackery

One issue around which the divided nineteenth-century medical profession was able to unite was the campaign against fringe medicine. The profession's opposition to quackery was consistent (and apparently largely ineffective)[73] throughout the century. It was a favourite topic in medical journals and publications of the period, and medical societies were generally opposed to all fringe practices, giving their absolute support to the allopathic system of medicine. One of the main tenets that the campaign against the unqualified rested on was that fringe practitioners used unreliable and even dangerous remedies, and therefore put at risk the health and lives of those they treated. Unqualified practice was also, quite rightly, seen as a threat to the pockets of regular doctors. The medical profession itself was overcrowded and competitive, and fringe personnel (lacking any formal training) provided extra and, in the eyes of regular practitioners, unfair competition. The medical fringe was the most important obstacle in the way of the closure of the profession. Once the fringe was eliminated, regular practitioners would obtain a monopoly over medical treatment.

Nineteenth-century medical journals (and the press) were quick to report alleged cases of malpractice on the part of quack doctors, the reports frequently being supplied in the first place by local medical men. For example, in 1854 both *The Lancet* and the *Medical Times and Gazette* seized on 'a deplorable instance of the evils resulting from the unrestrained usurption of the deep responsibilities of medical practice by ignorant pretenders . . .', which occurred at Meltham, near Huddersfield.[74] Jane Taylor, the wife of a Huddersfield weaver, was seized with haemorrhage in the eighth month of pregnancy, and an unqualified local practitioner, John Lingards Rawcliffe, was called in by her family. *The Lancet* commented that Rawcliffe

. . . was not only unqualified in the technical sense of possessing no diploma, but also absolutely unqualified by his gross ignorance of the duties he had the rashness to undertake.[75]

Rawcliffe attended the patient and supplied her with medicines, but when labour commenced the haemorrhaging increased and Jane Taylor died. The statements of two Huddersfield surgeons, Messrs W. Greenwood and Tatham (the two individuals who later clashed over Infirmary appointments), who carried out post-mortems on the woman, concluded that prompt action by a qualified practitioner would have saved her life.[76]

Strictly speaking, it was not only quack doctors who came under attack in medical journals. Regular practitioners, who had defected from the allopathic system of medicine, to embrace (even partially)

one of the 'pseudo-sciences', such as homoeopathy, hydropathy or mesmerism, were liable to similar treatment. In 1849 *The Lancet* reported a case of 'Homoeopathic Quackery in Huddersfield'.[77] Several men had been bitten by a rabid dog in Halifax, and two of them had died of hydrophobia, one of them while under the care of two 'regular' Halifax surgeons, Messrs Inglis and Fawthorp. The third case was treated by Mr Ramsbotham, a homoeopathic practitioner, 'who was once practising as a surgeon at Bradford, but with whom legitimate physic did not agree . . .'. (Presumably the John Hodgson Ramsbotham, who, homoeopathist or not, was recorded in the 1851 *Medical Directory* as holding the MRCS England and LSA (1832), and as practising in Huddersfield. By 1856 he had also acquired a medical degree (Erlangen and Lambeth).)[78] Ramsbotham was reported as being engaged in the practice of homoeopathy in the Huddersfield area. He claimed that hydrophobia could be cured by homoeopathic methods, and indeed the third man recovered under his care. Messrs Inglis and Fawthorp defended their own failure, and denied Ramsbotham's success, by claiming the case he had treated had not been one of hydrophobia. Rather, the man Ramsbotham had 'cured' was merely drunk and exhausted, and the homoeopathic practitioner had, they claimed, practised wilful deceit by pretending to effect a cure. *The Lancet*, naturally enough, supported the contentions of the regular practitioners, and concluded their account of the case with a warning:

We refer to the matter in question, in order to exhibit to the profession the tricks and tactics of homoeopathists. In other places, as well as in Halifax, honest medical men should be on their guard against the practices common to these people . . . and we only wish, that on all occasions in which legitimate medicine needs to be defended, and quackery attacked, the champion may be equal to Dr. INGLIS in tact, temper, and courage. We should then not have our provincial cities and towns overrun, as they now are, by a vagrant pack of homoeopathists and mesmerists.[79]

Not surprisingly, the majority of reports on unqualified practice which reached the medical journals involved alleged malpractice, which had resulted in death or injury, or cases of fraud or deceit. Cases of successful treatment by fringe practitioners were not reported. Nor was the possible value of fringe methods examined by the medical journals.

Wakefield and Huddersfield medical men joined with the rest of their medical brethren in producing papers on the subject of quackery, often for the benefit of the general reader, rather than their professional colleagues. For example, in 1855 Samuel Knaggs, later honorary surgeon to the Huddersfield Infirmary, produced *Common Sense versus Homoeopathy*, a short pamphlet designed for those 'who, from their want of medical knowledge, require it to be presented in a medium more condensed and popular'.[80] Knaggs expressed anxiety about the fact that many of the public, while not understanding homoeopathy, were favourable to its use. All the arguments contained in the pamphlet were, in Knaggs's own words, 'directed against the system of homoeopathy'.

My aim has been to show that homoeopathy is nothing more than leaving the disease to nature, and acting upon the imagination of the patient: . . . But when he (the homoeopath) professes and practises a species of jugglery, as the infinitesimal nonsense most assuredly is, he must not be surprised that medical men hold aloof and will not sanction, . . . what they conceive to be downright imposition.[81]

In a lecture to the Wakefield Mechanics' Institute, which was published in pamphlet form in 1843,[82] one of the town's most eminent physicians, Dr T. G. Wright, discussed the more general subject of quack medicines. The purpose of the lecture was, as he put it, to enable the working class, who formed the majority of the Institute's membership, to 'think correctly on a subject highly important to personal health and comfort, and yet on which a vast amount of ignorance and prejudice generally prevails . . .'. Wright vigorously attacked quacks and their medicines, which he suggested were at best useless, and at their worst extremely harmful. He pointed in particular to Morison's Pills, which were sold in the Wakefield marketplace, and which to his knowledge alone had caused attacks of paralysis and mental derangement. His parting words of advice on the issue were

Endeavour to acquire, and to act upon, such knowledge, as shall assist you to preserve health, to prevent disease, or to detect its first approaches . . . When you are ill, do not tamper with your complaint, but obtain medical assistance without delay; which, depend upon it, is the best economy in the end: . . . Lastly, as you value your own health, and that of those dear to you; as you would (such as are parents) see your children grow up robust and well; and as you would avoid trouble, suffering, and expense, prefer short doctors' bills to long ones, or, if possible, do without them altogether; AVOID THAT FRUITFUL SOURCE OF ALL THESE EVILS,

QUACK MEDICINES![83]

Despite exposure of the misdemeanours and neglect of the unqualified, the dangers of quack medicines and other adverse publicity, the medical profession failed to destroy quackery. Fringe practitioners did in fact present a formidable opposition. There was a long tradition of fringe practice, there were large numbers of unqualified medical men, they were cheap and popular (and not just with the poorer classes).[84] The regular doctor enjoyed little protection by the state, for unless the quack had broken the law, he could not be penalised for practising medicine. Although the 1858 Act had formally given qualified medical men a monopoly to practise, there was no way this provision could be enforced. Meanwhile, the layman did not fully support the regular doctor's claim to a monopoly position. 'Scientific medicine' did not produce valid therapeutic results until late in the century, and, as Peterson has pointed out, much of the available medical treatment was of questionable value, even by the standards of the day.[85] Moreover, the expansion of the medical market during the nineteenth century actually bred competition, the widespread need for medical services representing 'a tremendous asset for a category of professional producers only *after* they have succeeded in establishing a monopolistic hold on their market'.[86] The medical profession was in no condition to launch an attack on unqualified practice until it had put its own house in order. In 1839 a report of the Provincial Medical and Surgical Association, the forerunner of the BMA, declared

All active measures in relation to the suppression of quackery had better be delayed in the hope that a better organisation of the profession may render the suppression of quackery a more practicable undertaking than it appears at present to be.[87]

In Wakefield and Huddersfield the nineteenth century saw some movement towards this better organisation and the creation of professional unity. However, efforts to enhance the status and authority of the medical profession met with limited success, and the profession was unable to deal with two fundamental problems which beset qualified medical men for much of the nineteenth century: the survival of the fringe practitioner and the continuation of intra-professional conflict. Because of the failure to resolve these problems, the status of the profession remained dubious, its monopoly position far from assured. However, medical society activity did help mitigate these problems. The activities of the various associations encouraged increased social, intellectual and professional contact between medical men. By so doing, they may have taken some of the heat out of intra-professional conflict, and helped counteract these usually individualistic disputes before they were made public. The societies also provided forums for attacks upon quack medicine in the locality, an activity around which all medical men were able to unite. The high level of participation in medical society activity (the memorial presented to the Royal College of Surgeons in 1853 was, for example, signed by *all* Wakefield surgeons,[88] while the Huddersfield Medico–Ethical Society was supported by the majority of the town's practitioners), and the formulation of a strict code of ethics, provided a framework within which unity became possible.

8.2 Social activities: doctors and laymen

Wakefield and Huddersfield medical men involved themselves in a wide variety of civic activities during the nineteenth century. Some were concerned with public health reform; others were active in the provision of medical relief for the poor (via Poor Law agencies, medical charities or private philanthropy). A small number of medical men became involved in politics, in most cases at a local level, while probably the most common form of civic activity to attract doctors was participation in voluntary societies. All these forms of activity brought medical practitioners into direct contact with the lay communities of Wakefield and Huddersfield, in particular the middle classes. These contacts were of vital importance in an era when the personality and social attributes of medical men could be seen as crucial determinants of the success of their careers.

In this Section the different forms of civic activity which attracted medical men will be examined. The discussion will centre very much around voluntary societies, including charitable, religious, social and cultural organisations. Emphasis will be placed, naturally enough, on the involvement of doctors in the major medical charities, which served as 'institutional foci for the medical community'.[89] Other civic and public functions which interested doctors will be examined, in particular public health and its reform.

The Section will also look at a sample of individual medical men who become particularly active in the affairs of the two towns during the nineteenth century. An analysis of the involvement of medical men in voluntary societies could prove to be interesting for a number of reasons. Their activities in this sphere tell us something about their concerns and interests, and in some cases their social, political and religious backgrounds. Association with local élites through these mediums could be seen as an indication of a fairly high level of social acceptability and status. It could also indicate, especially where involvement in such activities implied financial contributions, reasonably high levels of income.

The actual number of medical men involved in voluntary society activity was not necessarily large. However, in Wakefield doctors seem to have experienced far higher levels of involvement than their Huddersfield contemporaries, not only in voluntary society activity, but also in other civic functions. In some Wakefield societies, particularly those linked to educational pursuits, medical practitioners made up a significant proportion of the membership, especially in relation to their numbers. In a few cases they comprised the most active group of supporters. In other Wakefield societies involvement was limited to the 'top' medical men of the community – those with the best practices and appointments, who were well known locally. In Huddersfield, meanwhile, participation in civic activities was generally restricted to the local medical élite. This was especially the case when involvement went beyond the payment of a financial contribution, to committee work or appointment to an official post. Towards the end of this Section an attempt will be made to relate medical men's degree of participation in civic activities to the differing social and economic structures of the two communities.

The activities which medical men became involved in tended to reflect their specialised knowledge and interests. They played a key role in the medical charities of the two towns, not only as the providers of medical treatment, but also as managers of the institutions. In provincial towns such as Wakefield and Huddersfield medical men formed the core and main representatives of a 'scientific community', and at many points the medical and scientific communities overlapped.[90] Doctors were interested in the promotion of societies with a scientific bias: in Wakefield, for example, the Microscopic Society[91] and the Museum. They also (especially in

Wakefield) became active in other educational societies, which apparently lacked any strong scientific, or at least medical, leanings: the Mechanics' Institutes, Philosophical and Literary Societies, and Newsroom Societies. They became involved in missionary and non-medical charitable work to a lesser extent. Participation in these areas seemed to be more a matter for individual conscience, rather than a group activity.

Medical charity

One of the first types of activity which medical men became involved in was the promotion (through publicity and fund-raising) and support of local medical charities. In Wakefield two of the town's most influential medical men, Drs Richardson and Dawson, were active in promoting the Dispensary from its establishment in 1787. During the first half of the nineteenth century the surgical staff of the Dispensary, Messrs Horsfall and Dawson, with the support of Dr Gilby, honorary physician to the charity, pressed for the addition of wards for accident cases (although this proposal was opposed by the senior physician to the Dispensary, Dr Crowther). In Huddersfield Dr Walker, the town's leading physician, campaigned for the foundation of the General Dispensary, which was set up in 1814. In the 1820s Walker, joined by Dr Turnbull, another eminent local physician and medical officer to the Dispensary, also advocated the need for the addition of in-patient facilities. Both physicians produced pamphlets outlining the necessity for such a provision.[92]

Once the medical charities were established, the leading medical men of the towns were prepared, or rather eager, to give their services free of charge and involve themselves in the administration of the institutions. In addition to attending once or twice a week to dispense medical treatment, the medical officers took a large part in the day-to-day management of the charities, serving on committees and sub-committees, compiling reports, supervising the appointment of paid staff and apprentices, and fund-raising. The newly-appointed medical staff of the Huddersfield Dispensary, for example, became involved in the preparations for its official opening in 1814. They were responsible for directing the repair and alteration of the Dispensary building, ordering tables, counters, drawers, utensils, surgical instruments and drugs, preparing a register of patients, and for making arrangements for the supply of leeches to the institution 'at as cheap a rate as they can'.[93] In 1815 Dr Walker, together with three lay officers, was made responsible for writing letters to the ministers of local churches and chapels requesting them to preach sermons and make collections in aid of the Dispensary. In 1824 Dr Walker was requested to draw up an appeal to the ladies of Huddersfield asking them to provide flannel for the patients.[94]

The medical staff of the Dispensary were also very much involved in the preparations for the opening of the Infirmary at its new site on the New North Road in 1831. They were made responsible for giving estimates of the accommodation thought necessary and the costs of running the proposed institution, and for checking the suitability of plans submitted by the architect. The medical staff helped draw up new rules, ordered beds and other furniture for the rooms and wards, and assisted in the appointment of additional staff, including a matron, an apothecary and several nurses.[95] In 1848 the medical officers were co-opted on to the newly-established House Committee, set up to superintend annual expenditure and to guard against extravagance. In the following year the medical staff were made responsible for supervising the provision of new drains at the Infirmary together with the Huddersfield Improvement Commissioners. In 1869 a sub-committee of three gentlemen and the honorary medical staff was appointed to report on the best mode of warming and ventilating the Infirmary, and in the same year the medical officers were requested to make any alterations that they thought necessary to the patients' diet tables.[96] The staff of the Wakefield Dispensary and Infirmary had similar obligations. Most of the responsibility for the governance of the Wakefield House of Recovery, meanwhile, devolved on the Ladies Committee. The medical officers were, however, responsible for the medical administration and for drawing up annual reports. The physicians also assisted the Ladies Committee with arrangements for the annual charity ball.

As R. J. Morris has pointed out, medical charities could have become sites of conflict between the lay supporters, who funded the institutions, and the medical officers, with their perhaps differing conception of the purposes of medical charity.[97] However, conflicts between the medical staff and the lay administrators appear to have been rare in the Wakefield and Huddersfield institutions.[98] Although the lay officers do seem to have been the dominant force in decision-making, the two groups co-operated well at committee and general meetings, presenting a uniform front on such important issues as admission policies, organisation and funding. As the medical officers became involved in the administration of the charities, they also became aware of their financial limitations. The lay and medical supporters of the charities, meanwhile, shared an interdependent relationship with each other, which ensured a high degree of consensus. The medical charities would have been unable to function without the active co-operation of local medical men. On the other hand, the advantages derived from an honorary medical post at a dispensary or infirmary, in terms of social and professional rewards and practice-building opportunities, were sufficient to ensure that there was always an over-abundance of medical practitioners ready and willing to fill these posts and to supply the medical needs of the lay managers of these institutions.[99]

Whenever lay officers expressed an opinion on the work of the honorary medical staff, it was usually couched in terms of approbation and gratitude. For example, at the Annual General Meeting of subscribers to the Huddersfield Dispensary, held in June, 1821, it was resolved

That the most cordial thanks of this meeting be given to the medical and surgical officers of this Institution for the *valuable service they have professionally rendered* to the numerous afflicted objects of its charity and for *their personal sanction and support* of its interests (my emphasis).[100]

Similarly, the committee of the Wakefield Infirmary remarked in their annual report for 1870–1871

. . . that it is due to the Honorary Medical officers to acknowledge their grateful sense of the very kind and efficient service so constantly rendered by those gentlemen in their treatment of the sick and the suffering, both in the house and at their own homes. *It is clear that the benefits conferred on the poor of our town and neighbourhood through this charity depends in a large measure on their skill and gratuitous attention* (my emphasis).[101]

Given that the medical officers were hand-picked by the lay governors, the consensus which existed between lay and medical supporters becomes less surprising. Although candidates for posts were vetted by the medical officers, who checked their testimonials and qualifications, the real task of electing the medical staff devolved upon the general body of subscribers, who were in fact responsible for judging the medical skills and competency of the applicants. In this way, the involvement of doctors in medical charities differed fundamentally from their participation in other voluntary society activity, which was less likely to be regulated by their peer (or socially superior) groups. The election of medical officers aroused a great deal of interest amongst subscribers; the majority participated in the elections, even if they had little other involvement in the functioning of the charity.[102]

Successful candidates were normally drawn from the medical élites of the two towns – those with the best qualifications and practices. In theory the posts were limited to 'pure' physicians and surgeons.[103] The holders of honorary medical posts were selected, however, not just on the basis of any medical knowledge and skills that they might have been seen to possess, but also on the basis of their social acceptability and personal bearing. The medical officers of the charities were to be first and foremost 'gentlemen', and as such representative of the middle-class lifestyle and interests. In the words of Inkster, 'a physician or surgeon to the Infirmary was not simply the holder of a medical office, but also the approved representative of the local middle class'.[104] His wife and other family members frequently participated in the medical charities, as fundraisers, subscribers, 'donors of useful articles' or visitors.[105]

Local men, who had practised in the town, in particular the sons of established medical practitioners, stood a greater chance of being elected. This applied especially to surgeons, who were more likely to have completed at least part of their training in the locality. In Huddersfield there even appears to have been a residency requirement for appointment to honorary Dispensary and Infirmary posts. The qualifications required by the institutions, meanwhile, tended to be lower for local men than for 'foreigners'. When Thomas Abbey Bottomley applied for the post of surgeon to the Huddersfield Infirmary in 1865, he placed the following advertisement in the local newspaper:

TO THE GOVERNORS OF THE HUDDERSFIELD AND UPPER AGBRIGG INFIRMARY . . .

I trust that my being a townsman, also having for a period of more than three years discharged the duties of House-Surgeon to your valuable institution, and since then being engaged in extensive private practice in the town and neighbourhood, will ensure me your vote and personal interest.

T. A. Bottomley
MRCSL, LSA[106]

His candidature was in fact successful, although two previous attempts to seek appointment in 1862 and 1863 had failed. (Two out of the three honorary surgeons elected in these years had also been born and trained in Huddersfield. All three had practised in the town for a number of years).

The post of honorary medical officer was not only confined to an élite, but also to a small number of medical men. Initially the Wakefield Dispensary appointed only two physicians. In 1823 two surgical posts were created, and, following a 'sharp contest' between four applicants, Messrs Horsfall and Dawson were appointed.[107] The number of honorary posts remained the same for the rest of the nineteenth century, in spite of a considerable expansion in the number of patients treated and the addition of in-patient facilities in 1854. In 1814 two physicians and two surgeons were appointed as medical officers to the Huddersfield Dispensary. In 1820 an additional surgeon was elected, and in 1853 two further surgical appointments were created, making seven posts in all.

Honorary medical posts were permanent and doctors tended to hang on to them for many years, even if they were no longer fit to practise. Medical men who had served the charities for long periods (in the region of twenty to thirty years) were given the opportunity to act as consulting physicians or surgeons upon their retirement from the normal duties of medical officer. Many medical practitioners retained their hospital posts until death. For example, John Horsfall filled the post of surgeon to the Wakefield Dispensary and Infirmary for a period of over thirty years, from 1823 until 1856. In 1856 he accepted the office of consulting surgeon and served the institution in this capacity until his death in 1859. Dr Caleb Crowther rendered his services as physician to the Wakefield Dispensary from 1795 until his death in 1849 (54 years).[108]

Dr John Kenworthy Walker served the Huddersfield Dispensary and Infirmary, an institution he had been especially active in promoting, from its initiation in 1814 until 1846, when he was forced to resign on account of poor health. In his letter of resignation Walker declared

It has been a main object of my wishes to see the Infirmary a real benefit to the poor, as well as honour to the town and I do hope under providence, it may continue to be more and more useful every year.

The Board received his resignation with 'deep regret'; during the 32 years he had served the institution 'by his medical skill, unwearied energies and Benevolent disposition the usefulness of this charity was widely extended, . . .'.[109] Walker, however, continued to serve the institution in the capacity of consulting physician. William Greenwood, the son of a Cleckheaton medical practitioner, acted as house surgeon to the Huddersfield Dispensary between 1820 and 1823.[110] After completing his studies at Guy's and St Thomas's Hospitals, he returned to Huddersfield, where he practised for almost forty years. Greenwood was honorary surgeon to the Infirmary from 1834 to within a few weeks of his death in 1862. In 1862 he had taken up the post of consulting surgeon. George Robinson was appointed one of the first surgeons to the Huddersfield Dispensary in 1814. He relinquished his active duties in 1853 on account of 'failing health', but continued to serve as consulting surgeon until his death in 1865. In recording his death in the annual report for the year 1865–1866, the Board were

at a loss to convey an adequate expression of their sense of the valuable services, which, for a period extending over more than fifty years, he rendered to the charity. He discharged his duties ably and faithfully and was revered and respected by all.[111]

William Turnbull had perhaps the most impressive record of service during this period, acting as physician to the Huddersfield Dispensary and Infirmary from 1816 until within a few weeks of his death in 1876, a period of sixty years! In 1871 he was appointed consulting physician, and in the same year it was agreed that one ward of the proposed new building should be called the 'Turnbull Ward'.[112] Appointment to the honorary posts of the charities was, therefore, limited to a few medical men in both Wakefield and Huddersfield. The posts were awarded to an élite group. The appointment then tended to reaffirm this status.

In most circumstances if a doctor failed to be chosen as a medical officer, he also withheld his financial and organisational support from the charity. Few doctors without honorary posts paid subscriptions or donations to the medical charities; fewer still served on committees or in any other official capacity. For example, only three medical men were recorded as having made donations to the fund for the building of the Huddersfield Infirmary. One, Dr J. K. Walker, was honorary physician to the Dispensary. Another, Dr Bradley, had been honorary physician to the charity between 1814 and 1816, but had been forced to resign on account of ill health. The third medical man to make a contribution was Dr Crowther, physician to the Wakefield Dispensary.[113] The only two medical men to subscribe in 1863 to the Prince Albert Memorial Fund to build an additional ward in the Wakefield Infirmary were Drs Holdsworth and Kendell, the two honorary physicians to the charity.[114]

Those doctors who felt in some way excluded from or maltreated by the medical charities could be very critical of their governance, although they seem to have objected more to the system of appointments, rather than to playing second fiddle in decision-making and the admission of patients (medical officers still being only allowed to have one or two patients on the books at a time in the 1870s). The comments of Brady and Tatham on election procedures and the operation of patrimony in the Huddersfield Infirmary have been referred to in Section 8.1 (and this subject was also fiercely de-bated by the Select Committee on Medical Education in 1834, when nepotism and patronage were claimed to be rife in hospitals). Tatham resigned his post as surgeon to the Infirmary in 1863 after nine years in office. Shortly after he sent a series of letters to the Infirmary Committee complaining of the favouritism shown to some of the medical officers. Tatham maintained, probably with some justification, that the governors of the Infirmary were not influenced by considerations of merit or experience, but by social and family concerns. With respect to the election of Frederick Greenwood as surgeon in 1862, Tatham remarked 'Was it not broadly asserted and publicly reported a son was to be elected out of respect for long services rendered by his father?' Tatham also attacked the committee for not acknowledging his services on his retirement from office. Tatham claimed that 'to omit to mention the *resignation* of a *Medical Officer* is a departure from *customary etiquette*, by which *omission* the *ordinary duty*, pertaining to a Public Institution is *subverted*, to make room for the *display* of a *malicious* and *vindictive feeling*' (his emphasis).[115]

The Infirmary Committee maintained that the omission was not intentional, and that Tatham's services had been fully recognised in a resolution of the committee when he announced his departure from Huddersfield.[116] Tatham's complaints continued, however, and finally in June, 1865 the committee further acknowledged his services at the Annual Meeting of Governors.[117] A copy of the resolution was forwarded to Tatham by David Marsden, Honorary

Secretary, together with an extraordinary piece of correspondence. The letter stated

You are a poor miserable person, an enemy to yourself and family; you came to Huddersfield with an excellent prospect before you, and you have made a wreck of yourself . . . You have quarrelled with your Medical Brethren . . . you have insulted the Infirmary Board, as if you considered them all to be your enemies . . . A word of praise to others appears to cut you to the quick, you take it as an oversight of your great abilities and services . . . I fear your condition is hopeless; any one who may read your disgraceful productions cannot fail to come to a very decided conclusion as to the state of your mind . . . You may depend upon it, that I would much sooner play a Game at Chess, than reply to one of your filthy compositions . . . You may print this letter if you think it likely to serve your purpose.!![118]

At the Annual General Meeting of the Huddersfield Infirmary in 1859 Mr Samuel Knaggs, a Huddersfield general practitioner, proposed a resolution suggesting that the governors should investigate the possibilities of self-help medical provisions for the poor of the town as an alternative to medical charity.[119] In the same year Knaggs wrote to the *Medical Times and Gazette* proposing the setting up of insurance societies for the poor and working classes, to which every qualified, regular doctor could be attached.[120] Knaggs's suggestion to the Infirmary governors was rejected out of hand, and Knaggs appears to have overcome any scruples he felt about the nature of medical charity when he was appointed to the post of honorary surgeon in 1863.[121] On the whole attacks by medical practitioners on either the nature of medical charity or on the particular administration of the Wakefield and Huddersfield institutions were rare, and seem to have been easily overcome by appointment to the sought-after honorary posts.

Other voluntary society activity
Medical practitioners in both Wakefield and Huddersfield showed an interest in cultural and educational societies, including those designed for their own intellectual improvement and those intended to provide some form of education for the lower classes. Involvement in societies of this nature, however, was more particularly the preserve of the local medical élite, especially in Huddersfield, and when it is considered that, in theory at least, doctors represented one of the best-educated groups in the two towns, their participation in some organisations was rather limited. Involvement in

associations set up to study natural history or science, for example, tended to be patronised for the most part only by those medical men with the best practices and honorary appointments.

The Wakefield Microscopic Society, founded in 1854 by and for medical men, opened its doors to interested laymen in 1858. This move appears to have coincided with a fall off in the support of medical practitioners. In 1858 ten medical practitioners were members of the Society (almost half of the Wakefield medical profession). By 1871 the number had dwindled to four, namely Dr Samuel Holdsworth (physician to the Wakefield Dispensary and Infirmary), Dr T. G. Wright (late physician to the Wakefield House of Recovery and consulting physician to the West Riding Lunatic Asylum) and Messrs Thomas Walker and James Fowler (honorary surgeons to the Wakefield Dispensary and Infirmary).[122] In the mid-nineteenth century Mr Henry Dunn was appointed Treasurer to the Wakefield Museum, while Dr William Thomas served on the council.[123] Both men held honorary posts, Dunn as surgeon to the House of Recovery, Thomas as physician to the Dispensary, House of Recovery and Lunatic Asylum. No other medical men appear to have participated.

A larger group of medical men became active in the town's two main educational societies, the Philosophical and Literary Society and the Mechanics' Institute, although the right to act in an official capacity was normally confined to the local medical élite. Dr T. G. Wright and Mr Dunn, for example, were both elected several times between 1825 and 1838 (when the Society was disbanded) to the post of President of the Phil. and Lit. Society. A wider cross-section of the Wakefield medical profession became members, and indeed this group came to dominate the Society, including Drs Gilby and Alexander and Messrs W. R. Milner, W. Statter, Starkey and J. Horsfall. Medical men offered lectures on a wide variety of subjects, of which only a small proportion could be classified as medical or scientific. In the late 1820s and 1830s, for example, Mr Dunn lectured on such topics as the varieties of human race, on the play *Cymbeline*, gymnastics, the Thames tunnel, deaf and dumb institutions, apparitions, pastimes, 'science', prison discipline, the supply of water to towns and 'The Deluge'![124]

Medical men were also involved in the Liberal-dominated Wakefield Mechanics' Institute, set up originally in 1820 and reconstituted in 1841. In 1841 books were donated to the Institute by Drs

Wright and Crowther and Messrs Dawson and Ebenezer Walker. Several medical men served as officers or committee members – Dr J. G. Atkinson (VP), Dr T. G. Wright (VP), Ebenezer Walker, Junior (VP), W. R. Milner (committee), Dr Samuel Holdsworth (committee) and Mr William Dyson Wood (committee). In addition to serving as officers and supplying books and equipment, members of the Wakefield medical profession spoke frequently at meetings or offered courses. In the year 1867–1868, for example, Dr T. G. Wright gave a talk on the origin of the English language, Mr W. R. Milner spoke on the subject of 'A Visit to Switzerland' and Lawson Tait lectured on Britain during the Stone Age. In 1870–1871 Mr R. Creane, house surgeon to the Infirmary, lectured on the subject of the human body, J. Fowler discussed astrological medicine and fortune-telling, while J. Crichton Browne, Esq., MD, Medical Superintendent of the Asylum, gave a talk entitled 'Observations on Obsequies'![125]

In Huddersfield only two medical men, Messrs Wilks and Houghton, were included amongst the 42 founder members of the Subscription Library, which was set up in 1807.[126] A handful of doctors also participated in the activities of the Huddersfield Mechanics' Institute after its establishment in 1844. Only one medical man, Dr R. Cameron, served the Institute in any official capacity: he was appointed Honorary Secretary in the 1850s and was one of the nine Life Members. Between 1844 and 1870 (when this survey ends) a few other doctors became involved in the work of the Institute – Mr William Greenwood, Mr Samuel Knaggs, Dr Ramsbotham[127] and Mr T. A. Bottomley.[128] (With the exception of Ramsbotham, all were honorary surgeons to the Infirmary.) In terms of membership their participation was insignificant. In 1855, for example, two doctors were listed as annual members out of a total of approximately 150.[129] Meanwhile, George Sargent, one of the town's most eminent surgeons, was the only medical man to play a significant role in the founding of the Huddersfield College in 1838. He was also involved in its subsequent management, serving on the Council of the College and acting as an examiner. Two other medical practitioners, Thomas R. Tatham and William Turnbull (honorary Infirmary officers), were governors of the College.[130]

Similarly, only three medical men were recorded as being involved in the Huddersfield Archaeological Association (forerunner of the Yorkshire Archaeological Society), founded in 1863, a society which enjoyed much aristocratic patronage. The Patron of the Association was the Earl of Dartmouth; Vice-Patrons included Sir John William Ramsden, Sir George Armytage, Sir Joseph Radcliffe and T. P. Crosland, Esq., MP. Dr William Turnbull, physician to the Infirmary, was elected President for the year 1866; J. K. Walker, MD, consulting physician, was one of the Vice-Presidents and G. W. Rhodes, honorary surgeon, an ordinary member.[131] Walker was one of the society's most prolific members, a regular lecturer and publisher on the subject of topography. As early as the 1820s Walker had published a topographical account of Huddersfield, relating it to the mortality of the town.[132]

Medical men seem to have become prominent in the field of public speaking during the nineteenth century, and not just within the confines of the various educational institutes. It was an activity which brought them into contact with and to the notice of middle- and upper-class groups. Appearance in the public eye offered doctors the chance not only to demonstrate their scientific knowledge, but also to show themselves to be gentlemen of many accomplishments and interests. They were able to capitalise on a growth of interest in science, which may have been given a boost by the setting up of medical charities in the two towns. Sometimes their talks were published in pamphlet form, directed mainly at a lay public.

When Dr Alexander donated the profits of his pamphlet on phrenology to the Wakefield Dispensary in 1827, for example, it was not only remarked on as an 'instance of literary kindness'; it also brought Alexander's name and opinions into the homes of many wealthy Wakefield families. The list of subscribers to the pamphlet was impressive, including many important local families: for instance, the Gaskells, Ridsdales, Leathams and Tootals (all potential and wealthy clients).[133] The editor of the *Wakefield and Halifax Journal* remarked that it was his wish that the author would be 'induced' to present the public with his remaining essays.[134]

The interests of James Fowler, honorary surgeon to the Wakefield Infirmary, extended far outside the medical field, to encompass water pollution and supply, agriculture, archaeology and history. He published a number of papers in the *Yorkshire Archaeological and Topographical Journal*, including a piece 'On Mural Paintings and other Antiquities at All Saints, Wakefield'.[135] He was a regular speaker at the Mechanics' Institute on the subjects of archaeology and history. In 1865 Fowler gave a series of lectures on phrenology at the Wakefield Music Saloon, covering such topics as 'Love, Courtship and Marriage', 'Self-knowledge and Self-culture' and 'The Location, Definition and Natural Language of the Organs', medical science popularised! At the final session Mr Fowler devoted two hours to a public examination of persons and a delineation of characters, which were 'in general' correct. All the lectures were reported as being well attended.[136]

Samuel Knaggs, a Huddersfield GP, published several pamphlets during the mid-nineteenth century directed primarily at an educated lay audience – *On the Unsoundness of Mind considered in relation to the question of responsibility for Criminal Acts* (1853), *Common Sense versus Homoeopathy* (1855) and *Some Thoughts on the Rights and Duties of the Individual in his Social and National Life* (n.d.). Samuel Booth of Huddersfield, an active temperance reformer, offered a series of talks and pamphlets in the 1850s and 1860s on the dangers of alcohol drinking and smoking, and on self-help medicine. (He also published widely in medical journals on similar subjects.)[137]

Meanwhile, during Lawson Tait's short stay in Wakefield he proved himself to be an enthusiastic public speaker and author. His lectures and publications, aside from his enormous outpourings on medical subjects, covered the fields of anthropology, natural history and pre-historic archaeology. Tait, a disciple of Darwin, was active in the International Congress of Pre-historic Archaeology and a Fellow of the London Anthropological Society.[138] While in Wakefield he became involved in both the Mechanics' and Church Institutes. In 1867 Tait delivered his piece on 'Britain in the Stone Age' to the latter Institute. The lecture, which went on for two hours, created a certain amount of scandal, the Chairman chiding Tait for expressing opinions about the origin of man which contradicted Old Testament teaching. In 1868 the *Wakefield Journal and Examiner* reported on Tait's 'voluminous' lecture to the Mechanics' Institute on the subject of alcohol, which had lasted for four hours. Tait suggested that crime and disease were not related to alcohol, and that it was in fact a useful food, on this occasion incurring the wrath of the temperance reformers. One critic commented that Tait, noted for his dogmatism, should abandon medicine and exercise his talents from 'the pulpit or in the law courts'![139]

The range of societies which could be examined in the context of this Section was by no means exhaustive. But medical men appear to have involved themselves rather less in non-medical charitable activities. Only a small group of medical men, for example, subscribed to the Wakefield Benevolent Society in the 1830s. Dr Corsellis, Medical Superintendent of the West Riding Lunatic Asylum, was a committee member, and Drs Crowther and Thomas and Mr Henry Dunn annual subscribers,[140] representing less than one-sixth of all medical practitioners in the town. The inter-denominational Wakefield Town Mission, a visiting society set up in 1840, which in a limited number of cases gave medical assistance to the sick poor, was supported by only a small proportion of the town's medical practitioners from its initiation up to 1870 – Drs Holdsworth, Julius and Kendell and Messrs Dunn, Ross and William Statter, plus two doctors' wives, Mrs Crowther and Mrs Corsellis. Several medical men were appointed by the charity as honorary medical officers. The first consulting physician was Dr Crowther; the first surgeons Messrs E. Walker and Son, members of the old Wakefield surgical family. Following Crowther's death in 1849, Dr T. G. Wright was appointed consulting physician. In 1870 Mr Jennings, former house surgeon to the Wakefield Infirmary, took over the post of honorary surgeon.[141]

In Huddersfield there appears to have been an even greater exclusivity, with a very small number of doctors involving themselves in the activities of non-medical charities and voluntary societies. For example, Dr William Turnbull seems to have been the only medical practitioner active in the Huddersfield Benevolent and Visiting Society during the first decades of the nineteenth century, and George Sargent the only one to serve on the committee of the Huddersfield Auxiliary Peace Society (set up in 1823 to circulate religious tracts). During the course of the nineteenth century, meanwhile, just a small group of medical men played an active role in the Huddersfield Temperance Society – Thomas Wrigley, James Astin, Samuel Booth and Norman Porritt.[142]

Public health

One area of civic activity which captured the interest of large numbers of the medical profession was public health and its reform. This was a natural enough extension of the work of medical men concerned with disease prevention and the effects of urban filth, sanitation, housing and water supply on the health of the population. During the late eighteenth and early nineteenth centuries medical practitioners became more and more involved in what could be loosely labelled 'social medicine', including industrial medicine and sanitary reform. Large towns and cities could all boast of medical practitioners eminent in these fields: in London Southwood Smith, Neil Arnott, William Farr and John Simon, in Manchester Thomas Percival, John Ferriar, James Phillips Kay and Peter Gaskell, in Leeds Robert Baker and Charles Turner Thackrah, and in Sheffield George Calvert Holland.[143] As M. E. Rose has pointed out, it is probable that examples of doctors who were actively concerned with social medicine, including public health reform, could be found in most urban communities during this period.[144]

In Wakefield and Huddersfield the interest of medical men in public health, and in particular its relationship to disease prevention, was illustrated by a considerable outpouring of literature on the subject. The cholera epidemics of 1832 and 1849 excited particular interest. Medical men in both towns offered their interpretations of how cholera was caused and spread, and, more importantly, how to cure and prevent the disease. Henry Dunn, visiting surgeon to the House of Correction, published a piece in *The Lancet* in 1833 on outbreaks of cholera and diarrhoea in the institution. In 1850 Dr T. G. Wright, physician to the Wakefield Asylum, made an attempt to explain the devastating epidemic of cholera which had broken out in the Asylum in the previous year.[145] Drs Turnbull and Taylor and Mr Samuel Booth of Huddersfield contributed papers to medical journals describing their experiences in the 1832 and 1849 cholera outbreaks, suggesting preventative measures. Taylor's piece is of particular interest, giving a case-by-case breakdown of 93 cholera (and diarrhoea) victims in Huddersfield, who had fallen prey to the 1849 epidemic.[146]

But it was not just epidemics which excited the interest of Wakefield and Huddersfield doctors. Throughout the nineteenth century there was a steady outpouring of literature on the sanitary condition of the towns, water supply and cleanliness, and the effects which improvement in these areas could have on the more 'everyday' diseases of the period: typhus, typhoid fever, smallpox, influenza and the contagious diseases of childhood. Samuel Booth published a number of papers on these subjects in the 1850s and 1860s – 'Precautions for the Prevention of Cholera' (1851), 'Essays on Sanitary Measures for the Prevention of Diseases' (1857), 'On

Fever in the Provinces' (1862) and 'Vaccination and Re-Vaccination' (1863).[147] In the late 1860s Mr James Fowler of Wakefield contributed a 'Report on the Condition of the Calder and its Tributaries in the Wakefield District' to the Third Report of the Royal Commission on the Pollution of Rivers.[148] In 1870 Dr James Crichton Browne and Lawson Tait assisted Dr Radcliffe, Medical Officer to the Privy Council, in the compilation of his report on the state of the sanitation, housing and water supply of Wakefield.[149]

For the first three-quarters of the nineteenth century the medical profession of Wakefield and Huddersfield normally acted in a consultative rather than official capacity in the field of public health. In 1873 the first Medical Officer of Health, John Benson Pritchett, was appointed in Huddersfield, followed by Dr J. S. Cameron.[150] In the late 1860s Mr William Swift Wade was appointed Officer of Health to the Borough of Wakefield. Previous to this a few medical men had served on the various official bodies set up in the towns to regulate water supply, sewerage, nuisance removal, scavenging, and so on. Messrs Wrigley and Bradshaw of Huddersfield were elected Street Commissioners, and Messrs B. Walker and W. Statter and Dr Wood served in the same capacity in Wakefield. William Dean was appointed Chairman of the Slaithwaite Board of Health in the 1860s. These men, however, did not necessarily represent the interests and concerns of the profession as a whole, apparently taking on 'another hat' when acting in their official capacity, expressing as much concern with rate saving as improving the sanitary state of the towns.

Poor Law medical officers were in a somewhat better position than their colleagues to attempt at least to insist on the provision of special facilities for fever cases, in particular isolation hospitals, on the removal of nuisances, and the encouragement of vaccination amongst the poor, although their efforts in these areas could be severely handicapped by the parsimonious attitude of the Boards of Guardians.[151] The medical staff of the Wakefield and Huddersfield medical charities, meanwhile, were able to monitor the effects of low standards of public health on the local communities. The treatment of large numbers of home cases gave the medical officers of the dispensaries and infirmaries the chance to observe the relationship between poor living and sanitary conditions and the incidence of epidemic disease. One of the tasks of the medical staff of the House of Recovery was to visit the homes of patients' families following their removal to the hospital to advise them on how best to prevent the spread of disease, usually typhus, to other family members, authorising financial assistance if it was believed necessary.

Peter Razzell has suggested that the dispensary movement helped in the diffusion of principles of personal hygiene, which he claims had some significance in reducing mortality rates in the first half of the nineteenth century.[152] The medical officers of the Huddersfield Dispensary and Infirmary did apparently see the necessity of impressing the rudiments of health care and hygiene on the patients (and their families) who came under their care. In-patients were ordered to bring with them supplies of clean linen, and those well enough assisted the nurses with washing and cleaning the wards. They also recognised the importance of pointing out special trouble spots to the appropriate authorities, and in some cases the officers of the institution took action themselves to clean up these areas of town.

A resolution of the AGM of June, 1824, for example, recommended to the newly-appointed committee that they '. . . appoint one or two of their number to make occasional visitations to the different Lodging Houses and report the state in which they find them to be'.[153] In 1837 the Reverend J. R. Oldham read a report to the Infirmary Committee on the state of lodging houses in Huddersfield. He claimed that out of the fifteen Irish lodging houses in the town, which together contained eighty beds, there had been 67 recent cases of typhus fever. The medical officers suggested that the best preventative measure would be to institute a twice-yearly whitewashing, and a public subscription was initiated by the committee to pay for this and the further cleansing of the lodging houses.[154] Another form of preventive medicine encouraged by both the committees and medical officers of the medical charities was vaccination, a service which was offered to the poor gratis. There were repeated vaccination drives during the nineteenth century: between 1814 and 1818, for example, 700 poor persons in the Huddersfield area availed themselves of this service. 331 were vaccinated in the year 1815–1816 alone, when a severe smallpox epidemic prevailed in the region.[155]

Doctors were also called in occasionally, usually in a crisis situation, to give practical assistance with health problems, or more commonly to help treat outbreaks of epidemic disease. During the cholera epidemics of 1832 and 1849, for example, additional medical men were drafted in to assist the medical officer to the Wakefield House of Correction. During the severe outbreak of 1832, when cholera and diarrhoea raged for two months, resulting in a total of 151 cases and 21 deaths, Drs Gilby and Thomas and Mr Starkey were engaged to assist Mr Dunn. Similarly, in 1849, when cholera struck again, Dr Thomas and Mr Marshall were called in to relieve the two regular medical officers, Messrs Milner and Dunn. Both the permanent staff and relief doctors were remunerated for their services. Dr Thomas received £25, Messrs Milner and Dunn £21 and Mr Marshall fifteen guineas.[156]

The Boards of Guardians employed additional medical men to relieve their medical officers or summoned expert advice, although usually only in cases of great emergency. In 1843, for example, Dr Turnbull was called in to consult with Mr Helliwell, the medical officer to the Huddersfield Workhouse. Helliwell had been unable to eradicate a serious infectious disorder, which had attacked half the Workhouse inmates. Turnbull identified the disease as 'the Itch' and suggested a remedial treatment.[157] Dr Taylor, honorary physician to the Huddersfield Infirmary, was called in to assist in the Huddersfield Workhouse during the 1847 outbreak of typhus fever. He was paid three guineas for his services.[158] During the 1849 cholera epidemic Dr Taylor was summoned again to act in an advisory capacity to the Guardians. The rest of the Huddersfield medical profession were given *carte blanche* to attend upon cholera cases at the Board of Guardians' expense (an extravagance later very much regretted by the Board).[159]

It was not uncommon for medical men to be consulted by the various official bodies in Wakefield and Huddersfield on matters relating to the health of the towns. In 1841, for example, the magistrates of the West Riding requested five Wakefield medical men to inspect and report on the healthiness of several sites adjacent to the House of Correction, which had been suggested as suitable locations for an extension of the institution. The magistrates consulted medical men who had practised for many years in Wakefield, and who, therefore, could be expected to be most familiar with the state of health of different parts of the town: Dr William Thomas (a resident practitioner in Wakefield for twenty years), Mr Benjamin Walker (a practising surgeon in Westgate Common, in the immediate vicinity of the prison, for 34 years), Joseph Bennett (a practising surgeon in the town for 24 years, and a pupil of the late

Mr W. Walker, prison surgeon, for six years), Mr William Starkey (a Wakefield practitioner for fifteen years) and Mr Henry Dunn (a practising surgeon in the town for sixteen years, and prison surgeon for fourteen). Dr Crowther also sent a 'very long letter' on the subject to the magistrates. The medical men were in almost complete accord about the suitability of the various sites, recommending the most elevated location, Site C, with Site B, on the North side of the prison, as a good second.[160]

Medical practitioners were also consulted when public health inquiries were held in the towns. In 1851 an inquiry into the sewerage, drainage, water supply and sanitary condition of Wakefield was held in consequence of a petition being presented to the Board of Health by the newly-founded Wakefield Town Council.[161] Over a third of all Wakefield medical practitioners were asked to supply evidence – Drs Wood and Wright and Messrs W. R. Milner, W. Statter, Marshall, Dawson, Burrell, Ebenezer Walker and Benjamin Walker, the latter giving evidence both in his capacity as a medical practitioner and as a Street Commissioner.[162] The medical witnesses examined cases of sickness in various districts of the town, paying special attention to the recent outbreak of cholera, its origins and spread. They covered most of the town during the course of their inquiries, looking at the general condition of the inhabitants and their homes, the state of the streets, drainage and sewerage, water supply and the ventilation of the streets and dwellings. The medical men proved to be valuable witnesses. They were able to back up their statements with statistical evidence, and they had more experience in dealing with the poor than many of the other witnesses. The Union medical officers and the honorary medical staff of the Dispensary, and more particularly the House of Recovery, were in a special position to monitor both epidemic (for example, influenza, measles, smallpox and cholera) and endemic (for example, typhus and typhoid fever, diarrhoea and chest infections) outbreaks of disease. The evidence of the medical witnesses was quite damning, and critical of the lack of effort on the part of the Street Commissioners to remedy the many evils in the town's sanitary arrangements.

In their reports the medical witnesses pointed to strong links between poor sanitary conditions and outbreaks of disease. They also concurred in their identification of particular trouble spots. The report summed up

It is especially worthy of notice how enormously in excess is the mortality of New-street, Nelson-street, and of some few other courts and yards, as compared with that of the rest of the locality, these places being, it must be observed, those specially alluded to by the medical men as the most wanting in all sanitary appliances and arrangements.[163]

Dr William Wood, medical inspector of the factories, for example, reported that the most common locations of fever cases were New Street, Nelson Street and Wrengate.[164] John Burrell also drew particular attention to the state of Nelson Street, which 'was densely inhabited, chiefly by low Irish, and was undrained, ill ventilated, ill supplied with water, and imperfectly paved'. In 1847 there had been a large number of cases of typhus in the street, and two years after 'the cholera broke out in the same street and in the same house, and was, in his opinion, mainly attributable to the defects he had already named'. Meanwhile, Mr William Statter reported that the whole of the drainage in the East Moor district was on the surface, and that many of these open drains

were half full of decomposing sewerage. The district was one hardly ever free from fever. The drainage of Westgate Common was, he believed, equally imperfect. There was a surface-drain in Pincheon-street, but it only extended half way up the street, and it was no uncommon thing to see the surface of the road covered with offensive matter'.[165]

Even Dr T. G. Wright, medical witness to the Street Commissioners, severely criticised them for permitting waste disposal depots to be sited in the town centre.[166]

In Huddersfield a similar inquiry was held in 1848, connected with the application by a portion of the inhabitants for an Improvement Act for the town.[167] Only one medical witness was invited to give evidence, Mr T. R. Tatham, in his capacity as Union medical officer for the Northern District of Huddersfield. Tatham pointed in particular to the problem of the town's lodging houses. Outbreaks of fever in the town, he claimed, were 'greatly attributable' to the overcrowding of 'low' lodging houses. Fever also resulted from poor drainage in certain parts of the town, a lack of privy accommodation, and nuisances, which the various official bodies had failed to remove. The problems were most severe in damp cellar accommodation and where housing conditions were especially cramped and overcrowded.[168]

The only other medical men to give evidence were Mr Thomas

Wrigley and Mr Bradshaw, who did so in the capacity of Street Commissioners (rather than medical witnesses). They gave a very different picture of the town's state of health to that provided by Tatham and other more critical witnesses. Wrigley agreed that there was some fever in the town, but blamed it on the influx of Irish into Huddersfield and their lack of adequate nutrition, which resulted in a low state of health – 'Huddersfield I do not consider an unhealthy Town at all – I see very few cases of Typhus Fever originating among the Inhabitants of the Town itself'.[169] Although, under the pressure of questioning, Wrigley did admit there was a shortage of privies in some parts of the town and problems with the drainage and sewerage, he tried to defend the position of the Commissioners, claiming much had been done in the last few years to remove filth and nuisances. His evidence was supported by that of Mr Bradshaw. Thomas Wrigley died one year after the 1848 Inquiry, and was given a glowing obituary in the *Leeds Mercury*, not least on account of his Reformist sympathies. But the paper also stressed Wrigley's significant role as a Street Commissioner. He had served in this capacity for 26 years, and the *Mercury* claimed that Wrigley had been largely responsible for the construction of the public waterworks in Huddersfield.[170]

Political and public activities
Few medical men in Wakefield and Huddersfield became actively involved in political affairs, or indeed professed strong political sentiments. Men such as Dr Crowther of Wakefield, an ardent Liberal and Reformer, and Mr Wrigley of Huddersfield, who 'was from an early period of life steadily attached to the reform party, and bore the name Reformer when it was anything but fashionable, and when Reformers had really to endure the heat and burden of the day',[171] were exceptional. Another individual with strong political opinions was Dr John Kenworthy Walker of Huddersfield, an outspoken critic of the factory system and supporter of Oastler, who, with his close knowledge of the factory districts and of conditions in the mills, lent practical support to the Factory Movement. Writing in 1831, Dr Walker condemned those who treated man as 'a manufacturing animal' and urged masters to act as the 'moral guardians of this great family', and in the same year he described the 'competitive system' as 'a state of Commercial cannibalism, or suicidal system of commerce!'.[172]

A few Wakefield medical men were involved in local politics, some being chosen as Councillors and Aldermen. For example, Ebenezer Walker, Liberal and member of the Wakefield surgical family, was elected as Councillor for the North Westgate Ward at the first local elections in May, 1848. His brother, Benjamin Walker, also a surgeon by trade and a Liberal, was chosen as Councillor for the South Westgate Ward in 1848, and elected Alderman in 1848 and 1850. Finally, in 1851 he became Mayor of Wakefield. In the 1860s Dr Samuel Holdsworth (Liberal) was elected Councillor for the Kirkgate Ward and Mr William Dawson (Conservative) was chosen as Alderman.[173] It was not until 1868 that Huddersfield received its Charter of Incorporation. At the first elections of a Council, which took place in the same year, no medical man was chosen as a Councillor or Alderman. This situation was apparently not untypical. E. P. Hennock found that the number of council members drawn from the medical profession during the nineteenth century was generally small. Three doctors, for example, sat on the old unreformed Leeds Corporation in 1835 (7.9 per cent of the Corporation); by 1842 there were four (6.2 per cent), but in the second half of the nineteenth century the medical profession made up an insignificant percentage of the Council or were not represented at all.[174]

The politics of Huddersfield were dominated by Liberalism;[175] its religion by Non-Conformity, particularly Methodism. Not surprisingly a large proportion of medical men shared in this Liberal/dissent mix (particularly those most active in the affairs of the town). For example, eight medical men, about half those in practice in Huddersfield, voted in the 1834 Borough elections. Two medical practitioners, Messrs Hudson and Newhouse, voted for the Tory Reformer, Mr Sadler; the remainder, Messrs Bradshaw, Astin, Sargent, Robinson, Wrigley and Wilks, for the Whig candidate, Mr Blackburne. None voted for the Radical Captain Wood, although John Moxon, surgeon and druggist, subscribed to defray the expenses of Wood's committee. At the polls Blackburne received 234 votes (48 per cent), Sadler 147 (30 per cent) and Captain Wood 108 (22 per cent). The voting behaviour of medical men, therefore, seemed to be less radical than that of the Huddersfield electorate as a whole. While three-quarters of the medical profession supported the Whig Blackburne, he polled less than half the total number of votes in the town.[176] The 1837 Borough election was a more closely-run affair. Edward Ellice, the Whig candidate, polled 340 (54 per cent) of the total votes, while Richard Oastler, standing as a Tory candidate, took 290 (46 per cent). Seven medical men voted for Ellice, only four for Oastler.[177]

In Wakefield the picture was quite different. Wakefield was an isolated centre of Anglican influence in the West Riding during the nineteenth century, and had a high Conservative poll. Although Conservatives won most elections, however, the contests were normally closely fought between the Liberal and Conservative candidates. However, the medical profession of the town did not mirror this almost 50:50 split in voting behaviour. The medical vote was predominantly Conservative. In 1837, for example, the Conservative candidate, Lascelles, was returned with a small majority of 307 to 281. Yet of the sixteen medical men voting (most of those in practice in the town), eleven voted for Lascelles and only five for Daniel Gaskell, the Liberal candidate.[178] Again in 1862 the Tory candidate won by only a small majority of 456 to 425. Four medical men voted for the Liberal candidate, eleven supported the Conservative. Two of the medical men entitled to vote abstained, Drs J. G. Atkinson and T. G. Wright.[179] It is likely that some medical men chose to remain neutral at elections, especially when they were to be closely-fought contests. By so doing, they could avoid offending patients or their potential clientele by voting the wrong way. For example, T. G. Wright, a man with apparently Liberal leanings, tended to remain neutral at elections. A note in the 1840 Register of Electors remarked that Wright was 'rather an uncertain Bird – but having Patients on both sides – is very likely to remain neutral'.[180]

In both towns there are examples of medical men being elected to official posts. Again this seems to have been more common in Wakefield, especially with respect to important appointments. Medical men were, for example, occasionally elected to serve on the Boards of Guardians. In 1840 Benjamin Bradshaw of Huddersfield was chosen as Guardian for Upperthong Township in the Huddersfield Union,[181] while Benjamin Walker of Wakefield served as Guardian to the Township of Alverthorpe-with-Thornes from the formation of the Union until his death in 1855, being elected several times as Chairman and Vice-Chairman. In marking his death the Board of Guardians noted that Walker had been

Constant in his attendance at the meetings of the Board – thoroughly conversant with the poor of his district – possessed of great kindness of heart and sympathy with the deserving poor, whilst acting with firmness against the idle and disorderly, his services were indeed most valuable, and his loss will be sensibly felt.[182]

In 1827 Squire Statter, surgeon, was elected Chairman of the Vestry of the Parish Church, Wakefield, and in the same year William Holdsworth was chosen as Constable.[183] In the mid-nineteenth century Drs Kendell and Wright served in a semi-official capacity as Governors of the Wakefield Charities. In 1870 Mr William Statter, nephew of Squire Statter, and Samuel Holdsworth, MD were elected as Justices of the Peace for Wakefield.[184]

The same names crop up repeatedly in connection not only with voluntary society activity, but also with respect to other civic involvement and election to public office. Those who became involved in the affairs of the communities tended to have practised for a number of years in their town. In Wakefield those families with a long tradition of medical practice tended to be especially active: for example, the Walkers, the Holdsworths and the Statters. Doctors with good practices and appointments, which typically coincided with wealth and high social status, were also best represented in local affairs. Wealth and a stable practice could be seen as fundamental prerequisites for involvement in voluntary society or civic activities, which was open only to those individuals who could afford to sacrifice money and time to their public interests. In addition, the Liberal and Non-Conformist elements of the medical profession were well represented. This tendency was most distinctive in Wakefield, in spite of the fact that the majority of medical men appear to have had Tory/Establishment sympathies. The Holdsworths and Walkers, for instance, were Non-Conformists and Liberals. In Wakefield Liberal/Non-Conformist doctors were represented in civic activities out of all proportion to their numbers.

Prominent medical men

Disney Alexander, MD (1769–1844), a leading local Methodist, came to be an active member of the Wakefield community following his arrival in the town from Halifax early in the nineteenth century. While he apparently had no ties with Wakefield, he was descended from an important Halifax medical family. In 1820, following the death of Dr James Richardson, he took over his posts as honorary physician to both the Dispensary and the West Riding Lunatic Asylum. Dr Alexander gave up his Dispensary appointment in 1829, but served as a Life Governor to the charity until his death. He acted as Superintendent of the Wakefield Asylum between 1831 and 1836, as successor to the distinguished asylum doctor and phrenologist, Sir William Ellis. He was also active in the Royal Medical Society, Edinburgh. He was a zealous member of the dissenting community, attending at the Westgate Wesleyan Chapel in Wakefield. Alexander preached on many occasions to local Non-Conformists, in some cases dedicating his sermons in aid of good causes. In 1800, for example, before taking up residence in the town, he preached a sermon at the Methodist Chapel, Wakefield, for the benefit of the Benevolent Society.[185] In 1835 he gave a course of six lectures at the Westgate Chapel on the 'Internal Evidences of Christianity'.[186]

Alexander was an ardent phrenologist, and greatly influenced the movement, especially in Wakefield and the district. He gave frequent lectures on the subject, was active in the Wakefield Phrenological Society and other local societies with an interest in phrenology (including the Leeds Phil. and Lit.), and was a corresponding member of the London Phrenological Society. In 1827 he donated £10, the profits arising from the publication of his pamphlet on phrenology, to the Wakefield Dispensary.[187] Alexander was indeed a typical representative of the body of men attracted by phrenology, as outlined by Roger Cooter, a Liberal, reformer and Non-Conformist, 'firmly imbued with an Enlightenment faith in Progress and the improvement of mankind through the application of science', *and* a member of the local medical and social élite.[188]

Alexander gave his support to many other Wakefield societies, including the Benevolent Society, the Bible Society, the Phil. and Lit. Society, the Mechanics' Institute and the Working Men's Association. In addition to more strictly 'scientific' subjects, he was also interested in raising standards of health amongst the population through the limited application of self-medication. He was particularly active in the fields of writing and lecturing, often raising money for his favourite charities by these means. In 1831, for example, he gave two lectures at the Wakefield Music Saloon on the subjects of the education of children and the conduct of men to animals, the profits of both talks being in aid of the London Society for the Prevention of Cruelty to Animals.[189] In 1837, following his retirement from medical practice, Alexander capped his previous literary achievements by publishing a book of poems.[190]

Apparently (perhaps due to over-exposure) his talks did not always go down well. In October, 1832 Clara Clarkson attended one of his lectures on the character of Napoleon Bonaparte and the evils of war, which was given for the benefit of the Mechanics' Institute. She remarked in her diary that the talk was 'very long and very dry'. In 1838 Dr Alexander preached at a special service in aid of the Working Men's Association, the text being 'The rich and the poor meet together and the Lord is the parent of them all'. After disclaiming all intention of meaning equality of station and circumstance, Alexander attempted to show that all men were equal in physical and moral structure, and, in the eyes of God, all were the joint heirs of immortality. Clarkson later remarked that some of the congregation (although unfortunately she did not specify which part) thought it a 'poor fawning sort of lecture'.[191]

Perhaps one of the most outstanding individuals to practice medicine in Wakefield during the nineteenth century was Dr Caleb Crowther (1772–1849). Crowther, who originated from Gomersal in the West Riding, qualified as MD at the University of Edinburgh in 1793, and immediately after came to Wakefield to set up in practice. In 1795 he was appointed honorary physician to the Wakefield Dispensary, a post which he held for 54 years, until his death in 1849. He acted as visiting physician to the Wakefield Asylum from 1818 to 1826. Crowther was able to build up the largest medical practice in the town, inheriting many of the patients of Drs Amory and Richardson, following their deaths in 1805 and 1820. In 1825, at the age of 53, he married Sophia Smithson, the sister of a wealthy railway owner. The marriage was childless, their only son dying in infancy.

Crowther was active in many of the civic affairs of the town. He served not only as an honorary medical officer to the Dispensary, but also in the capacities of committee member, benefactor and Life Governor. He subscribed to the Wakefield Town Mission and acted as its honorary consulting physician between 1840 and 1849. In 1804 he donated the sum of £21 to the Wakefield Volunteer Fund.[192] He was also involved in the Bible Society and Mechanics' Institute, and served on the committees of the Newsroom Society and the Benevolent Society. Crowther was a dedicated Non-Conformist, and in 1844 he lent £1,000 for the building of the Zion Congregationalist Chapel in Wakefield.

Crowther also donated large sums of money for the establishment of an Almshouse for Dissenters and a Fever Hospital in the town. By 1848 he had expended £4,592 on his project to erect Almshouses. By his will he bequeathed a further £11,200 and over three acres of valuable land for the purposes of building and maintaining the Almshouses and Fever Hospital.[193] Crowther stipulated that the charities were to be managed by trustees selected from the principal dissenting congregations of the town, excluding 'Catholics, Attorneys and Solicitors'! Each governor, following his election, was to declare in writing 'that he is not, and never intends to become, a member of the Church of England, and that he does not profess or act in supporting and never intends to profess or act in support of, those opinions in politics which are commonly called Tory or Conservative opinions'.[194] The first trustees to be elected included the prominent Liberal MP, William Henry Leatham, and other representatives of the Liberal/Non-Conformist community, the Holdsworths, Clarksons and Lawtons, Rowland Hurst and John Craven. In the 1860s Mr Thomas Clayton, founder of the Infirmary, and himself an important local Non-Conformist and Liberal, became Chairman of the Trustees.[195] The proposal to found a Fever Hospital eventually came to nothing: the first Union Workhouse, erected in 1852, complete with hospital wards, was thought to be a sufficient provision for the declining number of fever cases in the town and district. But Almshouses were erected in George Street and occupied by sixteen poor dissenters.

Crowther's strong opinions on the subjects of religion and politics (and apparently everything else) and his want of diplomacy led him into conflict with both members of the medical community[196] and other local inhabitants. One Wakefield historian noted that 'Dr. Crowther was better known for his eccentricities, which were almost proverbial, and for the active part he took in local and political affairs than as a medical man'.[197] And as Crowther himself remarked, 'During a long and active life I can truly say that Popularity has never been my polar star. I have uniformly acted from the impulse of my own judgement without reference to the opinion of others'.[198] Crowther had, for example, very firm views on charity, stating that many of those supporting philanthropic enterprises did so from incorrect motives; vanity or a hope to atone for a wicked life. Crowther changed his mind several times about the nature of the charitable bequests he would make. He considered leaving a sum of money for the establishment of an asylum for admitting tradesmen or 'that class of people who are just above paupers' either gratuitously or on very low terms. This project was later abandoned because Crowther believed that there would be too many difficulties attending the management of such an institution. Following on from this decision, Crowther bequeathed large sums of money to various local dispensaries and infirmaries, bequests which were later revoked from the belief that he should injure rather than benefit such charities by providing them with major legacies – '. . . if they were to be supported by permanent funds, I am persuaded that they would soon cease to excite the vigilance and sympathy of the public, they would soon be neglected and abused'.[199]

In 1840 Crowther's strong Liberal bias served to offend the proprietor of the local newspaper, the *Wakefield Journal*. Crowther had received a letter from the former Liberal member for Wakefield, Daniel Gaskell, who was then touring Europe, expressing his intention of subscribing £1,000 towards the erection of a public baths in Wakefield. Instead of forwarding the letter to the *Journal*, Crowther sent it to the Liberal *Leeds Mercury* for publication. The editor of the Tory *Journal* commented that Gaskell, who was now retired from political affairs, did not wish his schemes to be subject to any party bias, and

That the sum is very safely hazarded, for the whole scheme has been at the outset knocked on the head by that ancient mass of impenetrable prejudice, Caleb Crowther, Esq. M.D. and D.M. who received Mr. Gaskell's well-meant epistle on Wednesday, and serves it up in a Whig-Radical paper in a town at a distance on the Saturday, well knowing that the writer of the letter intended that the project should be unfettered by considerations of party, unbiased by the meannesses of any men or set of men, whether doctors or tinkers.[200]

Crowther also spoke at Reform meetings in the town in the early 1830s, at a time when even the notion of moderate political reform was anathema to many of the wealthier classes. Dr Crowther was apparently in the fortunate position of having sufficient private means to make him largely independent of people's opinions. He could well afford to lose patients or potential patients because of his religious or political views. In this Crowther differed from the majority of medical practitioners in both towns. Although several other doctors were possessed of considerable means, they still relied on the wealthier and more influential part of their clientele for the continuation of their medical practice and income. As already suggested, in some cases doctors must have been prepared to compromise politically, or on religious issues, to avoid offending their patients.

In some respects Crowther's position in the community was taken over after his death by Dr Thomas Giordani Wright. Wright was, however, far more moderate in both his political and religious views. While having Liberal and dissenting sympathies, he tended to steer a middle course in both matters, remaining neutral at elections. Like Crowther, Dr Wright received his MD from Edinburgh University (1831), plus the LSA (1830) and MRCS (1831), and settled in Wakefield immediately after. Following the departure of Dr Gilby from the town in 1833, he was appointed honorary physician to the Asylum and the Wakefield House of Recovery. He was also Medical Visitor of Licensed Houses for the Insane in the West Riding. Like Crowther, he enjoyed considerable wealth and a large private practice, which later in the century included many members of the local gentry.

While avoiding a strong Liberal commitment, his social activities brought him into contact with several eminent Liberal families, including the Leathams and the Gaskells, and similarly his medical practice seems to have been made up largely of members of the local Liberal community. Wright became a Vice-President of the Liberal-controlled Mechanics' Institute in the 1860s, and was Chairman of the exclusive Archery Club, membership of which appeared to be dominated by the local Liberal élite, including the Leathams, the Gaskells and George Ridsdale.[201] On the other hand, Wright also managed to be elected as a Governor of the Wakefield Charities, a notoriously Establishment/Conservative grouping.

For several years Wright was President of the Wakefield Phil. and Lit. Society, and he succeeded Crowther as honorary physician to the Wakefield Town Mission in 1849. Dr Wright was also responsible, together with Dr Thomas, for the organisation of the annual charity ball. For over twenty years Wright acted on behalf of the Ladies Committee of the House of Recovery as MC. When the arrangements for the ball were taken over by the Dispensary in

1852, following the winding up of the House of Recovery, Wright continued to act as Treasurer to the Ball Committee. Wright joined the staff of the Wakefield Infirmary in 1873 as honorary physician, and was still Treasurer to the Ball Committee in 1885 (altogether a period of over fifty years), with Mr Walker as Secretary and Dr Holdsworth and Mr Fowler as committee members.[202]

The diaries of Clara Clarkson, wealthy spinster and Unitarian, and, judging by the number of entries on the subject of her medical complaints, also something of a hypochondriac, provide us with some insight into the relationship she enjoyed with her medical attendant, Dr Wright. Wright acted as her medical attendant for a period of over 45 years (from around 1840), over which time they, not surprisingly, built up a friendly relationship. For example, when Dr Wright's daughter, Nellie, married in 1876 Clara Clarkson bought her an afternoon tea set as a wedding present. Dr Wright also confided in her following the serious illnesses and deaths in quick succession of two of his sons. Wright attended Clara Clarkson at frequent intervals in 1875 and 1876 during one of her many illnesses. While she was not entirely confident about Wright's advice and treatment, Clarkson felt a certain amount of loyalty to him, and resisted the urging of her friends to seek a second opinion. Her friend 'Alex', daughter of the late Dr Alexander, encouraged Clara to consult her nephew, Dr Reginald Alexander, but she felt 'reluctant to change to so young a man'. Finally, in December, 1876 Alex brought her nephew to examine Clara. He advised her to have morphine injections when her pain became severe, and suggested she recommended the treatment to Dr Wright, 'as if I would dare to do so!' Despite her doubts about Wright, Clara Clarkson retained him as her usual medical attendant until her death in 1889, aged 78.[203]

Rowland Houghton and George Sargent were two of the most important medical men in early nineteenth-century Huddersfield, in terms of both medical practices and participation in the affairs of the town. Both were staunch Liberals and leading members of the dissenting community. Rowland Houghton (1768–1820) was possibly the only doctor in practice early in the nineteenth century to be descended from an old Huddersfield family and to have been born in the town. His ancestors had been linen drapers, and the family had enjoyed a long tradition of charitable work in Huddersfield. They were Wesleyans and had taken a lead in Huddersfield's move to Non-Conformity, the older members of the Houghton family having been associates of Venn.[204]

In 1814 Houghton stood for election as surgeon to the newly-inaugurated Huddersfield Dispensary. He was, as a result of the unpleasant disputes surrounding the campaign, initially unwilling to stand, but a meeting of 'the Friends' of Houghton, anxious the charity should have the benefit of the most experienced surgeons, nominated him for the post.[205] Houghton's apparently half-hearted election bid failed, although his last-minute campaign resulted in him polling 161 votes (while the successful candidates, Wilks and Robinson, polled 209 and 174 respectively). Houghton placed a notice in the *Leeds Mercury* thanking his supporters – 'The very great Number of Votes they obtained after determining to bring him forward only after Days before the Close of the Poll, is to him most flattering, and he feels sensible of the Claims they have to his best Services in that benevolent Institution, whenever an Opportunity shall offer him to show it'.[206] Houghton did in fact act in an advisory capacity to the Dispensary (to the annoyance of the Dispensary's medical staff), and his failure to be elected surgeon does not seem to have affected his career. He became a surgeon of 'considerable eminence in the Town', continuing to practise in Huddersfield until his death in 1820. Houghton was a frequent attender at the Highgate Chapel and an ardent supporter of the Bible, Tract and Missionary Societies. His obituary in the *Leeds Mercury* remarked that

In the populous town and district in which he resided, his loss will be longly and deeply lamented by his numerous friends, among whom, for a period of thirty years, he discharged his professional duties with an ability, an assiduity, and a success, which are rarely exceeded. He was not less distinguished for the qualities of his heart than for his mental endowments . . . In the death of such a man society suffers no common loss, religion no common friend; . . . .[207]

More is known of Houghton's protégé, George Sargent (1792–1840), who took up surgical practice in Huddersfield shortly before Houghton's death in 1820. He was born in Tetney-haven, Lincolnshire, and was the son of the Reverend G. Sargent, a Wesleyan minister and contemporary of Wesley. George Sargent had a deeply religious upbringing. At the age of seven he taught in his father's Sunday school. He later studied at the Kingswood School and subsequently was apprenticed to a Hull surgeon. During his apprenticeship Sargent also attended at the London hospitals. He first came to Huddersfield in 1815 as assistant to Mr Houghton. The two shared a common religious background, and Sargent apparently worshipped with the Houghton family in their home. In 1818 Sargent moved for a short time to Halifax to practise, but early in 1820 he returned to Huddersfield to become Houghton's partner, and, following the latter's death later in 1820, his successor. In 1821 Sargent married Houghton's eldest daughter.[208]

Despite a succession of severe illnesses, which caused him to curtail his medical practice, Sargent became very active in the affairs of the town. Like Houghton, he was especially interested in promoting religious societies and in serving the Wesleyan community. He was Co-Secretary, together with the Reverend W. C. Madden, of the Huddersfield Auxiliary of the British and Foreign Bible Society, Treasurer of the Religious Tract Society and of the Missionary Society, and one of the Trustees of the Wesleyan Chapel. He was also on the committee of the Huddersfield Peace Society and on the Council of the Huddersfield College.

Although the Liberal/Non-Conformist elements of the medical profession were apparently far more involved than the rest of their medical brethren in the affairs of the two communities, this is not to say that doctors who worshipped in the Established Church and who had Conservative sympathies took no part in voluntary societies and other civic activities. For example, Squire and William Statter, staunch Conservatives and attenders at the Parish Church, Wakefield, were very active in civic life, both holding important official posts. Similarly, Henry Dunn (1804–1858), a Tory and Churchman, took a very keen interest in the civic affairs of Wakefield. Dunn was born in Norwich in 1804 and commenced his professional career with Mr Blakey, a surgeon in 'good practice' in Bradford. He qualified in 1824 and came to Wakefield in the same year, taking up the post of apothecary to the Dispensary. Shortly after Dunn was recommended by Dr Crowther, physician to the Dispensary, to Mr Thomas Stott, an established Wakefield surgeon. Stott was in bad health and wished to reduce his workload, and Dunn was taken on as his partner in practice.[209] In 1826 Dunn was appointed honorary surgeon to the House of Recovery, and in 1828 took over his father-in-law's post as surgeon to the House of Correction. The advantage of being the son-in-law (and 'heir apparent') of the previous prison surgeon was shown at the elections for the post. Dunn, a relative newcomer to the town, received 31 votes, Mr Horsfall two and Mr Dawson one. Three other candidates stood, none of whom received any votes.[210] Thomas Stott died in 1828 and Dunn inherited much of his private practice. In 1831 he married Thomas Stott's second daughter.

Henry Dunn became involved in the affairs of the town soon after his arrival. He was on the committee of the Wakefield Benevolent Society, a subscriber to the Town Mission, Treasurer of both the Newsroom and Museum, and a member, and in several years President, of the Phil. and Lit. Society. Upon his death in 1858 the *Provincial Medical Directory* noted in its obituary section that

During a long and useful life Mr. Dunn succeeded in gaining the confidence of his patients and of the magistrates of the riding, and the love and esteem of a very large circle of friends, among whom may be mentioned the whole of the medical men of Wakefield and the neighbourhood; indeed few men had more friends, and none fewer enemies.[211]

Reputation and social estimation

Although this Section has been concerned basically with the involvement of the medical profession with middle- and upper-class groups, it would appear to be useful to make a short comment on the relationship of the profession with the poorer classes. This is an interesting side-issue because the degree of social acceptability enjoyed by medical men in Wakefield and Huddersfield was apparently reflected in their relations with the poor. In Wakefield there is little sign of the tension which existed in many of the larger urban communities of the period, which was especially associated with the Anatomy Bill and cholera epidemics,[212] and the anti-vivisection, anti-vaccination and anti-Contagious Disease Act movements, which aroused much hostility against the medical profession, all became activated at a rather later period. There is no evidence, for example, of opposition to medical men during the cholera outbreaks of 1832 and 1849.

The medical profession and their lay colleagues in the medical charities, however, appear to have approached their relations with the poor with some caution. The officers of the Wakefield Dispensary, for example, expressed concern about 'winning the confidence' of the poor. The character of the resident house surgeon was seen as being of vital importance, for it was he who came into most regular contact with the charity's patients. In 1830, for example, the committee and medical men expressed extreme regret at the loss of their apothecary, William Holdsworth. Dr Crowther (who, as seen in Section 8.1, was not always inclined to praise his colleagues) wrote that during his 35 years as honorary physician he had never seen the office 'more regularly or diligently attended to'. Holdsworth had won 'the respect, the esteem and the confidence of all the medical officers', and more importantly had

... succeeded in obtaining the esteem and entire confidence of the poor by listening patiently to their complaints, by regular and diligent attendance (upon) them when seriously ill, by his mild and kind behaviour to them, ...[213]

Wakefield did not escape the visitations of the resurrectionists, who appear to have been especially active in the 1830s.[214] Their activities presumably heightened tensions between the medical profession and the poor. At the elections for the replacement of Holdsworth one of the candidates, Kemplay, had been recently associated with a charge of body stealing in Huddersfield. Although the charges against Kemplay had been dropped (and on all other counts he was eligible for the post), the officers of the charity felt unable to run the risk of employing him. They believed that if someone who had been associated with body stealing was elected apothecary, it would render the charity 'null and void'.[215]

In Huddersfield the relationship of the medical profession with the poor appears to have been more shaky. The officers of the Huddersfield Infirmary took great care to dissociate the institution from any connection with the 1832 cholera outbreak, refusing to allow the Board of Health to use their fever ward as a cholera hospital.[216] More serious was the link, as perceived by the Huddersfield populace, between voting behaviour and the medical profession's support of the Anatomy Bill, which would allow the bodies of unclaimed paupers to be used for dissection. During the 1834 election campaign attempts were made to turn popular opinion against the Whig candidate, Blackburne, who was associated very much with Macaulay, a supporter of the Anatomy Bill.[217] As shown above, the medical profession voted overwhelmingly in support of Blackburne, and by so doing also linked themselves very closely to the fierce debate over the Bill, and indirectly to the lobby opposed to factory reform. The 'reactionism' of the Huddersfield medical profession was remarked upon in the introduction to the 1834 Poll Book:

Who does Lawyer Blackburne represent? Why, not the Men of Huddersfield, but the Whigs, under the *haggard* form of a few Dead Body-Bill Doctors, FACTORY MONGERS, *Mushroom Merchants*, and their Myrmidons, who are *instinctively* against the PEOPLE , as the *shark* is against the herring (their emphasis).[218]

A series of anonymous poems and broadsheets were circulated in Huddersfield, drawing attention to the 'Yellow Doctor', designed to turn popular opinion against the profession. For example, around 1834 the following poem was circulated in the town.

<blockquote>
The Yellow Doctor
A brave yellow Doctor who lives in this Town,
And wish'd very much to increase his renown,
Adorn'd his Costume, like a spirited fellow,
In good taste, with an extra proportion of Yellow,
At the close of the day, when Squire Flax was first parting,
Doctor Bolus approach'd to take leave at departing,
Quoth Squire Flax 'I admire very much your array,
'For you bear o'er your fellows the bell far away,
'But the next time I come, whatever may fall up,
'I advise you to swallow a less dose of Jalap'.[219]
</blockquote>

The records of the medical charities and the Poor Law authorities describe a number of disputes between doctors and patients and accusations of neglect or cruelty, but these were rare incidents, and based usually on personal conflict. The local press, meanwhile, carried occasional reports describing attacks, sometimes physical, on individual practitioners. In 1815, for example, Edward Batty and Thomas Lancaster of Wakefield, shoemakers, broke into the house of Mr Squire Statter, surgeon, and assaulted and threatened him.[220] In 1852 Joseph Firth of Sheepridge, Huddersfield, violently attacked Mr Clough, surgeon, 'whipping him in a most savage and brutal manner with a whip similar to that used by horsebreakers'. Firth charged Clough with neglecting to attend upon his father when he was ill,[221] a fairly frequent complaint, but usually not backed up with such drastic action.

Medical men in Wakefield and Huddersfield were more likely to be well known in their communities than was the case in larger urban centres. This increased exposure to the public eye could work both ways. If doctors were able to win the confidence of their patients, and the support and approval of their social peers and superiors, all went well. Any benevolent gestures on the part of medical men were, for example, likely to be remarked upon. In 1842 the *Wakefield Journal* reported a case of

TRUE LIBERALITY. – Mr. William Rowlandson, of this town, surgeon, has kindly distributed to the poor of his neighbourhood, a large quantity of coals, which have been received at this Inclement Season, with the deepest gratitude. This is an example worthy of imitation.[222]

Those who practised and socialised successfully were rewarded with glowing obituaries in the local press. In recording the death of Dr James Richardson in 1820 the *Wakefield and Halifax Journal* stated

The regrets of a numerous acquaintance, who sincerely esteemed and valued him, have followed him to the tomb. This esteem he richly deserved; for as a professional man, a gentleman, a neighbour, and a friend, he was indeed exemplary; and we believe all who knew him will join us in saying,
'We scarce shall look upon his like again'.[223]

Increased exposure to the public eye could also be disastrous for a medical practitioner. If he was suspected of neglect, poor treatment or of committing a social or personal blunder he could lose his reputation overnight. For example, in 1825 a new physician, Dr Gilby, came to Wakefield to establish a practice. He had 'influential connections' and soon acquired a 'good standing' in the town. He was appointed as physician to the House of Recovery and the Asylum, and was taken in hand by Mr John Lee, solicitor, and other important Wakefield families. However, in 1833, following an 'unfortunate circumstance' for which Gilby was blamed, a 'blight' fell on his prospects and he was forced to leave town.[224] The occurrence was the death of a child chimney-sweep who got wedged in one of Gilby's chimneys and suffocated. The chimney-sweep's employer claimed that Gilby delayed rescuing the boy because he did not want any damage done to the house, and this testimony was supported by several other witnesses. Another group of witnesses claimed that Dr Gilby wished to obtain the advice of the builder of the house as to how the flues were constructed in order to free the boy quickly. At the inquest the Jury returned a verdict of 'Accidental death',[225] but Gilby's career in Wakefield was ruined by this incident, and he left the town for Bristol a short time afterwards. Clara Clarkson remarked in her diary that she was sorry that Gilby would leave Wakefield, '. . . but he has been very unpopular here since the sad affair of the little chimney boy'.[226]

Incidents such as these re-emphasise how important the personality and social behaviour of medical men was in determining their careers. As P. Starr has proposed, up until the late nineteenth century 'physicians' (and I would suggest all other medical practitioners) 'might win personal authority by dint of their character and intimate knowledge of their patients',[227] while Peterson has argued what little authority medical men had 'came not from their medical knowledge but had its origins in connection, social origins, or social style'.[228] Medical men were judged just as much on their social merits as on any medical skill that they might have been seen to possess. If one wished to succeed in practice, it was important to cultivate social contacts through the medium of voluntary societies and other forms of civic activity. Only more prestigious members of the profession tended to be admitted to civic organisations; membership, affiliation or office in these organisations then served to reinforce this status. Involvement brought the doctor into direct contact with a potential clientele, and on a wider basis proved his good character and social suitability as a medical attendant to the wealthier classes. Doctors, after all usually members of the middle class, also participated in civic affairs for the same reasons as others of their class, be they altruistic or pragmatic. On the whole it is likely that doctors shared in the creeds and ideologies held by the rest of the middle class. However, because they had more contact with the poor, they could attempt to act as translators of their needs, and influence and moderate the opinions of their contemporaries in such fields as medical charity, public health reform and the operation of the Poor Law, although, as has been seen, the layman usually remained dominant in determining the policies of the organisations dealing with these functions.

Within the confines of this chapter it has proved impossible to carry out an exhaustive survey of all forms of potential civic involvement.[229] However, it is possible to make a few tentative remarks regarding the activities of medical men in the communities in which they practised. Those medical men who fulfilled certain social and professional criteria were most likely to be active: important local (preferably medical) family connections, a well-established practice, medical-élite status and Liberal/Non-Conformist leanings. A combination of medical-élite status and a suitable family background was especially promising. Newcomers to the towns had more difficulty breaking into civic activities. Those who managed this tended to over-compensate for their status as 'foreigners' in some other way: for instance, by intermarrying with established medical families (as with Sargent and Dunn) or acquiring a string of impressive qualifications.

Overall Wakefield medical men broke into a wider range of civic affairs in greater numbers. Indeed, several played important roles in local government and voluntary society activities. Yet even in Wakefield the criteria outlined above were applicable. Although a larger group was involved in civic life, this did not constitute a majority of medical men. For example, with regard to voluntary society activity, out of the seventy or so medical men to pass through the town between 1840 and 1870, only about a dozen became involved in the work of the Town Mission, only six served in the Mechanics' Institute in any official capacity.[230]

These conclusions bring into question Inkster's concept of the 'social marginality' of medical men and their success in establishing 'a definite, identifiable social image'[231] by building up alliances with the lay community, by means, for example, of the voluntary society. By the beginning of the nineteenth century Wakefield medical men as a group could not be considered marginal. Provided that they fulfilled the normal requirements linked to social acceptability, they could become well integrated socially and active in civic life. The most eminent physicians and established surgical families enjoyed especially high levels of social status. Nor could the Wakefield medical profession be considered as being occupationally marginal. As shown in Chapter 2, Wakefield was noted throughout the century as a service and trading centre, rather than as a manufacturing town. There was a high concentration of professional and service groups, sharing a similar background and status to that of medical men. In Wakefield, and possibly in other provincial towns with similar social and economic backgrounds, the medical profession, in particular the medical élite, was well established and integrated.

The concept of marginality is apparently more applicable to towns such as Huddersfield, which, like Inkster's Sheffield, shared in the rapid industrial expansion common to many Northern manufacturing communities. There was a parallel growth in the town's commercial elements, in particular textile merchants and manufacturers, who outnumbered and outclassed professional and service groups. More medical men came to Huddersfield during the century, in part at least in response to an increased demand from these commercial groups for medical attendance. Yet in Huddersfield, with the exception of a small élite group, the medical profession appear to have been unable to break into voluntary society activity or other aspects of civic life. In Wakefield the medical profession seems never to have been marginal; in Huddersfield this group remained marginal for much of the nineteenth century.

Concluding remarks

This and the preceding chapter have demonstrated that a wide range of influences determined the career and social prospects of medical men. Professional criteria, education and qualifications, affected practice-building and job opportunities. Medical men sought to acquire status-conferring qualifications (many of which were acquired in mid-career). Successful practice often led to pluralism and a monopolisation of appointments. Professional furtherment, in particular via the medium of medical societies and publication, could also lead to improved career prospects.

Social factors had even more influence on the success of medical careers. Family background and wealth determined the kind of training that could be afforded in the first place, the type of practice a medical man could purchase or enter, and the standard of living he could adopt in the first crucial practice-building years. The best-placed individuals were clearly those who had an auspicious medical background, good connections or, alternatively, sufficient money to make up for a shortage of social advantages. High social status helped in the acquisition of posts and in gaining acceptance by the local community.

All these factors are so closely interrelated that it is impossible to place them in any clear order of importance. All acted upon each other. The same individuals who started out with good connections and wealth were most likely to win the best appointments and practices.[232] Social factors, however, perhaps deserve more weight than they have received in the past. In a similar way to Peterson's London medical élite, the top medical men of Wakefield and Huddersfield made their claims to status 'not because of their profession but by virtue of their prestigious association, university education, prosperity, and the "paraphernalia of gentility".'[233] The fact that social influences were so significant serves to re-emphasise the importance of looking at the development of individual practitioners and medical communities within the context of the environment in which they practised (and of examining the impact of urbanisation upon medical practice). Moreover, medical men in the two towns (and presumably other provincial practitioners) do seem to have been most concerned with local issues and their standing as professionals in the community. As John Pickstone has remarked, 'Provincial groups seem to have paid less attention to the metropolitan élite and more to their own local prestige and economic status'.[234] This was reflected in medical society and other professional activities, most of which were basically preoccupied with local concerns (while not precluding an interest and involvement in wider regional and national events). Professional activities were paralleled by efforts on the part of medical men to enter into community life and to forge alliances with local élite groups, a natural enough activity – their source of custom was predominantly local, their practices and appointments dependent upon the support and approval of important local groupings and individuals. This and the preceding chapter have attempted to provide a detailed study of the formation of the medical profession within the context of the two provincial communities of Wakefield and Huddersfield, and it is hoped that this survey has offered a useful 'counterbalance' to the more general analyses of the structure and activities of the nineteenth-century medical profession, made on a nationwide basis, such as those of the Parrys and Waddington, and to Peterson's study of medical practice in Victorian London.[235]

Wakefield and Huddersfield opened up very different career prospects to medical men. By the turn of the nineteenth century there was a well-established, albeit small, medical community in Wakefield. Around the same period, as seen in Chapter 7, a considerable number of paid and honorary posts became available. The fact that Wakefield had a high proportion of middle-class inhabitants may have also resulted in better practice-building opportunities. As pointed out in Section 8.2, Wakefield medical practitioners integrated themselves more successfully into the local community. Overall, they were also wealthier and of a higher social and professional status. Meanwhile, intra-professional relationships appear to have been more relaxed in Wakefield: posts as medical society officers, for instance, seem to have been widely distributed and meetings often took place in the informal setting of members' homes. In Huddersfield practice-building posts and job opportunities were less favourable. Despite the town's larger population and greater wealth, there were fewer possibilities for building up a successful medical practice. Huddersfield medical practitioners tended to be new and comparatively late arrivals, and throughout the century the medical community remained small (especially as a proportion of the population), and medical men occupationally and socially isolated. These factors may have made it more difficult for Huddersfield doctors to break into civic activities. This comparative isolation also appears to have influenced intra-professional relationships, which were more strident than those experienced by their Wakefield counterparts.

On the whole the social and professional position of Wakefield medical men and their relationship with other social groups appears hardly to have changed. A status quo was reached early in the century. By the third quarter of the nineteenth century Huddersfield had begun to duplicate the pattern long established in Wakefield. At the beginning of the century very few Huddersfield practitioners had been born in or had connections with the town; by mid-century this was no longer the case. Medical families, who had long been a feature of medical life in Wakefield, began to make their appearance, represented, for example, by the Greenwoods, Robinsons and Cloughs.[236] Other mid- to late-century Huddersfield practitioners were the sons of eminent professional or commercial families. As the Huddersfield middle class began to create a demand for medical treatment, in part they came forward to fill that demand, sending their sons into medical practice. Those setting up in practice later in the century tended to have the attributes of local connections, wealth and high social standing, and employment opportunities and possibilities for social integration began to improve. It is likely that late nineteenth-century Huddersfield medical men found their entrance into medical practice (and perhaps into civic life) somewhat easier than their early nineteenth-century predecessors.

9

Conclusion

This study has outlined the establishment and development of the most important forms of medical provision in the two West Riding communities of Wakefield and Huddersfield during the period 1780 to 1870. The chief mediums through which medical care was made available have been discussed, namely the medical profession, represented most significantly by the general practitioner, the 'institutional' services of the Poor Law and of medical charity, and the 'self-help' forms of fringe practice and the friendly society. Here an attempt will be made to compare the value and effectiveness of the various medical services and options (in terms of availability and accessibility rather than success rate).[1] Some of the findings of the survey have challenged the 'traditional wisdom' of the medical historian, in particular questioning the stress which has been placed on institutional services, and this will be re-emphasised. The leading role of laymen as both consumers and producers of medical facilities will also be re-emphasised, as will the significance of looking at medical care and options for treatment within the context of the local economy and society.

Developments in the provision of medical services during the eighteenth and nineteenth centuries appear to have augured well, especially for the poorer classes. As M. C. Buer has remarked for the eighteenth century '. . . one of the outstanding results of the advance in medicine was the foundation of hospitals and dispensaries', which '. . . attempted to bring such knowledge as it (medicine) had to the service of the mass of the people'.[2] The nationwide spate of hospital building continued into the nineteenth century, albeit at a steadier rate, and large numbers of dispensaries continued to be established as supplements to the infirmaries, so that by the mid-nineteenth century a network of charitable foundations for the poor had spread itself across the country, and most

particularly the North.[3] During the middle decades of the
nineteenth century a medical service for the poor, or rather paupers,
which set down uniform procedures for the application and giving
of relief, was created under the auspices of the New Poor Law. The
century also saw a tremendous rise in the membership of friendly
societies and sick clubs, and in some regions of the country (particularly the Midlands and the South), the creation of self-supporting
dispensaries. During the early decades of the nineteenth century the
number of qualified medical practitioners rose impressively
(between 1824 and 1833 the number of persons holding the MRCS
increased by 62 per cent from 5,000 to 8,125, while the average
number of licences granted by the Society of Apothecaries doubled
between 1815 and 1830 to just over 400 per annum),[4] and this
resulted in a ready supply of trained men to staff medical institutions
and to respond to an accelerated middle-class demand for their
services. Meanwhile, during the century there appears to have been
no diminution in the number of fringe practitioners; rather the
reverse in terms of the range of 'alternative' facilities and options.

On closer examination many of these medical options, particularly the 'institutional' provisions, appear to be less feasible. To take
the number of qualified doctors, for example. Following the passing
of the 1858 Medical Act the increase in the number of medical
practitioners was minimal, and was far outstripped by the population growth. In 1861 there were 14,415 qualified medical men, and
between 1861 and 1871 their numbers rose by only 269 or 1.8 per
cent. In 1861 there was one medical practitioner for every 1,392
persons; by 1871 one for every 1,547.[5] Meanwhile, qualified medical men, while attending upon the poor via the mediums of local
medical charities, the Poor Law medical services and friendly
societies, catered more specifically for a middle- and upper-class
demand than for a poorer clientele, and in most cases their private
practices were based on middle-class consumers. A small number
of medical men (as seen in Chapter 7) were forced by necessity to
concentrate on a lower middle-class/working-class practice.
Others, although the extent to which this took place is not clear,
treated the poor gratis or at much reduced rates as a 'philanthropic'
gesture. However, for the greatest proportion of the poorer classes,
resort to a private, qualified medical attendant was not a viable
alternative, especially on a regular or long-term basis. Medical
charities, meanwhile, were not necessarily founded in periods or

centres where the demand was greatest, and 'infirmaries which were found adequate when grazing small cathedral towns proved to be so small, and so widely scattered that their facilities were swamped by the embarrassing hordes of sick poor of the industrial towns'. In the eighteenth century, 'even with a restricted admissions policy the trustees of those hospitals in growth centres found that they were not able to meet local demand',[6] and this situation grew worse with the rapid population growth of the nineteenth century. Poor Law medical services were also slow to expand to meet the demands placed upon them, and it was not until the final quarter of the century that definite moves were made towards the establishment of a nationwide, non-pauperising health service.[7] Meanwhile, towards the end of the nineteenth century friendly societies began to run into financial difficulties, which presumably curtailed their ability to offer medical relief.

To return again more specifically to Wakefield and Huddersfield, dispensary and infirmary charities were set up during the late eighteenth and early nineteenth centuries. Intake to these charities (in common with similar foundations) was strictly regulated. Access was limited by two factors, the first one of necessity, the second one of policy. Firstly, the scale upon which these charities came to operate meant that there were consistently more applicants for relief than could be accommodated. Lack of funds prohibited expansion, and this was especially relevant with regard to in-patient facilities and the feebly-supported Wakefield institution. Secondly, access to the charities was strictly regulated by rules determining the social acceptability of patients and by the governors' tickets of recommendation. Admission was restricted to the 'deserving poor', in effect usually those who had some role to play in the functioning of the local economy. Paupers or better-off members of the working class (and of course the wealthy classes, who in some cases may well have benefited from hospital treatment) were excluded.[8] Moreover, there is little evidence to suggest that the supporters of these charities had any desire to expand their facilities beyond a fixed level, determined by the resolve to create a system of care designed to deal with accident and epidemic disease cases, and the fulfilment of various practical, social, religious and philanthropic ambitions.[9]

The Poor Law authorities also limited their services by means of both financial constraints and a policy of narrowly defining the class of patient eligible for this form of assistance. Under the Old Poor Law administration an informal and apparently 'compassionate' system of medical relief had allowed for a certain amount of flexibility in determining how assistance should be given and to whom, although it should be re-emphasised that this form of relief was given on only a very small scale. The regimented system heralded by the passing of the New Poor Law forestalled this flexibility, strictly limiting medical assistance to the pauper. Only in the final years of the nineteenth century did the Poor Law authorities move back to providing what had in essence existed before 1834, albeit in a rudimentary form, a non-pauperising health service.

What then did the 'institutional' services provided by the Poor Law authorities and medical philanthropists mean for the poor of Wakefield and Huddersfield during the late eighteenth and nineteenth centuries? For a large part of this period, apparently, not a great deal. Restrictive policies and financial limitations meant that many of the poorer classes could not gain access to these provisions, although it must be said that overall the position gradually improved during the nineteenth century. Of the two forms of institutional provision, the Poor Law medical services were the slowest to enlarge and improve (particularly in Huddersfield). Indeed, with the notable exception of provision for the mentally ill, Poor Law facilities hardly expanded before 1870. In terms of numbers treated and expenditure, the passing of the 1834 Poor Law Amendment Act had little impact. The most significant change resulting from the Act was a narrowing of the range of services available, to cut out, for example, the use of unqualified practitioners and midwives, the non-contracted surgeon and the friendly society. After 1834 Poor Law medical services via the workhouse and outdoor relief rarely reached more than a small percentage, usually below 3 per cent, of the Union populations; expenditure, meanwhile, rarely exceeded 2d per head. Workhouse facilities remained inadequate, especially in Huddersfield, provision for outdoor medical care small scale, intervention in epidemics largely ineffective and assistance in midwifery cases virtually non-existent.

The medical charities of both towns did expand the scale of their operations at a faster rate. By mid-century they admitted increased numbers of patients in both absolute terms and expressed as a percentage of the population. Admissions to the Huddersfield Dispensary increased rapidly from its foundation in 1814, and in 1831 the Infirmary was initiated as a new, purpose-built institution, with wards catering for the admission of several hundred in-patients per annum. In-patient facilities were first provided on a small scale in Wakefield in 1854, seventy years after the setting up of the Dispensary, and by the late 1850s the institution, experiencing a new financial stability, became capable of increasing its intake, especially in the out-patient department. By 1870–1871 admissions to the Wakefield Dispensary and Infirmary totalled 3,024 (or approximately 14.4 per cent of the population); in the same year 6,231 patients were treated by the medical officers of the Huddersfield Infirmary as in-, out- or home-patients (approximately 10.6 per cent of the population of Huddersfield).[10] In no year did the proportion of the populations of Wakefield and Huddersfield admitted to the towns' out-patient departments fall below 4 and 8 per cent respectively. Surprisingly enough both contemporaries and historians have concentrated in their analyses of the value of hospital provisions on in-patient admissions. Both the dispensary movement and hospital out-patient facilities have been relatively neglected, the implication being that these aspects of medical relief do not merit serious attention as medical services in their own right, or as influences on community health and mortality rates. Yet in Wakefield (and similarly in many other provincial towns) the Dispensary was the only form of charitable medical provision in existence for a period of almost seventy years, and even after the establishment of in-patient facilities, numerically the out-patient department remained far more significant. In Huddersfield too, the dispensary department was of great importance, treating several thousand persons annually. The dispensary services also dealt with a wider range of complaints than the in-patient wards, including epidemic disease, medical and chronic cases.[11]

In theory, Poor Law medical services and medical charities were designed specifically to deal with separate and clearly-defined classes of patients. In practice the relationship between the two agencies could be close, and it is misleading 'to suppose that the official Poor Law machinery and unofficial philanthropy existed in two different spheres'.[12] Many impoverished workers on the borderline between need and pauperisation were admitted to the medical charities, which in this way acted as a relief on the poor rate (and this seems to have been of particular importance in Huddersfield). In addition, as seen in Chapter 3, procedures did exist for the admission of persons recommended by Poor Law officials to the medical charities of the two towns, albeit on a small scale.

Of the two agencies, the medical charities appear to have been of more importance in terms of numbers treated, especially in Huddersfield and the surrounding area. In 1844 Rumsey computed that only 1,600 pauper patients were treated annually in the Huddersfield Union, in both the Union workhouses and as domiciliary cases by the Poor Law medical officers. Meanwhile, in this year 5,905 cases had been admitted as out-, home- and in-patients to the Huddersfield Infirmary. Throughout the Union as a whole only 1.47 per cent of the population had received Poor Law medical assistance, compared with the 5.2 per cent treated by the Infirmary's medical staff.[13] In the half-year ending March, 1861 the Huddersfield Board of Guardians estimated that their medical officers had given assistance in a total of 1,277 cases, 105 in the Union workhouses and 1,172 in the patients' homes (altogether 1.94 per cent of the Union population). By way of comparison, in the year 1860–1861 6,031 cases were admitted to the Huddersfield Infirmary, 5,680 as out-patients and 351 as in-patients. Halving these figures, to facilitate a true comparison with the totals for Poor Law medical relief, the Infirmary was percentage-wise treating well over twice as many patients as the Poor Law agencies in the Union as a whole (and calculated for the Huddersfield Township alone the difference would be much greater).[14]

In 1863 the total medical expenses (excluding an unknown, but probably small, amount spent on out-payments to the sick) of the Huddersfield Township amounted to just £296 (or less than 2d per head of the population). In the same year the expenses of the Huddersfield Infirmary amounted to over £1,900 (over 1s per head of the Township population).[15] In terms of capital expenditure, the Huddersfield Board of Guardians spent practically nothing during the first three-quarters of the nineteenth century, continuing to rent five old parish poorhouses, rather than build new workhouse accommodation. Finally, in 1872 a new workhouse was erected at the cost of £26,000,[16] but even this institution contained virtually no facilities for the sick poor. Meanwhile, the cost of erecting a new Infirmary building in Huddersfield in 1831 amounted to £7,500. A South wing was added in 1861 at a cost of £2,300.

In Wakefield the picture was somewhat different. Unlike the Huddersfield Infirmary, which took patients from a catchment area which covered much of the Huddersfield Union (and beyond), the Wakefield Dispensary and Infirmary limited its intake almost exclusively to the Township boundaries. Its impact on the area beyond was virtually nil. Rumsey's calculation that in 1844 the Poor Law medical officers treated 3 per cent of the Union population, while together the Wakefield House of Recovery and Dispensary only admitted 1.7 per cent (1,282 and 728 cases respectively) is somewhat misleading.[17] While we can dismiss the Wakefield medical charities' impact on the Union as minimal, their role in the town itself was more significant, and compared favourably with Poor Law medical relief. Between March, 1850 and May, 1851 (a fourteen-month period), for example, the surgeon to the Wakefield Medical District claimed to have treated a total of 791 cases, or 5 per cent of the population of his District (which in effect comprised most of the Wakefield Township). Meanwhile, between 1850 and 1851 (a twelve-month period) the Wakefield Dispensary treated 1,115 cases or 6.56 per cent of the Township population.[18]

The gap between the impact of the two agencies was less striking in Wakefield than in Huddersfield. As suggested in Chapter 3, the Wakefield Board of Guardians moved with greater rapidity towards the establishment of a more effective system of medical relief. (Compare Rumsey's figures for 1844, when only 1.47 per cent of the population of the Huddersfield Union received Poor Law medical relief, while in the Wakefield Union the figure was 3 per cent.) This can perhaps be seen in part as a response to the failure of the town's medical charities to expand to meet the needs of Wakefield and the surrounding district. After 1852 the newly-constructed Union Workhouse provided a rudimentary hospital service for the poor of the district, and in so doing took over the task of isolating and treating infectious disease cases from the House of Recovery. The Guardians also moved to fill the gaps left by the Wakefield Dispensary, which failed to provide in-patient care until 1854, and then only on a minimal scale, which limited its intake to the Township population, and which rigorously excluded paupers for much of the century. Although both the Wakefield and Huddersfield medical charities increased their intake during the century, the percentage of the population treated by the Huddersfield Infirmary was of a greater magnitude for much of this period. In

1850–1851, for instance, the Huddersfield Infirmary admitted 14.2 per cent of the Township population; in Wakefield the figure was half this, 6.6 per cent. By 1860–1861 the gap was smaller, 11.4 and 8.5 per cent respectively, but the Huddersfield Infirmary still had the edge by more than a small margin.[19]

For much of the nineteenth century the balance in expenditure on medical relief in Wakefield was in favour of the official Poor Law agencies, although neither the spending of official nor charitable agencies was particularly impressive. In 1830–1831, for example, the total expenditure of the Wakefield Dispensary amounted to only £236. In the year 1834–1835 the medical expenses of the Wakefield Township (excluding payments of out-relief to the sick) totalled £358. In 1858 the Township of Wakefield spent approximately £400 on medical relief; the Wakefield Dispensary and Infirmary, now enjoying increased financial support, £349.[20] With regard to capital expenditure, the Wakefield Board of Guardians opted to build a new Union Workhouse in 1851 at the cost of £8,000. The committee of the Wakefield Dispensary, on the other hand, continued to rent premises until 1854, when a small number of properties were purchased for a few hundred pounds. It was not until 1879 that a new purpose-built Infirmary was opened at the cost of £25,000.

Towards the final quarter of the nineteenth century an improvement can be detected in both the availability and standard of Poor Law medical relief. Although evidence is limited, it is possible to distinguish a small increase in the number of cases treated by the Union medical officers and a bettering of workhouse facilities for the sick. Meanwhile, admissions to the medical charities of the two communities also increased, especially during the middle decades of the century. However, whatever the balance between official and charitable provisions, and despite an extension of their fields of operation, it is safe to say that for much of the nineteenth century large numbers of the inhabitants of Wakefield and Huddersfield would have been unable, on social or medical grounds, or simply because of an inability to accommodate them, to obtain medical relief through these agencies.

It should not be automatically assumed, however, that the local population wished to obtain medical relief through these institutional channels. For the wealthier classes of the two communities, resort to these agencies was of course unnecessary, and 'institutional' treatment would be shunned by all but the poorest classes until late in the century. The wealthy obtained the medical assistance that they required from private medical attendants. As seen in Chapter 7, the middle class in particular created an increased demand for medical care during the nineteenth century, a demand fulfilled largely by the general practitioner. Middle- and upper-class groups, however, as illustrated in Chapter 6, were not averse to resorting to the services of fringe practitioners, local healers, chemists and druggists or to self-medication as a substitute for or supplement to regular medical attendance. The examples of Wakefield and Huddersfield have demonstrated that it should not be assumed that the use of alternative medicine was a practice confined to the poor, or that its usage was determined primarily by financial criteria.

For the poorer classes, for whom the choice of calling in a private medical attendant did not exist, there were a number of options (apart from applying for Poor Law medical relief or to a medical charity). The first option was to let their complaints go untreated, which presumably occurred in many (especially less serious and chronic) cases. The second possibility was to apply for another category of 'medical charity', in the form of free treatment from a regular medical practitioner. This option certainly existed, and according to doctors it was common practice to treat the poor gratis, although little evidence exists to confirm the extent to which this was carried out, at least with respect to Wakefield and Huddersfield. Akin to this option, some doctors offered cut-price treatment, making charges of a few shillings or even pence to the poor, or giving free advice while charging for medicines.[21] A further option, more likely to be taken up by better-off members of the working class, was to join a friendly society, and to thus provide themselves with a form of sickness insurance and in some cases medical treatment. The final option, or rather set of options, was to apply some form of self-medication or to seek relief from fringe personnel, local healers, itinerant quacks or chemists and druggists.

It has been suggested in Chapters 5 and 6 that the last two alternatives, friendly society medical provisions and fringe practices, not only went a long way towards filling the gap left by institutional services, but may also have been preferred options for many people. Self-help medicine it seems should not be regarded in a negative light, as a stopgap for institutional treatment, but as an important set of options in its own right. As Roy Porter has maintained, 'a great deal of healing in the past (as, of course, in the present) has involved professional practitioners only marginally, or not at all, and has been primarily a tale of medical self-help, or community care',[22] the sufferer playing '. . . an active and some-times a decisive role in interpreting and managing his own state of health'.[23] Medical men did after all seem to offer some 'cheap-rate' treatment and free medical advice to the poor, and the fact that this could be rejected in favour of 'alternative' medicine suggests that this constituted a preferred form of treatment and/or that self-help ideals had a strong influence in the region. (The rejection of 'institu-tional care' by the poor was also testified to by the frequency with which they chose to discharge themselves from the medical charities of the two towns before the completion of their course of treat-ment.) The friendly society specialised to some extent in the relief of long-term, chronic complaints, and many alternative forms also catered for this category of illness, and other medical groups least welcomed by the medical charities and Poor Law agencies (and in some cases by regular practitioners), 'incurables', medical, obstetric and VD cases, for example.

Little reliable numerical evidence is available to show the extent to which these two types of option were utilised, but it appears that both flourished during the nineteenth century. The number of friendly societies and members greatly increased in both towns – as early as 1815 approximately 7.5 and 12.2 per cent of the populations of Wakefield and Huddersfield were said to have joined a friendly society.[24] The greatest part of friendly society expenditure went on the payment of sickness money (and later in the century, although to a smaller extent, on medical treatment), and this form of relief was considered as the most important benefit conferred by these fraternities. Given these factors, it can be assumed that a large proportion of those joining friendly societies did so in order to provide themselves with assistance in the case of sickness. By the mid-nineteenth century spending on medical relief by friendly societies compared very favourably with that of the Poor Law administration. Between circa 1840 and 1850 approximately £305 per annum was spent on sick relief and medical attendance by just three Wakefield friendly societies. Roughly 104 sick members were assisted annually, the average number of days sickness per man sick being 22.5 days. In 1858 expenditure by the Poor Law Guardians on medical relief in the Wakefield Township amounted to only £400 (plus an unknown figure for out-relief of the sick).[25]

In a similar way fringe practices appear to have flourished during the late eighteenth and nineteenth centuries. As suggested in Chapter 6, the range of options and number of personnel involved in fringe medicine evidently increased in this period. New forms of fringe practice, often bolstered by commercial techniques, arrived to supplement older forms, and self-medication also continued to be a favoured form of treatment amongst all classes. To give just a few examples of the growing popularity of fringe practices. At the beginning of the nineteenth century there were only a handful of druggists in both communities, but by 1844 Rumsey could estimate that one-third of the population of Wakefield, that is, 4,000 to 5,000 people, resorted annually to the druggist's shop.[26] By the 1860s there were as many chemists and druggists as qualified medical practitioners in both towns.[27] In addition, a wide range of local healers, itinerant quacks, medicine salesmen and botanic practitioners made their livings from the retail of drugs and medical advice. By 1861 there were no less than six resident medical botanic practitioners in Huddersfield, whose services were supplemented by itinerants and vendors of botanic preparations.[28] The increasing popularity of hydropathic medicine, meanwhile, was reflected in the revival of old bathing establishments and the creation of new ones, while more distant spas also remained in favour. Examples of the popularity of fringe practice could be multiplied.[29] But it suffices to say here that throughout the nineteenth century many people (and not just the poor) continued to resort to these options. Taken together, friendly society membership and the utilisation of fringe personnel and practices point to a high level of self-help with respect to medical relief, and it could be suggested that in effect '. . . there was little informal or formal control over the kind of medical attention which the poor (and wealthy) got or did not get'.[30] While the wealthy classes retained control over the Poor Law medical services and medical charities, the working class and the poor created their own solutions to the treatment of sickness.

Gaps in the sources and in particular a lack of statistical data, make it difficult to talk about definite trends and results (a problem which could perhaps be resolved by drawing on evidence from any future studies on the development of medical agencies with a localised bias). However, it could be said tentatively that there seems to have been a wider range of medical options available to the various classes of society in Wakefield and Huddersfield by the final quarter of the nineteenth century. The continuing, even growing, importance of fringe medical practices and of friendly societies has just been referred to. Overall, the number of qualified doctors increased during the century, and, while their numbers did not keep pace with the population growth of the two communities, it is likely that they kept up with the demand for their services, a factor which is evidenced by the continuing high level of competition for posts and quality practices. The nineteenth century also witnessed an expansion in charitable facilities for the poor, with the out-patient department playing an especially significant role, although it should be re-emphasised that the supporters of these institutions did not base their efforts to any great extent on the real demand for medical care in the community. Meanwhile, towards the final quarter of the century, the Poor Law medical service began to develop into a viable relief agency and to provide, albeit in a very basic form, non-pauperising hospital facilities.

It would appear to be useful here to re-emphasise two subjects, first raised in the introduction (Chapter 1) and referred to repeatedly throughout the volume, which perhaps constitute two of the most vital themes of the survey, and which lend support to the hypothesis which stresses the value of local studies to medical history. The first theme refers to the leading role played by laymen in the provision of medical services in Wakefield and Huddersfield, a topic which can be examined in some detail within the context of local studies. The second relates to the significance and value of examining the development of medical options at the level of the known community and against a social and economic backdrop.

During the late eighteenth and nineteenth centuries laymen both created a demand for medical treatment and went much of the way towards fulfilling that demand, with respect to *both* 'orthodox' and 'institutional' medicine and self-help forms of relief. For example, it goes without saying that medical men were vital to the servicing of the Wakefield and Huddersfield medical charities. In addition, many doctors were actively involved in the foundation and organisation of these institutions. However, their role was in many senses secondary and 'inferior' to that of the lay managers of the charities, who provided the spur for the establishment of these facilities, the funding and organisational energy, and who made the key policy decisions.[31] Medical charities were seen by the lay subscribers and officers as 'rational' and 'economical' means of treating active components of the labour market and of preventing the spread of epidemic disease in the communities, and it is fair to say that up until the final quarter of the nineteenth century social and economic criteria and the aims of the lay supporters took precedence over medical concerns regarding both the scale upon which the charities came to be conducted and their admission policies. Laymen dominated admission policies, firstly, because they provided most of the financial support, and, secondly, because they controlled the actual intake via the ticket of recommendation and weekly board of admissions. Doctors were given only nominal discretion in the admission of patients, who continued to be selected largely on social rather than medical grounds. The medical officers, meanwhile, were seen very much as employees, who, while unpaid, showed in their competitiveness for appointments how much they were dependent upon obtaining them, and the support of the lay subscribers who elected them.[32]

In a similar way, lay administrators directed the Poor Law medical services from the top downwards, through the Poor Law Commission and Board, the Boards of Guardians, down to the relieving officer – the allocation of money, and the nature and extent of these services. The Poor Law medical officers were again seen merely as the 'appointees' of the lay overseers and the Boards of Guardians. After 1834 the authority of the medical man in the allocation of medical care was reduced still further.[33] Medical relief came to be strictly limited to paupers, applicants for assistance being judged almost solely on social and financial criteria. The lay Boards of Guardians, via the relieving officer, retained absolute responsibility for authorising medical relief. The emphasis placed on economy (or rather cheapness) proved to be a further problem for medical men. Their salaries were low, and unless the medical officers were prepared to supplement them out of their own pockets, the treatment they gave was dictated by this inadequate remuneration. Once admitted to the dispensary and infirmary charities, the medical staff were given *carte blanche* to treat cases how they wished (within certain time and cost limits). The Poor Law Guardians, by means of their stringent regulations and parsimony, even impinged upon that prerogative. The friendly society surgeon, meanwhile, was an employee of the working-class membership who elected him (and replaced him if he proved unsatisfactory). The membership determined the amount of dole to be given in the case of sickness and the scope of medical treatment offered.

The medical profession seems to have been overcrowded for much of the nineteenth century, and this exaggerated the extent to which medical men became dependent upon obtaining posts created almost exclusively by lay groups, whether they be the prestigious infirmary appointments or poorly-paid and low-status friendly society and Poor Law posts. The evolution of the general practitioner of medicine in the nineteenth century was very much influenced by the growth in middle-class demand for the services he offered, rather than a result of internal professional and structural developments. Over-subscription to this form of medical practice again led to a scramble for paying patients, and to an acute dependence on the layman.[34] In a similar way, fringe medical personnel were very much subject to lay demands and expectations, which determined their survival and success.[35]

Finally, it would seem to be useful to re-emphasise the advantages of examining medical provisions within the context of local communities. Combining this with a survey of a wide range of source material gives a detailed insight into the medical options available and their relative importance. This approach has also thrown light on previously neglected options, friendly society facilities and fringe medical practices. By looking closely at the functioning of medicine in a known locality, material for comparison with other communities becomes available, which may even, as John Pickstone optimistically remarks, '. . . transcend national boundaries',[36] and which helps build up a picture of the development of modern medical services and the medical profession. Such a survey also gives a greater insight into the reasoning behind the establishment of medical facilities; an idea of motivations and perceived needs, and of how local groups, and not just the wealthy and influential, responded to these needs. Population changes, the economic situation, class structure, and the activities of local government in the fields of public health and housing determined the kind and level of medical problems which would arise in a community. In turn, it can be seen how local élite groups, and the poor and working-class, via their self-help agencies, reacted to these problems. Perhaps one of the most interesting conclusions to result from such an analysis is that there appeared to be a limited response to many of the communities' most demanding health problems, shown most particularly by institutional medicine's failure to create viable systems of medical care. In many ways self-help forms (which paralleled a general striving for independence and a high level of activity in working-class movements in the region) catered in a more realistic way for health problems. The examination of medical facilities and practices in local communities not only gives us more information about the scale and range of options; it also enables us to learn more about the relationship between medicine, history and society.

APPENDICES

Appendix 1. Deaths in Wakefield Township from 1 July, 1837 to 30 June, 1847.

Sub-divisions of Wakefield Township	Under five years of age					Above five years of age					Total deaths at all ages
	Deaths from fever	Deaths from other zymotic diseases	Deaths from consumption and scrofula	Deaths from all other causes	Total deaths under five years	Deaths from fever	Deaths from other zymotic diseases	Deaths from consumption and scrofula	Deaths from all other causes	Total deaths above five years	
Westgate, South	2	66	18	130	216	18	22	71	198	309	525
Westgate, North	–	30	5	66	101	9	9	29	81	128	229
Northgate, West	–	39	7	83	129	6	18	60	226	310	439
Northgate, East[a]	11	97	16	182	306	7	26	97	206	336	642
Wrengate, North	1	14	1	42	58	4	1	15	37	57	115
Wrengate, South	–	15	1	18	34	7	3	15	18	43	77
Kirkgate, West	2	78	22	142	244	12	27	70	174	283	527
Kirkgate, East	5	39	9	75	128	10	14	40	86	150	278
Primrose Hill	2	62	12	110	186	13	13	45	72	143	329
Totals	23	440	91	848	1,402	86	133	442	1,098	1,759	3,161
		463		939			219		1,540		3,161
The prison, workhouse and those parts of Wakefield not mentioned above		149		150			82		341		722
Total deaths		612		1,089			301		1,881		3,883

[a] Including Nelson Street (see Appendix 4 and Chapter 2, Section 2.3 and p. 347).
Source: W. Ranger, *op. cit.,* Evidence of W. R. Milner, Esq., p. 84.

Appendix 2(a). Mortality in the Township of Wakefield in the years 1845, 1847, 1849[a] and 1850.

Causes of death	1845 Age				1847 Age				1849 Age				1850 Age			
	0–15	15–60	60+	Total	0–15	15–60	60+	Total	0–15	15–60	60+	Total	0–15	15–60	60+	Total
Specified causes:																
1. Zymotic diseases	88	12	3	103	42	16	12	70	89	76	16	181	22	7	9	38
2. Sporadic diseases, including dropsy, cancer, ulcer, gout	4	5	5	14	4	10	7	21	3	6	1	10	3	7	10	20
3. Tubercular diseases, including scrofula, phthisis, hydrocephalus	27	44	2	73	24	43	2	69	27	49	4	80	20	41	–	61
4. Diseases of brain, spine, nerves and senses	28	4	7	39	24	18	18	60	30	15	12	57	29	13	9	51
5. Diseases of heart and blood vessels	–	4	1	5	2	5	4	11	–	9	4	13	1	8	9	18
6. Diseases of lungs and other organs of respiration, including bronchitis, pleurisy, pneumonia, asthma	23	4	14	41	18	9	17	44	29	8	14	51	16	10	19	45
7. Diseases of stomach, liver and other organs of digestion	18	6	1	25	20	12	8	40	19	7	7	33	14	20	8	42
8. Diseases of kidneys, etc.	1	1	1	3	–	1	–	1	1	2	1	4	–	2	4	6
9. Childbirth, diseases of uterus, etc.	–	3	–	3	–	1	–	1	–	–	–	–	–	4	–	4
10. Rheumatism, diseases of bone, joints, etc.	–	1	–	1	1	–	1	2	–	4	1	5	–	–	1	1
11. Diseases of skin, etc.	–	–	–	–	–	–	–	–	–	1	–	1	–	–	–	–
12. Malformations	–	–	–	–	1	–	–	1	–	–	–	–	2	–	–	2
13. Premature birth and debility (infant deaths)	33	–	–	33	26	–	–	26	23	–	–	23	17	–	–	17
14. Old age	–	–	39	39	–	–	32	32	–	–	27	27	–	–	30	30
15. Violence, privation, cold and intemperance	7	15	6	28	5	13	3	21	2	7	5	14	3	14	1	18
All causes	229	99	79	407	167	128	104	399	223	184	92	499	127	126	100	353

Appendix 2(b). Mortality from zymotic diseases in the Township of Wakefield in the years 1845, 1847, 1849[a] and 1850.

Zymotic diseases – causes of death	1845 Age				1847 Age				1849 Age				1850 Age			
	0–15	15–60	60+	Total	0–15	15–60	60+	Total	0–15	15–60	60+	Total	0–15	15–60	60+	Total
Smallpox	8	–	–	8	–	–	–	–	–	–	–	–	1	–	–	1
Measles	43	–	–	43	1	–	–	1	33	–	–	33	–	–	–	–
Scarlatina	16	1	–	17	22	3	–	25	8	–	–	8	3	–	–	3
Hooping cough	–	–	–	–	6	–	–	6	1	–	–	1	7	–	–	7
Croup	6	–	–	6	2	–	–	2	2	–	–	2	2	–	–	2
Thrush	1	–	–	1	1	–	–	1	2	–	–	2	1	–	–	1
Diarrhoea	6	2	2	10	3	–	5	8	14	4	5	23	1	1	5	7
Dysentery	–	–	–	–	2	1	4	7	2	5	1	8	1	–	–	1
Cholera	–	–	–	–	–	2	1	3	19	61	7	87	1	–	1	2
Influenza	–	–	–	–	1	1	2	4	–	–	2	2	–	–	–	–
Purpura and scurvy	1	–	–	1	–	–	–	–	–	–	–	–	–	–	–	–
Remittent fever	3	1	–	4	2	–	–	2	2	–	–	2	1	–	–	1
Typhus	4	7	1	12	2	8	–	10	6	3	1	10	2	3	3	8
Rheumatic fever	–	–	–	–	–	–	–	–	–	–	–	–	–	2	–	2
Erysipelas	–	–	–	–	–	–	–	–	–	3	–	3	1	1	–	2
Syphilis	–	1	–	1	–	1	–	1	–	–	–	–	1	–	–	1
Total	88	12	3	103	42	16	12	70	89	76	16	181	22	7	9	38

[a] Year of cholera epidemic.
Source: W. Ranger, *op. cit.*, Appendix, pp. 80–84.

Appendix 3. A statement of the number of in and out patients attended by T. R. Tatham, from March 25, 1843 to March 25, 1844, inclusive; with an account of journies, medicines, etc. during the year.

Patients in the workhouse, 127. Out-patients, 180. Total, 307.

Number of written orders for attendance, etc., 166.

Total number of journeys and visits, 1633, at 6d. each, amount to £40 16s 6d.

	£	s	d
584 Mixtures, at 6d. per bottle	14	12	0
2225 Powders, or 185 doz., at 6d. per doz.	4	12	6
2736 Pills, or 228 doz., at 3d. per doz.	2	17	0
166 Bottles of Lotion, at 6d. per bottle	4	3	0
460 Ounces of Ointment, at 2½d. per oz	4	15	10
41 Blisters, at 9d. each	1	10	9
59 Leeches, at 4d. each	0	19	3
35 Ounces of Castor Oil, at 2d. per oz	0	5	10
38 Ounces of Lint, at 3s. 6d. per oz [*sic*]	6	13	0
93 Pounds of Linseed Meal, at 3d. per pound	1	3	3
18 Ounces of Carbonate of Iron, at 2d. per oz	0	3	0
Bandages	0	5	6
Toll Bars	2	2	0
	£37	18	2

24 Bleedings. 209 Dressings of Wounds. 20 Examination of persons for the board of Guardians, besides the extraction of teeth.

Source: Mr Tatham's Case against The Huddersfield Board of Guardians, Letter No. 2, To the Board of Guardians for the Huddersfield Union, dated 1844, p. 7, HPL (Tomlinson Collection).

Appendix 4. Return of cases treated by Mr E. Walker, jun., as surgeon to the poor of the Township of Wakefield, from March 25, 1850 to May 26, 1851.

Districts	Continued fever	Erysipelas	Smallpox	Hooping cough	Dysentery	Diarrhoea	Other diseases	Total
North Westgate	27	2	13	7	2	10	78	139
South Westgate	28	–	4	3	–	13	47	95
West Northgate	4	–	–	–	–	3	6	13
East Northgate[a]	61	–	2	16	4	31	92	206
West Kirkgate	30	–	4	2	2	11	70	119
East Kirkgate	39	1	7	–	–	17	86	150
North Kirkgate	12	–	–	2	–	5	17	36
South Kirkgate	1	–	–	–	–	–	5	6
Thornes-lane	5	–	–	1	1	4	11	22
Doncaster-road	–	–	–	–	–	–	2	2
Barnsley-road	–	–	–	–	–	1	2	3
Total	207	3	30	31	9	95	416	791

[a] Including Nelson Street (see Appendix 1 and Chapter 2, Section 2.3 and p. 347).
Source: W. Ranger, *op. cit.*, Appendix, p. 87.

Appendix 5. Abstracts of the accounts of the Wakefield and Huddersfield Dispensaries and Infirmaries.

a) Wakefield Dispensary, 1830–1831

Receipts

	Amount £ s d	Percentage of income
Balance in hand, July 1, 1830	278 8 0	
Items of income		
Annual subscriptions	178 19 0	72.8
Half proceeds of the charity ball	16 13 8	6.7
Miss Lumb, a donation	25 0 0	10.2
Dr Alexander, a donation	3 16 6	1.6
Fines, compromises, etc.	6 7 6	2.6
Vagrant office	0 5 0	0.1
Interest allowed by the Treasurer	9 15 7	4.0
Miscellaneous	5 1 6	2.0
Total	245 16 9	100%

Expenses

Items of expenditure	Amount £ s d	Percentage of expenditure
Apothecary's salary	84 9 0	35.9
Matron's salary	12 0 0	5.1
Drugs	72 5 4	30.7
Trusses, etc.	3 0 0	1.3
Leeches	11 11 6	4.9
One year's rent	16 16 0	7.1
Stationery, printing, etc.	12 2 7	5.1
Coal	2 0 9	0.8
Groceries, candles, etc.	4 3 6	1.8
Sundry repairs, cleaning, etc.	15 6 8	6.5
Miscellaneous	1 17 9	0.5
Total	235 13 1	100%

Balance in the hands of
the Treasurer, July 1, 1831   £288 13s 10d

Source: 44th AR WD, 1830–1831.

Appendix 5 (*contd*)

b) Huddersfield Dispensary, 1830–1831

Receipts

	Amount			Percentage of income
	£	s	d	
Balance in hand, June 21, 1830	85	16	6	
Items of income				
Annual subscriptions	291	18	0	59.0
Donations and legacies				
Mr George Senior £1				
Timothy Bentley, Esq., deceased				
£45	46	0	0	9.3
Fines ordered by magistrates	52	17	0	10.7
Congregational collections	96	5	6	19.5
Sale of trusses	3	2	6	0.6
Interest	3	5	4	0.7
Total	493	7	4	100%

Expenses

Items of expenditure	Amount			Percentage of expenditure
	£	s	d	
Salaries	146	14	6	34.7
Drugs and leeches	217	0	7½	51.3
Instruments and trusses	9	18	0	2.4
Rent, taxes and repairs	26	5	0	6.2
Stationery	17	18	8	4.3
Coals and candles	1	7	2	0.3
Miscellaneous	3	12	4½	0.8
Total	422	16	4	100%

Balance in the hands of
the Treasurer, June 24, 1831   £156 8s 6d

Source: 17th AR HD, 1830–1831.

c) Wakefield Infirmary, 1865–1866

Receipts

	Amount			Percentage of income
	£	s	d	
Balance in hand, June 30, 1865	82	7	11	
Items of income				
Annual subscriptions	515	2	0	33.4
Donations	75	16	0	4.9
Surplus of Lancashire (Cotton Relief) Fund	637	4	0	41.4
Congregational collections	140	3	10	9.1
Charity ball	43	0	6	2.8
Fines	2	0	0	0.1
Interest from National Investment Society	5	0	0	0.3
Interest on railway investments	104	14	2	6.8
Banker's interest	1	11	7	0.1
Rent of property belonging to Dispensary	15	17	11	1.0
Total	1,540	7	0	100%

Expenses

Items of expenditure	Amount			Percentage of expenditure
	£	s	d	
Salary of house surgeon	96	4	2	10.5
Salary of dispenser	65	0	0	7.1
Matron's wages	44	13	4	4.9
Nurse's wages	5	18	6	0.7
Messenger's wages	4	15	0	0.5
Drugs, etc.	188	10	6	20.6
Leeches	1	15	3	0.2
Trusses and implements	25	1	2	2.7
Wine and brandy	3	8	6	0.4
Patients' diet	115	13	8	12.7
House expenses, including furniture	193	15	8	21.2
Water and gas	11	17	0	1.3
Coal	16	2	0	1.8
Repairs, painting, etc.	33	5	0	3.6
Stationery, printing and advertising	73	15	8	8.1

Appendix 5 (*contd*)

Expenses (contd)

Insurance	1	17	6	0.2
Collector's commission and				
postages	10	14	10	1.2
Miscellaneous	20	15	4	2.3
Total	913	3	1	100%

Balance in the hands of
the Treasurer, June 30, 1866   £709 11s 10d

Invested on behalf of the institution by 1866

	£
National Investment Society, 4 shares	100
Great Western Railway, Debentures	600
Great Eastern Railway, Debentures	200
Lancashire and Yorkshire Railway £5 Guaranteed Stock	1,000
South Eastern Railway Preference Stock	1,000
Midland Railway Preference Stock	1,800
London and Brighton Railway Preference Stock	1,000
Total	£5,700

Source: 79th AR WI, 1865–1866.

d) **Huddersfield Infirmary, 1865–1866**

Receipts

	Amount			Percentage of income
	£	s	d	
Balance in hand, June 30, 1865	225	14	6	
Items of income				
Annual subscriptions	1,155	12	0	22.9
Legacies	1,087	1	0	21.5
Donations	37	2	10	0.7
Surplus of Cotton Relief Fund	1,831	1	0	36.3
Congregational collections	66	6	10	1.3
Charity boxes	1	5	5	0.02
Fines	12	11	6	0.2
Interest on investments	831	4	11	16.5
Miscellaneous	26	6	6	0.5
Total	5,048	12	0	100%

Expenses

Items of expenditure	Amount			Percentage of expenditure
	£	s	d	
Salaries	229	1	7	11.8
Wages	151	18	8	7.9
Collector's commission and expenses	63	8	7	3.3
Drugs and oil	322	7	1	16.7
Surgical instruments, bandages, plaster, etc.	46	5	0	2.4
Spirits of wine	11	18	4	0.6
Trusses, etc.	33	19	6	1.8
Patients' diet	551	14	5	28.5
Alcoholic stimulants	116	9	0	6.0
Coal	72	5	2	3.7
Gas	33	19	0	1.8
Garden	36	16	3	1.9
Linen	18	5	5	0.9
Shaving in-patients	12	0	0	0.6
Soap and ammonia	23	14	0	1.2
Furnishing, repairs and painting	118	14	11	6.1
Printing and stationery	28	19	6	1.5

Appendix 5 *(contd)*

Expenses (contd)

Rates and insurance	12	9	4	0.6
Law charges	12	1	0	0.6
Miscellaneous	37	9	4	1.9
Total	1,933	16	1	100%

Balance in the hands of
the Treasurer, June 28, 1866   £3,340 10s 5d

Invested on behalf of the institution by 1866

	£	s
On the Huddersfield Waterworks at 4.5 per cent	9,000	0
On the Woodhead Road at 3 per cent	1,274	18
On Great Western Railway Debenture at 4.5 per cent	1,000	0
On Mersey Docks/Harbour Debenture at 4.5 per cent	1,500	0
On North London Railway Preference Shares at 4.5 per cent	1,000	0
On Victoria Government Debentures for £2,000 at 6 per cent for 21 years running from October 1st, 1862	2,215	0
On North British Railway Company for £900, Border Union Guaranteed Stock at 5.5 per cent	1,049	1
On North Eastern Railway Company Debenture at 4.75 per cent	1,000	0
On the Brecon and Merthyr Tydfil Junction Railway Company Debenture at 5 per cent	1,000	0
On the Cambrian Railway Company Debenture at 5 per cent	1,000	0
Total	£20,038	19

Source: 35th AR HI, 1865–1866.

Appendix 6. Number of patients treated, cured and relieved, and mortality rates in the Wakefield and Huddersfield Dispensaries and Infirmaries.

a) Wakefield Dispensary (out-patients), 1790–1870

Period	Average number treated per annum	Average percentage cured	Average percentage cured and relieved	Average mortality rate
1790–1795[a]	425	85.88	91.29	2.24
No annual reports or patient figures were available for the period 1795 to 1810.				
1810–1815[a]	482	85.05	91.48	4.36
No annual reports or patient figures were available for the period 1815 to 1830.				
1830–1835[a]	1,180	79.24	86.69	3.73
1835–1840[a]	790	72.28	88.67	4.11
1840–1845[a]	669	71.90	88.12	3.81
No annual reports or patient figures were available for the period 1845 to 1850.				
1850–1855	1,278	62.18	80.94	3.97
1855–1860	1,320	59.64	81.01	2.99
1860–1865	1,973	56.94	77.04	3.31
1865–1870	2,904	62.66	80.82	2.98

b) Huddersfield Dispensary (out-patients), 1815–1870

Period	Average number treated per annum	Average percentage cured	Average percentage cured and relieved	Average mortality rate
1815–1820[a]	1,727	—	74.03	2.23
1820–1825	2,372	69.52	83.35	1.73
1825–1830	2,369	64.98	72.27	2.08
1830–1835	2,858	67.39	79.83	1.84
1835–1840	3,906	67.43	85.15	1.30
1840–1845[a]	4,692	65.81	86.17	0.43
1845–1850[a]	7,095	63.92	84.78	2.16
1850–1855[a]	6,271	59.64	75.63	1.15
1855–1860	5,572	50.31	70.56	2.06
1860–1865	5,884	54.43	68.30	2.44
1865–1870	5,904	60.57	74.14	2.36

Appendix 6 (*contd*)

c) Huddersfield Infirmary (in-patients), 1831–1870

Period	Average number treated per annum	Average percentage cured	Average percentage cured and relieved	Average mortality rate
1831–1835	165	46.28	70.41	3.49
1835–1840	303	52.71	75.17	4.95
1840–1845[a]	384	43.75	78.39	4.95
1845–1850[a]	406	39.90	67.98	6.16
1850–1855[a]	373	50.40	65.15	5.90
1855–1860	357	38.84	73.75	7.05
1860–1865	368	35.31	55.02	8.47
1865–1870	406	48.79	76.96	7.43

d) Wakefield Infirmary (in-patients), 1854–1870

Period	Average number treated per annum	Average percentage cured	Average percentage cured and relieved	Average mortality rate
1854–1855	39	53.85	79.49	12.82
1855–1860	19	75.00	77.08	11.46
1860–1865	43	71.43	75.58	8.29
1865–1870	73	76.65	81.59	8.79

[a] Periods where data were extracted from an incomplete set of reports.

The data are subject to a number of irregularities, which go some way towards explaining fluctuations in the figures given for the percentages of patients cured, cured and relieved, and mortality rates. Hospital statistics during this period were notoriously inaccurate, and the Wakefield and Huddersfield institutions were no exceptions. As Dr Walker of the Huddersfield Infirmary maintained, 'I know so much of the manner of making up lists of diseases, from now 30 years' experience in our medical charity, where we have from 5,000 to 6,000 patients annually, that I have little confidence in the accuracy of any such lists.'[1] It is possible that in some years patients were counted twice or more. (On the expiration of their first term of admission, usually a period of three months, they were readmitted and recounted.) Meanwhile, the category 'cured and relieved' often covered patients whose time had expired. It is not clear whether this group had received any benefits from their treatment. A proportion of in-patients classified as relieved were transferred to the out-patient departments, but in many years the actual number falling into this category does not show up in the reports.

It will be noted that there is often a large gap between the figures for patients cured and relieved plus the death rate and the total number treated. The difference was made up by a number of smaller categories: patients discharged as irregular, improper objects or at their own request, those dismissed as incurable or sent to other institutions (for example, the Wakefield House of Recovery, the Leeds Infirmary or the County Asylum at Wakefield), those transferred to the Poor Law medical officers and those remaining on the books at the end of the year.

Sources: Annual Reports of the Wakefield Dispensary and Infirmary for the years 1790–1792, 1812–1813, 1814–1815, 1830–1831, 1836–1837, 1839–1840, 1841–1843, 1850–1870, and of the Huddersfield Dispensary and Infirmary for the years 1814–1818, 1820–1841, 1846–1847, 1851–1852, 1855–1870.

[1] SCMPR 1844, Evidence of H. W. Rumsey, Esq., p. 560. Q.9166.

Appendix 7. Biographies of prominent Wakefield and Huddersfield medical philanthropists.

Colonel J. C. D. Charlesworth (Wakefield), 1815–1880

Occupation: Senior partner in Messrs J. and J. Charlesworth, one of the county's largest coal proprietors. Major landowner.
Religion: Rigid Churchman (Wakefield Parish Church and Sandal Church).
Politics: Conservative. In 1857 returned as MP for Wakefield. In 1859 defeated by Liberal candidate, W. H. Leatham.
Contributions to medical charity: Trustee, Life Benefactor and President, 1855–1880 (d). Made a large number of donations to the charity – 1859 £46 in aid of a Special Improvement Fund, 1863 £50 towards the Prince Albert Memorial Fund, 1871 £500 towards the Endowment Fund for the new hospital building. In 1865 acted as Patron to the Grand Concert in aid of the Endowment Fund of the Clayton Hospital. Active in campaign to establish larger, purpose-built accommodation, and in 1879 laid foundation stone of new building. On several occasions added a contribution to the Hospital Saturday Fund – in 1876 made up Fund from £712 to £1,000; in 1877 from £428 to £500. Steward of Wakefield Charity Ball. Several other members of the Charlesworth family funded the charity.
Contributions to other voluntary activities: President Wakefield Men's Conservative Association. President of the Cricket Club and Chairman of the Hunt Committee. Liberal benefactor to the Parish Church and Sandal Church. Past Master Wakefield Lodge of Freemasons (No. 495).
Public appointments: JP, Deputy Lieutenant. Member West Riding Police Committee. Visitor of Private Lunatic Asylums. Colonel of the Wakefield Volunteers.

Mr Thomas Clayton (Wakefield), 1786–1868

Occupation: Entered his father's (also Thomas Clayton) tallow chandler's concern. Very successful businessman, and in 1826 Thomas Clayton, junior, was able to retire, then aged forty. Thereafter no occupation and lived as a gentleman.
Religion: Until 1854 Clayton had not attended any place of worship on a regular basis. Practised as a Bible Christian, studying the scriptures at home. Following his marriage in 1854 to Eliza Stead, the sister of William Willans, an eminent Huddersfield Congregationalist, Clayton became a regular attender at the Zion Congregational Chapel in Wakefield. Although a strong Non-Conformist, also something of a 'liberal' with regard to his religious opinions. One of the stipulations of his legacy to the Wakefield Dispensary and Infirmary was that clergymen of all persuasions should be given free access to the institution.

Politics: Liberal-Reformer. Supporter of Lord Morpeth and Edward Baines.

Contributions to medical charity: Long-standing subscriber and committee member. 1854 bought three houses in Dispensary Yard, Northgate, and presented them to the Dispensary Committee. 1858 contributed £120 towards cost of the land and buildings required to add in-patient facilities. 1860 gave a further £150 to defray the entire cost of the purchase. 1863 donated £40 to fund to build 'Prince Albert Memorial Ward'. 1864 donated £100 on opening of the 'Albert Memorial Ward' for the purchase of surgical instruments. 1865 headed an Endowment Fund with a contribution of £1,000. 1867 presented £100 to the Infirmary Committee to purchase an adjacent cottage. By his will a legacy provided for the annual payment of £300 to the Infirmary. Served in capacity of Vice-President, Auditor and Patron. In 1854 name of charity changed to 'The Wakefield General Dispensary and Clayton Hospital', in 1862 to 'The Clayton Hospital and Wakefield General Dispensary'. In 1867 a special subscription was set up to procure a portrait of Clayton – displayed in Infirmary Board Room.

Contributions to other voluntary activities: Subscriber to Wakefield Town Mission, British and Foreign Bible Society and Ragged School. Liberal supporter of Zion Chapel and its Sunday School – contributed £200 to Sunday School in 1867 and laid foundation stone of new building. During his lifetime gave large proportion of his income to charity. By will bequeathed £1,000 to British and Foreign Bible Society, £500 to London Missionary Society, £500 to Doncaster Deaf and Dumb Institution, £500 to York School for the Blind, £500 to Friendless Children's Institute, Reedham, £500 to London Orphan Asylum, £25 to Port of Hull Society, £250 to Royal National Lifeboat Association, £100 to Harrogate Bath Hospital. Large sum of money vested in trustees to be given in sums of £10 or upwards to poor, old and 'deserving' men regardless of their religious creed.

Public appointments: Until 1848 little involvement in civic affairs. On incorporation of Wakefield in 1848 elected Alderman: between 1854 and 1855 served as Mayor.

Mr Robert Hodgson (Wakefield)

Occupation: Merchant/gentleman.
Religion: Church of England.
Politics: Conservative. Elected Alderman in the first municipal elections, 1848.
Contributions to medical charity: Annual subscriber. Committee member for many years and Collector of subscriptions. President 1850–1854.
Contributions to other voluntary activities: Gave land on which Holy Trinity

Church built in 1838. Life Member and committee member Wakefield
Auxiliary Bible Society, subscriber Town Mission.
Public appointments: Watch and Street Commissioner.

Mr W. Leatham (Wakefield), 1784–1842

Occupation: Banker (links with Barclay family).
Religion: Quaker.
Politics: Liberal.
Contributions to medical charity: Annual subscriber, Auditor and Life
Governor. Treasurer, together with other members of the Leatham
family, during middle decades of century.
Contributions to other voluntary activities: Liberal private benefactor. Trea-
surer Wakefield Auxiliary Bible Society. Subscriber Wakefield Benevolent
Society and Town Mission. Treasurer Lancastrian School. On committee
and Chairman of Newsroom. Member Phil. and Lit. Society. Vice-Presi-
dent Wakefield Museum.
Public appointments: Treasurer Waterworks Company.

Mr W. H. Leatham (Wakefield), 1815–1889

Occupation: Banker, with connections by marriage to Gurney banking
family.
Religion: Quaker.
Politics: Liberal. Elected MP for Wakefield 1865 (after two previous
attempts in 1852 and 1859). Brother-in-law of John Bright.
Contributions to medical charity: Life Benefactor, committee member and
Treasurer, 1850–1852. In 1859 donated £10 to Building Fund and in 1863
£5 to Prince Albert Memorial Fund.
Contributions to other voluntary activities: President and Treasurer Wakefield
Town Mission. Active in Mechanics' Institute. Donated books and lec-
tured to members. For a number of years acted as Vice-President and
President to the Institute. Member Phil. and Lit. Society. Vice-President
Wakefield Museum. Governor of the Wakefield Grammar School.
Member of Wakefield Archery Club.
Public appointments: None recorded.

Mr Edward Tew (Wakefield), 1877 (d)

Occupation: Banker.
Religion: Churchman.
Politics: Reputedly Conservative. Never voted, and a note in the Register
of Electors for 1840 stated '. . . never has voted – but is yellow – being now
a magistrate is not like to oppose the son of the Lord Lieutenant'.

Contributions to medical charity: Annual subscriber. 1859 donated £21 to Wakefield Infirmary. 1863 donated £10 to the Prince Albert Memorial Fund. Trustee, Life Governor, committee member and Vice-President. Left legacy of £4,000 to the Infirmary.

Contributions to other voluntary activities: Governor of the Wakefield Charities, 1830–1870. Governor and Honorary Treasurer to Green Coat Charity School.

Public appointments: JP.

Sir Joseph Armitage (Huddersfield), 1778–1860

Occupation: Woollen manufacturer. Built a mill at Milnsbridge in 1822 and Burdett Mill, Huddersfield, in 1838.

Religion: Church of England (Huddersfield Parish Church).

Politics: Whig.

Contributions to medical charity: Annual subscriber from initiation of Dispensary in 1814. In 1814 also donated ten guineas. Donated £150 towards Infirmary Building Fund. In 1831 elected Vice-President. 1831–1860(d) President of Infirmary. Patron of charity. Left legacy of £100 to Infirmary. In 1861 Messrs Armitage Broths., Huddersfield, donated £50 for a portrait of their father, the late Joseph Armitage, which was hung in the Infirmary Board Room upon completion.

Contributions to other voluntary activities: Built Milnsbridge Church. Founder member of Huddersfield Subscription Library.

Public appointments: JP and Deputy Lieutenant of the West Riding. In 1848 appointed Improvement Commissioner. Magistrate for Lancashire, Chester, Derby and the West Riding. Rewarded baronetcy because of services as a magistrate during the Luddite risings and Plug Riots.

Mr Charles Brook (Huddersfield), 1792–1869

Occupation: Cotton thread and silk manufacturer. Partner in Meltham Mills (Jonas Brook and Broths.) and Charles Brook and Son.

Religion: Church of England (Huddersfield Parish Church).

Politics: Not known, probably Whig. Opposed to Factory Acts. In 1831 signed petition to Parliament against proposed Bill to reduce hours of labour for factory children.

Contributions to medical charity: Annual subscriber. Donated fifty guineas to Building Fund of Huddersfield Infirmary, 1831. Vice-President 1831–1869 (d). Donated £30,000 and site for establishment of Convalescent Home in connection with Infirmary in 1869. Other family members were also liberal benefactors and annual subscribers. After death of Charles Brook, continued to support the charity – in 1873, for example, Jonas Brook and Broths. of Meltham Mills donated £250 towards the fund to extend the Infirmary.

Contributions to other voluntary activities: Erected Church at Helme and parsonage Meltham Mills. On committees of Bible Society and Auxiliary Peace Society. Supporter of Mechanics' Institute – subscribed £100 towards new building in 1861. Said to have subscribed to many other local charities and to have been an active private philanthropist.
Public appointments: Not very active in public affairs. JP.

Mr Thomas Pearson Crosland (Huddersfield), 1816–1868

Occupation: Woollen manufacturer/gentleman.
Religion: Initially Methodist New Connexion. In later life became a Churchman.
Politics: Staunch Whig. MP 1865–1868(d) for Huddersfield. Supporter of Free Trade, opponent of Factory Acts.
Contributions to medical charity: Together with other family members, subscribed to Huddersfield Infirmary. Liberal benefactors.
Contributions to other voluntary activities: Member of Mechanics' Institute and Patron of the Penny Bank. Proprietor of Huddersfield College. Patron of Naturalist Society. Involved in the administration of the local fund during the 'cotton famine'. Oddfellow and Master Freemason.
Public appointments: Improvement Commissioner 1848–1852. Waterworks Commissioner. Appointed JP 1852 and Deputy Lieutenant 1864. Active supporter of Volunteer Movement. Captain of the 2nd Co. 1860, Major of Battalion 1862, Lieutenant-Colonel 1864, Honorary Colonel 5th Battalion of West York Rifle Volunteers 1866. Active in campaign for a charter of incorporation. Active in Chamber of Commerce; in 1863 appointed President.

Mr C. H. Jones (Huddersfield), 1800–1884

Occupation: Manchester draper, who came to Huddersfield in 1841. Director of several railway companies, including Lancs. and Yorks. and Midland Railway Companies.
Religion: Congregationalist. Attended at Ramsden Street Chapel – Deacon, Trustee and Treasurer.
Politics: Staunch Liberal. Participant at Peterloo. Active in Anti-Corn Law League. Chaired Liberal Registration Association in Huddersfield. Friend of Leatham and Cobden. Great uncle of Asquith.
Contributions to medical charity: Annual subscriber and committee member of Huddersfield Infirmary. Auditor. Trustee Meltham Mills Convalescent Home till 1884 (d).
Contributions to other voluntary activities: Interested in both religious and secular education. President of Council of Huddersfield College. Trustee of British Schools at Outcote Bank until handed over to School Board.

1847–1877 member of School Board. Member and Vice-President British and Foreign Bible Society and member Tract Society. Active in Mechanics' Institute.

Public appointments: 1853–1857 Improvement Commissioner – Chairman 1854–1855 and 1856. Elected Alderman for West Ward in first municipal elections. First Mayor of Borough 1868–1872. Borough Magistrate. Agitator for Waterworks Act and active in campaign to rid town of Church Rate. Member of Chamber of Commerce.

Mr James Campey Laycock (Huddersfield), 1796–1885

Occupation: Solicitor and banker.

Religion: Staunch Church of England (Huddersfield Parish Church – Churchwarden 1834–1836).

Politics: No active political involvement. Initially a Whig; in later life become a moderate Conservative. Gave legal assistance to anti-Factory Act lobby.

Contributions to medical charity: Annual subscriber to Huddersfield Dispensary and Infirmary. In 1831 donated thirty guineas to the Infirmary Building Fund. For fifty years was responsible for the voting of an annual donation of 25 guineas by the Huddersfield Banking Company. Joint Secretary 1821–1837, Honorary Secretary 1837–1860 and President 1860–1885(d). Active committee member and business manager. Active in campaign to establish an infirmary in Huddersfield – served on Infirmary Committee and organised fund-raising, the building and staffing of the institution. 1858 specially commissioned portrait of Laycock placed in Board Room. 1873 donated £50 to Infirmary Extension Fund.

Contributions to other voluntary activities: Largely instrumental in rebuilding of Huddersfield Parish Church in 1836 and in founding of Parish Schools. Secretary and Treasurer to the Managers of the Day Schools 1841–1884. For over forty years teacher and superintendent of Parish Church Sunday Schools. Donated £300 towards building of new Parish Schools and laid the foundation stone of them in 1879. Treasurer Church Missionary Society, President of Huddersfield Branch of British and Foreign Bible Society. On committee of Benevolent and Visiting Society. Founder, Trustee and Governor of Huddersfield Collegiate School. On committee of Ragged and Industrial School. Treasurer of Newsroom.

Public appointments: Clerk to Justices 1828, Clerk to Borough Bench 1868. Chairman Huddersfield Gas Company.

Mr William Willans (Huddersfield), 1800–1863

Occupation: Woolstapler. Self-made man, who began life in Huddersfield as a commercial clerk.

Religion: Congregationalist. First attended Highgate Chapel. After 1825 active supporter of Ramsden Street Chapel – lay minister and Deacon, 1833–1863 (d).

Politics: Liberal-Radical. Associate of Edward Baines. 1831 Reformer. Founder Huddersfield Anti-Corn Law League 1839. 1852 stood as Liberal candidate for Huddersfield – defeated by the Whig candidate, W. R. C. Stansfield. Chaired Cobden Committee in 1857 election – Cobden defeated by Whig, Edward Akroyd. Grandfather of Asquith.

Contributions to medical charity: Annual subscriber, committee member and liberal benefactor.

Contributions to other voluntary activities: Supporter of British School. Member and Vice-President Mechanics' Institute – 1861 subscribed £21 towards new building in Northumberland Street. Supporter and Patron of Penny Bank. Active supporter of non-sectarian education. On first Council and President of Huddersfield College. On committees of Huddersfield Auxiliary Peace Society and Temperance Society. Supporter of Bible, Tract and Missionary Societies. Very active in promotion of Ramsden Street Chapel – on organising committee and first Secretary to the committee. Organiser of Bible classes. Established Congregational Mission in Huddersfield. Inspired building of Hillhouse Congregational Church. Active in support of Model Lodging House – held Sunday evening services there, organised Christmas dinner, etc. Reputedly gave one-tenth of his income to charity. Strong believer in voluntary principle and personal service – frequently visited sick and poor.

Public appointments: JP. President Huddersfield Chamber of Commerce, 1861–1863 (d).

Appendix 8. Poems written in celebration of the opening of the Huddersfield Infirmary.

a)   **Anonymous Lines Written for THE LADIES' BAZAAR, in aid of the HUDDERSFIELD INFIRMARY** (n.d., circa 1831)[a]

> I wandered to the poor man's cot,
> I stood beside his bed,
> Where a pale sickly woman strove
> To raise his aching head.
> And there his weeping children stood,
> In hopeless misery;
> Whilst every object which I saw
> Spoke abject poverty.
>
> And famine on each infant cheek
> Had left full many a trace,
> But deeper suffering I could read
> In that poor mother's face.
> A dreadful accident the cause –
> No hand of skill was there,
> And on his wretched couch he lay
> The victim of despair
>
>   ★   ★   ★   ★
>
> Again I visited that house,
> But what a change I found,
> Disease and want had fled the cot,
> And plenty smil'd around.
> I ask'd what caused this altered scene?
> They said with grateful eye,
> That under heaven, the mighty cause
> Was – the INFIRMARY!
>
> Daughters of England hear this tale,
> and your kind aid impart;
> Do the best work that woman can –
> Relieve the poor man's heart.
> And, sons of Britain, oft we know
> For woman's smiles ye sue;
> Come, show your gallantry, and prove
> Those smiles are still for you.

[a] HPL (Tomlinson Collection).

Assist by kind and generous aid
This branch of charity,
And purchase for some favoured one
A pledge of gallantry.
You've nobly raised the outward pile,
Now, woman claims her share;
The minor comforts of the rest
Must fall to female care.

Assist us then; without your aid
The great design will fail;
Oh! never be it said of you
The sex could not prevail
To gain your help in virtue's cause: –
Refuse! – you never can!
Still prove your title to the name
Of our superior man.

b) **Anonymous Poem IN MEMORY of Mr SAMUEL CLAY, OF HUDDERSFIELD, Who died Feb. 11, 1833, in his 54th Year** (n.d., circa 1833)[a]

How bright was life's morning! – what cheering delusion!
　　Which gladden'd the hours, and rais'd hope in thine heart, –
When braving the billows of worldly confusion
　　Thou bad'st each unwelcome foreboding depart!
Eccentric, yet friendly, – loquacious, yet pleasing, –
Philanthropy's efforts were early increasing.
Though humble thy sphere, – mortals' woes to be easing: –
　　And Wretchedness hail'd the approach of – S. CLAY.

Unaw'd by contagion, regardless of danger,
　　Obeying the impulse ennobling to man,
Thy pity befriended the Poor and the Stranger,
　　And lasting relief was deriv'd from THY PLAN! –
To raise the Samaritans' beautiful large pile, ⋆
By aid from the wealthy, with Charity's sweet smile;
E'en churls own'd thy pleas, – often jocund, without guile. –
　　Humanity honour'd her champion, – S. CLAY.

To different objects thy views were extending,
　　Political struggles thy mind could elate;
But, while for the blessing of freedom contending,
　　The patriot's warmth met the patriot's fate! –
Beflatter'd and cheer'd, revil'd and neglected,
Not merely by foes, but by some long respected:
Still Liberty glow'd, – the pure flame was ejected!
　　For Britain's wellwisher was injur'd – S. CLAY.

Thou wast indiscreet, but from motives thought blameless;
　　Thy suff'rings, in various quarters, not few:
With horror avoiding such deeds as were shameless,
　　Unwilling each cause of offence to renew.
Thou hast left us, we trust, for th'abodes of the blessed! –
Many numerous friends now assist the distressed;
That weeping survivors be not sore oppressed, –
　　The WIDOW and ORPHANS of worthy – S. CLAY.

T.S.

⋆ The division of Upper-Agbrigg is much indebted to Mr C. for the erection of that house of mercy, the Huddersfield Infirmary, which may be considered a lasting monument of his exertions.

LM

[a] HPL (Misc. Pamph., B.920 CLA).

Appendix 9. Medical licensing bodies and licences and degrees in the United Kingdom in the nineteenth century

Medical Corporations	Licences
England	
The Royal College of Physicians of London	FRCP, MRCP, LRCP, Extra-Lic., RCP
The Royal College of Surgeons of England	FRCS, MRCS, Lic., Midwifery (LM)
The Society of Apothecaries (London)	LSA
Archbishop of Canterbury	MD Lambeth – granted prior to 1 August, 1858
Scotland	
Royal College of Physicians of Edinburgh	FRCP Edin., MRCP Edin.
Royal College of Surgeons of Edinburgh	FRCS Edin., LRCS Edin.
Faculty of Physicians and Surgeons of Glasgow	FFPSG, LFPSG
Ireland	
King's and Queen's College of Physicians of Ireland	FKQCP Ire., LKQCP Ire.
Royal College of Surgeons of Ireland	FRCS Ire., LRCS Ire.
Apothecaries' Hall, Dublin	LAH

Universities		Degrees
England	Oxford	
	Cambridge	
	London	
	Victoria	
	Durham	
Scotland	Edinburgh	MB, MD, and BCh, Mch, and
	Aberdeen	Lic. Med.
	Glasgow	
	St Andrew's	
Ireland	Dublin	

F – Fellow, M – Member, L or Lic. – Licentiate.
Source: W. E. Steavenson, *The Medical Act (1858) Amendment Bill and Reform; a paper read before the Abernethian Society* . . . (1880), pp. 30–31. Cited in M. J. Peterson, *op. cit.*, pp. 289–290.

Appendix 10. Places of training of medical men in practice in Wakefield and Huddersfield in 1851, 1861 and 1871.

Places where training completed[a]	1851	1861	1871
Wakefield			
Scotland	9	11	16
London	7	12	11
Ireland	1	2	1
Paris	1	2	3
Leyden	1	1	1
Pisa	1	1	1
Cambridge	1	1	0
Leeds	1	2	6
Not known	14	11	8
Total number of practitioners	26	24	17
Huddersfield			
Scotland	4	11	13
London	14	12	12
Ireland	2	1	0
Paris	0	1	0
New York	0	1	0
Cambridge	0	1	1
Erlangen (Germany)	1	0	0
Leeds	0	1	1
Manchester	1	1	0
York	0	0	1
Not known	4	9	2
Total number of practitioners	21	23	21

[a] Where more than one place of training was given, they have each been recorded in the table, provided the training led to a major qualification. Data were not available on all medical practitioners, and where data were available, they were not necessarily complete.
Sources: Census Enumerators' Books, Wakefield and Huddersfield, 1851, 1861 and 1871; *Provincial Medical Directories*, 1852–1872.

Appendix 11. Biographies of Wakefield and Huddersfield medical men

Mr James Fowler (Wakefield)

Born: Winterton, Lincolnshire, 1839.

Family background and social characteristics: Resided South Parade, Wakefield, with his wife and three children. Fowler employed five resident servants – two nursemaids, a housemaid, a cook and a groom.

Qualifications: LSA 1861 (St Thomas's), MRCS Eng. 1861, LM 1862.

Appointments and practice: Appointed house surgeon to St Thomas's Hospital 1861 and resident accoucheur 1862. Elected honorary surgeon Wakefield Infirmary 1863. Also held appointments as assistant surgeon to the 5th West Riding Yorkshire Royal Volunteers, as surgeon to the Wakefield District of the GNR and as medical examiner to several assurance societies. Described himself as a general practitioner.

Involvement in professional organisations and publications: Fellow and Honorary Local Secretary of the Obstetrical Society. Member of the Wakefield Microscopic Society. Expert on obstetrics. Published on diverse subjects, including the action of alcohol on the body, diphtheria, ligature of arteries and obstetrics.

Religion: Church of England.

Politics: Not known.

Involvement in charitable work, civic affairs, a.s.o.: Fellow of the Society of Antiquities and Local Secretary for Yorkshire, Honorary Secretary University of Cambridge Local Examining Board, Member of the Council of the West Riding of Yorkshire Educational Board, Council Member of the Industrial and Fine Arts Institute, Vice-President Mechanics' Institute, Wakefield. In 1865 delivered a series of lectures on phrenology in the Wakefield Music Saloon. On Charity Ball Committee. Author of 'Report on the Condition of the Calder and its Tributaries in the Wakefield District', *Third Report Royal Commission on the Pollution of Rivers*, 'Water, its Natural uses, etc.', 'On the Scientific Principles in Agriculture', 'On Mural Painting and other Antiquities at All Saints, Wakefield', and several communications in the *Proceedings of the Antiquarian and Topological Journal*.

Dr Samuel Holdsworth (Wakefield)

Born: Wakefield, 1813–1896 (d).

Family background and social characteristics: Son of Samuel Holdsworth, a local gentleman (1777–1842). Member of an eminent Liberal family. In 1850s resided in Grove House, Kirkgate, with wife and one female domestic servant. By the 1860s had moved to the auspicious West Parade, where he resided with his wife and three children. Attended on by three servants. Eldest son, Samuel R. Holdsworth, followed his father into the medical profession.

Qualifications: Served his apprenticeship with Mr Bennett, a successful Wakefield surgeon (who in turn had been a pupil of Mr W. Walker of Wakefield). MRCS Eng. and LSA 1835 (Guy's, St Thomas's and Paris), MD Pisa 1839, MRCP London 1859.

Appointments and practice: 1836 appointed house surgeon to the Dispensary at a salary of £80 per annum. Resigned after usual three-year term in 1839. 1863 appointed honorary physician to the Wakefield Dispensary and Infirmary. Practised as a physician and built up large private practice.

Involvement in professional organisations: Founder member Wakefield Microscopic Society.

Religion: Methodist (Westgate Chapel). In 1858 acted as host to delegates attending the Annual Service of the West Riding Home Missionary Society and Congregational Union.

Politics: Strong Liberal. In 1860s served as Councillor and Alderman for the Kirkgate Ward.

Involvement in charitable work, civic affairs, a.s.o.: Subscriber and Life Benefactor to the Wakefield Dispensary and Infirmary. In 1863 subscribed £5 to the Prince Albert Memorial Fund to build an additional ward. On Charity Ball Committee. Subscriber to Wakefield Town Mission and Bible Society. Committee Mechanics' Institute. Appointed JP in 1870. West Riding County Councillor.

Mr W. R. Milner (Wakefield)

Born: Wakefield, 1813.

Family background and social characteristics: Son of Richard Milner (1782–1825), a Wakefield surgeon, and Sarah Halliley, daughter of a Wakefield cornfactor. Father, Richard, practised in the town from 1809 until his death, and built up a successful private practice. In youth William Milner resided at the house of Colonel Tottenham in Kirkgate. After appointment as prison surgeon took up residence in prison quarters with his unmarried sister and one female servant. No other family.

Qualifications: LSA 1831, MRCS Eng. 1838.

Appointments and practice: 1832 appointed apothecary to the Dispensary. In 1840s appointed resident surgeon to the Wakefield House of Correction at a salary of £200 per annum.

Involvement in professional organisations: Founder member of Wakefield Microscopic Society. Secretary and active member of the Wakefield Medical Society.

Religion: Methodist (Westgate Chapel).

Politics: No record of his voting.

Involvement in charitable work, civic affairs, a.s.o.: Member Phil. and Lit. Society. Committee of Mechanics' Institute. Gave extensive evidence to the 1851 Wakefield health inquiry on mortality rates in the town, the state of the streets and houses and on sickness in friendly societies. Served on the committee of the Wakefield Dispensary in the 1860s. Subscriber to Wakefield Town Mission.

Mr Squire Statter (Wakefield)

Born: Yorkshire, 1766–1839 (d).
Family background and social characteristics: Resided in Kirkgate. No family. Employed one female servant. In will bequeathed property to nephew, William Statter – messuages, lands, tenements and real estate in Wakefield and Sandal Magna. Also bequeathed pews, seats and sittings in Wakefield Parish Church.
Qualifications: Qualified as a surgeon.
Appointments and practice: Surgeon under the Old Poor Law to Township of Stanley-cum-Wrenthorpe.
Involvement in professional organisations: Not known.
Religion: Church of England (Wakefield Parish Church).
Politics: Conservative.
Involvement in charitable work, civic affairs, a.s.o.: Street Commissioner. 1827 appointed Chairman of the Vestry of the Parish Church. Treasurer Newsroom. In 1836 resolved that a portrait be placed in the Newsroom and that a piece of plate be presented to Statter as a token of 'respect and esteem' for his long services.[1]

Mr William Statter (Wakefield)

Born: Wakefield, 1807.
Family background and social characteristics: Son of John Statter, a Wakefield linen draper (died 1830). Nephew of Squire Statter, surgeon of Wakefield. Married Elizabeth Watson of Islington, eldest daughter of late B. Watson, in 1831. Wife died in childbirth 1832. Son William Squire Statter died in 1833, aged ten months. Remarried in 1840s and had five children. Lived with second wife in South Parade, and in 1850s moved to Thornhill House, Almshouse Lane. During the 1850s and 1860s Statter employed four servants – a groom, cook, housemaid and nursemaid. Uncle bequeathed to him messuages, lands, tenements and real estate in Wakefield and Sandal Magna and sittings in Wakefield Parish Church.
Qualifications: LSA 1828 (Guy's), MRCS Eng. 1829, FRCS Eng. 1854.
Appointments and practice: Entered practice of uncle, Squire Statter, on qualification. Upon death of his uncle in 1839, he inherited his practice. In early 1840s entered into a partnership with Edward Watson, which was dissolved by the end of the decade. In 1840s served as Poor Law medical

officer in the District of Warmfield-cum-Heath. Till end of our period (1870s) practised generally in Wakefield. Medical attendant to several important local families. 1850 appointed medical examiner to Legal Life and Fire Assurance Society.

Involvement in professional organisations: Member Wakefield Microscopic Society. Steward to the West Riding Medical Charitable Society in the 1830s, on the committee in the 1860s.

Religion: Church of England (Wakefield Parish Church).

Politics: Conservative.

Involvement in charitable work, civic affairs, a.s.o.: Member Wakefield Phil. and Lit. Society. Subscriber to Town Mission. Appointed JP in 1870. Street Commissioner – in 1851 gave evidence to Wakefield public health inquiry.

Mr Lawson Tait (Wakefield)

Born: Edinburgh, 1845–1899 (d).

Family background and social characteristics: Son of a vintner (status uncertain, probably humble). Lodged with Mr B. Kemp, surgeon, at Westgate End House during stay in Wakefield. 1871 married Miss Sybil Stewart, daughter of a Wakefield solicitor.

Qualifications: Entered Edinburgh University in 1859, aged fourteen. Pupil of Syme, Fergusson and Simpson. Acted as assistant to Simpson. Qualified as LRCS Edin. 1866, FRCS 1870.

Appointments and practice: Appointed house surgeon to Wakefield Infirmary in 1867, and remained in post until 1871. Undertook bulk of operating. During Wakefield period became a pioneer in the removal of ovarian cysts and began to specialise in gynaecology. Called in for consultations in both medicine and surgery as far away as Castleford.

Involvement in professional organisations and publications: Attended meetings of the Medical Society of London and the Obstetrical Society, London. Member Irish Medical Society, Dublin. Honorary Member (late President) Hunterian Medical Society, Edinburgh. Member BMA. Lectured to Leeds Medical Club while in Wakefield. Published widely during Wakefield period on such subjects as fractures of the femur, head injuries, the treatment of cleft palate and hairlip, thyroid diseases and abdominal abscesses.

Religion: Supposedly born into a Roman Catholic family. Likely Churchman, but not active. Follower of Darwin.

Politics: Not known.

Involvement in charitable work, civic affairs, a.s.o.: Active in Mechanics' Institute and Church Institute – enthusiastic lecturer. Member International Congress of Pre-historic Archaeology. Fellow Anthropological Society, London. Author on the subjects of anthropology, natural history and pre-historic archaeology. Great interest in Darwin. In 1870 assisted Dr Radcliffe, Medical Officer to the Privy Council, to draw up a report on the health of Wakefield.

Mr Samuel Booth (Huddersfield)

Born: Huddersfield, 1810.

Family background and social characteristics: Resided Queen Street, Huddersfield, with his wife and nine children. Employed one or two female domestics between 1841 and 1871. Son, James Webb Booth, entered medical practice and set himself up in Huddersfield. In 1861 took on nephew, Joseph Riley Booth of Manchester, as a pupil.

Qualifications: LSA 1832 (Univ. Coll.), MRCS Eng. 1857.

Appointments and practice: Surgeon Huddersfield Police Force and Prison, medical examiner to eighteen assurance companies.

Involvement in professional organisations and publications: Member Huddersfield Medico-Chirurgical Society and Medical Library. 1853 member of a committee to revise rules of Medical Library, 1854 Auditor, 1855 Honorary Secretary. Treasurer Huddersfield Medico–Ethical Society. Author of 'Essay on Physiological Effects of Alcohol', 'Precautions for the Prevention of Cholera', 1851, 'Lockwood Spa Baths and their Medicinal Effects', 1855–1856, 'The Sanitary measures necessary for the Prevention of Typhus Fever, Cholera, etc.', 1857, 'Essay on the Diseases produced by Smoking Tobacco', 1857, 'Dr Marshall Hall's Ready Method for Cases of Drowning', 1858, 'Maltreatment of Lunatics in Workhouses', 'Drunkenness and Medical Relief, etc.', 1860, 'Advantages of the Turkish Bath', 'Bathing, etc. and its influence on the Animal Economy', 'On Drs Lallemand, Perin and Duroy's New Discoveries on the Action of Alcohol', 1861, 'The Temperance Movement', 1862, 'Vaccination and Re-Vaccination', 1863, 'On the Russian Pestilence', 1865.

Religion: Non-Conformist.

Politics: Liberal.

Involvement in charitable work, civic affairs, a.s.o.: Member Philosophical Society and Lit. Sci. Society. Very active temperance reformer, and member of the Huddersfield Temperance Society.

Mr Samuel Knaggs (Huddersfield)

Born: Peckham Rye, Surrey, 1828.

Family background and social characteristics: Married with four children. In 1870s resided in Ramsden Street. Employed two female domestics. Also employed an assistant, William Pinck, an undergraduate of Glasgow University. Two of Samuel's sons, Francis Henry Knaggs and Lawford Knaggs, followed their father into successful medical careers.

Qualifications: MRCS Eng. and LSA 1850 (Guy's).

Appointments and practice: In the 1860s employed as Poor Law medical officer for the South District of Huddersfield Township at a salary of £27 per annum. Honorary medical officer Huddersfield Ragged and Industrial School. Honorary surgeon to the Huddersfield Infirmary 1863. Employed as a general practitioner.

Involvement in professional organisations and publications: Member Huddersfield Medical Library. Member of committee to revise rules in 1853. Fellow of the London Medical Society. Author of 'Some Suggestions for Diminishing the Abuses of Medical Charities', *Medical Times and Gazette*, 1859, the pamphlet *Common Sense versus Homoeopathy* (1855), *On the Unsoundness of Mind considered in relation to the question of responsibility for Criminal Acts* (1853), 'Letters on Homoeopathy and its Fallacies' and 'The Sanitary Condition of Huddersfield in 1857'.

Religion: Church of England (Huddersfield Parish Church).

Politics: Not known, likely Conservative.

Involvement in charitable work, civic affairs, a.s.o.: 1859 proposed to Huddersfield Infirmary Committee that a self-help provision be set up for the poor of town – proposal rejected out of hand. Annual subscriber to the Infirmary. In the years 1875 and 1880 Knaggs donated ten guineas to the charity. Member Huddersfield Mechanics' Institute. Author of *Some Thoughts on the Rights and Duties of the Individual in his Social and National Life* (Huddersfield, n.d.).

Mr T. R. Tatham (Huddersfield)

Born: Nottingham, 1804.

Family background and social characteristics: Resided Queen Street, Huddersfield, with his wife and four children. In 1861 employed two female domestics, a housemaid and a cook, and one male servant, a groom and house servant.

Qualifications: LSA 1826 (Westminster Hospital and London Univ.), MRCS Eng. 1832, MD 1862 (St Andrew's).

Appointments and practice: Resident surgeon to St Mary's Parish Hospital and Dispensary, Nottingham, 1827–1831. In early 1830s arrived in Huddersfield and entered practice of George Sargent. After death of Sargent in 1840, Tatham practised alone in Queen Street. In 1843 appointed medical officer to the Northern District of the Huddersfield Union and the Huddersfield Workhouse. Held appointment for nineteen years, until 1862. In 1833 stood for election to the post of honorary surgeon to the Infirmary – defeated by John Bradshaw (291 votes to 225). In May, 1853 stood again, but failed to be selected. Finally, in June, 1853 elected surgeon along with W. J. Clarke, following an increase in the number of surgical posts from three to five. In 1863 resigned post and returned to Nottingham.

Involvement in professional organisations and publications: Member Huddersfield Medical Society. Published 'Remarkable Case of Lithotrity', *London Med. Surg. Journ.*, 19 July, 1834. Claimed to have performed first lithotrity in Yorkshire. Also published 'Excess of Fatty matter in the Blood. Deficiency of the Rectum', *The Lancet*, 1835–1836. In 1848 produced a collection of correspondence between himself, the Huddersfield Board of Guardians, and the Poor Law Commission and Board, *Mr Tatham's Case against The Huddersfield Board of Guardians* (Huddersfield, 1848). In 1864 published a collection of correspondence on the subject of the administration of the Huddersfield Infirmary, with special reference to medical appointments and his own victimisation, *Strictures on the Administration of Affairs Pertaining to the Huddersfield & Upper Agbrigg Infirmary* (Nottingham, 1864).

Religion: Not known, probably Non-Conformist.

Politics: Liberal.

Involvement in charitable work, civic affairs, a.s.o.: Governor of the Huddersfield College. For two years President of the Huddersfield Lit. Sci. Society. In 1848 gave extensive evidence to the public health inquiry held in Huddersfield – only medical witness.

Dr John Taylor (Huddersfield)

Born: Not known, 1811–1852 (d).

Family background and social characteristics: Resided Fitzwilliam Street.

Qualifications: MD 1839 (London Univ.), MRCP 1842, FRCP 1847 (at same time Fellowship conferred on Sir George Magrath, Drs Kingston and Leeson of London, and Dr Southwood Smith).[2]

Appointments and practice: Professor of Clinical Medicine, University College, Physician University College Hospital, London. 1846 elected honorary physician Huddersfield Infirmary. Acted in advisory capacity to Huddersfield Board of Guardians.

Involvement in professional organisations and publications: Member Huddersfield Medical Library. Fellow Royal Medical and Chirurgical Society. Published widely in the *The Lancet*, *Medical Times* and other journals. His speciality was the treatment of pericarditis. Papers included 'On the Causes of Pericarditis', *Transactions Royal Medical and Chirurgical Society*, Vol. XXVIII, 'A series of 40 cases of pericarditis', *The Lancet*, 1845–1846, 'On a Case of Gangrene of the Upper Extremity', *The Lancet*, 1848, 'University College and Hospital – The late Appointments and Resignations', *The Lancet*, 1848, 'On the frequency of Pericarditis', *Medical Times*, 1851, 'On the Mode of Origin and Propagation of the Epidemic Cholera, in Huddersfield and the Neighbourhood, in the Autumn of 1849', *Medical Times*, 1851.

Religion: Church of England (Huddersfield Parish Church).

Politics: Not known.

Involvement in charitable work, civic affairs, a.s.o.: No records of involvement. The *Huddersfield and Holmfirth Examiner*, recording Taylor's death in 1852 at the age of 41, remarked 'Huddersfield and the West Riding of Yorkshire will deeply feel and regret the loss of this eminent and inestimable man, who was very highly and deservedly respected by all classes of society. In the prime of life, and in the midst of his benevolent and professional career, he has been snatched away. . . '.[3]

Dr John Kenworthy Walker (Huddersfield)

Born: Yorkshire, 1786?–1873 (d).

Family background and social characteristics: No family. Resided South Parade, Huddersfield, in 1840s, with two female domestic servants. In 1850s moved to Springhall, Deanhead, near Huddersfield.

Qualifications: MB 1811 (Edin. and London), MD 1820 (Caius College, Cambridge).

Appointments and practice: Appointed honorary physician to the Huddersfield Dispensary in 1814. Town's leading physician. Held Dispensary and Infirmary appointments until resignation on account of ill health in 1846. Was very active in establishment of both the Dispensary and Infirmary. In 1846 took up post of consulting physician. Following retirement from practice, Walker continued to give advice to his neighbours.

Involvement in professional organisations and publications: Steward West Riding Medical Charitable Society. Originated plan to establish a sea bathing infirmary on the Western coast, and organised campaign, also producing a pamphlet on the subject, *Reasons for Establishing a Sea Bathing Infirmary, on the Western Coast, for the Benefit of the Poor* (Huddersfield, 1840). Also author of 'On the Medical Act among the Jews'.

Religion: Church of England (Huddersfield Parish Church). Subscribed £50 to rebuilding of Parish Church in 1836. After retirement held pew in Scammondon Church. Assisted in its rebuilding in 1865. In 1868 helped collect £400 towards repair of Church.

Politics: Conservative. Supporter of Chartist movement and of Oastler, critic of factory system.

Involvement in charitable work, civic affairs, a.s.o.: Annual subscriber to Infirmary. Donated £30 to Infirmary Building Fund in 1831, and assisted in organisation of bazaar in same year. Vice-President and founder of Huddersfield Archaeological and Topographical Association (later the Yorkshire Archaeological Society). Said to be a great scholar, especially in subjects of archaeology and Hebrew. Published papers on the mortality of Huddersfield as related to its topography in the 1820s. 1867 published *Etymology applied to topography*. Fellow of the Society of Antiquities, London. Scammondon Sunday School doubled in size due to financial support of Dr Walker.

1 *WRH*, 1 January, 1836.
2 *WJ*, 30 July, 1847.
3 *HHE*, 3 July, 1852.

Notes

Chapter 1

1 For example, the classic studies of H. F. Garrison, *An Introduction to the History of Medicine* (4th ed., Philadelphia, 1929); D. Guthrie, *A History of Medicine* (London, 1945) (hereafter all books published in London unless otherwise stated); C. Singer and E. A. Underwood, *A Short History of Medicine* (2nd ed., Oxford, 1962).

2 J. Woodward and D. Richards, 'Towards a Social History of Medicine' in J. Woodward and D. Richards (eds), *Health Care and Popular Medicine in Nineteenth Century England. Essays in the Social History of Medicine* (1977), p. 17.

3 P. Starr, 'Medicine, Economy and Society in Nineteenth-Century America' in P. Branca (ed.), *The Medicine Show. Patients, Physicians and the Perplexities of the Health Revolution in Modern Society* (New York, 1977), p. 51.

4 J. Woodward, *To do the sick no harm. A Study of the British Voluntary Hospital System to 1875* (1974). An important exception is John Pickstone's recent study of hospital development in Manchester and its Region between 1752 and 1946. This comprehensive work, which covers voluntary hospitals, dispensaries, workhouse infirmaries, isolation and special hospitals in both Manchester and its satellite towns, relates hospital development to the economic, social and political structures of the communities they evolved in, and examines how and why differing patterns of medical services have developed. J. V. Pickstone, *Medicine and industrial society. A history of hospital development in Manchester and its Region, 1752–1946* (Manchester, 1985).

5 G. Rosen, 'Social variables and health in an urban environment: the case of the Victorian city', *Clio Medica*, Vol. 8, 1973, p. 1. Quoted in J. Woodward and D. Richards, *op. cit.*, p. 15.

6 P. Branca, 'Towards a Social History of Medicine' in P. Branca (ed.), *op. cit.*, p. 92.

7 W. A. Armstrong, 'The Census Enumerators' Books: a Commentary' in R. Lawton (ed.), *The Census and Social Structure. An Interpretative Guide to Nineteenth Century Censuses for England and Wales* (1978), p. 28.

8 R. S. Roberts, 'The Use of Literary and Documentary Evidence in the History of Medicine' in E. Clarke (ed.), *Modern Methods in the History of Medicine* (1971), pp. 36–57.

9 Within the context of this study it has proved impossible to undertake a wider regional survey. However, an extension of this project to cover more urban and rural communities within the West Riding would be an interesting proposition. The West Riding has, after all, been depicted as being a microcosm of the country as a whole. The region contained rapidly expanding cities such as Leeds, Bradford and Sheffield; smaller textile towns, Huddersfield, Halifax, Dewsbury and Batley; market and service towns of which Wakefield forms a prime example, and large rural areas of rich farming country and moorland pasture. A region of such contrasts presumably presented a variety of medical and social problems and methods of dealing with them.

10 The book has concentrated on the treatment of bodily ailments, rather than mental illness, which is looked at only briefly in connection with Poor Law medical services (Chapter 3). Public health provision has been examined in the context of the development of local government agencies (Chapter 2, Sections 2.2 and 2.3), the role of the Poor Law authorities in implementing measures connected with preventive medicine (Chapter 3) and the involvement of the medical profession in this field (Chapter 8, pp. 341–348).

Chapter 2

1 J. Aikin, MD, *A Description of the Country from Thirty to Forty Miles Round Manchester* (1795, reprinted Newton Abbot, 1968), p. 579.
2 White, 1837, p. 323. For a complete reference and listing of trade directories used throughout the book, see Bibliography.
3 Reverend C. E. Camidge, MA, *A History of Wakefield and its Industrial and Fine Art Exhibition* (London and Wakefield, 1866), p. 8.
4 *Ibid.*, p. 7.
5 White, 1837, pp. 360–361.
6 *Supplement to the Morning Chronicle*, 18 January, 1850. Cited in J. T. Ward, *The Factory System* (Newton Abbot, 1970), pp. 162, 164.
7 E. Parsons, *The Civil, Ecclesiastical, Literary, Commercial, and Miscellaneous History of Leeds, Halifax, Huddersfield, Bradford, Wakefield, Dewsbury, Otley, and the Manufacturing District of Yorkshire*, Vol. I (Leeds, 1834), p. 314.
8 R. Porter, *English Society in the Eighteenth Century* (Harmondsworth, 1982), p. 357.
9 Comparative Account of the Population of Great Britain in the Years 1801, 1811, 1821, and 1831, PP, 1831, XVIII (348), p. 407.
10 A. Briggs, *Victorian Cities* (1963), pp. 86, 140; S. E. Finer, *The Life and Times of Sir Edwin Chadwick* (1952), p. 213.
11 R. Dennis, *English industrial cities of the nineteenth century. A social geography* (Cambridge, 1984), pp. 36, 222.
12 W. Page, *op. cit.*, p. 525. (Hereafter all population figures are extracted from W. Page.)
13 *Ibid.*
14 F. J. Glover, 'The Rise of the Heavy Woollen Trade of the West Riding of Yorkshire in the Nineteenth Century', *Business History*, Vol. IV, 1961–62, p. 3.
15 White, 1837, p. 328.
16 J. W. Walker, *Wakefield. Its History and People* (2nd ed., Wakefield, 1939), Vol. II, p. 398.
17 Broadcloths – fine twilled woollen or worsted cloths. Tammies – thin worsted materials in which warp and weft were made from combed wool.
18 White, 1837, p. 323.
19 Reverend C. E. Camidge, MA, *op. cit.*, p. 8.
20 F. J. Glover, *op. cit.*, p. 3.
21 R. G. Wilson, *Gentlemen Merchants. The merchant community in Leeds 1700–1830* (Manchester, 1971), pp. 126–127. The early nineteenth century was also punctuated by banking failures. In 1811 the bank of Ingram, Kennet and Ingram failed, and there was a severe run on the bank of Townend and Rishworth a year later. In 1825 the collapse of the extensive banking house of Messrs Wentworth, Chaloner and Rishworth was linked closely to the bankruptcy of the Naylor family's cloth business.
22 D. T. Jenkins, *The West Riding Wool Textile Industry 1770–1835* (Edington, Wiltshire, 1975), p. 24.
23 T. Baines, *Yorkshire, past and present: a history and description of the 3 ridings of the great county of Yorks, from the earliest ages to the year 1870, . . .* (1871–1877), Vol. II, p. 465.
24 White, 1866, p. 824.

25 W. B. Crump and G. Ghorbal, *History of the Huddersfield Woollen Industry* (Huddersfield, 1935), p. 80.

26 G. S. Phillips, *Walks Round Huddersfield* (Huddersfield, 1848), p. 1.

27 J. Aikin, MD, *op. cit.*, pp. 554, 552. D. Wholmsley relates Huddersfield's development in the late eighteenth century very much to the positive influence of the Ramsden family, rather than to market forces. D. Wholmsley, 'Market Forces and Urban Growth: The Influence of the Ramsden Family on the Growth of Huddersfield 1716–1853', *The Journal of Regional and Local Studies*, Vol. 4, No. 2, Autumn, 1984, pp. 27–56.

28 White, 1837, p. 360.

29 D. T. Jenkins, *op. cit.*, p. 24.

30 W. B. Crump and G. Ghorbal, *op. cit.*, pp. 82, 84, 90.

31 Report from the Factories Inquiry Commission, PP, 1834, XX (167), Supp. II, 793 *et seq.* and Factory Inspectors' Reports, PP, 1839, XLII (42), 272 *et seq.* Cited in F. J. Glover, *op. cit.*, p. 10.

32 Report from the Select Committee on Manufactures, PP, 1833, VI (690), Q. 1289. Cited *ibid.*, p. 10.

33 For more on the development of the Yorkshire woollen industry, see E. Baines, *Account of the Woollen Manufacture of England* (reprinted from T. Baines, *op. cit.*), with an introduction by K. G. Ponting (New York, 1970); D. Gregory, *Regional Transformation and Industrial Revolution. A Geography of the Yorkshire Woollen Industry* (1982); D. T. Jenkins, *op. cit.*

34 The 1871 census listed the occupations of the inhabitants of Huddersfield as wool and cloth manufacturers 11,292 males and 6,005 females (all above twenty years), engine and machine makers 334, spindle makers 141, woollen dyers 332, worsted manufacturers 232 males and 84 females, silk manufacturers 108 males and 148 females, cotton manufacturers 938 males and 1,223 females, coal miners 569, stone quarriers 627 and iron manufacturers 404. Cited in T. Baines, *op. cit.*, p. 438.

35 A. Briggs, *op. cit.*, p. 150.

36 C. Binfield, 'Asquith: The Formation of a Prime Minister', *The Journal. United Reformed Church History Society*, Vol. 2, No. 7, April, 1981, p. 219.

37 *LM*, 3 May, 1845. For a complete list of newspaper abbreviations, see List of abbreviations.

38 For the influence of the Ramsden Estate upon urban development, see J. Springett, 'Landowners and urban development: the Ramsden Estate and nineteenth-century Huddersfield', *Journal of Historical Geography*, Vol. 8, No. 2, 1982, pp. 129–144.

39 D. F. E. Sykes, *Huddersfield and Its Vicinity* (Huddersfield, 1898), p. 385.

40 T. Dyson, *The History of Huddersfield and District from the earliest times down to 1932* (Huddersfield, 1932), pp. 452–453.

41 The qualifications required by the Commissioners were either £30 rental or possession of £1,000 personally. The electors' qualifications were under £50 rating one vote, between £50 and £100 two votes, and so on up to six votes if rated above £250 per annum. O. Balmforth, *Jubilee History of the Corporation of Huddersfield 1868 to 1918* (Huddersfield, 1918), p. 7.

42 *Ibid.*, pp. 8–9.

43 J. W. Walker, *op. cit.*, p. 480.

44 W. Ranger, Report to the General Board of Health on a Preliminary Inquiry into the Sewerage, Drainage, and Supply of Water, and the Sanitary Condition of the Inhabitants of the Borough of Wakefield in the County of York (Public Health Act 11 & 12 Vict. Cap. 63), 1852, pp. 8–13.

45 For the social class and employment of medical men in both towns, see Chapter 7.

46 K. A. Cowlard, 'The identification of social (class) areas and their place in nineteenth-century urban development', *Transactions Institute of British Geographers*, New Series, Vol. 4, 1979, pp. 239–257. Cited in R. Dennis, *op. cit.*, p. 189. These figures compare with 8 and 14 per cent for York in 1851, 5 and 12 for Hull in 1851, and 1 and 15 per cent for Liverpool in 1871.

47 Poll Book of the Wakefield Borough Election, 1865, p.v, WDA (Local Collection W.324).
48 R. Brook, *The Story of Huddersfield* (1968), p. 171; D. F. E. Sykes, *op. cit.*, p. 371; C. P. Hobkirk, *Huddersfield: Its History and Natural History* (2nd ed., London and Huddersfield, 1868), p. 3.
49 R. Dennis, *op. cit.*, p. 215.
50 H. Pelling, *Social Geography of British Elections 1885–1910* (1967), p. 301.
51 See Chapter 4, pp. 123–130 for the founding of the Wakefield and Huddersfield medical charities.
52 D. F. E. Sykes, *op. cit.*, p. 430.
53 Kelly, 1877, p. 419.
54 Reverend C. E. Camidge, MA, *op. cit.*, p. 24.
55 E. Baines, *The Social, Educational, and Religious State of the Manufacturing Districts* (1843, reprinted 1969), Table No. II, Sunday Schools and Day Schools. See also Table 2.2.
56 For the Wakefield Female Benefit Society, a combination of philanthropic enterprise and self-help medical relief, see Chapter 5, Section 5.3.
57 Address of the Huddersfield Benevolent and Visiting Society. Instituted December 13, 1830, Huddersfield, n.d., c. 1830, HPL (Tolson Collection).
58 The Twelfth Annual Report of The Wakefield Town Mission, 1852, p. 8, WDA (Local Collection, Box 4B).
59 B. Greaves, *Methodism in Yorkshire 1740–1851*, unpublished PhD thesis, Liverpool, 1968, pp. 32–34, 41. Greaves's figures are extracted from the 1851 religious census and may not be completely accurate. However, they do indicate the main trends and patterns of growth amongst each denomination.
60 *Ibid.*, p. 36.
61 D. Defoe, *Tour through England and Wales*, Vol. II, p. 186. Cited in S. H. Waters, *Wakefield in the Seventeenth Century. A Social History of the Town and Neighbourhood From 1550 to 1710* (Wakefield, 1933), p. 90.
62 B. Greaves, *op. cit.*, pp. 36, 45.
63 R. Brook, *op. cit.*, p. 128.
64 B. Greaves, *op. cit.*, p. 237.
65 E. P. Thompson, *The Making of the English Working Class* (1963), pp. 48–49.
66 E. J. Hobsbawm, *Labouring Men. Studies in the History of Labour* (1968), p. 29.
67 B. Greaves, *op. cit.*, p. 46.
68 *Ibid.*
69 R. Brook, *op. cit.*, p. 129; White, 1853, p. 597.
70 H. Pelling, *op. cit.*, p. 301.
71 In the 1834 Huddersfield election 74 merchants and manufacturers voted. Out of these 44 voted for the Whig candidate, Blackburne, twenty for the Tory-Reformer, Sadler, and ten for Captain Wood, a Radical standing on a Liberal ticket. J. R. Vincent, *Pollbooks. How Victorians Voted* (Cambridge, 1967), p. 111.
72 D. F. E. Sykes, *op. cit.*, p. 373.
73 *Ibid.*, pp. 362–383 for the politics of Huddersfield.
74 H. Pelling, *op. cit.*, p. 306.
75 J. W. Walker, *op. cit.*, p. 477.
76 White, 1847, p. 387.
77 F. Engels, *The Condition of the Working Class in England* (Panther ed., 1969, first published Leipzig, 1845, first published in Great Britain, 1892), p. 74; C. P. Hobkirk, *op. cit.*, p. 1; T. Baines, *op. cit.*, p. 431.
78 R. Dennis, *op. cit.*, pp. 175, 237–238.
79 Baines, 1822, p. 205.
80 *Supplement to the Morning Chronicle*, 18 January, 1850. Cited in J. T. Ward, *op. cit.*, p. 161.
81 W. Ranger, *op. cit.*, Appendix, p. 67.
82 *WJ*, 23 February, 1849. Mortality rates calculated for the country as a whole during this period were generally less than 21 per 1,000. For the years 1836–1846, for

example, Talbot Griffith gives an estimate of 20.8 per 1,000. In 1840 the death rates for Birmingham, Leeds, Bristol, Manchester and Liverpool averaged 30.8 per 1,000 compared with a national average of 22.9. G. Talbot Griffith, *Population Problems of the Age of Malthus* (2nd ed., 1967, first published Cambridge, 1926), pp. 36, 186.

83 White, 1853, p. 595.

84 Second Report of the Commissioners for inquiring into the State of Large Towns and Populous Districts, PP, 1845, XVIII (602), App., Part II, Report on the Condition of the Town of Huddersfield. By James Smith, Esq., p. 311.

85 F. Engels, *op. cit.*, pp. 74–75.

86 See note 84.

87 The Minutes of Proceedings on a Preliminary Inquiry on the Huddersfield Improvement Bill, Held February, 1848 (Huddersfield, 1851), Evidence of William Stocks (former Inspector of Nuisances), pp. 16–17, Ms HPL (KHT9/1).

88 'The Sanitary Movement. Article III. Proposed Increase to the Town of Huddersfield', *LM*, 15 December, 1849 (Supplement).

89 White, 1853, p. 594.

90 The Sanitary Inspector's First Annual Report on the Sanitary Condition of the Borough of Huddersfield, for the Year ending August 31st, 1869 (Huddersfield, 1870), p. 12, HPL (Misc. Pamph: Hudd. Corp. Sanitary Dept.).

91 W. Sheardown, *Pamphlets* (three volumes of extracts from the *Doncaster Gazette*, c. 1840–1870), Vol. 2, p. 558, Doncaster Public Library (Local Studies); A. Briggs, *op. cit.*, p. 19.

92 The Sanitary Inspector's First Annual Report on the Sanitary Condition of the Borough of Huddersfield, pp. 4, 15, HPL (Misc. Pamph: Hudd. Corp. Sanitary Dept.).

93 Medical Officer's Reports to the Sanitary Committee, June 1873 to March 1876. Second Report, July 1873, p. 3, Ms HPL (Unclassified).

94 See Chapter 3, Section 3.2 for the activities of the Boards of Guardians in the field of public health. For the involvement of medical men in public health, see Chapter 8, pp. 341–348.

95 W. Ranger, *op. cit.*

96 *Ibid.*, p. 44.

97 *Ibid.*, p. 60.

98 *Ibid.*, pp. 16–17.

99 'The Sanitary State of Wakefield', *The Lancet*, 1870, Vol. I, p. 59.

100 'The Sanitary Condition of Wakefield', *Medical Times and Gazette*, 1870, Vol. I, pp. 36–37.

101 *Ibid.*, p. 36.

102 W. Ranger, *op. cit.*, Evidence of W. R. Milner, Esq., p. 84.

103 The Minutes of Proceedings on a Preliminary Inquiry on the Huddersfield Improvement Bill, Evidence of Mr Joshua Hobson, pp. 8–10, Ms HPL (KHT9/1).

104 See Chapter 4 for the House of Recovery.

105 The Minutes of Proceedings on a Preliminary Inquiry on the Huddersfield Improvement Bill, Evidence of Mr Joshua Hobson, p. 8, Ms HPL (KHT9/1).

106 See Chapter 4, especially pp. 134–136 and Chapter 3.

107 J. W. Walker, *op. cit.*, p. 545.

108 W. Ranger, *op. cit.*, Appendix, p. 80.

109 *WJ*, 23 February, 1849. For further details of causes of death in Wakefield, see Appendices 1 and 2.

110 W. Ranger, *op. cit.*, p. 15.

111 The total number of deaths recorded from cholera during the 1832 epidemic in the West Riding was given as 1,416. In Leeds the total was 702, Sheffield 402, Hull 300 and York 185. Other towns got off more lightly; only 34 deaths were recorded in Rotherham, 30 in Bradford and 26 in Doncaster. Figures taken from C. Creighton, *A History of Epidemics in Britain* (2nd ed., 1965, first published Cambridge, 1894), Vol. II, p. 822.

112 J. W. Walker, *op. cit.*, p. 543.
113 *WHJ*, 29 June, 1832.
114 J. W. Walker, *op. cit.*, p. 543.
115 *LM*, 25 August, 1832.
116 *WHJ*, 21 September, 1832.
117 *LM*, 21 July, 1832.
118 *LM*, 28 July, 1832.
119 *LM*, 14 September, 1849.
120 'The Cholera at the Wakefield Lunatic Asylum', *London Medical Gazette*, Vol. IX, 1849, p. 865.
121 C. Creighton, *op. cit.*, p. 844. Total deaths in the West Riding during the 1849 epidemic are given by Creighton as 4,151.
122 J. Taylor, MD, 'On the Mode of Origin and Propagation of the Epidemic Cholera, in Huddersfield and the Neighbourhood, in the Autumn of 1849', *Medical Times*, Vol. 23, 1851 (pp. 256–259, 340–344, 399–402), p. 341.
123 See, for example, R. A. E. Wells, *Dearth and Distress in Yorkshire 1793–1802* (Borthwick Papers No. 52) (York, 1977).
124 D. F. E. Sykes, *op. cit.*, pp. 263–264.
125 R. A. E. Wells, *op. cit.*, p. 12.
126 A. J. Brooke, 'Jacobinism and Unrest in the Huddersfield Area 1799–1803', *Old West Riding*, Vol. 11, No. 1, 1982, pp. 22–25.
127 *London Gazette*, 27 December, 1800. Cited in R. A. E. Wells, *op. cit.*, p. 19.
128 E. P. Thompson, *op. cit.*, pp. 518, 548.
129 *WHJ*, 28 January and 21 April, 1820.
130 *WHJ*, 14 January, 1820.
131 *WHJ*, 28 January, 1820.
132 O. Balmforth, *Huddersfield Past and Present; in its Social, Industrial and Educational Aspects* (Huddersfield, 1893), p. 10, HPL (Local Pamphlets, Vol. 14).
133 W. B. Crump and G. Ghorbal, *op. cit.*, pp. 120–121.
134 E. P. Thompson, *op. cit.*, p. 319.
135 Report of the Committee . . . for the relief of the Distressed Manufacturers (1844), p. 19. Cited in E. J. Hobsbawm, *op. cit.*, p. 75.
136 O. Balmforth, *Huddersfield Past and Present*, p. 11, HPL (Local Pamphlets, Vol. 14).
137 J. Mayhall, *The Annals of Yorkshire, From the Earliest Period to the Present Time*, Vol. I (1862), p. 200.
138 O. Balmforth, *Huddersfield Past and Present*, p. 11, HPL (Local Pamphlets, Vol. 14).
139 E. Baines, *Account of the Woollen Manufacture of England*, p. 93.
140 G. D. H. Cole and R. Postgate, *The Common People 1746–1946* (4th ed., 1961, first published 1938), p. 302.
141 E. Baines, *Account of the Woollen Manufacture of England*, p. 115.
142 J. Addy, *The Textile Revolution* (1976), p. 46.
143 E. P. Thompson, *op. cit.*, p. 610.
144 Details of the Luddite uprising were taken largely from E. P. Thompson, *op. cit.*, pp. 608–618 and D. F. E. Sykes, *op. cit.*, pp. 273–287.
145 All supporters of the Huddersfield Infirmary. For Plug Riots in Huddersfield, see D. F. E. Sykes, *op. cit.*, pp. 299–301.
146 D. Fraser, 'The Agitation for Parliamentary Reform' in J. T. Ward (ed.), *Popular Movements c.1830–1850* (1970), p. 46.
147 G. D. H. Cole and R. Postgate, *op. cit.*, p. 261.
148 For more on the Anti-Poor Law Movement, see N. C. Edsall, *The anti-Poor Law movement, 1834–44* (Manchester, 1971) and M. E. Rose, 'The Anti-Poor Law Movement in the North of England', *Northern History*, Vol. I, 1966, pp. 70–91.

Chapter 3

1 See, for example, M. W. Flinn, 'Medical Services under the New Poor Law' in D. Fraser (ed.), *The New Poor Law in the Nineteenth Century* (1976), pp. 45–66; R. G. Hodgkinson, *The Origins of the National Health Service* (1967); S. and B. Webb, *English Poor Law History: Part I, The Old Poor Law* and *Part II, The New Poor Law* (Vols 7 and 8 of *English Local Government*) (1927 and 1929, reprinted 1963); J. E. O'Neill, 'Finding a Policy for the Sick Poor', *Victorian Studies*, Vol. VII, No. 3, March, 1964, pp. 265–283; M. A. Crowther, *The Workhouse System 1834–1929* (1981).

2 This Act required the Poor Law Board to amalgamate the medical services of the metropolitan unions into larger units. The Metropolitan Asylums Board became the unified hospital authority for all of Greater London with respect to the treatment of typhus, smallpox and insanity. It was financed by a Common Poor Fund to which all member unions contributed. For other forms of medical treatment, the London unions were grouped into 'sick asylum districts' in which the sick poor were to be treated in hospitals separated from the workhouse.

3 M. W. Flinn, *op. cit.*, p. 64.

4 S. and B. Webb, *op. cit.*, *Part II*, p. 314.

5 See, for example, D. Ashforth, *The Poor Law in Bradford c. 1834–1871. A Study of the relief of poverty in mid-nineteenth century Bradford*, unpublished PhD thesis, Bradford, 1979, especially Chapters 5 (ii) and 11.

6 With the exception of the Township of Mirfield which, although situated midway between Wakefield and Huddersfield, came to be included in the Dewsbury Union after 1837.

7 The minute books of the Wakefield Board of Guardians are no longer extant.

8 Especially the Report from the Select Committee on Medical Poor Relief. Third Report, PP, 1844, IX (531) and the Report from the Select Committee on Medical Relief, PP, 1854, XII (348). Hereafter referred to as SCMPR 1844 and SCMR 1854.

9 Sturges Bourne's Act of 1819 gave powers to parishes to appoint a salaried assistant overseer and to establish a select vestry to control poor relief. The adoption of the Act was most widespread in the North.

10 M. E. Rose, *Poor Law Administration in the West Riding of Yorkshire (1820–1855)*, unpublished DPhil thesis, Oxford, 1965, p. 16.

11 Account Book of the Overseers of the Poor of South Crosland, 1814–1830, Ms HPL (CP/SC/OP).

12 M. E. Rose, *Poor Law Administration in the West Riding of Yorkshire (1820–1855)*, p. 19; M. E. Rose, 'The New Poor Law in an Industrial Area' in R. M. Hartwell (ed.), *The Industrial Revolution* (Oxford, 1970), p. 124.

13 A. Ure, *Philosophy of Manufactures* (1835), p. 477. Cited in M. E. Rose 'The New Poor Law in an Industrial Area', p. 126; M. E. Rose, *Poor Law Administration in the West Riding of Yorkshire (1820–1855)*, p. 36.

14 M. E. Rose, *Poor Law Administration in the West Riding of Yorkshire (1820–1855)*, pp. 30, 35. This policy was continued after 1837. In 1839, for example, at the request of the Street Commissioners, workhouse paupers were employed in cleaning the streets. The Guardians were allowed £50 per annum in return for this service. Minute Book of the Huddersfield Board of Guardians, Vol. 2, 14 June, 1839, Ms HPL (P/HU/M).

15 For more on the background to the 1834 Act, see A. Brundage, *The Making of the New Poor Law 1832–39* (1978).

16 D. F. E. Sykes, *op. cit.*, p. 301. See Chapter 2, Section 2.4 for more on depression in the region.

17 See Chapter 2, Section 2.4 for opposition to the New Poor Law.

18 Report of the Select Committee on the Poor Law Amendment Act, PP, 1837–1838, XVIII (518), Part III, p. 245.

19 SCMPR 1844, Evidence of G. C. Lewis, Poor Law Commissioner, p. 76, Q.846.

20 See Chapters 5 and 6.

21 Report of the Poor Law Commissioners on the Further Amendment of the Poor Laws, PP, 1840, XVII (253), App. B, Reports of Arrangements for Medical Relief, No. 6, III, Mr Power's Report – Lancashire and the West Riding of York, pp. 164–165.

22 *Ibid.*, p. 164.

23 SCMPR 1844, Evidence of G. C. Lewis, p. 8, Q.13.

24 Account Book of the Overseers of the Poor of South Crosland, 1814–1830, Ms HPL (CP/SC/OP).

25 Township of Mirfield, Overseers Accounts, 1805–1826, Ms HPL (P/M).

26 Accounts of the Overseers of the Poor of Wakefield Township, 1738–1790, Ms WDA (JGC). This appears to be a generous payment for a contract surgeon, and compares well with figures of £2 to thirteen guineas a year cited for Warwickshire parishes between the years 1750 to 1800. J. Lane, 'The Provincial Practitioner and his Services to the Poor, 1750–1800', *The Society for the Social History of Medicine Bulletin*, 28 June, 1981, p. 11. (Extracts from overseers' account books, vestry minute books, etc. are transcribed as they appear in the original document.)

27 Township of Mirfield Vestry Minute Book, Vol. I, 1758–1834. Meeting of 4 November, 1813, Ms HPL (P/M).

28 *Ibid.*, Meetings of 7 March, 1816, 26 March, 1818, 29 October, 1820, 2 May, 1822.

29 *Ibid.*, Meeting of 23 December, 1813.

30 *Ibid.*; Township of Mirfield, Overseers Accounts, 1816–1818, Ms HPL (P/M).

31 Account Book of the Overseers of the Poor of South Crosland, 1790–1801, Ms HPL (CP/SC/OP).

32 The title 'doctor' is used with great frequency in Poor Law accounts. Only very rarely does it refer to a medical man possessing a medical degree. The title serves as a useful indication of a qualified medical man.

33 Stanley Township Accounts, 1795–1801, Ms WDA (JGC).

34 Township of Mirfield, Overseers Accounts, 1772–1803, Ms HPL (P/M).

35 See Chapter 6, note 14 for the activities of the Whitworth doctors.

36 Account Books of the Overseers of the Poor of South Crosland, 1790–1801, 1814–1830, Ms HPL (CP/SC/OP).

37 Huddersfield Town Book, 1784–1793, Ms HPL (P/HU/M). See Chapter 6, Section 6.2 for more on midwives and their activities, and for more details of the employment of fringe personnel by the overseers of the poor.

38 Accounts of the Overseers of the Poor of Wakefield Township, 1738–1790, Ms WDA (JGC).

39 Township of Mirfield, Overseers Accounts, 1805–1826, Ms HPL (P/M).

40 Horbury Overseers Account Book, 1821–1834, Ms WDA (JGC).

41 Receipt of Subscription of Six Guineas to Leeds Infirmary from the Overseers of Ossett, 13 July, 1830, WDA (JGC).

42 The Annual Statement of the Receipts and Payments of the Overseers of the Poor of the Township of Wakefield, 1834–1835, WDA (JGC).

43 Accounts of the Overseers of the Poor of Wakefield Township, 1738–1790, Ms WDA (JGC); 3rd AR WD, 1790–1791 (see List of abbreviations), WYCRO (C235/1/37–41). (The same location applies throughout, unless otherwise stated.)

44 Rules and Regulations of the Huddersfield and Upper Agbrigg Infirmary, 1834, p. 8, HPL (B.362).

45 1st AR HI, 1831–1832 (see List of abbreviations), WYCRO (C500). (The same location applies throughout, unless otherwise stated.)

46 The Accounts of Matthew Ash Overseer of the Poor of Horbury for the Year 1775. Printed as K. Bartlett, *A Year in the Life of Horbury 1775* (Wakefield, n.d.), WDA (Local Collection).

47 S. and B. Webb, *op. cit.*, *Part I*, p. 30.

48 Horbury Overseers Account Book, 1821–1834, Ms WDA (JGC).

49 Ossett Overseers West York Lunatic Asylum Half-Yearly Account for January to June, 1830, WDA (JGC).

50 Township of Mirfield, Overseers Accounts, 1832–1839, Ms HPL (P/M).

51 The Annual Statement of the Receipts and Payments of the Overseers of the Poor of the Township of Wakefield, 1834–1835, WDA (JGC).
52 See Chapter 5, Section 5.1.
53 Horbury Overseers Account Book, 1821–1834, Ms WDA (JGC).
54 Township of Mirfield, Overseers Accounts, 1805–1826, Ms HPL (P/M).
55 See Chapter 5, Section 5.3.
56 P. H. J. H. Gosden, *The Friendly Societies in England 1815–1875* (Manchester, 1961), p. 199.
57 Township of Mirfield, Overseers Accounts, 1772–1803; Township of Mirfield, Workhouse Expenses Book, 1804–1830, Ms HPL (P/M).
58 Township of Mirfield, Workhouse Diary and Account Book, 1777–1779, Ms HPL (P/M).
59 A service of thanksgiving performed after childbirth.
60 Township of Mirfield, Overseers Accounts, 1772–1803, House Book, Ms HPL (P/M).
61 Presumably for treatment at the Lockwood Spa. For spa treatment in the Wakefield and Huddersfield areas, see Chapter 6, pp. 229–234.
62 Most likely an unqualified local healer. In this set of accounts most qualified medical men were referred to as 'doctor'.
63 Huddersfield Town Book, 1784–1793, Ms HPL (P/HU/M).
64 Township of Mirfield, Overseers Accounts, 1805–1826, Ms HPL (P/M).
65 The Annual Statement of the Receipts and Payments of the Overseers of the Poor of the Township of Wakefield, 1834–1835, WDA (JGC).
66 See Chapter 6, especially pp. 218–222.
67 Huddersfield Town Book, 1784–1793, Ms HPL (P/HU/M).
68 *Ibid.*
69 *Ibid.*
70 Godfrey Bottles and other infant calmatives constituted frequent items of expenditure. See Chapter 6, pp. 239–240 for details of the widespread use of these medicaments.
71 Township of Mirfield, Overseers Accounts, 1772–1803, Ms HPL (P/M).
72 *Ibid.*, House Book, Ms HPL (P/M).
73 Township of Mirfield, Overseers Accounts, 1805–1826, Ms HPL (P/M).
74 For a discussion of medical services under the Old Poor Law in Berkshire, Essex and Oxfordshire, circa 1720 to 1834, see E. G. Thomas, 'The Old Poor Law and Medicine', *Medical History*, Vol. 24, No. 1, January, 1980, pp. 1–19.
75 White, 1837, pp. 324, 361; White, 1853, pp. 345, 594.
76 Minute Books of the Huddersfield Board of Guardians, Vol. 7, 19 April, 1850, Vol. 13, 22 April, 1870, Ms HPL (P/HU/M).
77 The Annual Statement of the Receipts and Payments of the Overseers of the Poor of the Township of Wakefield, 1834–1835, WDA (JGC); Township of Wakefield. Statement of the Accounts, For the Half-Year Ending Twenty-Ninth September, 1858, WDA (Local Collection, Box 8).
78 A Statement of the Accounts of the Huddersfield Union, 1861–1873. The Township of Huddersfield in Account with the Huddersfield Union, for the Year ended March 25th, 1863, HPL (P/HU/Cfo).
79 See P. H. J. H. Gosden, *op. cit.*, pp. 205–210.
80 For more on Poor Law medical officers, their duties and conditions of appointment, see R. G. Hodgkinson, 'Poor Law Medical Officers of England 1834–1871', *Journal of the History of Medicine*, Vol. 11, 1956, pp. 299–338 and M. A. Crowther, *op. cit.*, especially Chapters 5 and 7.
81 Honley Civil Township Records. Certificate from Thomas Martin, Surgeon of Holmfirth, re Jonathan Crosland of Gully, Wooldale, 29 March, 1833, Ms HPL (CP/HO/OP/72).
82 Minute Book of the Huddersfield Board of Guardians, Vol. 4, 17 February and 17 March, 1843, Ms HPL (P/HU/M).
83 *Ibid.*, Vol. 7, 24 and 31 December, 1847, 21 January, 1848, Vol. 8, 2 March, 1855.

84 A detailed account of the dispute is contained in the pamphlet *Mr Tatham's Case against The Huddersfield Board of Guardians* (Huddersfield, 1848), HPL (Tomlinson Collection).

85 Minute Book of the Huddersfield Board of Guardians, Vol. 5, 16 July, 1847, Ms HPL (P/HU/M).

86 *Mr Tatham's Case against The Huddersfield Board of Guardians*, Letter No. 14, To the Board of Guardians for the Huddersfield Union, dated September 24th, 1847, p. 15, HPL (Tomlinson Collection).

87 Minute Book of the Huddersfield Board of Guardians, Vol. 6, 31 December, 1847, Ms HPL (P/HU/M).

88 For the efforts of the medical profession to improve the status, conditions of service and remuneration of the Poor Law medical officers, see P. Vaughan, *Doctors' Commons. A Short History of the British Medical Association* (1959), Chapter 2; F. B. Smith, *The People's Health 1830–1910* (1979), pp. 346–362.

89 Minute Book of the Huddersfield Board of Guardians, Vol. 7, 19 April, 26 July and 18 October, 1850, 24 January, 1851, Ms HPL (P/HU/M); A Return 'of the Medical Officers under the Poor Law Acts, . . .', PP, 1856, XLIX (434).

90 Minute Book of the Huddersfield Board of Guardians, Vol. 4, 17 February, 1843, Ms HPL (P/HU/M).

91 *Provincial Medical Directories* (hereafter referred to as *PMD*), 1848, 1852, 1856, 1860, 1870. See Appendix 11 for biographies of Knaggs and Tatham.

92 For Tatham's dispute with the Huddersfield Infirmary Committee, see Chapter 8, pp. 322, 335–336.

93 *WJ*, 12 March, 1841.

94 *WJ*, 19 March, 1841.

95 For more on the dominance of medical families in the two towns, see Chapter 7, pp. 293–298.

96 Minute Book of the Huddersfield Board of Guardians, Vol. 4, 17 March, 1843, Ms HPL (P/HU/M).

97 *Ibid.*, Vol. 5, 31 January, 1845.

98 For more on medical appointments, see Chapter 7, pp. 274–280.

99 Minute Book of the Huddersfield Board of Guardians, Vol. 3, 11 June, 1841, Ms HPL (P/HU/M).

100 *Ibid.*, Vol. 6, 20 October, 1 and 29 December, 1848.

101 *Ibid.*, Vol. 9, 7 May, 1858.

102 For a full account of Tatham's expenditure for the year 1843–1844, see Appendix 3.

103 *Mr Tatham's Case against The Huddersfield Board of Guardians*, Letters No. 2, 4 and 7, To the Board of Guardians for the Huddersfield Union, dated 1844, February 26th and July 2nd, 1847, pp. 7–8, 10, HPL (Tomlinson Collection).

104 W. Ranger, *op. cit.*, Appendix, p. 87. For a full breakdown of cases treated by Mr Walker in the different areas of the Wakefield Township in this year, see Appendix 4. See also Appendix 1 for causes of death in the Wakefield Township between 1837 and 1847.

105 Census Enumerators' Books (hereafter referred to as C.) Wakefield, 1851.

106 White, 1853, p. 345.

107 Report of the Committee inquiring into the necessity of erecting a New Union Workhouse, 23 February, 1849, Ms HPL (P/HU/Cfo).

108 Minute Book of the Huddersfield Board of Guardians, Vol. 5, 11 December, 1846, Ms HPL (P/HU/M).

109 *LM*, 5 February, 1848.

110 Newspaper cuttings enclosed in Huddersfield Correspondence, May to June, 1848, PRO, MH12/15070.

111 Huddersfield Correspondence, July, 1848, PRO, MH12/15070. Quoted in M. E. Rose, *Poor Law Administration in the West Riding of Yorkshire (1820–1855)*, pp. 171–172. A report of the Overseers of the Poor made to the ratepayers of the Huddersfield Township in May, 1848 confirmed the above findings. 'Report of the Overseers of the Poor of the Township of Huddersfield to the Rate-Payers of

the said Township, in Vestry Meeting Assembled, on Monday, May 1st, 1848' in Minute Book of the Ratepayers of Township of Huddersfield, 1835–1878, Ms and Printed, HPL (KHT1/2/2).

112 Minute Book of the Huddersfield Board of Guardians, Vol. 9, 8 May, 1857, Ms HPL (P/HU/M). For more on workhouse conditions for the sick, see N. Longmate, *The Workhouse* (1974), Chapters 16 and 17; A. Digby, *Pauper Palaces* (1978), Chapter 9; B. Abel-Smith, *The Hospitals 1800–1948* (1964), Chapters 4, 5 and 6.

113 Inquiry instituted by the Poor Law Board, 15 April, 1867. Cited in R. G. Hodgkinson, *The Origins of the National Health Service*, p. 525.

114 Minute Books of the Huddersfield Board of Guardians, Vol. 4, 8 September and 24 November, 1843, 2 February, 26 April and 2 August, 1844, Vol. 7, 19 April, 26 July and 18 October, 1850, 24 January, 1851, Ms HPL (P/HU/M); Wakefield Union. Extracts from the Half-yearly Abstract of the Separate Accounts of each Township, . . . for the Half-year ending 29th September, 1850, WDA (JGC).

115 C. Wakefield and Huddersfield, 1851.

116 A Statement of the Accounts of the Huddersfield Union, 1861–1873. Statement of the Number of the Several Classes of Persons Relieved in the Workhouses, during the Half-Year Ended 25th March, 1861, HPL (P/HU/Cfo); C. Huddersfield, 1861.

117 W. Ll. Parry-Jones, *The Trade in Lunacy. A Study of Private Madhouses in England in the Eighteenth and Nineteenth Centuries* (1972), p. 58.

118 Minute Book of the Huddersfield Board of Guardians, Vol. 7, 23 August, 1850, 21 February, 1851, Ms HPL (P/HU/M).

119 *Ibid.*, Vol. 10, 23 March, 1860.

120 A Statement of the Accounts of the Huddersfield Union, 1861–1873. Summary of Receipts and Expenditure by the Guardians during the Half-Year Ended 25th March, 1861, Analysis of Common Charges For the Year ended 25th March, 1868, HPL (P/HU/Cfo).

121 Township of Wakefield. Statement of the Accounts, For the Half-Year Ending Twenty-Ninth September, 1858, WDA (Local Collection, Box 8).

122 68th AR WI, 1854–1855.

123 73rd AR WI, 1859–1860, Annual Address, p. 1.

124 In 1851, following a number of disputes between the Huddersfield Board of Guardians and the Infirmary Committee over the payment of maintenance for pauper patients, the weekly charge was lowered from 5s to 2s 6d. A year later the Board of Guardians resolved to refuse to pay any weekly maintenance for paupers. In 1853 the intransigence of both sides resulted in the death of Eliza Bowker, who was turned away from the Infirmary, 'whilst suffering from a dreadful calamity', because her father had received 5s from the relieving officer. Finally, in 1854 the rule concerning the admission of paupers was modified to allow for the immediate admission of emergency cases without the usual recommendation and financial undertakings from the Guardians. Minute Book of the Huddersfield Infirmary, Vol. II, Meetings of the Monthly Board, 23 June, 1851, p. 201, 4 October, 1852, p. 227 and 7 November, 1853, pp. 254–255, Special General Meeting, 7 July, 1854, p. 272, Ms WYCRO (C500). (The same location applies throughout.)

125 13th Report of the Wakefield House of Recovery, for the year 1838, *WJ*, 1 February, 1839; Wakefield House of Recovery. Register of Patients, 1826–1854, Ms WYCRO (C235/5/1).

126 Wakefield House of Recovery. Register of Patients, 1826–1854, Ms WYCRO (C235/5/1).

127 Wakefield Union. Extracts from the Half-yearly Abstract of the Separate Accounts of each Township, . . . for the Half-year ending 29th September, 1850, WDA (JGC).

128 Minute Book of the Huddersfield Board of Guardians, Vol. 10, 1860 (subscriptions and payments to medical charities), Ms HPL (P/HU/M).

129 Township of Wakefield. Statement of the Accounts, For the Half-Year Ending Twenty-Ninth September, 1858, WDA (Local Collection, Box 8).

130 Minute Book of the Huddersfield Board of Guardians, Vol. 3, 4 June, 1841, Ms HPL (P/HU/M).
131 *Ibid.*, Vols 7, 10–13 (vaccination accounts).
132 *WJ*, 5 October, 1849; W. Ranger, *op. cit.*, p. 88.
133 See Chapter 2, Section 2.3 for more on public health and its reform in Wakefield and Huddersfield.
134 Minute Book of the Huddersfield Board of Guardians, Vol. 6, 21 and 24 September, 1849, Ms HPL (P/HU/M).
135 *Ibid.*, Vol. 7, Meetings of October to November, 1849.
136 See, for example, E. G. Thomas, *op. cit.*; J. Lane, 'Disease, Death and the Labouring Poor, 1750–1834: the provision of parish medical services in Warwickshire under the Old Poor Law', unpublished paper, University of Warwick, May, 1980.
137 G. W. Oxley, *Poor Relief in England and Wales 1601–1834* (Newton Abbot, 1974), pp. 65–66.
138 Many parliamentary inquiries into medical relief indicate this tendency; for example, witnesses to both the SCMPR 1844 and SCMR 1854.
139 Report of the Poor Law Commissioners on the Further Amendment of the Poor Laws, PP, 1840, XVII (253), App. B, Reports of Arrangements for Medical Relief, No. 6, III, Mr Power's Report – Lancashire and the West Riding of York, p. 165. See also Poor Law Commission, Ninth Annual Report, PP, 1843, XXI (468), p. 11.
140 See Chapter 4, especially Section 4.4, for more on the Wakefield House of Recovery.
141 Minute Book of the Huddersfield Board of Guardians, Vol. 12, 21 September, 1866, Ms HPL (P/HU/M).
142 SCMPR 1844, Evidence of H. W. Rumsey, Esq., Appendix, Schedules 1, 2 and 3.
143 *Ibid.*
144 See Chapters 5 and 6.
145 For a comparison of Poor Law medical facilities with other forms of medical provision, see Chapter 9.

Chapter 4

1 W. Dearden, *Lines Written on Witnessing the Laying of the Foundation Stone of the Huddersfield and Upper Agbrigg Infirmary, June 29, 1829* (Huddersfield, 1829), HPL (HC OLT).
2 D. Owen, *English Philanthropy 1660–1960* (1965). For a useful criticism of Owen's study, see B. Harrison, 'Philanthropy and the Victorians', *Victorian Studies*, Vol. IX, No. 4, June, 1966, pp. 353–374.
3 D. Fraser, *The Evolution of the British Welfare State* (1973), pp. 115–123.
4 G. Best, *Mid-Victorian Britain 1851–70* (1971), pp. 153–154.
5 R. J. Morris, *Organisation and Aims of the Principal Secular Voluntary Organisations of the Leeds Middle Class, 1830–1851*, unpublished DPhil thesis, Oxford, 1970.
6 F. M. L. Thompson, 'Social Control in Victorian Britain', *Economic History Review*, 2nd Series, Vol. XXXIV, No. 2, 1981, p. 189. Thompson's article provides us with both a summary and a criticism of some of the arguments used by social historians who over the last decade have embraced the concept of social control, with particular reference to working-class education and leisure, and law and order. See also A. P. Donajgrodzki (ed.), *Social Control in Nineteenth Century Britain* (1977). For paternalism see, for example, D. Roberts, *Paternalism in Early Victorian England* (1979); P. Joyce, *Work, Society and Politics. The culture of the factory in later Victorian England* (1980).
7 For example, Woodward's pioneering study of the voluntary hospital movement in the eighteenth and nineteenth centuries was based largely on the earliest and

most prestigious institutions. J. Woodward, *op. cit.* John Pickstone's recent study of hospital development provides an exception to this tendency. Based on the period 1752 to 1946, it looks at the development of medical charities (and other hospital facilities) in both Manchester and its surrounding communities. J. V. Pickstone, *op. cit.*

8 C. Webster, 'The crisis of the hospitals during the Industrial Revolution' in E. G. Forbes (ed.), *Human implications of scientific advance* (Edinburgh, 1978), p. 214.

9 M. J. Peterson provides us with an interesting account of the struggle between medical and lay officers in the London hospitals in the nineteenth century, and of how doctors secured more power and influence within these institutions, in M. J. Peterson, *The Medical Profession in Mid-Victorian London* (Berkeley, 1978), pp. 136–193.

10 The reports of these institutions are unfortunately far from complete, especially for the Wakefield Dispensary in the first half of the nineteenth century. The printed reports of the charities have been supplemented as far as possible with annual press reports. For a complete list of available reports, see Bibliography and Appendix 6.

11 J. Woodward, *op. cit.*; B. Abel-Smith, *op. cit.*; W. B. Howie, 'The Administration of an Eighteenth-Century Provincial Hospital: The Royal Salop Infirmary, 1747–1830', *Medical History*, Vol. 5, No. 1, January, 1961, pp. 34–55 and 'Finance and Supply in an Eighteenth-Century Hospital, 1747–1830', *Medical History*, Vol. 7, No. 2, April, 1963, pp. 126–146.

12 Annual subscribers and benefactors of ten guineas or upwards.

13 See, for example, J. Woodward, *op. cit.*, pp. 36–44; H. W. Hart, 'Some Notes on the Sponsoring of Patients for Hospital Treatment under the Voluntary System', *Medical History*, Vol. 24, No. 4, October, 1980, pp. 447–460.

14 T. G. Wright, MD, *Reminiscences of the Charity Ball* (Wakefield, 1895) in Wakefield Charity Ball Scrapbook, c. 1818–1898, WYCRO (C235/2/1).

15 1st AR HI, 1831–1832.

16 *WHJ*, 28 April, 1820.

17 *WHJ*, 12 and 19 July, 1822.

18 *WHJ*, 19 January, 1827; D. Alexander, MD, *A Lecture on Phrenology, as Illustrative of the Moral and Intellectual Capacities of Man* (London, Edinburgh and Wakefield, 1826), WDA (Local Collection, Box 14).

19 35th AR HI, 1865–1866.

20 46th AR HI, 1876–1877. See pp. 158–59 for more on the Hospital Saturday Fund.

21 1st AR HD, 1814–1815.

22 *WJ*, 23 June, 1815.

23 4th AR HI, 1834–1835.

24 69th AR WI, 1855–1856.

25 84th AR WI, 1870–1871; 40th AR HI, 1870–1871. For breakdowns of the annual incomes of the medical charities, see Appendix 5.

26 The most active proponents of the pessimistic view of hospital treatment are McKeown and Brown, who claim that these institutions actually resulted in a rise in mortality rates in the late eighteenth century. T. McKeown and R. G. Brown, 'Medical Evidence Related to English Population Changes in the Eighteenth Century', *Population Studies*, Vol. 9, Part 2, November, 1955, pp. 119–141. For more optimistic interpretations of the value of eighteenth- and nineteenth-century hospitals see, for example, S. Cherry, 'The Role of a Provincial Hospital: The Norfolk and Norwich Hospital, 1771–1880', *Population Studies*, Vol. 26, Part 2, July, 1972, pp. 291–306; E. M. Sigsworth, 'Gateways to death? Medicine, Hospitals and Mortality, 1700–1850' in P. Mathias (ed.), *Science and Society 1600–1900* (Cambridge, 1972), pp. 97–110.

27 30th AR HI, 1860–1861.

28 74th and 84th ARs WI, 1860–1861, 1870–1871.

29 1st to 40th ARs HI, 1831–1871; 67th to 84th ARs WI, 1854–1871. See also Figures 4.2(a) and (b).

30 2nd AR HI, 1832–1833, Annual Address, p. 4; *WJ*, 18 July, 1862.
31 I. S. L. Loudon also points to the increased expectations of the sick poor, confident of being treated by out-patient departments gratis. What became in effect a serious problem for these departments, also triggered off a major conflict between the hospitals and general practitioners in the late nineteenth century. The GPs believed that, as a result of the growth in out-patient services, they were being deprived of paying patients. I. S. L. Loudon, 'Historical importance of outpatients', *British Medical Journal*, Vol. I, No. 6118, April, 1978, pp. 975–976.
32 Especially when compared with Poor Law medical facilities. For a comparison of official and charitable medical services in the two towns, see Chapter 9.
33 64th AR WD, 1850–1851.
34 76th AR WI, 1862–1863.
35 84th AR WI, 1870–1871.
36 1st AR HD, 1814–1815.
37 6th–7th and 8th ARs HD, 1819–1821, 1821–1822.
38 20th AR HI, 1850–1851.
39 24th to 39th ARs HI, 1855–1870.
40 SCMPR 1844, Evidence of H. W. Rumsey, Esq., p. 560, Q.9166.
41 1st AR HD, 1814–1815. For more on the kind of treatment offered by dispensaries, see H. Marland, *The Provision of Medical Treatment for the Sick Poor. The Doncaster Dispensary 1792–1867*, unpublished MA thesis, Warwick, 1980, Chapter 5.
42 40th AR HI, 1870–1871.
43 Annual Reports of the Huddersfield Dispensary and Infirmary.
44 3rd AR WD, 1790–1791.
45 84th AR WI, 1870–1871.
46 Annual Reports of the Wakefield Dispensary and Infirmary.
47 73rd to 83rd ARs WI, 1860–1870; 29th to 39th ARs HI, 1860–1870.
48 Annual Reports of the Wakefield and Huddersfield Infirmaries.
49 T. Holmes's 1864 report on the Huddersfield Infirmary, for example, stated that cases of pyaemia (blood poisoning) had occurred occasionally in the institution's oldest wards, which he blamed on poor ventilation and overcrowding. With the addition of new wards during the second half of the century these problems largely disappeared. Sixth Report of the Medical Officer of the Privy Council, PP, 1864, XXVIII I (3416), App. 15, 'Reports on the Hospitals of the United Kingdom', by J. S. Bristowe and T. Holmes, p. 649.
50 1st AR HI, 1831–1832.
51 35th AR HI, 1865–1866.
52 For more on rates of admission, cure and mortality in the Wakefield and Huddersfield Dispensaries and Infirmaries, see Appendix 6. For a comparison with other medical facilities, see Chapter 9.
53 For more on typhus fever see, for example, G. M. Howe, *Man, Environment and Disease in Britain. A Medical Geography through the Ages* (Newton Abbot, 1972), especially pp. 145–147, 164–165.
54 Wakefield House of Recovery. Register of Patients, 1826–1854, Ms WYCRO (C235/5/1).
55 The term 'men' is used advisedly. Women were not eligible to serve on committees or to fill honorary posts, and, although many women were subscribers and benefactors, or were active in fund-raising efforts, few could match the enormous contributions of hundreds or even thousands of pounds made by a small group of men during the nineteenth century. The role of women in the medical charities will be discussed in Section 4.4.
56 For an analysis of a larger sample of individuals prominent in the running and financing of the Wakefield and Huddersfield Infirmaries, see Appendix 7.
57 'Death of Mr J. C. Laycock', *HE*, 21 February, 1885; C. A. Hulbert, *Supplementary Annals of the Church and Parish of Almondbury, July, 1882, to June, 1885* (London and Huddersfield, 1885), pp. 133–136.
58 *A Sermon Preached at the Parish Church, Huddersfield, On Sunday, February 22nd,*

1885, On the Occasion of the Death of J. C. Laycock, Esq., By the Rev. J. W. Bardsley, MA, Vicar (Huddersfield, 1885), HPL (Local Pamphlets, Vol. 2).
59 *HE*, 21 February, 1885.
60 38th AR HI, 1868–1869, Annual Address, p. 9.
61 'Huddersfield Convalescent Home. Laying of the Foundation Stone', *HE*, 31 October, 1868.
62 41st AR HI, 1871–1872, Annual Address, p. 6.
63 34 gentlemen became Vice-Presidents on the inauguration of the Infirmary in 1831 in acknowledgement of their large donations to the Building Fund. Most of them played little part in the government of the charity.
64 'Death of Charles Brook, Esq., of Healey House', *HC*, 20 November, 1869.
65 72nd and 76th ARs WI, 1858–1859, 1862–1863; Letter from J. C. D. Charlesworth to Mr John Binks, re. endowment of the proposed new hospital, dated February 16, 1871, Ms WDA (Local Collection, Box 8).
66 'Death of Colonel Charlesworth', *WH*, 25 March, 1880.
67 For a biography of William Willans, see Appendix 7.
68 'Death of Thomas Clayton, Esq.', *WE*, 24 October, 1868.
69 67th AR WI, 1853–1854, Annual Address, pp. 5–6.
70 The hospital retains Clayton's name as its founder up to the present day.
71 78th AR WI, 1864–1865, Annual Address, p. 3.
72 81st AR WI, 1867–1868, Annual Address, pp. 4–5; Printed appeal for subscriptions for a portrait of Thomas Clayton, Esq., dated 24 October, 1867, WYCRO (C235/4/1).
73 Report of the Charity Commissioners on Endowed Charities of the West Riding, Vol. V, 1899, pp. 665–668.
74 W. Read, 'The Story of the Clayton Hospital, Wakefield', *Wakefield Historical Society Journal*, Vol. 2, 1975, p. 12.
75 For a more complete list of Clayton's charitable contributions (and for more detailed biographies of the individuals discussed here), see Appendix 7. For Clayton's biography I have also referred to the *Programme of Centenary Celebrations of The Clayton Hospital, 1854–1954* (Wakefield, 1954), WYCRO (C235/6/5) and W. Read, *op. cit.*, pp. 5–13.
76 4th AR HI, 1834–1835; 79th AR WI, 1865–1866. See Appendix 5 for examples of the charities' incomes.
77 B. Harrison, *op. cit.*, p. 374.
78 F. K. Prochaska, 'Women in English Philanthropy 1790–1830', *International Review of Social History*, Vol. 19, 1974, pp. 426–445.
79 The task of identification was made more difficult, especially in the case of Huddersfield, because of the large number of subscribers sharing the same surname. For example, fourteen Haighs and 35 Brookes are included on the subscription list of the Huddersfield Infirmary in the year 1865–1866. 35th AR HI, 1865–1866.
80 C. Huddersfield, 1851, 1861. For more on the social and economic status of shopkeepers, see T. Vigne and A. Howkins, 'The Small Shopkeeper in Industrial and Market Towns' in G. Crossick (ed.), *The Lower Middle Class in Britain 1870–1914* (1977).
81 For example, the 1866 directory for Huddersfield listed two subscribers to the Infirmary, Mr H. K. Beaumont and Mr Abraham Graham, as an 'oil merchant, drysalter and wood grinder' and a 'mason, builder and farmer'. The occupation of Mr George Beaumont, subscriber to the Wakefield Infirmary, was given as 'auctioneer, builder, undertaker and agent to the Metallic Coffin Co. etc.'. Mr Joseph Leighton was described as a 'gardener and victualler'. White, 1866.
82 In the year 1865–1866, for example, over sixty subscriptions or donations were received by the Treasurer of the Huddersfield Infirmary from individuals living at a considerable distance from Huddersfield, including York, Leeds, Liverpool, London, Suffolk and Worcestershire. In many cases these were former residents of the town, who had moved or retired to other areas of the country.

83 Rules and Regulations for The Government of the Wakefield General Dispensary and Clayton Hospital, 1854, p. 7, WYCRO (C235/1); Rules and Regulations of the Huddersfield and Upper Agbrigg Infirmary, 1834, p. 3, HPL (B.362).

84 44th AR HI, 1874–1875.

85 66th AR WD, 1852–1853; White, 1853.

86 *Ibid.*

87 M. C. Buer, *Health, wealth, and population in the early days of the industrial revolution* (2nd ed., New York, 1968, first published 1926), p. 258; G. D. H. Cole and R. Postgate, *op. cit.*, pp. 21–22.

88 See Chapter 2, Section 2.4.

89 See Chapters 3 and 5.

90 *WHJ*, 22 October, 1813.

91 For example, Robert Bell, a Wakefield MD, argued in a letter to the local newspaper that a change should be made in the management of the '. . . well-intentioned, but misconducted Charity', and complaints were also heard about a lack of economy on the part of the Dispensary's officers. *WHJ*, 2 July, 1824.

92 *WS*, 27 July, 1810.

93 *Ibid.*

94 *WHJ*, 16 August, 1816, 13 July, 1827.

95 *WHJ*, 23 June, 1815; *WJ*, 7 July, 1843.

96 64th AR WD, 1850–1851, Annual Address, p. 3.

97 *WHJ*, 3 April, 1829, 2 March, 1832.

98 *WJ*, 4 September, 1840.

99 *WJ*, 11 June, 1840.

100 Clayton's gift coincided with the closure of the Wakefield House of Recovery. The committee of this institution offered their furniture and equipment to the Dispensary, and this offer gave further impetus to the idea of setting up in-patient wards.

101 77th and 78th ARs WI, 1863–1864, 1864–1865, Annual Addresses, pp. 1, 3–4.

102 For example, the following members of the local hierarchy became Patrons to the Grand Concert in Aid of the Endowment Fund of the Clayton Hospital, held in April, 1865: Sir J. C. D. Hay, Bart., MP, W. B. Beaumont, Esq., MP and Lady Beaumont, Colonel J. G. Smyth, MP, Sir Lionel Pilkington, Bart. and Lady Pilkington, Colonel J. C. D. Charlesworth and the Vicar of Wakefield, the Reverend Camidge. *WE*, 8 April, 1865.

103 82nd AR WI, 1868–1869.

104 1st AR HD, 1814–1815.

105 2nd AR HD, 1815–1816, Annual Address, p. 4.

106 10th AR HD, 1823–1824.

107 9th AR HD, 1822–1823.

108 Minute Book of the Huddersfield Dispensary, Vol. I, Meeting of the Committee, 6 September, 1824, p. 140.

109 *LM*, 30 April, 7 May, 1825.

110 *LM*, 28 May, 1825.

111 On Clay's death in 1833 a poem was dedicated to him, commemorating his fund-raising efforts. See Appendix 8.

112 W. Turnbull, MD, *An Appeal, in Behalf of the Intended Hospital at Huddersfield* (Huddersfield, n.d., c. 1825), HPL (Tolson Collection).

113 Report of the General Meeting of the Inhabitants of the Town and Neighbourhood of Huddersfield, held at the George Inn, on Friday the 17th of October, 1828, for the purpose of receiving the Report of the Committee, relative to the Establishment of an Infirmary, HPL (Tolson Collection).

114 14th AR HD, 1827–1828, Annual Address, p. 1.

115 *The Huddersfield & Upper Agbrigg Infirmary. Laying of the First Stone* (Huddersfield, 1829), p. 2, HPL (Tomlinson Collection).

116 This emphasis on accident cases was shared by many other dispensaries and infirmaries during the nineteenth century, especially after the 1840s. Even in the

more rural area served by the Norfolk and Norwich Hospital, Cherry points to a growth in casualty admissions, which '. . . reflected population growth and the increased mechanization of agriculture and industry'. S. Cherry, *op. cit.*, p. 301. The nearby Leeds Infirmary also admitted large numbers of accident cases during the century. For details of accident cases admitted to the Leeds charity between 1823 and 1824, see S. T. Anning, *The History of Medicine in Leeds* (Leeds, 1980), pp. 100–134, 202–212.

117 Rules of the Huddersfield Dispensary, 1821, p. 12, WYCRO (C500). Mrs Gaskell emphasised the priority placed on accident cases in *Mary Barton*, when a serious typhus case was refused an in-patient's order to the infirmary by Mr Carson, a local manufacturer, with the remark that 'they're always wanted for accidents'. E. Gaskell, *Mary Barton. A Tale of Manchester Life* (Harmondsworth, 1970, Penguin ed., first published 1848).

118 1st AR HI, 1831–1832.

119 16th AR HI, 1846–1847.

120 26th and 33rd ARs HI, 1856–1857, 1863–1864, Annual Addresses, pp. 6, 7.

121 Sixth Report of the Medical Officer of the Privy Council, PP, 1864, XXVIII I (3416), App. 15, pp. 649–650.

122 43rd and 50th ARs HI, 1873–1874, 1880–1881.

123 Rules and Regulations for The Government of the Wakefield General Dispensary and Clayton Hospital, 1854, p. 18, WYCRO (C235/1).

124 79th AR WI, 1865–1866.

125 77th to 84th ARs WI, 1863–1871.

126 6th–7th AR HD, 1819–1821, Annual Address, p. 4.

127 *LM*, 1 May, 1847.

128 16th AR HI, 1846–1847, Annual Address, p. 5.

129 72nd and 74th ARs WI, 1858–1859, 1860–1861; 32nd AR HI, 1855–1856.

130 43rd AR WD, 1830–1831; 17th AR HD, 1830–1831; 79th AR WI, 1865–1866; 35th AR HI, 1865–1866.

131 *HE*, 28 July, 1860.

132 2nd AR HD, 1815–1816.

133 10th AR HD, 1823–1824.

134 13th AR HD, 1826–1827.

135 27th AR HI, 1857–1858.

136 43rd AR HI, 1873–1874.

137 C. Crowther, MD, *Notes on Proposed Alms House for Dissenters & Fever Hospital* (Wakefield, 1842), Ms WDA (JGC).

138 2nd Report of the Wakefield House of Recovery, for the year 1827, *WHJ*, 11 January, 1828.

139 See A. S. Wohl, *Endangered Lives. Public Health in Victorian Britain* (1984), pp. 1–2.

140 A. K. Jacques, *Merrie Wakefield* (based on some of the Diaries of Clara Clarkson (1811–1889) of Alverthorpe Hall, Wakefield) (Wakefield, 1971).

141 6th Report of the Wakefield House of Recovery, for the year 1831, *WHJ*, 3 February, 1832.

142 Wakefield House of Recovery. Register of Patients, 1826–1854, Ms WYCRO (C235/5/1).

143 5th AR HI, 1835–1836, Annual Address, p. 4.

144 32nd AR HI, 1862–1863, Annual Address, p. 7.

145 8th AR HI, 1838–1839, Annual Address, p. 17.

146 36th AR HI, 1866–1867, Annual Address, p. 7.

147 65th AR WD, 1851–1852, Annual Address, p. 5.

148 37th AR HI, 1867–1868, Annual Address, p. 8.

149 See Chapter 7, pp. 274–280 and Chapter 8, pp. 329–336.

150 66th AR WD, 1852–1853.

151 Minute Book of the Huddersfield Dispensary, Vol. I, Meeting of the Monthly Committee, 7 October, 1816, p. 37.

152 Minute Book of the Huddersfield Dispensary and Infirmary, Vol. I, Memorandum, 9 May, 1817, p. 44, Meetings of the Infirmary Committee, 8

October, 1831, p. 289 and 22 December, 1831, p. 294.

153 Minute Books of the Huddersfield Dispensary and Infirmary, Vols I and II, 1825–1826, 1855–1856, 1865–1866; 12th AR HD, 1825–1826; 25th and 35th ARs HI, 1855–1856, 1865–1866.

154 By 1870 an annual subscription of one guinea or a donation of ten guineas entitled the benefactor to have one out-patient on the books of the Huddersfield Infirmary at a time. For an annual subscription of two guineas or a donation of twenty guineas a subscriber was able to have one in-patient or two out-patients on the books, and so on progressively, to a limit of five in-patients or ten out-patients. 40th AR HI, 1870–1871.

155 C. Webster, *op. cit.*, p. 214.

156 T. G. Wright, MD, *Wakefield Charity Ball*, letter dated January, 1885 in Wakefield Charity Ball Scrapbook, c. 1818–1898, WYCRO (C235/2/1).

157 See Appendix 8.

158 L. Davidoff, *The Best Circles. Society Etiquette and the Season* (1973), p. 71.

159 J. V. Pickstone, 'The Professionalisation of Medicine in England and Europe: the state, the market and industrial society', *Journal of the Japan Society of Medical History*, Vol. 25, No. 4, October, 1979, p. 542.

160 For patterns of denominational support in the two towns, see Chapter 2, pp. 26–31.

161 See Chapter 2, pp. 31–34 for voting behaviour in Wakefield and Huddersfield.

162 Incidently, the committee of the Huddersfield Infirmary seem to have been very much opposed to Socialists. In June, 1840, for example, it was recorded in the minutes 'That Mr. Laycock the Secretary having recently issued Adverts declining to accept of any funds to be realised from the Lectures or Diversions held in the Building occupied by the persons calling themselves "Socialists". This Board hereby sanction the steps adopted by Mr. Laycock on that occasion, and thanks him for the spirited manner in which he rejected the proposed contribution to the funds of this Institution'. Minute Book of the Huddersfield Infirmary, Vol. I, Meeting of the Board, 22 June, 1840.

163 D. Fraser, 'Voluntaryism and West Riding politics in the mid-nineteenth century', *Northern History*, Vol. XIII, 1977, p. 199.

164 J. V. Pickstone, 'What were Dispensaries for? The Lancashire Foundations during the Industrial Revolution', unpublished paper, UMIST, Manchester, 1980, p. 3.

165 A 'rival' dispensary known as the 'Regular Dispensary' did exist in Huddersfield for a short period (circa 1814 to 1820). Very little is known of this institution, or the support it commanded. The two dispensaries amalgamated in 1820, on apparently amicable terms. Minute Book of the Huddersfield Dispensary, Vol. I, 1814–1820.

166 R. J. Morris, *op. cit.*

167 32nd AR HI, 1862–1863, Annual Address, p. 8.

168 See, for example, J. Woodward, *op. cit.*, pp. 36–37.

169 8th AR HI, 1838–1839.

170 See Chapter 3 for the admission of paupers to medical charities. See Chapter 5, pp. 195–196 for the relationship between friendly societies and medical charities.

171 16th AR HD, 1829–1830, Annual Address, p. 1.

172 Minute Book of the Huddersfield Infirmary, Vol. II, Meeting of the Monthly Board, 20 June, 1853, p. 245.

173 The 1841 census enumerated all hospital patients in Great Britain on census day. A very high proportion were servants (18 per cent of those classified), while various manufacturing groups were also well represented. 1841 Census, Occupation Abstract, PP, 1844, XXVII (587). Abstract of Occupations of Persons enumerated as Inmates of the following Public Institutions of Great Britain on the night of 6th June 1841: 2. Hospitals. For a full reference, see Bibliography.

174 43rd AR WD, 1830–1831, Set of Rules, pp. 18–19.

175 Rules and Regulations of the Huddersfield and Upper Agbrigg Infirmary, 1834, pp. 18–19, HPL (B.362).

176 66th AR WD, 1852–1853, Annual Address, p. 4.

177 38th and 39th ARs HI, 1868–1869, 1869–1870, Annual Addresses, pp. 7–8, 7.

178 J. Hart, 'Religion and Social Control in the mid-Nineteenth Century' in A. P. Donajgrodzki (ed.), *op. cit.*, pp. 108–133.

179 *The Huddersfield & Upper Agbrigg Infirmary. Laying of the First Stone* (Huddersfield, 1829), p. 2, HPL (Tomlinson Collection).

180 See Section 4.4.

181 Minute Book of the Huddersfield Infirmary, Vol. II, Annual Meeting of Subscribers, 24 June, 1859, p. 367.

182 See Chapter 2, pp. 26–31.

183 2nd AR HD, 1815–1816, Annual Address, p. 4 (my emphasis).

184 12th AR HD, 1825–1826, Annual Address, p. 3.

185 68th AR WI, 1854–1855, Annual Address, p. 6.

186 See Chapter 2, Section 2.4 for more on working-class unrest in Wakefield and Huddersfield.

187 G. Stedman Jones, *Outcast London. A Study in the Relationship between Classes in Victorian Society* (Oxford, 1971).

188 R. Dennis, *op. cit.*, pp. 236, 239.

189 P. Joyce, *op. cit.*; D. Roberts, *op. cit.*, especially Chapter VII.

190 P. Joyce, *op. cit.*, p. xxi.

191 *WJ*, 26 March, 1841.

192 Report of the Commissioner Appointed under the Provisions of the Act 5 & 6 Vict. c. 99, to Inquire into the Operation of that Act, and into the State of the Population in The Mining Districts, PP, 1845, XXVII (670), Report of Seymour Tremenheere on the West Riding of Yorkshire, pp. 21–26, 29–30.

193 W. R. Croft, *The History of the Factory Movement* (Huddersfield, 1888), pp. 32–34.

194 *WRH*, 17 November, 1837.

195 J. T. Ward, *The Factory Movement 1830–1855* (1962), pp. 136–137.

196 Cited in D. F. E. Sykes, *op. cit.*, pp. 307–313. In September, 1851 the *Huddersfield and Holmfirth Examiner* cited the case of Samuel Milnes, a dyer of Upper Mill, near Huddersfield, whose apron was accidentally caught in some shafting, whereby he was drawn into the cog-wheels and before the machine could be stopped his head 'was most dreadfully mangled and his neck twisted in a most shocking manner so as to produce instantaneous death'. In the same month the paper reported on the inquest of a fourteen-year-old mine worker, Henry Oldroyd. The Jury found he had been 'accidentally killed' from an accumulation of smoke in the works of High Close Pit, which smoke could not have so collected if the mine had been well ventilated. The Jury 'hoped' that Messrs Jagger would in future keep a more efficient check on the pit, as it was the second accident to occur in a month. In December of the same year another mining accident occurred in Field House Colliery, when a miner fell down a shaft. He broke both legs and sustained other 'serious injuries', and was immediately conveyed to the Huddersfield Infirmary, where he was reported to be in a 'precarious state'. *HHE*, 13 and 27 September and 6 December, 1851.

197 J. V. Pickstone, 'What were Dispensaries for?', p. 3.

198 A. Summers, 'A Home from Home – Women's Philanthropic Work in the Nineteenth Century' in S. Burman (ed.), *Fit Work for Women* (1979), p. 43.

199 In 1810 the committee of the Wakefield Dispensary calculated that out-patients cost on average nearly 4s to treat. In 1833 the Huddersfield Infirmary Committee claimed in-patients cost £3 7s per head, out-patients 3s. *WS*, 27 July, 1810; 2nd AR HI, 1832–1833, Annual Address, p. 4.

200 67th AR WI, 1853–1854, Annual Address, p. 7.

201 See Chapters 5 and 6.

202 For complaint procedures, see W. B. Howie, 'Complaints and Complaint Procedures in the Eighteenth- and early Nineteenth-Century Provincial Hospitals in England', *Medical History*, Vol. 25, No. 4, October, 1981, pp. 345–362.

203 25th to 40th ARs HI, 1855–1871.

204 86th AR WI, 1872–1873, Annual Address, p. 5.

205 89th AR WI, 1875–1876, Annual Address, pp. 5, 8.

206 90th AR WI, 1876–1877, Annual Address, p. 4.

207 94th AR WI, 1880–1881, Annual Address, p. 7.

208 42nd AR HI, 1872–1873, Annual Address, p. 7.

209 46th AR HI, 1876–1877, Annual Address, p. 5.

210 50th AR HI, 1880–1881.

211 See, for example, F. K. Prochaska, *Women and Philanthropy in 19th Century England* (Oxford, 1980); M. B. Simey, *Charitable Effort in Liverpool in the Nineteenth Century* (Liverpool, 1951); A. Summers, *op. cit.*

212 H. More, *Coelebs in Search of a Wife* (1809). Quoted in P. Hollis (ed.), *Women in Public: The Women's Movement 1850–1900* (1979), p. 230.

213 A. Summers, *op. cit.*, p. 33.

214 D. Fraser, *The Evolution of the British Welfare State*, p. 118.

215 For middle-class incomes, see, for example, J. F. C. Harrison, *The Early Victorians 1832–51* (1971), p. 131 and G. Best, *op. cit.*, p. 110.

216 In 1858 a correspondent to *The Times* with an income of £300 per annum claimed that he allocated £20 yearly to 'Church and Charity' out of a total expenditure of £230, for himself, his wife, one woman servant and one nursery girl. Another letter to *The Times*, again published in 1858, gave the annual expenditure for a couple, three children and three servants as £393 14s. Of this, £26 15s 4½d was spent on subscriptions to charity. *The Times*, 15 and 25 January, 1858. Cited in J. A. Banks, *Prosperity and Parenthood* (1954), pp. 41–42, 61–63.

217 For women's role in the middle-class household, see P. Branca, *Silent Sisterhood. Middle-Class Women in the Victorian Home* (1975).

218 5th Report of the Wakefield House of Recovery, for the year 1830, *WHJ*, 14 January, 1831; 43rd AR WD, 1830–1831.

219 *Ibid.*; 16th Report of the Wakefield House of Recovery, for the year 1841, *WJ*, 18 February, 1842.

220 See J. A. Banks, *op. cit.*, pp. 32–47.

221 *LM*, 10 February, 1849; Wakefield Charity Ball Scrapbook, c. 1818–1898 (newspaper cuttings), WYCRO (C235/2/1).

222 5th Report of the Wakefield House of Recovery; Parson and White, 1828; White, 1837.

223 F. K. Prochaska, *Women and Philanthropy in 19th Century England*, p. 142.

224 8th AR HI, 1838–1839.

225 C. Cappe, *Thoughts on the Desirableness and Utility of Ladies visiting the Female Wards of Hospitals and Lunatic Asylums* (1816), p. 376. Quoted in F. K. Prochaska, *Women and Philanthropy in 19th Century England*, p. 141.

226 25th AR HI, 1855–1856.

227 F. K. Prochaska, *Women and Philanthropy in 19th Century England*, pp. 155–160.

228 29th, 34th and 36th ARs HI, 1859–1860, 1864–1865, 1866–1867.

229 17th AR HD, 1830–1831; 43rd AR WD, 1830–1831; 35th AR HI, 1865–1866; 79th AR WI, 1865–1866.

230 69th and 70th ARs WI, 1855–1856, 1856–1857; Minute Book of the Huddersfield Dispensary and Infirmary, Vol. I, Meeting of the Infirmary Committee, 23 April, 1829, p. 209, Vol. II, Meeting of the Monthly Board, 4 December, 1843, p. 58.

231 *Ibid.*, Vol. I, Meeting of the Infirmary Committee, 23 April, 1829, p. 209; 31st and 35th ARs HI, 1861–1862, 1865–1866.

232 28th AR HI, 1858–1859.

233 3rd Report of the Wakefield House of Recovery, for the year 1828, *WHJ*, 30 January, 1829; Wakefield Charity Ball Scrapbook, c. 1818–1898, WYCRO (C235/2/1).

234 1st AR HI, 1831–1832; *HHEx*, 7 May, 1831.

235 T. G. Wright, MD, *Reminiscences of the Charity Ball*, WYCRO (C235/2/1).

236 *WHJ*, 25 April, 1828.

237 16th Report of the Wakefield House of Recovery; *WJ*, 8 July, 1842.

238 F. K. Prochaska, *Women in English Philanthropy 1790–1830*, pp. 430–431.

239 Annual subscribers of 10s or more and benefactors of £5 or upwards automatically became trustees of the charity. 2nd Report of the Wakefield House of Recovery.

240 5th and 16th Reports of the Wakefield House of Recovery.

241 6th and 15th Reports of the Wakefield House of Recovery, for the years 1831 and 1840, *WHJ*, 2 March, 1832, *WJ*, 15 February, 1841.

242 T. G. Wright, MD, *The Wakefield House of Recovery* (Wakefield, 1895), WYCRO (C235/5/1).

243 *Ibid.*

244 C. Crowther, M.D., *op. cit.*, Ms WDA (JGC).

245 In 1838, for example, 57 patients were admitted to the House of Recovery. Fifteen were men (aged over eighteen), sixteen women, eighteen boys and eight girls. In 1847 out of the 71 patients admitted there were 26 adult males, 23 adult women, twelve boys and ten girls. Wakefield House of Recovery. Register of Patients, 1826–1854, Ms WYCRO (C235/5/1).

246 See Chapter 5, p. 190 for more on the activities of the Female Benefit Society.

247 See Chapter 2, Section 2.1 and pp. 22–23.

248 For the role of medical charities in the field of public health, see Chapter 8, pp. 343–344.

249 1st AR HD, 1814–1815, Annual Address, p. 4.

250 C. Webster, *op. cit.*, p. 214.

251 See Chapter 8, pp. 329–336 for the relationship between laymen and doctors in the medical charities.

Chapter 5

1 B. B. Gilbert, *The Evolution of National Insurance in Great Britain. The Origins of the Welfare State* (1966), p. 165.

2 W. R. Greg, 'Investments for the Working Classes', *Edinburgh Review*, Vol. XCV, 1852, p. 407. Cited in H. Perkin, *The Origins of Modern English Society 1780–1880* (1969), pp. 381–382.

3 E. P. Thompson, *op. cit.*, p. 460; H. Perkin, *op. cit.*, p. 119.

4 P. H. J. H. Gosden, *op. cit.*, pp. 33–34, 24.

5 Abstracts of the quinquennial returns of sickness and mortality experienced by Friendly Societies for periods between 1855 and 1875, PP, 1880, LXVIII (517). Hereafter referred to as QRSM 1880.

6 In Chapter 9 the amount and quality of medical relief provided by friendly societies will be put into context, by means of a comparison with other forms of medical relief in the two towns.

7 See E. Hobsbawm, 'Friendly Societies', *The Amateur Historian*, Vol. 3, No. 3, Spring, 1957, pp. 95–101. The plea Hobsbawm makes for further research into friendly societies in this article, published almost thirty years ago, has apparently largely gone unanswered. See also D. Neave, 'The local records of affiliated Friendly Societies: A plea for their location and preservation', *The Local Historian*, Vol. 16, No. 3, August, 1984, pp. 161–167.

8 H. Perkin, *op. cit.*, p. 381.

9 In these areas the 'benefit societies' were more likely to take the form of organisations supported only in part by the subscriptions of the poor. They also involved a large degree of upper-class patronage, control and financial support, resulting in a combination of self-help, with a large measure of paternal control and philanthropy. Local clergymen or gentry typically became officers to these societies. These types of societies, however, remained small and few throughout the nineteenth century. There were less than 90,000 out of 1,857,896 registered members in 'paternal' benefit societies in 1872. Cited *ibid.*

10 SCMPR 1844, Evidence of H. W. Rumsey, Esq., p. 535, Q.9077.

11 E. P. Thompson, *op. cit.*, p. 460.

12 This may explain the relative neglect of friendly societies by historians of the eighteenth and nineteenth centuries. The most complete surveys to date of friendly societies are provided in P. H. J. H. Gosden, *op. cit.* and *Self-Help Voluntary Associations in the 19th Century* (1973). These accounts concentrate on the progress of the affiliated orders, for which there is far more statistical and qualitative evidence.

13 Abstract of Returns relative to the Expense and Maintenance of the Poor, PP, 1803–1804, XIII (175).

14 *Ibid.*; Abstract of Returns Relative to the Expense and Maintenance of the Poor, PP, 1818, XIX (82). The figures give percentages of the total population, rather than of the adult population, which would result in a more precise and larger estimate. Population figures were taken from W. Page, *op. cit.*, p. 525.

15 *Ibid.*

16 SCMPR 1844, Evidence of H. W. Rumsey, Esq., p. 537, Q.9087. In nearby Gomersal it was reported in 1854 that approximately two-thirds of the working class were members of a friendly society. SCMR 1854, Evidence of Joseph Ellison, Esq., p. 169, Q.2594.

17 White, 1866, p. 292; 'Return of Number of Societies which have deposited their Rules with the Registrar of Friendly Societies', PP, 1867, XL (75); Returns of all Societies whose Rules have been deposited with the Registrar of Friendly Societies in England, PP, 1868–1869, LVI (359). Huddersfield was also noted for its high proportion of building societies to the population and high level of home ownership by working men. See J. Springett, *op. cit.*, p. 135.

18 The Court Directory of the Order of Ancient Foresters, 1840, WDA (Local Collection W.334.7); Register of Shepherds Sanctuaries containing 139 sanctuaries in the West Riding, Lancashire and Cheshire, 1817–1859, Ms HPL (S/RS 3/1); M. A. Jagger, *The History of Honley* (Honley, 1914), p. 260. By 1850 the Yorkshire division of the Ancient Order of Foresters had the largest number of both courts and members. There was a total of 364 courts in this district, with 20,202 members. Directory of the Ancient Order of Foresters, Compiled up to January 1st, 1850, WDA (Local Collection W.334.7).

19 Archives of the Grand United Order of Oddfellows, Charity Lodge, No. 97, Cleckheaton, Membership Book, 1824–1839, Ms HPL (S/CL 12); Register of Shepherds Sanctuaries containing 139 sanctuaries in the West Riding, Lancashire and Cheshire, 1817–1859, Ms HPL (S/RS 3/1).

20 Wakefield British Friendly Union Society, Annual Reports, Nos. 1–20, 1842–1862, WDA (Local Collection, Box 2C).

21 *The Lancet*, 1868, Vol. I, p. 17.

22 H. Perkin, *op. cit.*, p. 144.

23 B. B. Gilbert, *op. cit.*, p. 166.

24 H. Levy, 'The Economic History of Sickness and Medical Benefit Since the Puritan Revolution', *Economic History Review*, Series 1, Vol. XIV, 1944, p. 147.

25 P. H. J. H. Gosden, *The Friendly Societies in England 1815–1875*, pp. 74–76.

26 E. P. Thompson, *op. cit.*, pp. 458, 460.

27 SCMPR 1844, Evidence of H. W. Rumsey, Esq., p. 536, Q.9078.

28 See Chapter 3, pp. 64–65 for more on the utilisation of friendly societies by overseers of the poor as a cheap form of medical relief.

29 Contribution Book of the Royal Shepherds Sanctuary, No. 99, Huddersfield, 1832–1881; Rules for the Royal Shepherds Order, No. 99, Branch of the Royal Foresters of Court Silence, n.d., Ms HPL (S/RS 4/1, 2/1); Independent Order of Oddfellows Manchester Unity Friendly Society Huddersfield District. Perseverance Lodge, c. 1846–1870 Contribution Book; Victory Lodge, 1875 Rule Book, Ms and Printed, HPL (KC45 10/9, 12/2).

30 Report from His Majesty's Commissioners for Inquiring into the Administration and Practical Operation of the Poor Laws, 1834 (1905 ed.), p. 232. Quoted in M. E. Rose, *Poor Law Administration in the West Riding of Yorkshire (1820–1855)*, p. 262.

31 Anon., *Observations on Friendly Societies* (Huddersfield, 1830), HPL (Local Pamphlets, Vol. 21).
32 Deighton Lodge of Oddfellows, No. 156, Misc. Correspondence, Ms HPL (Unclassified).
33 *HHEx*, 2 July, 1831.
34 49th AR HI, 1879–1880, p. 6.
35 H. Perkin, *op. cit.*, p. 381.
36 Two exceptions will be given in Sections 5.3 and 5.4 of societies which were partly supported and organised by the upper and middle classes, namely the Wakefield Female Benefit Society and the West Riding of Yorkshire Provident Society. Friendly societies enjoying patronage by the wealthy classes, however, seem to have been in a minority.
37 E. P. Thompson, *op. cit.*, p. 457.
38 Rules for the Regulation of a Friendly Society called A Free Gift instituted at Wakefield May 16th, 1808, p. 1, Ms WDA (JGC).
39 Rules of the Friendly Society of Oddwomen held at the Kirkgate Hotel in Wakefield in the County of York, n.d. Ms WDA (JGC).
40 Rules for the Regulation of a Friendly Society called A Free Gift, p. 22, Ms WDA (JGC).
41 Articles to be Observed by the Members of the Benevolent Brief, Holden at the House of Mr Thomas Huscroft, The Hammer and Hand, in Kirkgate, Wakefield, 1816, pp. 8, 11–12, WDA (Local Collection, Box 8).
42 For example, at the termination of sickness members were expected to send written notices to the officers of their friendly society, informing them of their recovery and thanking them for the allowances they had received. The notes forwarded by friendly society members differed little in tone from those sent to the governors of medical charities, giving thanks for treatment.
43 Certification of sickness by medical practitioners or other witnesses generally took the form used by Benjamin Hudson, surgeon to the Huddersfield Shepherds Sanctuary, No. 99, dated 14 March, 1837: 'I hereby certify that John Walker is ill of an inflammatory fever from cold, and that he is entirely unable to do any kind of work. Benjn Hudson, surgeon'. Notices of illness of members of the Royal Shepherds Sanctuary, No. 99, Huddersfield, c. 1833–1879, Ms HPL (S/RS 3/2).
44 General Laws of the Golden Fleece Lodge, of Loyal Ancient Shepherds, Wakefield, n.d., p. 4, WDA (JGC).
45 Articles to be Observed by The Members of the Friendly Society at Almondbury. Revived the Twenty-fifth Day of July, 1810, p. 7, HPL (Tomlinson Collection).
46 Minute Book of the Wakefield Female Benefit Society, Committee Meeting, 9 April, 1810, Ms WDA (Local Collection W.334.7).
47 Rules for the Regulation of a Friendly Society called A Free Gift, p. 4, Ms WDA (JGC).
48 General Laws of the Golden Fleece Lodge, of Loyal Ancient Shepherds, Wakefield, p. 11, WDA (JGC).
49 Articles to be Observed by the Members of the Benevolent Brief, Wakefield, p. 9, WDA (Local Collection, Box 8).
50 Rules of the Friendly Society of Oddwomen, Ms WDA (JGC); Articles to be Observed by The Members of the Friendly Society at Almondbury, p. 6, HPL (Tomlinson Collection); General Laws of the Golden Fleece Lodge, of Loyal Ancient Shepherds, Wakefield, p. 3, WDA (JGC).
51 Rules for the Regulation of a Friendly Society called A Free Gift, p. 3, Ms WDA (JGC).
52 Minute Book of the Wakefield Female Benefit Society, Committee Meetings, 12 January, 1818, 30 June, 1831, Ms WDA (Local Collection W.334.7).
53 For example, in 1811 it was ordered 'That the President do pay Francis Paget of Pot ovens a Beneficiary member in consideration of her Lying in of Twins, the sum of five shillings as a Donation out of the Private Fund'. Again in 1812, one guinea was paid out of the private fund to Mary Tyson, a beneficiary member,

who had been ill for a considerable time, but who had neglected to apply for the relief she was entitled to. *Ibid.*, Committee Meetings, 8 July, 1811, 13 July, 1812.

54 Rules of the Huddersfield Co-operative Trading Friendly Society, Established, April 20, 1829. Revised and Enrolled April 12th, 1838, especially pp. 13–15, HPL (Misc. Pamph: Co-op. Trading Friendly Society).

55 Rules of the West Riding of Yorkshire Provident Society, 1857, p. 7, HPL (Unclassified).

56 Prince Albert Lodge of the Ancient Order of Druids, Thurstonland, Sick Rules, 1856–1863, pp. 5–6, Ms HPL (S/TD 4).

57 Articles to be Observed by The Members of the Friendly Society at Almondbury, p. 8, HPL (Tomlinson Collection).

58 Rules of the West Riding of Yorkshire Provident Society, 1857, p. 8, HPL (Unclassified).

59 Deighton Lodge of Oddfellows, No. 156, Misc. Correspondence, Ms HPL (Unclassified).

60 P. H. J. H. Gosden, *The Friendly Societies in England 1815–1875*, p. 143. See Chapter 3 for a discussion of Poor Law medical relief in the area.

61 SCMPR 1844, Evidence of H. W. Rumsey, Esq., p. 536, Q.9086.

62 SCMR 1854, Evidence of Joseph Ellison, Esq., p. 169, Q.2606.

63 SCMPR 1844, Evidence of H. W. Rumsey, Esq., p. 536, Q.9086.

64 For an example of a conflict between two Wakefield surgeons in competition for friendly society appointments, see Chapter 8, pp. 312–313.

65 *PMD*, 1852, 1860, 1870.

66 P. S. Brown, 'The vicissitudes of herbalism in late nineteenth- and early twentieth-century Britain', *Medical History*, Vol. 29, No. 1, January, 1985, p. 86.

67 The rules of the Huddersfield Infirmary, for instance, provided that any officer of a society on subscribing three guineas annually could have on the books one in-patient or two out-patients at a time, provided an engagement was entered into to remove any such patient on notice being given, or to take away the body or to pay the funeral expenses in the case of death. Rules and Regulations of the Huddersfield and Upper Agbrigg Infirmary, 1834, p. 8, HPL (B.362).

68 1st, 24th and 34th ARs HI, 1831–1832, 1855–1856, 1865–1866.

69 Minute Book of the Huddersfield Infirmary, Vol. II, Meetings of the Monthly Board, 3 January, 1859, p. 358 and 5 November, 1866, p. 510.

70 72nd and 79th ARs WI, 1858–1859, 1865–1866. If a member of a club which did not subscribe to the infirmaries was admitted as a patient, he was normally expected to make a contribution towards his keep while receiving treatment. In 1833, for example, the committee of the Huddersfield Infirmary inquired into the case of George Brook, an in-patient, who was found to have 6s a week coming in from a friendly society. It was resolved that he pay 3s a week to the Infirmary as long as he remained an in-patient. Minute Book of the Huddersfield Infirmary, Vol. I, Meeting of the Infirmary Committee, 4 February, 1833, p. 318.

71 Royal Shepherds Sanctuary, No. 99, Huddersfield, Treasurer's Book, 1832–1870; Notices of illness of members, Ms HPL (S/RS 4/2, 3/2).

72 Wakefield British Friendly Union Society, Annual Report, No. 20, 1861–1862, WDA (Local Collection, Box 2C).

73 Deighton Lodge of Oddfellows, No. 156, Misc. Correspondence (especially doctors' notes), Ms HPL (Unclassified).

74 Grand United Order of Oddfellows, Charity Lodge, No. 97, Cleckheaton, Membership Book, 1824–1839 (Sick Brothers list); First to Eighth Annual Reports, 1863–1871, Ms and Printed, HPL (S/CL 12, 15).

75 For example, Col. J. C. D. Charlesworth and J. Barff of Wakefield, and T. P. Crosland, Esq. and George Armitage of Huddersfield. John Barff and George Armitage were both important woollen merchants and manufacturers. T. P. Crosland was an MP for Huddersfield and an eminent man in the affairs of the town. J. C. D. Charlesworth was one of the largest coal proprietors in the West Riding, also playing an active role in the public and political affairs of Wakefield. For more on Crosland and Charlesworth, see Appendix 7.

76 Rules of the West Riding of Yorkshire Provident Society, 1857; Abstract of the Tables of the West Riding Provident Society, c. 1857, HPL (Unclassified). In the same period the wages of the best-paid workers in the textile industry, the slubbers, averaged 27s per week in the Leeds area. Meanwhile, most other adult male textile workers received something in the region of 15s to 24s a week. E. Baines, *Account of the Woollen Manufacture of England*, p. 93. For more on wages in the woollen industry, see Chapter 2, Section 2.4.

77 Abstract of Returns of Sickness and Mortality, and of Reports of Assets, etc., of Friendly Societies in England and Wales, during the Five Years ending 31st December 1850, PP, 1852–1853, C (31). For details of mortality and sickness rates amongst different classes of occupation, based on friendly society returns, see H. Ratcliffe, *Observations on the rate of mortality and sickness existing amongst friendly societies* (Manchester, 1850) in W. Farr, *Mortality in Mid 19th Century Britain* (reprinted, with an introduction by R. Wall, Amersham, 1974).

78 QRSM 1880.

79 First Report of the Commissioners for Inquiring into the State of Large Towns and Populous Districts, PP, 1844, XVII (572), Report on the Sanatary Condition of Preston by the Rev. J. Clay, p. 48. These figures compare with an average of 9.1 work-days lost per man per year (in employment) in the UK due to illness or injury in 1971. For skilled and unskilled manufacturers the rate was higher, 9.3 and 18.4 days respectively. *Encyclopaedia of Occupational Health and Safety* (3rd ed., Geneva, 1983), Vol. I, p. 7.

80 See, for example, P. H. J. H. Gosden, *The Friendly Societies in England 1815–1875*, pp. 94–114.

81 Wakefield British Friendly Union Society, Annual Report, No. 20, 1861–1862, WDA (Local Collection, Box 2C); Prince Albert Lodge of the Ancient Order of Druids, Thurstonland, Annual Reports, 1872–1873, 1875–1876, HPL (S/TD 10).

82 B. B. Gilbert, *op. cit.*, p. 171.

83 *Ibid.*, pp. 167–180, for reasons for the decline of friendly societies during the last quarter of the nineteenth century.

Chapter 6

1 See Chapter 7, Section 7.1 for details of the numbers and practices of 'regular' medical practitioners in Wakefield and Huddersfield.

2 R. Porter, 'Quacks: An Unconscionable Time Dying', unpublished paper, Wellcome Institute for the History of Medicine, London, 1983, p. 1.

3 With the exception perhaps of the chemists and druggists, who were slowly organising and taking on some features of a professional group by the second half of the nineteenth century. The setting up of the Pharmaceutical Society in 1841, the establishment of the *Pharmaceutical Journal*, and the development of uniform standards of training and examination, which became compulsory under the 1868 Pharmacy Act, were important aspects of this process. For more on these developments, see G. E. Trease, *Pharmacy in History* (1964). Friendly societies and sick clubs offered an 'alternative' source of medical treatment, in the sense that they were substitutes for the relief supplied by agencies of the wealthy, a form of self-help on the part of the working classes. But the friendly society and medical club differed in a fundamental way from other alternative forms, in that the treatment made available by these organisations was given by a qualified member of the medical profession. For this reason, friendly societies have been discussed separately in Chapter 5.

4 The amount spent on Poor Law medical relief before 1834 in the North was estimated as being one-sixth of that spent in Southern and Midland counties. SCMPR 1844, Evidence of G. C. Lewis, p. 9, Q.13.

5 'Quackery in the Manufacturing Districts', *The Lancet*, 1857, Vol. II, p. 326.

6 C. Huddersfield, 1851, Wakefield, 1861; *LM*, 1 June, 1839.

7 1841 Census, Occupation Abstract, PP, 1844, XXVII (587).

8 E. M. Sigsworth and P. Swan, 'Para-medical provision in the West Riding', *The Society for the Social History of Medicine Bulletin*, 29 December, 1981, pp. 37–39. These figures compare dramatically with evidence given on the extent of unqualified practice in a district of Lincolnshire in 1806. In a district which included five market towns there were five physicians, eleven surgeon–apothecaries, five druggists, forty unqualified practitioners and 63 midwives. E. Harrison, *Remarks on the Ineffective State of the Practice of Physic in Great Britain* (1806), pp. 38–39. Cited in S. W. F. Holloway, 'Medical Education in England, 1830–1858: A Sociological Analysis', *History*, Vol. 49, 1964, p. 313. For a comparison with a still earlier period, see M. Pelling and C. Webster, 'Medical Practitioners' in C. Webster (ed.), *Health, Medicine and Mortality in the Sixteenth Century* (Cambridge, 1979), pp. 165–235.

9 For a complete listing of the trade directories referred to, see Bibliography.

10 Baines, 1822; C. Wakefield and Huddersfield, 1861.

11 White, 1847; White, 1866.

12 C. Wakefield and Huddersfield, 1841, 1861.

13 White, 1861; C. Huddersfield, 1861.

14 Huddersfield Town Book, 1784–1793, Ms HPL (P/HU/M). The reference is presumably to one of the Taylor family of Whitworth, Lancashire, who were famed throughout the North for their bonesetting and other surgical skills for much of the eighteenth and nineteenth centuries. Later in the nineteenth century some of the Whitworth Taylors obtained licences in medicine and surgery; others (including some of their wives, who also practised) remained unqualified. All were 'unorthodox' in their methods of treatment. For an account of the activities of the Taylor family, see J. L. West, *The Taylors of Lancashire. Bonesetters and Doctors 1750–1890* (Worsley 1977).

15 Mirfield Town Book, 1717–1795, Ms HPL (P/M).

16 Township of Mirfield, Overseers Accounts, 1805–1826, Ms HPL (P/M). The practice of granting lump sums to paupers for medical treatment dated back a long way. In 1662, for example, the Yorkshire magistrates ordered a voluntary collection to be made in parish churches to enable a poor Wakefield widow 'afflicted with the evil' to be sent to London to be touched by the king. S. H. Waters, *op. cit.*, pp. 62–63. See Chapter 3, Section 3.1 for further examples of the employment of fringe personnel by the overseers of the poor.

17 G. Wilson, 'On the State of the medical Profession in England, and on Quackery in the manufacturing Districts', *The Lancet*, 1854, Vol. I, p. 458.

18 R. J. Cooter, 'Phrenology and British alientists, c. 1825–1845', Part I, 'Converts to a doctrine', *Medical History*, Vol. 20, No. 1, January, 1976, pp. 4–5, 17.

19 D. Alexander, MD, *A Lecture on Phrenology*, WDA (Local Collection, Box 14).

20 *HHE*, 24 and 31 July, 1852.

21 R. Porter, 'Lay medical knowledge in the eighteenth century: the evidence of the *Gentleman's Magazine*', *Medical History*, Vol. 29, No. 2, April, 1985, p. 138.

22 A. K. Jacques, *op. cit.*

23 R. Aldington, *The Strange Life of Charles Waterton 1782–1865* (1949), p. 35. Waterton was an acknowledged eccentric, whose exploits were also recorded in E. Sitwell, *The English Eccentrics* (1933), pp. 262–285.

24 Letter to George Ord, 24 October, 1847. In R. A. Irwin (ed.), *Letters of Charles Waterton of Walton Hall, near Wakefield* (1955), p. 64.

25 This action resulted in a verbal conflict with Henry Horsfall, a Wakefield surgeon, following the death of a patient he had been called to visit. The patient had declined to seek medical assistance, continuing to rely on Waterton's powders, which he believed to be infallible. Horsfall sharply attacked Waterton for his interference. The final upshot, however, was that Horsfall was forced to apologise for his remarks in order to avoid a legal suit. Waterton's wealth and position apparently excused his dabblings into medical practice, a crime not so easily pardoned in the case of the less fortunate quack doctor. *LM*, 8 September, 1849, Supplement.

26 J. Hirst, *Notable Things of various Subjects, 1836–c.1892*, Ms HPL (Diary: Ms/f).

27 J. Woodhead, *Netherthong, recipe book, 1818*, Ms HPL (KC 190/1). For more on folk healing practices, see, for example, K. Thomas, *Religion and the Decline of Magic* (1971), Chapter 7; J. Camp, *Magic, Myth and Medicine* (1973); W. Henderson, *Notes on the Folk-Lore of the Northern Counties of England and the Borders* (1879), Chapter 5.

28 *WS*, 20 July, 1804.

29 *WJ*, 4 January, 1839.

30 *WE*, 7 April, 1855.

31 R. Porter, 'Lay medical knowledge in the eighteenth century', pp. 149, 141.

32 W. Buchan, *Domestic medicine; or the Family Physician* (Edinburgh, 1769). The first edition of the book was priced just 6s. The success of the book was immediate and great: nineteen large editions, amounting to at least 80,000 copies, were sold in Great Britain in the author's lifetime alone (1729–1805). For more on W. Buchan and the background to his work, see C. J. Lawrence, 'William Buchan: medicine laid open', *Medical History*, Vol. 19, No. 1, January, 1975, pp. 20–35.

33 Anon., *The Villager's Friend & Physician: Or, A Familiar Address on the Preservation of Health, and the Removal of Disease on its first Appearance; Supposed to be Delivered by a village Apothecary* (Huddersfield, 1811) (first published under the authorship of J. Parkinson in 1804), HPL (Local Pamphlets, Vol. 20).

34 D. Alexander, MD, *An Answer to the Enquiry, if it be the duty of Every Person to study the preservation of his Health, what means are the most likely to answer that end, and to which recourse may be had by all Classes of People?* (Manchester, 1804), Wellcome Institute Library.

35 *Ibid.*, pp. 26–27.

36 *The Villager's Friend & Physician*, p. 39, HPL (Local Pamphlets, Vol. 20).

37 T. G. Wright, MD, *A Lecture on Quack Medicines, Delivered to the Wakefield Mechanics' Institution, February 20th, 1843* (London and Wakefield, 1843), Wellcome Institute Library.

38 M. A. Jagger, *op. cit.*, pp. 100–101.

39 J. Sykes, *Slawit in the 'Sixties* (Huddersfield and London, n.d., c. 1926), pp. 127–128.

40 *Ibid.*, p. 130.

41 For the most thorough history of midwives to date, see J. Donnison, *Midwives and Medical Men* (1977). See also E. Shorter, *A History of Women's Bodies* (1983), especially Chapters 3 and 4.

42 Huddersfield Town Book, 1784–1793, Ms HPL (P/HU/M); Township of Mirfield, Overseers Accounts, 1772–1803, Ms HPL (P/M); Account Book of the Overseers of the Poor of South Crosland, 1790–1801, Ms HPL (CP/SC/OP).

43 See Chapter 3, Section 3.2.

44 Township of Mirfield, Workhouse Diary and Account Book, 1777–1779; Township of Mirfield, Overseers Accounts, 1772–1803, Ms HPL (P/M). For female practitioners, see A. L. Wyman, 'The surgeoness: the female practitioner of surgery 1400–1800', *Medical History*, Vol. 28, No. 1, January, 1984, pp. 22–41.

45 Letter to George Ord, 25 April, 1851. In R. A. Irwin (ed.), *op. cit.*, p. 82; G. Phelps, *Squire Waterton* (Wakefield, 1976), p. 132.

46 Callus – hard tissue, formed at the site of a broken bone, which is gradually converted into new bone.

47 G. Phelps, *op. cit.*, pp. 132–133.

48 Letter to George Ord, 31 May, 1851. In R. A. Irwin (ed.), *op. cit.*, pp. 83–84.

49 The literature on quack medicine is limited and concentrates on the most famous or rather notorious quack doctors, James Graham, 'Chevalier' John Taylor, Sally Mapp, Dr Solomon, etc. See, for example, E. Maple, *Magic, Medicine and Quackery* (1968).

50 J. Sykes, *op. cit.*, p. 129.

51 *LM*, 28 August, 1847.

52 *WRH*, 6 April, 1836.

53 *LM*, 4 May, 1850.

54 *Northern Star*, 4 April, 1840; *LM*, 1 June, 1839.
55 For example, the Royal College of Surgeon's dental licence was not created until 1859. In the same year the first dental school was set up in England, and by 1900 there were eleven schools throughout the country. Between 1841 and 1881 the number of dentists in England increased from 522 to 3,583. For more on the professionalisation of dentistry, see E. G. Forbes, 'The professionalization of dentistry in the United Kingdom', *Medical History*, Vol. 29, No. 2, April, 1985, pp. 169–181.
56 *WS*, 19 April, 1810.
57 *WJ*, 12 March, 1841.
58 *LM*, 13 and 20 January, 1849.
59 *LM*, 6 November, 1841.
60 *LM*, 1 June, 1839.
61 *HHEx*, 5 March, 1831.
62 *WE*, 6 May, 1854.
63 Cases of malpractice involving fringe practitioners have been discussed in connection with the medical profession's opposition to the unqualified in Chapter 8, pp. 322–324.
64 *The Lancet*, 1857, Vol. II, pp. 282–283; West Riding Quarter Sessions Indictment Book, March, 1857–January, 1858, Leeds Sessions, 20 October, 1857, pp. 236–238, Ms WYCRO (Q54/86).
65 P. S. Brown, 'Herbalists and medical Botanists in mid-Nineteenth-Century Britain with special Reference to Bristol', *Medical History*, Vol. 26, No. 4, October, 1982, pp. 405–420.
66 A. I. Coffin, *The Botanic Guide to Health* (5th ed., Manchester, 1846). Another very popular handbook was W. Fox, MD, *The Working Man's Model Family Botanic Guide or Every Man His Own Doctor* (11th ed., Sheffield, 1887). Fox's book, like many other guides, set out the main principles of botanic practice and the most useful methods of treating common ailments in easily comprehensible terms.
67 J. V. Pickstone, 'Medical Botany (Self-Help Medicine in Victorian England)', *Memoires of the Manchester Literary and Philosophical Society*, No. 119, 1976–77, p. 90.
68 A. I. Coffin, *op. cit.*, pp. 333–334.
69 *HE*, 9 January, 1864, 25 March, 1865; *Tindall's Huddersfield Directory and Year Book, for 1866*, p. 222.
70 C. Huddersfield, 1861; White, 1861.
71 *HE*, 13 July, 1861.
72 *HE*, 2 March, 1861.
73 *HE*, 13 July, 1861.
74 *HE*, 16 May, 1868.
75 John Pickstone also dates the decline of medical botany to the 1860s. The father of Jesse Boot was a follower of Coffinism and a Wesleyan lay preacher, devoted to good works. It is symptomatic that Jesse Boot converted his father's business into a proprietary medicine store, retailing medicines by modern methods. J. V. Pickstone, 'Medical Botany', pp. 94–95. For the future progress of medical botany and herbalism, see P. S. Brown, 'The vicissitudes of herbalism in late ninteenth- and early twentieth-century Britain, pp. 71-92.
76 See, for example, W. Addison, *English Spas* (1951); P. J. N. Havins, *The Spas of England* (1976).
77 M. A. Jagger, *op. cit.*, p. 168; *WE*, 16 December, 1939; E. N. Steele, *Glimpses of Stanley's Past* (Wakefield, 1974), p. 34, WDA.
78 J. W. Walker, *op. cit.*, p. 523.
79 J. Smedley, *Practical Hydropathy* (4th ed., 1861), p. iii. Smedley, a hosiery manufacturer, was proprietor of the Matlock Hydro, one of the chief nineteenth-century hydropathic establishments. For more on hydropathic techniques, see R. Price, 'Hydropathy in England 1840–70', *Medical History*, Vol. 25, No. 3, July, 1981, pp. 269–280.
80 *LM*, 18 August, 1832.

81 A. B. Granville, *Spas of England. 1: the North* (1841, reprinted Bath, 1971), p. 37.
82 A. K. Jacques, *op. cit.*, pp. 156–158, 163.
83 Misc. Medical Bills to Mr Whitely of Wakefield. The Spa Hydropathic Establishment, Ilkley, 25 August, 1884, WDA (JGC).
84 D. F. E. Sykes, *op. cit.*, pp. 404–405.
85 *HHEx*, 14 May, 1831.
86 A. B. Granville, *op. cit.*, p. 405.
87 *HE*, 1 May, 1852, 18 May, 1860.
88 E. Parsons, *op. cit.*, Vol. II, p. 395; C. P. Hobkirk, *op. cit.*, p. 10.
89 J. Sykes, *op cit.*, p. 157.
90 *HE*, 18 May, 1861.
91 *HE*, 1 May, 1852; J. Sykes, *op. cit.*, p. 158.
92 Baines, 1822; White, 1837.
93 A. B. Granville, *op. cit.*, p. 406.
94 *Ibid.*, pp. 406–407.
95 Minute Book of the Huddersfield Infirmary, Vol. II, Meeting of the Monthly Board, 5 September, 1853, p. 251.
96 *HE*, 4 June, 1870.
97 See, for example, J. Lowerson and J. Myerscough, *Time to Spare in Victorian England* (Hassocks, Sussex, 1977), Chapter 2; J. Walvin, *Beside the Seaside: A Social History of the Popular Seaside Holiday* (1978); J. K. Walton, *The English Seaside Resort. A Social History 1750–1914* (Leicester, 1983), especially Chapter 2.
98 J. K. Walker, MD, *Reasons for Establishing a Sea Bathing Infirmary, on the Western Coast, for the Benefit of the Poor* (Huddersfield, 1840), HPL (Misc. Pamph: Sea Bathing Infirmary).
99 For more information on these developments, see, for example, B. Hamilton, 'The Medical Professions in the Eighteenth Century', *Economic History Review*, 2nd Series, Vol. IV, No. 2, 1951, pp. 159–169; S. W. F. Holloway, 'The Apothecaries' Act, 1815: A Reinterpretation', Parts I and II, *Medical History*, Vol. 10, Nos 2 and 3, April and July, 1966, pp. 107–129, 221–236; G. E. Trease, *op. cit.*, pp. 169–174, 181–182, 185–189; Kremers and Urdang, *History of Pharmacy* (4th ed., Philadelphia, 1976), pp. 102–117.
100 T. Dyson, *op. cit.*, p. 467; White, 1837, 1870.
101 'Unqualified Medical Practitioners', *Medical Times and Gazette*, 1853, Vol. II, p. 143.
102 *WS*, 5 January, 1810; *WJ*, 6 October, 1842.
103 In the 1830s and 1840s a good class family business in Highgate, which dispensed prescriptions for several eminent London doctors, including four Presidents of the Royal College of Surgeons, found it necessary to prescribe for customers and to sell a range of non-pharmaceutical goods in order to make a profit. Even a large business concern like this was making up only an average of 350 prescriptions per annum in the 1830s. A. E. Bailey, 'Early nineteenth century pharmacy', *Pharmaceutical Journal*, Vol. 185, 1960, pp. 208–212.
104 *WS*, 20 July, 1804; *WJ*, 13 December, 1850; *WE*, 27 May, 1854.
105 White, 1853.
106 *WE*, 3 June, 1854.
107 The township populations were considered to constitute a fair basis of comparison as most chemists and druggists' shops were situated within the township boundaries, in fact, usually in the town centres. Meanwhile, most of the outlying villages, especially the larger ones, had their own chemists' shops. In 1866, for example, the village of Meltham, situated five miles from Huddersfield, had one druggist's shop for its population of 4,046. Horbury, just two and a half miles from Wakefield, with only 3,246 inhabitants, supported three druggists' shops in 1866 (1 : 1 082). White, 1866. Most towns in England recorded an improvement in the ratio of chemists' shops to the population in the first half of the nineteenth century. A survey of eight provincial and manufacturing towns resulted in a figure of one shop for every 1,720 people in 1850. D. Alexander, *Retailing in England during the Industrial Revolution* (1970), p. 101.

108 'The Pharmaceutical Society and the Medical profession', *Medical Times and Gazette*, 1853, Vol. I, p. 60.

109 SCMPR 1844, Evidence of H. W. Rumsey, Esq., p. 547, Q.9121.

110 G. Wilson, *op cit.*, *The Lancet*, 1854, Vol. I, p. 458.

111 See V. Berridge and G. Edwards, *Opium and the People* (1981); V. Berridge, 'Opium Over the Counter in Nineteenth Century England', *Pharmacy in History*, Vol. 20, No. 3, 1978, pp. 91–100.

112 Second Report of the Commissioners for inquiring into the State of Large Towns and Populous Districts, PP, 1845, XVIII (602), p. 5. For the dosing of infants with opiates, see also M. Hewitt, *Wives and Mothers in Victorian Industry* (1958), Chapter X.

113 In 1845 Dr Lyon Playfair described how far the practice of purchasing opium preparations had extended among the working classes of Lancashire. Three druggists in one district of Manchester, '. . . all of acknowledged respectability . . .', sold a total of nine gallons of laudanum weekly. A surgeon based in Wigan, who also kept a druggist's shop, certified to Playfair '. . . that he is in the habit of selling various preparations of opium under the forms of infants' mixture, Godfrey's cordial, paregoric elixirs, and laudanum; also, crude opium, combined with other substances, according to popular receipes'. *Ibid.*, (610), App., Part II, Dr L. Playfair, Report on the Sanatory Condition of the Large Towns in Lancashire, pp. 62, 65.

114 First Report of the Commissioners for Inquiring into the State of Large Towns and Populous Districts, PP, 1844, XVII (572), App., J. R. Coulthart, Esq., Report upon the Sanatory Condition of the Town of Ashton-under-Lyne, pp. 78–80.

115 T. G. Wright, MD, *A Lecture on Quack Medicines*, p. 26, Wellcome Institute Library.

116 For more on abortion as a form of birth control in the manufacturing districts, particularly in the late nineteenth century, see P. Knight, 'Women and Abortion in Victorian and Edwardian England' and A. McLaren, 'Women's Work and Regulation of Family Size: the question of abortion in the nineteenth century', both in *History Workshop*, No. 4, Autumn, 1977, pp. 57–68, 70–81.

117 *LM*, 8 June, 1839.

118 *WHJ*, 19 January, 1827.

119 *HE*, 28 July, 1860.

120 *WS*, 2 February, 1810.

121 *WHJ*, 16 November, 1832.

122 For an interesting survey of the vendors of patent medicines in the Bath area, see P. S. Brown, 'The vendors of medicines advertised in Eighteenth-Century Bath Newspapers', *Medical History*, Vol. 19, No. 4, October, 1975, pp. 352–368 and 'Medicines advertised in Eighteenth-Century Bath Newspapers', *Medical History*, Vol. 20, No. 2, April, 1976, pp. 152–168.

123 *WJ*, 17 May, 1839.

124 *Pharmaceutical Journal and Transactions*, Vol. 5, 1845–1846, p. 193. Quoted in J. K. Crellin, 'The Growth of Professionalism in Nineteenth-Century British Pharmacy', *Medical History*, Vol. 11, 1967, p. 223.

125 *WHJ*, 16 February, 1816, 12 January, 1827.

126 *William's Directory of the Borough of Huddersfield* (1845), p. 15.

127 *Pharmaceutical Journal and Transactions*, Vol. 3, 1843–1844, p. 101. Quoted in J. K. Crellin, *op. cit.*, p. 222.

128 C. Wakefield and Huddersfield, 1871.

129 *WJ*, 25 October, 1850.

130 *WHJ*, 7 January, 1820.

131 *WE*, 24 October, 1868; *HE*, 1 January, 1870.

132 M. Ramsey, 'Medical Power and Popular Medicine: Illegal Healers in Nineteenth-Century France' in P. Branca (ed.), *The Medicine Show*, p. 192.

133 T. G. Wright, MD, *A Lecture on Quack Medicines*, p. 10, Wellcome Institute Library. For the medical profession's campaign against quack medicine, see Chapter 8, pp. 322–327.

134 'Quackery in the Manufacturing Districts', *The Lancet*, 1857, Vol. II, p. 326.
135 *William's Directory* (1845), p. 15.
136 *LM*, 4 January, 1840.
137 The continued usage of self-medication in Britain to date is illustrated, for example, by a survey made in 1972, where over a two-week period the ratio among adults of self-prescribed to prescribed medicines was roughly two to one. Two-thirds of the sample had taken a self-prescribed medicine during the period, while about 41 per cent had taken 'aspirin or other pain-killers'. Nineteen per cent of babies had been given 'an indigestion remedy or gripe water'. K. Dunnell and A. Cartwright, *Medicine Takers, Prescribers and Hoarders* (1972). Cited in V. Berridge and G. Edwards, *op. cit.*, p. 238. Another survey made in the 1970s claimed that only one person in four experiencing symptoms or feeling unwell sought medical advice. In the UK 40 per cent of the population had regular recourse to pain-killers, only 10 per cent of these on prescription. J. Camp, *op. cit.*, p. 60.
138 For the cost of regular and fringe medical care as financed out of the poor rate, see Chapter 3, Section 3.1.

Chapter 7

1 With the important exception of M. J. Peterson's study of the mid-Victorian medical profession in London (1858–1886). M. J. Peterson, *op. cit.*
2 For discussions of this aspect of medical life, see, for example, W. D. Foster, 'Dr William Henry Cook: The Finances of a Victorian General Practitioner', *Proc. Royal Society of Medicine*, Vol. 66, January, 1973, pp. 46–50; I. S. L. Loudon, 'A Doctor's Cash Book: The Economy of General Practice in the 1830s', *Medical History*, Vol. 27, No. 3, July, 1983, pp. 249–268; M. J. Peterson, *op. cit.*, Chapter 5.
3 Again with the exception of the work of Ian Inkster, which analyses the efforts of early nineteenth-century Sheffield medical men to legitimise their professional and social status through social action. I. Inkster, 'Marginal Men: Aspects of the Social Role of the Medical Community in Sheffield 1790–1850' in J. Woodward and D. Richards (eds), *op. cit.*, pp. 128–163. For more on Inkster's arguments, see Chapter 8, Section 8.2.
4 S. F. Simmons, *Medical Register for the Year 1780*, pp. 160, 165.
5 Baines, 1822; White, 1853, 1861, 1870. To some extent this decline was offset by the tendency for a small number of medical men to take up residence in suburbs and villages outside the Townships, and who, therefore, fall out of the range of this survey. This tendency, as shown pp. 287–290, was more prevalent in Huddersfield.
6 See Chapter 2, Section 2.1 for the population growth of the two towns. This fits in with the general tendency for the number of qualified medical men to decline following the passing of the 1858 Medical Act, which tightened up recruitment. Between 1861 and 1881 the number of qualified practitioners increased by just 676 from 14,415 to 15,091 in 1881. This represented an increase of less than 5 per cent compared with a 29 per cent rise in the population during the same period. I. Waddington, 'Competition and monopoly in a profession. The campaign for medical registration in Britain', *Amsterdams Sociologisch Tijdschrift*, No. 2, October, 1979, p. 314.
7 1841 Census, Occupation Abstract, PP, 1844, XXVII (587).
8 Excluding the 83 individuals recorded as being under twenty years of age. Presumably most of these were as yet unqualified (although lack of formal qualifications did not entirely preclude the practice of medicine). The usual age of qualification for Wakefield and Huddersfield medical men was between the ages of 21 and 25. C. Wakefield and Huddersfield, 1841, 1851, 1861, 1871; *PMD* 1847–1872.
9 The figures cited for Wakefield and Huddersfield differ from those given in Tables 7.1. The discrepancies can be explained by the fact that trade and medical

directories were also utilised to arrive at the number of practitioners in Tables 7.1, which hopefully gives a more accurate computation of the number of doctors practising in the towns.

10 E. M. Sigsworth and P. Swan, *op. cit.*, pp. 37–39.

11 H. Clarkson, *Memories of Merry Wakefield* (1887, reprinted Wakefield, 1969, from the 2nd ed., published in 1889), pp. 166–167.

12 See pp. 287–290 for more on the residential patterns of Wakefield and Huddersfield medical practitioners.

13 *The Journal of Dr John Simpson of Bradford, 1825*, ed. E. Willmott (Bradford, 1981).

14 R. Aldington, *op. cit.*; G. Phelps, *op. cit.*

15 Meanwhile, many of the larger villages in the Wakefield and Huddersfield areas had their own resident medical attendants. In 1847 Horbury, situated two miles from Wakefield and with a population of just 2,500, had one resident surgeon, Mr William Walker Kemp. Meltham, six miles from Huddersfield, with a population of 3,262, had two resident surgeons, Messrs Eastwood and Rawcliffe. Mirfield, lying midway between Wakefield and Huddersfield, had four surgeons for its 6,919 inhabitants in 1847 (1:1730). White, 1847.

16 See Chapter 2 for the economies and social make-up of Wakefield and Huddersfield.

17 By the late 1850s consultants, that is, those specialising in a medical or surgical practice, charged upwards of three guineas per visit compared with the general practitioner's charge of between 5s and 10s. *The Lancet*, 1858, Vol. I, p. 78. Cited in F. B. Smith, *op. cit.*, p. 369.

18 J. Lane, 'The medical practitioners of provincial England in 1783', *Medical History*, Vol. 28, No. 4, October, 1984, pp. 361–362.

19 *The Journal of Dr John Simpson of Bradford, 1825,* p. 13. The 'Peace' he refers to is that arranged at the Congress of Vienna in 1815, which brought the Napoleonic Wars to an end.

20 G. Wilson, *op. cit.*, *The Lancet*, 1854, Vol. I, p. 458.

21 *WS*, 24 February, 1809; *WJ*, 6 October, 1842. This seems to have been a nationwide practice. In the early 1850s William Henry Cook of Tunbridge Wells (where there was one doctor to every 557 persons) set aside his mornings for seeing poor patients gratis. In 1856 he instituted the practice of charging 6d per consultation, and within two months his morning practice had completely dissolved. W. D. Foster, *op. cit.*, pp. 47–48.

22 Huddersfield Medical Society. Minute Book, 1825–1834. Medical Regulations dated 1825, p. 1, Ms HRI. See Chapter 8, Section 8.1 for more on the activities of the Huddersfield Medical Society.

23 For careers in general practice in London, see M. J. Peterson, *op. cit.*, Chapter 3.

24 *WS*, 27 January, 1809.

25 *WHJ*, 2 March, 1832; *PMD*, 1848.

26 *WHJ*, 29 November, 1822.

27 The stock of drugs and all fixtures and instruments were to be divided between the two. William Holdsworth was empowered to receive for his own use all debts owed to the partnership. He was also to deliver to George Holdsworth a bond to pay £154 10s payable with interest at 4 per cent. Articles of agreem[t] made this 28 day of April 1837 Bet[n] Geo. Holdsworth of Wakef[d] in the Co. of York Surgeon & Apothecary Wm. Holdsworth of the same place Surgeon & Apothecary, Ms WDA (JGC).

28 *PMD*, 1848, C. Wakefield, 1841. For more on Henry Dunn, see Chapter 8, pp. 359–360.

29 M. J. Peterson, *op. cit.*, p. 12.

30 Holloway suggests that as early as the mid-eighteenth century the apothecary had assumed the functions of a general practitioner of medicine. The majority of town apothecaries and practically all those with country practices attended patients of the poorer and lower middle classes, prescribing and supplying medicines to them. S. W. F. Holloway, 'The Apothecaries' Act, 1815', Part I, p. 107. See also I. S. L. Loudon, 'The nature of provincial medical practice in eighteenth-century

England', *Medical History*, Vol. 29, No. 1, January, 1985, pp. 1–32. For similarities with medical practice in a still earlier period, see M. Pelling and C. Webster, *op. cit.*

31 M. J. Peterson, *op. cit.*, p. 8.

32 *Ibid.*, pp. 10–11; Report from the Select Committee on Medical Education, PP, 1834, XIII (602) (hereafter referred to as SCME 1834), Part III, Society of Apothecaries, Evidence of John Ridout, Member of the Society of Apothecaries and Court of Examiners, p. 72, Q. 1003.

33 J. W. Wilcock, *The Laws Relating to the Medical Profession* (1830), pp. 30–31. Quoted in I. Waddington, 'General Practitioners and Consultants in Early Nineteenth-Century England: The Sociology of an Intra-Professional Conflict' in J. Woodward and D. Richards (eds), *op. cit.*, p. 165.

34 I. S. L. Loudon, 'The nature of provincial medical practice in eighteenth-century England', p. 1.

35 J. Lane, 'The medical practitioners of provincial England in 1783', pp. 354–355.

36 SCME 1834, Part III, Evidence of John Nussey, Master of the Apothecaries' Company and Apothecary to the King's Household, p. 1, Q. 12.

37 I. S. L. Loudon, 'A Doctor's Cash Book: The Economy of General Practice in the 1830s', p. 257.

38 SCME 1834, Part I, Royal College of Physicians, pp. 301–302, Q. 4384–4385.

39 Perhaps first suggested by Holloway in S. W. F. Holloway, 'Medical Education in England, 1830–1858'.

40 J. Lane, 'The Early History of General Practice, 1700–1850: Sources and Methods', *The Society for the Social History of Medicine Bulletin*, 30–31, June and December, 1982, pp. 19–21.

41 For a detailed discussion of the doctors' registration movement, see N. and J. Parry, *The Rise of the Medical Profession. A Study of Collective Social Mobility* (1976), Chapter 6 and I. Waddington, 'Competition and monopoly in a profession. The campaign for medical registration in Britain'. Waddington's paper stresses the monopolistic and anti-monopolistic elements of the campaign for registration.

42 I. Waddington, 'General Practitioners and Consultants in Early Nineteenth-Century England', pp. 164–188, especially pp. 170–173.

43 Only those who were in practice prior to 1815 were exempt from this obligation.

44 SCME 1834, Part II, Royal College of Surgeons, App. 44, p. 87.

45 First and Second Reports from the Select Committee on Medical Registration and Medical Law Amendment, PP, 1847–1848 (210), Q. 1215. Cited in I. Waddington, 'General Practitioners and Consultants in Early Nineteenth-Century England', p. 168.

46 C. Wakefield and Huddersfield, 1851; *PMD*, 1852.

47 *PMD*, 1848, 1860.

48 C. Wakefield and Huddersfield, 1851; *PMD*, 1852.

49 *Medical Register for the Year 1780; PMD*, 1848, 1860, 1870.

50 C. Wakefield and Huddersfield, 1871; *PMD*, 1872. The problem of reading too much into small samples is heightened by possible inaccuracies in the medical practitioners' returns to the *Medical Directories*. For example, many of those holding the LSA may not have acknowledged it. G. M. Stansfield remarked in 1856 that some holders of the LSA '. . . seem to be ashamed of it . . .' and did not mention it in their returns to the compilers of the *Medical Directories*. G. M. Stansfield, 'Statistical analysis of the medical profession in England and Wales', *Associated Medical Journal*, 1856, pp. 253–254. Cited in P. S. Brown, 'The Providers of Medical Treatment in Mid-Nineteenth-Century Bristol', *Medical History*, Vol. 24, No. 3, July, 1980, p. 302.

51 During the nineteenth century a large proportion of Wakefield and Huddersfield medical practitioners were educated and qualified in Scotland. Scottish universities offered higher standards of training, involving the study of medicine, surgery, anatomy, botany, pharmacy and midwifery. Indeed, they offered a more 'practical' training for those wishing to enter general practice. Of the nine MDs in practice in Huddersfield in 1861, seven were graduates of Scottish universities (and

Scottish MDs typically functioned as general practitioners). (The two others had qualified at Cambridge and New York.) Eight of the ten individuals with medical degrees or licences in Wakefield in the same year had received a Scottish training. By 1871 Scotland had taken over the lead from London as the most common place of training of *all* Wakefield and Huddersfield medical practitioners. Others received their medical educations in Cambridge, Ireland, Paris and Germany, and later in the century, Manchester and Leeds. Many practitioners had of course received their medical educations in a number of different universities, hospitals and medical schools. C. Wakefield and Huddersfield, 1861, 1871; *PMD*, 1862, 1872. For details of the places of training of Wakefield and Huddersfield medical practitioners, see Appendices 10 and 11.

52 C. Wakefield, 1851; *PMD*, 1860, 1870. See Appendix 11 for a biography of Holdsworth.

53 *WHJ*, 27 June, 1823, 4 January, 1833.

54 *WS*, 1 December, 1809; *WJ*, 5 January, 1810.

55 See Chapter 6, pp. 234–237 for the chemist's takeover of the dispensing business.

56 For example, the 1851 census returns for Huddersfield Township described Thomas Hick as 'practicing as an apothecary, but not a member of any college'. C. Huddersfield, 1851.

57 C. Wakefield and Huddersfield, 1841, 1851.

58 For example, the rules of the Wakefield Infirmary stipulated 'That no gentleman shall be considered eligible for the office of physician who has not obtained his degree or license in medicine, at one of the Universities or chartered colleges of the United Kingdom; or who practices surgery, or shall dispense his own medicines. And that no gentleman shall be eligible for the office of surgeon, who has not received a diploma from one of the Incorporated colleges of surgeons of the United Kingdom'. Rules and Regulations for The Government of the Wakefield General Dispensary and Clayton Hospital, 1854, p. 12, WYCRO (C235/1). The rules of the Huddersfield Infirmary were even more stringent, excluding from the office of physician all those who practised in the following branches of medicine: 'surgery, pharmacy, or midwifery; or who is in any way connected with such practice'. Rules and Regulations of the Huddersfield and Upper Agbrigg Infirmary, 1834, p. 10, HPL (B.362).

59 SCME 1834, Part I, p. 229, Q. 3534–3535.

60 Information on the total expenditure and the proportion of the middle-class family budget spent on medical care is limited. P. Branca gives some indication of expenditure on this item in samples of two budgets for families with incomes of £150 per annum, extracted from household manuals published in 1828 and 1874. In 1828 expenditure on illness and amusement (classified together!) was budgeted at £3 14s (2.5 per cent of total estimated expenditure). In 1874 the two items were estimated at £10 (6.7 per cent of expenditure). P. Branca, *Silent Sisterhood*, p. 26.

61 A. K. Jacques, *op. cit.*.

62 Bill of Messrs Stott & Walker to Mrs J. Lee, dated 1816; Bill of Messrs Milner & Bennett to John Lee, Esq. for the years 1822–1824, WDA (JGC); H. Clarkson, *op. cit.*, p. 168.

63 Misc. Medical Bills to Mr Whitely of Wakefield, WDA (JGC).

64 A few individuals who were taken as apprentices did return to Wakefield and Huddersfield to practise. In 1840, for example, George Winter Rhodes, the son of a prosperous Huddersfield cloth dresser, was taken as an apprentice to the Huddersfield Infirmary for five years 'with the privilege of attending the lectures in London during the last 2 years at a pm of £150'. He became an MRCS in 1846 and LSA in 1847, and returned shortly after to Huddersfield to practise. In 1863 he was elected honorary surgeon to the Infirmary. Minute Book of the Huddersfield Infirmary, Vol. II, Meeting of the Monthly Board, 5 October, 1840, p. 7, Special General Meeting, 27 February, 1863, p. 442; *PMD*, 1851.

65 For more on the relationship between lay supporters and medical officers to the dispensaries and infirmaries, see Chapter 8, pp. 329–336.

66 A small number of doctors were less dependent upon their incomes from medical practice, and could be selective in choosing both their clientele and type of practice, confining themselves to consulting work if they so desired. See Section 7.2 for more on this wealthy group of practitioners.

67 Letter from John Thomson of Halifax to Mr Wilks, surgeon, dated May 5, 1814, Ms HRI.

68 *WHJ*, 10 January, 1823.

69 The Eighth Annual Report of The Wakefield Town Mission, 1848, WDA (Local Collection, Box 4B).

70 *PMD*, 1865.

71 *HE*, 28 January, 1860.

72 For Poor Law and friendly society appointments, see Chapters 3 and 5. Pre-1834 Poor Law appointments seem to have offered more in terms of income and perhaps status.

73 It was also common practice to pay well-thought-of house surgeons gratuities, which could be as much as £20. In 1830 William Holdsworth resigned his post as house surgeon to the Wakefield Dispensary. The subscribers to the institution presented him with the sum of 21 guineas to purchase an instrument case as a mark of respect for his four years of 'diligent attention' to his duties. *WHJ*, 31 December, 1830.

74 *PMD*, 1852, 1865, 1870; Minute Book of the Huddersfield Infirmary, Vol. II, Special General Meeting, 19 November, 1851, p. 208, Meeting of the Monthly Board, 1 January, 1855, p. 280, General Meeting, 15 December, 1865, p. 496, Vol. III, General Meeting, 19 November, 1869, p. 18.

75 *Ibid.*, Vol. II, Special General Meeting, 29 October, 1856, p. 316, Meeting of the Monthly Board, 5 October, 1863, p. 455; *PMD*, 1859, 1866.

76 J. A. Shepherd, *Lawson Tait. The Rebellious Surgeon (1844–1899)* (Lawrence, Kansas, 1980), Chapter 2; N. L. Maxwell Reader, 'An Ancient Practice Alive and Well Today', *Practitioner*, Vol. 206, 1971, p. 693.

77 J. Horsfall Turner, *Wakefield House of Correction* (Bingley, 1904), pp. 147–148, 205, 219.

78 A Return 'of the Medical Officers under the Poor Law Acts, . . .', PP, 1856, XLIX (434) (Wakefield Union). See Chapter 3, Section 3.2 for more on the salaries of medical officers under the New Poor Law.

79 *PMD*, 1848, 1861, 1866, 1871. For a useful survey of job opportunities and the development of pluralism amongst the Glasgow medical profession in the nineteenth century, see O. Checkland and M. Lamb (eds), *Health Care as Social History. The Glasgow Case* (Aberdeen, 1982), pp. 21–43.

80 *WE*, 6 January, 1855.

81 *WJ*, 1 October, 1841, 13 May, 1842.

82 For biographies of individual practitioners, including their posts, qualifications and type of practice, see Appendix 11.

83 P. S. Brown, 'The Providers of Medical Treatment in Mid-Nineteenth-Century Bristol', pp. 297–314. Brown in turn bases his interpretation and description of household size and composition on the definitions suggested by Laslett. P. Laslett, 'Introduction: the history of the family' in P. Laslett and R. Wall (eds), *Household and Family in Past Time* (Cambridge, 1972), pp. 1–89.

84 *Ibid.*, pp. 28–32.

85 C. Wakefield, 1861, Huddersfield, 1851.

86 In fiction, George Eliot's Dr Lydgate faced the dilemma as to whether he should marry Rosamond Vincy, or first establish himself in practice in Middlemarch and begin the pursuit of his medical research interests. At the age of 27 he had just set up in practice and was forming important connections with the newly-established infirmary. He had determined not to take a wife until he had built up a good practice and income. He broke his resolve, and marriage to Rosamond proved disastrous. Her extravagance and dissatisfaction with her status as a doctor's wife led to debts, poverty and the loss of Lydgate's reputation. Finally, he abandoned

his professional and scientific ambitions to become a prosperous spa doctor, but a failure in his own estimation. G. Eliot, *Middlemarch* (Harmondsworth, 1965, Penguin ed., first published 1871–1872). For more on Lydgate and other Middlemarch doctors, see A. Briggs, 'Middlemarch and the Doctors', *The Cambridge Journal*, Vol. I, No. 12, September, 1948, pp. 749–762.

87 *WJ*, 3 March, 1843, 21 October, 1842 (Marriages).

88 Sigsworth and Swan's analysis of servant employment by West Riding doctors in 1851 yielded the following results. 86.9 per cent of household heads employed servants; 64 per cent of servant-employing doctors had one or two servants, an additional 27 per cent employed three. E. M. Sigsworth and P. Swan, *op. cit.*, p. 39.

89 C. Wakefield, 1851, 1861.

90 In 1857 the maintenance of a man servant was calculated at £30 a year, at least twice the cost of keeping a female domestic servant. By the 1870s a man servant was costing between £50 and £60 for board and salary. J. H. Walsh, *A Manual of Domestic Economy* (1857), p. 226 (2nd ed., 1873), p. 224. Cited in J. A. Banks, *op. cit.*, p. 73.

91 H. Perkin, *op. cit.*, p. 143.

92 I. W. Beeton, *The Book of Household Management* (1861), p. 8. Cited in J. A. Banks, *op. cit.*, p. 76.

93 For example, P. Branca, *Silent Sisterhood*, p. 54.

94 *A New System of Practical Domestic Economy: founded on modern Discoveries, and the private communications of Persons of Experience* (3rd ed., 1823), Appendix of Estimates of Household Expenses, Part 2. Cited in J. A. Banks, *op. cit.*, p. 74.

95 Only those at the peak of the profession left a record of their earnings, which often ran into several thousand pounds a year. For example, in some years the leading surgeon Abernethy earned £10,000 and Liston almost £7,000. During the 1820s and 1830s Sir Henry Halford, for many years President of the Royal College of Physicians, made £10,000 per annum. I. Waddington, 'General Practitioners and Consultants in Early Nineteenth-Century England', p. 172.

96 R. D. Baxter, *The Taxation of the UK* (1869), pp. 105–106. Cited in G. Best, *op. cit.*, p. 110.

97 C. Wakefield, 1841; First Factory Doctor's Personal Accounts. George Holdsworth, of St John's Square Household Accts, May, 1839 to December, 1844 and January, 1845 to August, 1846, Ms WDA (JGC).

98 C. Wakefield, 1861.

99 C. Huddersfield, 1841, 1851.

100 The procedures of advertising for apprentices in the local press and of drawing up articles of agreement between surgeons and parents or guardians, regulating the training and conduct of apprentices, remained unchanged well into the nineteenth century. Premiums ranged between £100 and £200 in the first half of the nineteenth century, moving towards the higher figure by mid-century. In 1819, for example, John Brook was apprenticed to Messrs Stott and Walker of Wakefield for a term of six years on the payment of a premium of £80. In 1833 Charles Walker Wood, surgeon and apothecary of Wakefield, was paid £199 for taking on Thomas Halliwell Roby for a period of five years. Brook to Messrs Stott & Walker. Articles of Apprenticeship for 6 Years, 25 Sept^r, 1819; Mr Roby & his Son to Mr Wood. Articles of Apprenticeship, 1833. Wakefield Apprenticeship Indentures, Nos 717 and 719, Ms WDA (JGC, App. Indents.).

101 C. Wakefield and Huddersfield, 1861.

102 J. W. Walker, *op. cit.*, p. 468.

103 P. Joyce, *op. cit.*, p. 27.

104 Kelly, 1857.

105 *WJ*, 1 May, 1840; C. Wakefield, 1841.

106 N. L. Maxwell Reader, *op. cit.*, pp. 691–697.

107 *WHJ*, 7 February, 1812, 30 September, 1831 (Marriages).

108 N. L. Maxwell Reader, *op. cit.*, p. 693.

109 *WHJ*, 10 December, 1813; *WJ*, 7 June, 1839 (Marriages).

110 *A Brief Memoir of the Late Mr Sargent, Surgeon, Huddersfield* (Huddersfield, n.d., c. 1840), HPL (Local Pamphlets, Vol. 30).

111 *WHJ*, 21 October, 1831 (Marriages); C. Wakefield, 1841. For more on Dunn, Houghton and Sargent, see Chapter 8, pp. 357–360.

112 Memorandum of an Agreement made the sixth day of April One Thousand seven hundred and ninety six, Between Thomas Smith of Wakefield Merchant of the one part and Edward Taylor of the same Place Surgeon and Apothecary of the other part, Ms WDA (JGC).

113 *WHJ*, 27 March, 1823; *WS*, 5 December, 1806; Minutes respecting the property of the late George Holdsworth of Wakefield Surgeon – who died 31ˢᵗ August 1846, Ms WDA (JGC).

114 J. Springett, *op. cit.*, p. 135.

115 Memorial HD 743 790, dated March 30, 1820, Ms WYCRO (Registry of Deeds).

116 Memorial RB 474 733, dated September 9, 1839, Ms WYCRO (Registry of Deeds).

117 1863 Wills, Vol. IV. Her Majesty's Court of Probate, Wakefield District Registry. (Died July 28, 1863, Will proved November 28, 1863), Ms WYCRO (Registry of Deeds).

118 C. Huddersfield, 1871; *PMD*, 1871. The medical career of Dr John Simpson of Bradford may not have been completely untypical. He started out in practice in 1822 after taking his MD at Edinburgh University. After only three years in practice his wealthy uncle died, leaving Simpson a large property at Malton. Simpson left Bradford to take possession of his estate in 1825, and thereafter lived the life of a country gentleman. Even in the three years in which he practised medicine, he seems to have limited himself to treating a few wealthy families and to attendance as honorary physician at the local dispensary. *The Journal of Dr John Simpson of Bradford, 1825.*

119 C. Crowther, MD, *op. cit.*, Ms WDA (JGC). See Chapter 8, pp. 353–356 for a biography of Crowther.

120 George Gissing, himself the son of a Wakefield chemist, provides us with a literary example of a failed medical practitioner in *New Grub Street*. Victor Duke, a minor character in the novel, had been 'comfortably established' in practice in Wakefield, but his capital ran out, and the practice, never large, 'fell to nothing'. By the time he appears in the novel he has fallen into the direst poverty, is living in a poor lodging house in London and is reduced to begging. He apparently had no hopes whatsoever of re-establishing himself in practice. G. Gissing, *New Grub Street* (Harmondsworth, 1968, Penguin ed., first published 1891), pp. 442–445.

121 *WHJ*, 14 July, 1837.

122 *The Lancet*, 1846, Vol. II, p. 202, 1855, Vol. II, p. 94.

123 Nor was the West Riding Society unique. The Society for the Relief of Widows and Orphans of Medical Men reported in the early 1840s that 'one in four of the members of the Society left a widow or orphans claimant on its funds'. At the end of the century there were three charitable societies in London alone which aimed at 'relieving cases of pecuniary distress among medical men, their widows and orphans'. The number relieved by the London societies amounted to between 450 and 500 per annum, and there were always more applicants than could be satisfied by the funds. *The Lancet*, 1841–1842, Vol. II, p. 100; H. N. Hardy, *The State of the Medical Profession in Great Britain and Ireland in 1900* (Dublin, 1901), p. 70. Cited in I. Waddington, 'General Practitioners and Consultants in Early Nineteenth-Century England', p. 174.

124 C. Huddersfield, 1861, Wakefield, 1861, 1871.

125 Mr Thos. Alder & his son to Mr Price. Indenture of Apprenticeship, 22nd Aug 1845. Wakefield Apprenticeship Indentures, No. 697, Ms WDA (JGC, App. Indents.).

126 C. Wakefield and Huddersfield, 1861; *PMD*, 1864, 1866.

127 C. Wakefield, 1861.

128 G. W. Tomlinson, *History of Huddersfield (Home Words) 1885–1887* (Huddersfield, 1887), pp. 22–23.
129 C. Wakefield, 1851; *PMD*, 1860, 1870.
130 C. Wakefield, 1861; *PMD*, 1867, 1868, 1871.
131 C. Wakefield and Huddersfield, 1861, 1871; *HE*, 30 June, 1917.
132 M. A. Jagger, *op. cit.*, p. 102.
133 *WHJ*, 7 April, 1814.
134 C. Wakefield, 1841, 1851; *PMD*, 1848, 1860. For biographies of Squire and William Statter, see Appendix 11.
135 *PMD*, 1851, 1856; Annual Reports of the Huddersfield Dispensary and Infirmary; *HE*, 2 November, 1912. The operation of patrimony did not always go ignored or uncriticised. See Chapter 8, pp. 322, 335–336 for the opinion of T. R. Tatham, a Huddersfield practitioner, on the subject.
136 *WS*, 29 March, 1805; *WJ*, 24 May, 1839; C. Wakefield, 1851, Huddersfield, 1841, 1861.
137 *WHJ*, 3 May, 1822, 11 January, 1839 (Marriages).
138 C. Huddersfield, 1841, 1851, 1861, Wakefield, 1871; *PMD*, 1856, 1863; *WE*, 1 October, 1870.
139 Irvine Loudon has estimated that the total amount paid out for the education of Henry Peart, a Worcestershire general practitioner, between 1828 and 1831 was at least £500. This covered the costs of apprenticeship, of sitting for the LSA and MRCS in London and of a three-month-long trip to Paris. The expenses of maintaining Peart during his first two years in practice brought the figure up to approximately £1,000. His income as a general practitioner in his first eighteen months in practice, meanwhile, amounted to only £53. I. S. L. Loudon, 'A Doctor's Cash Book: The Economy of General Practice in the 1830s', pp. 250–251, 254.
140 J. C. Hudson, *The parent's hand-book – or, guide to the choice of employments, professions, etc.* (London, 1842), p. 89. Cited *ibid.*, p. 259.
141 *The Lancet*, 1864, Vol. I, pp. 285, 29, 1868, Vol. I, p. 300. Cited in F. B. Smith, *op. cit.*, p. 367. See also M. J. Peterson, *op, cit.*, pp. 209–224 for the incomes of medical men.
142 Income during the course of a professional career was also subject to great variation. In 1854 William Henry Cook, then practising in Tunbridge Wells, earned only £174; in 1859, following a move to London, his income after expenses amounted to £377, in 1865, after entering into partnership with an established Hampstead practitioner, £576. W. D. Foster, *op. cit.*, pp. 47, 49.
143 I. S. L. Loudon, 'A Doctor's Cash Book: The Economy of General Practice in the 1830s', p. 263.
144 For biographies of doctors, including their social characteristics, see Appendix 11.

Chapter 8

1 With the recent exception of Holmes, who suggests that the medical profession developed most significantly in the period between 1680 and 1730, linked closely to the rise of the surgeon-apothecary, improvements in medical education and the formation of a corporate identity. G. Holmes, *Augustan England. Professions, State and Society, 1680–1730* (1982).
2 J. V. Pickstone, 'The Professionalisation of Medicine in England and Europe: the state, the market and industrial society', p. 544.
3 E. Greenwood, 'Attributes of a Profession', *Social Work*, Vol. 2, 1957, pp. 45–55.
4 C. Rosenberg, 'The medical profession, medical practice and the history of medicine' in E. Clarke (ed.), *op. cit.*, p. 27.
5 E. Durkheim, for example, originally identified the professions as a means of redressing the balance against individualism. Professional ethics were seen as a counterbalance in industrial society to the impact of individualism, which was

leading to moral decline. Others choosing a micro-sociological approach, to include Ben-David and Sorokin, saw the professions as vehicles utilised for individual social mobility. The centrality of power to an understanding of the professions is stressed by Johnson and Friedson. Johnson defines professionalisation as control over clients, while Friedson stresses the importance of control over organisations and institutions. N. and J. Parry have suggested that the defining characteristic is the control which professional associations themselves developed over professional colleagues. N. and J. Parry, *op. cit.*, pp. 247–248. More recently P. Starr has suggested that the rise of the American medical profession was due to a growth in professional and cultural authority. The kind of authority claimed by the profession involved not only skill in performing a service, validated by a peer group, but the ability to judge the needs of clients and make them dependent on professional competence. P. Starr, *The Social Transformation of American Medicine* (New York, 1982).

6 S. E. D. Shortt, 'Physicians, Science, and Status: Issues in the Professionalization of Anglo–American Medicine in the Nineteenth Century', *Medical History*, Vol. 27, No. 1, January, 1983, p. 52.

7 I. Inkster, *op. cit.*, p. 130.

8 M. Ramsey, *op. cit.*, p. 183.

9 Literature on the growth and activities of medical societies is extremely sparse. D'Arcy Power has provided us with a survey of major medical societies and professional organisations in Sir D'Arcy Power (ed.), *British Medical Societies* (1939). See also W. H. McMenemey, 'The Influence of Medical Societies on the Development of Medical Practice in Nineteenth-Century Britain' in F. N. L. Poynter (ed.), *The Evolution of Medical Practice in Britain* (1961), pp. 67–79.

10 P. Swan, 'A Brief Survey and Summary of the Role and Position of Medical Societies in the early Nineteenth Century Medical Profession', *The Journal of Local Studies*, Vol. 2, No. 2, Autumn, 1982, p. 46.

11 M. J. Peterson, *op. cit.*, p. 18.

12 See P. Vaughan, *op. cit.* for the founding and activities of the Association.

13 Sir D'Arcy Power (ed.), *op. cit.*, pp. 130, 109.

14 I. Inkster, *op. cit.*, pp. 141–142. See also W. S. Porter, *The Medical School in Sheffield, 1828–1928* (Sheffield, 1928).

15 For more on the activities of the Huddersfield medical associations, see H. Marland, 'Early Nineteenth-Century Medical Society Activity: The Huddersfield Case', *The Journal of Regional and Local Studies*, Vol. 6, No. 2, Autumn, 1985, pp. 37–48.

16 Minute Book of the Wakefield Microscopic Society, 1854–1858. First meeting of the Society, held at Saml Holdsworths, October 26, 1854, Ms WDA (Local Collection, Box 2C).

17 Proceedings of the Huddersfield Medical Library, 1852–1883, Ms HRI.

18 Minute Book of the Huddersfield Infirmary, Vol. II, Meeting of the Monthly Board, 7 November, 1853, p. 255.

19 Rules of The Wakefield Medical Book Club, Jan. 5th, 1830, Ms WDA (JGC). For more on medical libraries and book clubs, see W. J. Bishop, 'Medical Book Societies in England in the Eighteenth and Nineteenth Centuries', *Bulletin of the Medical Library Association*, Vol. 45, 1957, pp. 337–350 and R. Guest-Gornall, 'The Warrington Dispensary Library', *Medical History*, Vol. 11, 1967, pp. 285–296.

20 Huddersfield Medical Society. Minute Book, 1825–1834. Medical Regulations dated 1825, pp. 1–9, Ms HRI. Charges were also drawn up for pills, mixtures, powders and linctus, etc., a further indication of the practice of physic by surgeons.

21 *Ibid.*, Meeting of May 29, 1828.

22 *Ibid.*, Meetings of February 27, March 27 and September 24, 1829 and August 29, 1833.

23 Minute Book of the Wakefield Microscopic Society, 1854–1858, Meeting of December 21, 1854, Ms WDA (Local Collection, Box 2C).

24 *Ibid.*, Meeting of October 27, 1858. See p. 337.

25 *Ibid.*

26 Minute Book of the Huddersfield Dispensary, Vol. I, Special Meeting of the Infirmary Committee, 7 December, 1829, p. 231.

27 *HHE*, 29 November, 1851.

28 See S. J. Rogal, 'A Checklist of Medical Journals Published in England during the Seventeenth, Eighteenth and Nineteenth Centuries', *British Studies Monitor*, Vol. IX, No. 3, Winter, 1980, pp. 3–25.

29 D. Alexander, MD, *A Treatise on the Nature and Cure of the Cynanche Trachealis, Commonly called the Croup* (Huddersfield, n.d.), HPL (Local Pamphlets, Vol. 20); *An Answer to the Enquiry, if it be the duty of Every Person to study the preservation of his Health, . . .* , Wellcome Institute Library; *A Lecture on Phrenology*, WDA (Local Collection, Box 14).

30 *PMD*, 1851, 1856.

31 W. J. Clarke, 'Surgical Cases Treated in the Huddersfield Infirmary', *The Lancet*, 1855, Vol. II, pp. 165–166.

32 *PMD*, 1851. For more details of Taylor's publications and those of a sample of Wakefield and Huddersfield medical men, see Appendix 11.

33 'Medical Ethics in the Provinces', *Medical Times and Gazette*, 1852, Vol. II, p. 544.

34 Ivan Waddington has demonstrated this imbalance, citing the work of Thomas Percival, whose *Medical ethics*, published in 1803, was arguably one of the most important and influential books to appear on the subject in the nineteenth century. Excluding Percival's last chapter, which dealt with medical jurisprudence, out of a total of 48 pages only half a dozen discussed the ethical problems involved in the doctor–patient relationship, which was tackled in a very general and traditional way. T. Percival, *Medical ethics* (1803). Cited in I. Waddington, 'The Development of Medical Ethics – A Sociological Analysis', *Medical History*, Vol. 19, No. 1, January, 1975, pp. 38–40.

35 *Ibid.*, pp. 37–38.

36 *PMD*, 1860, pp. 913–914 (Section on Medical Societies).

37 'Medical Ethics in the Provinces', *Medical Times and Gazette*, 1852, Vol. II, p. 545.

38 *PMD*, 1860, p. 913.

39 'Unprofessional Conduct – Degrading Offer of a Qualified Surgeon', *The Lancet*, 1851, Vol. I, p. 559.

40 Incidentally, Thornton appears to have been more than adequately qualified, being an MRCS England (1849), LSA (1850) and MB London (1850). In 1853 Thornton added an MD London to his qualifications. William Kemp, his adversary, held only the double qualification of MRCS/LSA (1844). *PMD*, 1848, 1852, 1860.

41 'The Degrading Club System', *The Lancet*, 1851, Vol. I, p. 586.

42 *PMD*, 1860, 1865, 1870.

43 'The Case of Mr Housley', *The Lancet*, 1854, Vol. I, p. 377.

44 *Ibid.*

45 *Medical Times and Gazette*, 1852, Vol. I, p. 99.

46 'Memorial from Wakefield and Its Vicinity to the Royal College of Surgeons', *Medical Times and Gazette*, 1853, Vol. I, p. 221.

47 *WJ*, 5 March, 1841; J. K. Walker, MD, *op. cit.*, HPL (Misc. Pamph: Sea Bathing Infirmary).

48 *WRH*, 8 July, 1836. See Chapter 7, p. 293 for the purposes of the West Riding Medical Charitable Society.

49 *PMD*, 1854, 1861, 1871.

50 *PMD*, 1870.

51 J. A. Shepherd, *op. cit.*, p. 24.

52 'Medical Ethics in the Provinces', *Medical Times and Gazette*, 1852, Vol. II, p. 544.

53 N. and J. Parry, *op. cit.*

54 'Medical Ethics in the Provinces', *Medical Times and Gazette*, 1852, Vol. II, p. 544.

55 P. Brady, 'The Status of the Medical Profession Considered in Connection with its Educational System', *Medical Times*, Vol. 17, 1847–1848, pp. 224–225.

56 *Ibid.*, p. 224.

57 *Ibid.*, p. 225.

58 Huddersfield Medical Society. Minute Book, 1825–1834, Meeting of January 26, 1832, Ms HRI.

59 Proceedings of the Huddersfield Medical Library, 1852–1883, Half Yearly Meeting, December 1, 1865, Ms HRI.

60 *LM*, 25 June, 1814. For an account of the power struggles between various pressure groups, lay and medical, within the Manchester Infirmary between 1788 and 1792, see J. V. Pickstone and S. V. F. Butler, 'The politics of medicine in Manchester, 1788–1792: hospital reform and public health services in the early industrial city', *Medical History*, Vol. 28, No. 3, July, 1984, pp. 227–249.

61 Minute Book of the Huddersfield Dispensary, Vol. I, General Meeting of the Governors, 27 June, 1814, p. 8.

62 Letter from John Thomson of Halifax to Mr Wilks, surgeon, dated May 5, 1814, Ms HRI.

63 *Ibid.* Houghton was also a Huddersfield practitioner and a rival for the post of surgeon to the Huddersfield Dispensary. As shown by the election results, Houghton's bid for appointment failed. This did not, however, appear to be a setback for Houghton, who built up one of the best practices in the town. See pp. 357–359 for more on Houghton.

64 Minute Book of the Huddersfield Infirmary, Vol. I, Special Committee Meeting, 14 October, 1833, p. 331.

65 *Ibid.*, Vol. II, Special Meeting of the Monthly Board, 4 July, 1853, p. 248.

66 *WHJ*, 3 April, 1829.

67 *WHJ*, 2 March, 1832.

68 For more details on the setting up of surgical wards in the Wakefield Dispensary, see Chapter 4, pp. 125–127.

69 J. W. Walker, *op. cit.*, pp. 569–570. For more on Crowther, see pp. 353–356.

70 *PMD*, 1866; *HE*, 6 June and 7, 14 and 28 July, 1860.

71 T. R. Tatham, MD, *Strictures on the Administration of Affairs Pertaining to the Huddersfield & Upper Agbrigg Infirmary* (Nottingham, 1864), pp. 9, 35, HPL (Tomlinson Collection).

72 *Ibid.*, p. 11. For more on Tatham's dispute with the lay officers of the charity, see pp. 335–336.

73 For more on the survival and strength of fringe medicine in the nineteenth century, see Chapter 6.

74 'Illegal Practice: A Recent Verdict at Huddersfield', *The Lancet*, 1854, Vol. I, p. 645; 'Malpraxis by Unqualified Practitioners', *Medical Times and Gazette*, 1854, Vol. I, pp. 624–625.

75 *Ibid.*, p. 645.

76 The Coroner's Jury, held at Meltham, concluded that Jane Taylor had 'died of haemorrhage'. *The Lancet* reported that the Jury had taken no account of the fact that had proper skill been employed, in all probability she would not have died, and had concluded that Rawcliffe used the 'best skill' he had. The Coroner in his summing up declared that it was 'no part of their duty to consider whether or not the deceased had been attended by a properly qualified Practitioner'. *The Lancet* concluded the piece by stating, with some satisfaction, that the Huddersfield magistrates subsequently charged Rawcliffe with having, through carelessness and ignorance, caused the death of Jane Taylor, and had committed him to be tried at York for manslaughter. The verdict of the York trial apparently was not reported in the medical journals.

77 'Homoeopathic Quackery in Huddersfield', *The Lancet*, 1849, Vol. II, pp. 405–406.

78 *PMD*, 1851, 1856.

79 'Homoeopathic Quackery in Huddersfield', *The Lancet*, 1849, Vol. II, pp. 405–406.

80 S. Knaggs, *Common Sense versus Homoeopathy* (1855), Wellcome Institute Library.
81 *Ibid.*, p. 43.
82 T. G. Wright, MD, *A Lecture on Quack Medicines*, Wellcome Institute Library.
83 *Ibid.*, p. 40.
84 See Chapter 6, especially the Concluding remarks.
85 M. J. Peterson, *op. cit.*, p. 130.
86 M. S. Larson, *The Rise of Professionalism. A Sociological Analysis* (Berkeley, 1977), pp. 20–21.
87 P. Vaughan, *op. cit.*, p. 89.
88 'Memorial from Wakefield and Its Vicinity to the Royal College of Surgeons', *Medical Times and Gazette*, 1853, Vol. I, p. 221.
89 I. Inkster, *op. cit.*, p. 140.
90 I. Inkster, *Studies in the Social History of Science in England During the Industrial Revolution, circa 1790–1850*, unpublished PhD thesis, Sheffield, 1977, p. 162.
91 The Wakefield Microscopic Society initially confined its membership to medical men. See p. 307.
92 For the setting up of the Wakefield and Huddersfield medical charities, see Chapter 4, pp. 123–130.
93 Minute Book of the Huddersfield Dispensary, Vol. I, Meetings of the Committee, 29 June, 1814, p. 8, 2 July, 1814, p. 9 and 7 November, 1814, p. 13.
94 *Ibid.*, Meetings of the Committee, 3 April, 1815, p. 18 and 5 January, 1824, p. 129.
95 *Ibid.*, Meetings of the Committee and Infirmary Committee, 1828–1832.
96 Minute Book of the Huddersfield Infirmary, Vol. II, Meetings of the Monthly Board, 9 June, 1848, p. 146, 6 August, 1849, p. 168 and 1 February, 1869, Vol. III, 7 June, 1869, p. 7.
97 R. J. Morris, *op. cit.*, p. 182.
98 This lack of conflict apparently typified the relationships between lay and medical officers in most nineteenth-century medical charities. See, for example, B. Abel-Smith, op. cit., pp. 32–45.
99 See Chapter 7, pp. 274–280.
100 Minute Book of the Huddersfield Dispensary, Vol. I, Annual Meeting of Subscribers, 21 June, 1821, p. 105.
101 84th AR WI, 1870–1871, Annual Address, p. 4.
102 For example, at the election of a surgeon to the Huddersfield Infirmary in 1833 a total of 580 votes were cast for the three candidates. (John Bradshaw received 291, T. R. Tatham 225 and Mr Astin 64.) The number of votes approximated very closely to the total number of subscribers to the charity. Minute Book of the Huddersfield Infirmary, Vol. I, General Meeting of Subscribers, 30 October, 1833, p. 333.
103 See Chapter 7, note 58.
104 I. Inkster, 'Marginal Men: Aspects of the Social Role of the Medical Community in Sheffield 1790–1850', p. 140.
105 For example, in 1857 Mrs Frederick Greenwood, wife of the former house surgeon and future honorary surgeon, donated two testaments and linen to the Huddersfield Infirmary, and in 1870 Mrs Turnbull, wife of the honorary physician, donated Bibles and prayer books. 26th and 40th ARs HI, 1856–1857, 1870–1871.
106 *HE*, 9 December, 1865.
107 *WHJ*, 10 January, 1823.
108 Annual Reports of the Wakefield Dispensary and Infirmary; *PMD*, 1850 (Obituary Section).
109 Minute Book of the Huddersfield Infirmary, Vol. II, Special Meeting of the Monthly Board, 15 June, 1846, p. 100.
110 In recognition of Greenwood's services as apothecary, he was adjudged a gratuity of £20 'in testimony of his merits'. At a committee meeting in September, 1823 it was recorded 'That this Committee Sensible of the value of moral principles to society and especially of the benefit of their practical operation in the personal

conduct of the Apothecary to this Institution, deem it requisite to express its high approbation of the moral and correct deportment which has been maintained by Mr Wm Greenwood for more than three years during which period he has discharged with assiduity & ability the official duties of apothecary to the Huddersfield Dispensary'. Minute Book of the Huddersfield Dispensary, Vol. I, General Meeting of Subscribers, 20 June, 1823, p. 124, Meeting of the Committee, 1 September, 1823, p. 126.

111 35th AR HI, 1865–1866, Annual Address, p. 8.
112 Annual Reports of the Huddersfield Dispensary and Infirmary.
113 1st AR HI, 1831–1832. See Chapter 4, pp. 118–119, 121 for more on the financial contributions of doctors to the medical charities.
114 76th AR WI, 1862–1863.
115 T. R. Tatham, MD, *op. cit.*, pp. 35, 9, HPL (Tomlinson Collection).
116 Minute Book of the Huddersfield Infirmary, Vol. II, Meeting of the Monthly Board, 4 January, 1864, p. 462.
117 *Ibid.*, General Meeting of the Governors, 30 June, 1865, p. 489.
118 To the Governors of the Huddersfield and Upper Agbrigg Infirmary, The Official Letter, from David Marsden, Esq., Honorary Secretary; also a Reply by Thos. Robt. Tatham, MD (Nottingham, 1865), p. 3, HPL (Tomlinson Collection). For Tatham's dispute with the Huddersfield Board of Guardians, see Chapter 3, Section 3.2. For a biography of Tatham, see Appendix 11.
119 Minute Book of the Huddersfield Infirmary, Vol. II, Annual Meeting of Subscribers, 24 June, 1859, p. 367.
120 S. Knaggs, 'Some Suggestions for Diminishing the Abuses of Medical Charities', *Medical Times and Gazette*, 1859, Vol. II, p. 442.
121 Minute Book of the Huddersfield Infirmary, Vol. II, Special General Meeting, 27 February, 1863, p. 442. See Appendix 11 for a biography of Knaggs.
122 Minute Book of the Wakefield Microscopic Society, 1854–1858; Wakefield Microscopic Society. List of Meetings for 1871, Ms and Printed, WDA (Local Collection, Box 2C).
123 The Laws and Regulations of the Wakefield Museum, 1830, WDA (Local Collection, Box 2C).
124 Wakefield Philosophical and Literary Society. List of Essays Read during Former Sessions, n.d., c. 1836, WDA (JGC).
125 Reports of the Wakefield Mechanics' Institution, For the Years 1842–1843, 1849–1850, 1862–1868, 1870–1871, WDA (Local Collection, Box 11B).
126 Laws for the Regulation of the Huddersfield Subscription Library, Established in March 1807, HPL (Local Pamphlets, Vol. 16).
127 Of homoeopathist fame. See p. 324.
128 Reports of the Huddersfield Mechanics' Institution, 1844–1870, HPL (Misc. Pamph: Mechanics' Institute).
129 Fourteenth Report of the Committee of the Huddersfield Mechanics' Institution, Jan. 27th, 1855, HPL (Misc. Pamph: Mechanics' Institute).
130 A List of The Proprietary of Huddersfield College, n.d., c. 1838, HPL (Misc. Pamph: Huddersfield College).
131 Transactions of the Huddersfield Archaeological and Topographical Association, Vol. I, Part I, 1866; Huddersfield Archaeological Association. Papers Read at the Annual meeting on the 30th January, 1867, to which are Prefixed the Rules of the Association and List of Officers for 1867, HPL (Misc. Pamph: Societies: Arch. and Top.).
132 Baines, 1822, p. 205.
133 D. Alexander, MD, *A Lecture on Phrenology* (List of Subscribers), pp. iii–vi, WDA (Local Collection, Box 14).
134 *WHJ*, 19 January, 1827. For more on Alexander, see pp. 351–353.
135 *PMD*, 1870.
136 *WE*, 14 October, 1865.
137 *PMD*, 1856, 1861, 1866.

138 *PMD*, 1870.
139 J. A. Shepherd, *op. cit.*, pp. 27–28.
140 Report of the Wakefield Benevolent Society, Instituted in the Year 1791, Wakefield, Nov. 30th, 1836; Subscriptions to the Benevolent Society, c. 1832–1844, Printed and Ms WDA (JGC).
141 Annual Reports of The Wakefield Town Mission, 1848, 1849, 1852, 1870, WDA (Local Collection, Box 4B).
142 Address of the Huddersfield Benevolent and Visiting Society. Instituted December 13, 1830, Huddersfield, n.d., c. 1830, HPL (Tolson Collection); First Annual Report of the Huddersfield Auxiliary Peace Society, for the Circulation of Tracts, 1823, HPL (Misc. Pamph: Peace Society); *1832–1932. Souvenir of the Centenary Celebrations of the Huddersfield Temperance Society* (1932), p. 11, HPL (S/HTe 8).
143 For discussions on the involvement of medical men in public health reform, see, for example, M. W. Flinn's introduction to E. Chadwick, *Report on the Sanitary Condition of the Labouring Population of Great Britain* (1842, reprinted Edinburgh, 1965), especially pp. 18–26; W. M. Frazer, *A History of English Public Health 1834–1939* (1950), Part I; M. Pelling, *Cholera, Fever and English Medicine 1825–1865* (Oxford, 1978).
144 M. E. Rose, 'The doctor in the Industrial Revolution', *British Journal of Industrial Medicine*, Vol. 28, 1971, p. 22.
145 H. Dunn, 'The malignant Cholera in the House of Correction at Wakefield', *The Lancet*, 1833–1834, Vol. I, pp. 787–789; T. G. Wright, MD, *Cholera in the Asylum. Reports on the Origins and Progress of Pestilential Cholera, In the West-Yorkshire Lunatic Asylum, During the Autumn of 1849, and on the previous State of the Institution. A Contribution to the Statistics of Insanity and of Cholera* (London and Wakefield, 1850), Wellcome Institute Library..
146 W. Turnbull, MD, 'Examples of Cholera Spreading by Contagion', *London Medical Gazette*, Vol. 9, 1832, pp. 823–825; J. Taylor, MD, *op. cit.*, *Medical Times*, Vol. 23, 1851, pp. 256–259, 340–344, 399–402; S. Booth, 'Precautions for the Prevention of Cholera', 1851 and 'The Sanitary measures necessary for the Prevention of Typhus Fever, Cholera, etc.', 1858. *PMD*, 1852, 1856, 1861.
147 *PMD*, 1856, 1866, 1871. For more on Booth and his publications, see Appendix 11.
148 *PMD*, 1870.
149 J. A. Shepherd, *op. cit.*, p. 17; 'The Sanitary Condition of Wakefield', *Medical Times and Gazette*, 1870, Vol. I, pp. 36–37.
150 For the work of Dr Cameron as Medical Officer in Leeds and public health issues in the town during the late nineteenth century, see E. P. Hennock, *Fit and Proper Persons. Ideal and reality in nineteenth-century urban government* (1973), pp. 231–236, 247–252.
151 For the public health activities of the Boards of Guardians, see Chapter 3, Section 3.2.
152 P. E. Razzell, 'An Interpretation of the Modern Rise of Population in Europe – A Critique', *Population Studies*, Vol. 28, Part 1, March, 1974, p. 13.
153 Minute Book of the Huddersfield Dispensary, Vol. I, Annual Meeting of Subscribers, 16 June, 1824, p. 136.
154 Minute Book of the Huddersfield Infirmary, Vol. I, Meetings of the Monthly Board, 4 September, 1837, p. 389 and 2 October, 1837, p. 390.
155 1st to 4th ARs HD, 1814–1818.
156 J. Horsfall Turner, *op. cit.*, pp. 185, 211.
157 Minute Book of the Huddersfield Board of Guardians, Vol. 4, 20 January and 3 February, 1843, Ms HPL (P/HU/M).
158 *Ibid.*, Vol. 5, 21 May, 1847.
159 *Ibid.*, Vol. 7, 15 March, 1850. The charges made by medical men for attendance on cholera cases totalled £270.
160 *WJ*, 10 September, 1841.
161 W. Ranger, *op. cit.* See Chapter 2, Section 2.3 for more on public health in Wakefield and Huddersfield.

162 There is no record of the evidence of Benjamin Walker being included in the Report.
163 W. Ranger, *op. cit.*, p. 77.
164 *Ibid.*, Appendix, Medical Evidence, p. 79.
165 *Ibid.*, pp. 78–79.
166 *Ibid.*, p. 89.
167 The Minutes of Proceedings on a Preliminary Inquiry on the Huddersfield Improvement Bill, Ms HPL (KHT 9/1).
168 *Ibid.*, Evidence of T. R. Tatham, pp. 27–36.
169 *Ibid.*, Evidence of Mr Thomas Wrigley, pp. 37–43.
170 *LM*, 2 June, 1849.
171 *Ibid.*
172 J. T. Ward, *The Factory Movement 1830–1855*, p. 39; R. Oastler, *Humanity Against Tyranny, Being An Expose of a Petition, Presented to the House of Commons, By Lord Morpeth, August 3rd, 1831 From Ten Factory-Mongers, Resident in Huddersfield and its Neighbourhood, Against Sir J. C. Hobhouse's Factories Bill* (Leeds, 1831), p. 5. For more on the involvement of doctors in Chartism and the Factory Movement, see, for example, J. T. Ward, pp. 23, 38–40, 177, 294; M. Hovell, *The Chartist Movement* (2nd ed., Manchester, 1925), pp. 36–38, 91.
173 White, 1853, p. 866; J. W. Walker, *op. cit.*, p. 554; Poll Book of the Wakefield Borough Election, 1865, WDA (Local Collection W.324).
174 E. P. Hennock, *op. cit.*, pp. 194, 206.
175 See Chapter 2, pp. 31–34 for more on the politics of the two towns.
176 A Copy of the Poll. Borough of Huddersfield, 1834, HPL (B.324).
177 J. R. Vincent, *op. cit.*, pp. 112–113.
178 For Lascelles Joseph Bennett, William Dawson, Henry Dunn, John Horsfall, Thomas Ross, William Rowlandson, William Starkey, Squire Statter, William Statter, Edward Taylor and William Thomas, MD; for Gaskell Caleb Crowther, William and George Holdsworth, and Benjamin and Ebenezer Walker. Wakefield Borough Election. Poll Book, 1837, WDA (Local Collection W.324).
179 Poll Book of the Wakefield Borough Election, 1862, WDA (Local Collection W.324).
180 Register of Electors for the Borough of Wakefield, 1840, WDA (Local Collection W.324).
181 Minute Book of the Huddersfield Board of Guardians, Vol. 2, 27 March, 1840, Ms HPL (P/HU/M).
182 *WE*, 7 July, 1855.
183 *WHJ*, 12 October, 1827.
184 J. W. Walker, *op. cit.*, p. 129.
185 *LM*, 11 January, 1800.
186 Westgate Chapel. Announcement of a Course of Lectures on the Internal Evidences of Christianity, to be delivered by D. Alexander, 1835, WDA (JGC).
187 *WHJ*, 19 January, 1827.
188 R. J. Cooter, *op. cit.*, Part I, pp. 5, 11–12. See also R. J. Cooter, *The cultural meaning of popular science. Phrenology and the organization of consent in nineteenth-century Britain* (Cambridge, 1984).
189 *WHJ*, 18 and 25 March, 1831.
190 D. Alexander, *Horae Poeticae or Poems, with Notes By a Retired Physician* (1837), WDA (JGC).
191 A. K. Jacques, *op. cit.*, pp. 48, 125.
192 *WS*, 24 February, 1804.
193 C. Crowther, MD, *op. cit.*, Ms WDA (JGC).
194 Rules and Regulations Respecting Dr Crowther's Charities, Wakefield, 1839, pp. 6–7, WDA (Local Collection, Box 8).
195 *Ibid.*, p. 21.
196 For Crowther's relationships with his medical brethren, see pp. 320–321.
197 J. W. Walker, *op. cit.*, p. 570.
198 C. Crowther, MD, *op. cit.*, Ms WDA (JGC).

199 *Ibid.*
200 *WJ*, 16 October, 1840.
201 Wakefield Archery Club; Established June 25th, 1834. Report of 1st meeting, 25th June, 1834, WDA (Local Collection, Box 2C).
202 T. G. Wright, MD, *Reminiscences of the Charity Ball*, WYCRO (C235/2/1).
203 A. K. Jacques, *op. cit.*, pp. 155, 161–162, 169–170.
204 G. W. Tomlinson, *Some Account of the Founders of the Huddersfield Subscription Library* (Huddersfield, 1875), pp. 51–54.
205 *LM*, 25 June, 1814.
206 *LM*, 2 July, 1814.
207 *LM*, 20 May, 1820.
208 *A Brief Memoir of the Late Mr Sargent, Surgeon, Huddersfield*, HPL (Local Pamphlets, Vol. 30).
209 'The Late Mr Henry Dunn, of Wakefield', *Medical Times and Gazette*, 1858, Vol. II, pp. 254–255.
210 J. Horsfall Turner, *op. cit.*, p. 172.
211 *PMD*, 1859 (Obituary Section). For interesting biographies of eighteenth-century Sheffield medical practitioners, see M. C. Hamilton, *The Development of Medicine in the Sheffield Region up to 1815*, unpublished MA thesis, Sheffield, 1957, Chapter VII. See also B. and D. Payne (eds), 'Extracts from the Journals of John Deakin Heaton, MD, of Claremont, Leeds', *Publications of the Thoresby Society*, Vol. 53, 1972, Part II, pp. 95–153. For further biographies of Wakefield and Huddersfield medical men, see Appendix 11.
212 For a study of the impact of the 1832 cholera epidemic on various sections of society and the medical profession, see M. Durey, *The Return of the Plague. British Society and the Cholera 1831–2* (Dublin, 1979).
213 *WHJ*, 3 December, 1830.
214 J. W. Walker, *op. cit.*, pp. 540–543.
215 *WHJ*, 3 December, 1830.
216 Minute Book of the Huddersfield Infirmary, Vol. I, General Meeting of the Governors, 12 July, 1832, p. 311.
217 R. J. Morris points to a similar expression of mistrust and opposition towards the Leeds medical profession. R. J. Morris, *op. cit.*, pp. 179–180.
218 A Copy of the Poll. Borough of Huddersfield, 1834, HPL (B.324).
219 Bolus – large pill. Jalap – strong purgative. Misc. Broadsheets on the 1834 Huddersfield election campaign, HPL (Tomlinson Collection).
220 *WHJ*, 28 April, 1815.
221 *HE*, 10 April, 1852.
222 *WJ*, 21 January, 1842.
223 *WHJ*, 24 March, 1820.
224 H. Clarkson, *op. cit.*, p. 168.
225 *WHJ*, 18 May, 1832.
226 A. K. Jacques, *op. cit.*, p. 48.
227 P. Starr, *The Social Transformation of American Medicine*, p. 19.
228 M. J. Peterson, *op. cit.*, p. 134.
229 It has also been impossible to give a numerical breakdown of the participation of medical men in comparison with other social and occupational groups. A comparison of the doctors' civic activities with those of the legal profession, for example, could prove interesting.
230 Annual Reports of The Wakefield Town Mission, 1848–1870, WDA (Local Collection, Box 4B); Reports of the Wakefield Mechanics' Institution, 1842–1871, WDA (Local Collection, Box 11B).
231 I. Inkster, 'Marginal Men: Aspects of the Social Role of the Medical Community in Sheffield 1790–1850', p. 129.
232 See Appendix 11; for example, the biographies of Samuel Holdsworth and William Statter of Wakefield.
233 M. J. Peterson, *op. cit.*, p. 194.

234 J. V. Pickstone, 'The Professionalisation of Medicine in England and Europe: the state, the market and industrial society', p. 529.
235 N. and J. Parry, *op. cit.*; I. Waddington, *The Medical Profession in the Industrial Revolution* (Dublin, 1984); M. J. Peterson, *op. cit.*
236 See Chapter 7, pp. 295–297.

Chapter 9

1 For the separate findings of the survey with respect to the different forms of provision, see the Concluding remarks to Chapters 3 to 8. The only indications of the success (or failure) of medical treatment are provided by the dispensary and infirmary charities, and the figures cited are far from reliable. For more on this subject, see Chapter 4, Section 4.1 and Appendix 6.
2 M. C. Buer, *op. cit.*, pp. 126, 136.
3 For the spread of the dispensary movement, see I.S.L. Loudon, 'The Origins and Growth of the Dispensary Movement in England', *Bulletin of the History of Medicine*, Vol. 55, Part 3, 1981, pp. 322–342 and H. Marland, *The Provision of Medical Treatment for the Sick Poor. The Doncaster Dispensary 1792–1867*, Chapter 3.
4 I. Waddington, *The Medical Profession in the Industrial Revolution*, p. 140.
5 I. Waddington, 'Competition and monopoly in a profession. The campaign for medical registration in Britain', p. 314.
6 C. Webster, *op. cit.*, p. 215.
7 See, for example, M. W. Flinn, *op. cit.*; R. G. Hodgkinson, *The Origins of the National Health Service*; M. A. Crowther, *op. cit.*, especially Chapters 3 and 6.
8 Most hospitals had similar regulations. For example, the first county hospital to be founded, for Hampshire, was established in Winchester in 1736. It was stated in an account of its foundation that it was intended to relieve the 'useful and industrious instead of only *the Poor*' (their emphasis). M. C. Buer, *op. cit.*, p. 127.
9 See Chapter 4, especially pp. 130–145.
10 84th AR WI, 1870–1871; 40th AR HI, 1870–1871.
11 For more on the relative importance of out-patient care, and for details of rates of admission and cure, see Chapter 4, Section 4.1.
12 N. McCord, 'The Implementation of the 1834 Poor Law Amendment Act on Tyneside', *International Review of Social History*, Vol. XIV, 1969, p. 100. Quoted in D. Ashforth, *op. cit.*, p. 213.
13 SCMPR 1844, Evidence of H. W. Rumsey, Esq., Appendix, Schedule 2.
14 A Statement of the Accounts of the Huddersfield Union, 1861–1873. Medical Cases and Vaccinations during the Half-Year ended March, 1861, HPL (P/HU/Cfo); 30th AR HI, 1860–1861.
15 A Statement of the Accounts of the Huddersfield Union, 1861–1873. The Township of Huddersfield in Account with the Huddersfield Union, for the Year ended March 25th, 1863, HPL (P/HU/Cfo); 33rd AR HI, 1863–1864.
16 D. F. E. Sykes, *op. cit.*, p. 409.
17 SCMPR 1844, Evidence of H. W. Rumsey, Esq., Appendix, Schedule 2.
18 W. Ranger, *op. cit.*, Appendix, p. 87; 64th AR WD, 1850–1851.
19 20th and 30th ARs HI, 1850–1851, 1860–1861; 64th and 74th ARs WI, 1850–1851, 1860–1861. These figures do not include patients admitted to the Huddersfield institution from beyond the Township boundaries.
20 44th AR WD, 1830–1831; The Annual Statement of the Receipts and Payments of the Overseers of the Poor of the Township of Wakefield, 1834–1835, WDA (JGC); Township of Wakefield. Statement of the Accounts, For the Half-Year Ending Twenty-Ninth September, 1858, WDA (Local Collection, Box 8); 71st AR WI, 1857–1858.
21 These practices were reputed to exist in connection with the Old Poor Law and private practice. For a brief discussion of this theme, see the Concluding remarks to Chapter 3 and Chapter 7, p. 262.

22 R. Porter, 'The Patient's View. Doing Medical History from Below', *Theory and Society*, Vol. 14, 1985, p. 175.

23 R. Porter, 'Lay medical knowledge in the eighteenth century', p. 138.

24 Abstract of Returns Relative to the Expense and Maintenance of the Poor, PP, 1818, XIX (82).

25 W. Ranger, *op. cit.*, Evidence of W. R. Milner, Esq., p. 88; Township of Wakefield. Statement of the Accounts, For the Half-Year Ending Twenty-Ninth September, 1858, WDA (Local Collection, Box 8).

26 SCMPR 1844, Evidence of H. W. Rumsey, Esq., p. 547, Q.9121.

27 White, 1861.

28 *Ibid.*

29 See Chapter 6.

30 J. V. Pickstone, 'The Professionalisation of Medicine in England and Europe: the state, the market and industrial society', p. 540.

31 See Chapter 4.

32 See Chapter 7, pp. 274–278 and Chapter 8, pp. 329–336.

33 See the Concluding remarks to Chapter 3.

34 See Chapter 7, Section 7.1.

35 See the Concluding remarks to Chapter 6.

36 J. V. Pickstone, 'The Professionalisation of Medicine in England and Europe: the state, the market and industrial society', p. 550.

Bibliography

List of abbreviations used in Bibliography

HPL   Huddersfield Public Library (Kirklees District Archives and Local Studies
          Department)
HRI   Huddersfield Royal Infirmary (Postgraduate Library)
WDA   Wakefield District Archives (JGC Private Collection of Mr John Goodchild,
          District Archivist)
WYCRO West Yorkshire County Record Office
Ms   Manuscript source (all sources are printed unless otherwise stated).
          All books and pamphlets, etc. are published in London unless otherwise stated.

Primary sources

Official sources

Census Enumerators' Books, Wakefield and Huddersfield Townships, 1841, 1851, 1861
    and 1871, Ms.
Report of the Charity Commissioners on Endowed Charities of the West Riding, Vol. V,
    1899.
West Riding Quarter Sessions Indictment Books, Ms WYCRO (Q54).
Ministry of Health Papers. Correspondence between the Poor Law Unions and Poor Law
    Commission, and after 1847 Poor Law Board. Wakefield and Huddersfield Unions, Ms
    Public Record Office (Category MH12/).
Annual Reports of the Poor Law Commission, 1834–1846.
Annual Reports of the Poor Law Board, 1847–1870.
The Minutes of Proceedings on a Preliminary Inquiry on the Huddersfield Improvement
    Bill, Held February, 1848 (Huddersfield, 1851), Ms HPL (KHT9/1).
W. Ranger, Report to the General Board of Health on a Preliminary Inquiry into the
    Sewerage, Drainage, and Supply of Water, and the Sanitary Condition of the Inhabitants
    of the Borough of Wakefield in the County of York (Public Health Act 11 & 12 Vict.
    Cap.63), 1852.
The Sanitary Inspector's First Annual Report on the Sanitary Condition of the Borough of
    Huddersfield, for the Year ending August 31st, 1869 (Huddersfield, 1870), HPL (Misc.
    Pamph: Hudd. Corp. Sanitary Dept.).
Medical Officer's Reports to the Sanitary Committee, June 1873 to March 1876. Second
    Report, July 1873, Ms HPL (Unclassified).

Local sources

a) *Poor Law*
Accounts of the Overseers of the Poor of Wakefield Township, 1738–1790, Ms WDA
    (JGC).

The Annual Statement of the Receipts and Payments of the Overseers of the Poor of the Township of Wakefield, 1834–1835, WDA (JGC).

The Accounts of Matthew Ash Overseer of the Poor of Horbury for the Year 1775. Printed as K. Bartlett, *A Year in the Life of Horbury 1775* (Wakefield, n.d.), WDA (Local Collection).

Horbury Overseers Account Book, 1821–1834, Ms WDA (JGC).

Stanley Township Accounts, 1795–1801, Ms WDA (JGC).

Miscellaneous Accounts and Correspondence, Ossett Township, c. 1830, Ms and Printed, WDA (JGC).

Huddersfield Town Book, 1784–1793, Ms HPL (P/HU/M).

Township of Mirfield Poor Law Archive, c. 1718–1838, Ms HPL (P/M).

Honley Civil Township Records, c. 1709–1838, Ms HPL (CP/HO).

Account Books of the Overseers of the Poor of South Crosland, 1790–1841, Ms HPL (CP/SC/OP).

Wakefield Union. Extracts from the Half-yearly Abstract of the Separate Accounts of each Township, . . . for the Half-year ending 29th September, 1850, WDA (JGC).

Township of Wakefield. Statement of the Accounts, For the Half-Year Ending Twenty-Ninth September, 1858, WDA (Local Collection, Box 8).

Minute Books of the Huddersfield Board of Guardians, Vols 1–13, 1837–1871, Ms HPL (P/HU/M).

Minute Book of the Ratepayers of Township of Huddersfield, 1835–1878, Ms and Printed, HPL (KHT1/2/2).

Report of the Committee inquiring into the necessity of erecting a New Union Workhouse, 23 February, 1849, Ms HPL (P/HU/Cfo).

A Statement of the Accounts of the Huddersfield Union, 1861–1873, HPL (P/HU/Cfo).

b) *Medical charities*

Annual Reports of the Wakefield Dispensary and Infirmary (1790–1792, 1830–1831 (including set of rules), 1850–1881), WYCRO (C235/1/37–41).

Thirty Years of Hospital Work. A Record of the Growth and Management of the Clayton Hospital & Wakefield General Dispensary During the Period when John Binks was Honorary Secretary, 1894 (press cuttings, photographs and handwritten reports of annual meetings, etc.), WYCRO (C235/6/2).

Rules and Regulations for The Government of the Wakefield General Dispensary and Clayton Hospital, 1854, WYCRO (C235/1).

Rules and Regulations for The Government of The Clayton Hospital and Wakefield General Dispensary, 1864, WYCRO (C235/1).

Printed appeal for subscriptions for a portrait of Thomas Clayton, Esq., dated 24 October, 1867, WYCRO (C235/4/1).

Letter from J. C. D. Charlesworth to Mr John Binks, re. endowment of the proposed new hospital, dated February 16, 1871, Ms WDA (Local Collection, Box 8).

Programme of Centenary Celebrations of The Clayton Hospital, 1854–1954 (Wakefield, 1954), WYCRO (C235/6/5).

Minute Books of the Huddersfield General Dispensary and Infirmary, 3 Vols, 1814–1840, 1840–1869, 1869–1887, Ms WYCRO (C500).

Annual Reports of the Huddersfield General Dispensary and Infirmary (1814–1818, 1820–1841, 1846–1847, 1855–1881), WYCRO (C500).

Rules of the Huddersfield Dispensary, Instituted May 12, 1814, 1821, WYCRO (C500).

Rules and Regulations of the Huddersfield and Upper Agbrigg Infirmary, 1834, HPL (B.362).

Letter from John Thomson of Halifax to Mr Wilks, surgeon, dated May 5, 1814, Ms HRI.

Report of the General Meeting of the Inhabitants of the Town and Neighbourhood of

Huddersfield, held at the George Inn, on Friday the 17th of October, 1828, for the purpose of receiving the Report of the Committee, relative to the Establishment of an Infirmary, HPL (Tolson Collection).

The Huddersfield & Upper Agbrigg Infirmary. Laying of the First Stone (Huddersfield, 1829), HPL (Tomlinson Collection).

Anon., *Lines Written for The Ladies' Bazaar, in aid of the Huddersfield Infirmary* (Huddersfield, n.d., c. 1831), HPL (Tomlinson Collection).

Anon., *In Memory of Mr Samuel Clay, of Huddersfield, Who died Feb. 11, 1833, in his 54th Year* (Huddersfield, n.d., c. 1833), HPL (Misc. Pamph., B.920 CLA).

W. Dearden, *Lines Written on Witnessing the Laying of the Foundation Stone of the Huddersfield and Upper Agbrigg Infirmary, June 29, 1829* (Huddersfield, 1829), HPL (HC OLT).

In Affectionate Remembrance of William Willans, Esq., J.P. (This Sermon was preached in Highfield Chapel, On Sunday Evening, September 20th, 1863, By the Rev. R. Bruce) (Huddersfield, n.d., c. 1863), HPL (Local Pamphlets, Vol. 2).

A Sermon Preached at the Parish Church, Huddersfield, On Sunday, February 22nd, 1885, On the Occasion of the Death of J. C. Laycock, Esq., By the Rev. J. W. Bardsley, MA, Vicar (Huddersfield, 1885), HPL (Local Pamphlets, Vol. 2).

Huddersfield Royal Infirmary. An Epitome (Oldham, n.d., c. 1921), HPL (Tomlinson Collection).

Wakefield House of Recovery. Register of Patients, 1826–1854, Ms WYCRO (C235/5/1).

Wakefield Charity Ball Scrapbook, c. 1818–1898 (newspaper cuttings), WYCRO (C235/2/1). Includes T. G. Wright, MD, *Reminiscences of the Charity Ball* (Wakefield, 1895) and *Wakefield Charity Ball*, letter dated January, 1885.

c) *Friendly societies*

The Court Directory of the Order of Ancient Foresters, 1840, WDA (Local Collection W.334.7).

Directory of the Ancient Order of Foresters, Compiled up to January 1st, 1850, WDA (Local Collection W.334.7).

Rules of the Friendly Society of Oddwomen held at the Kirkgate Hotel in Wakefield in the County of York, n.d., Ms WDA (JGC).

General Laws of the Golden Fleece Lodge, of Loyal Ancient Shepherds, Wakefield, n.d., WDA (JGC).

Minute Book of the Wakefield Female Benefit Society, 1 July, 1805 to 4 April, 1864, Ms WDA (Local Collection W.334.7).

Rules for the Regulation of a Friendly Society called A Free Gift instituted at Wakefield May 16th, 1808, Ms WDA (JGC).

Articles to be Observed by The Members of the Friendly Society at Almondbury. Revived the Twenty-fifth Day of July, 1810, HPL (Tomlinson Collection).

Articles to be Observed by the Members of the Benevolent Brief, Holden at the House of Mr Thomas Huscroft, The Hammer and Hand, in Kirkgate, Wakefield, 1816, WDA (Local Collection, Box 8).

Archives of the Royal Shepherds Sanctuary, No. 99, c. 1817–1881, Ms. and Printed, HPL (S/RS).

Archives of the Grand United Order of Oddfellows, Charity Lodge, No. 97, Cleckheaton, 1824–1875, Ms and Printed, HPL (S/CL).

Achives of the Deighton Lodge of Oddfellows (Woolpack Inn), No. 156, 1829–1868, Ms HPL (Unclassified).

Archives of the Independent Order of Oddfellows Manchester Unity Friendly Society Huddersfield District. Perseverance and Victory Lodges, 1842–1875, Ms and Printed, HPL (KC45).

Rules of the Huddersfield Co-operative Trading Friendly Society, Established, April 20,

1829. Revised and Enrolled April 12th, 1838, Huddersfield, 1838, HPL (Misc. Pamph: Co-op. Trading Friendly Society).

Wakefield British Friendly Union Society, Annual Reports, Nos 1–20, 1842–1862, WDA (Local Collection, Box 2C).

Archives of the Prince Albert Lodge of the Ancient Order of Druids, Thurstonland, c. 1851–1907, Ms and Printed, HPL (S/TD).

Rules of the West Riding of Yorkshire Provident Society, 1857, HPL (Unclassified).

Abstract of the Tables of the West Riding Provident Society, c. 1857, HPL (Unclassified).

Anon., *Observations on Friendly Societies* (Huddersfield, 1830), HPL (Local Pamphlets, Vol. 21).

d) *Charities and voluntary societies/churches and chapels*

Report of the Wakefield Benevolent Society, Instituted in the Year 1791, Wakefield, Nov. 30th, 1836, WDA (JGC).

Subscriptions to the Benevolent Society, c. 1832–1844, Ms WDA (JGC).

Annual Reports of The Wakefield Town Mission, 1848, 1849, 1852, 1870, WDA (Local Collection, Box 4B).

Reports of the Wakefield Auxiliary Bible Society (with lists of subscribers and benefactors), 1815–1832, WDA (Local Collection, Box 2C).

Rules and Regulations Respecting Dr Crowther's Charities, Wakefield, 1839, WDA (Local Collection, Box 8).

The Rules and Regulations of the Literary and Philosophical Society, at Wakefield, Established in 1825, Wakefield, 1834, WDA (Local Collection, Box 2C).

Wakefield Philosophical and Literary Society. List of Essays Read during Former Sessions, n.d., c. 1836, WDA (JGC).

The Laws and Regulations of the Wakefield Museum, 1830, WDA (Local Collection, Box 2C).

Reports of the Wakefield Mechanics' Institution, For the Years 1842–1843, 1849–1850, 1862–1868, 1870–1871, WDA (Local Collection, Box 11B).

First Annual Report of the Wakefield Mechanics' Institution. Natural History Department, Wakefield, 1857, WDA (Local Collection, Box 11B).

Wakefield Archery Club; Established June 25th, 1834. Report of 1st meeting, 25th June, 1834, WDA (Local Collection, Box 2C).

First Report of the State of the Huddersfield Benevolent Society, For the Relief of The Indigent, Sick, and Distressed, of every Description, for the Year 1798, HPL (Tolson Collection).

Address of the Huddersfield Benevolent and Visiting Society. Instituted December 13, 1830, Huddersfield, n.d., c. 1830, HPL (Tolson Collection).

Huddersfield Benevolent and Visiting Society. Appeal to Subscribers and Public, 1837, HPL (Tolson Collection).

First and Third Annual Reports of the Huddersfield Auxiliary Peace Society, for the Circulation of Tracts, 1823 and 1825, HPL (Misc. Pamph: Peace Society).

The Tenth Report of the Huddersfield Temperance Society, 1843, HPL (Misc. Pamph: Temperance).

1832–1932. Souvenir of the Centenary Celebrations of the Huddersfield Temperance Society (1932), HPL (S/HTe 8).

Laws for the Regulation of the Huddersfield Subscription Library, Established in March 1807 (Leeds, 1807) (including a list of members in 1807), HPL (Local Pamphlets, Vol. 16).

Reports of the Huddersfield Mechanics' Institution, 1844–1870, HPL (Misc. Pamph: Mechanics' Institute).

List of Subscribers for the Erection of the New Building in Northumberland-Street, Huddersfield, 1861, HPL (Misc. Pamph: Mechanics' Institute).

Huddersfield Ragged & Industrial School Fitzwilliam Street East. Report of the Thirteenth Year, Huddersfield, 1874, HPL (Misc. Pamph: Schools).

A List of The Proprietary of Huddersfield College, n.d., c. 1838, HPL (Misc. Pamph: Huddersfield College).

Preparatory School of Huddersfield College, 1838 (printed announcement), HPL (Misc. Pamph: Huddersfield College).

Transactions of the Huddersfield Archaeological and Topographical Association, Vol. I, Part I, 1866, HPL (Misc. Pamph: Societies: Arch. and Top.).

Huddersfield Archaeological Association. Papers Read at the Annual meeting on the 30th January, 1867, to which are Prefixed the Rules of the Association and List of Officers for 1867, Huddersfield, 1867, HPL (Misc. Pamph: Societies: Arch. and Top.).

Westgate Chapel. Announcement of a Course of Lectures on the Internal Evidences of Christianity, to be delivered by D. Alexander, 1835, WDA (JGC).

Westgate Chapel, Wakefield. Pew Rents Register, Vol. 2, 1834–1913, Ms WDA (JGC).

Register of Internments, 1829–1913. Wesleyan Chapel, West Parade, Wakefield, Ms WDA (JGC).

Ministers and Delegates attending the Anniversary Services of the West-Riding Home Missionary Society & Congregational Union, Held in Wakefield, April, 5th, 6th, and 7th, 1858, With Their Temporary Places of Abode, WDA (JGC).

Circular of the Committee for conducting the rebuilding of the Parish Church of Huddersfield. Jan., 1836, HPL (Misc. Pamph: St Peter's Church).

Circular of Committee appointed to superintend the repairing and repewing of St Paul's Church, Huddersfield, 1857, HPL (Misc. Pamph: St Paul's Church).

Huddersfield Parish Church. Abstract of the Churchwarden's Accounts for the Years 1854 and 1870, HPL (Misc. Pamph: St Peter's Church).

e) *Medical profession: medical societies, legal agreements, accounts, memoirs*
Rules of The Wakefield Medical Book Club, Jan. 5th, 1830, Ms WDA (JGC).

Minute Book of the Wakefield Microscopic Society, 1854–1858, Ms WDA (Local Collection, Box 2C).

Wakefield Microscopic Society. List of Meetings for 1871, WDA (Local Collection, Box 2C).

Huddersfield Medical Society. Minute Book, 1825–1834. Ms HRI.

Proceedings of the Huddersfield Medical Library, 1852–1883, Ms HRI.

Huddersfield Medical Library. Account Book, 1849–1926, Ms HRI.

Memorandum of an Agreement made the sixth day of April One Thousand seven hundred and ninety six, Between Thomas Smith of Wakefield Merchant of the one part and Edward Taylor of the same Place Surgeon and Apothecary of the other part, Ms WDA (JGC).

Articles of agreem[t] made this 28 day of April 1837 Bet[n] Geo. Holdsworth of Wakef[d] in the Co. of York Surgeon & Apothecary Wm. Holdsworth of the same place Surgeon & Apothecary (partnership dissolution), Ms WDA (JGC).

Miscellaneous Wakefield Apprenticeship Indentures (re. medical apprentices), Ms WDA (JGC, App. Indents.).

First Factory Doctor's Personal Accounts. George Holdsworth, of St John's Square Household Accts, May, 1839 to December, 1844 and January, 1845 to August, 1846, Ms WDA (JGC).

Minutes respecting the property of the late George Holdsworth of Wakefield Surgeon – who died 31st August 1846, Ms WDA (JGC).

Miscellaneous Medical Bills to Mr and Mrs John Lee of Wakefield, c. 1816–1824, WDA (JGC).

Miscellaneous Medical Bills to Mr Whitely of Wakefield, c. 1872–1888, WDA (JGC).

Memorials 1820 (HD 743 709) and 1839 (RB 474 733), Ms WYCRO (Registry of Deeds).
Her Majesty's Court of Probate, Wakefield District Registry. 1858 Wills, Vol. I, 1863 Wills, Vol. IV, WYCRO (Registry of Deeds).
A Brief Memoir of the Late Mr Sargent, Surgeon, Huddersfield (Huddersfield, n.d., c. 1840), HPL (Local Pamphlets, Vol. 30).
The Great Object of the Christian's Life and the Advantages of his Death. The Substance of A Sermon preached In Highfield Meeting-House, Huddersfield, on Sunday, the 28th Day of May, 1820, Occasioned by the lamented death of Mr Rowland Houghton, Surgeon (Sermon by the Rev. B. Boothroyd) (Huddersfield, 1820), HPL (Misc. Pamph: Sermons and Addresses).

f) *Poll Books, etc.*
A Copy of the Poll. Borough of Huddersfield, 1834, HPL (B.324).
Wakefield Borough Election. Poll Book, 1837, WDA (Local Collection W.324).
Wakefield Borough Election. The Poll Book, 1852, WDA (Local Collection W.324).
Poll Book of the Wakefield Borough Election, 1862, WDA (Local Collection W.324).
Poll Book of the Wakefield Borough Election, 1865, WDA (Local Collection W.324).
Register of Electors for the Borough of Wakefield, 1840, WDA (Local Collection W.324).
Miscellaneous Broadsheets on the 1834 Huddersfield election campaign, HPL (Tomlinson Collection).

Parliamentary papers and returns

a) *Returns*
Comparative Account of the Population of Great Britain in the Years 1801, 1811, 1821 and 1831. 1831, XVIII (348).
Abstract of the Answers and Returns made Pursuant to Acts 3 & 4 Vict.c. 99, and 4 Vict.c.7, entitled respectively 'An Act for taking an Account of the Population of Great Britain' and 'An Act to amend the Acts of the last Session for taking an account of the Population'. Occupation Abstract, Part 1. England and Wales, and Islands in the British Seas. 1844, XXVII (587).
A Return 'of the Medical Officers under the Poor Law Acts, . . .'. 1856, XLIX (434).
Abstract of Returns relative to the Expense and Maintenance of the Poor. 1803–1804, XIII (175).
Abstract of Returns Relative to the Expense and Maintenance of the Poor. 1818, XIX (82).
A Return relating to Friendly Societies enrolled in the Several Counties of England and Wales. 1842, XXVI (73).
Abstract of Returns of Sickness and Mortality, and of Reports of Assets, etc., of Friendly Societies in England and Wales, during the Five Years ending 31st December 1850. 1852–1853, C (31).
'Return of Number of Societies which have deposited their Rules with the Registrar of Friendly Societies, in England, Scotland, and Ireland, respectively under the Act 18 & 29 Vict.c.63,s.44, with the Name and Objects of each, and when Established'. 1867, XL (75).
Returns of all Societies whose Rules have been deposited with the Registrar of Friendly Societies in England, under the 18 & 19 Vict.c.63,s.44, and the Date when Deposited. 1868–1869, LVI (359).
Abstracts of the quinquennial returns of sickness and mortality experienced by Friendly Societies for periods between 1855 and 1875. 1880, LXVIII (517).

b) *Reports*
Report from the Select Committee on Medical Education. 1834, XIII (602).
Report of the Select Committee on the Poor Law Amendment Act. 1837–1838, XVIII (518).
First Annual Report of the Registrar – General. 1839, XVI (187).

Report of the Poor Law Commissioners on the Further Amendment of the Poor Laws. 1840, XVII (253).

Report from the Select Committee on Medical Poor Relief. Third Report. 1844, IX (531).

First Report of the Commissioners for Inquiring into the State of Large Towns and Populous Districts. 1844, XVII (572).

Second Report of the Commissioners for inquiring into the State of Large Towns and Populous Districts. 1845, XVIII (602) (610).

Report of the Commissioner Appointed under the Provisions of the Act 5 & 6 Vict.c.99, to Inquire into the Operation of that Act, and into the State of the Population in The Mining Districts. 1845, XXVII (670).

Report from the Select Committee on Medical Relief. 1854, XII (348).

Sixth Report of the Medical Officer of the Privy Council. 1864, XXVIII I (3416), App. 15, 'Reports on the Hospitals of the United Kingdom', by J. S. Bristowe and T. Holmes.

Newspapers

Halifax and Huddersfield Express
Huddersfield and Holmfirth Examiner
Huddersfield Chronicle
Huddersfield Examiner
Leeds Intelligencer
Leeds Mercury
Northern Star
Wakefield and Halifax Journal
Wakefield Express
Wakefield Journal and West Riding Herald
Wakefield Star
West Riding Herald and Wakefield Commercial and Agricultural Journal
The London Times
Newspaper Cuttings Book (Obituaries), No. II, 1868–1916, HPL (A920).
Newspaper Cuttings Books, Vols 2, 14, 18, 87, 88, 93, WDA (Local Collection).

Nineteenth-century medical journals

Birmingham Medical Review
Cholera Gazette
Edinburgh Medical Journal
The Lancet
London Medical Gazette
London Medical and Surgical Journal
Medical Times
Medical Times and Gazette
Pharmaceutical Journal and Transactions

Medical and trade directories

S. F. Simmons, *Medical Register for the Year 1780.*
Provincial Medical Directories, 1847–1872.
E. Baines, *History, Directory and Gazetteer of the County of York*, Vol. I, *The West Riding* (1822, reprinted Wakefield, 1969).
Huddersfield Directory and Year Book, 1868 (Huddersfield, 1868).
Kelly and Co., *Post Office Directory of Yorkshire* (1857).
E. R. Kelly, *The Post Office Directory of the West Riding of Yorkshire (1877).*
Our Ancestors; or Huddersfield 1818. 62 Years Ago (reprinted from the *Commercial Directory* for

1818–1820, published by J. Pigot and R. and W. Dean, Manchester, 1818) (Huddersfield, 1880).

W. Parson and W. White, *West Riding Yorkshire Directory* (Leeds, 1828).

W. Parson and W. White, *Directory of the Borough of Leeds, The City of York, and the Clothing District of Yorkshire* (Leeds, 1830).

Slater, *Royal Directory of Yorkshire* (1848).

Tindall's Huddersfield Directory and Year Book, for 1866 (Huddersfield and London, 1866).

F. White, *General and Commercial Directory of Sheffield, And official Guide, with Separate Historical, Statistical, and Topographical Descriptions of all the Boroughs, Towns, Parishes, Villages & Hamlets in a large District of Yorkshire, Nottinghamshire, & Derbyshire* (Sheffield, 1872).

W. White, *History, Gazetteer, and Directory, of the West Riding of Yorkshire* (Sheffield, 1837 (Vol. I), 1838 (Vol. II)).

W. White, *Directory and Topography of Leeds, Bradford, Halifax, Huddersfield, Wakefield, and the whole of the Clothing Districts of the West Riding of Yorkshire* (Sheffield, 1847).

W. White, *Directory and Gazetteer of Leeds, Bradford, Halifax, Huddersfield, Wakefield and the Whole of the Clothing Districts of Yorkshire* (1853, reprinted Newton Abbot, 1969).

W. White, *Directory and Topography of the Borough of Leeds, Wakefield, Bradford, Huddersfield, etc.* (Sheffield, 1861).

W. White, *Directory of Leeds, Bradford, Huddersfield, Halifax, Wakefield, Dewsbury* (Sheffield, 1866).

W. White, *General and Commercial Directory of Leeds, Huddersfield, Wakefield, Dewsbury, Batley, Heckwondwike, Holmfirth, Morley, Pudsey, and all the Parishes and Villages in and near those Populous Districts of the West Riding, forming the Seat of the great woollen manufacture, Being Part 1 of the Clothing District Directory* (12th ed., Sheffield, 1870).

William's Directory of the Borough of Huddersfield (1845).

Publications of Wakefield and Huddersfield medical men

D. Alexander, MD, *A Treatise on the Nature and Cure of the Cynanche Tracealis, Commonly called the Croup* (Huddersfield, n.d.), HPL (Local Pamphlets, Vol. 20).

D. Alexander, MD, *An Answer to the Enquiry, if it be the duty of Every Person to study the preservation of his Health, what means are the most likely to answer that end, and to which recourse may be had by all Classes of People?* (Manchester, 1804), Wellcome Institute Library.

D. Alexander, MD, *A Lecture on Phrenology, as Illustrative of the Moral and Intellectual Capacities of Man* (London, Edinburgh and Wakefield, 1826), WDA (Local Collection, Box 14).

D. Alexander, *Horae Poeticae or Poems, with Notes By a Retired Physician* (1837), WDA (JGC).

C. Crowther, MD, *Notes on Proposed Alms House for Dissenters & Fever Hospital* (Wakefield, 1842), Ms WDA (JGC).

S. Knaggs, *Common Sense versus Homoeopathy* (1855), Wellcome Institute Library.

Mr Tatham's Case against The Huddersfield Board of Guardians (a collection of correspondence between Mr T. R. Tatham, the Huddersfield Board of Guardians, and the Poor Law Commission and Board) (Huddersfield, 1848), HPL (Tomlinson Collection).

T. R. Tatham, MD, *Strictures on the Administration of Affairs Pertaining to the Huddersfield & Upper Agbrigg Infirmary* (Nottingham, 1864), HPL (Tomlinson Collection).

To the Governors of the Huddersfield and Upper Agbrigg Infirmary, The Official Letter, from David Marsden, Esq., Honorary Secretary; also a Reply by Thos. Robt. Tatham, MD (Nottingham, 1865), HPL (Tomlinson Collection).

W. Turnbull, MD, *An Appeal, in Behalf of the Intended Hospital at Huddersfield* (Huddersfield, n.d., c.1825), HPL (Tolson Collection).

J. K. Walker, MD, *Reasons for Establishing a Sea Bathing Infirmary, on the Western Coast, for the*

Benefit of the Poor: Addressed to The Governors of Medical Charities, to the Poor Law Guardians, and to The Friends of the Poor, In General, Resident in North Wales, Cheshire, Lancashire, and the West-Riding of Yorkshire; with an Appendix, containing the opinions of various eminent Medical authorities (Huddersfield, 1840), HPL (Misc. Pamph: Sea Bathing Infirmary).

T. G. Wright, MD, *A Lecture on Quack Medicines, Delivered to the Wakefield Mechanics' Institution, February 20th, 1843* (London and Wakefield, 1843), Wellcome Institute Library.

T. G. Wright, MD, *Cholera in the Asylum. Reports on the Origins and Progress of Pestilential Cholera, In the West-Yorkshire Lunatic Asylum, During the Autumn of 1849, and on the previous State of the Institution. A Contribution to the Statistics of Insanity and of Cholera* (London and Wakefield, 1850), Wellcome Institute Library.

T. G. Wright, MD, *The Wakefield House of Recovery* (Wakefield, 1895), WYCRO (C235/5/1).

Secondary sources

Local sources (Wakefield and Huddersfield)

O. Balmforth, *Huddersfield Past and Present; in its Social, Industrial and Educational Aspects* (Huddersfield, 1893), HPL (Local Pamphlets, Vol. 14).

O. Balmforth, *Jubilee History of the Corporation of Huddersfield 1868 to 1918* (Huddersfield, 1918).

R. Brook, *The Story of Huddersfield* (1968).

A. J. Brooke, 'Jacobinism and Unrest in the Huddersfield Area 1799–1803', *Old West Riding*, Vol. 11, No. 1, 1982, pp. 22–25.

Reverend C. E. Camidge, MA, *A History of Wakefield and its Industrial and Fine Art Exhibition* (London and Wakefield, 1866).

S. Chadwick, '*A Bold and Faithful Journalist'. Joshua Hobson 1810–1876* (Huddersfield, 1976).

H. Clarkson, *Memories of Merry Wakefield* (1887, reprinted Wakefield, 1969, from the 2nd ed., published in 1889).

W. B. Crump and G. Ghorbal, *History of the Huddersfield Woollen Industry* (Huddersfield, 1935).

T. Dyson, *The History of Huddersfield and District from the earliest times down to 1932* (Huddersfield, 1932).

C. P. Hobkirk, *Huddersfield: Its History and Natural History* (2nd ed., London and Huddersfield, 1868).

J. Horsfall Turner, *Wakefield House of Correction* (Bingley, 1904).

C. A. Hulbert, *Supplementary Annals of the Church and Parish of Almondbury, July, 1882, to June, 1885* (London and Huddersfield, 1885).

A. K. Jacques, *Merrie Wakefield* (based on some of the Diaries of Clara Clarkson (1811–1889) of Alverthorpe Hall, Wakefield) (Wakefield, 1971).

M. A. Jagger, *The History of Honley* (Honley, 1914).

N. L. Maxwell Reader, 'An Ancient Practice Alive and Well Today', *Practitioner*, Vol. 206, 1971, pp. 691–697.

R. Oastler, *Humanity Against Tyranny, Being An Expose of a Petition, Presented to the House of Commons, By Lord Morpeth, August 3rd, 1831 From Ten Factory-Mongers, Resident in Huddersfield and its Neighbourhood, Against Sir J. C. Hobhouse's Factories Bill* (Leeds, 1831).

G. S. Phillips, *Walks Round Huddersfield* (Huddersfield, 1848).

W. Read, 'The Story of the Clayton Hospital, Wakefield', *Wakefield Historical Society Journal*, Vol. 2, 1975, pp. 5–13.

J. Springett, 'Landowners and urban development: the Ramsden Estate and nineteenth-century Huddersfield', *Journal of Historical Geography*, Vol. 8, No. 2, 1982, pp. 129–144.

E. N. Steele, *Glimpses of Stanley's Past* (Parish Church of St Peter, Stanley. Commemorative Brochure to Celebrate 150 Years' Jubilee, 1824–1974) (Wakefield, 1974), WDA.

A. W. Sykes, *The Founders and Early History of Ramsden Street Chapel, Huddersfield* (Huddersfield, 1901).

A. W. Sykes, *Ramsden Street Independent Chapel Huddersfield. Notes and Records of A Hundred Years 1825–1925* (Huddersfield, 1925).

D. F. E. Sykes, *Huddersfield and Its Vicinity* (Huddersfield, 1898).

J. Sykes, *Slawit in the 'Sixties* (Huddersfield and London, n.d., c. 1926).

G. W. Tomlinson, *Some Account of the Founders of the Huddersfield Subscription Library* (Huddersfield, 1875).

G. W. Tomlinson, *History of Huddersfield (Home Words) 1885–1887* (Huddersfield, 1887).

J. W. Walker, *Wakefield. Its History and People* (2nd ed., Wakefield, 1939), Vol. II.

S. H. Waters, *Wakefield in the Seventeenth Century. A Social History of the Town and Neighbourhood From 1550 to 1710* (Wakefield, 1933).

D. Wholmsley, 'A Landed Estate and the Railway: Huddersfield 1844–54', *The Journal of Transport History*, New Series, Vol. II, No. 4, 1974, pp. 189–213.

D. Wholmsley, 'Market Forces and Urban Growth: The Influence of the Ramsden Family on the Growth of Huddersfield 1716–1853', *The Journal of Regional and Local Studies*, Vol. 4, No. 2, Autumn, 1984, pp. 27–56.

P. Wintersgill, 'A Huddersfield surgeon. William Wilks and the Old Dispensary', *Practitioner*, Vol. 216, 1976, pp. 352–355.

Contemporary sources (books and pamphlets, pre-1900)

Anon., *The Villager's Friend & Physician: Or, A Familiar Address on the Preservation of Health, and the Removal of Disease on its first Appearance; Supposed to be Delivered by a village Apothecary* (Huddersfield, 1811) (first published under the authorship of J. Parkinson in 1804), HPL (Local Pamphlets, Vol. 20).

J. Aikin, MD, *A Description of the Country from Thirty to Forty Miles Round Manchester* (1795, reprinted Newton Abbot, 1968).

E. Baines, *The Social, Educational, and Religious State of the Manufacturing Districts* (1843, reprinted 1969).

E. Baines, *Account of the Woollen Manufacture of England* (reprinted from T. Baines, *Yorkshire, past and present*), with an introduction by K. G. Ponting (New York, 1970).

T. Baines, *Yorkshire, past and present: a history and description of the 3 ridings of the great county of Yorks, from the earliest ages to the year 1870, . . .* (1871–1877), Vols I and II.

W. Buchan, *Domestic medicine; or the Family Physician* (Edinburgh, 1769).

E. Chadwick, *Report on the Sanitary Condition of the Labouring Population of Great Britain* (1842, reprinted, with an introduction by M. W. Flinn, Edinburgh, 1965).

A. I. Coffin, *The Botanic Guide to Health* (5th ed., Manchester, 1846).

W. R. Croft, *The History of the Factory Movement* (Huddersfield, 1888).

G. Eliot, *Middlemarch* (Harmondsworth, 1965, Penguin ed., first published 1871–1872).

F. Engels, *The Condition of the Working Class in England* (Panther ed., 1969, first published Leipzig, 1845, first published in Great Britain, 1892).

W. Fox, MD, *The Working Man's Model Family Botanic Guide or Every Man His Own Doctor* (11th ed., Sheffield, 1887).

E. Gaskell, *Mary Barton. A Tale of Manchester Life* (Harmondsworth, 1970, Penguin ed., first published 1848).

G. Gissing, *New Grub Street* (Harmondsworth, 1968, Penguin ed., first published 1891).

A. B. Granville, *Spas of England. 1: the North* (1841, reprinted Bath, 1971).

W. Henderson, *Notes on the Folk-Lore of the Northern Counties of England and the Borders* (1879).

J. Hirst, *Notable Things of various Subjects, 1836–c.1892*, Ms HPL (Dairy: Ms/f).

G. C. Holland, MD, *The Vital Statistics of Sheffield* (London and Sheffield, 1843).

J. Mayhall, *The Annals of Yorkshire, From the Earliest Period to the Present Time*, Vol. I (1862).

F. Oppert, *Hospitals, Infirmaries and Dispensaries* (1867).

E. Parsons, *The Civil, Ecclesiastical, Literary, Commercial, and Miscellaneous History of Leeds, Halifax, Huddersfield, Bradford, Wakefield, Dewsbury, Otley, and the Manufacturing District of Yorkshire*, Vols I and II (Leeds, 1834).

H. Ratcliffe, *Observations on the rate of mortality and sickness existing amongst friendly societies* (Manchester, 1850) in W. Farr, *Mortality in Mid 19th Century Britain* (reprinted, with an introduction by R. Wall, Amersham, 1974).

W. Sheardown, *Pamphlets* (three volumes of extracts from the *Doncaster Gazette*, c. 1840–1870), Doncaster Public Library (Local Studies).

J. Smedley, *Practical Hydropathy* (4th ed., 1861).

The Journal of Dr John Simpson of Bradford, 1825, ed. E. Willmott (Bradford, 1981).

J. Woodhead, *Netherthong, recipe book*, 1818, Ms HPL (KC 190/1).

Books

B. Abel-Smith, *The Hospitals 1800–1948* (1964).

W. Addison, *English Spas* (1951).

J. Addy, *The Textile Revolution* (1976).

R. Aldington, *The Strange Life of Charles Waterton 1782–1865* (1949).

D. Alexander, *Retailing in England during the Industrial Revolution* (1970).

S. T. Anning, *The General Infirmary at Leeds* (Edinburgh and London, 1963), Vol. I.

S. T. Anning, *The History of Medicine in Leeds* (Leeds, 1980).

J. A. Banks, *Prosperity and Parenthood* (1954).

V. Berridge and G. Edwards, *Opium and the People* (1981).

G. Best, *Mid-Victorian Britain 1851–70* (1971).

P. Branca, *Silent Sisterhood. Middle-Class Women in the Victorian Home* (1975).

P. Branca (ed.), *The Medicine Show. Patients, Physicians and the Perplexities of the Health Revolution in Modern Society* (New York, 1977).

A. Briggs, *Victorian Cities* (1963).

W. Brockbank, *Portrait of a Hospital 1752–1948* (1952).

A. Brundage, *The Making of the New Poor Law 1832–39* (1978).

M. C. Buer, *Health, wealth, and population in the early days of the industrial revolution* (2nd ed., New York, 1968, first published 1926).

J. Camp, *Magic, Myth and Medicine* (1973).

F. F. Cartwright, *A Social History of Medicine* (1977).

O. Checkland and M. Lamb (eds), *Health Care as Social History. The Glasgow Case* (Aberdeen, 1982).

E. Clarke (ed.), *Modern Methods in the History of Medicine* (1971).

G. D. H. Cole and R. Postgate, *The Common People 1746–1946* (4th ed., 1961, first published 1938).

R. J. Cooter, *The cultural meaning of popular science. Phrenology and the organization of consent in nineteenth-century Britain* (Cambridge, 1984).

C. Creighton, *A History of Epidemics in Britain* (2nd ed., 1965, first published Cambridge, 1894), Vol. II.

G. Crossick (ed.), *The Lower Middle Class in Britain 1870–1914* (1977).

M. A. Crowther, *The Workhouse System 1834–1929* (1981).

Sir D'Arcy Power (ed.), *British Medical Societies* (1939).

L. Davidoff, *The Best Circles. Society Etiquette and the Season* (1973).

R. Dennis, *English industrial cities of the nineteenth century. A social geography* (Cambridge, 1984).

A. Digby, *Pauper Palaces* (1978).

A. P. Donajgrodzki (ed.), *Social Control in Nineteenth Century Britain* (1977).

J. Donnison, *Midwives and Medical Men* (1977).

M. Durey, *The Return of the Plague. British Society and the Cholera 1831–2* (Dublin, 1979).

N. C. Edsall, *The anti-Poor Law movement 1834–44* (Manchester, 1971).

Encyclopaedia of Occupational Health and Safety (3rd ed., Geneva, 1983).

S. E. Finer, *The Life and Times of Sir Edwin Chadwick* (1952).

D. Fraser, *The Evolution of the British Welfare State* (1973).

D. Fraser (ed.), *The New Poor Law in the Nineteenth Century* (1976).

W. M. Frazer, *A History of English Public Health 1834–1939* (1950).

H. F. Garrison, *An Introduction to the History of Medicine* (4th ed., Philadelphia, 1929).

B. B. Gilbert, *The Evolution of National Insurance in Great Britain. The Origins of the Welfare State* (1966).

P. H. J. H. Gosden, *The Friendly Societies in England 1815–1875* (Manchester, 1961).

P. H. J. H. Gosden, *Self-Help Voluntary Associations in the 19th Century* (1973).

D. Gregory, *Regional Transformation and Industrial Revolution. A Geography of the Yorkshire Woollen Industry* (1982).

G. Talbot Griffith, *Population Problems of the Age of Malthus* (2nd ed., 1967, first published Cambridge, 1926).

D. Guthrie, *A History of Medicine* (1945).

C. Hadfield, *The Canals of Yorkshire and North East England* (Newton Abbot, 1972), Vols I and II.

J. F. C. Harrison, *The Early Victorians 1832–51* (1971).

P. J. N. Havins, *The Spas of England* (1976).

E. P. Hennock, *Fit and Proper Persons. Ideal and reality in nineteenth-century urban government* (1973).

M. Hewitt, *Wives and Mothers in Victorian Industry* (1958).

E. J. Hobsbawm, *Labouring Men. Studies in the History of Labour* (1968).

R. G. Hodgkinson, *The Origins of the National Health Service* (1967).

P. Hollis (ed.), *Women in Public: The Women's Movement 1850–1900* (1979).

G. Holmes, *Augustan England. Professions, State and Society, 1680–1730* (1982).

M. Hovell, *The Chartist Movement* (2nd ed., Manchester, 1925).

G. M. Howe, *Man, Environment and Disease in Britain. A Medical Geography through the Ages* (Newton Abbot, 1972).

I. Inkster and J. Morrell (eds), *Metropolis and Province. Science in British culture, 1780–1850* (1983).

R. A. Irwin (ed.), *Letters of Charles Waterton of Walton Hall, near Wakefield* (1955).

E. Jameson, *The Natural History of Quackery* (1961).

D. T. Jenkins, *The West Riding Wool Textile Industry 1770–1835* (Edington, Wiltshire, 1975).

P. Joyce, *Work, Society and Politics. The culture of the factory in later Victorian England* (1980).

Kremers and Urdang, *History of Pharmacy* (4th ed., revised by G. Sonnedecker, Philadelphia, 1976).

M. S. Larson, *The Rise of Professionalism. A Sociological Analysis* (Berkeley, 1977).

P. Laslett and R. Wall (eds), *Household and Family in Past Time* (Cambridge, 1972).

R. Lawton (ed.), *The Census and Social Structure. An Interpretative Guide to Nineteenth Century Censuses for England and Wales* (1978).

N. Longmate, *The Workhouse* (1974).

J. Lowerson and J. Myerscough, *Time to Spare in Victorian England* (Hassocks, Sussex, 1977).

E. Maple, *Magic, Medicine and Quackery* (1968).

J. Money, *Experience and Identity. Birmingham and the West Midlands 1760–1800* (Manchester, 1977).

D. Owen, *English Philanthropy 1660–1960* (1965).

G. W. Oxley, *Poor Relief in England and Wales 1601–1834* (Newton Abbot, 1974).

W. Page, *The Victorian History of the Counties of England. A History of the County of York*, Vol. III (1913).

N. and J. Parry, *The Rise of the Medical Profession. A Study of Collective Social Mobility* (1976).

W. Ll. Parry-Jones, *The Trade in Lunacy. A Study of Private Madhouses in England in the Eighteenth and Nineteenth Centuries* (1972).

H. Pelling, *Social Geography of British Elections 1885–1910* (1967).

M. Pelling, *Cholera, Fever and English Medicine 1825–1865* (Oxford, 1978).

H. Perkin, *The Origins of Modern English Society 1780–1880* (1969).

M. J. Peterson, *The Medical Profession in Mid-Victorian London* (Berkeley, 1978).

G. Phelps, *Squire Waterton* (Wakefield, 1976).

J. V. Pickstone (ed.), *Health, Disease and Medicine in Lancashire 1750–1950* (Dept. of History of Science and Technology, UMIST, Occasional Publications, No. 2, Manchester, 1980).

J. V. Pickstone, *Medicine and industrial society. A history of hospital development in Manchester and its Region, 1752–1946* (Manchester, 1985).

R. Porter, *English Society in the Eighteenth Century* (Harmondsworth, 1982).

W. S. Porter, *The Medical School in Sheffield, 1828–1928* (Sheffield, 1928).

F. N. L. Poynter (ed.), *The Evolution of Medical Practice in Britain* (1961).

F. K. Prochaska, *Women and Philanthropy in 19th Century England* (Oxford, 1980).

W. J. Reader, *Professional Men. The Rise of the Professional Classes in Nineteenth-Century England* (New York, 1966).

D. Roberts, *Paternalism in Early Victorian England* (1979).

M. E. Rose (ed.), *The English Poor Law 1780–1930* (Newton Abbot, 1971).

J. A. Shepherd, *Lawson Tait. The Rebellious Surgeon (1844–1899)* (Lawrence, Kansas, 1980).

E. Shorter, *A History of Women's Bodies* (1983).

R. H. Shryock, *The Development of Modern Medicine* (Madison, Wisconsin, 1979, first published 1936).

M. B. Simey, *Charitable Effort in Liverpool in the Nineteenth Century* (Liverpool, 1951).

C. Singer and E. A. Underwood, *A Short History of Medicine* (2nd ed., Oxford, 1962).

E. Sitwell, *The English Eccentrics* (1933).

F. B. Smith, *The People's Health 1830–1910* (1979).

P. Starr, *The Social Transformation of American Medicine* (New York, 1982).

G. Stedman Jones, *Outcast London. A Study in the Relationship between Classes in Victorian Society* (Oxford, 1971).

K. Thomas, *Religion and the Decline of Magic* (1971).

E. P. Thompson, *The Making of the English Working Class* (1963).

G. E. Trease, *Pharmacy in History* (1964).

P. Vaughan, *Doctors' Commons. A Short History of the British Medical Association* (1959).

J. R. Vincent, *Pollbooks. How Victorians Voted* (Cambridge, 1967).

I. Waddington, *The Medical Profession in the Industrial Revolution* (Dublin, 1984).

J. K. Walton, *The English Seaside Resort. A Social History 1750–1914* (Leicester, 1983).

J. Walvin, *Beside the Seaside: A Social History of the Popular Seaside Holiday* (1978).

J. T. Ward, *The Factory Movement 1830–1855* (1962).

J. T. Ward (ed.), *Popular Movements c. 1830–1850* (1970).

J. T. Ward, *The Factory System* (Newton Abbot, 1970).

S. and B. Webb, *English Poor Law History: Part I, The Old Poor Law* and *Part II, The New Poor Law* (Vols 7 and 8 of *English Local Government* (1927 and 1929, reprinted 1963).

R. A. E. Wells, *Dearth and Distress in Yorkshire 1793–1802* (Borthwick Papers No. 52) (York, 1977).

J. L. West, *The Taylors of Lancashire. Bonesetters and Doctors 1750–1890* (Worsley, 1977).

R. G. Wilson, *Gentlemen Merchants. The merchant community in Leeds 1700–1830* (Manchester, 1971).

A. S. Wohl, *Endangered Lives. Public Health in Victorian Britain* (1984).

R. Woods and J. Woodward (eds), *Urban Disease and Mortality in Nineteenth-Century England* (London and New York, 1984).

J. Woodward, *To do the sick no harm. A Study of the British Voluntary Hospital System to 1875* (1974).

J. Woodward and D. Richards (eds), *Health Care and Popular Medicine in Nineteenth Century England. Essays in the Social History of Medicine* (1977).

E. A. Wrigley (ed.), *Nineteenth-century society. Essays in the use of quantitative methods for the study of social data* (Cambridge, 1972).

Articles and papers

A. E. Bailey, 'Early nineteenth century pharmacy', *Pharmaceutical Journal*, Vol. 185, 1960, pp. 208–212.

V. Berridge, 'Opium Over the Counter in Nineteenth Century England', *Pharmacy in History*, Vol. 20, No. 3, 1978, pp. 91–100.

C. Binfield, 'Asquith: The Formation of a Prime Minister', *The Journal. United Reformed Church History Society*, Vol. 2, No. 7, April, 1981, pp. 204–242.

W. J. Bishop, 'Medical Book Societies in England in the Eighteenth and Nineteenth Centuries', *Bulletin of the Medical Library Assocation*, Vol. 45, 1957, pp. 337–350.

A. Briggs, 'Middlemarch and the Doctors', *The Cambridge Journal*, Vol. I, No. 12, September, 1948, pp. 749–762.

P. S. Brown, 'The vendors of medicines advertised in Eighteenth-Century Bath Newspapers', *Medical History*, Vol. 19, No. 4, October, 1975, pp. 352–368.

P. S. Brown, 'Medicines advertised in Eighteenth-Century Bath Newspapers', *Medical History*, Vol. 20, No. 2, April, 1976, pp. 152–168.

P. S. Brown, 'The Providers of Medical Treatment in Mid-Nineteenth-Century Bristol', *Medical History*, Vol. 24, No. 3, July, 1980, pp. 297–314.

P. S. Brown, 'Herbalists and medical Botanists in mid-Nineteenth-Century Britain with special Reference to Bristol', *Medical History*, Vol. 26, No. 4, October, 1982, pp. 405–420.

P. S. Brown, 'The vicissitudes of herbalism in late nineteenth- and early twentieth-century Britain', *Medical History*, Vol. 29, No. 1, January, 1985, pp. 71–92.

S. Cherry, 'The Role of a Provincial Hospital: The Norfolk and Norwich Hospital, 1771–1880', *Population Studies*, Vol. 26, Part 2, July, 1972, pp. 291–306.

R. J. Cooter, 'Phrenology and British alientists, c.1825–1845', Part I 'Converts to a doctrine' and Part II 'Doctrine and practice', *Medical History*, Vol. 20, Nos 1 and 2, January and April, 1976, pp. 1–21, 135–151.

J. K. Crellin, 'The Growth of Professionalism in Nineteenth-Century British Pharmacy', *Medical History*, Vol. 11, 1967, pp. 215–227.

M. W. Flinn, 'Medical Services under the New Poor Law' in D. Fraser (ed.), *The New Poor Law in the Nineteenth Century* (1976), pp. 45–66.

E. G. Forbes, 'The professionalization of dentistry in the United Kingdom', *Medical History*, Vol. 29, No. 2, April, 1985, pp. 169–181.

W. D. Foster, 'Dr William Henry Cook: The Finances of a Victorian General Practitioner', *Proc. Royal Society of Medicine*, Vol. 66, January, 1973, pp. 46–50.

D. Fraser, 'Voluntaryism and West Riding politics in the mid-nineteenth century', *Northern History*, Vol. XIII, 1977, pp. 199–231.

F. J. Glover, 'The Rise of the Heavy Woollen Trade of the West Riding of Yorkshire in the Nineteenth Century', *Business History*, Vol. IV, 1961–62, pp. 1–21.

E. Greenwood, 'Attributes of a Profession', *Social Work*, Vol. 2, 1957, pp. 45–55.

R. Guest-Gornall, 'The Warrington Dispensary Library', *Medical History*, Vol. 11, 1967, pp. 285–296.

B. Hamilton, 'The Medical Professions in the Eighteenth Century', *Economic History Review*, 2nd Series, Vol. IV, No. 2, 1951, pp. 141–169.

B. Harrison, 'Philanthropy and the Victorians', *Victorian Studies*, Vol. IX, No. 4, June, 1966, pp. 353–374.

H. W. Hart, 'Some Notes on the Sponsoring of Patients for Hospital Treatment under the Voluntary System', *Medical History*, Vol. 24, No. 4, October, 1980, pp. 447–460.

E. Hobsbawm, 'Friendly Societies', *The Amateur Historian*, Vol. 3, No. 3, Spring, 1957, pp. 95–101.

R. G. Hodgkinson, 'Poor Law Medical Officers of England 1834–1871', *Journal of the History of Medicine*, Vol. 11, 1956, pp. 299–338.

S. W. F. Holloway, 'Medical Education in England, 1830–1858: A Sociological Analysis', *History*, Vol. 49, 1964, pp. 299–324.

S. W. F. Holloway, 'The Apothecaries' Act, 1815: A Reinterpretation', Parts I and II, *Medical History*, Vol. 10, Nos 2 and 3, April and July, 1966, pp. 107–129, 221–236.

W. B. Howie, 'The Administration of an Eighteenth-Century Provincial Hospital: The Royal Salop Infirmary, 1747–1830', *Medical History*, Vol. 5, No. 1, January, 1961, pp. 34–55.

W. B. Howie, 'Finance and Supply in an Eighteenth-Century Hospital, 1747–1830', *Medical History*, Vol. 7, No. 2, April, 1963, pp. 126–146.

W. B. Howie, 'Complaints and Complaint Procedures in the Eighteenth- and early Nineteenth-Century Provincial Hospitals in England', *Medical History*, Vol. 25, No. 4, October, 1981, pp. 345–362.

I. Inkster, 'Marginal Men: Aspects of the Social Role of the Medical Community in Sheffield 1790–1850' in J. Woodward and D. Richards (eds), *Health Care and Popular Medicine in Nineteenth Century England. Essays in the Social History of Medicine* (1977), pp. 128–163.

P. Knight, 'Women and Abortion in Victorian and Edwardian England', *History Workshop*, No. 4, Autumn, 1977, pp. 57–68.

J. Lane, 'Disease, Death and the Labouring Poor, 1750–1834: the provision of parish medical services in Warwickshire under the Old Poor Law', unpublished paper, University of Warwick, May, 1980.

J. Lane, 'The Provincial Practitioner and his Services to the Poor, 1750–1800', *The Society for the Social History of Medicine Bulletin*, 28, June, 1981, pp. 10–14.

J. Lane, 'The Early History of General Practice, 1700–1850: Sources and Methods', *The Society for the Social History of Medicine Bulletin*, 30–31, June and December, 1982, pp. 19–21.

J. Lane, 'The medical practitioners of provincial England in 1783', *Medical History*, Vol. 28, No. 4, October, 1984, pp. 353–371.

C. J. Lawrence, 'William Buchan: medicine laid open', *Medical History*, Vol. 19, No. 1, January, 1975, pp. 20–35.

H. Levy, 'The Economic History of Sickness and Medical Benefit Since the Puritan Revolution', *Economic History Review*, Series 1, Vol. XIV, 1944, pp. 135–160.

I. S. L. Loudon, 'Historical importance of outpatients', *British Medical Journal*, Vol. 1, No. 6118, April, 1978, pp. 974–977.

I. S. L. Loudon, 'The Origins and Growth of the Dispensary Movement in England', *Bulletin of the History of Medicine*, Vol. 55, Part 3, 1981, pp. 322–342.

I. S. L. Loudon, 'A Doctor's Cash Book: The Economy of General Practice in the 1830s', *Medical History*, Vol. 27, No. 3, July, 1983, pp. 249–268.

I. S. L. Loudon, 'The nature of provincial medical practice in eighteenth-century England', *Medical History*, Vol. 29, No. 1, January, 1985, pp. 1–32.

H. Marland, 'Early Nineteenth-Century Medical Society Activity: The Huddersfield Case', *The Journal of Regional and Local Studies*, Vol. 6, No. 2, Autumn, 1985, pp. 37–48.

T. McKeown and R. G. Brown, 'Medical Evidence Related to English Population Changes in the Eighteenth Century', *Population Studies*, Vol. 9, Part 2, November, 1955, pp. 119–141.

A. McLaren, 'Women's Work and Regulation of Family Size: the question of abortion in the ninteenth century', *History Workshop*, No. 4, Autumn, 1977, pp. 70–81.

D. Neave, 'The local records of affiliated Friendly Societies: A plea for their location and preservation', *The Local Historian*, Vol. 16, No. 3, August, 1984, pp. 161–167.

J. E. O'Neill, 'Finding a Policy for the Sick Poor', *Victorian Studies*, Vol. VII, No. 3, March, 1964, pp. 265–283.

B. and D. Payne (eds), 'Extracts from the Journals of John Deakin Heaton, MD, of Claremont, Leeds', *Publications of the Thoresby Society*, Vol. 53, 1972, Part II, pp. 95–153.

M. Pelling and C. Webster, 'Medical Practitioners' in C. Webster (ed.), *Health, Medicine and Mortality in the Sixteenth Century* (Cambridge, 1979), pp. 165–235.

J. V. Pickstone, 'Medical Botany (Self-Help Medicine in Victorian England)', *Memoirs of the Manchester Literary and Philosophical Society*, No. 119, 1976–77, pp. 85–95.

J. V. Pickstone, 'The Professionalisation of Medicine in England and Europe: the state, the market and industrial society', *Journal of the Japan Society of Medical History*, Vol. 25, No. 4, October, 1979, pp. 550–520.

J. V. Pickstone, 'What were Dispensaries for? The Lancashire Foundations during the Industrial Revolution', unpublished paper, UMIST, Manchester, 1980.

J. V. Pickstone and S. V. F. Butler, 'The politics of medicine in Manchester, 1788–1792: hospital reform and public health services in the early industrial city ', *Medical History*, Vol. 28, No. 3, July, 1984, pp. 227–249.

R. Porter, 'Quacks: An Unconscionable Time Dying', unpublished paper, Wellcome Institute for the History of Medicine, London, 1983.

R. Porter, 'Lay medical knowledge in the eighteenth century: the evidence of the *Gentleman's Magazine*', *Medical History*, Vol. 29, No. 2, April, 1985, pp. 138–168.

R. Porter, 'The Patient's View. Doing Medical History from Below', *Theory and Society*, Vol. 14, 1985, pp. 175–198.

R. Price, 'Hydropathy in England 1840–70', *Medical History*, Vol. 25, No. 3, July, 1981, pp. 269–280.

F. K. Prochaska, 'Women in English Philanthropy 1790–1830', *International Review of Social History*, Vol. 19, 1974, pp. 426–445.

P. E. Razzell, 'An Interpretation of the Modern Rise of Population in Europe – A Critique', *Population Studies*, Vol. 28, Part 1, March, 1974, pp. 5–17.

S. J. Rogal, 'A Checklist of Medical Journals Published in England during the Seventeenth, Eighteenth and Nineteenth Centuries', *British Studies Monitor*, Vol. IX, No. 3, Winter, 1980, pp. 3–25.

M. E. Rose, 'The Anti-Poor Law Movement in the North of England', *Northern History*, Vol. I, 1966, pp. 70–91.

M. E. Rose, 'The New Poor Law in an Industrial Area' in R. M. Hartwell (ed.), *The Industrial Revolution* (Oxford, 1970), pp. 121–143.

M. E. Rose, 'The doctor in the Industrial Revolution', *British Journal of Industrial Medicine*, Vol. 28, 1971, pp. 22–26.

S. E. D. Shortt, 'Physicians, Science, and Status: Issues in the Professionalization of Anglo-American Medicine in the Nineteenth Century', *Medical History*, Vol. 27, No. 1, January, 1983, pp. 51–68.

E. M. Sigsworth, 'Gateways to death? Medicine, Hospitals and Mortality, 1700–1850' in P. Mathias (ed.), *Science and Society 1600–1900* (Cambridge, 1972), pp. 97–110.

E. M. Sigsworth and P. Swan, 'Para-medical provision in the West Riding', *The Society for the Social History of Medicine Bulletin*, 29, December, 1981, pp. 37–39.

A. Summers, 'A Home from Home – Women's Philanthropic Work in the Nineteenth Century' in S. Burman (ed.), *Fit Work for Women* (1979), pp. 33–63.

P. Swan, 'A Brief Survey and Summary of the Role and Position of Medical Societies in the early Nineteenth Century Medical Profession', *The Journal of Local Studies*, Vol. 2, No. 2, Autumn, 1982, pp. 43–47.

E. G. Thomas, 'The Old Poor Law and Medicine', *Medical History*, Vol. 24, No. 1, January, 1980, pp. 1–19.

F. M. L. Thompson, 'Social Control in Victorian Britain', *Economic History Review*, 2nd Series, Vol. XXXIV, No. 2, 1981, pp. 189–208.

I. Waddington, 'The Development of Medical Ethics – A Sociological Analysis', *Medical History*, Vol. 19, No. 1, January, 1975, pp. 36–51.

I. Waddington , 'General Practitioners and Consultants in Early Nineteenth-Century England: The Sociology of an Intra-Professional Conflict' in J. Woodward and D. Richards (eds), *Health Care and Popular Medicine in Nineteenth Century England. Essays in the Social History of Medicine* (1977), pp. 164–188.

I. Waddington, 'Competition and monopoly in a profession. The campaign for medical registration in Britain', *Amsterdams Sociologisch Tijdschrift*, No. 2, October, 1979, pp. 288–321.

C. Webster, 'The crisis of the hospitals during the Industrial Revolution' in E. G. Forbes (ed.), *Human implications of scientific advance* (Edinburgh, 1978), pp. 214–233.

A. L. Wyman, 'The surgeoness: the female practitioner of surgery 1400–1800', *Medical History*, Vol. 28, No. 1, January, 1984, pp. 22–41.

Unpublished theses and dissertations

D. Ashforth, *The Poor Law in Bradford c.1834–1871. A Study of the relief of poverty in mid-nineteenth century Bradford*, PhD thesis, Bradford, 1979.

K. A. Cowlard, *The urban development of Wakefield, 1801–1901*, PhD thesis, Leeds, 1974.

R. J. Dennis, *Community and interaction in a Victorian city: Huddersfield, 1850–1880*, PhD thesis, Cambridge, 1975.

B. Greaves, *Methodism in Yorkshire 1740–1851*, PhD thesis, Liverpool, 1968.

M. C. Hamilton, *The Development of Medicine in the Sheffield Region up to 1815*, MA thesis, Sheffield, 1957.

I. Inkster, *Studies in the Social History of Science in England During the Industrial Revolution, circa 1790–1850*, PhD thesis, Sheffield, 1977.

H. Marland, *The Provision of Medical Treatment for the Sick Poor. The Doncaster Dispensary 1792–1867*, MA thesis, Warwick, 1980.

H. Marland, *Medicine and Society in Wakefield and Huddersfield 1780–1870*, PhD thesis, Warwick, 1984.

R. J. Morris, *Organisation and Aims of the Principal Secular Voluntary Organisations of the Leeds Middle Class, 1830–1851*, DPhil thesis, Oxford, 1970.

M. E. Rose, *Poor Law Administration in the West Riding of Yorkshire (1820–1855)*, DPhil thesis, Oxford, 1965.

R. J. Springett, *The Mechanics of Urban Land Development in Huddersfield 1700–1911*, PhD thesis, Leeds, 1979.

Index